The Economic History
of the Middle East
1800–1914

The Economic History of the Middle East 1800–1914

A BOOK OF READINGS

Edited and with Introductions by
CHARLES ISSAWI

THE UNIVERSITY OF CHICAGO PRESS
CHICAGO AND LONDON

THE UNIVERSITY OF CHICAGO PRESS, CHICAGO 60637
THE UNIVERSITY OF CHICAGO PRESS, LTD., LONDON

International Standard Book Number: 0-226-38609-0
Library of Congress Catalog Card Number: 66-11883

To Sir Hamilton Gibb

Preface

Few aspects of the history of the Middle East in the last two hundred years have received less attention than the economic. The paucity of literature on the subject may be easily ascertained by referring to the standard bibliographies or to the articles listed in *Index Islamicus* and its *Supplement*. Yet it is clear that without some grasp of the economic changes that occurred during this period, no real understanding is possible either of the course of events in other fields of Middle Eastern history during these two centuries or of economic developments in the region during recent decades. This book is an attempt to fill one of the many gaps in this field by presenting a selection of articles and extracts from reports, articles, and books on various aspects of the economic history of Turkey and the eastern Arab countries; as such it may be useful not only to students of the Middle East but also to those working in the general area of economic development. It is presented essentially as an aid in teaching and research. If it serves to arouse interest in this neglected subject and stimulates further study, it will have fulfilled its main objective.

The region under review consists of Anatolia, Arab Asia, and the Nile Valley. The period covered is 1800–1914, but in certain selections the narrative continues beyond 1914; literature on the period after the First World War is relatively abundant and easily accessible. Within these limits, emphasis varies from country to country, depending on the particular nature of its history.

The nineteenth century, which is the object of study, forms a transition between the "medieval" and "modern" periods in the history of the Middle East. The emphasis of the selections is therefore on the gradual transformation that took place during that century: the integration of the region in the international commercial and financial network, the investment of foreign capital, the development of mechanical transport, the transition from a subsistence to a market-oriented agriculture, the decline of the handicrafts, the growth of the population, and the attempts to establish modern industries. Of course this transformation was part of the wider changes in the political, social and cultural life of the region.

The primary aim in selecting the material has been to include the best and most interesting texts available. Within this framework, four criteria have been applied:

First, no passage written in English has been reproduced if it was originally published in a book. This has led to the exclusion of important writings by such authors as Bonné, Crouchley, Gaitskell, Gibb and Bowen, Hoskins, Landes, Bernard Lewis, Longrigg, Rivlin, Stanford Shaw, and others, an exclusion justified, however, by the ready availability of the books written by these authors.

Second, preference has been given to texts in non-Western languages over texts in Western languages, and within the latter group, to non-English texts over English.

Third, priority has been given to articles, reports, and pamphlets over books, and to older books over more recently published ones.

Last, since the main laws, treaties, and concessionary and other agreements affecting economic activity have been reproduced in J. C. Hurewitz, *Diplomacy in the Near and Middle East* (Princeton, 1956), no attempt has been made to include such documents here, with a single, short exception.

Of the sixty-two selections, seven are published here for the first time, and one of them was written specially for this book. They cover two centuries, the earliest having been written in the 1760's and the latest in the 1960's, and they are drawn from English, French, Arabic, German, Russian, Turkish, Hebrew, and Italian. Twenty-nine were originally written in English, and published translations of two others were available. The Hebrew passage was translated by Professor Gerson D. Cohen, my colleague. Some three-quarters of the others were translated by me, and I have checked all the remaining ones against the original text and revised the draft. Each part of the book is preceded by a short essay; these essays are somewhat longer for those countries where material is scarcest. Each selection is preceded by an introductory note, with bibliographical references. The selections and introductions have been arranged so as to provide a more or less consecutive narrative and bring out the salient features of the economic history of the country concerned.

Appendixes on weights and measures and on currencies, a brief glossary of the Arabic and Turkish terms used most frequently in this book, and a selected bibliography are also provided. A few explanatory words or sentences, as well as cross-references, have been inserted in the text or footnotes; all such additions in the text are enclosed in brackets; added footnotes are indicated by "Translator" or "Editor." Otherwise, except for some omissions, no attempt has been made to·edit the selections—thus the numbering of tables in the original texts has not been changed and references to passages not included in this book have been kept.

No book on the Middle East can avoid a mention in the preface of transliteration. I have made little attempt to change the fanciful spelling of Arabic, Persian, and Turkish words used by some of the authors included, or to correct their inconsistencies. In the translated passages and introductions I have used a reasonably consistent system, following Turkish practice in Part II and Arabic in the others, omitting diacritical marks other than the Arabic *'ain* and the Turkish ç and ş, and paying due respect to usage; in these passages Arabic and Turkish words have been italicized, except terms meaning weights and measures and currencies. I believe the result should be intelligible to the reader.

I should like to thank the following colleagues and friends who read parts of the manuscript and gave me the benefit of their comments and criticisms: Shepherd B. Clough, D. M. Dunlop, P. H. Holt, A. H. Hourani, J. C. Hurewitz, George Rentz, and F. H. Stoakes; Mrs. Judy Marsh, Miss Marilyn Sjoberg, Miss Isabel Ludeman, and Miss Lily Venn, who typed the manuscript; and above all my wife, whose help at every stage was invaluable. Dr. C. Zurayk read the proofs and made many helpful suggestions.

Lastly, I wish to express my gratitude to the John Simon Guggenheim Memorial Foundation and the Social Science Research Council, which granted me fellowships in 1961–62 for research on the economic history of the Arab countries, and to the School of International Affairs at Columbia University, whose financial assistance made it possible for me to carry out much of the work that went into this book.

Contents

xi

PART I

General Introduction

General Introduction: Decline and Revival of the Middle Eastern Economy

The long history of the Middle East has witnessed several cycles of growth and decay. The last of these shows a slow and prolonged decline from about the twelfth century until the nineteenth, followed by a sharp recovery and steady growth to the present day.[1]

The causes of the economic decline of the Arab countries in the medieval period have still to be determined, but the fact of the decline itself stands plain. By the eighteenth century the cultivated area in Iraq had shrunk to a minute fraction of what it had been in the tenth, and the population had correspondingly diminished. In Syria, for whose population under the Romans a figure of ten million has been declared "by no means improbable"[2] and which may perhaps more realistically be estimated at five to six million,[3] the total had dropped to perhaps two million by the end of the eighteenth century. The margin of cultivation had moved much nearer the coast than in Roman or early Arab times, and in some spots it actually reached the sea. In southern Arabia the prosperity of former times survived only in legend. Even Egypt had fallen very low although, thanks to the regularity of the Nile and to the strength of the Mamluk army, it had been spared the worst calamities that befell its neighbors. Its population, which is reliably put at eight million in Roman times, is estimated to have fallen to not more than four million[4] by the fourteenth century and by 1800 stood at about two and a half million. The cultivated area had also appreciably diminished.

Urban life had suffered less than rural, since the breakdown of the state had never been complete and since the government always retained some authority

[1] Perhaps the best single study of the economy of any medieval Arab country at its peak is 'Abd al-'Aziz al-Duri, *Tarikh al-'Iraq al-iqtisadi* (Baghdad, 1948), covering tenth-century Iraq. See also, on Fatimid Egypt, Rashid al-Barawi, *Halat Misr al-iqtisadia fi 'ahd al-Fatimiyyin* (Cairo, 1948).

[2] F. M. Heichelheim, "Roman Syria," in Tenney Frank (ed.), *An Economic Survey of Ancient Rome* (Baltimore, 1927), IV, 158. Throughout this book, unless otherwise indicated, the term Syria denotes "natural" or "greater" Syria, i.e., the area now composing the states of Syria, Lebanon, Israel, and Jordan.

[3] Julius Beloch, *Die Bevölkerung der griechish-römischen Welt* (Leipzig, 1886), cited in Heichelheim, *op. cit.*

[4] Gibb and Bowen, *Islamic Society and the West*, I, 209.

over the main towns. But one has only to compare the industrial products of the eighteenth century with those made a few hundred years earlier to realize that the handicrafts had not only stagnated but had actually retrogressed; moreover, the number of craftsmen must have greatly diminished in such towns as Baghdad, Mosul, and, to a lesser extent, Cairo. As for the seaports—Alexandria, Basra, Antioch, Beirut, Tripoli—they were only a shadow of their former selves; their trade had been reduced to a trickle, and the advanced and complex financial transactions which accompanied it[5] had all but disappeared. Needless to say, economic decline was accompanied by social and cultural retrogression.

Many factors helped bring about this deterioration. By the beginning of the twelfth century the scientific and intellectual life of Islamic society was already showing signs of fatigue and rigidity, and its religion was becoming more dogmatic and intolerant. The prolonged warfare with the Crusaders, Mongols, and Tatars caused much destruction in Iraq and Syria; and, what was no less serious, in the course of repelling these invaders the Arab countries transformed themselves into militaristic, "feudal" societies whose institutions were much less conducive to economic and social development. The Turco-Persian wars, which dragged on for nearly three centuries, impeded the economic recovery of Iraq. The breakdown of authority in the Ottoman Empire in the seventeenth century, the emergence of petty dynasties and quasi-independent governors, and the growing depredations of the beduins dealt further blows to economic and social activity.[6]

As for the strictly economic factors, attention should be drawn, first of all, to the grave deficiencies in three major resources of the Arab Middle East: forests, minerals, and rivers. In the Arab countries, and to a lesser extent in neighboring Anatolia and Iran, forests had always been sparse, and they shrank steadily and rapidly with the passage of time. The magnitude of the resulting handicap can be realized only by remembering that in pre-industrial societies, wood—a bulky product to transport—provided almost the sole source of fuel and by far the most important material for the construction of implements, machines, bridges, ships, and houses, not to mention furniture and a host of other consumer goods.[7] The shortage of minerals was a less severe obstacle in such societies, mainly because

[5] See, for example, the use of bank checks in eleventh-century Basra as described in Nasir-i Khusrau, *Safarnameh* and that of bills of exchange in A. Mez, *The Renaissance of Islam* (London, 1937), p. 478. On the availability of gold and silver in medieval Islam, see M. Lombard, "L'or musulman du VII au X siècles," *Annales* (Paris), 1947, and Sture Bolin, "Mohammed, Charlemagne and Ruric," *Scandinavian Economic History Review*, I (1953).

[6] Another factor that may conceivably have contributed to the decline of medieval Arab civilization was the climate cycle. There is much evidence to show that the period A.D. 700–1000 was an exceptionally humid one and was followed by a dry period lasting over 200 years. See Karl. W. Butzer, "Late Glacial and Postglacial Climatic Variation in the Near East," *Erdkunde*, XI (1957).

[7] The scarcity of wood has, from the earliest times, forced the peoples of the Middle East to rely on other materials. Thus, houses were built of clay or stone and bridges of stone, and boats made of inflated skins were used in Mesopotamia. One has only to study the architecture of ancient Egypt to see how far the substitution of stone for wood can be carried. But, needless to say, the labor and other costs of such a substitution must have been very high.

much smaller quantities were used, and therefore domestic supplies could be more easily supplemented by imports. But it is worth noting that except for oil, the utility of which was negligible until about a hundred years ago, the eastern Arab countries seem to be very poorly endowed with minerals. And the rivers being sparse and few constituted a double handicap. In the first place, of all Middle Eastern rivers only the Nile, Tigris, and Euphrates are navigable over a significant stretch; one has only to recall the part played by water transport in the economic development of Europe, North and South America, Russia, China, and India to realize the importance of this factor. Moreover, the Middle Eastern rivers are silt-laden and therefore do not have those estuaries which in other regions have formed many of the world's great ports; this, however, was not a serious consideration in the days of small sailing ships, which could use even the small and poor natural harbors of the Arab countries without undue hardship. Another consequence of the lack of swift rivers with a fairly constant year-round flow, like those of Western Europe, was that the Middle East was deprived of the main source of motive power available to man until the advent of the steam engine. The scarcity of navigable rivers was, to a certain extent, offset by the fact that a large part of the Middle East consists of hard gravel, over which the camel can move swiftly and easily. The Arabs thus had at their disposal a pack animal far superior to those available in medieval Europe.[8] But camel transport was, of course, always several times more expensive than water transport.

The subject of waterpower suggests another cause of retardation, the lack of mechanical inventiveness of the Islamic civilization. It is true that some important new processes and products were developed or adopted in the Middle East during the eighth through the thirteenth centuries. These were particularly conspicuous in the following fields: irrigation and hydraulics; cultivation of high-value crops such as cotton, linen, silk, sugarcane, citrus, and other fruits; sugar refining; steel production; ceramics and glassware; paper milling; distillation; the making of soap, nitric acid, sulfuric acid, and other chemical products; and, above all, textile production.[9] But Islam has nothing comparable to the remarkable technical advance of the Greco-Roman civilization in the period 400 B.C.–A.D. 100 or to the no less impressive progress registered in Western Europe in the eleventh and twelfth centuries.

---

[8] In principle the standard camel load was equal to 244 kilograms, but in practice it varied widely according to the locality, the terrain, and the nature of the goods transported; thus for Syria at the end of the eighteenth century a figure of over 300 kilograms has been quoted, and for the middle of the nineteenth century one of over 250 kilograms. In Arabia today a load of 400–500 kilograms is fairly common. These weights considerably exceed those carried by pack horses in Europe and elsewhere. They are also distinctly greater than those drawn by horses until the invention of the improved harness, around the ninth century. (See Lefebvre des Noëttes, *La force motrice animale à travers les âges* [Paris, 1924].) The camel has greater endurance than the horse, a fact that must be set against its slower walking pace—2.5 miles an hour in a caravan. In the Middle East, where horses are very seldom used as pack animals, the typical mule load is 100–150 kilograms and the donkey load 50; the horse load is somewhat smaller than that of the mule.

[9] See Charles Singer (ed.), *A History of Technology* (London, 1957), II, 57, 191, 199, 285, 327, 356–57, 372, 738.

More particularly, the Middle East did not keep pace with Europe in the utilization of non-human sources of energy, a development that was to have incalculable consequences in the future. Three examples may be given.

One was the improved harness, which increased several-fold the amount of animal energy at man's disposal. This was an early medieval European invention or adaptation with no Islamic counterpart.[10]

A more important development was the water mill, which provided the bulk of Europe's non-human energy until well into the nineteenth century. Water wheels were used, of course, in the Middle East for milling and irrigation and occasionally for other industrial purposes, but their number was small and declined rapidly in the late Middle Ages. Moreover, the Muslims continued to use the more primitive "Greek" or "Norse" water mill, as distinct from the far superior "Vitruvian" type used in Europe from Roman times onward. In the words of the leading authority: "Apart from its use in irrigation, the water-wheel never became a principal prime-mover in the Muslim world, as economic conditions did not stimulate further developments."[11]

Still more striking is the history of the windmill. Windmills seem to have been invented in Iran, in "early Muslim or even pre-Muslim times," but although they came to be used in the Islamic society "to grind corn, to pump water, to crush sugar cane, and so on," their number remained very small and, except in Iran, they had practically disappeared by the late Middle Ages. And although it seems that the windmill entered Europe by way of Morocco and Spain, the construction of the western windmill "is entirely different from that of its eastern counterpart. Thus it does not seem to derive from the Greek water-mill and may have some completely different origin."[12] Both the development and the diffusion of the windmill in Europe were very rapid, and windmills came to constitute a major source of motive power.

The advances registered in the use of animate and inanimate power, in metallurgy, and later in shipbuilding tilted the technical balance sharply in favor of Europe. Combined with the latter's advantages in wood, minerals, waterpower, and navigable rivers, they ensured its economic predominance over the Middle East. "The frontier region of Mediterranean civilization," to use C. E. Ayres's expressive phrase, drew ahead of its older competitors.

A third set of factors is connected with sea navigation and foreign trade. Arab control of the Mediterranean in the latter half of the ninth and in the tenth century led to much commercial activity in that sea.[13] Still earlier the Muslims

[10] The history and consequences of the improved harness are brilliantly discussed in Lefebvre des Noëttes, op. cit.

[11] R. J. Forbes, in Singer, op. cit., II, 614.

[12] Ibid., pp. 616–17. In Europe, the working rates of various forms of power available before the steam engine were: a man 0.1 horsepower, a donkey 0.25, a mule 0.5, an ox 0.66, a camel 2, an overshot water wheel 2 to 5, and a post windmill 2 to 8 (A. R. Ubbelohde, Man and Energy [London, 1963] pp. 50–51).

[13] See Archibald Lewis, Naval Power and Trade in the Mediterranean (Princeton, 1951).

had established their domination over the Indian Ocean and set up important trading posts in Malaya, Indonesia, and China; until the sixteenth century the "Arabs remained the leading traders and mariners of the Indian Ocean."[14] The income earned from navigation, trade, and piracy must have been great and must have contributed substantially to the economic prosperity of the Middle East. In the eleventh century, however, a Byzantine counteroffensive in the eastern Mediterranean, and an Italian thrust in the western, transferred control to the Christians, and Europeans soon became the main carriers and traders in that sea. Thus in 1192 Ibn Jubair had to use a Christian ship to travel from Ceuta to Alexandria, and the European—mainly Italian—colonies established in Constantinople, along the Syrian coast, and in Alexandria and Damietta monopolized trade between the Middle East and Europe. The attempts of Salahuddin and his successors to reduce the power of the Christians and to establish a Muslim monopoly of the valuable spice trade merely stimulated Europe to find an alternative route to the Indian Ocean, around the Cape of Good Hope.[15] Even the temporary naval domination of the Mediterranean by the Turks in the sixteenth century failed to wrest the control of trade and navigation from the Europeans, and in the seventeenth and eighteenth centuries this control was complete, except for occasional attacks by Barbary pirates. Meanwhile, in the sixteenth century, the Portuguese had established their naval and commercial hegemony over the Indian Ocean, and in the seventeenth they were succeeded by the Dutch. Arab navigation and trade in that area, whether with India and Indonesia or with East Africa, was reduced to a surreptitious trickle. Although the prohibitions on local shipping and trade so rigidly enforced by the Portuguese and Dutch were relaxed by the British, the Arabs profited little from this: their primitive craft could no longer compete with the splendid sailing ships—and, later, steamers—of Europe nor their petty traders with the organized western companies. In other words, trade between the Middle East and other parts of the world—and indeed much of the coasting trade—formerly mainly in Arab hands, was conducted almost solely by Europeans, to whom the bulk of the income accrued. And, to make matters worse, the local merchants with whom the Europeans dealt came mainly from the minority groups, Christian and Jewish,[16] whose higher educational level, keener business sense, and greater readiness to accept foreign ways made them more suitable partners for the Europeans.

This secular process of decline was arrested in the nineteenth century, with the beginning of an upward movement which has steadily gained in momentum and scope. Indeed, it is no exaggeration to say that during the last 150 years the Middle

---

[14] George F. Hourani, *Arab Seafaring in the Indian Ocean* (Princeton, 1951), p. 83.

[15] See Subhi Labib, "Al-tujjar al-karimia," *Majallat al-jam'ia al-misria li al-dirasat al-tarikhia* (Cairo), May, 1952, and Charles Issawi, "Crusades and Current Crises in the Near East: A Historical Parallel," *International Affairs* (London), July, 1957.

[16] See Gibb and Bowen, I, 308–9.

East has compressed, in some regions and branches, the process through which Europe passed between the Middle Ages and the end of the nineteenth century. In both regions the economy was quickened by the impact of trade with an alien and more advanced civilization. In both, the initial effects were first felt in a few Mediterranean ports—Pisa, Venice, and Genoa, and Istanbul, Smyrna, Alexandria, and Beirut—and spread from there along the principal trade routes. In both, the economic transformation was accompanied by profound social changes and an intellectual awakening.

But the differences are as great as the similarities. In the first place, the Middle East, although much more stagnant technologically and intellectually than Europe on the eve of the Crusades, was more urbanized, made much wider use of money in its internal transactions, and had less of a subsistence economy—with obvious consequences for its future course of development. Second, the high technical level and the great economic and political power of Europe, when it impinged on the Middle East in the nineteenth century, not only accelerated but also drastically changed the nature of the evolution of the latter. Lastly, whereas the agents of economic change in Europe were natives, in the Middle East they were primarily foreigners. This not only gave a particular character to economic relations but meant that whereas in the medieval period the capital accumulated, the experience gained, and the external economies achieved benefited the backward area (Europe), in the modern period they accrued to the more advanced area (again Europe) and not to the Middle East. As a result, in several parts of the Middle East most "middle-class" economic activities were performed by foreigners and a "national bourgeoisie" emerged, slowly and painfully, only in the last few decades.

The rapid development of some sectors of the economy accompanied by stagnation, or almost imperceptible progress, in others has brought about in some societies the phenomenon known as "economic dualism."[17] In the Middle East this can be seen most clearly in the oil-producing countries of the Arabian Peninsula, where one of the largest and technologically most advanced industries in the world coexists with a nomadic or seminomadic society that is only just beginning to change. In the other parts of the region, however, the gap between the "advanced" and "backward," or "modern" and "traditional," sectors is not so wide, and the term "lopsided" or "export-oriented" economy seems to describe the situation better than that of "dual economy" (see Part VI, chap. 1).

The transformation of the largely self-sufficing subsistence economy into an export-oriented one required the development of both "directly productive activities" and "social overhead capital," to use the convenient terms coined by

[17] See J. H. Boeke, *Economics and Economic Policy of Dual Societies* (New York, 1953); W. A. Lewis, "Economic Development with Unlimited Supplies of Labour," *Manchester School of Economic and Social Studies*, May, 1954; and Benjamin Higgins, "The Dualistic Theory of Underdeveloped Areas," *Economic Development and Cultural Change*, January, 1956. For an interesting study of the Chinese experience, see Chi-Ming Hou, "Economic Dualism: The Case of China, 1840–1937," *Journal of Economic History*, September, 1963.

Hirschman.[18] In all the underdeveloped countries in the nineteenth century, directly productive activities were equated with primary production; since, until the exploitation of oil on the eve of the First World War, the Middle Eastern Arab countries—unlike Anatolia—had little in the way of mineral resources, the development of the directly productive sector came to mean, in fact, the expansion and improvement of agriculture.

Expansion was made possible by bringing under cultivation the vast areas of cultivable land which had lain unused for centuries. In Anatolia and Syria and parts of Iraq all that this required was the establishment of law and order, which was immediately followed by individual reclamation and cultivation of the rain-fed land. In other parts of Iraq and the Sudan, and in Egypt, the extension of cultivation necessitated the building of irrigation works, which were provided by the government. The improvement of agriculture consisted of the introduction or expansion of certain cash crops grown for export: cotton in Egypt, the Sudan and Western Anatolia, silk in Lebanon, tobacco in Syria, dates in Iraq, coffee in Yemen, and wheat and barley in most of these countries. But practically no progress was made in the use of improved methods or instruments of cultivation, the introduction of better seeds or varieties, or the application of chemical fertilizers until the beginning of this century, at the very earliest. The switch-over from subsistence to cash crops did, however, help to bring about a profound change in land tenure. At the risk of oversimplification, this change may be described as the breakdown of the system of communal or tribal ownership of land and its replacement by individual ownership.

The only serious attempt at industrial development was made by Muhammad Ali, who governed Egypt between 1805 and 1849. For various reasons his endeavor failed, and thereafter progress in industrialization was negligible until the 1930's. Meanwhile the old handicrafts, which had played a vital part in the traditional economy, were faced with the increasingly powerful competition of machine-made goods. Many were wiped out, a few managed to survive by modernizing some of their equipment and methods of work, and others were enabled to linger on because of the low wage rates that prevailed.

The expansion of the agricultural sector was mainly the work of the Middle Easterners themselves, including both the government (e.g., the Aswan and Hindiyya dams) and private sectors, and both the Muslim majority and the Christian and other minorities. The bulk of the social overhead capital was provided by foreign investors, either in the form of direct investment or through loans to the Ottoman, Egyptian, and other governments. Thus, foreign enterprise dug the Suez Canal; developed the ports of Port Said, Beirut, Haider Pasha, Mersin, and Alexandretta; built the Berlin–Baghdad and Syrian railways, as well as the light railways in Egypt; and provided gas, electricity, and water in Istanbul, Alexandria, Cairo, Beirut, Damascus, Baghdad, and other cities. The standard-

[18] Albert O. Hirschman, *The Strategy of Economic Development* (New Haven, 1958).

gauge railways built in Egypt before the First World War, as well as the Hijaz Railway, were financed by the local governments, which also installed the telegraphs and almost all the telephones operating in the region. Other railway systems owed their origins to wartime military construction, as in the Sudan, Palestine, and Iraq, supplemented by government action after the war. With the exceptions noted above, the ports built in the region, both before and after the First World War, were also financed by the local governments.

Social overhead, in the form of educational and health services, was also provided mainly by the government and foreigners. Thus the Egyptian and Ottoman governments founded the first modern schools of medicine in the 1820's, built army hospitals, and set up a few quarantine and other public health services; other medical schools, hospitals, and dispensaries were established by foreign missionaries, chiefly American and French. Similarly in education the slender network of government schools was reinforced by foreign missionary schools, again mainly French and American, as well as by private schools run by the various local religious communities. An idea of the scope of the foreign contribution in the social field is given by the following estimate of American expenditure, made in 1919: "We have invested $20,000,000 in founding colleges, $40,000,000 in feeding the hungry and $50,000,000 in preaching, instruction and free medicine." [19]

The remaining indispensable activities, trade and finance, as well as the technical and business skills, were conducted by foreign businessmen, sometimes acting through the intermediary of members of minority groups, and by foreign professional men. Thus, in the first half of the nineteenth century, as before, British, French, and other traders exported such produce as grains, cotton, silk, tobacco, and dates, but now they started to advance to merchants—and occasionally directly to farmers—the funds required for growing and marketing the crops; a few went further and set up the necessary processing plants, e.g., for the ginning of cotton and the reeling of silk. Similarly European businessmen, or local Christian or Jewish merchants, accounted for the bulk of the trade in textiles, sugar, hardware, coal, petroleum, and other commodities imported from Europe. Except in a few places, such as Damascus, Muslims continued to play a very minor part in foreign trade, apart from some traditional branches such as soap and spices, until the last two decades or so.

The next and principal phase of foreign financial penetration began around the 1850's. In the preceding two or three decades British and other private bankers had established themselves in the various seaports.[20] There then followed the

---

[19] Talcott Williams, quoted in Eliot Grinnell Mears (ed.), *Modern Turkey* (New York, 1924), pp. 361–62. The exact geographical coverage of the figures is not clear.

[20] A list of foreign bankers in 1846 "shows an English private banking firm in every Mediterranean port, forty in all, from Gibraltar to Jerusalem" (Leland H. Jenks, *The Migration of British Capital to 1875* [New York, 1938], p. 188). By 1848 there were seven British private bankers in Alexandria—(A. S. J. Baster, *The International Banks* [London, 1935], p. 39).

founding of incorporated banks such as the Bank of Egypt in Alexandria in 1855, the Ottoman Bank in Constantinople in 1856, the Anglo-Egyptian Bank in Alexandria in 1864, and the London and Baghdad Association, in the same year. Thereafter progress was rapid, new banks were established and branches of powerful European banks such as Barclay's, Crédit Lyonnais, Comptoir d'Escompte, Deutsche Bank, and Banco di Roma were opened in the various countries. European banks completely dominated the field; the first truly Egyptian, Arab, and Turkish banks were not established until after the First World War, and such banks did not account for a large proportion of total business until after the Second World War. As for the governments, their role until 1914 was confined to attempts, more or less successful, to establish and maintain sound currencies (see Appendix II).

At the same time that it was setting up banks, European capital was advancing huge sums to the spendthrift Ottoman sultans and Egyptian viceroys who were modernizing their countries on a lavish scale. By the time the Ottoman Empire was declared bankrupt, in 1875, it had contracted a debt with a nominal value of £200 million, which was reduced by settlement to £106.4 million. The corresponding process in Egypt ended with the Law of Liquidation of 1880, which fixed the consolidated debt at £98.4 million. In both countries further loans were contracted in the years preceding the First World War, but this time, thanks to the vigilance of the international bodies set up to protect foreign bondholders, the capital so raised was used mainly for productive purposes.

As mentioned before, during this period European capital also established railways, ports, and other public utilities. A small amount went into mining and a tiny amount into manufacturing. It was only after the First World War that European capital participated significantly in the process of industrialization and that the large-scale development of the Middle Eastern oil industry by British, American, Dutch, and French capital began. It may be added that the history of European finance in North Africa shows much the same sequence of stages.

All these factors helped to draw the Middle East into the network of international trade and finance. The measure of the involvement is given by the fact that, in the hundred years preceding the First World War, the foreign trade of the principal countries covered in this study increased, in real terms, between twenty- and fifty-fold. But the extent to which the economy came to be connected with the world market varied considerably from country to country. Thus in Egypt cotton soon spread all over the land, bringing millions of cultivators in contact with the market, and the same process occurred in Lebanon thanks to the breeding of silkworms and the provision of goods and services to summer vacationers. In the Sudan and Arabia, on the other hand, practically the whole rural population continued in its age-old subsistence economy. In Syria and Iraq the orientation of agriculture toward the world market began several decades later than in Egypt and developed to a much smaller degree.[21]

But irrespective of the extent of the transformation from subsistence into a cash economy, the countries of the Middle East continued to combine "economic development" with "economic backwardness," to use Myint's illuminating distinction.[22] That is to say, the natural resources of the region were opened up essentially by foreign enterprise and capital; the function of the local population remained basically unchanged, except for the part played by certain minority groups (see Part II, chap. 13). To quote Myint: "In spite of the striking specialization of the inanimate productive equipment and of the individuals from the economically advanced groups of people who manage and control them, there is really very little specialization, beyond a natural adaptability to the tropical climate, among the backward peoples in their roles as unskilled labourers or peasant producers." This condition prevailed in the Middle East during most of the nineteenth century, and there were very few signs at the beginning of the present century to indicate that a radical change would occur in the relations between the indigenous and foreign groups, and between the rather inert majority and the more differentiated and economically active minorities.

Yet in fact the main economic trend prevailing during the period covered in this study—the development by foreign capital and enterprise of an economy oriented primarily toward the world market—had in the more advanced countries reached its climax by the First World War. In the Middle East, as elsewhere, that war marks a turning point. On the one hand, the rapid growth in international trade characterizing the nineteenth century slowed down drastically, the price of raw materials fell sharply, and for most countries of the region the volume of foreign trade in the 1930's was no larger than in 1913. On the other hand, the achievement of political and fiscal independence by most of the Middle Eastern governments enabled them to initiate new economic policies. Generally speaking, three objectives were pursued: the subjection of economic and social activities to greater government control; diminution of the foreign hegemony; and the development of manufacturing and other neglected sectors of the economy. The Second World War saw an acceleration of these trends. And in the postwar period two new developments blended with and further hastened these economic

[21] The expansion of agricultural production and exports in the Middle East seems to have conformed to the pattern noted by Myint in tropical Asia and other underdeveloped regions. His contention is that when these regions were drawn into the network of international trade they started with a surplus productive capacity in the form of unused land and partly unemployed labor. The provision by Europeans of mechanical transport and modern economic organization made it possible to utilize this surplus capacity and, for several decades, greatly to increase output and exports. Expansion, however, was not accompanied by any great increase in physical productivity per worker, and therefore when the initial surplus had been fully utilized, the increase in output and exports slowed down drastically.

This process may be clearly discerned in Egypt, but in Syria, Iraq, and the Sudan it started considerably later and is therefore much less advanced. See Hla Myint, "The Classical Theory of International Trade and the Underdeveloped Countries," *Economic Journal* (London), June, 1958.

[22] Hla Myint, "An Interpretation of Economic Backwardness," *Oxford Economic Papers*, June, 1954.

and social changes: the phenomenal growth of the oil industry and the income it produced and the inflow of huge amounts of foreign aid from the United States, the Soviet Union, the United Kingdom, West Germany and others (see Epilogue). This set the economy of the Middle Eastern countries on a new path, the end of which is not yet in sight.

PART II

Ottoman Empire

OTTOMAN EMPIRE
Introduction

At the beginning of the period under review the northern borders of the Ottoman Empire stretched from the Save to the Dniester, and the sultan claimed suzerainty over the whole of North Africa except for Morocco. By 1914 all the African possessions were under foreign control and almost all the European provinces had achieved independence; during the First World War, Arab Asia also shook off Ottoman rule. As population was growing in most parts of the empire, the decline in the number of inhabitants was much smaller than the loss of territory; the total fell from perhaps thirty million in 1800 to about twenty million in 1914.[1]

This shrinking was accompanied by a decline in the relative economic as well as political importance of the Empire. Thus the share of the Levant in total French foreign trade, which had been about 50 per cent in the seventeenth century, had fallen to about 6 per cent in 1789 and 4 per cent in 1846. Nevertheless, the large absolute increase in the foreign trade of the Ottoman Empire (see Part II, chap. 2) meant that it still retained considerable importance. In 1876 it was the tenth largest trader in the world,[2] and about the same time it was Britain's fifth or sixth most important customer.

[1] No reliable figures are available before the census of 1927, which put the total at 13,648,000. The 1831 census put the number of adult males in Rumelia at 1,370,000 and in Anatolia at 2,384,000, giving total populations of about 6.2 million and 10.7 million, respectively (Karal, *Osmanli imparatorlugunda ilk nufus sayimi, 1831,* p. 215). In 1833, David Urquhart (*Turkey,* p. 270) put the population of European Turkey at 12,150,000 inhabitants. An estimate by some missionaries, in 1841, for European Turkey was 7 million (Bailey, *British Policy and the Turkish Reform Movement,* p. 7). John MacGregor (*Commercial Statistics,* IV, 7) put the population of European Turkey in the 1840's at 7.1 million (plus 1.8 million for Serbia, Moldavia, and Wallachia), that of Asia Minor and Syria at 10.5 million, and that of Arabia at 12 million. A. Ubicini (*Letters on Turkey,* I, 18–25), apparently using the 1844 census, put the total at 35.3 million, of whom 12.8 million were Turks, 6.2 million Slavs, 4.7 million Arabs, and 4.0 million Rumanians; a figure of 40 million was quoted for 1867, also based on government statistics; each of these estimates presumably covers all countries acknowledging the suzerainty of the sultan. But for the years immediately preceding the First World War estimates are much lower, and probably more accurate. Thus A. Philippson (*Das türkische Reich,* p. 101) gives a total of 21.2 million, of whom 1.9 million were in European Turkey, 10.6 in Anatolia, 2.4 million in Armenia, 5.3 million in Syria and Mesopotamia, and 1 million in Arabia. An estimate of 20,973,000, broken down by provinces, was given in the *Statesman's Yearbook, 1921* (reproduced in Mears [ed.], *Modern Turkey,* pp. 580–81).

[2] Gordon, *American Relations with Turkey, 1830–1930,* p. 52.

The growth in foreign trade was greatly facilitated by the changes brought about by the Anglo-Turkish Commercial Convention of 1838 (see Part II, chap. 3). The abolition of prohibitions on exports, and gradually of duties, stimulated exports of agricultural and mineral raw materials. The reduction of import duties opened the way for a flood of machine-made consumer goods, especially when transport began to improve. Naturally, these imports dealt a severe blow to local handicrafts, many of which were wiped out in the following decades (see Part II, chap. 4). Attempts to arrest this decline and to promote the establishment of modern industries were half-hearted and ineffective (see Part II, chap. 5). In the first place, "Even among the second generation of Tanzimat men we cannot find a single one who really had a clear understanding of economic issues or a sincere interest in them."[3] It is true that in 1859 Mehmet Şerif, who taught political economy at Istanbul, advocated industrialization; similarly Namik Kemal, the essayist and journalist, wanted his country to industrialize but, since it lacked capital and technical knowledge, urged it to concentrate on agriculture and use European techniques.[4] However, these were rare exceptions, and the dominant Ottoman attitude toward economic life continued to be that it was an inferior activity, best left to the subject races (see Part II, chap. 13). But even had it wanted to, the Ottoman government could hardly have extended much help, given its administrative and technical weakness on the one hand and the very severe limitations put on it by the Capitulations and other international treaties and conventions on the other. Lastly, the intense international rivalries, which led each European government to oppose schemes proposed by nationals of another country, further hampered development. The industrial backwardness of Turkey may be judged from official figures relating to 1913–15; although these are incomplete, covering only Constantinople and the main centers of western Anatolia, they give a fairly accurate idea of the limited extent of industrialization, since manufacturing was in fact concentrated in that area. They enumerate 269 enterprises with 16,975 workers; the largest industry was textiles, with 75 enterprises and 7,765 workers, followed by food processing, with 76 and 4,281, respectively.[5] The value of industrial production on the eve of the First World War was £T6,500,000.[6]

Mining, which produced mainly for export, was somewhat more developed. In 1913 the value of the mineral output of Anatolia was £T2,040,000, or $9 million.[7] The most important product was coal, extracted mainly from the Eregli basin by a French company founded in 1896; in 1912–13 output averaged 840,000 tons. Other minerals produced in appreciable quantities, usually by foreign firms, included lead (14,000 tons), emery (40,000 tons), borax (18,000 tons),

3 Ward and Rustow, *Political Modernization in Japan and Turkey*, p. 153.
4 Aktan, "Agricultural Policy of Turkey," p. 62.
5 See details in Novichev, *Ocherki ekonomiki Turtsii*, pp. 109, 272–73.
6 Hershlag, *Introduction to the Modern Economic History of the Middle East*, p. 72.
7 Mears, p. 313.

and chrome (25,000 tons).[8] The vast petroleum resources of the Empire were just beginning to attract attention in the prewar years (see Part III, chap. 9).

While manufacturing declined, agriculture began slowly to revive. One of the most important causes was the improvement in security, following the re-establishment by the central government of its authority over various provinces (see Part II, chap. 1). Another favorable factor was the gradual change in land tenure. The attempt to replace the existing system by one which simultaneously asserted the rights of the government and gave greater scope to individual property and initiative proved to be disastrous in the Arab provinces, where it ran counter to both the exigencies of the natural environment and the prevailing social structure (see Part II, chaps. 8 and 9). But in the Balkans and Anatolia, where rainfall was more abundant and European property relations were more appropriate, the reforms met with greater success. Although the landed aristocracy, the *a'yan*, managed to keep sizable estates, even after the formal abolition of the *timar* in 1831, and continued to play an important part in local and national politics down to the present, the bulk of the land seems to have passed into the hands of the peasants: "Small holdings take in seventy-five per cent of all cleared land in Asia Minor."[9] Peasants also benefited from such measures as the abolition of forced labor and the scaling-down of debts by Reşid pasha in the late 1840's.[10] Repeated attempts to abolish tax-farming and to improve the efficiency and equity of taxation were unsuccessful, and the burden borne by the peasants continued to be very heavy until the establishment of the Republic (see Part II, chaps. 9 and 12), but some of the worst abuses seem to have been curbed.

The main stimulus to Turkish agriculture, however, was foreign demand for various products, which rose sporadically until the First World War. The American Civil War led to a sharp increase in the output of Turkish tobacco, which soon became the country's leading export item (see Part II, chap. 6). Cotton cultivation, which had been declining, also received a temporary stimulus in the 1860's, but then resumed its downward trend until the end of the century, when it began to expand rapidly (see Part II, chap. 7); from 2,000 bales in 1896, output rose to 135,000 in 1914.[11] Production and export of grains also increased appreciably, as did those of raisins, figs, and other cash crops.

Both the penetration of foreign manufactures into the Turkish market and the export of Turkish agricultural and mineral produce were facilitated by the spread of railways. The first Turkish railways, the Smyrna-Aydin line (begun in 1856) and the Smyrna-Kasaba line (begun in 1863), served the rich hinterland of Anatolia's leading port (see Part II, chap. 10). Shortly afterward, railways began to be laid down in European Turkey, and by 1888 a connection had been established between Constantinople and Western Europe. This pointed up still more

[8] *Ibid.*, p. 325, and Novichev, p. 105.
[9] Mears, pp. 295–96.
[10] Ward and Rustow, p. 59.
[11] *Istatistik Yilligi*, 1931.

clearly the absence of railways serving the interior of Anatolia and, a government attempt to supply the lack having been given up in 1873 after the construction of only 93 kilometers, in 1888 a concession was given to a German firm. Construction started immediately and by 1899 over 1,000 kilometers had been opened to traffic.[12] But attempts to extend the Anatolian railways eastward and to build the Berlin-Baghdad line ran into great diplomatic obstacles, which were not overcome until 1914.[13]

By 1913 Turkey had 480 kilometers of railways in its much reduced European part and 5,433 in Asia.[14] Of the latter, 1,465 constituted the Hijaz Railway, 789 kilometers were in Syria, and the rest were in Anatolia or belonged to the Syrian part of the Berlin-Baghdad line: practically all the latter group was of standard gauge.[15] Except for the Hijaz Railway, the cost of which ran to about ninety-five million francs, all the lines were built by private capital, with government subventions. In the earlier concessions these consisted of kilometric guarantees: the government undertook to guarantee to the company a minimum annual revenue—usually 10,000 to 15,000 francs—per kilometer of line open to traffic, and was to take a share—usually 25-50 per cent—of any excess revenue.[16] The concession for the Berlin–Baghdad line, in 1903, provided for a kilometric guarantee of only 4,500 francs, but in addition the government agreed to issue to the company 275,000 francs of Ottoman 4 per cent bonds per kilometer; this represented an additional revenue of 11,000 francs; moreover the company was given broad fiscal exemptions and the right to exploit the natural resources adjacent to the line.[17] The revenues of certain provinces were assigned for the payment of these subsidies.

The capital raised by the railway companies of Turkey in Asia amounted to 840 million francs; construction costs were somewhat lower.[18] Of the total, 46.3 per cent belonged to German interests, 38 per cent to French, and 15.6 to British; these figures closely correspond to each country's share of railway mileage.[19]

The kilometric guarantees granted to the earlier lines had proved burdensome to the state; however, the German-controlled Anatolian and Baghdad railways, which were very efficiently constructed and run, not only greatly stimulated the economic development of the adjacent regions (see Part II, chap. 7) and doubled the yields of the tithes between 1889 and 1908, but also brought in an appreciable amount of revenue to the government.[20] The change was symptomatic

---

12 Pressel, *Les chemins de fer de Turquie*, p. 56.
13 See Earle, *Turkey, the Great Powers, and the Baghdad Railway*, and Part III, chap. 2, Part IV, chap. 4, below.
14 There were also 6,500 kilometers of road, almost all in very poor condition (Hershlag, p. 74).
15 Hecker, "Die Eisenbahnen in der asiatischen Türkei," *Archiv für Eisenbahnwesen*, XXXVII (1914), 754-57.
16 For details, see *ibid.*, p. 1087.
17 See Earle, pp. 77-80, and Part II, chap. 11, below.
18 See Hecker, pp. 1087-1310. The nominal capital of the European railways was £T2,000,000 (Mears, p. 367).
19 Hecker, p. 1084.
20 Earle, pp. 232-34.

of the altered conditions in Turkey and of the beginnings of greater awareness and purpose shown by both the government and foreign investors. In the earlier period the vast amounts borrowed abroad had been almost entirely squandered (see Part II, chap. 11). After 1881, however, the Public Debts Administration exercised vigilant control and made sure that loans were used for productive purposes, but it could not prevent the huge expenditures on the Balkan and Italian wars. Moreover foreign capital began to flow into various sectors of the economy: mining, port improvement, banking,[21] electricity, telephones, and other municipal utilities.[22] Particularly noteworthy was the Konya irrigation scheme, implemented in 1913 at a cost of 19.5 million francs by the Anatolian Railway Company in partnership with the government;[23] in 1911 a similar scheme was started in Cilicia,[24] and the Hindiyya dam was built in Iraq in 1913 (see Part III, chap. 8). Among the first signs of interest in economic affairs taken by Muslim Turks was the foundation of two small shipping lines, one of which proved unprofitable and was taken over by the government and later turned over to a British firm.[25] Another was the establishment of the Commercial Islamic Bank of Adapazar, in 1914.

The government also began to promote economic development in other ways: by changing the tariff to secure more revenue and greater protection for Ottoman industries (see Part II, chap. 3); by granting, in 1913, various exemptions and privileges to newly founded industries;[26] by greater expenditure on education,[27] roads, and other economically productive activities (see Part II, chap. 12); by founding the Agricultural Bank in 1888; by certain important reforms in the land tenure system, extending to *miri* land almost all the privileges enjoyed by owners of *mulk*, in matters of mortgage, inheritance, and land use (see Part II, chap. 9); by setting up commissions to survey the land, register titles, and base tax assessments on more accurate and equitable land valuations; and by improving budgetary procedures and structures (see Part III, chap. 7). Earlier in the 1870's the codification of law had somewhat facilitated transactions.[28]

The First World War and the subsequent War of Independence inflicted enormous hardships on the Turkish people but also speeded up the process of economic change and Turkification (see Part II, chap. 13). The work of reform

[21] Until 1914 banking in Turkey was carried on exclusively by foreigners, or minority groups such as the Galata bankers who began to achieve prominence at the beginning of the eighteenth century. In 1856 the Ottoman Bank, renamed Imperial Ottoman Bank in 1863, was founded by British and French interests and continued to function as a state bank until the Republic. In 1871 the Crédit Lyonnais opened branches in Turkey, as did several German (notably the Deutsche Bank), British, French, and other banks during the next decades, particularly after 1900.

[22] See Mears, chap. xvi.
[23] *Ibid.*, p. 275.
[24] Earle, p. 117.
[25] Verney and Dambmann, *Les Puissances étrangères dans le Levant, en Syrie et en Palestine*, p. 619; Novichev, pp. 168–70.
[26] Novichev, p. 112.
[27] See Ward and Rustow, pp. 213–16, and Davison, *Reform in the Ottoman Empire*, pp. 246–50.
[28] Davison, pp. 252–56.

was taken up again, and pursued with greater energy, under the Republic. In the interwar period basic social reforms were carried out: the westernization of the legal system, the Latinization of the alphabet, the emancipation of women, and the spread of education, which raised the literacy rate from about 10 per cent in the early 1920's to 20 per cent in the late 1930's and about 40 per cent in the mid-1950's. The hard-pressed peasants were given a long respite from war as well as tax relief (see Part II, chap. 12) and more direct assistance and price supports. The foreign-owned railways were bought out by the state, which doubled the mileage; other foreign concessions were also taken over. Vigorous attempts were made to industrialize the country, and the government-owned Sumer and Eti banks founded and managed several new enterprises in manufacturing and mining. It is estimated that, thanks mainly to the increase in agricultural output, per capita income rose by over 50 per cent between the mid-1920's and 1938.

The Second World War caused some disruption in Turkey's economy, owing to the need for keeping some 500,000 men under arms. In the postwar period, however, helped by large-scale financial and technical assistance from the United States, the country has made considerable progress in the economic and social fields.

CHAPTER I

The Political and Social Background in the Eighteenth Century

At its height, in the fifteenth and early sixteenth centuries, the Ottoman Empire was probably the best-governed state the world had seen since the decline of Rome. A clear picture of the high administrative and fiscal standards achieved and of the control exercised by the central government over both its officials and the "feudal" (*timar*) lords is given by the many registers (*defter*) that have survived.

The political changes of the sixteenth through the eighteenth centuries outlined in the following selection were accompanied, and to a large extent caused, by more far-reaching economic, social, and military transformations: the halting of the Ottoman advance in Europe and the consequent cessation of the acquisition of new territories and spoils of war; the diversion of trade caused by the circumnavigation of Africa; the inflationary effects of the influx of precious metals from America; the intellectual sclerosis and religious conservatism which prevented not only innovation but even the adoption of such western inventions as the printing press; and the consequent decline in agriculture, industry, and trade.

No progress could be expected until the authority of the central government had been re-established. In the central parts of the Ottoman Empire this was achieved by Mahmud II (reigned 1808–39), in Egypt by Muhammad Ali (1805–49), in Iraq following the reconquest of the country by Ottoman troops in 1831, and in Syria after the withdrawal of the Egyptian troops in 1841 (see Part IV, chap. 5). In the Sudan, order was introduced by Muhammad Ali after 1820, but the system he established collapsed during the Mahdist revolt and a new beginning had to be made after the Anglo-Egyptian reconquest of 1896. As for the Arabian peninsula, the opening of the Suez Canal in 1869 enabled the Ottoman Empire to increase its authority in that region, but, in spite of prolonged fighting, the Porte did not succeed in imposing its rule on Yemen; it was not until after the First World War that Ibn Saud (reigned 1901–53) subdued and unified most of the Arabian peninsula and only now is Yemen beginning to establish a government of the modern type.

With the imposition of central control came an opening-up to foreign economic and social influences and an attempt by such westernizers as Muhammad Ali, Mahmud II, and Midhat pasha (governor of Iraq in 1869–72) to modernize the army, the administration, and certain segments of education and the economy. One consequence of this transformation, as noted in this selection, was greatly to increase the power and influence of certain non-Muslim groups, who showed greater acceptance of western ideas and methods.

(See also Part II, chap. 13, and Epilogue; and works by Gibb and Bowen, Lewis, Karal, Rafi'i ['Asr Isma'il], and Longrigg [Four Centuries], listed in the Bibliography.)

[From A. H. Hourani, "The Fertile Crescent in the Eighteenth Century," Studia Islamica (Paris), No. 8, 1957, pp. 91–118; reproduced by kind permission of the author and the editor.]

. . . By the beginning of the eighteenth century, Asia Minor, the Balkans, the Arab countries of the Fertile Crescent, Egypt and the North African coast had been part of the Ottoman Empire for three hundred years. Regions so distant from one another, and peoples so varied in beliefs and ways of life, could not have been held together in political unity by anything less than a tour de force. The institutions of the great Ottoman age—the Sultanate, the slave-household, the Janissaries, the "feudal" cavalry, the religious hierarchy—have been often described, and aroused, at their height, the wonder of those who saw them; so much so indeed that here too we are in danger of a false historical perspective. We tend to think of the Empire of Suleiman the Magnificent as the "true" Empire, and judge all that came before and after in terms of it. Seen in this light, what came after was sheer decline; and in saying this, we are indeed only reflecting what the Ottomans themselves believed, or at least what they were in the habit of saying. From Khoja Bey onwards, it was the custom for Ottoman writers to put their proposals for reform in the shape of exhortations to return to the great days of Sultan Suleiman. But like any institution which lasts for five hundred years, the Empire changed radically in course of time, although the degree of change was sometimes obscured by the liking which Ottomans shared with Englishmen for formal continuity. We can indeed

—without imposing on the history of the Empire a greater degree of artificial order than is involved in our thinking about it at all—distinguish clearly several phases in Ottoman history. The Turkish frontier-state of the first phase was succeeded by the universal Sultanate ruled by slaves, and this in its turn virtually disappeared in the troubles of the seventeenth century. The whole machinery of government depended, in the last resort, on the political skill and virtue of the Sultan; and when the long line of splendid princes, whose eyes stare at us with confidence and unchallenged authority from the portraits in the Old Serai, began to weaken, the motive-force of the machine was diminished. There began a long struggle for power, to fill the vacuum at the heart of the Empire. Different groups in the Palace and different groups among the slave-officials, interlocked with each other in elaborate embrace, competed for control of the Sultan, with the doctors of law (Ulema) and the slave-corps in the Army playing a certain role as instruments or supports. This "age of the women" ended with the Ottoman Government recovering some of its strength, towards the end of the seventeenth century and the beginning of the eighteenth. But although the Empire emerged from the crisis, it did so in a new form, and with its foundations permanently weakened. In so far as a single hand now controlled the Government, it was not that of the Sultan but that of the Grand Vizir, who had behind him the élite of the palace-schools, the solid and loyal group which held the Empire together. From the eldest Koprulu onwards, a succession (although by no means an unbroken one) of strong and vigorous Vizirs gave impetus to the Government; the Vizir's household became the central organ of control, and his own officials—his *Kehya* or chief lieutenant, his *Reis ul-Kuttab* or chief clerk—came to be ranked among the greatest of Imperial officials. This change was significant of a shift in the whole structure of political power. The permanent officials in the bureaus of the government, the "men of the pen," came to play a decisive part in the Empire, and they were now drawn from a different class. Although the fiction was preserved that they were slaves of the Sultan, in fact the old system of recruiting slaves into the ruling group had virtually died out. Black slaves from East Africa, and white slaves from the Caucasus in smaller numbers, were still recruited for the service of the Palace, but the major sources of recruitment—the periodical levy of Christian boys for the Turkish army (*devshirme*) and the renegades—had more or less dried up, and officials of the government, whether trained in the palace-schools, or in the religious schools (*madaris*) were for the most part free-born Moslems, drawn from the Turkish population of Asia Minor and the Balkans, or at least absorbed into the community of Ottoman Turkish culture.

Thus a new centre of authority and a new ruling group appeared, and gave to the Empire a direction and a strength which, in the chaos of the seventeenth century, it seemed to have lost. But this revival came too late to restore to the Government that control over the whole Empire which it had possessed in an earlier age. The power of the Vizir could never be wholly a substitute for that of the Sultan, because its basis was different. His tenure of office was uncertain. He was appointed and dismissed by the Sultan; he could therefore be made and broken by the caprice of the Sultan, and those who had his ear—his mother, his concubines, or the Kizlar Agha, chief of the Black Eunuchs and the sole intermediary between the Sultan and his Government. Moreover, during the long crisis of the seventeenth century the control of the central Government over the provinces of

the Empire had largely disappeared. This control had depended on three factors: an administration more precise and honest than any other of its age, ruling on the basis of full and accurate statistical knowledge and in accordance with regulations which took account of the rights of each community and the ancient customs of each region; the slave-army, loyal to the Sultan and the Empire, strictly disciplined and maintaining firm and impartial order; and the "feudal" cavalry, having the right to collect the land-tax, being virtual landowners of their districts, and serving also as the network throughout which the Government controlled the countryside. By the eighteenth century all three had lost their efficacy. Officials were no longer honest, the Janissaries were no longer disciplined, or soldiers, or slaves; they were more dangerous to the Sultan than to his enemies, and more a threat to public order than the force which maintained it. The feudal cavalry too had lost their military importance, and as feudal tenures fell in they were replaced by a new sort of tenure, the tax-farms which were given for life and finally made hereditary, and which created a new class of virtual landowners, whose exactions and whose very existence increased the distance between Government and people.[1]

Since the central Government could no longer control the Empire, it could no longer serve as the focus of loyalty and solidarity. Thus we can observe in the course of the eighteenth century a strengthening of the communal loyalties which had always formed the basis of Ottoman society, and a regrouping of the peoples of the Empire around those authorities which could give them what the Imperial Government no longer gave: a defence against disorder and a system of law regulating the relations of man and man.

In the steppe and the countryside, the Beduin challenge reasserted itself, and society regrouped itself around new tribal

[1] For the changes in the Ottoman system of government, see H. A. R. Gibb and H. Bowen, *Islamic Society and the West*, vol. I, part I (London, 1950), chaps. i–iii.

authorities. In the Syrian Desert, the spread of the Shammar and Anaza tribes from central Arabia into Syria and Iraq destroyed the power of the Mawali, who had been the strongest tribe of the early Ottoman centuries, and had lived in relative harmony with the Imperial Government. It destroyed also the trade-routes across the desert, which the control of the Mawali prince, and his good relations with the Government, had kept open. Even large caravans were plundered; in 1700, 1703, and 1757 the Beni Sakhr plundered the pilgrims' caravan from Damascus to Medina; in 1774 the Anaza plundered that from Damascus to Baghdad. What was more important still, in regions of settled life—near the coasts, the great rivers and the great cities—the tribes established their predominance. In some places this meant that settled life ceased—in the Tigris for example north of Baghdad, and on the Euphrates north of Hilla—; even where it continued, it did so under the protection of the more peaceable and sedentary Beduin chiefs, not under that of the Government. The annals of the countryside are scanty, but we hear of Ibn Habib protecting trade and agriculture in the Egyptian Delta; and of the Muntafiq dominating vast regions of southern Iraq. In the Muntafiq districts, sedentary tribesmen cultivated dates on the banks of the Euphrates, and merchants met in the little tribal centre of Suq al-Shuyukh, under the protection of the princes of the family of Shabib. The ruling family maintained its own customs-houses on the rivers, to levy tolls on boats passing from Basra to Hilla and Baghdad; and after the Persian occupation of Basra (1775–79), when it had shown itself to be the only force on which the Government could rely, it dominated the port, and even occupied it for a time (1785–87). A Christian merchant of Basra records that "respect and fear were given to the chiefs of the Arabs, and as for the Ottoman, nobody goes in awe of him."[2] In northern Palestine, again, a sheikh of Beduin origin, Dhahir al-'Umar, built up a little kingdom,

where the Beduin at first gave him power, but he used it to protect the peasants and encourage French merchants to move from Saida to his new capital at Acre.[3]

It was only in the hills and near the great garrison-towns that peasant life could hold out against the Beduin. In the hills, there was a strengthening of the power and autonomy of the local chieftains. In Jebel Druze on the edge of the Syrian Desert, Druzes from Lebanon were settling and building up their independent societies under the Hamdans and other leading families; and here, by exception, it was the Druze peasants who dominated the Beduin, not the Beduin who extorted tribute from the peasants. In Mount Lebanon, the Shihabi princes strengthened that control over the whole mountain, north and south, which they had inherited from Fakhr al-Din; but there already existed, beneath the surface of unity and freedom, the tendencies which were to lead, in the nineteenth century, to the break-up of the unity of the mountain—the spread of the Maronite peasantry southwards, the increase in the power of their hierarchy, the gradual transfer of Shihabi favour from Druzes to Maronites, and the growth in influence of the great Druze families, Jumblatt and Bellama, through the extension of their control over the fertile lands of the Biqa. In Kurdistan, the old ruling families were giving place to a new, more powerful house, that of Baban, and the Kurdish sheepbreeders of the Milli group, gathered in a new unity around a new chieftain family at the end of the eighteenth century, spread southwards from the foothills of Asia Minor towards the eastern bank of the Tigris.

It was in the towns that the grouping of the population around local centres of loyalty and defence was carried furthest, for it was here that the weight of Ottoman exactions and the effects of Ottoman decay were most fully felt. In the towns too, the closeness of man to man, and the relative freedom of individual choice in a society too

[2] Ya'qub Sarkis, *Mabahith 'Iraqiyya*, vol. I (Baghdad, 1948), p. 21.

[3] For the life of Dhahir al-'Umar, see Mikhail Sabbagh, *Tarikh al-shaikh Dhahir al-'Umar al-Zaidani*, ed. Qustantin Basha (Harissa, n.d.).

complex to be wholly governed by custom, made possible the development of voluntary organizations. Already before the Ottoman conquest, such groupings had given to the Moslem city a complex unity: the craft-guilds, the associations not so much of the ordinary citizens as of the productive middle-class, the skilled merchants and craftsmen who formed the basis of urban economic life; the Christian and Jewish communities, living in accordance with their own religious law and custom under the authority of their own spiritual heads; the quarter, the association of those living in the same part of the city, and whose link of propinquity was often backed by that of common belief or common origin; the *turuq*, brotherhoods of mystics following the path towards union with God taught by a master of the spiritual life, which served as a link between different classes and races in the Moslem community. Now, as the Ottoman order decayed, the old forms of organization acquired a more specifically "political" purpose, of defence against the Ottoman authorities, and new ones with the same purpose arose by their side. The quarter was a real community, with its maze of narrow streets, its whole life turned inwards, its heavy doors barred at night, its headman and watchman. The religious hierarchy, too, acquired a new importance, as leader and spokesman of "public opinion" against the Ottoman Governor and the civil officials. The judge or Qadi, the head of the religious organiza-tion in each city, was appointed from Istanbul, and normally held office for a year only; but most of the other religious officials —the *Naibs* or deputy judges, the *Naqib* or head of the *Sharifs*, the *Muftis* of the different religious schools—tended to be drawn from local families with a tradition of learning or social influence. Their political position was strong, not only because of public respect for them but also because of their essential part in the life of the Empire, as upholders of the *shari'a*, as members of the councils of the Vizir and the local governors, and as belonging to a corps which was spread throughout the Empire, and whose influence

reached to the ear of the Sultan. They could at times control and even depose the governor, either by action inside the city, or by petition sent to the Imperial authorities. Even the Qadi would at times use his influence to rescue the local population from an unloved Pasha.

The *Ulema* were drawn mainly from families of local standing. It was indeed the practice for such families to send their sons into the corps of *Ulema*, not only for the social influence it gave, but also because it provided some guarantee against the con-fiscation of property; Muradi tells us, for example, of a family who were soldiers to begin with but turned into a family of *Ulema*. Although the *Ulema* spoke in general for local interests, they tended to speak more specifically for the more prosperous and influential classes. In northern Syria those classes—for reasons which are obscure —also found a defence in the organization of the *Sharifs* or *Ashraf*, the privileged corps of those who claimed descent from the prophet. This was the only recognized hereditary aristocracy, and its privileges, and the respect in which it was held, were inducements to those who had property or position to protect to secure admission to it even by false pretences. In Cairo, a *Naqib* was accused of entering the names of Copts in the register of *Ashraf*;[4] and in Aleppo and the neighbouring towns the numbers were enormous by the end of the eighteenth century. As they grew they came to play an important political role, and indeed for a generation after 1770 they virtually con-trolled Aleppo and its government.[5]

Sharifs might be drawn from any social class, but they had a tendency to be drawn from families of some wealth, culture, and standing. Those from a lower stratum of society looked for protection to another organization. As the Janissaries declined as a military force, they became more important as a political body. When the soldiers

[4] 'Abdal-Rahman al-Jabarti, *'Ajaib al-athar* (Cairo, 1879), vol. IV, p. 194.
[5] For the role of the Sharifs and Janissaries in the politics of Aleppo, see H. L. Bodman, *Political Factions in Aleppo, 1760–1826* [Chapel Hill, N.C., 1963].

became craftsmen, it was a simple step for craftsmen to enrol themselves as soldiers. Thus not only in Istanbul but in the great provincial centres, there grew up bodies of Janissaries affiliated with the various regiments, giving military service (albeit of doubtful quality) when the Sultan was engaged in major wars, but otherwise serving no military purpose. They served two other purposes, however. They provided an essential aid and protection for the poorer section of the population, and particularly those whom the depopulation of the countryside was driving into the towns, and it was protection the more effective because of the legal privileges which the Janissaries enjoyed, and their connection with each other in all the cities of the Empire. They also provided ambitious popular leaders with an instrument by which they could establish their influence in town and government. Divided as they were into corps, the rivalry of leaders and quarters could easily lead to civil conflict; and in Damascus and perhaps elsewhere, there was conflict, too, between the locally enrolled "auxiliary" Janissaries (*Yerliyya*) and the full members of the Imperial corps, directly responsible to the central government and occupying the Citadel (*Kapikouli*).[6] Their conflicts often threatened public order and prosperity, and sometimes—as in Aleppo in the first years of the nineteenth century—they succeeded in dominating the government.

In the Near East, landownership is an urban phenomenon, not only in the obvious sense that the landowner usually lives in the town and not on his estate, but also in the sense that his claim on the land is usually created and made effective by urban processes. It was the urban government which created the landowning classes of "feudal" cavalry and tax-farmers; and there gradually developed another class with claims on the land in those districts under the protection of

the urban government and where the Beduin had not yet planted their authority. The peasants put themselves under the protection of city notables, who managed their business with the government and protected them as far as possible from its exactions; and in course of time the protectors became virtual landlords. The religious families were particularly well-placed to perform this function; they had a voice in the governor's council (*Diwan*), and the annual auction of tax-farms took place in the religious court and under the supervision of the religious judge who had to register the results. Thus the town gave to the countryside around it —but at a price—that protection which it could not give itself.[7] . . .

European trade with the Empire also underwent a change. The Venetians, Dutch, and Portuguese, who had played so large a part in earlier days, had now lost their importance, and although Italian remained the *lingua franca* of the Levant, and was not replaced by French until the middle of the nineteenth century, England and France by now had begun their two hundred years' career as representatives of the West in the Near East. The Red Sea and the Fertile Crescent offered them if not the safest, certainly the quickest routes between India and Europe; the old British and French communities in Syria, the newer ones in Mesopotamia, were to play an essential role in the conflicts of British and French Imperial power, above all in the transmission of news. As industrial and commercial powers, too, they were concerned with the local markets, and here also there was a change. The import of luxury goods—fine cloths of England and Provence and Bohemian glass—still continued, but something new was now added to it, a trade in the staples, no longer in the luxuries alone,

6 See Muhammad Khalil al-Muradi, *Silk al-durar*, vol. IV, p. 97; Mikhail Breik, *Tarikh al-Sham*, ed. Qustantin Basha (Harissa, 1930), pp. 9 ff.; Salah al-Din al-Munajjid, *Wulat Dimashq* (Damascus, 1949), p. 79.

7 Much insight into the interplay of social forces in the political life of the towns and the surrounding countryside, at a slightly later period, can be obtained from the register of the *majlis* set up by Ibrahim Pasha in Aleppo. The MS. is in the library of the American University of Beirut. Long extracts are printed in A. Rustum, *Al-usul al-'arabiyyah li-tarikh Suriya fi 'ahd Muhammad 'Ali Basha*, vols. III–IV (Beirut, 1934), pp. 76, 100, 107–226.

of life. "Colonial goods"—the sugar, coffee and indigo of the West Indies—gradually replaced local products in the Near Eastern market; by 1800 Syria was drinking West Indian coffee, not the Southern Arabian.[8] The time was not far distant when the machine-made cottons of Manchester would enter the market, replace other local products, and in the process bring about a profound change in social and economic power.

The growth of trade had a double influence on social development. Around the foreign colonies there gathered a Levantine bourgeoisie of brokers and employees, who had learned the technique of international trade and finance. In the late eighteenth century, when the European merchants began to desert the Levant—because of the insecurity of life, the wars of Persia and Turkey, the exactions of the Egyptian Mamlukes, the attractions of the Cape route, and the greater profits to be derived from investment in other parts of the world—it was these Levantine auxiliaries who largely took their place, and sometimes even took over the names and trading connections of the European houses, because of the lower rate of duty which European merchants paid. The rise of the ports of Livorno and Trieste to dispute the monopoly of Marseilles, where less favourable terms were given to foreign than to French shippers, gave them a chance to extend their connections and take an initiative. In the first half of the nineteenth century they were to install their own agents in the centres of manufacture, and found the Greek, Syrian, and Armenian communities in England. Moreover, the disturbances caused by the American War of Independence and the Revolutionary Wars gave Greek ships an opportunity to acquire the local sea-trade

of the eastern Mediterranean, and to indulge in discreet piracy as well.

It was to protect trade and merchants first of all that consuls were appointed, but they came to serve another purpose. For the Christian and Jewish population of the commercial cities the embassies and consulates fulfilled a function similar to that of *Ashraf* and Janissaries among the Moslems. Similarity of religion made it possible for the European Powers to put forward claims to protect those of the same religion as themselves, and the Capitulations gave some ground to these claims. The French Capitulations gave them the right to protect Latin priests and chapels, and Europeans of Latin Catholic faith, and from the middle of the seventeenth century they began to extend this right to Eastern Catholics, and to a lesser extent to Eastern Christians as a whole. The French government supported the missions which were building up and educating the Uniate communities, although some more than others; the Franciscans of Terra Santa looked more to Spain than to France. In the long struggle of Catholics and non-Catholics for possession of Churches and bishoprics, French influence was always on the side of the Catholics, as also it was when, pushed by the Orthodox, the Ottoman authorities persecuted the Catholics. It was the French Ambassador who arranged that the persecuting Armenian Patriarch, Avedik, should be kidnapped and smuggled over to France, where he spent the rest of his life in the Bastille, and may—or may not —have been the Man in the Iron Mask.[9] Such intervention was most effective when the relations of France with the Ottoman Government were best; when they were bad, her protégés might well be regarded as traitors....

[8] J. L. Burckhardt, *Travels in Arabia* (London, 1829), p. 17.

[9] A. Rabbath, *Documents Inédits*, vol. II (Paris, 1910), p. 548.

CHAPTER 2

Ottoman Trade with Europe, 1784

Until the massive flow of European capital into the Middle East began in the second half of the nineteenth century, foreign trade was the sole economic link between that region and the outside world. The establishment of friendly relations between the Ottoman Empire and France in the sixteenth century led to a rapid growth of trade between the two countries. Thereafter the volume of trade fluctuated sharply, being determined mainly by the political conditions and the degree of security prevailing in the Mediterranean, but the general trend was slightly upward. In 1783 the French Ministry of Marine put total European trade with the Ottoman Empire at 110 million livres, or £4.4 million, an estimate that tallies with the one given in the following selection and may, indeed, have been based on the same sources.

The French Revolutionary and Napoleonic Wars disrupted trade in the Mediterranean, and even by 1829 Ottoman trade with the United Kingdom and France—which between them accounted for the greater part of the total—amounted to only £2.6 million.

After that, however, progress was swift, the combined total for these two countries reaching £12.2 million in 1845. By 1876 total Ottoman foreign trade was estimated at $270 million, or £54 million, by the United States Department of Commerce and Labor.[1] It should be noted that this gain was registered in spite of considerable loss of territory in Europe, as well as the exclusion of Egypt, and that the price level in 1876 was not significantly different from what it had been in 1829. By 1911 total trade had risen to £T69.4 million, or £63.5 million, again in spite of further loss in territory and little change in price levels. From the middle of the century until 1914 imports greatly exceeded exports, the average deficit for 1880–1900 being about £T10,000,000 and for 1900–1914 £T20,000,000.

In the early sixteenth century most Ottoman trade was conducted with the

---

[1] The official Ottoman figures, which may considerably underestimate the total, put it at £T26,300,000 in 1880, £T35,800,000 in 1890, and £T38,500,000 in 1900 (Hershlag, *Introduction to the Modern Economic History of the Middle East*), p. 76.

Italian states, but France soon became the leading trade partner and, with brief interruptions, retained that position until the Revolutionary Wars. After Waterloo, Britain drew far ahead of its rivals, but by the 1890's it began to lose ground steadily to Germany; however, it retained its leading position until 1914. Between them, Britain, Germany, and France accounted for the bulk of Ottoman and Egyptian trade.

(See also works by Gibb and Bowen, Masson, Wood, Bailey, Gordon, Mears, Novichev, and Hershlag listed in the Bibliography.)

["Etat du commerce du Levant en 1784, d'après les régistres de la chambre de commerce de Marseille," in *Oeuvres de C. F. Volney* (Paris, 1825), III, 321-40.]

Generally speaking, trade is always difficult to ascertain and estimate because it is a variable thing, being sometimes greater and sometimes smaller according to the needs of a country, the state of its crops, its supplies, and its deficiencies, all of which are subject to the changing influence of the seasons, government, war, epidemics, and so on. This is particularly true of the Levant, because that region is the scene of continual revolutions. Another difficulty in the way of estimating the annual volume and composition [*objet*] of this trade is that the value of goods changes as they are moved from place to place. In this study, evaluation will be based on prices at Marseilles for both outgoing and incoming goods.

The term Levant trade covers transactions in the various ports of Turkey and a few towns in Barbary; to this has been added trade with the African countryside along the Barbary coast. The commercial ports of Turkey are Constantinople, Salonica, Smyrna, the ports of Morea [Peloponnesus], Candia [Crete], Cyprus, Syria and Egypt, and Tunis, Algiers, and the factories of the company [Compagnie d'Afrique] in La Calle, Bone, and Collo.

Our [French] exports consist of: woolen cloth, caps, cloths and braids, paper, haberdashery, hardware; some French agricultural produce; produce from America such as coffee, sugar, indigo, cochineal; spices from the Indies; French metals—iron, lead, and tin; French liquor; Spanish piastres, Venetian sequins, dahlers, and so on.

In return we import: cotton and woolen yarn, wool, silk, silk cloth, goat and camel hair, wax, hides, drugs, cotton and linen cloth, rice, oil, Arabian coffee, gums, copper, gallnuts, pulse [*légumes*], wheat, and so on. These materials supply our industries; thus cotton from the Levant is used by all the factories of what were formerly known as Picardy, Normandy, and Provence. These are used to make camlets, woolen cloth [*bourancans*], cotton cloth [*siamoises*], velvets, linen cloth, and caps. These factories provide a livelihood for a great number of workmen and merchants; the transport of these goods maintains and trains sailors for the navy; their purchase gives employment to a host of agents and factors in the Levant; and all this is at the expense of the Orientals. Let us examine each port in detail.

CONSTANTINOPLE

The competition of French woolen cloth has reduced British and Dutch trade in this port by more than half. The Venetians cannot make similar cloth at the same price.

Constantinople imports[1] 1,500 bales of woolen cloth a year which, at 1,200 francs a bale, amounts to 1,800,000 livres.[2] All other items together hardly reach that figure; the most important is coffee from the West Indies, in view of the prohibition of Mocha coffee on the Black Sea.

Formerly, the Armenian and Greek cloth merchants formed an association, through

[1] *Consommer* is translated throughout as import, where this is the obvious meaning.—Translator.

[2] The terms *livre* and *franc* are used interchangeably, to designate the same unit of currency.—Translator.

which they made all their purchases, thus imposing their terms on the French. The Grand Signor has destroyed this association by severe penalties.

French purchases are very small, hardly attaining 700,000 francs. The balance is made up either by purchases in Smyrna and the Archipelago or by bills of exchange drawn on Constantinople itself.

SMYRNA

This port is the main market for most of Asia [Minor]; it is the entrepôt for Anatolia, Karamania, Tokat, Erzurum, and even Persia. Formerly caravans from Persia came twice a year, but at present they stop at Erzurum because, this way, merchants manage to conceal the quantity of goods they have for sale and gain advantages in both selling and buying.

Smyrna imports 2,500 bales of woolen cloth a year which, on the basis of 1,200 francs a bale, amounts to 3,000,000 francs. This sum accounts for half the total trade, estimated at 6,000,000 francs a year. The other items are the same as those sold in Constantinople.

The main export is raw cotton. Annual output is 42,000–44,000 bales, of which 12,000–13,000 are sent to France, 5,000 to Italy, 8,000 to Holland, 3,000 to England, and the rest stays in the country. Wool and mohair are also produced, as well as other varieties [*laine de chevron*] which are bought almost entirely by foreigners. Exports, including orders from Constantinople, exceed imports by at least a third. The balance is used for purchases of oil in Metellin and wheat in Volo, the Gulf of Cassandra, Sanderli, Menemen, Mosrouissi, and so on, which are paid for in sequins or Turkish piastres. The balance is also used to settle bills of exchange as in Constantinople; bills are seldom drawn on any but those two cities. However, Smyrna is certainly the leading commercial center in the Levant.

SALONICA AND ITS DEPENDENCIES

This port, the outlet for all Macedonia, is daily gaining in importance because its merchandise is beginning to penetrate Albania, Dalmatia, Bosnia, Bulgaria, Wallachia, and Moldavia. Imports range between 1,000 and 1,200 bales of woolen cloth, and in the four peaceful years 1770 through 1773 were higher. Sales of other goods are correspondingly large. Formerly it exported gold bars; the bulk of exports consists of wool, cotton, wheat, leather, tobacco, silk, fine sponges, woolen mantles, vermillion seed, alum, wax, aniseed, and oil.

Kavalla, twelve leagues away from Salonica, is an entrepôt through which most of these goods first pass. Sales take place during the fairs, which are held in various locations: there is one in Selminia, twelve days by camel from Salonica, in May [O.S.]; another at Ouzourkova in September; and one at Deglia, two days' journey from Salonica, in October. At these times the Armenians, who are the traders of this region, make their purchases and sales in peacetime. Total imports of this port and of Kavalla amount to 3,000,000 francs and exports to 3,500,000; the balance is sometimes paid for in bills of exchange.

MOREA AND ITS DEPENDENCIES

The trade of this region is constantly decreasing, because the troubles of the last few years and the daily depredations of the Albanians have been destroying its crops and reducing its import capacity. The main commercial ports are Tripoli, Naples of Romania [Nauplia?], Coron, Modon, Patras, Oustiche [Vastitza?], and Corinth. Imports consist of coarse cloth, caps, a little cochineal, indigo, coffee, and especially Venetian sequins. Oil and wheat are bought there at low prices. Exports [to Morea] do not exceed 400,000 francs, while imports are above 1,000,000 francs.

CANEA AND ITS DEPENDENCIES [CRETE]

Trade with this region is like that with Morea. Oil and a little wax are the only produce of Candia, and are paid for in specie, either Turkish piastres or imperial dahlers. Few manufactured goods are exported [to Crete], the total value being below 400,000 francs, while imports exceed 700,000 francs.

SATALIA [ANTALYA] AND KARAMANIA

Satalia has not been able to support a regular trading establishment. Commerce is carried on by means of irregular voyages of ships from Smyrna or Cyprus, which load silk and cotton and pay for it in cash. The value of this trade is less than 100,000 francs.

CYPRUS

By ruining Cyprus, the pashas have destroyed its trade. This island is one of the *malikane*, or private life fiefs [tax farms granted for life], which are always oppressed. It serves as entrepôt or meeting place [*point de réunion*] for Syria and Egypt, and as such is important in wartime. Imports may be as high as 80 bales of woolen cloth. The main towns are Larnaca, Nicosia, and Famagusta. It has an industry which processes almost all the silk and cotton [grown on the island] but which is hampered by the daily *avania* [arbitrary fines] imposed on the workers. Exports [to Cyprus] are estimated at 300,000 francs and imports at 500,000.

ALEXANDRETTA AND ALEPPO

Aleppo is one of the trade centers for all neighboring countries, as far as Persia. Caravans from this kingdom come to Aleppo twice a year, bringing silk, muslins, wool, rhubarb, and drugs and taking back our cloth, cochineal, and indigo as well as West Indian coffee. Formerly, all Persian caravans came to this market, but the disturbances have diverted them to Erzurum.

In Aleppo, Diyarbakir, and the surrounding region there are many linen and cotton textile factories which use our dyes, such as indigo and cochineal; Aleppo also buys 1,000 bales of woolen cloth. Total exports to Aleppo amount to 2,500,000 francs and imports to 2,600,000; the balance is settled in Constantinople, by bills of exchange.

TRIPOLI OF SYRIA

Tripoli's trade consists almost entirely of raw silk, used for braids. Trade is highly variable; at times this town buys much and sells little, and at others the opposite is true; exports to it average 400,000 francs and imports 500,000; the Maronites and the [traders of the] Hama region make their purchases in Tripoli.

SAIDA, ACRE, AND THEIR DEPENDENCIES

The dependencies of Saida are Sur [Tyre] and the towns of Palestine such as Ramleh, Jerusalem, Lydda, and Majdal. This area is one of the most important, importing 800–900 bales of woolen cloth for which it pays in raw cotton and cotton yarn. Here the French face no competition. In Saida they have one or two agents who buy cotton yarn every Monday or Tuesday. They wished to do the same in Acre, but the pasha cornered all cotton stocks, forbade all sales, and became sole master of the market; since the merchants needed to buy goods in return for what they sold, he put a duty of 10 piastres on each quintal of cotton. Exports to Saida and Acre amount to 1,500,000 francs and imports to 1,800,000.

EGYPT

Alexandria is the only port in which there is a factory [*comptoir*]; Damietta has only agents, Rosetta is an entrepôt, and Cairo is the great consuming center.

Egypt imports a large amount of woolen cloth, cochineal, spices, iron, potters' lead, and liquor; much of the cloth and cochineal is re-exported to Jidda, as are Venetian sequins and dahlers. The French community, with its consul, left Cairo in 1777, but a few agents have remained at their own risk; 10,000 francs a year are given to them to pay the *avania* to which they are subjected. Damietta is a poor roadstead; from it rice is exported in contraband, being ostensibly sent to a port in Turkey;[3] ten to twelve ladings are sent to Europe each year. (The author of the memoir says nothing about Egypt's exports. They consist of Mocha coffee, rough cotton piecegoods used by

---

[3] The export of foodstuffs outside the Ottoman Empire was prohibited.—Translator.

Negroes in the West Indies, saffron, cassia, senna, and so on.[4]) Egypt's trade fluctuates considerably: average exports to it are estimated at 2,500,000 francs, and imports from it at 3,000,000.

BARBARY; TRIPOLI

The anarchic and vexatious government of Tripoli impedes the development of trade to the extent commensurate with the fertility of the country. The Arabs dominate and devastate the countryside. Caravans from Fezzan and Murzuk come to Tripoli twice a year, bringing with them male and female Negroes, gold dust, elephant tusks, and a few other items. The French have tried to establish business, but the dishonesty of the inhabitants, by cheating on their payment, has forced the abandonment of this project. Trade is conducted exclusively by caravan ships [i.e., coasting vessels] which carry rough woolen cloth, hardware, silk cloth, and liquor, for a total value of some 50,000 francs. In return they bring back wheat, barley, pulse, senna, dates, and barilla, for 70,000 francs.

TUNIS

The Tunisians, who were formerly corsairs, have in the last fifty years devoted themselves entirely to trade, thanks to the good policy of their beys, who have protected merchants and abolished all vexations.

This country produces in abundance wheat, pulse, oil, wax, wool, hides, and ashes. To it are exported the same goods as to the Levant, together with Spanish wool, vermillion, and so on. Tunis has a cap factory which formerly supplied the whole of Turkey, but our competitive merchandise has dealt it a blow.

French trade with this country amounts to 1,500,000 francs of sales and 1,600,000 of purchases. The agents complain that the indigenous people are encroaching on their business by dealing directly with Marseilles, which a fairly large number of Tunisians visit on our ships.

[4] Paragraph presumably added by Volney.—Translator.

CALLE, BONE, AND COLLO

The trade of these three factories (concessions given to the Africa Company) is exploited by a company established by an edict in February, 1741; its capital was fixed at 1,200,000 francs, divided into 1,200 shares of 1,000 francs each, of which the chamber of commerce of Marseilles took a quarter. This company replaced, in perpetuity, the one that had been set up in 1730 to trade in grain for ten years. Owing to retrocessions, relinquishments, and local transport by the India Company, the Africa Company pays to the *divan* (Council of the Dey) of Algiers, to the *divan*'s of Bone, and Collo, and to the Arabs living near La Calle, the dues agreed upon by another company and the *divan* of Algiers under a treaty of 1694. It maintains in its factories about three hundred persons —officers, soldiers, coral fishermen, and workers. The governor of La Calle is the inspector-general.

This trade is kept alive solely by sending Spanish piastres, which the company disposes of in standard units [*que la compagnie réduit à des pieds (poids?) determinés*]. With these it buys wheat, wool, wax, and hides. In order to withdraw these goods it has to engage in perpetual intrigues at the Regency of Algiers, which holds it to ransom and makes it buy authorizations—even for the provisioning of the factories which was agreed upon at 2,000 loads of wheat. An important article of purchase is coral, which comes from the neighboring sea; the company buys it from the masters of its boats at an agreed upon price per pound. This coral is used to buy Negro slaves in Guinea, and thus promotes agriculture in our sugar islands; shipments are also made to China and India. Attempts have been made to remove coral from the Sea of Bizerta; but, notwithstanding the concession given to us by the bey of Tunis, the Neapolitans and the Trapanians, who were there before us, have prevented us by force of arms.

The company's trade varies greatly, but may be put at an average of 800,000–900,000 francs of sales and 1,000,000 of purchases.

ALGIERS

Algiers' trade, which is considerably less than that of Tunis, nevertheless offers great possibilities in view of the richness of the soil. For some time the inhabitants have been showing signs of awakening industry, and many have come to trade in Marseilles. Formerly we had three establishments in Algiers, but, owing to competition from the Jews, two have had to close.

Exports to Algiers are of the same kind as those to the Levant; excluding the Spanish piastres sent there, the total value may be put at 100,000 francs. Imports are the same as from Tunis, and amount to 300,000 francs.

The foregoing account shows that annual French sales to the Levant amount to 23,150,000 francs; and annual French purchases from the Levant amount to 26,800,000 francs. The registers for 1776–82 show very different figures, but it should be noted that this period includes five years of war which, as always, resulted in sharp decreases.

The chamber of commerce has based its calculations on the value of exports of woolen cloth, since it almost equals that of all other goods combined. Annual exports have ranged from 7,000 to 8,000 bales. From 1762 to 1772—that is, in the ten years of peace—exports averaged 7,000 bales. Assuming a unit price of 1,200 francs, which is the average for all qualities, a sum of 9,600,000 francs per annum is obtained. Allowing an equal sum for other goods gives a total of 19,200,000 francs. But to this should be added some 3 or 4 million francs, to take account of smuggling and of undervaluation in customs declarations, thus reaching a total of 23 million.

The amount of trade may also be estimated on the basis of the number of factories; in the Levant they total 78, where Constantinople has 11, Smyrna 19, Salonica and Cavalla 8, Morea 5, Canea 2, Cyprus 2, Aleppo 7, Tripoli of Syria 3, Saida and Acre 10, Alexandria of Egypt 4, Tunis 6, and Algiers 1. Assuming that each, on the average, has a turnover of 100,000 écus, a total of a little over 23 million [francs] is obtained.

As for imports, one may be certain of their quantity, since they have to pass through quarantine where nothing escapes. The ten years 1762–72 have averaged 26 million [francs].

FOREIGN SPECIE TAKEN TO THE LEVANT

Mention has repeatedly been made of specie shipped to the Levant, such as Spanish piastres, Venetian sequins, and German dahlers. These vary greatly in quantity and value. Formerly an astonishingly large amount of Turkish sequins was brought into Marseilles. In 1773 and 1774, Marseilles being in the midst of a bankruptcy crisis, the merchants withdrew considerable sums in Turkish money, which was melted down; afterward European currency, to a value of nearly 4 million a year, was sent back. But since 1781 no more coins have been sent to the Levant, and coins have disappeared there, owing to the fact that they are melted down in Constantinople. The prohibitions in Spain regarding piastres, or rather the fact that they are melted down there, has led to their disappearance in Marseilles; then too, such shipments no longer pay, since the exchange would involve a loss. The Turks have debased their currency by almost one-fourth; the cost of goods has risen, so that prices are now 25 per cent more than in the past; the notables and the rich have hidden their gold. Nevertheless an estimate of our shipments of currency at about 1,000,000 [francs] would probably be fairly accurate.

BARS AND OBJECTS MADE OF GOLD

Trade in gold objects occurred only briefly. It was brought into being by the edict of Mustafa, who decried the sequins that had been debased by the Jews, and ordered them to be melted down. Since the rate offered by the mint was lower than that prevailing in France, our merchants offered a more advantageous one, which attracted much precious metal [*une quantité de matières*] without the government's prohibiting these transactions. The same cause led to the reappearance of much gold that had been buried in the ground—the difference between silver and gold was 5 to 6 per cent, in favor of the former [*de bénéfice*]. In addition, the war with Russia having spread misery in Greece, the Greeks melted down

Holland, and Germany, which proves that these countries import more goods [from the Levant] than they export; since the goods we send also do not cover the value of our imports, we have recourse to foreigners to make up the balance. One may therefore estimate total sales at 24,150,000 francs, and

RECAPITULATION OF THE EXPORTS OF MARSEILLES TO THE LEVANT AND BARBARY DURING THE YEAR 1784

Centers	Value of Merchandise (Livres)	Number of ships	Sailors
Constantinople	3,495,960	21	315
Salonica and Cavalla	1,938,425	38	530
Morea and dependencies	233,979	23	276
Candia and Canea	242,019	18	216
Smyrna	5,134,220	42	630
Alexandretta.	2,560,507	22	330
Syria	1,198,403	18	270
Alexandria	2,311,637	28	420
Barbary	1,356,847	39	312
Coasting	102,203	28	224
Total	18,574,200	277	3,523

This table has been drawn from the registers showing consular duties; the estimated values used for this purpose are 15 per cent below the real price of the merchandise; thus, the total shown in the table must be raised to 21,360,330 livres. To this should be added merchandise smuggled out, without the payment of duty, which can hardly be less than 3 million; assuming it is 2,639,670, the exact total would be 24,000,000 livres.

RECAPITULATION OF IMPORTS FROM THE LEVANT AND BARBARY TO MARSEILLES DURING THE YEAR 1784

Centers	Value of Merchandise (Livres)	Number of Ships	Sailors
Constantinople	682,043	17	255
Salonica and Cavalla	2,674,818	35	490
Morea and dependencies	1,098,218	19	228
Candia and Canea	801,527	15	180
Smyrna	6,025,845	49	735
Alexandretta	2,815,391	13	195
Syria and Palestine	1,604,020	16	240
Alexandria	2,465,630	18	270
Barbary	695,657	37	370
Total	18,863,149	219	2,963

This table has been drawn from the registers of consular duties. The estimated values used for the purpose are 25 per cent below the real price of merchandise; thus, the real value of exports in 1784 was 23,578,936, but no consular duties are levied on wheat, rice, legumes, or other grains from the Levant or Barbary; nevertheless, in an ordinary year, the value of such exports may amount to two or three million. Assuming value of 2,500,000, the total would be 26,078,936 livres.

their jewelry; and in Albania there is a small amount of gold washed down by the rivers.

BILLS OF EXCHANGE

It is impossible to estimate the amount represented by bills of exchange. It often happens that Marseilles draws bills of exchange from the Levant on England,

disbursements [*retraits*], including cash [*fonds*] and bills of exchange, at 30,000,000, of which duties, freight, and costs of operation amount to 4,000,000, leaving 26,000,000 francs.

NAVIGATION IN THE LEVANT

In normal years two hundred vessels leave Marseilles for Barbary and Turkey, not including those of the Africa Company. Several of these ships make two trips a year, which would suggest that the annual total may be put at 350. Between 1764 and 1773, inclusive, there were 2,662 departures, which gives an annual figure of 266, but this does not include ships loaded with food-stuffs, which go to Toulon for quarantine. The years of the last war [the American Revolution] cannot serve as a guide. From this it may be deduced that this trade supports 4,000 sailors, at twelve per ship; some allowance should however be made for double counting.

CARAVAN

The caravan, or coasting, trade is a valuable branch of industry in that, by becoming carriers for the Turks and their merchandise, we earn—without undergoing any risks—the upkeep and wages of our ships and their sailors. This trade is carried out on either a wage or a share basis. In the former case, the owner pays the wages of the crew and gets all the profit or loss; in the latter, profits are shared, after deduction of expenses. The 1756 war reduced our sailings, to the advantage of the people of Ragusa who succeeded in putting to sea up to a hundred coasting ships; but the war of 1769 [the Russo-Turkish war of 1768–74] restored our superiority. The number of coasting ships sailing each year from Marseilles, Agde, Martigues, Ciotat, or Antibes is estimated at 150. They are sent out for two years; assuming that 100 return each year, with profits of 20,000 francs, a total of 2,000,000 is reached.

FREIGHT

Freight should not be included in the profits of trade, since it already figures in the price of merchandise. It may be estimated at 1,728,000 francs; the only part of the total which returns to us is that on goods resold to foreign countries.

GOODS FROM THE LEVANT RE-EXPORTED ABROAD

In 1781 and 1782, 4,522 bales of raw cotton, weighing 1,583,728 pounds, left Marseilles in transit for Switzerland, Geneva, and so on; to this should be added 617 bales of cotton yarn and dyed yarn, weighing 148,000 pounds, and 500 bales of wool, weighing 52,562 pounds. Assuming a price of 85 francs a quintal for raw cotton, 135 for yarn, and 60 for wool, a total of 1,576,595 livres tournois is obtained for the two years, or 788,297 per annum. However, these two years cannot be used as a basis for generalization.

TRADE OF OTHER EUROPEANS IN THE LEVANT

Dutch imports are about a quarter of ours, but their exports fall short of their imports. The English and the Venetians together may account for another quarter. Thus, the French carry on four-eighths of the trade, the Dutch two-eighths [sic.], and the English and Venetians one-eighth each.

CHAPTER 3

Anglo-Turkish Commercial Convention of 1838

Until the nineteenth century the Ottoman Empire made no attempt to stimulate local production by means of a protective tariff. After the Capitulations of 1673, both exports and imports were taxed at a uniform rate of 3 per cent ad valorem, a practice that had its counterpart in Manchu China. Buyers of foreign goods paid a supplementary duty of 2 per cent, while exporters often had to pay even higher duties and were subjected to many prohibitions (e.g., on wheat and rice) and to monopoly restrictions. In addition, the internal duty on goods carried by land (the *mururiye*) was 8 per cent.

By the early 1830's the Ottoman government was trying to renegotiate the Anglo-Ottoman tariff treaty of 1820, which was due to lapse in 1834. Its objective was to raise the basis on which taxes were levied, in view of the general rise in prices, and also to protect its woolen handicrafts against the rapidly increasing foreign competition. For their part foreign, especially British, merchants complained of export prohibitions, of very high duties on exports—amounting on certain items to 33 per cent—and of the fact that they were being subjected to the same taxes as Ottoman subjects when they moved their merchandise into the interior; formerly, foreign merchants did not go beyond the ports and therefore did not have to pay internal duties.

The Convention of 1838, reproduced below, set up the framework for Ottoman fiscal policy that prevailed until the First World War. It removed all monopolies, allowed British merchants to purchase goods anywhere in the Empire, and imposed duties of 5 per cent on imports, 12 per cent on exports, and 3 per cent on transit. It was to apply to all parts of the Empire, and specifically to Egypt, where Muhammad Ali had set up an elaborate system of monopolies (see Part VI, Chap. 1). Other European powers soon acceded to the Convention.

The realization that such a system put Ottoman producers at a disadvantage compared with foreign competitors, and the desire for more revenue, led the Porte to seek repeatedly to modify the rates. In 1861–62 new treaties were signed raising import duties to 8 per cent and providing for the gradual reduction of export duties to 1 per cent (see Part III, chap. 7). Further attempts at modification were thwarted by the opposition of one or the other of the powers—whose consent was necessary, under the Capitulations, for any change—until 1907, when import duties were raised to 11 per cent and in 1914 to 15 per cent. Following Turkey's entry into the war, the Capitulations were abolished, and in 1916 the uniform ad valorem tariff was replaced by differentiated specific duties designed to yield more revenue and provide greater protection.

(See also works by Bailey, Gordon, Puryear, and Mears listed in the Bibliography.)

[Great Britain, *Parliamentary Papers*, 1839, L, 291–95.]

Art. I. All rights, privileges, and immunities which have been conferred on the subjects or ships of Great Britain by the existing Capitulations and Treaties, are confirmed now and for ever, except in as far as they may be specifically altered by the present Convention: and it is moreover expressly stipulated, that all rights, privileges, or immunities which the Sublime Porte now grants, or may hereafter grant, to the ships and subjects of any other foreign Power to enjoy shall be equally granted to, and exercised and enjoyed by, the subjects and ships of Great Britain.

Art. II. The subjects of Her Britannic Majesty, or their agents, shall be permitted to purchase at all places in the Ottoman Dominions (whether for the purposes of internal trade or exportation) all articles, without any exception whatsoever, the produce, growth, or manufacture of the said Dominions; and the Sublime Porte formally engages to abolish all monopolies of agricultural produce, or of any other articles whatsoever, as well as all *Permits* from the local Governors, either for the purchase of any article, or for its removal from one place to another when purchased; and any attempt to compel the subjects of Her Britannic Majesty to receive such *Permits* from the local Governors, shall be considered as an infraction of Treaties, and the Sublime Porte shall immediately punish with severity any Vizirs and other officers who shall have been guilty of such mis-

conduct, and render full justice to British subjects for all injuries or losses which they may duly prove themselves to have suffered.

Art. III. If any article of Turkish produce, growth, or manufacture, be purchased by the British merchant or his agent, for the purpose of selling the same for internal consumption in Turkey, the British merchant or his agent shall pay, at the purchase and sale of such articles, and in any manner of trade therein, the same duties that are paid, in similar circumstances, by the most favoured class of Turkish subjects engaged in the internal trade of Turkey, whether Mussulmans or Rayahs.

Art. IV. If any article of Turkish produce, growth, or manufacture, be purchased for exportation, the same shall be conveyed by the British merchant or his agent, free of any kind of charge or duty whatsoever, to a convenient place of shipment, on its entry into which it shall be liable to one fixed duty of nine per cent. *ad valorem*, in lieu of all other interior duties.

Subsequently, on exportation, the duty of three per cent., as established and existing at present, shall be paid. But all articles bought in the shipping ports for exportation, and which have already paid the interior duty at entering into the same, will only pay the three per cent. export duty.

Art. V. The regulations under which Firmans are issued to British merchant vessels for passing the Dardanelles and the Bosphorus, shall be so framed as to occasion to such vessels the least possible delay.

Art. VI. It is agreed by the Turkish

Government, that the regulations established in the present Convention, shall be general throughout the Turkish Empire, whether in Turkey in Europe or Turkey in Asia, in Egypt, or other African possessions belonging to the Sublime Porte, and shall be applicable to all the subjects, whatever their description, of the Ottoman Dominions; and the Turkish Government also agrees not to object to other foreign Powers settling their trade upon the basis of this present Convention.

Art. VII. It having been the custom of Great Britain and the Sublime Porte, with a view to prevent all difficulties and delay in estimating the value of articles imported into the Turkish Dominions, or exported therefrom, by British subjects, to appoint, at intervals of fourteen years, a Commission of men well acquainted with the traffic of both countries, who have fixed by a tariff the sum of money in the coin of the Grand Signior, which should be paid as duty on each article; and the term of fourteen years, during which the last adjustment of the said tariff was to remain in force, having expired, the High Contracting Parties have agreed to name conjointly fresh Commissioners to fix and determine the amount in money which is to be paid by British subjects, as the duty of three percent upon the value of all commodities imported and exported by them; and the said Commissioners shall establish an equitable arrangement for estimating the interior duties which, by the present Treaty, are established on Turkish goods to be exported and shall also determine on the places of shipment where it may be most convenient that such duties should be levied.

The new tariff thus established, to be in force for seven years after it has been fixed, at the end of which time it shall be in the power of either of the parties to demand a revision of that tariff; but if no such demand be made on either side, within the six months after the end of the first seven years, then the tariff shall remain in force for seven years more, reckoned from the end of the preceding seven years; and so it shall be at the end of each successive period of seven years.

CHAPTER 4

Decline of Ottoman Industry in the 1840's

The following selection describes very clearly a process that took place in the Ottoman Empire, as in many other parts of the world, in the first half of the nineteenth century: the decline of the handicrafts. (See also Part II, chap. 5, Part III, chap. 7, and Part IV, chaps. 2, 3, and 7.) In the Middle East this decline began in the twelfth or thirteenth century and was accelerated by such disasters as the sack of Baghdad by the Mongols in 1258 and the deportation of Syrian handicraftsmen to Samarkand by Timur Lenk in 1401. By the sixteenth century the Middle East, whose former industrial pre-eminence is shown by such loan words as damask, damascene, muslin, gauze, alcohol, and arsenic, had become a heavy importer of manufactured goods from Europe.

The only industrial goods that continued to be exported to Europe were textiles, notably certain kinds of silk cloth and cotton yarn and cloth. But a high protective duty on imports of cotton yarn to France in 1761, followed by the growth of machine spinning in England, struck heavy blows at Middle Eastern exports of this commodity and led to a shift to exports of raw cotton. Similarly, exports of cotton cloth, which were restricted by import duties designed to protect the woolen industry in Britain and France, began to suffer in the mid-eighteenth century from the competition of finer Indian cloth and then from that of machine-made goods. In the nineteenth century cotton yarn and cloth became the principal articles of import, together with woolens, which had been bought in large quantities from Europe for a long time.

Already in the 1830's a British consular report from Syria vividly described the flooding of the local market with imported textiles; it also pointed out the effect of imports of cotton yarn, which destroyed local spinning but enabled hand weaving to survive for another hundred years:

The articles of British manufacture forming the bulk of trade are longcloths or grey domestics, cotton yarn, muslins and some nankins. The first two are of large importation for consumption; the former interferes with the manufacture of similar goods formerly made in Syria, and has entirely superseded the importation via the Persian Gulf of a similar quality from the East Indies.

Cotton yarn in its application for the manufactures of the country is, like a two-edged sword, cutting both ways; it being of great consequence as an article of production by the British manufactories, at the same time furnishing the manufacturers of cotton alone, and of cotton and silk goods of this country, with an article in general consumption.[1]

The competition of European factories was greatly aided by the opening of the country, following the Anglo-Turkish Commercial Convention of 1838 (see Part II, chaps. 3 and 5), and by the shift in tastes. The following, somewhat lyrical, account by Urquhart describes the process at work. It also brings out the difficulty non-industrialized countries had in paying for their rising imports of manufactured goods. For their exports soon came to consist almost exclusively of agricultural raw materials and foodstuffs, and many of these items were faced by high tariff walls in Europe.

It is on this that our hopes of commercial prosperity must rest, that notwithstanding eastern despotism, the means of exchanging commodities are open. It is established, that our cottons and muslins, calicoes, chintzes, etc., are, if not better, infinitely cheaper than those of the East. Taste is gradually directing itself to our manufactures, and money less expended than formerly on furs, jewels, Persian and Damascus blades, amber mouthpieces and shawls. We may calculate, at no remote period, if, indeed, political troubles are arrested, on supplying the necessaries as well as the luxuries of the whole of the eastern population, whose attention will thus be exclusively directed to agriculture, and the furnishing of raw produce; when we can take from them their produce in return for our wares, or find them the means of exchanging it. These changed circumstances are beginning to produce their effects. Persia, which lately drew raw silk from Turkey for its manufactures, now has commenced to import silk from England; and the current of precious metals, which a few years ago carried £5,000,000 towards the east, is now drawn backwards by the spinning mules and power looms of England. . . .

The manufacture of cotton is the principal in-door occupation of the greater portion of the East—of above sixty millions of men, with whom our future commerce will probably be carried on through the scales of the Levant—of men who are applying their labour to manufacture the cotton, and wool, and silk, that clothe them, while their fields lie uncultivated—under a climate producing all those articles which at present give the highest remuneration for labour. Throughout these vast and varied regions, these resources have lain dormant, as in the Turkish village; because hitherto the first object of necessity was not furnished to them cheap enough to induce them to forego its manufacture, and turn their attention to cultivation. How important, then, is it to establish the fact, that our cottons are at a sufficiently low price to induce them to forego the home manufacture! It is superfluous to follow out the vast consequences thence to be deduced; but it may not be uninstructive to remark, that perhaps a few pence diminution of price and charges in a pound sterling, may open or close the door of the market of a village, and for the same reason of a quarter of the globe, to our manufactures.

The village which was insulated before, now seeks to connect itself with the lines of communication with the principal marts; cultivation extends, wealth accumulates, instruction follows, desire for new objects increases, produce is raised; England's looms have called this prosperity into existence, but she herself imposes restrictions on the only return the Turkish peasant can make, and therefore cripples his ability to purchase.

[1] MacGregor, *Commercial Statistics*, IV, 156.

From the year 1827 to 1830, our exports have increased from £531,704 to £1,139,616,[2] but there is no corresponding increase in our returns. England, like a large haberdashery and hardware store, displays to the longing eyes of the peasantry of the world, calicoes, long cloths, ginghams, zebras, scissors, and razors; but if the merchant will not use the peasant's produce—nay, will not allow him to leave it, until exchanged, at his warehouse, the peasant, without money or credit, must wish in vain, and return home empty-handed." [3]

(See also works by Gibb and Bowen, Atsamba, MacGregor, Bonné, and Novichev listed in the Bibliography.)

[2] Of these sums cottons formed, in the first year, £464,873, and in the last, £1,037,160. Yet notwithstanding this rapidly increasing importation of our woven cottons, the demand for twist, to mix with home-spun cotton yarn or silk, has advanced as rapidly. While this confirms our superiority, even in the most elementary portion of the manufacture, it proves that our present supply has, comparatively speaking, little affected the home manufacturer, and leaves us to infer the vastness of the demand which we shall soon have to meet. From 1828 to 1831 the exportation of cotton yarn to Turkey has been as follows: £10,834, £39,930, £95,355, £105,615. However, the year 1828 is far below the general average.

[3] Urquhart, *Turkey*, pp. 141–44.

[From M. A. Ubicini, *Letters on Turkey*, translated by Lady Easthope (London, 1856), II, 339–44.]

...Manufacturing industry has greatly declined from what it formerly was in the Ottoman Empire. At present the greater part of the exports of Turkey consist in raw material, which it hands over to Europe, and which the latter returns to Turkey in a manufactured form. The numerous and varied manufactures, which formerly sufficed not only for the consumption of the empire, but which also stocked the markets of all parts of the Levant, and of several countries of Europe, no longer exist or have completely declined. The forges of Samakov and of Fognitza in Bulgaria and Bosnia, the manufactories of arms at Mostar and Travnik in the latter province,[1] are almost the only large manufacturing concerns in European Turkey. At Scutari and Tirnova there were two thousand looms of muslin in operation in 1812, whereas there were only two hundred in 1841. Five years ago Salonica possessed from twenty-five to

twenty-eight silk-looms; this number has been reduced to eighteen, producing about 88,000 lbs. of fine silk per annum. In Anatolia, Diarbekir, and Broussa, which were formerly so renowned for their velvets, satins, and silk-stuffs, do not now produce a tenth part of what they yielded from thirty to forty years ago. The latter scarcely manufactures 400,000 piastres' worth of silk annually, whilst its exports of raw silk and of dry cocoons amount to a value of nearly nine million piastres.

The same decay is observable in the old manufacturing towns of Syria and of Arabian Irak. Baghdad was once the centre of very flourishing manufactories, especially occupied with calico-printing, tanning, and preparing leather, pottery, jewellery, etc. The combined produce of all these branches of industry, which formerly supplied a great part of the trade of the Levant, attains now scarcely a value of three or four millions. Aleppo was still more flourishing than Baghdad. Its manufactures of gold thread, of cotton tissues, silk and gold, cotton and silk, and pure cotton, called *nankeens*, gave occupation to more than 40,000 looms and manufactured yearly an amount estimated at a hundred millions; the present yearly value produced does not exceed seven or eight millions. The industry of the islands has not declined so much: Candia still produces

[1] The Turks always excelled in the tempering of steel for the fabrication of arms. Witness the fine Damascus blades, and those manufactured at Travnik, at Constantinople, and in some other parts of the empire. But their exorbitant price, which converts them into articles of luxury, prevents their being demanded in foreign parts, and has greatly contributed in causing the decline of this branch of industry.

soap and tissues to the value of six millions; Cyprus manufactures printed calicoes, which are used to cover the divans in Turkey, light silks, gold and silk embroideries, and quilted counterpanes, highly esteemed in the Levant.

To these chief articles of native industry, it is proper to add the camlets of Angora, and the goat-hair stuffs, known in the Levant trade by the name of Châly, the sandals of Chios, the printed calicoes of Tokat, the crepes and gauzes of Salonica, the carpets of Smyrna, and those which are manufactured in certain districts of Bulgaria, especially at Jaskoi; lastly, saddlery, a branch of industry which has never been emulated in Europe.

Besides the general causes which I pointed out whilst treating of agriculture, two special causes appear to me to have influenced the existing state of manufacturing industry among the Turks. The first is an inveterate custom, which inclines them always to employ the same processes of manufacture; the other results from the reforms themselves, which, by the changes that they introduced in costume, made Turkey tributary to Europe for the new stuffs which it borrowed from the latter, and which it was unable to manufacture at so low a price: and thus these reforms destroyed at a blow the most important branches of native manufacturing industry. Nevertheless, instead of learning a lesson from this inferiority, which was a necessary consequence of its position, and instead of directing all its efforts to agriculture, so as to maintain the balance of commerce, Turkey fell into that error, so common to young states or nations in the process of transformation, of endeavouring to produce all things necessary for its own consumption. Though it is essentially agricultural country, as we have seen, instead of favouring to the uttermost the productions and cultivation of its soil, and of handing over its raw materials to foreign industry, which sends them back in a manufactured state, it committed the error of trying to become a manufacturing country itself, when it had everything to create, and could only proceed slowly, and as it were by groping. Nor was there any assignable cause for this foolish mistake, save the puerile satisfaction of being able to say that Turkey could manufacture cloths as well as Europe—iron and glass as they do in Europe. But the operatives came from Europe, and the machines too came from Europe. Hence the share that accrued to Turkey in the merit and labour of the manufactures was very small.

Still, it might have been excusable if it had succeeded. But the Sultan only repeated, at his own cost, the experiment of Mohammed Ali; and if Turkey had not possessed admirable resources, it would have succumbed like Egypt.

I shall here mention a fact extracted from a number of others.

A few years ago the Government judged it more convenient, and probably also less expensive, to have a foundry and forges at Constantinople, instead of obtaining its iron from England. They began by expending eight or nine millions for the construction of their works; after this they called in an English engineer, and English mechanics to work them. The material and the machines, which were also brought from England, swallowed up several millions more. On the other hand, and as a set-off, the Government possessed a superb establishment, situated not more than half a league from the capital, on the sea-shore, and the brightest hopes were entertained of its success. The ore was brought from the Prinkipo islands, eighteen miles distant; and the mines of Heraclea, distant about thirty miles, furnished the coal; and both the ore and the coals were transported to the furnaces by water. Still, on comparing accounts, it was found that the iron it yielded came to more than fifty piastres the quintal (220 lbs.), while the same quantity is habitually sold for forty-two piastres in the market at Constantinople.

Another foundry, which was established at a great cost at Beschik-tash, on the Bosphorus, has been abandoned, and is now used, I believe, as a victualling magazine.

And this has been done whilst the richest produce of the soil is neglected, as if intentionally—when the country possesses the richest copper mines, perhaps, in Europe, since the ore of Argana-Maden yields 30 per cent. of metal, whereas the best English mines only yield 10; and these mines are little, if at all worked. Eighty-four mines were formerly in full operation in Asia Minor, whereas now only fourteen are worked, and these scarcely yield one-third of what they ought to do.

The same result has attended the attempts of the Government to introduce foreign branches of manufacture into Turkey. The manufacture of printed calicoes at San Stefano, and the imperial manufactories of cloth and silk at Ismid (Nicomedia), have great difficulty in keeping a footing. There are only two branches of manufacture recently introduced into Turkey which have yielded satisfactory results: the paper factory at Smyrna, and the fez-Khane, where fez caps[2] are manufactured at Eyoub. The latter establishment was founded in 1832, by Sultan Mahmoud, in consequence of a decree promulgated at that period, which directed that the fez should be worn as a national head-dress instead of the turban. Placed in dependence on the mint, it manufactures annually 300,000 caps, a part of which are destined for the use of the troops, whilst the remainder are handed over to the bazaars, at the rate of 180 piastres per dozen,

[2] These are the caps of red wool which serve as a headdress in Turkey and in almost all Musulman countries: they were originally manufactured at Fez, in Morocco, whence they received their appellation. A considerable quantity is now exported from Tunis, from France, and especially from Austria.

besides about 16,000 or 17,000 yards of cloth. Native wool only enters as one-third into the material used in this manufacture; two-thirds being derived from Saxony, Spain, and Russia.

The other unfortunate attempts that have been made, have absorbed, for some years past, more than a hundred millions of piastres; a sum which if it had been devoted to the improvement of the roads, and of agriculture generally, would have doubled in the same interval the tithes and the returns of the customs.

It results from these facts united, that Turkey should learn two lessons from the past: first that she ought to give up, for the present, all attempts at competing with Europe for the main objects of manufacture, and to confine herself to bringing forth the natural riches of her soil, or to several special branches of native manufacture, destined to give life to her inland trade, such as carpets, shawls, morocco leather, gold embroidery, sadlery, arms, soap, etc. Nor should she spare any cost to issue from the false road that she is following. And if she fears becoming impoverished by drawing more from foreign countries than they take in return, I repeat that it is in her power to restore the balance by turning the riches of her soil to account. Cereals alone, without speaking of the other branches of culture, might easily furnish an equivalent to more than 100,000,000 of francs per annum. With this sum there would not be much difficulty in paying for many quintals of iron, many barrels of sugar, many ells of cloth, many yards of calico and muslins....

CHAPTER 5

Ottoman Industrial Policy, 1840–1914

The decline in the handicrafts described in the preceding selection is discussed more fully in the following one. Among the reasons for the disappearance of the old industries and the lack of new ones was the change in taste mentioned in both selections. Another factor was the general insecurity of life and property throughout much of the period. The strict regulation of craftsmen by the guilds and the government until the end of the nineteenth century constituted a further handicap.[1] The subordination of many craftsmen to merchants, who supplied them with credit or raw materials and bought their output, also diminished the former's incentive to improve and modernize. But perhaps the most important single factor was the massive influx of European machine-made goods following the Anglo-Turkish Commercial Convention of 1838 (see Part II, chaps. 3 and 4). The effect of the Convention was thus described by the Austrian consul: "The treaty of 1838 is more hostile to Ottoman industry than the treaty of Adrianople. At least the 1829 treaty did not give any preference to foreign manufacturers over the indigenous industry. . . . Now a Belgian merchant pays 5% on goods sold in Turkey; a Turkish merchant pays 12% for exports or even for transport from one of the Ottoman states to another."[2] When, in the following decades, the improvement of transport removed the last natural protection enjoyed by the craftsmen of the interior, their ruin was consummated.

The following selection describes some attempts to establish a modern factory industry. Here too the 1838 Convention presented a great obstacle, which was only partly surmounted by the gradual changes in tariff (see Part II, chap. 3). No less important was the general incompetence of the government and the unwieldiness, inefficiency, and corruption of the bureaucracy.[3] Another handicap was the absence of a native middle class with capital and enterprise; this gap might have been filled by the minority groups or even by foreigners, but both were diverted from investment in industry by the attractions of rival fields that promised

---

[1] Novichev, *Ocherki Ekonomiki Turtsii*, pp. 98–99.
[2] Puryear, *International Economics and Diplomacy in the Near East*, p. 127.
[3] See Mears, *Modern Turkey*, p. 325, on the mining laws.

quicker returns, such as loans to governments, speculation, trade, or the purchase of real estate in the rapidly growing towns. International rivalries also played their part, by preventing the granting of concessions for railways, mines, and public utilities.

Another important factor was the lack of managers and technicians, which might have been remedied by requiring the numerous foreign experts hired by the government to train replacements, but this was seldom done.

As an instance in point, I may mention the case of another foreigner, a Mr. Kellie, who manages the two steamboats in the service of the sultan. He has been nearly five years in Turkey, and yet when I left Constantinople, there was not in the whole empire a single Turk who was competent to start or to stop a steam-engine. His salary is sufficiently large, no extra exertions are required, and of course it would be perhaps too much to expect of him to give such instructions as would at some future day enable the Turks to dispense with his services. This case is alluded to as illustrating the defects of the system, and has no reference to the merits of the individual in question.[4]

But even with the best intentions on the part of the foreign technicians, training would have presented great difficulties, as may be seen from MacFarlane's version of the same incident:

Two young Turks, selected for their superior capacity and docility, who were placed on board the steam-boat to learn the nature of the machinery and management of the vessel, remained there more than three months without going into the engine-room more than twice during the whole time. They protested that the thing was magical, far too abstruse for their intellects. . . . The difficulty of an explanation to men wholly ignorant of the elements of physics will be readily conceived; the Turkish language offered no medium for the conveyance of novel ideas. . . .[5]

Lastly, mention must be made of the baleful effects of the laissez-faire philosophy that was urged on the Ottoman government both by well-wishers and by interested parties. In 1873, the distinguished Orientalist Vanbery stated that "European factories can only exist on the basis of the climatic and social relationships of Europe," and gave his opinion that the spirit of application and hard work which had made possible Europe's factories: "never have been nor ever will be conceivable amongst Moslems of Asia."[6]

In addition to measures the government took to encourage industry which are described in the following selection, mention may be made of the *iradeh* of 1873 exempting machines from customs duties and the law of 1913 offering privileges to persons establishing new industries or expanding existing ones.

(See also works by Gibb and Bowen, MacGregor, Urquhart, Grothe, Mears, Novichev, and Bonné listed in the Bibliography.)

---

[4] Kay, *Sketches of Turkey in 1831 and 1832*, p. 120.
[5] Charles MacFarlane, *Constantinople in 1828* (London, 1829), II, 231.
[6] Quoted by Kurt Grunwald, "Industrializing the Middle East," *New Outlook*, January, 1961.

[Omer Celal Sarç, "Tanzimat ve Sanayimiz" ("The Tanzimat and Our Industry"), in *Tanzimat* (Istanbul, 1941), pp. 423–40; reproduced by kind permission of the author.]

OTTOMAN INDUSTRY AT THE END OF THE EIGHTEENTH CENTURY

Despite the existence of many documents and studies concerning the organization and structure of old Ottoman industry and its legal problems in general, its economic and commercial aspects are still rather unexplored. Our knowledge is especially limited on such points as methods of production, the division of labor within factories, the amount of production, the level of local consumption, and the export and import of products. Therefore, unfortunately, it is impossible to explain with any precision and detail when the various branches of industry, which we know existed at one time in the Ottoman Empire, began their decline and just what were the phases in their decline.

According to several documents, at the end of the eighteenth century Ottoman industry was as yet in no serious crisis. In particular, cotton and silk—the most important branches of industry—were essentially maintaining their position. Our country was producing enough of the principal cotton and silk products not only to meet its domestic needs at this date but also to export a large amount, as the trade (exports and imports) between France and Turkey at the end of the eighteenth century would indicate.

According to Masson, in the year 1788 France imported from Turkey cotton goods worth 2.3 million livres. Despite very heavy customs duties, French imports of Turkish-made silk textiles reached 187,000 livres in 1789.[1] On the other hand, French exports

of cotton goods to Turkey were almost nonexistent. In the years 1788 and 1789, no muslin was imported into our country from France. In the same years, the value of cotton goods exported to Turkey did not exceed 42,000 livres a year. And although during these years there was an export of silk goods to Turkey valued at 400,000 livres annually, this is very insignificant when compared to the total silk exports of France, which amounted to 26 million livres.[2]

In this period the empire was exporting, aside from textiles, cotton yarn in significant amounts. The town of Ambelakia[3] in Thessaly was the most important center of yarn manufacture. This town, the population of which had once risen to 4,000, had become like a formidable factory. All hands were at work. While the men and even the children were busy dying cotton in twenty-four dye houses, the women were preparing and spinning the cotton. Each year 250,000 kilograms of cotton yarn were sent from Ambelakia to foreign countries, especially to Germany and Austria. The textile factories of Vienna, Budapest, Leipzig, Dresden, Anspach, and Bayreuth were using yarn made in Ambelakia in large amounts.[4] Unfortunately, in spite of the fact that the industry of the Ottoman Empire still exported textiles and yarn in this period, it

---

[1] Paul Masson, *Histoire du commerce français dans le Levant au XVIIIe siècle* (Paris, 1911), p. 475. The cotton goods that France imported from Turkey in these years came from Egypt and Aleppo, and the Aleppo goods were produced in Aintab, Kilis, Diyarbakir, Mosul, Mardin, and elsewhere.

[2] *Ibid.*, p. 495. Unfortunately information concerning Ottoman cotton and silk trade with the most advanced industrial nation of that period, Great Britain, is not available. Even if there were no cotton exports from Turkey to Britain at this time, it is certain that no significant quantity of cotton goods was exported to Turkey from Britain. Indeed the increase in the import of British cotton yarn and textiles in the years 1828–31 is clearly shown both by Urquhart's statistics, published first, and by other explanations he gives in his book. It is also known that British exports of cotton goods gained importance only after the Napoleonic Wars. Hargreaves invented the spinning jenny only in 1777 and Cartwright the power loom only in 1786. While in 1820 British imports of raw cotton were about 144,818 tons, in 1782 they amounted to only 11,828 tons. See Cunow, *Allgemeine Wirtschaftsgeschichte*, IV (Berlin, 1931), 274.

[3] I have not been able to ascertain whether Ambelakia had a separate Turkish name....

[4] David Urquhart, *La Turquie, ses ressources, son organisation municipale, son commerce* (Brussels, 1837), pp. 75–78.

no longer had its former strength. A large amount of the products consumed in the country at this time was obtained from the outside. Despite the fact that industry had not yet declined, it had remained backward as a whole and could not keep abreast of new developments. It was especially obvious that some branches of industry, which were newly established in Europe or had developed there recently, could not be established in the country. Since the demand for the products of these new European industries was gradually increasing, many industrial items, such as woolen cloth, small wares, sugar, paper, and clocks were imported into Turkey. For example, in 1788 and 1789, whereas France was exporting to Turkey on the average 3.6 million livres worth of raw materials, her export of manufactured goods to Turkey was 8.14 million livres.[5] On the other hand, raw materials were leading exports of the Ottoman Empire. The export of raw cotton and raw wool was much more important than that of textiles.

In summary, Ottoman industry had lost its former importance in both fulfilling the country's needs and supplying exports, but it was not yet on the decline.

THE DECLINE OF THE OLD INDUSTRY

Probably Ottoman industry maintained the above level until the end of the Napoleonic Wars and entered the period of definite decline only after 1815–20. Despite the increasing use of machines in industry at the end of the eighteenth century, it is known that machine products began to conquer foreign markets only in the period of early "capitalist" development (1818–25), which followed the Napoleonic Wars. In any case, it is obvious that our industry was experiencing a serious crisis in the years 1825–30. The manufacture of cotton goods, which constituted the backbone of Ottoman industry, was exposed to the crushing competition of the Manchester factories. Urquhart, who visited our country in this

period, has given many examples of the effects of this crisis.

The factories of Ambelakia, partly because of disagreement between their managers but especially because of the effects of the industrial revolution taking place in Europe, became completely idle.[6] The city had been deserted for ten years. The export of the cotton goods of the country stopped. In response, there was a significant rise in imports. The value of British cotton goods imported by the Ottoman Empire increased from £465,000 in 1828 to £1,040,000 in 1831. In addition to yarn, finished products (fabrics) are included in these imports. We can see from the figures below how quickly importation of British cotton fabrics increased in those years.[7]

EXPORT OF COTTON FABRICS FROM ENGLAND TO
TURKEY
(In pounds sterling)

1828	10,834
1829	39,920
1830	95,355
1831	105,615

This increase in the importation of fabrics was a great blow not only to yarn manufacturing but also to cotton weaving. In Scutari, Albania, although there were 600 looms in operation in 1812, their number dropped to 40 in 1821. In Tirnova, in 1812 there were 2,000 looms, but in 1830 there were only 200.[8] Nevertheless, the decline of our industry at this date was not complete, and there were still many branches of industry which remained alive:

a) The cotton industry was particularly affected by the competition of European factories. On the other hand, some industries such as those of silk, embroidery, Moroccan leather, and cutlery were not affected seriously at the time. For example, Charles Texier, who visited our country at almost the same time as Urquhart, says that despite the competition of Chinese and Lyon silks, the price of Bursa products had not declined, and approximately 100,000

---

[5] Masson, *op. cit.*, p. 472.

[6] Urquhart, *op. cit.*, pp. 74–80.
[7] *Ibid.*, pp. 206–23.
[8] *Ibid.*, p. 215.

pieces of silk fabric were being exported.[9] Later studies show that some other branches of industry mentioned above were able to preserve their position, more or less, even in the years 1855–60.[10]

b) The European factories were not yet able to extinguish completely the Ottoman cotton industry. It was rather the small urban industries which were declining. The manufacturing of cotton within the family continued despite great hardships. Urquhart states: "The profits have been reduced to one-half, and sometimes to one-third, by the introduction of English cottons, which, though they have reduced the home price, and arrested the export of cotton-yarn from Turkey, have not yet supplanted the home manufacture in any visible degree."[11] Elsewhere in his book, Urquhart has calculated that if the peasant gave up cotton manufacturing and bought the cotton goods he used from the market, it would be possible to increase British exports of cottons to Greece and to European Turkey by £5 million.[12]

c) The decline of industry was more conspicuous in those parts of the country which maintained close contact with the outside, such as Istanbul and European Turkey. In the interior, probably owing to the high cost of transportation, domestic products still dominated the market.

After stating that the consumption of "eastern" products in Turkey was still very great, Urquhart publishes a list of the goods brought to Aleppo by the caravans coming from the various parts of the country.[13] This list indicates that, at this time, cotton yarn and goods were still coming to Aleppo from Mosul, Mardin, Urfa, Aintab, Kilis, Trebizond, and Malatya. On the industry of Maraş, Charles Texier states: "There

exists an active industry in Maraş. Here cloaks, mantles, and vests made from wool and embroidered with silk or silver-gilt thread are manufactured. The dyed cotton goods used by Turkmen women also constitute an item of heavy trade."[14]

However, in subsequent years, the decline of industry was accelerated as well as widened.

Soon industries other than cotton manufacturing also became stagnant. We may mention the silk industry as an example. About the middle of the century, a significant decline became observable in this branch of industry. Viquesnel, in his work covering the years 1848–55, writes that formerly there were a great many silk factories in cities like Damascus, Aleppo, Amasia, Diyarbakir, and Bursa. He goes on to say that these factories, which produced silks in a variety of weaving and design and composition of colors, now had to reduce gradually the number of their looms.[15]

According to Hommaire de Hell, the introduction of dyed cloth to all classes of the people had been dangerous for this industry. Viquesnel gives the following account concerning the Bursa silk industry in 1847: "A few years ago, Bursa had 1,000 looms using 25,000 okkas of silk. Today, the number of its looms is not more than 75, and the silk used does not exceed 4,000 okkas."[16]

In 1851 Mordtmann wrote that only 3,000 kilograms of silk was exported from Bursa. He stated that the estimates given by some other observers on the production of previous years could not be realistic because if these estimates were correct, exports of silk products should have been drastically lower. He continued by stating: "However, let us not forget that there are still in Istanbul many merchants who remember very well the time when practically no foreign silk fabric was imported into the country. But now every ship coming from Marseilles or Trieste brings loads of silk

[9] Charles Texier, L'Asie Mineure (Paris, 1882), p. 122. According to Mordtmann's calculations, the 100,000 pieces of silk cloth were equivalent to 50,000 okkas. See. A. D. Mordtmann, Anatolien (Hanover, 1925), p. 294.
[10] A. Viquesnel, Voyage dans la Turquie d'Europe (Paris, 1868), pp. 299–300.
[11] Urquhart, op. cit., p. 211. [English text pp. 147–48.]
[12] Ibid., p. 214.
[13] Ibid., pp. 215–17.

[14] Texier, op. cit., p. 586.
[15] Viquesnel, op. cit., p. 297.
[16] Ibid.

products from Milan, Lyon, and Switzerland."[17]

At this time the production of silk thread, which was essentially a village industry, was also declining. Concerning the silk industry of Amasia, Mordtmann explained:

For many years, in Amasia as well as in other parts of Turkey, the cocoons were bought by European firms. Although this was dangerous for Turkish industry, it could not be prevented as long as the producer profited from the sale of the cocoon more than from the manufacture of thread, or as long as the European thread manufacturer offered him more than the Turkish thread manufacturer. From this it is evident that the European thread manufacturer produces much more cheaply than the Turkish thread manufacturer. This situation is liable to create serious problems [for the future of Turkish industry]. As with many other things, the silk industry in Turkey is in a state of decline.[18]

Besides, many branches of industry such as tanning, silver-gilt thread embroidering, and the manufacture of cloth were also declining. A report published in *Takvimi Vakayi* in August, 1867 (1283 A.H.), stated that the embroiderers, who once were well organized, "for various reasons and causes, lost their skill gradually and by going excessively into debt faced total destruction and extinction."[19]

An Industrial Improvement Commission set up in 1866 (1282 A.H.) issued a report on the establishment of a leather company in Istanbul. This report mentioned that "the leather makers, who were once very prosperous and whose wealth and power had been superior to that of other guilds, have been gradually declining during the last thirty or forty years," and finally the leather factories reached a state of total idleness.[20]

Another report of the same commission, dated 1868, noted that during the last thirty or forty years the number of cloth-producing looms in Istanbul and Uskudar had decreased from 2,750 to 25, the number of brocade looms from 350 to 4, and the number of upholstery silk looms from 60 to 8.[21]

These examples, especially Mordtmann's statements on the silk industry of Amasia, show that the crisis of our industry was more than a local phenomenon limited to easily accessible regions like European Turkey and the Aegean and Mediterranean shores, and had spread to the interior. Other observations confirm this. According to Viquesnel, in the city of Aleppo in 1864 only 150 out of 300 cotton-textile factories were operating; only 80 out of 100 print-handkerchief factories remained; out of the 200 establishments manufacturing fabrics of silk mixed with cotton, only 150 were active.[22] The amount of organdy, muslin, and gauze produced in such cities as Aleppo and Musul was henceforth not even sufficient to meet local needs.[23] [See Part IV, chap. 3.]

Finally, the family industrial enterprises were also affected in time by the crisis, although they were not affected as much as the small commercial enterprises in the cities; and in definite crafts—especially weaving[24]—they have continued their importance even until our time. For instance, the end of silk-thread manufacture marked essentially the termination of family enterprises. Moreover, after a while even the manufacture of home-made cotton yarn stopped, and farmers started to sell their cotton in its raw, unspun form. In

[17] Mordtmann, *op. cit.*, pp. 293–94.

[18] *Ibid.*, p. 92. However, the decline of former silk-thread production does not imply that the country was deprived of this industry. As will be noted in subsequent pages, in the years 1845–55, in various sections of the country (especially in Bursa and Lebanon) many new machine-equipped silk-thread factories were established. In other words, the old declining industry was partly replaced by government-owned factories, and the domestic manufacture of silk thread continued for some time, even if not in its former proportions.

[19] Osman Nuri, *Mecellei Umuru Belediye*, I (Istanbul, 1922), 750.

[20] *Ibid.*, p. 755.

[21] *Ibid.*, p. 760.

[22] Viquesnel, *op. cit.*, p. 297.

[23] *Ibid.*, p. 294.

[24] The Belgian Duckerts, who visited Turkey early in the twentieth century, states: "The textile industry is diffused in the whole country, mostly in the form of home factories. It is possible to see looms even in the most remote villages." M. Duckerts, *Turquie d'Asie* (Brussels, 1904), p. 119.

fact, although books describing the condition of Turkish industry in the early nineteenth century contain detailed information on home-manufactured cotton yarn, books on the second half of the nineteenth century do not even mention cotton yarn as a product of Turkish industry. Moreover, while among the manufactured goods sent to the 1856 Paris World's Fair there were many samples of silk and cotton cloth, only four samples of cotton yarn, made at Istanbul and Serez, were sent.[25] This is another indication that this family-operated industry had almost gone out of existence at that date.

In this manner, the crisis brought about in our country by European industrial capitalism was gradually spreading to all branches of industry, one by one, thus making the decline of our industry complete by the second half of the century. "Now [1848–55], the many diverse factories of Turkey which used to export to all the East and to many sections of Europe, in addition to meeting home consumption, are either nonexistent or in complete decline."[26] Indeed, all that now operated in the country were the remnants of industries that had come down from earlier centuries. Except for such branches as shoemaking, tailoring, and bread-baking, whatever industry survived no longer played any role in the production of everyday products, which generally had to be imported from abroad. Basically, old forms of industry were able to survive only in those fields of manufacture which possessed esthetic value. Such were the knife and arms industry in Damascus and Erzurum; the manufacture of silk cloaks, jackets, and mother-of-pearl household goods of Damascus; and the jewelry industry of Erzurum, Van, and Diyarbakir. However, these products—which were expensive to manufacture, had limited consumption, and were purchased only by amateurs—were not of great economic value. Most of the remaining branches of production existed in name only, and their producers

were, for the most part, in great poverty. Totomjanz states: "Turkey's center of government and its environs are full of individuals who earn their livelihood by handicrafts—weavers, tinsmiths, coppersmiths, and others. Masters of small industry dwell exclusively in certain sections of Istanbul. This large army of workers ... either lives in semi-starvation or has begged for years."[27]

ATTEMPTS AT AID

The Ottoman statesmen were not indifferent to the deterioration of the industry of a nation which had formerly been so flourishing. On the contrary, the poverty being experienced by the artisans had attracted the attention of government officials from the first signs of crisis. From a document preserved in the archives of the Prime Ministry it is evident that even Selim III was closely interested in the difficulties of our industry. The cloth furnishings of the reception hall in Topkapi Palace had been renovated by the Sadrazam Halil Halid pasha with fabrics that were then in fashion in Istanbul. In his petition [to the sultan] describing the situation, the sadrazam stated that if textile dealers were encouraged further, they would be able to produce a variety of "printed, newly conceived designs" and thus "totally prevent the use of French designs." The sadrazam further beseeched the sultan to state where the fabrics could be displayed, if His Majesty desired to see them. In his memorandum the sultan replied: "My Vizir, there is no doubt that everything could be manufactured at its best in Istanbul, if encouraged. I like the fabrics of Istanbul, and I mostly wear clothes made in Istanbul. I wish that the people did the same. If you now send the materials to Silahdaraga, I will look at them."[28]

However, until the era of Abdul Aziz nothing was done to protect industry; only

---

[25] The Turkish goods shown at this fair and the prizes won are listed in Viquesnel, op. cit., pp. 302–16.
[26] Ibid., p. 292.

[27] V. F. Totomiants and E. Topchian, Die sozialökonomische Türkei (Leipzig, 1901), p. 191.
[28] Prime Ministry Archives, "The Era of Selim III," Box 56, line 165.

after his accession were steps taken in this direction.[29] With the aim of reviving industry, four measures were taken in this period: (1) the increase of customs duties; (2) the organization of fairs; (3) the opening of industrial schools in Istanbul and the provinces; (4) the formation of associations.

Customs duties were increased in 1862 (1278 A.H.) from 5 per cent to 8 per cent, and in 1863 a fair was opened in Sultan Ahmet Square, where foreign manufacturing machines and local goods were exhibited in a building erected at a cost of £30,000.[30] Following this, in 1867 (1283 A.H.) the School of Industrial Reform was established in Istanbul.

The most interesting of the measures adopted to safeguard industry were the attempts to unite the tradesmen in associations. Evidently the aim of this measure was to create producer cooperatives among the small-industry owners. We understand this from the third article of the instructions of the Second Commission on Industrial Reform.[31] This article states: "There is no basis for and no advantage in the individual and separate endeavor of the tradesmen as of old, and their attainment is dependent upon their common and united efforts in arranging for the organization of an association among their interests and skills, with as much capital as necessary."[32] According to Osman Nuri, in the years 1867–74, seven associations were formed among various groups of tradesmen in this manner.

The following privileges were granted to these companies: (1) a twelve-year concession; (2) exemption from certain taxes; (3) exemption from customs duties on imported tools and materials; (4) preference to be accorded to products of these companies by the buyers of governmental agencies.[33]

These companies, whose capital is understood to have been supplied by the tradesmen themselves, the treasury, and certain donors,[34] were not as successful as their European counterparts, and in 1874 (1290 A.H.) the Commission for Industrial Reform was abolished and its duties transferred to the city government.[35]

In a document on the abolition of this commission dated October, 17, 1874 (1290 A.H.), it is stated: "If, like their existing counterparts, the companies which the tradesmen will organize are to perform simple acts such as drawing up contracts among themselves, there will be no need for outside mediation [by the commission], since this can be accomplished among individuals. If it is desired to form joint stock companies, this can be accomplished under the auspices of the Ministry of Commerce and the Lending Council." The document further recommends that there should be no intervention in the internal functioning and management of these companies.[36] Evidently, the reasons for the lack of success of these companies were lack of capital, lack of experience, "lack of understanding of the advantages of collective commercial practices, as opposed to individual endeavor," and so on.[37] Such measures as the increase of customs duties to 8 per cent, the establishment of the Industrial School at Istanbul and of the fair, which were aimed at revitalizing the old industry in modern forms by uniting its professions in cooperatives, did not have a positive influence, and the process of decline continued with full force. In fact, as will be better understood from an examination of the causes of the decline of industry, all these measures were doomed to fail.

REASONS FOR THE DECLINE

The old type of industry, which produced goods on a small scale without benefit of

[29] Osman Nuri, *op. cit.*, p. 718.

[30] On this fair, see Osman Nuri, *op. cit.*, pp. 738–44, and M. Callas, *La Turquie en 1864* (Paris, 1864), pp. 188–96 and pp. 239–41.

[31] The First Industrial Reform Commission, organized in 1864–66, was not able to accomplish anything. A second commission was organized in 1868. See Osman Nuri, *op. cit.*, p. 718.

[32] *Ibid.*, p. 724.

[33] *Ibid.*, pp. 748–49.

[34] See the section in *Takvimi Vakayi* on the Saddlers' Association; Osman Nuri, *op. cit.*, p. 752.

[35] *Ibid.*, p. 727.

[36] This memorandum is included in *ibid.*, p. 728.

[37] See section on the Saddlers' Association, *ibid.*, p. 752.

division of labor and mechanization, declined not only in Turkey but also in the whole world, including the west European countries where the process of decline was more tragic than in Turkey, resulting in rebellions and incidents such as the destruction of machinery. Basically, the decline of Ottoman industry also was the result of those factors which caused the disappearance of the old industrial system in Europe. This industry, too, was crushed by capitalism, which developed in the latter part of the eighteenth century. In fact, after the emergence abroad of establishments which, by the application of machinery and the division of labor, were able to produce cheaper, more uniform and regular goods, there was one solution for the continuation of the old manufacturing systems existing in Turkey—absolute isolation, that is, severing every kind of commercial, political, and other relations with the outside world. This kind of isolation had become impossible in the nineteenth century. Even an island country like Japan was compelled to abandon isolation, and a country in the geographical and political position of the Ottoman Empire was totally unable to achieve it. Therefore, with the emergence of capitalism, the decline of the old Ottoman industry became a historical necessity.

Moreover, certain aspects of our country's structure at that time also had some influence on this decline. Among the conditions that accelerated and intensified this decline of industry, it is first necessary to mention the Capitulations. These Capitulations, which established import duties of 3 per cent until 1838,[38] 5 per cent in 1836–62 (including octroi taxes, etc.), and 8 per cent in 1862–1902, did not permit even the government to protect the national industry against capitalism.

A second factor was that wants changed in the first half of the nineteenth century. It is known that during the Tanzimat, first military and later civilian dress underwent a

change, and with this change of dress came the demand for many accessories. For instance, Sultan Mahmud changed not only the uniforms of the cavalry but also their saddles. And the people not only preferred European dress but also gradually showed preference for European furnishings. These changes narrowed the market for products of the old industry and struck a heavy blow against these institutions exactly at a time when they were in great distress because of the keen competition of European factories. All authors are unanimous in confirming the negative influence of the changes in wants.[39]

In addition, internal customs duties also had a destructive influence on certain sectors of Ottoman industry. After the payment of 5 per cent import duty, foreign products had complete freedom of movement within the country, while local products being transported from one locality to another were subject to duties such as *amediye*, *reftiye* (local export duty), *mururiye* (transit taxes), and *masdariye* (taxes of origin). According to Mordtmann, the internal duties imposed on silk goods shipped from Amasia to Istanbul or Bursa were, in 1847, 12 per cent of their value.[40] Engelhardt mentions that in some cases this percentage rose as high as 50 per cent.[41] When the difference in manufacturing costs between foreign and Turkish products was not great, the effects of these duties were not felt to any great extent. After European products were made cheaper by the use of machinery, these duties became an unbearable burden on our industry. Moreover, the industry most affected by these internal customs duties was the one whose products were shipped to other parts of the country, that is, which produced manufactured goods over and above local needs, and thus which would lend itself to progressive methods in general.

Nevertheless, neither the Capitulations

---

[38] Engelhardt states that this 3 per cent duty was actually worth 1 per cent, owing to the debasement of currency (*La Turquie et le Tanzimat*, II [Paris, 1884], 308).

[39] See Viquesnel, *op. cit.*, p. 292; Engelhardt, *op. cit.*, p. 308; Urquhart, *op. cit.*, p. 215.
[40] Mordtmann, *op. cit.*, pp. 92–93.
[41] Engelhardt, *op. cit.*, p. 309.

nor the changing wants nor internal customs duties were the basic factors necessitating the decline of the old Ottoman industry. Even if the Capitulations and the internal customs duties had not existed and wants had not changed, the old industrial methods would not have continued for long. Indeed, the Capitulations and internal customs duties were negative influences preventing the regeneration of the old industry and the formation of a modern industry in the country, rather than the cause of the decline of the old industry.

The fundamental point, which is bewildering and regrettable, is the following: whereas in the European countries it had been possible to replace the old declining industrial forms with an advanced system, in our country, with the decline of old forms of industry, almost all important industrial activity also ceased, and the country's economy lost all the major branches of industry; it was then necessary to import even the most basic products.

There were other attempts in the nineteenth century to equip the country with a modern industry. To comprehend the role the Tanzimat movement played in the history of the country's economy, these attempts must be examined.

The Industrialization Movement

It was learned during the Tanzimat that henceforth it would be impossible to prolong the old forms of industry; it was also understood that in order to keep alive industrial activity it would be necessary to organize a modern industry in the country. The proof of this is found in documents about attempts at industrial reform stating that tradesmen "in working individually and separately would not profit" and also in the attempts to unite industrial workers in associations.

With this aim, while the country was trying to reform the old industry, efforts were being made directly to establish a modern industry; and thus both the state and private individuals set up many factories. The history of this industrialization movement has not yet been written. There still has not been sufficient research on what factories were established or attempted, what programs were set up, and the technical quality, activities, and phases of development. It is desirable that this research be done without delay, since this will help us to succeed in our present industrialization drive, by enabling us to benefit from past experience. At this point we must limit ourselves to the mere mention of individual attempts to create a national industry during the Tanzimat.

STATE FACTORIES

Without doubt, industrial establishments with large production existed in the Ottoman Empire before the Tanzimat. For example, just as it is certain that cannon foundries and shipyards belonging to the state employed many workmen and that they took advantage of rather complex tools and means of production, so it is thought that these establishments also practiced division of labor, which is a distinctive characteristic of modern manufacturing methods. Nevertheless, industrial plants using machinery—and thus deserving the name "factories"—came into being only after the elimination of the janissaries and the establishment of a European-type army, especially concerned with providing new uniforms and supplies for this army. Thus, when it was decided to use the fez as a headgear for soldiers in 1826 (1242 A.H.), an order for 50,000 fezzes was placed with the Tunis Beylerbeyi; steps were also taken to manufacture the fez locally, and in 1835 (1251 A.H.) a fez factory was established.[42] It is known that cloth factories in Izmit and Islimiye were also established with the same purpose.[43] After Abdul Mecid's accession, factory construction was accelerated; and this sultan, whose aim was "to open a

[42] See Talat Mumtaz Yaman, "The Last Two Headgears of Ottomans," *Varlik Mecmuasi*, No. 140, pp. 266, 273.
[43] *Ibid.*, p. 273, and Ami Boue, *La Turquie d'Europe*, III (Paris, 1840), 101–2.

brilliant industrial era for Turkey,"[44] established many factories, including the Zeytinburnu factory.

It is possible to form an idea about the state factories existing around the mid-nineteenth century from the following list of establishments which displayed Ottoman products at the 1856 Paris Fair:[45]

Izmit factory: cloth, military uniforms.

Istanbul fez factory: cloth, fezzes, blankets, neckties.

Printing factory: flannel cloth.

Zeytinburnu factory: cotton cloth, calico, imprints, striped cloth [indiennes]; cotton, woolen, and lisle-thread stockings.

Hereke factory: velvet; silken, Damascus-style, flowered cloth; satin, taffeta, gauze, ribbons.

Military equipment factory of Beykoz: military shoes, boots, bandoliers, cartridge belts, etc.

Tophane (artillery) factory: rifles, pistols, etc.

Incekoy factory at Beykoz: porcelain, glass, demitasse cups, etc.

Nevertheless, the state factories surely did not consist only of these establishments. In fact, among the establishments enumerated, neither the factory in Islimiye nor the paper factory in Izmir[46]—which was also active at this time—is mentioned. Also, we understand from certain documents in the Archives of the Prime Ministry that at that time other state factories existed as well.[47]

Although the majority of these factories were built during Abdul Mecid's reign by foreign engineers and had partly foreign management and labor, they could not succeed. They became a heavy burden on the state and after a short time were compelled to curtail their activities. However, there were exceptions. Ami Boue, who toured the Islimiye factory in 1837, reports the successful operation of this establishment.[48] According to Viquesnel, in the years 1848–50 the fez manufacturing plant that annually produced 400,000 fezzes and 30,000 meters of cloth was also in a satisfactory condition.[49] Yet the majority of the factories did not justify their existence and became parasitic establishments that continuously consumed the state budget. Both in the founding and in the managing of these factories innumerable instances of waste and misuse are observed.

According to A. Boue, the French manager of one of the state factories had for a long time delivered to the state cloth that was imported from France as if it were the product of the state factory. As soon as he suspected exposure, he fled abroad with the receipts.

The irregularities committed during construction of the Zeytinburnu factory and "the ridiculous and tragic phases" through which this work passed are described in Ali Riza Seyfi's articles based on MacFarlane's memoirs.[50] The construction of this factory, built under the supervision of two Armenian brothers named Dadyan, dragged on for many years. The engineers, craftsmen, and workmen brought from Europe were kept idle for long periods and at times did not receive pay for months. The chimney, constructed by an Armenian craftsman who ignored the advice of specialists, collapsed during the construction of the factory, causing the death of thirty workmen. The problem of water supply was not properly considered, and the factory manager was forced to use salty water from newly dug wells in the boilers.

A large number of these factories, which

---

[44] Ali Riza Seyfi, "The Comedy of Industrialization in the Period of the Empire," *Cumhuriyet*, July 31 and August 5, 1939.

[45] See n. 25, above.

[46] See Viquesnel, *op. cit.*, p. 292. Also Archives of the Prime Ministry, the sections on commerce, industry, and agriculture (M. Cevdet's classification), Documents 329, 348, 801.

[47] See the archive sections on trade, industry, and agriculture (M. Cevdet's classification), Documents 424, 419, 434, 448, 449 (Bursa textile factory, Balikesir cloak factory, Samako cloth and iron factories). Moreover, according to Viquesnel, the state established a silk-thread factory in Bursa, which was ruined in the 1855 earthquake (Viquesnel, *op. cit.*, p. 295). Also MacFarlane speaks about the existence in 1828–29 of a paper factory in Beykoz (*Constantinople et La Turquie en 1828 et 1829*, III [Paris, 1830], 198). This paper factory is also mentioned in Document 472 of the Prime Ministry Archives on trade, industry, and agriculture (M. Cevdet's classification). However, I could not ascertain whether this factory was still in operation at the start of the Paris fair.

[48] A. Boue, *op. cit.*, pp. 100–101.

[49] Viquesnel, *op. cit.*, p. 292.

[50] See n. 44, above.

cost enormous sums of money (for instance, the paper factory in Izmir and the porcelain and glass factory in Beykoz) had to be closed after a while because there was no possibility of overcoming the continuous drain they made on the treasury. Thus the industrialization movement, which had started with great hopes, went bankrupt because of ignorance, mismanagement, and abuse, and partially also because of the Capitulations, which did not permit the protection of state factories. From this period until the Republic, the state did not undertake any important industrial construction and basically confined itself to keeping the status quo in the operation of factories left from the reigns of Mahmud and Abdul Mecid.

PRIVATE FACTORIES

In the Tanzimat era various private factories had been established, mostly by foreign capitalists, just as some had been established by the state. For, despite the fact that the Capitulations did not permit the state to protect national industry, the Ottoman economy offered certain conditions that encouraged enterprising individuals to set up establishments. Raw materials were ample. Experienced skilled workers were easy to find for a variety of jobs because, until a short time before, industry had been widespread in the country. Moreover, wages were low, and the market was vast. Finally, in the early stages of the Tanzimat, even European industry had not yet achieved a very high degree of development —that is, it had not reached a stage impossible to overtake. Some capitalists then thought that these favorable factors—in addition to the savings in transportation costs necessary for foreign goods coming to Turkey—would compensate for the negative conditions that prevented the progress of national industry, and it is natural that they should have attempted to open factories in the country.

It was in the manufacture of silk thread that private factories were initially dominant and played the most important role.

According to Mordtmann,[51] Falkeisen, a Swiss, established a factory powered by steam engine, in Bursa in 1845; until that time the products had been made by old methods. In the beginning this factory was confronted with great difficulties and could not find workers, because no one was willing to work in a factory using machinery. Later, it progressed quickly, and in a short time a number of silk factories were established in Bursa. Viquesnel states that, in 1855, there were eight to ten silk-thread factories in Bursa, modeled on their French counterparts.[52]

In this period the number of privately owned silk factories was also gradually increasing in Lebanon. In that country, in 1852, there existed nine reeling plants, five of which were French-owned, two British-owned, and two owned by natives. Five of these mills showed great activity. The most important of these factories had an annual production of 10,000 kilograms of silk cocoons and 50,000 kilograms of yellow silk. This French establishment, called Ayni Hamade, sold its products to France.[53]

In time private factories appeared in fields other than the silk industry. General information about these factories is given in a book by Duckerts, who was the former Belgian consul-general in Izmir and who made a journey of investigation throughout our country in the first years of the twentieth century.[54] For instance, at that date a few large carpet-weaving shops had been founded. There was in Izmir a large shop founded by Aliotti and Ispartali, which employed close to 1,000 workers. In addition the Gustiniani establishment had founded another rug-manufacturing plant in the vicinity of Konya. Moreover, in flour milling and olive-oil extraction, great strides were made in modern production methods. In the extraction of olive oil,

[51] Mordtmann, *op. cit.*, pp. 294–96.
[52] Viquesnel, *op. cit.*, p. 295. Mordtmann puts the number of silk-thread factories in Bursa in 1855 at twenty-three, but this may include small shops, which would not be classified as factories.
[53] Viquesnel, *op. cit.*, pp. 295–96.
[54] Duckerts, *op. cit.*, pp. 103–20.

especially in Syria and Midilli, various steam-driven hydraulic presses were being used. In addition, the following factories were established: in Paşabahçe on the Bosphorus, a large candle and stearin factory with French capital; in Kartal, a canning factory with Swiss-British capital; in Beykoz, around the 1890's, a new glass factory; again in Beykoz, a large paper factory by a British group with a capital of 7.5 million francs; in Beirut, another paper factory. At the same time, there existed in Adana and Tarsus, cotton-ginning plants; in Afyon and Izmir, carpet-thread factories; in Adana, Tarsus, and Izmir, cotton-yarn factories.

However, like the state's industrialization efforts, the founding activities of private individuals also remained basically fruitless and certainly did not yield positive results for the country. Most of the new factories closed down within a short time. For example, the candle factory in Paşabahçe, the paper factory in Beirut, and the glass factory in Beykoz ceased operations within a few years. As for the paper factory in Beykoz, it lasted only a few months after its opening. Moreover, the fact that almost all the factories established were controlled by foreigners indicates that the Turkish element was subjected to foreign economic control within its own country. Finally, the industry established was negligible in comparison with the needs of the country. In the manufacture of cotton and wool and metal articles—which were most important for the country—significant strides were not made, and the country remained totally dependent on imports for these products. The industries that developed involved mostly the first-stage processing of raw materials to be exported, and since they were not sufficient to meet the need even from this point of view, many of our raw materials were exported without being processed at all.

The Tanzimat and Our Industry

After these necessarily incomplete explanations about the phases through which nineteenth-century Ottoman industry passed, let us try to determine what effect the Tanzimat had on our industry.

It can be said that the Tanzimat movement, that tended to westernize the structure of Ottoman society which had come down from the time of Islam and the expansion of the empire, had an essentially negative influence on the industrial activity of the country. Above all, the Tanzimat had shaken our old industry by changing some of the needs of the population and thus had been instrumental in its decline. Perhaps, as we explained above, it is not fair to hold the Tanzimat directly and solely responsible for the decline of the industrial systems left over from past centuries. We should not forget that even if no new needs had developed within the country and demand for old-type products had continued, European factories would have either copied these products or produced equivalent ones. Thus the European factories would still have driven Ottoman industry to its doom. It is known that western factories have destroyed many branches of eastern industry by producing more cheaply with modern methods goods not used in Europe but only in the East. Moreover, as a result of the penetration of western customs in the country, a change had taken place in people's wants. This dealt a heavy blow to the already weakened Ottoman industry by reducing the demand for locally manufactured goods.

The Tanzimat, although instrumental in the decline of old industry, could not create a modern industry to take its place. Not only had it not been possible to reform and develop our industry toward modern ways, but also the efforts of the state and private individuals were not fruitful and could not have any significant results. As a result the country, which at the start of the Tanzimat era could provide many of these industrial goods with its own manufacture and was even able to export them, at the end of this era was almost totally dependent on foreign markets for necessary products.

We can state that the ultimate reasons for

the failure of the Tanzimat efforts to establish industry were ignorance and weakness. Ignorance had caused the state and individuals sometimes to pursue aims that could not possibly be attained. And at times ignorance prevented the full realization of the conditions that had to be satisfied in order to bring these efforts to fruition. It also prevented the effort that was necessary to supply what was missing. This ignorance manifested itself very tragically in the establishment and the administration of state factories, in efforts to establish associations among the tradesmen, and in many state measures completely contrary to economic principles, such as internal customs duties.

But the most important reason for the failure of the industrialization effort was the state's own weakness. During the Tanzimat period the Ottoman state displayed a strange and controversial picture. The Empire was trying to apply the policy of European mercantilism aimed at increased national production, but it did not possess even the most basic traits of mercantilist governments. In fact, unlike the mercantilist states which had complete sovereignty over their lands, the Ottoman Empire exhibited total incapacity. Its helplessness toward the outside world made it impossible for the Empire to protect its newly created industry even temporarily. The financial weakness of the state necessitated the use of such harmful means of obtaining revenue as the debasement of money and the levying of tithes and pre-

vented the state from taking the necessary steps to industrialize and to improve roads and schools. Moreover, the state was helpless against the outdated and other worldly mentality dominant in the country. Lacking the courage to combat this mentality, the state could not basically reform the laws and institutions that had come down from ancient times and were designed to fit only the needs of those times. The Empire was not capable even of maintaining internal order, which is a necessary condition for industrial development.

In spite of this, it would be unfair to consider the Tanzimat as having had no place in the historical evolution of our industry. Although the Tanzimat was not able to create anything significant in the field of industry, it did change some of the basic factors of our political and social structure and, by opening the road to western civilization, it prepared for the great Turkish Revolution, which did not finally occur until the Republic. The strides that we are making today in industry are actually the results of the Revolution. Indirectly the Tanzimat was of importance in the development of our industry, because it was a necessary phase in the social development of our society and because advances in industry are directly dependent on the development of the social structure. In this regard, on the one-hundredth anniversary of the Gulhane Hatti, the Tanzimat movement should be considered an early initiator of our present moves toward industrialization.

CHAPTER 6

The Expansion of Tobacco Growing in the Nineteenth Century

Both smoking and planting tobacco in the Ottoman Empire started at the end of the sixteenth century. As elsewhere, there were attempts to forbid smoking, especially by Murat IV (1623–70), under whom (in the words of Katib Çelebi) "many thousands of men were sent to the abode of nothingness." But capital punishment failed to have any effect, and taxation was tried instead, under Suleyman II (1687–91). By then cultivation was well established in Syria and the Smyrna region, as well as in the Balkans, and by the eighteenth century tobacco was being exported from Salonica (see Part II, chap. 2), Syria,[1] and Trebizond.[2] However, as late as 1845 Britain's exports to Turkey of tobacco and its products, 10,362 pounds worth £2,118, exceeded its imports from that country, 2,118 pounds worth £19.[3]

As stated in the following selection, which seems to be based mainly on contemporary French newspaper accounts, tobacco cultivation in Turkey was given a great stimulus by the American Civil War—just as was cotton in Egypt (see Part VI, chap. 8). At the same time, in 1860, tobacco was declared a state monopoly. In 1884 the monopoly was transferred to a foreign consortium, the Régie Cointeressée des Tabacs de l'Empire Ottoman, founded the previous year with a capital of 100 million francs by French, British, German, and Austrian interests. The Régie operated until 1925, when it was once more replaced by a state monopoly. Its effects on cultivation seem to have been unfavorable. In the words of Verney and Dambmann:

The immediate effect of the creation of the Ottoman Régie was to diminish considerably tobacco cultivation in Asiatic Turkey. This is a phenomenon that has been observed in several centers: in Beirut, Lebanon, Haifa, Mosul, Latakia and Smyrna . . . [see references in original]. This phenomenon is attributable either to the duties or vexations to which tobacco growers are subjected, or to the import of foreign tobacco by the Régie, or lastly to the reduction in exports of tobacco from Syria to Egypt. But if the establishment

[1] Gibb and Bowen, *Islamic Society and the West*, I, 304.
[2] Bailey, *British Policy and the Turkish Reform Movement*, p. 111.
[3] *Ibid.*, Appendix Tables 7 and 11.

of the Régie has hampered the development of tobacco cultivation, it has given birth to widespread smuggling.[4]

But other factors were also at work increasing foreign competition. In Egypt a cigarette industry was developed in the 1870's, largely by Greek immigrants from Turkey.[5] Moreover, "The then current high costs of tobaccos from Turkey and Egypt suggested to British entrepreneurs that they try those of Greece, Bulgaria, China, Japan, and elsewhere."[6] Turkey's production fell from an average of 22,800 tons in 1884–85 to 16,700 in 1887–88 but then picked up rapidly; one important cause of the recovery was the increasing demand, from American merchants, for blending. In 1911 the output reached a record 63,500 tons, and tobacco had become Turkey's leading export item. This position it has retained, thanks to a further growth in output: in 1938 tobacco exports amounted to 43,500 tons, or 27 per cent of total exports, and in 1949 to 80,000 tons, or 37 per cent.

(See also works by Philips, Günyüz, Kahyaoglou, and Brooks, listed in the Bibliography.)

4 Verney and Dambmann, *Les Puissances étrangères dans le Levant, en Syrie et en Palestine*, pp. 183–84.
5 Wright, *Twentieth Century Impressions of Egypt*, pp. 487–95.
6 Brooks, *The Mighty Leaf*, p. 240.

[From *Ziraat Tarihine bir Bakiş* (*A Look at Agricultural History*) (Istanbul, 1938), pp. 159–65.]

... Among the agricultural products which are displayed in the exhibition tobacco has attracted a great deal of attention because the yearly harvest is abundant and especially because of the great additional revenue that is assured for the state since the contracting of new trade agreements. Therefore it would not be useless to dwell upon this branch of agriculture, which the American [Civil] War caused to assume a great importance, as it did for cotton. [See Part II, Introduction and chap. 7.]

Tobaccos were exhibited by the orders and directives of the Minister of Taxation [*rusumat naziri*], Kani ·pasha. The tobaccos of six provinces were to be found in a particular room. These provinces were: in European Turkey: Salonica, Edirne, and Yanina; in Asian Turkey: Trebizond, Izmir, and Hudavendigar [Bursa area]; in Syria: Aleppo and Sidon. ...

In Asia the district which produces most tobacco is Trebizond province. The yearly tobacco crop of Samsun and Bafra is approximately 4,000,000 okkas. This tobacco is exported to the entire country and, on account of its cheapness, is easily sold there. It is especially used in blends, where it gives a pleasant color and a very strong taste.

In Trebizond the tobacco is grown in a manner different from that in Rumelia. In December the tobacco growers select a piece of land on the side of a hill, exposed to the sun and protected from wind. They dig this land two to three times, and in February they sow tobacco seeds mixed with ashes. If the weather is favorable the seeds sprout in twenty to twenty-five days, but when it is extremely cold they begin to sprout only after fifty to sixty days. During this time the tobacco growers' occupation consists of pulling up and throwing away the useless grass, which grows together with the tobacco, and watering the plants when they are dry.

By the beginning of May the young roots have germinated, and the growers transfer them to plots which have been manured. They sow the roots on lines at intervals of one arshin [a Russian and Turkish measure of length, about 71 centimeters] with a space opposite each one.

...ley water the roots at intervals, and at the end of twenty days they hoe the soil which covers them.

The tobacco remains in this situation until the month of August, namely, until the beauty of the opening of the flowers. When the flowers open the growers collect the seeds that are needed for the next sowing and abandon the others to the birds of the field. After one to fifteen days those of the leaves which have taken on a yellowish color are cut and hung on a string 1.5 meters long in a special place which is covered over from the two ends of the string, protected from rain, and called *salaş* [booth, temporary shed]. The other leaves are subjected to the same procedure.

When the leaves are dry they take grass and make a bunch of three strings [of tobacco]. These bunches remain suspended on the ceiling in the house of the person to whom they belong until the end of October. The humidity resulting from the November rains serves to soften the leaves. The softened leaves are brought to one place, fifteen to twenty at a time. They sort the leaves by size, not quality, and make bales of thirty to thirty-five okkas each.

These bales are bought by traders in the place of production and transported to a neighboring village. The traders who have paid the official toll in advance are able to take the bales directly to their warehouses. There they sort the leaves by quality and make up new bales to be sent to the centers of consumption. Every kind of tobacco is dispatched in a definite direction according to the desires and needs of the various districts.

As for the traders who have [not followed this procedure], because they do not possess the right to transport the goods directly to their warehouses, they go to a place which is shown them inside the building of the tax office, and there make their selection and classification of the leaves.

The districts of Trebizond province which grow the most tobacco are Bafra "inside Alaçam," Çarşamba, and Samsun. Tobacco also grows in a few places adjacent to Samsun but the quantity is small, approximately 15,000 okkas a year.

The yearly amount of tobacco of the districts mentioned above is estimated at 550–650 thousand batmans. At the rate of one batman equaling 6 okkas that means 3.3–3.9 million okkas. By using proper selection and classification 150–200 thousand of the 550–650 thousand are of average quality, and each batman is sold for 45–72 kuruş, i.e., each okka is sold for 7.5 kuruş. It is known that the Bafra and Alaçam tobaccos take on a beautiful color and acquire a pleasant flavor with time. On the contrary, the tobaccos of Samsun, Çarşamba, and other localities, which present in the first months a beautiful sight, lose much of their quality after a few years and must then be sold at much lower prices.

The [two] samples which Trebizond province sent consisted of tobaccos of a quality which surpassed that of new Samsun and Bafra. Each was of very good quality and an okka of each brought 12 kuruş. . . .

It is evident that the climate and the quality of the soil facilitate the growing of the tobacco plant, which is found in all of Turkey, on all the lands of the Empire, whether in Europe or Asia. In a great many of the provinces, especially in Macedonia, one-tenth of the land is assigned to tobacco. And the quality of the tobacco produced in these places is very popular. In addition, local consumption of tobacco in Turkey is greater than in any other country, and exports to Europe show a growth registered in all official statistics.

Considering the fact that the Ottoman Empire is a state most blessed and most suitable for every sort of crop, the tobacco growers, who are sowing their crop in suitable places in accordance with agricultural techniques, would increase the production of tobacco if it were certain that they would be able to sell their output locally. Above all, as is commonly known, there is no possibility of Turkish tobaccos being injured by competition with American and European tobaccos. Because tobacco cultivation in Europe has reached the highest state of development, no new development in tobacco there can be expected. As for America, the [Civil] war destroyed the crop, and it is not known when America will again be able to export tobacco. Since Turkey is a neighbor to the western states and since it is able to export tobacco freely, it is in a position to offer its tobacco, which is gradually being more appreciated in foreign markets, at a cheap price.

From the port of Kavalla alone, 2,300,000 okkas of tobacco were exported in 1860. The consignment to France from Syria was also very important. According to registration statistics, the value of tobacco consigned to French ports from Turkey, approximately 200,000 francs in 1857, was 500,000 francs in 1858 and 1,700,000 francs in 1859. Transactions are still increasing.

As for the tobacco consumed within the Empire, it can be claimed that the amount is relatively greater than that consumed in any other state, however large. The amount of tobacco smoked by all classes, local and foreign, is so great that it cannot be imagined. Without exception the men and most of the women and children use a great deal of tobacco. One-fourth of the 25 million people dependent on the Sublime Porte, namely, 6,000,000, smoke cigarettes. If we estimate at 6 okkas the yearly average tobacco consumption of one person, we find an approximate total for internal consumption of 36,000,000 okkas.

A point which attracts attention in France is the extraordinary revenue that the treasury derives from the tobacco monopoly, which operates through a Régie. From a [government] revenue of 1,800 million francs, 200 million francs, namely, one-ninth, represent the revenue from tobacco. In England tobacco produces approximately 140 million francs a year.

As for Turkey, the tobacco monopoly, which was established in favor of the state following the new trade agreement, has not as yet given the anticipated results. Nevertheless there is a manifest surplus in the revenues.

We cannot deny that with the creation of new sources of revenue for the state by the last trade agreement, the government, which had not as yet taken measures in this matter, was confused. The Tax Commission must select one of the three methods described below:

(a) To levy an indirect tax, in the form of an octroi in the centers of consumption and storage; (b) to hold the carryover [baki] on the lines of the Tobacco Régie and organize a competent and autonomous tobacco office; or [(c)] to buy the tobacco crop by means of a tobacco monopoly and offer it on the market after sorting, blending, and manufacture.

The commission which Kani pasha chaired temporarily accepted the octroi principle, after closely scrutinizing the advantages of every method. The reason for their preference was the consideration that the octroi method was more suitable for present needs, that slowness in application because of the complexity of the other two methods would give rise to difficulties, and, finally, that, because of the financial crisis caused by [the introduction of] paper money, the imperial government was not in a position to divert large sums of money—which the other operations would entail—from other affairs in favor of this one.

The form of the present octroi is a tax called *mururiye*. A *mururiye* tax of 24 kuruş is levied on each okka of tobacco which is worth 15–30 kuruş or more per okka, and 12 kuruş on each okka which is worth 2.5–15 kuruş per okka. It is estimated that this tax would assure an income of 100 million kuruş a year. It is necessary to check directly at the production places the amount of tobacco produced in order to counter all sorts of tricks [or], more correctly, the traders who play a central role between the consumer and the producer.

In order to achieve this result the fields which are to be sown in tobacco are assigned by the local administrations and the crop is collected in public warehouses, or it is handed over to the Ottoman Régie from there or offered to the public after the tax is paid.

The taxes of 6, 12, and 22 kuruş which are

taken now, according to the kind of tobacco, correspond to 12 kuruş per okka on
the average. By subjecting 36 million okkas
of the tobacco used in the various districts
of the Empire to a direct Régie system, we
find a minimum 230 [*sic*, read 432] million
kuruş revenue, if we estimate the revenue of
the government relying on this average
of 12 kuruş. If we calculate the expense of
collecting the tax, the salaries of the
officials, and other expenses at 130 million,
namely 30 per cent of this source, a surplus
of 300 million kuruş remains in favor of the
treasury even so. . . .

CHAPTER 7

The Development of Agriculture in Anatolia

In the nineteenth century the development of agriculture in Anatolia was held up by a number of interrelated elements, some of which are still in effect. First, rainfall is inadequate and variable; except in the heart of the central plateau, however, this handicap is less severe than in other parts of the Middle East. Second, there was the lack of security in many regions, the unfavorable system of land tenure (see Part II, chap. 9), and the crushing burden of taxation on farmers (see Part II, chap. 12); these conditions almost eliminated the incentive to improve the land or expand production. The absence of organized agricultural credit drove farmers into the hands of money lenders. Inadequate transport also presented a major obstacle, one that was particularly significant in view of the fact that the population of Anatolia is scattered in nearly 40,000 small villages. Lastly, farm techniques had remained almost unchanged for thousands of years; in fact, as late as 1952, in spite of the marked progress registered under the Republic, only 29 per cent of the farms had iron plows—the others still used wooden plows with iron tips. As a result, yields were very low and both crops and livestock continued to be at the mercy of droughts, pests, and disease.

But, as the following selection shows, during the second half of the nineteenth century seeds of progress were sown which bore fruit much later. The most important inducement for change was the rapid expansion of industry and incomes in Europe, which stimulated the demand for Turkish tobacco (see Part II, chap. 6), cotton, raisins, and other cash crops. This rise in demand would, however, have remained unsatisfied had European capital not provided the channel through which the required goods could flow, namely, railways and ports (see Part II, chap. 10). European capital and technology—particularly German—also provided some irrigation works, banks, and assistance in the development of certain crops (see Part II, Introduction). This external stimulus would not have resulted in any significant change but for the response of some sections of the Turkish farm population to the new opportunities. As noted in the selection, to a marked extent this response came from Greeks, Armenians, Syrians, and other minority groups.

(See also Part III, chap. 13, and works by Aktan, Hallauer, and Mears listed in the Bibliography.)

[From A. D. Novichev, *Ocherki ekonomiki Turtsii* (*Essays on the Economy of Turkey*) (Moscow-Leningrad, 1937), pp. 75–83.]

THE DEVELOPMENT OF COMMODITY-MONEY AND CAPITALISTIC RELATIONS IN AGRICULTURE

... The weakest capitalistic relationships were to be found in the interior regions, where the production of grain crops and raising of livestock were predominant. Nevertheless, even in these regions a breach was made in the natural economy, commodity-money relations began to develop and, together with them but to a markedly lower degree, capitalistic relationships. In this process the railways played a very important part. As the railway network spread, the districts lying near it became increasingly involved in the task of providing the more remote markets with bread grains and other agricultural produce. From year to year there was an increase in the sale of bread grains in markets, as is clearly shown by the data on the transport of cereals on the railways. For instance, the Haider-paşa-Ankara railway (i.e., the one linking the central regions with Istanbul) in 1893—when the line was opened to traffic—transported 51,390 tons of bread grains, but in 1911 it carried 262,146 tons; in other words in eighteen years the freight had risen fivefold.[1]

According to the data given by the tsarist consul in Konya in 1912, from the *vilayet* of Konya 6,242,000 puds [a pud equaled 16.4 kilograms] of wheat out of a crop of 23,616,000 puds were sent to Istanbul and Smyrna, and 1,606,500 puds of barley out of a crop of 6,280,000. In other words, the ratio of marketing (*tovarnost*, i.e., ratio of commodity output to total output) in the Konya *vilayet* was not below 26.4 per cent for wheat and 25.5 for barley—not lower because it is to be presumed that a

certain part of the grain crops must have been disposed of in the local markets.[2]

The *vilayet* of Konya, particularly in the part adjoining the Anatolia-Baghdad railway, was one of the regions that sent grains to the large consuming markets of Turkey. This is why we find there a high ratio of marketing of grains. For the whole of Turkey, however, the average ratio before the [First World] War was not high. For the territory lying within the present limits of Turkey it stood at 8 per cent for wheat and 10 per cent for barley.

Turkish livestock breeding similarly raised its ratio of marketing. In 1893, the value of exports of mohair was 35.5 million piastres but already by 1895 the figure was 73.3 million. The sharper rise in export of mohair, compared to that of bread grains, is due to the fact that mohair was exported to foreign markets, whereas grains were sent to internal markets, where the dominant commodity in the larger centers was the wheat and flour imported from abroad. Export of animals also increased, mainly of sheep and goats slaughtered for meat.

The rise in the marketed quantity of grains and livestock was to only a negligible degree attributable to an increase in the productive powers of these branches. In a few regions close to the railways a marked extension of cultivation and increase in output did take place. But for Turkey as a whole it was insignificant, since there was no progress in agriculture or improvement of methods of production. In 1899 and 1912–13, the area under the two main crops in Turkey was as follows:[3]

	Hectares	
	1899	1912–13
Wheat. . .	2,667,000	2,653,000
Barley. . .	1,042,300	1,236,000

Thus, in thirteen years, the area under wheat not only failed to increase but actually shrank by 1 per cent. The area under barley, however, expanded by 18 per cent, which is

[1] Hecker, "Die Eisenbahnen der asiatischen Türkei," *Archiv für Eisenbahnwesen*, 1914, p. 1539.

[2] "Sbornik konsulskikh donesenii za 1904," No. 36, p. 22.
[3] "Sbornik konsulskikh donesenii za 1901," p. 390 (for 1899), and Mears, *Modern Turkey* [p. 291] (for 1912–13).

explained by the fact that much of the barley was exported abroad.

The main supplier of bread grains to the markets was the exploiting section of the countryside which, having greater possibilities of marketing agricultural produce, pushed still further its exploitation of the Turkish peasantry.

The ratio of marketing of grains in Turkey would have been much higher if it had not been impeded by foreign capital, with its high railway rates and its dominant position in the grain markets of the Turkish towns. Russia showed particular fear of the increase in agricultural production in Turkey, apprehending the emergence of a powerful competitor in the export of bread grains to the Mediterranean markets. This fear was one of the main reasons why Russia impeded railway construction in Turkey. When the Germans started to build the main Anatolia-Baghdad railway [see Part II, chap. 10] one of the tsarist Russian agents wrote: "The greatest harm that can be inflicted by this German enterprise to the economic growth of Russia, as an agricultural country, is competition in the cereals markets of Europe."[4]

By contrast with grain crops, industrial and garden crops had a very high ratio of marketing; with few exceptions, they were almost wholly exported abroad. As the production of these crops was developed by foreign capital to meet its own needs, their export to foreign markets increased and with it the dependence on these crops of Turkish agriculture and the great mass of peasants, especially those living in the coastal regions and more particularly the ones along the Aegean Sea and the Sea of Marmara. The intensity of this process is shown by data on shipments from Turkey's leading exporting port, Smyrna. In 1839 its exports totaled 35,856,000 francs but already by 1865 they were 128,269,623 francs. In 1881 they fell to 104,600,000 francs.[5] In 1898

Smyrna exported 249,500 tons of goods and by 1906, 403,268 tons. Information on the volume of trade of Turkey's other important port—that of Mersin on the Mediterranean —shows that here too exports rose significantly. In 1890 they totaled 5.7 million rubles [the ruble equaled about 50 cents or 2 shillings] and in 1903, 8 million.[6]

Such a large rise in exports entailed a significant increase in the production of the goods exported. Thus, for example, in 1884 the total area planted in tobacco was 192,262 donums but in 1911 it was 814,162.[7] The output of tobacco was 22.5 million kilograms in 1884 and 63.5 million in 1911.[8] [See Part II, chap. 6.] The output of cotton in the main producing region, Adana, on the Mediterranean, amounted in 1896 to 400 tons but in 1914 to 33,750. Cotton production in Turkey passed through periods of expansion and contraction and once more started to increase at the end of the nineteenth century. At the beginning of the century Turkey was still one of the main suppliers of cotton for European textile factories. Particularly important as a cotton exporter was Macedonia. Later, however, cotton production in Turkey decreased because of the competition of American cotton. By the middle of the nineteenth century Turkey had lost its significance as a supplier of cotton, even for Europe. After the Crimean War cotton production began once more to revive in Turkey, but its greatest stimulus came at the time of the American Civil War, when English capitalists were compelled to tap new sources of raw materials [see Part VI, chap. 8]. Once more their attention turned to Turkey. In those Turkish provinces suited to cotton growing, seeds were distributed free of charge, as were farm implements and instructions on cotton cultivation. In the twentieth century, Germany played a leading part in the development of cotton cultivation in

---

[4] Tomilov, *Otchet o poezdke po Aziatskoi Turtsii*, Part 1, 1907, p. 356.
[5] Demetrius Georgiades, *Smyrne et l'Asie Mineure au point de vue économique et commercial* (Paris, 1885), p. 188.

[6] Tomilov, *op. cit.*, p. 43.
[7] A donum equals 1/12 of a hectare or 1/11 of a desiatin.
[8] *Istatistik yilligi* [*Annuaire statistique*], V (1931–32), 197.

Turkey, seeking to establish there a raw materials base for its cotton textile industry.

The production of raisins and figs also rose significantly: output of raisins was 36,000 tons in 1904 and 69,000 in 1913 and that of figs 18,000 and 32,000 tons, respectively.[9]

With the development of industrial and garden crops, i.e., of specialized agriculture, in Turkey, capitalistic relations began to appear. The production of these crops acted against the spread of share-cropping, for they demand many labor-consuming operations and careful attention in fields or gardens and thus entail the use of improved work tools, fertilizers, more intensive combatting of pests, and the investment of large amounts of capital. Hence the part of the cropper in such a system is very small, for all he can do is offer his labor power. The intensive labor methods of production of these crops necessitated hired labor, and agricultural machines made their appearance. And together with capitalistic relationships in agriculture came their carriers: the capitalist landowner and kulak, on the one hand, and the hired laborer, the farm hand, on the other. A German scholar, Bruck, stated: "In the last years preceding the war various large landowners—few of them pure Turks and mostly Greeks, Armenians, Syrians, and others—showed increasing understanding of more contemporary methods of production aimed at securing greater productivity. In the last prewar decade, in the *vilayet* of Adana, there were in use no fewer than 1,000 mowing machines, 100 steam threshers, 25 double steam plows, and 85 ordinary steam plows."[10]

An official Turkish publication, issued after the war, stated: "In contrast to other cotton-growing areas, where the system of renting out land prevails, in the Adana region large landholding is prevalent and labor is paid wages."[11]

In the wheat-growing areas, the most marked use of plows and agricultural machines took place in the *vilayet* of Konya, particularly in localities lying along the railway. But even there the demand for such machines was insignificant. According to the report of the tsarist consul in Konya, in 1912, sales of American, German, and Austrian plows in the *vilayet* totaled 400, with a total value of 1,000 Turkish liras; in addition Greek plows worth 650–700 liras were sold and local ones from Izmir and Ak-Şehir worth 1,000 liras. It is thus evident that the total value of plows sold in the *vilayet* of Konya in 1912 did not exceed £1,200–1,250 [*sic*]. The sale of reaping machines, mostly of American make, reached £250 in the same year. "The business transacted by the farm-implements store opened in Konya by a German company is still unsteady and does not cover the expenses incurred," reported the consul.[12]

The preceding data show that, before the war, the use of machinery in Turkish agriculture was extremely limited. The decisive factor in capitalist production continued to be the manual labor of the hired farm hands, which was paid for at extremely low rates. In western Anatolia, at the end of the last century, for example, laborers received from 20 to 50 kopeks for a working day of 15–16 hours. Female labor received still lower remuneration. Frequently, especially in cotton growing, wages were paid in kind. Food had to be provided by the workers and there were no lodgings—people slept in the fields.[13]

The majority of farm laborers were temporary workers who, especially during harvest time, left their villages in large crowds seeking work in the cotton areas. Often whole groups went from one locality headed by their elders, who served as intermediaries between the laborers and the employers and received the whole wage fund for distribution among the individuals;

[9] *Ibid.*, p. 200.
[10] Bruck, *Die türkische Baumwollwirtschaft* (Jena, 1919), p. 17.
[11] *Die Baumwolle*, issued by the Ministry of Commerce of Turkey, 1926, p. 3.
[12] "Sbornik konsulskikh donesenii za 1914," No. 32, p. 35.
[13] F. Rougon, *Smyrne* (Paris, 1892), p. 76.

taking advantage of their position, the elders thoroughly robbed their countrymen. The cotton region of Adana drew from 50,000 to 70,000 workers during harvest time.

Before the war many regions of Turkey complained of a shortage of labor. But this shortage was due not to the rapid development of capitalism in Turkish agriculture but, on the contrary, to its extreme weakness; thanks to this the mass of Turkish villages continued to practice *métayage* and did not throw on the market a large number of farmers ruined by capitalism, deprived of everything, and compelled to sell their labor. Furthermore, in the production of labor-absorbing industrial and garden crops *métayage* displayed its vitality, as we have shown above.

With respect to the considerable development of commodity-money relationships in the production of specialized crops and the marked growth of capitalistic relationships, we should once more emphasize that these were brought about not because of the demand of the internal market—i.e., as a consequence of the growth of its own industry—but because of the demand of foreign markets. The further this process developed, the greater became Turkey's dependence on foreign capital.

This defect in the development of commodity-money relationships in Turkey constituted an additional, powerful factor contributing to the immiserization and ruin of the peasant masses. Large landowners, tax farmers, and money lenders began to exploit the peasantry even more intensively, in order to have more produce for sale in the market. Furthermore, they began to be more interested in concentrating land in their own hands. An additional stimulus for this process came from the rise in the price of land. Thus already at the end of the last century vineyards in the valleys of the Gediz-çay and Buyukmenderes-çay, in western Turkey, were valued at 100 to 400 francs per donum, i.e., at 350 to 1,400 rubles per hectare. The price of fig plantations stood at a similar, or even higher level.

Cotton fields were worth 350 to 700 rubles per hectare. The price of land planted in cereals, in areas disposing of greater possibilities for the marketing of their produce, reached 150–180 rubles per hectare.[14]

Consequently, in regions connected with the market, together with the development of commodity-money relationships and the rise in land prices, there was an increase in the expropriation of peasant land. This process was particularly marked in the coast lands and in European Turkey, especially in Macedonia.

The power of money in the countryside became stronger, but the peasants had no means of offsetting this new factor aggravating their condition. Thus, for example, the newly built railroads increased imports of goods into many regions, striking a hard blow against peasant domestic industries, in spite of their vitality. The peasant was even forced to buy from the market several goods which he had formerly made for himself. His growing need for money strengthened his dependence on money lenders. To an increasing extent, peasant land passed over to money lenders and merchants in payment of debts, large landownership increased, and the number of landless peasants rose. At the beginning of the twentieth century a German scholar, Warburg, noted: "The number of peasant-proprietors is falling rather than rising. Peasant-owned land constitutes in several provinces 15 to 50 per cent of cultivated land. The rest belongs to *vakfs*, the government, or large landowners who, with rare exceptions, however, also have the land worked by share-croppers, for the most part former peasant-proprietors."[15] To a much more marked degree than before, land became an object of purchase and sale.

In this way the development of commodity-money relationships in Turkey, under the influence of foreign capital which was interested in the preservation of the

---

[14] *Ibid.*, p. 75.
[15] O. Warburg, "Die Landwirtschaft der Türkei," in *Das türkische Reich*, ed. J. Hallauer (1918), p. 182.

remnants of feudalism, resulted in the worsening of the condition of the broad peasant masses and, although it may seem strange, sometimes in the strengthening of the system of share-cropping.

From what has been said it is clear that an indispensable precondition of progress in Turkish agriculture was the overthrow of the rule of foreign imperialist capital and its internal feudal agents: the sultan's government, the temporal and spiritual feudalists and semi-feudalists, and the tax farmers, money lenders, and other representatives of the pre-capitalist social order. . . .

Land-Tenure Problems in the Fertile Crescent in the Nineteenth and Twentieth Centuries

The land-tenure system of the Middle East has a very long and complex history and shows the influence of the many civilizations that flourished before Islam— Egyptian, Persian, Byzantine, and others—as well as the influence of Arab, Mongol, and Turkish laws and customs. The basic legal distinction was between *mulk*, or freehold private property which applied to urban real estate and the site of village houses and immediately adjacent plots, and *miri* (or *arazi amiriye*), or crown lands. The latter applied to most of the land; under it ownership was vested in the state, while the occupant enjoyed the usufruct on payment of land tax. On crown lands a "feudatory" intermediary exercised the functions of the state, in return for military service. Alongside these categories were the tribal or village communal lands.

Under the Ottomans most of the crown land was given out to *sipahi*'s in the form of *ziamet*'s or *timar*'s, the former bringing in a revenue five to ten times as high as the latter. The *sipahi*'s constituted the "feudal" cavalry of the Empire, as distinct from the janissaries or house-hold slaves who were recruited from the Christian subjects and provided the shock troops. The *sipahi*'s farmed part of their "fief" directly and raised taxes from the peasants who worked the rest. But the state kept strict control over all *ziamet* and *timar* land, through carefully drawn registers, and by and large prevented abuse of power or extortion; when the *sipahi*'s failed to perform the required military and police duties, they could be dismissed.

Three aspects of the crisis that overtook the Ottoman Empire in the sixteenth and seventeenth centuries affected the system of land tenure. First, the influx of American silver caused prices to rise and hence greatly increased the government's need for revenue. Second, the introduction of firearms decreased the value of the cavalry; at the same time the *sipahi*'s began increasingly to evade their military duties, bribing their way out or sending unfit substitutes, and sought to transform their "fiefs" into private property. Third, the number of janissaries increased rapidly and their quality deteriorated even faster. As a result, the government increasingly began to take over the vacant "fiefs" and either grant them to courtiers, in return for payment or bribes, or else let them out to tax farmers. By the end of the eighteenth century a very large part of the land was under a system of tax farming called *iltizam*.

These farmers, or *multazim*'s, were supposed to raise from the peasants only a stipulated amount, but in fact they enjoyed great power and, owing to the increasing weakness and corruption of the government, the peasants had practically no legal redress. Their extortion was usually proportionate to the shortness of their tenure; this led the government to introduce, in the eighteenth century, a system of life farming of taxes, *malikane*, in the hope of checking abuses, but its application was not universal. There seems little doubt that the position of the peasants deteriorated considerably in the course of the seventeenth and eighteenth centuries. "The spread of tax-farming accounted more than any other cause for the disruption of the order that had formerly ruled in the provinces. But what rendered the pursuit of agriculture difficult, and in many cases finally impossible, was the provincial anarchy that resulted from the weakening of control by the central government, and the consequent emergence of petty dynasts."[1]

In the nineteenth century another factor gained importance: the growth of cash farming (see Part II, chap. 7, Part III, chap. 5, and Part IV, chap. 3). This led, as in other parts of the world, to an acceleration in the breakup of prevailing forms of communal tenure and to a tendency for village or tribal lands to be appropriated by some powerful individual, e.g., tribal *shaikh*'s, local landlords, or urban money lenders. The attempts of the Ottoman government to deal with the resulting situation in the Fertile Crescent are described in the two following selections, the second of which (chap. 9) compares the evolution of Egypt and the Crescent. The reforms carried out by Muhammad Ali in Egypt are further discussed in Part VI, chap. 3.

(See also works by Gibb and Bowen, Inalcik, Himadeh [*Syria* and *Palestine*], Barkan, Granott, Weulersse, Rivlin, and Baer listed in the Bibliography.)

[1] Gibb and Bowen, *Islamic Society and the West*, Part I, p. 256. See also Part II, chap. 1, above.

[From unpublished report by Doreen Warriner, "Land Tenure in the Fertile Crescent," presented to Middle East Supply Centre, 1944; printed by kind permission of the author.]

THE REAL MEANING OF THE OTTOMAN LAND CODE

When the mandatory powers took over the territories of these four countries [Palestine, Trans-Jordan, Syria, Lebanon, and Iraq] after the last war, the system of land tenure was based on the Ottoman Land Code. This was a body of civil law which had been put on the statute books during the nineteenth century. Its weakness was that it was never generally enforced owing to the well-known Turkish lack of administrative efficiency, but because it was the only legal pattern in existence it was necessarily adopted by the mandatory powers, and has since been modified by them in different directions. We must examine briefly its main outline in order to understand the purpose of their work in reforming conditions of tenure.

Descriptions of land tenure in the Near and Middle East usually begin by giving the main legal categories into which land was divided by the Ottoman Land Code (promulgated in 1858). These are five:

1. *Mulk land:* This is the land held in absolute freehold ownership. It is governed by the provisions of sacred law and not by those of the Civil Statute Law. Land-ownership comprises two rights: the *raqaba*, or right of absolute ownership, and the *tasarruf*, or right to the usufruct of land. In *mulk* tenure both rights belong to the individual.

2. *Miri land:* This is the land of which the *raqaba* or absolute ownership belongs to the state but the *usufruct* to the individual. It is a form of heritable leasehold ownership in which the state leases land to the individual.

3. *Waqf land:* This is land dedicated to some pious purpose and is not very important in this region.

4. *Matruka:* Land reserved for some public purpose as for example village threshing floors.

5. *Mawat land:* Dead or unreclaimed land.

Now in actual practice these divisions do not seem to have much significance. *Mulk* and *miri*, the two main categories so far as the use of land is concerned, come to much the same thing. The owner of the land on *miri* title, in theory a tenant of the state, is really in just the same position as the owner with the *mulk* title, since he pays no rent to the state and his title to the land can be inherited by his legal heirs; he can also sell the land. There are no restrictions on the way the land is farmed, with the one exception that if *miri* land is left uncultivated for five years the owner's title lapses.

Another surprising fact is that these different divisions do not cover the lease-hold tenancies between landlord and cultivator which are by far the most general form of tenure, and which affect the actual tillers of the soil more closely than do any of these muddled and rather meaningless legal categories. The Ottoman Land Code apparently does none of the things that a land-tenure code ought to do.

The question arises therefore what the

purpose of these categories of land really was. So purposeless are they at first sight that it is easy to conclude that they represent simply some oriental attitude unintelligible to the west. But a study of the development of the land code in the course of the nineteenth century suggests that these divisions of land really had an important purpose—the collection of revenue. The real purpose of the code was to tax every piece of land, and therefore to establish clearly the title to it by registering its legal owner as a *miri* owner. The state's claim to ownership really meant only that the state did not recognize ownership unless the title were registered and the land therefore taxable.

In general, the practice was to grant the title directly to the cultivator and to prevent any intermediary between the government and the small individual owner. Hence the theory that the legal ownership of *miri* land belongs to the state, and that title can be granted only to the usufruct of land, was an attempt to centralize the power of administration against the feudal or tribal forms of existence. The object was to establish a form of peasant ownership as against the tribal *shaikh*'s. There are, of course, instances of large estates which have arisen from direct grant of *mulk* land by Turkish sultans to their political supporters; there are also estates which have arisen from the farming-out of taxes under the Ottoman regime, and others which have arisen from the indebtedness of the peasantry. But to establish these was not the general intention of the law. The Turks wanted to create a strong central government, on top of a large number of small cultivators, in order to be able to extract the maximum revenue from the land. They were therefore, anti-*shaikh*, since the tribal power of the *shaikh*'s was a threat to the central government.

Consequently the Ottoman Land Law was also opposed to the recognition of any type of collective ownership. Article 8 of the code states: "The whole land of a village or of a town cannot be granted in its entirety to all of the inhabitants nor to one or two persons chosen from amongst them. Separate pieces are granted to each inhabitant and a title is given to each showing his right of possession."

In actual fact, as we shall see, this provision was evaded, owing to the failure of the administration to register land titles systematically. The intention, however, was to introduce a system of direct contact between the cultivator and the government. Most of the activity of the land-settlement departments in the last twenty years has had the same object in view and has been trying to rectify the defects of the Turkish administration, while adhering to its principles.

In practice this has not been easy, because the forms of agricultural organization and social structure still contain tribal elements. Between the legal conceptions of the land code and the realities of Arab society there is a conflict, and the result is a muddle which will take much effort and energy to straighten out.

The Influence of Arab Custom

The desert and tribal life have imprinted a distinctive stamp on the customary methods of Arab tenure, as a brief survey of the area will show.

The agricultural land which we are considering in this survey forms the so-called Fertile Crescent, a semicircle of cultivable land round the deserts of Syria and Saudi Arabia, in which rainfall is high enough to permit arable cultivation, because of the proximity either of the seacoast or of the mountains. The 20 centimeter (or 8 inch) rainfall line marks its limits, since with less rainfall wheat cultivation is impossible; and though crops of barley are grown on the desert border with only a 4 inch rainfall, they are uncertain or poor.

The cultivable land, as defined by this rainfall line, begins about at Beersheba in Palestine and at first is only a fringe along the coast. To the east, its limits are defined by the Hijaz Railway in Trans-Jordan, which roughly marks the boundary between

the desert and the sown land, up to the Syrian frontier. There the cultivable area widens to include the Hauran, and contracts back west to Damascus, which stands in its irrigated oasis, the Ghuta, on the edge of the desert. Thence northward the area widens again, under the influence of the Anti-Lebanon Mountains, and eastwards from Aleppo follows the line of the Taurus Mountains, along the Syrian-Turkish frontier, widening southward to cover the big region known as the Jezireh, which lies between Syria and Iraq, a region formerly productive but now only sparsely populated and partly uncultivated.

The rainfall zone continues into Iraq and ends at the edge of the alluvial plain of southern Iraq at a line between the two rivers from Hit to Samarra. South of this line begins the irrigated zone of Iraq, with very low rainfall, which depends on the irrigation supplies of the two rivers, in whose delta the Fertile Crescent ends.

Around the Crescent the rainfall declines, from west to east, away from the coast line, or from north to south away from the mountains, and the intensity of cultivation declines with it. The zone of really intensive cultivation is very narrow. It covers the coastal plain of Palestine and the Plain of Esdraelon, and Lebanon, which is densely populated and intensively cultivated, using the short rivers which descend from the Lebanon to the sea for small irrigation schemes.

But in all the regions not more than fifty miles east of the coast, and not irrigated, the types of farming are very extensive indeed. Fallow every second or third year is the usual rotation, wheat or barley being the main crop. Yields are low, between 50 and 80 kilograms per donum (0.5–0.8 tons per hectare or approximately 4–6 hundredweight per acre), and vary with the rainfall, to a far greater extent than in Europe. In the Jezireh, for instance, wheat gives a tenfold return in a good year, sevenfold in a normal year, and in a bad year gives back only the equivalent of the seed. Yields are in fact a function of a very irregular rainfall, and the

Fertile Crescent is fertile only in comparison with the desert which it surrounds.

All around the margin of the cultivated zone are regions of still greater uncertainty, where yields may be sufficient in a good year to give some return and where there is desert grazing in spring. These are the regions for tribal grazing, for the genuinely nomadic population. The process of settlement of the nomad tribes is still going on. The existence of the desert gives a continuous sense of uncertainty in the settled regions.

Because of the great instability of the crop yields, general poverty, and social insecurity, forms of tribal ownership tend to linger. Up the coast, and particularly in Lebanon, individual small ownership or small tenancies is the predominant system, because the cultivation of olives, citrus, and other fruits demands a long-term investment. Wherever irrigated crops or fruit trees are grown, stable ownership is also the rule (except in Iraq, where conditions are very peculiar indeed).

But in the cereal belt, among the settled population, a form of semicommunal ownership still exists which originated in tribal custom. As the tribes settled, they allotted the arable land to the tribal subgroups or clans on an equal basis, dividing up the land of the village into different zones according to its quality and allotting a section in each zone to the different subgroups, which in turn divided up the land in their section among their members. To maintain equality between tribes, and between members of the tribe, the land was realloted at intervals between the tribal subgroups and between the members of the group. In this way originated the *Musha'* (i.e., Arabic "shared") system, which is still fairly prevalent in Syria and parts of Palestine and Trans-Jordan, though in the two last it is tending to disappear.

Musha' ownership represents a stage of transition between the completely communal property system of the seminomadic tribe on the desert borders and the completely divided property system which

exists in the settled zone along the coast line; and it is limited to the rain-fed cereal zone. Its basic idea, the communal ownership of land, is clearly tribal in origin.

Among the Arabs, in so far as they are a nomadic people, the idea prevails that land lies outside commercial transactions. Private property is recognized for livestock, tents, and personal equipment, but land, since it is available only temporarily and is extensively cultivated, is regarded as tribal property, much as grazing grounds are regarded. Among some settled villages in Syria, in the Ansariehs, the completely communal concept still dominates: the land of the village is divided each year among all the families of the village in proportion to the numbers of male inhabitants; when an individual dies or leaves the village, his rights go back to the community, and when a new child is born he automatically acquires a share in the family's right to land. This type of ownership is prevalent only among the poorest villages, and among the beduin settled in the districts of Hauran and Palmyra.

Musha' ownership is a development from this more primitive system. Under *Musha'* the right to own land is expressed as a share in the total, and the land of the village is periodically redistributed among different owners in proportion to their share. But the shares are not necessarily equal, as under a communal system they are, and can be bought and sold, as under a communal system they cannot be.

Originally the land was divided on an equal basis among different families (or tribal units); in order to make an equitable share out of the land, the good and the bad lands of the village were divided into zones (*maqsam*'s or *mawqa*''s) and each family received a claim to an equal area or land in each zone.

As the original families or tribal units have broken up into individual households, and the shares subdivided by inheritance, inequality arises, and the shares held by the different cultivators vary considerably. The *musha'* share is expressed in Syria on the basis of *faddan*, which means not a definite area of land, but a fraction of the total land, and a cultivator is said to own 3 faddans, which means 3 out of the 60 or 100 or 500 shares into which the whole land of the village is divided.

Usually as numbers grow the system breaks down, the periodic redistribution of the strips of land between the different groups is abandoned, and individual ownership gradually establishes itself by prescriptive right. The division of holdings into many small strips remains. The *musha'* system has lapsed in most of Palestine and in Bekaa in Lebanon. As soon as intensive farming begins, the *musha'* system has to be abandoned.

Of course the system has great disadvantages, since it prevents any investment in the land and is an obstacle to any attempt at progress. The individual cultivator is precluded from manuring the land or undertaking any improvement such as terracing against erosion. *Musha'* can be tolerated only for a very extensive system with a biennial or even triennial rotation, and without any fruit cultivation. (Fruit plantations are always held as individual property, even in a village with the *musha'* system on the rest of the land.) Even for an extensive system it is a wasteful one and, according to M. Duraffourd (the former director of the Land Survey Office in Syria and Lebanon), means a loss of about 30 per cent in efficiency —10 per cent due to loss of time, in moving about the different strips, 10 per cent due to loss of land, and 10 per cent due to the excessive seeding rate.

It would, of course, be desirable to keep the communal type of landownership, as a basis for introducing large-scale development, on the village level, with machinery and irrigation, rather than to allow the communal form to break into a large number of very small holdings, most of which would be too small and too split up into parcels for any rational system. But in practice it would be very difficult to run the village as a communal unit, since once the *musha'* system has reached saturation point,

owing to the growth of the number of owners, the conflicts between the villagers prevent any agreement between producers. To carry through any general investment on a village basis would necessitate some form of communal administration in the village, and this would not be possible, since between the villagers who have title to land, there can be no permanent agreement to give up any point of their independence. The restrictions of the *musha'* system prevent any advance in the way of agricultural credit, improvement in seeds, and particularly in the way of investment in fruit production. There is no doubt, in the minds of all those who have seen it working, that it must be abolished before any real advance can be made.

THE CONFLICT BETWEEN LAW AND CUSTOM

The Ottoman government aimed at abolishing the *musha'* custom in individual holdings as long ago as 1858. In that year the Ottoman government carried out a census and introduced a compulsory registration of title. While in theory this census established title to divided holdings of land, by registering a claim under the name of the occupying owner, in fact the titles as they were then established did not correspond at all to reality. The villagers, fearing that the registration was a preliminary to a call for military service, or for taxation purposes, falsified the returns, registering the property either in the name of the head of the tribe or in the name of a member of the family who would not be liable for military service. In practice they disregarded the titles which were granted (the *sanad tapu*) and continued to farm on the *musha'* system, recognizing the customary quota-holders as the real owners. Thus complete confusion resulted, since there arose one situation established by law under which certain owners held titles to divided land and another situation, existing in fact, in which the persons cultivating the land had claims recognized by custom or presumptive right, which were not enforceable by law.

Obviously, a system of registration of title was the first reform the mandatory governments had to undertake. This immediately raised very difficult problems. Was it desirable to register land as a claim to a share, and so to recognize the *musha'* system, or was it preferable to establish title to individual divided ownership? Obviously there was everything to be said for divided ownership, provided that the peasants themselves recognized the disadvantages of *musha'* tenure and wanted it abolished. But on the other hand there was the warning example of the failure of the Ottoman government's attempt to introduce divided ownership because it conflicted with custom.

The mandatory governments have approached this problem in different ways. In Palestine, the *musha'* system has apparently lapsed to a very large extent (though there is no exact information on this point), and the Department of Land Settlement has registered titles to individual holdings which already existed before registration. In Trans-Jordan, titles have been settled both in *musha'* and *mafruz* (divided) villages, but mainly in the former, and settlement is invariably accompanied by a division of the land of the villages into individual holdings and the abolition of *musha'*. In Syria, the Survey Office has adopted the contrary practice, registering titles to *musha'* quotas, not to individual holdings unless these already exist or unless there is a marked demand for it. . . .

None of the departments concerned, except in Syria and Lebanon, have been able to deal with the fragmentation of individual holdings, which is almost as great an obstacle to progress as the *musha'* system, and sooner or later this will have to be tackled.

THE LANDLORD CLASS

The third factor that influences the land system is the existence of a parasitic landlord class, a result in part of the Turkish system in which grants of land were made to political supporters of the sultan or in which powerful chiefs seized the rights to farm taxes. But the more general cause for the rise of the city-notable type of landlord is the perpetual indebtedness of the peasants, which results from the uncertainty of grain yields. One or two years of bad harvests will impoverish the cultivators, force them to borrow even to buy seed, and after borrowing at high rates of interest, they are eventually forced to sell their holdings to wealthy merchants in the towns and to continue to exist as tenants of the big landowners. This process has gone very far in Syria and northern Iraq.

Usually the rent is fixed on a share basis, amounting to one-fifth of the produce if the landlord performs no service except that of paying taxes, two-fifths if the landlord provides seeds, four-fifths if the landlord pays all costs but labor. This system is common throughout Syria and is followed in most of these countries to some extent.

The landlords who have acquired land in this way are rarely farmers and may not even visit the villages they own. In Deir ez Zor, for example, on the Euphrates, one family is said to own thirty-two villages. The villagers continue their strip cultivation, even sometimes on the *musha'* system, without in any way changing their methods of production. Landownership is a credit operation and nothing more.

There are, of course, landowners who are also farmers in a big way, but usually only where there is irrigation, as in the date gardens of Iraq, which are really large farms, and on the coast of Lebanon where there are irrigation schemes on a small scale developed by local landowners. In this case the large landowner really invests capital in the estate and manages it, as in Europe, but in the rain-fed cereal zone he appears simply in the role of a money lender without responsibility to the land. This type of ownership is injurious, since it prevents constructive investment in the land.

None of the mandatory powers has attempted to regulate the relations of landlords and peasant cultivators; they have followed too much the conceptions of the Turkish code, in which registration of title was the be-all and end-all of the system. They have enormously improved on the efficiency of the Turkish system, but in following it have neglected all the things which it neglected. There has been no attempt to give tenant cultivators greater security of tenure, or to facilitate their desire to become owners. To do this, of course would need more than merely legal changes; it would involve the provision of a system of agricultural credit, a system of greater marketing stability, since otherwise the tendency of the peasant to borrow at excessive rates will never be checked. To some extent the official grain-collection schemes introduced during the [Second World] War have been a change in this direction and are therefore more popular with the smaller men than with the landlords. . . .

CHAPTER 9

Land Tenure in Egypt and the Fertile Crescent, 1800–1950

The differences between the agrarian structure of Egypt and that of the Fertile Crescent are numerous and far-reaching. Some are due to geographical factors: the prevalence of irrigated as contrasted with rain-fed agriculture; the regularity of the Nile as compared with the unpredictability of the Tigris and Euphrates (see Part III, Introduction); the utter barrenness of the Egyptian deserts, which cannot sustain so large a nomadic population as that of the Syrian desert and thus greatly diminished the beduin threat to Egypt; the flatness of Egypt, as against the very mountainous nature of Syria and northern Iraq; the presence of the magnificent waterway provided by the Nile, which puts the whole country within easy reach of the capital (see Part VI, chap. 6); and the relative isolation and greater capacity for defense of Egypt. From these and other factors, further differences have followed: the political unity of Egypt and the frequent breaking apart of the countries of the Fertile Crescent; the greater density of the population of Egypt during the last seven or eight centuries; and the high degree of control exercised by the central government over the remotest parts of the countryside, a control which is indicated by the cadastral surveys repeatedly undertaken both before and after the Muslim conquest.

The following selection traces the consequent divergence in the agrarian history of the two regions since the beginning of the nineteenth century. Since 1952 the contrasts have once more been sharply revealed. In Egypt the agrarian reform of that year—which was based on a sound understanding of the agricultural methods, the pattern of landownership, and the historical relationships prevailing in the country—must be pronounced a distinct success, for it both brought about a greater measure of social justice in the countryside and probably helped to increase productivity; the same may be true of the reform of 1961. In Syria on the other hand the land reform of 1958—a hastily drawn-up measure ill suited to an agriculture suffering from large fluctuations in rainfall and owing its rapid development to an active entrepreneurial group of landowners and merchant-cultivators—

failed signally and helped to dislocate the country's economy. The same applies to a still greater degree to the Iraqi land reform of 1958, whose implementation was thwarted or disorganized by the highly disturbed political conditions that followed the overthrow of the monarchy in that year.

(See also works by Karpat, Barkan, Warriner [*Land and Poverty* and *Land Reform*], and Issawi [Egypt in Revolution] listed in the Bibliography, and references for Part II, chap. 8.)

[Unpublished article by Gabriel Baer (1962), "The Evolution of Private Landownership in Egypt and the Fertile Crescent"; printed by kind permission of the author.]

In the Ottoman Empire and, after its disintegration, in the Arab countries of the Fertile Crescent private ownership of land developed during the nineteenth and twentieth centuries as it did in Egypt in the nineteenth century. There were however fundamental differences between the two developments with regard to both their pace and character. The analysis of these differences is essential for understanding the differences between the agrarian structure of these two areas, as well as between the conditions under which, today, land-reform measures are to be implemented in the various states of the Middle East.

THE ABOLITION OF FEUDALISM

The agrarian system of the Ottoman Empire in the eighteenth century was not uniform as it was in Egypt. As in Egypt, in remote and isolated districts of the Empire the *iltizam* prevailed, by which the land, theoretically owned by the state, was made over to tax farmers for the collection of its revenue. In the adjacent vicinity of Turkey, however, the remnants of a system of military feudalism survived, by which feudal estates (*timar*) were granted to the *sipahi*'s, the Ottoman cavalry. At the beginning of the nineteenth century feudalism was abolished in the Ottoman Empire and *iltizam* in Egypt, and an attempt was made to introduce ownership by the farmers over their lands and direct collection of taxes by the state. But many factors caused this development to be quicker and more thorough in Egypt than in the Fertile Crescent. The following are among the most important:

1. The government in Egypt was of a centralist character, stemming from its importance to the economy as a regulator of irrigation by the waters of the Nile.

2. The Nile enabled every government in Egypt to reach the most remote parts of the state with comparative ease, while the communications of the Ottoman Empire were rather deficient, not enabling the state to control efficiently all its territory. Without such an efficient control over every acre of state land it was impossible fully to abolish feudalism and to introduce a system of private individual ownership, since such a system requires registration of land and rights of ownership, the effective protection of these rights, systematic collection of taxes from every farmer, and so on.

3. The population of the Fertile Crescent was much more variegated than that of Egypt: it included beduins in Iraq and the Syrian desert, tribes in the mountains of Syria, Lebanon, Palestine, and Kurdistan, as well as ethnic and religious minorities. Of all these problems only that of the beduin tribes existed in Egypt, but conditions were much more favorable for its solution than in the countries of the Fertile Crescent; indeed, Egypt preceded the Fertile Crescent in its solution by about a century. It was thus much easier for the rulers of Egypt to introduce a new uniform system of private ownership of land than it was for the Ottoman government to do so.

4. From Muhammad Ali's time onward Egypt's irrigation network developed tremendously, and summer crops, especially cotton and sugar cane, became more and

more important. Thus the change-over to cash crops took place much earlier in Egypt than in the countries of the Fertile Crescent. This gave a strong impetus to the acquisition of land. Simultaneously, extensive ownership rights were granted to the new owners by Egypt's rulers as an incentive to agricultural development in which they were interested in order to increase the income of the state. Therefore land transactions and the development of mortgage credit, requiring a modern system of legislation, made much progress as early as the middle of the nineteenth century, while in the Fertile Crescent they did not evolve before the second quarter of the twentieth.

5. Political conditions in the Ottoman Empire during the Tanzimat period, both external (especially the wars with Russia) and internal (for instance, the Balkan and Lebanon problems) were not conducive to the efficient introduction of reforms even when Mahmud II and Abdul Mecid actually wished to bring them about. If similar problems existed in Egypt, they were much easier to overcome.

Muhammad Ali carried out his "agrarian reform" in a very short time: between 1811 and 1814 he destroyed the Mamluks, abolished the *iltizam* system, and appropriated all land held as *iltizam*. He seized all agricultural *waqf* land (called in Egypt *rizaq ahbasia*), i.e., land not subject to normal transactions, the income of which was assigned by the founder of the endowment to his offspring, to a family guest house, to a mosque, or to any other beneficiary in order to prevent its being confiscated by the ruler or its being split up among a large number of heirs. After having become the actual owner of almost all agricultural land in Egypt, Muhammad Ali carried out a cadastral survey and registered all land in the name of the villages to which it belonged.[1]

As against this, during the thirty-two years between the destruction of the janissaries in 1826 and the Ottoman Land

Law of 1858, Mahmud II and Abdul Mecid introduced only a part of these reforms in theory and in practice even less. A few days after the destruction of the janissaries (or, according to others, in 1831), Mahmud II ordered the reunification of lands held in the past by the *sipahi*'s as military feudal estates with those of the state.[2] The order was carried out in stages, first in the central districts and then in the more distant ones, until finally all feudal estates were abolished.[3] At the time of the Egyptian occupation, the revenue of the former *timar*'s of *sipahi*'s in the districts of Aleppo, Damascus, and Jaffa was apparently collected by the government.[4]

Compensation was paid to the former owners of *timar*'s throughout the nineteenth century, reaching very substantial proportions: the sum assigned for pensions to former timariots amounted to 120,000 purses.[5] At the same time, payment of the *faiz*, the *multazim*'s profit commuted into an annual pension, to the former *multazim*'s of Egypt, never constituted a serious problem for the treasury. There were two reasons for this: first, in Upper Egypt lands were seized from the Mamluk *multazim*'s (who offered resistance) without compensation; second, the *faiz* of the *multazim*'s in Lower Egypt was reduced at frequent intervals and paid only in part. Moreover, the *multazim*'s had in general contrived to

[1] For detailed treatment of this development see G. Baer, *A History of Landownership in Modern Egypt, 1800–1950* (London, 1962), pp. 1–7.

[2] M. Belin, "Du régime des fiefs militaires dans l'Islamisme," *Journal Asiatique*, March–April, 1870, pp. 293–94; B. Lewis, *The Emergence of Modern Turkey* (London, 1961), pp. 89–90. On 17 Rabi 'al-awwal 1247 A. H. (August 26, 1831) 'Abdallah pasha, the *wali* of Sidon and Tripoli, transmitted to the *mutasallim* of the *sanjaq* of Jerusalem the imperial decree about the dissolution of the *timar*'s (numbering 82 in that *sanjaq*), and ordered him to collect their revenue retroactively, beginning with 1829, for the imperial treasury. See A. Rustum, *Al-usul al-'arabiya li-tarikh surya fi 'ahd Muhammad 'Ali Basha*, I (Beirut, 1930), 36–37. For this and some other references in this section, I am grateful to Mr. Ori Standel, who permitted me to use his unpublished Seminar paper "Agrarian Relations in Syria and Palestine in the Nineteenth Century."

[3] According to Belin (*op. cit.*) in 1837; according to E. Engelhardt, *La Turquie et le Tanzimat* (Paris, 1882), I, 37 n. and 92, as late as in 1851.

[4] J. Bowring, *Report on the Commercial Statistics of Syria* (London, 1840), p. 22.

[5] Belin, p. 295; Lewis, p. 90; A. Granott, *The Land System in Palestine* (London, 1952), p. 31. (One purse = 500 piastres.)

reduce payments to the state by declaring a smaller income than they had had in fact. As a result, the compensation they received, based on their own assessments, was extremely small. It amounted to 6,000 purses in 1821, to 3,500 in 1833, and to 2,500 in 1835. Thereafter it became part of the general pension, until at the end of the century (1889–94) it was abolished in favor of a single, once-for-all payment.[6]

There was, however, a much more fundamental difference between Egypt and the Ottoman Empire in this respect. The Ottoman feudal estates taken from the *sipahi*'s were made over, in the first instance, to tax farmers (*multazim*'s or *muhassil*'s), which was exactly the system that had been abolished by Muhammad Ali in Egypt.[7] *Iltizam*, called in Syria *muqata'a*, thus became the prevailing method of tax collection in the Fertile Crescent. When Ibrahim pasha conquered Syria he tried to do away with *iltizam* there as his father had done in Egypt, but these experiments turned out to be among the causes for the uprising against him.[8] At the same time, in 1839, *iltizam* was officially abolished in the Ottoman Empire by the Hatti Şerif of Gulhane.[9] However, financial difficulties led to the reintroduction of the *iltizam* system in the Ottoman Empire in 1842,[10] to be again "finally" abolished in 1856 by the Hatti Humayun.[11]

Actually the system survived much longer.[12] In Lebanon, a fellah rebellion against the *muqata'ajiya* broke out in 1858, the rebels demanding the abolition of

feudal privileges, and it was found necessary to abolish once again all feudal privileges by the Regulation for the Administration of Lebanon of June 9, 1861.[13] In Palestine and Syria, the *a'shar* or tithes were farmed out to the highest bidder as late as in the 1890's, and, in some places, even at the beginning of the twentieth century. The following was written in 1891:

From all the produce of the farming lands of the empire a tithe is taken in kind. As, however, it would be a complicated and difficult process for the Government to collect these taxes directly, they are accustomed to let them out to tax farmers (*multazamin*), for a sum agreed upon by both parties... the government supplies them with soldiers to assist them in the collection of the taxes. . . . He has the power to quarter his horsemen and other animals without compensation on the poor villagers, who are glad to buy him off and get rid of him by paying two tenths or more.[14]

Moreover, in the Fertile Crescent the power of local dynasties (to be compared, to a certain extent, to the Turkish *derebey*'s whose power had been broken at the beginning of the century) survived much longer than elsewhere in the Middle East. Throughout the first half of the nineteenth century local families of *shaikh*'s virtually ruled large parts of Palestine and continued to do so even later in the century, though their power had been reduced during Ibrahim pasha's rule.[15] In the Syrian Jabal Druz (Hauran) the leading families exercised semi-feudal rights which were partly broken in the wake of a peasant revolt in 1886–87.[16] The strongholds of the remnants of feudal-

[6] F. Mengin, *Histoire de l'Egypte sous le gouvernement de Mohammed-Aly* (Paris, 1823), II, 338, 389; *Histoire sommaire de l'Egypte sous le gouvernment de Mohammed Aly* . . . (Paris, 1839), p. 153; Col. Campbell, "Report on Egypt," Public Record Office, F.O. 78/408 B; Egypt, No. 2, 1879, C. 2233, pp. 252–53; Ph. Gélat, *Répertoire de la législation et de l'administration égyptienne*, 2e période, I, 7–8, 3e période, I, 645–46.

[7] Lewis, *op. cit.*, p. 442.

[8] See A. D. al-'Aqiqi, *Thawra wa fitna fi lubnan* (Beirut, 1936), pp. 26 ff., and F. Perrier, *La Syrie sous le gouvernment de Mehemet-Ali* (Paris, 1842), pp. 358 ff.

[9] Cf. W. Padel and L. Steeg, *De la législation foncière Ottomane* (Paris, 1904), pp. 17, 23, and Lewis, p. 379.

[10] Engelhardt, *op. cit.*, I, 50–51, II, 52 (where the year 1841 is given). Cf. Lewis, p. 380.

[11] Engelhardt, I, 268–69.

[12] *Ibid.*, p. 52, and Granott, *op. cit.*, p. 58.

[13] Al-'Aqiqi, *op. cit.*, pp. 84, 161–63, 178, and *passim*. For text of the regulation see J. C. Hurewitz, *Diplomacy in the Near and Middle East* (Princeton, 1956), I, 165–68.

[14] G. E. Post, "Essays on the Sects and Nationalities of Syria and Palestine. Essay 2: Land Tenure," *Quarterly Statement of the Palestine Exploration Fund* (QPEF), 1891, pp. 106–7; cf. S. Bergheim, "Land Tenure in Palestine," *QPEF*, 1894, pp. 197–98; A. Ruppin, *Syrien als Wirtschaftsgebiet* (Berlin, 1920), p. 149.

[15] J. Finn, *Stirring Times* (London, 1878), I, 228–32, 240–41; L. Oliphant, *Haifa or Life in Modern Palestine* (2d ed.; London, 1887), p. 198; R. A. S. Macalister and E. W. G. Masterman, "Occasional Papers on the Modern Inhabitants of Palestine," *QPEF*, 1905, pp. 344, 352–56.

[16] M. Von Oppenheim, *Vom Mittelmeer zum persischen Golf* (Berlin, 1899), pp. 169–70, 175; A. Latron, *La vie rurale en Syrie et au Liban* (Beirut, 1936), p. 212.

ism and of *iltizam* were the hilly areas of Lebanon, Palestine, and northern Iraq, as well as the tribal marsh areas of southern Iraq. There were no provinces or areas in Egypt geographically or socially equivalent to these. This certainly was the main reason why the abolition of feudalism and *iltizam* in the Ottoman Empire took so much longer than in Egypt and why even after their abolition vestiges of the old agrarian system survived in the Fertile Crescent.

THE LAWS OF 1858

After Muhammad Ali's reforms, the next important stage in the evolution of the rights of private landowners in Egypt was Said's Land Law of 1858 (24 Dhu al-hijja 1274 A.H./August 5, 1858). The fact that Egypt was at that time part of the Ottoman Empire and that Said's law was promulgated only four months after the well-known Ottoman Land Law of the same year (7 Ramadan 1274 A.H./April 21, 1858) has misled a number of authors to believe that the former was no more than the application of the latter to Egyptian conditions. Thus Gatteschi wrote: "The order of the Viceroy of 1274 [Said's Land Law] applied the imperial law of 1858 [to the conditions of Egypt].... it was impossible to accept simply the laws of Constantinople for Egypt, where there did not exist a system parallel to that of Turkey.... it was therefore necessary to make special arrangements, which in taking into account these differences would carry out in Egypt the broad and liberal reforms of the imperial laws." [17]

This view seems to us to be completely mistaken. There certainly were some sections of the two laws which were partly or even entirely identical. Both draw a distinction between two kinds of land: one type over which the persons holding it have full ownership (in Egypt—*ib'adiya*; in the Ottoman Empire—*mulk*), and a second type whose *raqaba* (ownership without usufruct) is in the hand of the state and whose holders possess rights of usufruct only (in Egypt—

athariya or *kharajiya* lands; in the Ottoman Empire—*miri*). Both laws regulate the prescription of *kharajiya* (*miri*) lands; article 5 of the Egyptian law lays down that whoever has tilled a parcel of land for five years in succession cannot be deprived of his right of prescription, and article 20 of the Ottoman law states: "Actions concerning *miri* lands the occupation of which has continued without dispute for a period of ten years shall not be maintainable." [18] Both laws grant preferential rights in acquiring the holding of an heirless holder of *kharajiya* (*miri*) lands to the inhabitants of his village (article 3 in the Egyptian law; article 59 in the Ottoman law). [19] Both laws (article 9 in both) allow holders of *kharajiya* (*miri*) land to rent (although this right is limited differently in each of them).

However, in these common provisions no rights were granted that did not exist before that time. They were no more than a codification of the traditional rights of *kharajiya* (*miri*) landholders. In all other respects the two laws were completely different from one another not only in form but also in their intentions. In the Ottoman Empire vestiges of feudalism still survived, the state was weak, and, as we have seen, its rights over its lands were still challenged by local powers. Therefore, the Ottoman law aimed at consolidating these rights of the state, mainly by imposing severe restrictions on holders of *miri* lands and by listing exactly and in detail all rights held by them before its enactment which could not be denied them. [20] In Egypt, on the other hand,

---

[17] D. Gatteschi, *Des lois sur la propriété foncière dans l'Empire Ottoman* (Paris, 1867), p. 28.

[18] For the Ottoman Land Law see, for instance, the English translation by F. Ongley (London, 1892), in addition, the Arabic translation of Du'aybis al-Murr (in later references: Murr) in his *Kitab ahkam al-aradi* (Jerusalem, 1923), Part II, and the Hebrew translation in the appendix of M. Doukhan, *Dinei qarqaot beretz yisrael* (Jerusalem, 1925), have been consulted. Said's Land Law has been published separately in *Loi sur la propriété territoriale* (Alexandria, 1875). See also Y. Artin-Bey, *La propriété foncière en Egypte* (Cairo, 1883), *passim*.

[19] In the Ottoman law the inhabitants of the villages share the preference rights with other groups.

[20] See Engelhardt, *op. cit.*, I, 209; Granott, *op. cit.*, p. 87—as against Gatteschi, *op. cit.*, pp. 20 and 28, and N. H. Chiha, *Traité de la propriété immobilière en droit ottoman* (Cairo, 1906), p. 18.

the state had already gained satisfactory control over its lands long before. Private agricultural enterprise began to develop rapidly after the abolition of Muhammad Ali's monopolies, and a need was felt to facilitate land transactions in order to encourage the development of agriculture. Thus the principal purpose of Said's law was to expand the ownership rights of Egyptian landholders and to give their property security and stability.[21] Unlike the Ottoman law, Said's law was a far-reaching change in relation to the conditions of the past.

The different spirit permeating the two laws finds a very clear expression in the provisions concerning the erection of buildings and planting of trees on *kharajiya* (*miri*) land. Article 11 of Said's law granted full ownership rights to holders of *kharajiya* land who had erected buildings or set up a *saqiya* (water-raising apparatus for irrigation) or planted trees on it. In contrast, the Ottoman Land Law states: "Without the permission of the official, new buildings cannot be erected on *miri* land. If they have been erected the government can have them demolished." Article 25 states: "Without the permission of the official a person cannot make into a garden or vineyard the land he possesses by planting vines and different kinds of fruit trees. Even if he has done so without permission the government has the power during three years to make him pull them up." The purpose of the Egyptian law obviously was to encourage the development of agriculture. The Ottoman law, on the other hand, reflected the government's intention not to let out of its grasp any right or part of a right over *miri* land, for buildings and plantations were *mulk* property, and if they belonged to a person who was not the owner of the land on which they were established they invested this person with the right of pre-emption over the land.[22]

However, the differences between the two laws are not confined to provisions regarding buildings and plantations. The Egyptian law granted a number of new rights, while the Ottoman law imposed many restrictions on holders of *miri* land. Said's law provided for *kharajiya* lands to be inherited according to the Muslim laws of inheritance (like land in full ownership), and authorized their sale (without the necessity of obtaining prior permission from the state) and their mortgage. As against this, the Ottoman law laid down that leaving *miri* land fallow for three years was sufficient cause for confiscation by the state (arts. 68–71); prohibited the holder of *miri* land from using its soil for making bricks (art. 12); made its sale conditional on official consent (art. 36); and did not recognize pre-emption rights (*shuf'a*) over *miri* land (art. 46). Whoever cultivated *miri* land over which he had no right of usage and paid the taxes to the state was not required to pay an indemnity or rent to the owner but just to return it to him (art. 21). *Miri* land held in partnership might be divided only with the permission of the government (art. 17). The Ottoman law prohibited the mortgaging of *miri* land, although the owner was allowed, after having obtained a special permission from the authorities, to "alienate it to his creditor ... on condition that at the time he settles his debt the creditor will return the land to him," or to sell it in "a returnable sale [*faragh al-wafa*] on condition that whenever he returns the cost of the sale he has the right to claim the restitution of the land from the buyer" (art. 116). This last right had already been granted to Egyptian *kharajiya* holders in 1846 without the stipulation of a special permit from the authorities.[23]

There was only one point in which the Ottoman law was more "liberal" than the

[21] Artin, *op. cit.*, p. 105, and A. Crouchley, *The Economic Development of Modern Egypt* (London, 1938), p. 127.

[22] Article 44 of the Ottoman Land Law. This is Doukhan's explanation, which looks much more convincing than that given by Padel and Steeg.

[23] There is however a difference between *faragh al-wafa* and *rahn hiyazi* or *gharuqa* which was practiced in Egypt: *faragh al-wafa* transfers the ownership to the creditor, while *rahn hiyazi* transfers only cultivation rights. From this stems the provision in the Ottoman law which makes *faragh al-wafa* conditional on permission from the authorities.

Egyptian one: the 1858 Land Law and Ottoman legislation relating to immovable property in general[24] did not draw the same distinction between *miri* and *mulk* land as the Egyptian law did between *kharajiya* and *ib'adiya* lands with regard to rights of compensation in case of confiscation for public purposes. Thus the Ottoman law granted rights of compensation to holders of *miri* land confiscated for public use, while Egypt's rulers did not undertake such an obligation. The reason for this difference was the importance of public land in Egypt as a result of the extensive irrigation network. Said, and Egypt's rulers after him, did not wish to jeopardize the plans for development of irrigation and other works by placing obligations on the treasury, so long as they could prevent this by arguing that the *raqaba* of *kharajiya* lands belonged to the state. That Egypt differed fundamentally from the Fertile Crescent countries in this respect is shown by figures on the area of public domain (*matruka*)[25] in proportion to the total area: in Egypt this proportion rose from 7.9 per cent in 1922 to 10.8 per cent in 1949, while in Iraq it amounted to only 3.4 per cent in 1951 and in Trans-Jordan to only 1.5 per cent in 1950.[26]

1858–1950: MIRI AND MULK LAND REGISTRATION

The year 1858 had been a landmark in the history of landownership in the Middle East, after which the property rights of landowners continued to grow. They did so, however, with the same difference in pace and character between Egypt and the Fertile Crescent as before. In Egypt cash crops, especially cotton, became ever more important, land transactions multiplied, and foreign capital became interested in Egypt's landed property. Nothing comparable took place in the Fertile Crescent; only in the second quarter of this century did a slight change-over to cash crops begin to manifest itself, but it never attained the importance it did in Egypt. This difference in economic development was fully reflected in land legislation.

Throughout the second half of the nineteenth century the proportion of *mulk* land in Egypt, i.e., land held as full private property, grew steadily. From less than one-seventh of the total area in the 1850's, it increased to more than one-quarter in 1875, and it was approaching one-third in the 1890's. By that time, however (to be exact, in 1896),[27] *kharajiya* land was fully assimilated to *mulk*, so that in the twentieth century all agricultural land in Egypt was the full private property of its owners (except, of course, *waqf* land).

In the Ottoman Empire and the countries of the Fertile Crescent the proportion of agricultural *mulk* land did not increase at all. But here, too, ownership rights over *miri* were extended. This was done, however, much later than in Egypt: the first main group of laws in this direction was issued in 1913, and the second phase took place, in Syria and Iraq, in 1930 and 1932.

Moreover, in the Fertile Crescent *miri* land was never entirely assimilated to *mulk*, and some restrictions on *miri* land have remained in force to this day.

Although the state's right to demolish buildings erected on *miri* land without its permission was abolished by a special order in 1890,[28] the need for special authorization to erect buildings and to plant trees on *miri* land remained in force for another twenty years. It was abolished on 5 Jumada al-ula 1331 A.H./April 12, 1913, by article 5 of the Law of Transfer of Immovable Property,[29] which also permitted the transfer and sale of *miri* lands. Article 7 of the same law abolished the prohibition on the use of *miri*

[24] Cf. G. Young, *Corps de droit ottoman* (Oxford, 1906), VI, 127–31

[25] "Public domain" is land marked for special purposes, such as roads and irrigation canals, which cannot be sold by the state.

[26] The International Bank for Reconstruction and Development (IBRD), *The Economic Development of Iraq* (Baltimore, 1952), p. 179; Al-mamlaka al-urduniya al-hashimiya, *Al-nashra al-ihsaiya al-urdunniya 1950* (*Jordan Statistical Year-Book*).

[27] For details see Baer, *A History of Landownership*, pp. 10–12.

[28] Doukhan, *op. cit.*, p. 53.

[29] For text see Murr, *op. cit.*, Part II, pp. 119–23, and Doukhan, pp. 232–35.

land for making bricks. Article 14 required persons who cultivated other people's *miri* land to pay the owner rent, though not compensation for the depreciation of the land (the 1858 law required no payment of either kind). Mortgaging of *miri* land was permitted by the Law of Mortgages of 16 Rabi'al-thani 1331 A.H./March 25, 1913.[30] The need to obtain official permission for the division of *miri* land held in partnership was abolished by the Law of Division of Immovable Property of 4 Muharram 1332 A.H./December 13, 1913, which made such a division much easier.[31] All these rights, which were granted in the Ottoman Empire in 1913, had been granted for *kharajiya* lands in Egypt by Said in 1858 and partly even before that. Moreover, pre-emption rights in relation to *miri* land were not granted as long as the Ottoman Empire existed. They were granted in Syria and Lebanon in 1931,[32] but never in Palestine and Israel.[33] Another restriction which remained in force in all Fertile Crescent countries (more often than not in theory only) is the regulation that after a certain period of lying fallow *miri* land passes into the possession of the state: in Palestine (like the original provision of Ottoman times) after three years,[34] in Syria and Lebanon after five years,[35] and in Iraq after three to four years, according to different kinds of *miri* land.[36]

While these last-mentioned restrictions were of little practical importance, others had quite substantial influence on the development of landownership in the Fertile Crescent and its divergence from the course in which this development proceeded in Egypt. Originally the tilling of *kharajiya* lands in Egypt (formerly called *athariya*)

passed from father to son; in 1855 the right of inheritance was established for male heirs, and in 1858 Said ordered that *kharajiya* lands were to be inherited like *mulk* according to the Muslim law of inheritance. This provision remained in force except for the short period 1869–81, during which only the income from the land, but not the land itself, was divided in accordance with the Muslim inheritance law.[37] In the Ottoman Empire, too, the tilling of the peasants' land originally passed from father to son, but later other relations were included in the list of potential heirs, though their number was very small.[38] Subsequent enactments gradually expanded the number of potential heirs but never assimilated *miri* land to *mulk* in this respect. The laws containing such provisions were the Ottoman Land Law of 1858 (arts. 54–59), the Law on Expansion of Inheritance Rights in *miri* and *mawqufa* Lands of May 21, 1867,[39] and the Law on Inheritance of Immovable Property of March 12, 1913.[40] This last-mentioned law is still in force in the Fertile Crescent countries, where *miri* land is not subject to the Muslim law of inheritance.

The right to bequeath *kharajiya* lands by will was granted in Egypt in 1866.[41] From the 1890's onward, when they became *mulk*, they also could be endowed as *waqf* without prior permission from the khedive. These two rights were never granted to owners of *miri* land in the Ottoman Empire, and as late as 1913, in the Law of Transfer of Immovable Property, it was explicitly stated (art. 8) that "the holder of *miri* land is not permitted to endow it as a true *waqf*[42] and not to bequeath it by will except if the government had transferred the land to him as his own absolute property [*mulk*] by special order of the sultan in accordance with

[30] For text see Murr, Part II, pp. 86–92, and Doukhan, pp. 240–42.
[31] For text see Murr, Part II, pp. 97–101, and Doukhan, pp. 243–45.
[32] L. Cardon, *Le régime de la propriété foncière en Syrie et au Liban* (Paris, 1932), pp. 160–61.
[33] M. Doukhan, *Dinei qarqaot bimdinat yisrael* (Doukhan, *Israel*, in later references), (Jerusalem, 1953), p. 164.
[34] *Ibid.*, p. 475, and Granott, *op. cit.*, p. 20.
[35] Cardon, *op. cit.*, p. 150.
[36] IBRD, *Iraq*, p. 139.

[37] See Baer, *A History of Landownership*, pp. 38–39.
[38] See Padel and Steeg, *op. cit.*, pp. 213–14.
[39] Murr, *op. cit.*, Part II, pp. 113–15, and Doukhan, *op. cit.*, pp. 228–29.
[40] Murr, Part II, pp. 109–12, and Doukhan, pp. 230–31.
[41] For text see *Loi sur la propriété territoriale*, p. 41.
[42] Called *waqf sahih*. The ruler may endow as *waqf* the taxes from the land, or the rent may be assigned as a *waqf* to a specified beneficiary. Such a *waqf* is called *waqf ghayr sahih* or *takhsisat*.

the religious law."[43] This law remained partly in force in several of the Fertile Crescent countries. In Syria and the Lebanon permission was granted to bequeath *miri* land by will in 1930,[44] and in Iraq in 1932.[45] Palestine and the State of Israel retained the Ottoman provision in its entirety.[46] The prohibition on endowing *miri* land as *waqf* without special authority (i.e., without having it turned into *mulk* by the government) remained in force throughout the Fertile Crescent. *Miri lazma* land in Iraq cannot be endowed as *waqf* under any circumstances.[47]

To appreciate the significance of all these laws governing *miri* one has to take into account the fact that practically all agricultural land in the Fertile Crescent is *miri* and that *mulk* land amounts to a neglible quantity. Statistics distinguishing between these two categories are rather inadequate; the only exact figures are those pertaining to Iraq, which reveal that only 0.3 per cent of the area that had been registered up to February, 1951 (one-half of the total), was *mulk*.[48] The area of *miri* land in Syria is not known but "actually all agricultural land in Syria is *miri*."[49] Doukhan estimated *miri* land in Palestine to amount to "95 per cent of all cultivated lands."[50] Lebanon is the only exception: the greater part of its land is *mulk*. This seems to be the result of the autonomous status enjoyed by Lebanon in the Ottoman Empire for many centuries.[51]

There was, finally, another important difference between the development of landownership in Egypt and in the Ottoman Empire. Muhammad Ali and Said had already carried out a full, though primitive, cadastral survey in Egypt; and by 1907 a full modern land registration had been completed.[52] As against this, in the Ottoman Empire absolute confusion and anarchy reigned in the survey of lands and registration of ownership up to its distintegration. Instructions for the registration of lands issued in the wake of the Ottoman Land Law on February 29, 1860[53] were carried out only sporadically and most inaccurately because of administrative incompetence and because the major part of the agricultural land was held collectively by the villages in so-called *musha'* tenure to be periodically redistributed among the villagers; as long as the villagers were not ready to forgo the security of the village community or driven to do so by economic differentiation among its members, *musha'* prevented registration of individual ownership rights. In this respect too Egyptian practices differed completely: in Lower Egypt village lands apparently were never periodically redistributed among the villagers, while in Upper Egypt this custom had been abandoned by the middle of the nineteenth century.[54] To this day *musha'* tenure in the Fertile Crescent still constitutes a severe impediment to registration of land and, for that matter, to economic development in general. A third reason for the failure of registration in the Fertile Crescent was the tribal character of a substantial part of its population.[55]

[43] Doukhan, p. 233.

[44] Cardon, *op. cit.*, p. 151.

[45] *Qanun taswiyat huquq al-aradi*, No. 50, 1932. See S. Himadeh, *Al-nizam al-iqtisadi fil-'Iraq* (Beirut, 1938), p. 127.

[46] Doukhan, *Israel*, p. 250.

[47] *Ibid.*, p. 63; S. Himadeh, *Economic Organization of Syria* (Beirut, 1936), p. 53; Himadeh, *'Iraq*, pp. 127, 130. *Miri lazma* is land held by tribes which may not be transferred to anyone outside the tribe.

[48] IBRD, *Iraq*, p. 179.

[49] Himadeh, *Syria*, p. 53.

[50] Doukhan, *op. cit.*, p. 26.

[51] See *Rapport général sur les études foncières...* (Beirut, 1921), pp. 72–73. According to this, apparently official publication, nearly all immovable property in Mount Leganon is *mulk*. According to *Lubnan fi 'ahd al-istiqlal* (Beirut, 1947), p. 58, about 65 per cent of the land of the Republic of Lebanon is *mulk*.

[52] Cf. H. G. Lyons, *The Cadastral Survey of Egypt, 1892–1907* (Cairo, 1908).

[53] Doukhan, *op. cit.*, pp. 223–27.

[54] See G. Baer, "The Dissolution of the Egyptian Village Community," *Die Welt des Islams*, N.S., VI, No. 1–2, pp. 56–70.

[55] For the failure of nineteenth-century land registration in Iraq see S. H. Longrigg, *Four Centuries of Modern Iraq* (Oxford, 1925), p. 307; for Palestine: L. French, *Reports on Agricultural Development and Land Settlement in Palestine* (Jerusalem, 1931), p. 13; for Lebanon: T. al-Shidyaq, *Akhbar al-a'yan fi jabal lubnan* (Beirut, 1858), pp. 701, 718; A. Ismail, *Histoire du Liban*, IV: *Redressement et déclin du féodalisme libanais* (Beirut, 1958), pp. 303–7; on the situation of land registration in the various countries of the Fertile Crescent at the end

In the 1920's, the mandatory government in each of the Fertile Crescent countries set up an administration for the survey and registration of land, and in the 1930's registration was undertaken again, this time by modern methods. But the mandatory authorities too encountered part of the basic difficulties mentioned above, and new political ones on top of them. Nevertheless, land registration continued slowly under both mandatory rule and independence, but by the middle of this century not one of these countries had reached the position attained by Egypt at the beginning of it. The greatest progress was made in Trans-Jordan, where, up to 1950, two-thirds of the total area had been registered—6,279,850 dunums out of 9,428,835.[56] In Iraq about half had been registered by 1951—50,447,034 Iraqi dunums out of 107,032,725,[57] and in Syria in 1950 little more than 40 per cent—3,430,407 hectares out of 8,339,028.[58] The lack of a complete and exact registration of land is certainly one of the main difficulties encountered by Syria and Iraq in their efforts to implement reforms of their agrarian structure.

THE EFFECT OF UNLIKE DEVELOPMENT ON THE AGRARIAN STRUCTURE IN THE 1950's

We have dwelt at length on the legal development of landownership in Egypt and the Fertile Crescent and we must now ask the question: to what extent is this development relevant to the present structure of land tenure in these two areas of the Middle East, or rather to the structure of land tenure before the land reforms which are being

carried out today, and therefore to the problems which these land reforms intend to solve? Before answering these questions, one point must be stressed: as we have seen, differences in land laws reflected differences in geographical and social conditions as well as in economic development. It would be a grave mistake not to take these basic conditions into account as direct causes for different structures of land tenure; but it is our contention that the legal development had an important influence in shaping these different structures.

In the first place, the fact that for almost a century Egypt's landed property was sub-divided, generation after generation, according to the Muslim law of inheritance, while agricultural land in the Fertile Crescent, being *miri*, was not, certainly was of major significance. Under Muslim inheritance law an extremely large number of persons of varying degrees of kinship are entitled to share an estate, and not more than one-third of a person's property may be transferred by will. The result was extreme fragmentation of landownership in Egypt, hundreds of thousands of fellah families owning tiny plots, too little to make their living out of them. There were of course ways to circumvent the law, but they were used mainly by big landowners and very seldom by small or medium ones. It is very difficult to compare the fragmentation of landownership in Egypt with that in the Fertile Crescent, since no adequate statistics exist for any of the Fertile Crescent countries. But there can be no doubt that this problem is much more severe in Egypt than in any of the other Arab countries. That it has troubled Egypt and continues to do so is evident from the fact that Egyptian governments have tried twice to solve it by special legislation (while none of the Fertile Crescent countries has ever deemed it necessary to enact such legislation). The first attempt was the Five Faddan Law of 1912, according to which agricultural holdings of farmers who did not own more than five faddans could not be seized for debt. The second attempt was the Land Reform of 1952 which prohibited

of the First World War see, for Palestine: Doukhan, *op. cit.*, pp. 86–87, 166; for Syria and Lebanon: *Rapport général sur les études foncières*, pp. 136–43, and *passim*; for Iraq: Himadeh, *'Iraq*, pp. 159–60, and E. Dowson, *An Inquiry into Land Tenure and Related Questions* (Baghdad, 1932), p. 19 and *passim*.

[56] *Jordan Statistical Year-Book*, 1950.

[57] IBRD, *Iraq*, p. 179.

[58] Government of Syria, *Statistical Abstract of Syria*, 1950, p. 178; according to a later source, 3.54 million hectares had been registered up to the end of 1952 out of 7.82 million, i.e., 45.3 per cent; See IBRD, *The Economic Development of Syria* (Baltimore, 1955), p. 354.

the splitting-up of a unit of land by sale, transfer, inheritance, or attachment, below the size of five faddans. The Five Faddan Law, which tackled only the problem of indebtedness, failed because fellahs and money lenders found ways to evade it. According to Sayyid Mar'i, former Minister of Land Reform, the provisions of the land reform in this respect have also not been carried out.[59]

Second, since from the end of last century all land in Egypt was *mulk*, it could freely be endowed as *waqf*, while most agricultural land in the Fertile Crescent, being *miri*, could not. Egyptian landowners, particularly big ones, made ample use of this freedom in order to prevent the splitting-up of large estates and to keep them in the family and thus to maintain the family's power and social status. During the first half of the twentieth century the area of *waqf* land in Egypt doubled, reaching about 10 per cent of the total area (as against 1.2 per cent in Iraq at mid-century and less than 0.1 per cent in Trans-Jordan). There seem to exist quite extensive areas of *waqf* land in Lebanon (where land was *mulk* as in Egypt) and in Palestine (although there *waqf* was of the "untrue" kind, the so-called *waqf ghayr sahih*), but there are no statistics to show how large these areas were. Thus a strange situation was created: although she had lifted the burden of *waqf* from her lands at the beginning of the nineteenth century, Egypt found it a more acute problem in this century than any other successor state of the Ottoman Empire (which had not radically confiscated all agricultural *waqf* land at an earlier stage). In this respect, however, the radical cure of the recent Egyptian land reform seems to have been successful.[60]

Third, Egypt's more extensive ownership rights, her greater simplicity in classification of land, and her more exact and more complete registration of lands contributed decisively to another important distinction:

foreign capital became interested in purchasing land in Egypt and estates owned by non-Egyptians soon reached much larger dimensions than those of foreigners in any Arab country of the Middle East. Moreover, since Muhammad Ali's time Egypt's rulers had ignored Muslim law according to which strangers are not allowed to own landed property in the Muslim state, and Egypt's agricultural development in the nineteenth century and after induced them to acquire lands in Egypt rather than in other parts of the Middle East. By the 1920's foreign-owned land amounted to about 10 per cent of the total area; later, however, foreigners either sold much of their landed property for political reasons or else acquired Egyptian nationality, so that by 1950 the percentage had dropped to 3.6. Therefore, in so far as the land reform dealt with foreign-owned land, it was rather the land owned by the ruling Muhammad Ali family (of "Turkish" origin), extending as it did over a much larger area than the estates of foreigners of European origin. In any case, although no figures are known, it is evident that neither of these two kinds of foreigners owned nearly so much land in the Arab Fertile Crescent countries as they did in Egypt.[61]

The activity of land companies was another feature of the agrarian structure which distinguished Egypt from other Arab countries of the Middle East. Though joint stock companies bought, sold, and cultivated land in a number of Middle Eastern countries, they never attained such importance as they did in Egypt. During the peak period of the foundation of land companies in Egypt, i.e., the last decade of the nineteenth and the first decade of the twentieth century, no company was entitled to hold land in the Ottoman Empire—a right that was granted only in 1913.[62] But there were also economic and social reasons: land reclamation, a typical field of activity for companies, was carried out on a much larger

[59] Sayyid Mar'i, *Al-islah al-zira'i fi misr* (Cairo, 1957), pp. 183–91.

[60] Cf. G. Baer, *"Waqf* Reform in Egypt," *St. Antony's Papers, Middle Eastern Affairs,* No. 1 (London, 1958), pp. 61–76.

[61] A law was passed in 1962 expropriating land owned by foreigners.—Editor.

[62] Doukhan, *op. cit.,* pp. 69–70, and Murr, *op. cit.,* Part II, p. 94.

scale in Egypt than in the countries of the Fertile Crescent; and nowhere in the Middle East except in Egypt did there exist large plantations, especially sugar cane plantations, a type of economic activity undertaken in many countries by companies. In this connection it is interesting to note that Egyptian land companies which operated in other countries of the Middle East bought mainly urban land and property, not agricultural estates, even if their main concern in Egypt was agricultural land.

Earlier survey and registration of land in Egypt brought with it yet another important difference between its system of land-ownership and that of the Fertile Crescent countries: the much lower proportion of state land. While Egypt was already busy transferring cultivated and cultivable state lands into private hands, the Syrian and Iraqi governments, for instance, were still claiming and recovering lands illegally occupied and appropriated by various persons (the most prominent among them being beduin *shaikh's*). In addition, in the Fertile Crescent there are much larger cultivable but not yet cultivated reserves of land (which form the main part of lands registered in the name of the state), and therefore a lower density of population in relation to the cultivated and cultivable area. Thus pressure on the government to dispose of its lands was much higher in Egypt than in the other countries. Finally, the earlier development of cash crops as well as land reclamation by land companies accelerated the pace of transfer of state lands into private hands. The result was that in the early 1950's state land covered in Egypt only about 17 per cent of all registered land, as against 30 per cent in Trans-Jordan, more than 40 per cent in Syria, and as much as 62 per cent in Iraq.[63] It should therefore

[63] Cf. G. Baer, "Land Tenure in the Hashemite Kingdom of Jordan," *Land Economics*, XXXIII (August, 1957), 188-°⁻

be much easier in the Fertile Crescent to carry out a policy of creating a new class of small landowners by granting them state land than to do so in Egypt. Indeed, in the legislation of recent years in Syria and Iraq the distribution of state lands has always figured as a major item, while it did so in Egypt before the revolution mainly as an argument against the necessity to redistribute privately owned estates. In fact state land in Egypt was sold, generally by auction, to big landowners or to rich urban merchants who thus became big landowners.

This leads us to our final observation. Reserves of uncultivated state land granted or sold by the ruler or the government to officials, village notables, or urban merchants were the primary source for the formation of Egypt's large estates during the last 150 years. Big landownership in Egypt derived from the state, and Egypt's big landowners concentrated in Cairo. In the Fertile Crescent, on the other hand, many of the large estates evolved because of the weakness of the state: fellahs asked powerful notables for protection and paid for it in land; land registration being vague, socially influential families managed to have the land registered in their name; beduin *shaikh's* with power over their tribes succeeded, when title deeds were made out, to appropriate the tribal *dira* (area fixed for the pasture and agricultural activity of a tribe). [See Part III, chap. 5.] This does not mean that other factors for the concentration of land in few hands, as for instance peasant indebtedness, have not been operative in both areas, in Egypt as well as in the Fertile Crescent. But local power based on the control of vast tracts of land always was and has remained much stronger in Syria or Iraq than in centralized Egypt. This certainly is a factor which makes the implementation of any reform in the Fertile Crescent much more difficult than in Egypt.

CHAPTER 10

Railway Projects in Turkey, 1872–1900

The original impetus for the construction of railways in Turkey in Asia arose from the British desire to establish swift overland communications with India. The shortest route passes through Mesopotamia (see Part III, chap. 2), but the opening, first, of the Egyptian railways (see Part VI, chap. 7) and then of the Suez Canal met the requirements of international trade and obviated the need for a Mesopotamian line. However, these developments in no way diminished the need for railways to develop the huge resources of Anatolia. In 1856 British interests received a concession for the 130-kilometer Smyrna-Aydin railway, opened to traffic in 1867 and extended to a total of 516 kilometers by the end of the century. Another concession waš given, in 1863, also to a British company, for the 93-kilometer Smyrna-Kasaba line; this railway was eventually taken over by French interests and by the end of the century totaled 522 kilometers.

These lines opened up only a tiny fraction of Anatolia, and neither of them satisfied the Ottoman government's desire to link Constantinople with the various provincial capitals. On August 4, 1871, therefore, the construction of an Anatolian railway line, starting in Constantinople, was decreed. The following year a German engineer, Wilhelm von Pressel, drew up a ten-year master plan for a line extending from the Bosporus to the Persian Gulf, a distance of 2,700 kilometers, with feeder and branch lines adding another 1,800 kilometers. Thirty years later this plan was elaborated and modified in the book from which the following selection is taken.

A look at a railway map of present-day Turkey, Syria, and Iraq shows that many of von Pressel's proposals have been implemented, but not all of them. First, construction of the northern route, which he advocated, was blocked by Russia—which objected to having railways too close to its southern borders—and was not completed until the Republic. Second, the system of kilometric guarantees, to which von Pressel was strongly opposed, continued until the end of the Empire (see Part II, Introduction). Lastly, the gauge used was the standard 1,435-millimeter one and not the narrow 1,000-millimeter gauge, whose adoption he urged.

(See also works by Hecker, Rohrbach, Earle, Chapman, Wolf, Hüber, and Novichev listed in the Bibliography.)

[From W. von Pressel, *Les chemins de fer de Turquie* (Zurich, 1902), pp. 28–31.]

PRINCIPAL ROUTES

For half a century the construction of this railway has been preoccupying political, financial, and commercial circles. Its importance from the geographic point of view has drawn their attention, and from the time of Colonel Chesney in 1856 [see Part III, chap. 2] to this day many projects have been put forward. Of these only three deserve consideration: (a) from Tripoli (Syrian coast) to Baghdad, along the Euphrates, passing through Homs and Palmyra (Tadmor), and crossing the Syrian and Babylonian deserts; (b) from Smyrna to Baghdad, through Konya, Maraş, and Mosul; (c) from Constantinople to the Persian Gulf, through Boli, Amasia, Sivas, Kharput, Diyarbakir, Mosul, Baghdad, and Basra. Let us examine the utility of these projects and the result of their implementation in regard to the government, the people, and the capital which would be invested in them.

At the time when project (a) was presented, an exaggerated importance had been given to establishing rapid communications between Syria and the Persian Gulf—hence the choice of this route which, passing through two immense, sterile, and uninhabited deserts, would have swallowed up huge amounts of capital without bringing any profit. . . .

In establishing any railway, three main interests must be taken into consideration and reconciled: that of the government, that of the people, and that of the capital invested. Now project (a), which is at present being taken up again by a certain group, does not satisfy any of these three interests. The government's interest may be examined from the strategic, military, administrative, and fiscal points of view. Strategic, military, and administrative considerations demand that the main towns of the interior be linked together at first, and then with the capital. The fiscal point of view demands an increase in state revenues.

Project (a) goes against these considerations and hence runs counter to the interests of the state. As it runs counter to the interests of the state it is harmful to those of the people and of capital. Since project (a) must be set aside, it remains to compare the results expected from projects (b) and (c). In order to facilitate an understanding of this question, we shall designate project (b), i.e., Smyrna-Konya-Maraş-Mosul, as the southern route and project (c), i.e., Constantinople-Boli-Amasia-Sivas, etc., as the central one.

When called upon, by the imperial Ottoman government, in 1872, to give my opinion on the solution of the great question of the railways of Turkey in Asia, I proposed that during the first ten-year campaign the following lines should be built:

a) The main line starting from the east coast of the Bosporus, passing through Izmit, Eskişehir, Angora, Sivas, Kharput, Diyarbakir, Mosul, and Baghdad and reaching the Persian Gulf downstream of Basra.

b) Two main feeder lines: Samsun-Amasia-Tokat-Sivas and Suwaidia-Aleppo-Diyarbakir.

c) Two first-class branches: Eskişehir-Afyonkarahisar-Konya and Sivas-Ersincan-Erzurum.

I was able to draw up the preliminary projects for these routes, except for two sections: Sivas-Diyarbakir and Baghdad-Persian Gulf.

At that time, for reasons which it is not incumbent on me to disclose here, my project could not be carried out. The present situation being more favorable, I have taken up again the old 1873 project in its entirety, with the necessary modifications. My subsequent studies and a deeper knowledge of the country and its needs have led me to take as axiomatic that the primordial interest of the government, of the country, and of capital demand the following: the route of the western part of the main line should, after Adapazar, take a northerly direction to Sivas, passing through Boli and Amasia and crossing regions far more thickly inhabited and fertile than those lying along the Adapazar-Eskişehir-Angora line; this would make it possible, consequently, to anticipate considerable revenue from the very beginning of the exploitation of the line.

I believe the central route to be superior to the southern for the following reasons:

a) For any enterprise one must first of all seek to find the means of producing maximum utility. After Konya, the southern route crosses the vast, salty deserts of Lycaonia, grazes—so to speak—the rich plain of Adana, passes through the redoubtable gorges of the Taurus and enters the rich zone of Aintab-Urfa which, under the northern plan, would be served by the Suwaidia-Diyarbakir feeder line. On the other hand the northern route, from the Bosporus to Diyarbakir, would serve the finest regions of Anatolia, regions as fertile as those that feed the two Smyrna networks. Hence the construction costs of the southern route are considerably higher than those of the central route, and the benefits to be gained from exploitation considerably lower.

b) One should certainly not ignore [*Il est incontestable de méconnaitre* (*sic*)] the importance of establishing direct communication between the capital of the Empire and the principal provincial centers. The choice of the southern route will have the inevitable consequence of making Smyrna superior to Constantinople. For it is Smyrna which would thus become the railhead of the Anatolian railway network. . . .

The Ottoman Debt, 1850–1939

The process by which European capital penetrated each of the Muslim countries was remarkably similar. After the Napoleonic Wars, trading houses, private banks, and a few processing plants were established. This was followed, in the 1850's, by the foundation of incorporated banks (see Part I, Introduction) and the beginning of large-scale lending to the monarchs who, from Morocco to Iran, were modernizing their countries with little regard to cost or consequences. These efforts led, in the 1870's, to a series of bankruptcies, followed in turn either by formal foreign occupation—Tunisia in 1881, Egypt in 1882, and Morocco in 1912—or by *de facto* foreign control.

The following selection describes the growth of the public debt in the Ottoman Empire; the corresponding process in Egypt is described in Part VI, chapter 9. After the First World War the Ottoman public debt was divided among the successor states according to the ratio of the revenue collected in each state to the total revenue of the Ottoman Empire in the two fiscal years 1910–11 and 1911–12. The share of Turkey was 67 per cent, that of Syria and Lebanon 8.41 per cent, of Iraq 5.5 per cent, and of Palestine 2.5 per cent.

In the last decades of the nineteenth century private European capital investments in the Ottoman Empire increased sharply, and by November 1, 1914, totaled £63,444,000. Of this amount railways accounted for £39,163,000, banks for £10,210,000, manufacturing and mining for £5,495,000, and public utilities for £4,983,000. The leading investor was Germany, which had contributed 45.4 per cent of the total and accounted for 67.5 per cent of the capital invested in Ottoman railways and 22.1 per cent of that in banks. France had contributed 25.9 per cent of the total and accounted for 76.5 per cent of the capital invested in mining and 59.0 per cent of that in banks. Britain came third, with 16.9 per cent of the total and 75.6 per cent of the capital invested in manufacturing and 41.2 per cent of that in trade. Belgian capital, which accounted for 3.7 per cent of the total, went almost exclusively to public utilities, and United States capital, amounting to 1.8 per cent of the total, to trade.[1] Most of this investment was made in European Turkey or western Anatolia; very little went to the Arab countries,

---

[1] See table by Ismail Husrev, reproduced in Novichev, *Ocherki ekonomiki Turtsii*, p. 127.

except for some railways, some public utilities, and a few processing plants (see Part IV, Introduction).

In Egypt foreign investment in the private sector was greater than in the Ottoman Empire. By 1914, foreign holdings of shares and debentures in companies operating in Egypt was £E92,000,000; this figure excludes the Suez Canal. Three-quarters of the total was in mortgage banks and land companies. Of the total, £E46,267,000 was French capital, £E30,250,000 British, and £E14,294,000 Belgian. Another £E50,000,000 or more was invested in branches of foreign companies, private firms, and individual enterprises owned by foreigners. There are several discrepancies between the list of debts given in the following selection and the one in the *Fifty-fourth Annual Report of the Corporation of Foreign Bondholders, for the Year 1927* (London).

(See also Epilogue; for the Sudan, Part VII, Introduction and chap. 8; and works by Morawitz, Velay, Blaisdell, Roumani, Yeniay, Novichev, Hershlag, and Crouchley [*Investment of Foreign Capital in Egyptian Companies*] listed in the Bibliography.)

[Rafii-Şukru Suvla, "Tanzimat Devrinde Istikrazlar" ("Debts during the Tanzimat Period"), in *Tanzimat* (Istanbul, 1940), pp. 263–88.]

... The military alliance during the Crimean War of 1854, between the Ottoman Empire and France and Britain, was more responsible for giving the Ottomans an opportunity to receive credit from the West than were the promised but unrealized Tanzimat reforms. Immediately after this war, the Ottoman Empire availed itself of this opportunity to receive foreign credit. Thus, the public debt was utilized to meet the expenses of war and rebellions and the continuous deficits in the budget. Even the servicing of the debt itself was met by these apparently easy and convenient foreign loans. Indeed, no one thought about the future and everyone followed the rule of living from hand to mouth; the result was a rapid increase in foreign loans in a period of forty to fifty years. Reaching a very high sum, these debts became a source of trouble more serious than the Capitulations and periodically threatened the country's political independence.

In the field of public finance, and especially in relation to the public debt, the Tanzimat failed to register an improvement but, contrary to its name, created corruption. After passing through various phases, this serious problem, among others, was finally solved only by the Turkish Republic.

In order properly to study the public debt in the Tanzimat period, we find it necessary to present a four-part inquiry:

1. Public finance and loans before the Tanzimat
2. The financial reforms expounded in the Hatti Şerif of Gulhane
3. The loans of the Tanzimat period
4. A critical economic and financial analysis of the public debt

PUBLIC FINANCE AND LOANS BEFORE THE TANZIMAT

... After the Koprulus, who succeeded in postponing for a time the decline of the Empire, the country's finances had reached a state of confusion, in which a solution seemed almost inconceivable. The arbitrary [*orfi*] taxes which were created by way of supplement to the religious [*şeri*] and commercial [*ticari*] taxes, the whole of which were tax farmed [*iltizam*], were not sufficient to meet the expenditures of the palace and the government. Thus, sometimes it was necessary even to melt gold and silver plate of the palace and the vizirs, in order to distribute stipends to the janissaries [given by each sultan, on his accession to throne]. The most important affairs were also effected by bribes, given even to the palace, and high offices could be obtained in the same way. Personal interest was considered more important than that of the state treasury for the most part. Since the *sancak* governors could not be subjected to [effective] control, they always imposed taxes arbitrarily and sent only a small part of the *ayni* and *nakdi* taxes [in kind or cash] to the state treasury. On the other hand, corrupt and ignorant officials of the treasury—the *defterdar*'s—did not hesitate to waste the little money collected there. The reforms that Selim III wanted to initiate (such as to free the revenue sources of the state from tax farming and to establish a war treasury) could not be successfully implemented. Instead of applying radical fiscal measures to a perpetually troubled state treasury, only day-to-day remedies were considered, which worsened the situation. Since the treasury was in a perpetual state of emptiness, the sole method of meeting the state expenditures was through the public debt, in the form of bonds, the terms of which were sometimes indefinite. The holders of these bonds would transfer them to Galata brokers (Armenian, Greek, Jewish, Levantine) at exorbitant discount rates. The brokers attempted to cash the bonds by giving large bribes to the palace or the *defterdar*'s. When the bonds to be reimbursed became considerable, the vizirs and the *defterdar*'s, now unable to stand the pressure [of the brokers] on the one hand, and seeking their personal gain on the other, did not hesitate to auction the *iltizam* taxes of five to ten years, for various parts of the country. The *sancak* governors and the Galata brokers were accomplices in bringing about these auctions through fraud. They paid for the larger portion of the amounts [promised at the auction] in treasury bonds and the remaining small portion through money borrowed from the brokers. Moreover the governors, in co-operation with the brokers, for a long

period were exploiting the *sancak* population through unbearably high taxes.

Another measure to which the treasury resorted in times of trouble was the debasement of the currency. In earlier times, debasement was a primary source of revenue used by almost every state. Although this method (consisting of melting coins and reminting them, using a lower grade or lighter weight of metal) was convenient for the state, it quickly created complaints among the people and therefore was considered dangerous. After the Middle Ages, in advanced western countries the use of this method was generally abandoned. Those defending this method put forward an ill-founded doctrine stating that "because the absolute ruler is the owner of money, he can devalue it as he pleases." [1]

Throughout Ottoman history, the state has often debased the currency. Especially when money was needed to give stipends to the soldiers at times of accession to the throne, the hard-pressed treasury usually resorted to debasement and as a result faced janissary uprisings.

Another form of borrowing money, the banknote, was first initiated in the Ottoman Empire in 1830. However, we doubt that one could call this a real banknote. It was a hand-written treasury bond, of a minimum value of 100 kuruş, bearing 8 per cent interest. Because of the fact that these banknotes carried interest and had only a limited circulation, they cannot be considered real banknotes. Subsequently, in 1839, these bonds were printed and proclaimed "valid money." But since these were eight-year term bonds with an interest of 8 per cent, it is still doubtful that they can be called banknotes. These bonds, issued in the years 1830–39, kept their character as compulsory loans, even if they are not considered real banknotes.

In the period before the Tanzimat, we do not find that any state loans in the modern meaning of the term existed in the Ottoman Empire.

[1] See the disputes between the Canonists and their opponents.

A state loan can be either domestic or foreign. In order for a state to find credit by issuance of securities inside the country, two conditions are required: national savings must have reached a high level, and the people must have confidence in the state. Since these two conditions did not exist in the Ottoman Empire, it was impossible for the state to have recourse to domestic loans.

On the other hand, in order to acquire foreign loans, a borrowing state must show not only verbal but also some effective guarantees of its capacity for future repayment. It was only natural that no foreign creditor would advance loans to a state such as the Ottoman Empire, with its medieval mentality and inefficient state structure.

In order to suppress some internal revolts during the reign of Abdul Hamid I (1774–89), a foreign loan of 50,000 to 100,000 keses (1 kese is equal to 5 liras) was considered, but this project died in the *divan* (council of ministers) without results. Thus, the first attempt of the empire to acquire a foreign loan was unsuccessful.

To sum up, we have established that, until the Tanzimat, the Ottoman Empire resembled a medieval state in the field of public finance as well as in every other field. Instead of initiating reforms in financial affairs, new disorders were introduced, and every time the treasury was empty the easiest and worst borrowing methods learned from the West were utilized—such as the devaluation of money and the issuing of bonds and banknotes.

The Financial Reforms Promulgated in the Hatti Şerif of Gulhane

One of the important aspects covered in the Gulhane Hatti (1839) was public finance, which was the source of continuous complaints among the population. With the purpose of bringing the tax [structure] within the realm of justice, tne Hatti Şerif ordered that: the financial capacity of the taxed be considered fundamental; all races and religions in the Empire, without any distinction, be taxed equally; the collection of taxes be carried out not under the extremely troublesome and primitive *iltizam* system, but directly by the state; there be a transition from payment in kind to payment in cash in revenues and expenditures; finally, the preparation, execution, and control of state expenditures and revenues be set in a document equivalent to a budget. (The expenditures of the land and sea forces were to be regulated by special laws.)

In order to accomplish such great and important financial reforms, it was of course necessary to reorganize completely the state's administration of finance. Until a little before the Tanzimat, the public revenues and expenditures of the Empire were managed by the *defterdarlik* department, headed by a *başdefterdar* [head bookkeeper] who was, at the same time, a member of the *divan*. At the beginning of the nineteenth century the *defterdarlik* department was composed of thirty-two offices. Selim III tried to bring some modifications into this department, within the framework of his *nizami cedid* [new system]. But the man who really wanted to introduce radical reforms into the financial institutions before the Tanzimat was Mahmud II. After the suppression of the janissaries (1826) he established two new departments, called the ministry of expenditures and the ministry of farming out sources of revenue. In 1835 the ministry of expenditures was abolished and in its place two new *defterdarlik*'s—*hazinei amire* and *mansure*—were organized. On 3 Zilhicce 1258 A.H. (1837) a ministry of finance was established in the Ottoman Empire.

The Tanzimat also showed the necessity of adding a *divani muhasebat* [accounts and audit department] to the existing ministry of finance, but this department was not established until 1296 A.H. (1880). Since these financial reforms, initiated before the Tanzimat and continued throughout, were not based on serious study and research, they remained superficial in character and constituted mainly verbal changes. The ministry of finance was far from directly administering state revenues and expenditures, and by assigning a predetermined revenue to a predetermined expense, it prevented all possibility of control over finances.

Among other reforms, the Hatti Şerif of Gulhane sought to end the indirect abuses of the Galata brokers. When the taxes were given to the *iltizam* by auction, the Galata brokers used to pay some advance money to notorious *multezim*'s (tax farmers) and then proceed to collect the lion's share for themselves. In addition to this, when the state was in financial crisis, the brokers lent money to the treasury at very high rates of interest and commission, and at the end of the term of loan, they collected their money by giving bribes.

By abolishing the *iltizam* and by connecting treasury expenditure to prescribed laws —that is, by a budget—the Tanzimat aimed at obstructing the activities of the Levantine, Greek, and Armenian brokers of Galata. In order to assure the availability of low-cost credit to the treasury, in case of need, Reşid pasha even considered the possibility of creating a [national] credit institution, similar to the British and French national [central] banks. There is no clause relating to loans in the Hatti Şerif. The reason for this lack was that, with the exception of the bonds given to Galata brokers, the state was not yet able to conclude credit agreements in the full and complete sense of the word, and also that this method had not yet been discovered by those in charge of state finances.

The major part of the financial reforms planned by the Tanzimat could never be carried out. The little that was implemented —the abolishing of *iltizam*, for example— was abandoned within two or three years, because of poor results owing to faulty application. Then, the old worn-out system was brought back into operation—that is, arbitrary taxation and *iltizam*. In order not to exceed the scope of our subject, we are not going to treat at length here the financial reforms of the Tanzimat and their lack of success.

THE LOANS OF THE TANZIMAT PERIOD

Until the middle of the nineteenth century, the Ottoman Empire was able to meet its expenditures without directly resorting to foreign credit. However, as has been pointed out, expenditures were frequently covered by various means, such as the debasement of money and the issuing of bonds and banknotes, in addition to the normal tax revenues.

Wishing to take advantage of the interest created by the spectacular Tanzimat reforms among foreigners and of the seemingly favorable British and French attitudes toward the Tanzimat movement, Sadrazam Mustafa Reşid pasha signed in 1850 a loan agreement of 55 million francs with Bechet Dethomas et Cie. of Paris and Deveaux and Co. of London in order to repay the treasury debts to the Bank of Istanbul.[2] According to the agreement, 55,000 bonds with terms of 27 years were to be issued. These bonds were put on the market before the agreement was ratified by the sultan's *iradeh* and from the proceeds of the loan an amount of 20 million francs was deposited on account with the firm of Baltazzi, the London representative of the Bank of Istanbul. And when the loan agreement was submitted for ratification, Reşid pasha was once more removed from power. As a result the agreement was rejected. But in order to cancel the agreement, the treasury was compelled to pay an indemnity of 2.2 million francs, in addition to paying back the deposit of 20 million.

Whatever may be the reasons for the

[2] It is doubtful whether the Bank of Istanbul can be called a "bank" in the modern meaning of the term. No serious and powerful credit institution was established in the Ottoman Empire until 1856. In the Hatti Humayun (1856), promulgated during the reign of Abdul Mecid, projects of financial reforms were once again included, and in order to improve the monetary and financial systems, the establishment of banks and similar institutions was considered. Consequently, the Ottoman Bank was founded in 1856 in Istanbul with British capital, parallel to the project of the Hatti Humayun. Subsequently, by the *ferman* of 1863, the distinction of becoming the state bank was conferred upon the Ottoman Bank and its name was changed to Banki Osmanli Şahane—that is, Imperial Ottoman Bank.

cancellation of the loan agreement—viz., hostility toward Reşid pasha and his activities—it is interesting to note how an easily and successfully obtained foreign loan was given up. Indeed, a foreign loan obtained by a weak state will necessitate political concessions beforehand or subsequently. Although this decision was taken by a government hostile to Reşid pasha, it is praiseworthy and interesting to note that the successfully concluded agreement was rejected because of fear of foreign pressures, despite the treasury crisis in the Tanzimat period. (The British dispatch of a fleet to Piraeus, because of Greek inability to repay debts, was cited as a warning.)

The resistance of the Tanzimat period to domestic loans (in the form of issuing banknotes) and foreign loans did not last long. The great treasury crisis caused by the expenses of the Crimean War and the favorable attitude of our military allies, Great Britain and France, toward extending credit—because it would help their interests—were instrumental in pushing the Ottoman Empire into foreign indebtedness, which subsequently created great economic and political troubles for the state.

The Ottoman Empire signed its first real foreign loan agreement, with Britain, shortly after the start of the Crimean War in 1854. This loan, issued at 80 and carrying 6 per cent interest, provided the treasury with 2.5 million Ottoman gold pounds. The Egyptian tax revenue was pledged as security for the loan.[3] "There are things that are very quickly learned. The art of indebtedness is among them. As soon as the Ottoman Empire was initiated it made rapid progress in that direction."[4] We concur with this author's opinion.

Barely a year had elapsed after the first loan, when the empire signed in 1855 a second loan under circumstances which we may call extraordinary. This loan, issued at $102\frac{5}{8}$ and bearing 4 per cent interest, provided the treasury with 5.65 million Ottoman gold pounds. The remaining part of the Egyptian tribute and the customs revenues from Syria and Izmir were pledged as security for this loan.

Since the regular state revenues and the above-mentioned loans were not sufficient to meet the war expenses, the empire resorted to the issuing of banknotes, which is equivalent to a compulsory domestic loan. These banknotes, named "the New Shares" [*Eshami Cedide*], "Privileged Bonds," and "Privileged Shares" (all of which were termed *sergi*), were some kind of treasury bonds with various terms and 6 per cent interest. The amount of these various bonds on the market exceeded 5 million. In view of the annually increasing debt burden on the treasury and the confusion of the money market, Abdul Mecid ordered the establishment of a special commission to cut down expenses and prepare a well-balanced budget.

We have already noted, particularly in the financial field, that the reforms promised in the Hatti Şerif of Gulhane were either left unrealized or abandoned after a few superficial attempts at implementation. The result was a return to the old deficient methods—such as *iltizam* in tax collection [see Part II, chap. 9]. We also noted that Reşid pasha was several times removed from power and that various kinds of reactions against reform began to manifest themselves.

After the victorious end of the Crimean War and the initiation of peace negotiations, Britain and France gave the Sublime Porte their views on the sterility of the Tanzimat movement. After the signature of the Vienna Protocol of February 1, 1855 (which constituted the basis for the 1856 Treaty of Paris), the pressure of the allies at the Porte for reforms was accelerated. Thereupon, on February 18, 1856, Abdul Mecid proclaimed a new Hatti Humayun at the Sublime Porte, which promised the continuation of the social and financial reforms.

---

[3] The *ferman* sent to the khedive of Egypt, instructing him to deposit tax revenues at the Banks of France and England, is in the archives of the Bank of England. Additional information on this and subsequent loans is to be found in the following tables.

[4] Morawitz, *Les Finances de la Turquie* (Paris, 1902), p. 20.

TABLE 1

Year	Amount of Debt (in Ottoman liras)	Rate of Issue (per cent)	Amount Acquired (in Ottoman liras)	Interest (per cent)	Remarks
1854	3,300,000	80	2,514,913	6	Loan taken for the Crimean War. Contracted with Palmers Goltschmid. The Egyptian tribute pledged as security (in pounds sterling).
1855	5,500,000	102⅜	5,644,375	4	Loan also contracted for the Crimean War through Rothschilds. A commission was sent to supervise the use of the loan for war expenses. The Egyptian tribute, in addition to the customs revenues of Izmir and Syria, pledged as security (in pounds sterling).
1858 1859	3,300,000 2,200,000	85 } 62.5 }	4,056,250	6	Loan taken because, as a result of the Crimean War, the value of banknotes had dropped and the foreign exchanges needed support. Contracted with Dent, Palmers, and Co. The Istanbul octroi and customs given as security (in pounds sterling).
1860	17,600,000	53¾			Not ratified. The Mires loan (in francs).
1860	2,240,942	62.5	1,400,588	6	The money acquired by the Empire from the sale in France of some of the bonds of the loan contracted with Mires (taken to meet a budget deficit).
1862	8,800,000	68	5,984,000	6	Loan taken to withdraw the circulating banknotes. Contracted with the Ottoman Bank. The taxes on tobacco, salt, stamps, and profits pledged as security (in francs).
1863	8,800,000	71	6,248,000	6	Contracted with the Ottoman Bank, this loan was designed to pay off floating debts and to issue metal coins. The customs, silk, olive-oil, tobacco, and salt tithes were pledged as security and the equivalent of the amount of the loan was transferred to the Galata bankers in payment of debts (in francs).
1865	6,600,000	66	4,356,000	6	Taken to settle foreign loan payments and budget deficits. Contracted with the Ottoman Bank and Société Générale. The Ergani mines were pledged as security (in francs).
1865	40,000,000	50	20,000,000	5	Taken to cover the debts incurred under the first loan arrangement. Contracted with General Credit and Finance and Société Générale. No special security shown.
1869	24,444,442	54	13,200,000	6	Loan taken to cover budget deficits and to pay off various floating debts. Contracted with Comptoire d'Escompte. The tithes of various *vilayet*'s given as security (in francs).
1870	34,848,001	32⅛	11,194,820	3	Bonus loan, called Lot-Turc, taken for the construction of the Rumeli railway. Contracted with Baron Hirsch. Egyptian tribute pledged as security (in francs).
1871	6,270,000	73	4,577,100	6	Louis Kohensons was the contractor for this loan, taken out to cover budget deficits. Egyptian tribute given as security (in pounds sterling).
1872	12,238,820	98.5	10,403,004	9	Contracted with Ottoman Bank and Crédit Général Ostr. The revenues of the *vilayet*'s of Salonica, Edirne, and Danube, and the sheep tax of Anatolia were pledged as security (in francs).
1873	12,611,995	55	6,936,600	5	Taken to consolidate the treasury bonds issued in 1872.

TABLE 1—*continued*

Year	Amount of Debt (in Ottoman liras)	Rate of Issue (per cent)	Amount Acquired (in Ottoman liras)	Interest (per cent)	Remarks
1873	30,555,558	54	16,500,000	6	Taken to cover budget deficits, Contracted with Crédit Mobilier de Paris and Crédit Général Ottoman. The revenues of the Danubian and Aleppo *vilayet*'s and the animals-tax revenues of Anatolia pledged as security (in francs).
1874	44,000,000	43.5	19,140,000	5	Contracted with the Ottoman Bank. Taken to meet floating debts and the overlapping interests of other loans. No special security shown (in francs).
1877	. . .	. . .	. . .	. . .	Not concluded because of the war with Russia. Egyptian tribute pledged as security. The loan was to have amounted to 125 million francs, at par issue and 5 per cent interest.
1877	5,500,000	52	2,860,000	5	Loan taken to meet war expenses in the conflict with Russia. Contracted with the Ottoman Bank and Glyn Mills, Currie and Co. of London. Egyptian tribute given as security (in pounds sterling).

Knowledge and perseverance were necessary prerequisites to success in financial reforms; so was economy in public expenses, especially under the prevailing conditions of those days. Since none of these was present, no positive results were obtained despite the establishment, for this purpose, of many international financial reform commissions. The treasury, which used to find it difficult to meet even daily expenses, continued to borrow from foreign sources without any consideration for the future financial and political repercussions that these stiff conditions would bring.[5] In the meantime (1861–76) a total of over 50 million's worth of banknotes was issued.

Most foreign loans were concluded to pay the charges on previous loans or to meet budget deficits. In the short period of twenty-five years their total reached a huge sum. In 1875, it was necessary to pay as much as 14 million gold liras for yearly charges. Yet the total revenue of the Empire was only about 17 or 18 million gold liras.

Sadrazam Mahmud Nedim pasha, who was a tool of Russian diplomacy, partially suspended the debt payments in 1875. In 1875 he declared the Empire financially bankrupt and suspended all payments. At a time when, in this manner, because of Russian intrigue, we offended our European creditors and it became impossible to get [new] foreign credits, the war with Russia broke out (1877). In order to meet the war expenses, Mahmud Nedim pasha gave the remaining non-assigned state revenues to the Galata brokers and the Ottoman Bank, under the name of Rusumu Sitte, and managed to get 10 million liras in return.

Let us briefly examine the foreign loans contracted by the Ottoman Empire from 1854 to 1877 (see Table 1).[6] "The amount of the debt is 251,209,758 liras and the amount received is 135,015,751. The loan of 1873 was used for the consolidation of the treasury bonds issued in 1872, with which 6,936,600 liras' worth of bonds on the

[5] As understood from the preceding explanation, a very small amount of the revenues from the loans was invested in useful public works such as railroads, ports, and the founding of some educational, financial, and judicial institutions such as Galata Saray, *vilayet* reforms, and Şurayi Devlet. But the major part of loan revenues were used to meet expenses of wars, revolts, budget deficits, and, most unfortunately, for palace construction (such as the Saray of Dolmabahçe) and imperial visits (Abdul Mecid's Paris travel). Although some of the loan revenues were, from time to time, channeled to liquidate some of the troublesome banknotes, this was not done very often because the proceeds were assigned to other uses.

[6] *Maliye Vekaleti Mecmuasi* [*Journal of the Ministry of Finance*], No. 6, p. 5.

market were liquidated. Taking the latter into account, it should be assumed that the amount of the debt is 244,273,158 liras and the amount received is 128,079,151 liras. The ratio of the money received to the amount of the debt is 52 per cent."[7]

We have already noted the difficulties faced by the treasury in getting foreign credit, as a result of the hardships which the Russo-Turkish War of 1877 and its conclusion produced. We have further noted how Mahmud Nedim pasha took a loan of 10 million gold liras at very stiff terms from the Galata brokers and the Ottoman Bank, pledging the most lucrative sources of state revenue as security. In order to utilize the revenue sources thus pledged to meet the charges on foreign debts, the state established an agency called Rusumu Sitte. This agency, which was entitled to collect the revenue from salt, tobacco, alcohol, and stamp taxes, as well as the silk tithes of Istanbul and Bursa, and the fish tax of Istanbul and vicinity, was going to appropriate 1,100,000 liras of its revenue to paying the charges due to the Galata brokers and the rest to the charges on foreign debts. Unsatisfied with this payment arrangement, the foreign bondholders immediately began to complain, and in 1880 the powers presented a strongly worded note to the Sublime Porte, which bowed to the pressure and began to negotiate with representatives of the bondholders. The result was an agreement known as the Decree of Muharrem (1881) according to the terms of which all the revenues of the Rusumu Sitte agency were transferred to the newly organized Public Debts Administration. Having under its control certain other sources of revenue, the Public Debts Administration took over the task of paying both domestic (Galata brokers) and foreign debts.

By the Decree of Muharrem all the debts were unified under four categories (A, B, C, D). As shown in Table 2, the debts were considerably cut down, so that their nominal value was reduced to their issue value (except the loans of 1854, 1855, 1871, 1877).

[7] *Ibid.*, p. 8.

Moreover, the yearly charges of 1,100,000 liras on the loans taken from the Galata brokers and the Ottoman Bank were reduced to 590,000 liras. However, in return, the loans of the Galata bankers were recognized as having priority over others, and their bonds were called "privileged bonds."

The division of the debts into various categories—A, B, C, D—resulted from the differences in amortization. Although the consolidated debts were subject to the same treatment in the matter of interest, group A was to be amortized first and groups B, C, and D were to be amortized later on, if it was possible to do so. The Decree of Muharrem reduced the principal of the Ottoman debts from 237 million to 142 million, and the charges from 15 to 3 million (see Table 2).

The Decree of Muharrem removed the allocations stipulated in the debt agreements (except the allocations of the loans of 1854, 1855, 1871, 1877), and replaced them with new allocations, the collection of which was entrusted to the Public Debts Administration. The new allocations, in addition to the sources of the Rusumu Sitte, were, under certain conditions, composed of some customs revenues, the remainder of the Cyprus taxes, and other revenues.

The collection of this revenue was entrusted to the executive council of the Public Debts Administration (one member from the Ottoman Bank, one from Ottoman creditors, and the rest representatives of foreign creditors). This organization, which managed our finances and acted as a state within the state, was established in 1883. As an independent network, it operated without restraint and employed more than 6,000 foreigners and citizens.

The Decree of Muharrem was an important turning point in the history of the Ottoman Empire. In addition to the promised but unfulfilled Tanzimat financial reforms of the Abdul Mecid–Abdul Aziz period (1854–77), the acquisition of loans from foreign creditors continued without interruption, despite their clearly negative

TABLE 2

OTTOMAN DEBTS AFTER THE 1881 MUHARREM DECREE*
(IN TURKISH GOLD POUNDS)

Loans		Principal, Not settled on December 20, 1881	Charges	Principal Accepted by Decree of Muharrem	Final principal, after the Subsequent Reduction	Charges after Decree of Muharrem
Debts included in the decree of Muharrem						
Series A	1858	4,053,225	385,300	3,789,848	7,831,870	
	1862	5,407,490	704,000	4,112,411		
Series B	1860	1,808,730	152,000	1,148,621	11,049,307	
	1863–4	5,618,250	704,000	4,371,050		
	1872	5,302,220	477,199	5,745,482		
Series C	1865	4,437,950	556,930	3,212,784	33,604,176	1,463,474
	1869	22,715,000	1,711,110	14,174,160		
	1873	29,916,414	2,138,888	16,528,818		
General shares Series D		95,917,096	4,795,854	48,365,255	48,017,162	
Gratuity shares		34,652,640	1,231,649	15,635,548	15,632,548	
Ramazan securities		1,939,558	96,977	117,080,957	116,135,063	
Privileged securities (1881 Galata banker debts)		8,169,986	1,100,000	8,169,986	8,169,986	590,000
Total		219,938,559	14,054,507	125,250,943	124,305,049	2,053,474
Debts not included in the Decree of Muharrem						
Loan of 1854		1,925,660	108,917		1,925,660	108,917
Loan of 1855		4,196,720	275,000		4,196,720	275,000
Loan of 1871		5,783,140	251,453		5,783,140	251,453
Loan of 1877		5,294,740	302,500		5,294,740	302,500
Total		17,200,260	937,870		17,200,260	937,870
Grand total		237,128,819	14,992,377		141,505,309	2,991,344

* Heidborn, *Les Finances ottomanes* (Vienna-Leipzig, 1912), p. 241.

effects on the political independence of the state. The general characteristics of the debts are to be analyzed later. But it is necessary for us to clarify one point at this time: with the Decree of Muharrem (1881), the foreign creditors established, under the protection of their own governments, a sort of new state, called the Public Debts Administration, within the Ottoman Empire. The Administration spent the revenues of the state as it pleased and even interfered in the realm of the state's budget. It may almost be stated that there has never been an organization similar to the Administration in world history. This type of institution, that is, a complete contradiction of state sovereignty, can be found only in the administration of colonies.

The establishment of the Administration and its infraction upon the state's independence and dignity were not sufficient to teach the Ottoman government a lesson. As soon as there was an opportunity, additional loans were continuously taken from abroad, without considering the pressure of increasing stipulations. Even the Meşrutiyet (constitutional) administration, despite all its foresight, perseverance, and abstention, was not able to liberate itself from foreign debt.

In order to make a succinct judgment about the foreign loan problem initiated by the Tanzimat period, it is necessary for us

TABLE 3

Year	Amount of Loan (in Ottoman gold liras)	Rate of Issue (per cent)	Amount Received (in Ottoman gold liras)	Interest (per cent)	Remarks
1886	6,500,000	100	6,500,000	5	Taken to consolidate the advances received from the Ottoman Bank; contracted with the latter; 4.5 million given to the Ottoman Bank and 2 million given to the treasury. Customs and taxes pledged as security.
1888	1,617,647	70	1,132,352	5	Taken to pay for munitions bought from Germany. The Deutsche Bank acted as contractor. The remaining revenues of the Public Debts–administered fishing industry pledged as security (in marks).
1890	8,609,964	75	6,457,580	4	Taken to pay off the 1881 privileged bonds. Contracted with Ottoman and other banks. Of the net revenues, 6,425,386 liras paid in exchange of the old securities (in pounds sterling).
1890	4,995,500	76	3,796,580	4	Contracted for the settlement of floating debts, through the Ottoman and other banks. Cereals tithes of various *vilayet*'s and *sancak*'s pledged as security.
1891	6,948,612	90	6,253,750	4	Taken for the conversion of the 1877 loan. Contracted with Rothschilds; 4,713,896 liras paid for the conversion of bonds, and the rest to the treasury. Egyptian tribute as security (in pounds sterling).
1893	1,000,000	70	700,000	4	To cover a budget deficit. Contracted with Viscount Zogheb's group; tobacco tax given as security.
1894	1,760,000	73.5	1,293,600	4	Contracted to liquidate the debt for the Eastern Railways, by the Deutsche Bank group; 20,637,624 francs out of a net loan of 29,400,000 were given to the railways and the rest to the treasury (in French francs).
1894	9,033,574	91	8,220,552	3.5	Contracted with Rothschilds and Ottoman Bank. Egyptian tribute given as security. Of this loan 1,567,750 for the consolidation of the 1854 loan, and 5,378,700 for the 1871 loan. The rest given to the treasury (in pounds sterling).
1896	3,272,720	84	2,749,084	5	Contracted with Ottoman Bank. Used to repay loans for the Ottoman Bank and the Rumeli railways and to meet expenses of the Crete and Armenian incidents. Sheep taxes and tithes pledged as security.
1902	8,600,020	80	6,880,016	4	Contracted with Ottoman Bank. Customs and intermediary taxes given as security. Used to pay for the 1886 loan, of which securities worth 5,132,666 liras were in circulation. The rest of the money was given to the treasury.
1903	2,376,000	100	2,376,000	4	Contracted with Deutsche Bank (for Plan I of the Baghdad railway). The crop tithes of Aleppo, Urfa, Aydin, Baghdad, and Diyarbakir pledged as security. The securities given to the company as kilometric guarantees.
1903	2,640,000	80	2,112,000	4	Contracted with Deutsche Bank. Fishing revenues pledged as security. Used to exchange the circulating 18,042,400 mark bonds of the 1888 loan for new ones. The remaining 21,125,600 marks given to the treasury (in marks).

TABLE 3—*continued*

1903	32,738,772	100	32,738,772	4	Loan was taken to consolidate and exchange the circulating D, C, and B series created by the 1881 Muharrem Decree; 31,051,565 liras' worth of old bonds were exchanged and the rest—1,687,207 liras—left to the treasury.*
1904	2,750,000	78.5	2,158,750	4	Taken to cover budget deficits. Contracted with Ottoman Bank and Comptoire d'Escompte. The balance of the revenues the administration of which had been turned over to the Public Debts Administration was pledged as security.
1904	5,306,664	80	4,248,932	4	Contracted with Ottoman Bank to pay debts to the latter. The remaining 2,510,411 liras were turned over to the treasury. The remainder of customs—revenues of various *vilayet*'s with the 0.5 per cent addition made to the Public Debts–administered tithes (82,700 liras from the tithes of various *sancak*'s) pledged as security.
1905	2,640,000	79.5	2,098,800	4	Contracted with Deutsche Bank. Loan taken to pay for military equipment. The 6 per cent addition to the revenues managed by the Public Debts Administration and additional customs duties for military equipment were pledged as security.
1906	9,537,000	85.5	8,154,135	4	Contracted with Ottoman Bank. The sources shown in the Muharrem Decree pledged as security. The 6,786,164 liras' worth of (1890) "privileged bonds" securities that were still in circulation, were exchanged, at par, for new ones. The rest given to the treasury.
1908	9,988,000	100	9,988,000	4	Taken for Plans II and III of the Baghdad Railway. The remainder of Public Debts Administration revenues pledged as security. Securities were given to the Baghdad Railway Company as kilometric guarantees.
1908	4,711,124	82.5	3,069,455	4	Contracted with Ottoman Bank, to cover budget deficit; 180,000 liras from various customs revenues and 40,000 liras from Public Debts Administration revenues pledged as security.
1909	7,000,004	86	6,002,503	4	Contracted with Ottoman Bank; taken to cover budget deficits; 320,000 liras from various *vilayet* tithes and 32,000 liras from Aleppo *vilayet* sheep tax pledged as security.
1910	1,712,304	89	1,523,950	4	Taken to construct the Soma-Bandirma railway, through the intermediary of the Izmir-Kasaba Railway Company. The gross revenues of the railway and the guaranteed balance of the 1894–95 Izmir-Kasaba and Extension Loan pledged as security.
1911	1,000,010	84	840,008	4	Taken to build the Hudaida-San'a and Extension Railway. The customs revenues of Hudaida and Jabana pledged as security. [See Part V, chap. 8.]
1911	7,040,000	81.5	5,737,600	4	Taken to cover certain advances and budget deficits. Contracted with the Deutsche Bank Syndicate of Banks. The customs revenues of Istanbul *vilayet* pledged as security.
1913	818,970	100	818,970	5	Issued by the Anatolian Railway Company. Loan appropriated to the debt resulting from the Konya plain-irrigation project. The remaining tithes of this district, and those of the Public Debts Administration, and the revenues from drained and sold lands pledged as security.

TABLE 3—*continued*

Year	Amount of Loan (in Ottoman gold liras)	Rate of Issue (per cent)	Amount Received (in Ottoman gold liras)	Interest (per cent)	Remarks
1913	1,485,000	100	1,485,000	5.5	Contracted with Armstrong Vickers. Loan taken for the construction of docks and the improvement of the maritime arsenal. The tithes of Sivas pledged as security.
1914	22,000,000	88¾	19,525,000	5	Contracted with Ottoman Bank. Loan appropriated to the consolidation of the floating debts resulting from the Libyan and Balkan Wars. The balance of Public Debts Administration revenues and the remainder of the subsidy tithes and customs pledged as security.

* Those securities of D, C, and B series created by the Muharrem Decree of 1881 which were still in circulation were exchanged and consolidated as shown below. The principal of the loans subject to this operation was reduced by 53 per cent.

	Those in Circulation in 1903			Accepted as Result of Conversion and Consolidation		
A	cancelled					
B	4,158,023	100	old	70	new	2,910,616
C	27,354,470	100	old	42	new	11,488,877
D	44,405,526	100	old	37.5	new	16,652,072
	75,918,019					31,051,565

to present, in the form of a table (Table 3), the foreign loans contracted after the Decree of Muharrem (1881–1914).[8]

The loans taken between 1881 and 1908 amounted to 120,314,473 liras, of which 107,858,796 was actually received. It appears that in the conversions and consolidations made by the loans of 1890, 1891, 1894, 1902, 1903, and 1906, the debt amounted to 51.5 million and the amount received to 45 million. In the 1908–14 loans, a debt of 46 million was incurred, but only 39 million received.

We have already observed at the beginning of our study that the Tanzimat period —even the name of which is incompatible with reality—brought upon the country this chronic trouble [the debt] among others which were not solved until the advent of the Republic. A brief explanation of the form of solution of this trouble is not without benefit.

After the treaty of Lausanne, the creditors revealed that, of the Ottoman debts, 161 million gold liras were still unpaid. This debt was divided by the Public Debts Administration among the successor states

[8] *Maliye Vekaleti Mecmuasi*, No. 6, pp. 6 ff.

of the Empire, and 107.5 million was fixed as the obligation of the Turkish Republic. The government of the Republic began its task by abolishing the Public Debts Administration and then proceeded to settle these former injustices, through several agreements, in which the foreign creditors acquiesced. As a consequence of the last Paris Agreement (1933), the Turkish government's outstanding portion of the Ottoman debt was reduced to 962 million French francs (approximately 80 million present Turkish paper liras, according to the pre-1936 calculation in francs) and the yearly charge to 700,000 Turkish gold liras; because of the shortage of foreign exchange the charge is presently being paid in goods. As a consequence of the devaluation of the franc in 1936, our debt was again reduced by 40 per cent.

Because of the devaluation of foreign currencies, the orderly repayment of installments by the government of the Republic, the state's gradual purchase from the market, of Uni Turk securities (according to the latest understanding, "obligations" taken out for debts), and so on, today the nightmarish gift of the Tanzimat—the Ottoman debt—is almost completely repaid. . . .

The Burden of Taxation on the Peasants

In the Ottoman Empire, as in all pre-industrial countries, the burden of taxation rested squarely on the shoulders of the peasantry. Under the *timar* system they usually handed anything from a fifth to a half of their crops to their "feudal" lord, the *sipahi*. The gradual replacement of *timar* by tax farming (*iltizam*) (see Part II, Introduction and chap. 9) resulted in a further deterioration in the position of the peasants, since the state exercised much less control over the tax farmers than it had over the *sipahi*'s, leaving greater scope for extortion and abuse. The first attempt to abolish tax farming and replace it by direct collection of taxes by salaried state officials was made in the Gulhane Rescript of 1839, but shortage of trained personnel soon made a return to the old system necessary, and in fact tax farming continued, in a somewhat modified form, until the First World War.

As the following selection shows, the main taxes paid by farmers were tithes and the livestock tax. The proportion of gross output taken by tithes varied greatly, from around one-tenth in rain-fed lands to between a tenth and a fifth in lands irrigated by rivers or streams and one-fortieth in lands watered by wells; further variations existed, according to the locality and the nature of the crops.[1] In the latter half of the nineteenth century some uniformity was introduced in methods of assessment and collection, but the tax continued to be very defective (see Part III, chap. 7). The livestock tax was levied on sheep, goats, pigs, cattle, and camels. Animals under one year old were exempt, as were horses, mules, and donkeys unless raised for income purposes. The tax was collected in cash or kind, at the rate of one-fortieth of the value of the animals.

One of the first measures taken by Mustafa Kemal in favor of the Turkish peasants was the abolition of the tithes in 1925. The great relief thus given was only partly offset by the concurrent raising of the land tax and the livestock tax. The effect of these changes may be measured by comparing the proportion of taxes paid by farmers with the figures given in the following selection. Aktan estimates that in 1935 farmers, who constituted 76.5 per cent of the population, bore exclusively taxes amounting to 6.5 per cent of total tax receipts; paid more than a

---

[1] Aktan, "Agricultural Policy of Turkey," pp. 143–47.

proportional share of other taxes amounting to a further 11.3 per cent of the total; and paid a proportional share of a third group of taxes, amounting to a further 22.2 per cent—a subtotal of 40 per cent, compared with 77 per cent under the Empire; they paid 34.9 per cent less than proportionately and did not contribute at all to 25.1 per cent.[2] The accompanying changes on the expenditure side meant that 12.8 per cent of the total benefited farmers exclusively, 6.2 per cent benefited urban dwellers, and 81 per cent were of general benefit.

(See also works by Gibb and Bowen, Barkan, Belin, Engelhardt, Velay, Morawitz, Mears, Bursal, Webster, and Hershlag listed in the Bibliography.)

[2] *Ibid.*, pp. 443–51.

[From Reşat Aktan, "Agricultural Policy of Turkey" (Ph.D. dissertation, University of California, 1950), pp. 140–41, 162–73; printed by kind permission of the author.]

KINDS OF TAXES

. . . Since a great majority of the people were farmers, and since the most important economic activity was agriculture, the basis of taxation was agriculture, and the main contributors of government revenues were the peasants. For over six centuries the two most basic revenue sources of the Empire were tithes and livestock taxes.[1]

The chief taxes in existence until the Tanzimat reform can be classified in five groups. They were tithes, livestock taxes, *cizye*, tariff duties, and traditional taxes. In the following sections, tithes and livestock taxes will be discussed separately [see Part III, chap. 7]. *Cizye* was a poll tax collected from non-Muslim adult males. Since they were exempted from military service, they had to share the expenses of the army by this tax. It was differentiated into three degrees, according to the ability to pay.

Tariff duties, originally fixed at 3 per cent on foreign imports and exports, brought in considerable sums. There were also duties on internal shipments at bridges and gates of towns; excises and duties on alcoholic drinks, tobacco, gunpowder, coffee, and trade transactions in the town and city markets. . . .

[1] I. F. Pelin, *Science of Finance* (Istanbul, 1945), pp. 292–93.

FARMERS' TAX BURDEN

It is impossible to determine what portion of the state's expenses was carried by the peasants in the early period of the Empire because of the lack of data. On the one hand, the expenses were not great, since the organization of the government was simple and most of the officials were not directly and regularly paid by the state because they were assigned the revenues of *has* and *ziamet*'s. Thus, one may think that the tax burden in general was not too heavy.

On the other hand, the most important economic activity of the period was agriculture, and a large majority of the people were farmers. Therefore, the state naturally had to depend mainly on this resource for its revenue. Besides, certain classes of the people were either exempted from taxes or were taxed very lightly—for example, all foreigners, religious groups, the people of Istanbul (then the capital city), the traders, industrialists, businessmen, and others. The richest *sarraf* who managed a financial concern perhaps worth millions did not pay as much tax as the poorest farmer of very modest means.[2] Garnett has remarked that the "small agriculturist in Turkey is, indeed, perhaps the most highly taxed individual in the world."[3]

As a result of wastes in administration and the luxurious and extravagant life of the

[2] *History of Turkish Agriculture*, p. 213.
[3] L. M. J. Garnett, *Home Life in Turkey* (New York, 1909), p. 69.

ruling class,[4] enormous foreign loans were contracted by the government, especially during the later period of the Empire. For these debts the only collateral was agricultural produce. As the Turkish peasants were held responsible for these unproductive and wasteful loans, their modest, hard-earned incomes were squeezed more and more to maintain the outrageous excesses of the ruling class.

In the later part of its history, the Empire had regular budgets for the revenues and expenses of the state. On the revenue side, the largest item has always been the return from tithes, and livestock taxes are high on the list. The peasants' share in the government expenses did not consist solely of these two kinds of taxes. As was noted earlier in this chapter, farmers were subject to many other duties and taxes by both local and central governments. To get a clearer picture we give some concrete data in the first two tables. Table 1 applies to the whole

Empire and contains total revenue, tithes, and livestock tax figures for specific years. Table 2 presents the same kind of figures for selected provinces. All figures are rounded to the nearest tenth.

Table 1 shows that the proportion of the revenue received from two kinds of taxes in the total government revenues varies from 34 to 44 per cent. As there were many kinds of taxes, indeed sometimes over a hundred, it is obvious that this ratio is a very high one. Besides, the total revenues given here do not include local taxes levied by the provincial and municipal authorities. These local taxes, it should be remembered, amounted to great sums.[5]

It is also interesting to notice the continuous rise in the proportion of the two taxes in the total revenues. In fact, it rose from 34 to 44 per cent in nine years, representing approximately a 30 per cent increase.

Table 2 is more meaningful for showing the direct contribution of farming people to government expenses, since the provincial budgets did not include certain revenue

[4] "The poverty of the treasury was extreme and the government was reproached for collecting the taxes through bankers (*sarraf*'s) who absorbed the greater part. No one went back to the real causes of the crisis: a weakened monetary system, absence of budgetary control, and a wasteful administrative organization" (E. Engelhardt, *La Turquie et le Tanzimat* [Paris, 1884], I, 99).

A vizir of three pennants had a suite of at least 500 people and 200–300 horses. Some of them had as many as 2,000 people besides bodyguards and harem women. They also had to pay out in order to keep their offices (A. du Velay, *Essai sur l'histoire financière de la Turquie*, pp. 64–65, quoted in *History of Turkish Agriculture*, p. 64).

[5] The following remark made by Urquhart is significant although it seems to the present writer that it contains some exaggeration: "The local and municipal expenses amount, at least, to three times the sum received by the government; and I have no doubt the people would be benefited if the government were to quadruple its demands, allowing the municipal authorities the entire management of the finances" (David Urquhart, *Turkey* [London, 1833], p. 87).

TABLE 1

TOTAL REVENUES, TITHES, AND LIVESTOCK TAXES OF THE OTTOMAN EMPIRE IN SELECTED YEARS
(Million Kese)*

Fiscal Year	Total Revenue	Tithes	Livestock Taxes	Sum of (2) and (3)	Per cent of Tithes in Total Revenue	Per cent of Livestock Taxes in Total Revenue	Sum of (5) and (6)
	(1)	(2)	(3)	(4)	(5)	(6)	(7)
1863–64 . .	3.0	0.8	0.2	1.0	27	7	34
1864–65 . .	3.2	0.9	0.2	1.1	28	6	34
1868–69 . .	3.4	1.1	0.3	1.4	32	9	41
1869–70 . .	3.4	1.1	0.3	1.4	32	9	41
1871–72 . .	3.8	1.3	0.4	1.7	34	10	44
1872–73 . .	4.3	1.5	0.4	1.9	35	9	44
Averages .	3.5	1.1	0.3	1.4	31	8	39

SOURCE: *History of Turkish Agriculture*, Appendixes.
* Kese (purse) = 500 gold piastres.

TABLE 2

Revenues of Selected* Local Governments
(In Millions of Kuruş)†

Province	Year	Total Revenue	Tithes	Livestock Taxes	Sum of (2) and (3)	Per cent of Tithes	Per cent of Livestock Taxes	Sum of (5) and (6)
		(1)	(2)	(3)	(4)	(5)	(6)	(7)
Ankara . .	1883	40.1	16.1	8.8	24.9	40	22	62
Aydin . .	1895	110.1	40.6	11.7	52.3	37	11	48
Edirne . . .	1891	74.8	32.9	12.4	45.3	44	17	61
Erzurum . .	1872	42.9	23.1	10.4	33.4	54	24	78
Diyarbekir .	1897	15.5	6.1	4.9	11.0	39	32	71
Hudavendigar	1901	94.7	42.6	13.7	56.3	45	14	59
Konya . . .	1892	48.7	17.2	10.9	28.1	35	22	57
Sivas . . .	1907	47.6	21.3	7.2	28.5	45	34	79
Trebizond . .	1890	35.0	13.7	3.2	16.9	39	9	48
Averages . .	. .	56.6	23.7	9.2	32.9	42	21‡	63

Source: *History of Turkish Agriculture*, Appendixes.
* Selection is made on the basis of availability of data.
† Kuruş is one one-hundredth of a Turkish pound.
‡ *Sic*—Editor.

items such as tariff duties and outright taxes paid by semi-subject countries. As a matter of fact, we see that the proportion of the two taxes in the total revenues rose from 48 to 79 per cent, depending on the economic conditions of the province. On the average the two taxes comprise 63 per cent of the provincial revenues.[6]

There are two more computations made by S. N. Ilkmen concerning farmers' contributions to government expenditures.[7] He considered only direct taxes and found the following proportions for two different years: 1903—84.7 per cent; 1910—87.2 per cent. Thus the proportion rose again between 1903 and 1910 at the expense of the farming class.

For a more exact understanding of the farmers' contribution to government revenues, it would be well to analyze one year's budget more closely. In this analysis we shall break up the revenues of the fiscal year 1872–73 into five groups:

1. Revenues paid solely by farmers.
2. Revenues paid mostly by farmers.

[6] The writer admits that this statement is rather ambiguous, since the sample contains only a few observations and the figures belong to different years. However, the intention is to give a general idea about the farmers' contribution rather than to derive precise statistical conclusions.
[7] Ilkmen, pp. 15–17.

3. Revenues paid by farmers according to the ratio between farmers and the total population.
4. Revenues to which the farmers contributed less than a proportionate amount.
5. Revenues not related to the farming class.

We shall compare each of these types of revenues with one another and also with the population distribution of rural and urban sections. The fact that there are no data on functional and personal distribution of national expenditures makes it necessary to use such a cumbersome and primitive method of analysis.

Table 3 shows that farmers contributed 45 per cent of the total revenue directly, most of an additional 7 per cent in duties, and 25 per cent proportionately. On the average, their share in 77 per cent of the revenue is more than proportionate. They also contributed, though less than proportionately, to the group of taxes [4] which comprise 16 per cent of the total revenue. The remaining 7 per cent was not strictly a tax burden on the people of the country, since it was contributed mostly by semi-independent countries such as Egypt and Rumania.

There are no data on the total population and its distribution between urban and rural

TABLE 3

ANALYSIS OF THE REVENUES OF THE FISCAL YEAR 1872–73

Tax Group	Taxes Included in Group	Amount of Revenue (1,000 kese) (1)	Per cent of Total Revenue (2)	Cumulative Amounts (1,000 kese) (3)	Cumulative Percentages (4)
1	Tithes and livestock taxes	1,916	45	1,916	45
2	Duties on silk and tobacco production and on salt consumption	282	7	2,198	52
3	Excises on tobacco and alcohol, tax on properties, duties on registrations and government affairs, and miscellaneous duties . .	1,080	25	3,278	77
4	Tariff duties, payment for exemption from military service, certain duties on government affairs, etc.	711	16	3,989	93
5	Contribution from semi-subject countries, revenues from state enterprises, etc.	298	7	4,287	100

SOURCE: Computed from the budget of 1872–73 given in *History of Turkish Agriculture*, Appendixes.

areas for this period. However, a crude estimate of the proportion of rural population on the basis of later surveys[8] and on indications from the earlier period would be about 85 per cent. This figure must be reduced to account for those peasants who did not pay the two main taxes (i.e., tithes and livestock) directly to the government because they were settled on *vakif* lands. Their contribution was not included in the amounts given in Table 3. If we assume this allowance to be 15 per cent, there remains 70 per cent of the population contributing 77 per cent of the total revenue more than proportionately. In addition, the farmers also contributed to the remaining 23 per cent of the revenue. Furthermore, a glance at the distribution of wealth—movables and immovables—between rural and urban areas makes the disproportion of the division of the tax burden in that period even more obvious.

When we look at the expenditure side of the budget and analyze the main items of expense we get a better idea of the unjust treatment which the farming class received during this period. Table 4 gives the expenditure items and their proportions in the budget for the year 1872–73.

[8] The first population census in 1927 indicated that 82 per cent of the population were farmers.

According to Table 4 the largest item of expenditure, indeed almost half the budget, was payments and interest charges on public debts. Since most of these debts were contracted with foreign lenders, and since the loans were spent on unproductive activities rather than on development of the country's resources, paying them back at such a high rate would cripple the fiscal power of the Empire. The second and third items were military and civil expenditures comprising 22 per cent and 13.6 per cent of the total expense, respectively. The fact that the

TABLE 4

GOVERNMENT EXPENDITURES IN THE FISCAL YEAR 1872–73

Items	Amount of Expenditure (1,000 kese)	Per cent of Total Expenditure
1. Public debts.	1,891	44.2
2. Army and navy . . .	945	22.1
3. Civil administration . .	580	13.6
4. Royal family	262	6.1
5. Public works (i.e., postal and telegraph services, mines, highways, railroads, and harbors) . .	229	5.3
6. Financial administration .	198	4.6
7. Education (all grades) . .	16	0.4
8. Health and commerce (including agriculture) . .	13	0.3
9. Other	147	3.4

SOURCE: *History of Turkish Agriculture*, Appendixes.

TABLE 5

BENEFICIARIES OF PUBLIC EXPENDITURES, 1872–73

Class	Expenditures	Amounts (1,000 kese)	Per cent of Total Expenditures	Cumulative Amounts (1,000 kese)	Cumulative Percentages
		(1)	(2)	(3)	(4)
1	Health and commerce (including agriculture) .	13	0.3	13	0.3
2	Civil and financial administration, army and navy, public works	1,952	45.6	1,965	45.9
3	Education, public debts, royal family, misc.. .	2,316	54.1	4,281	100.0
Totals.		4,281	100.0	. . . .	. . . .

SOURCE: Table 3, above.

country covered a vast area and that it had to support a large army and navy may explain why these items were so great. However, this does not necessarily justify the relatively high proportion of these expenditures in the budget. These three items of expenditure took 79.9 per cent of the total.

The allowance of the royal family amounting to 6 per cent came fourth on the list; then came expenditures on public works, 5 per cent of the total. The expenses of the financial organization also took 5 per cent of the total. Owing to the fact that the financial and administrative organizations were separated in the Ottoman Empire, the expense of collecting taxes was relatively high.

The expenditures on education, health, and commerce comprised the smallest portion of the budget, being only 0.4 and 0.3 per cent, respectively. When one thinks of the importance of these services in the life of a nation, these ridiculously low ratios are shocking. It is impossible to excuse and justify the otherwise generous government of the period for its parsimoniousness in matters of vital importance such as these.

To get a clearer notion about farmers' benefits from the government's services, we may further analyze the expenditure of the government of the Empire. It is true that to determine the actual beneficiaries of any public outlay is very difficult, if not impossible. However, an attempt is made to draw rather crude estimates. In this analysis the expenditures are reclassified under three headings as follows:

1. Expenditures which benefit mostly the rural population.

2. Expenditures from which farmers benefit in proportion to their ratio of the population.

3. Expenditures which benefit mostly non-rural people.

A comparison is then made between the farmers' contribution to state revenues and the farmers' benefits from the public expenditures. Here the revenue groups of Table 3 are reclassified by combining tax groups 1 and 2 as Class 1, and tax groups 4

TABLE 6

COMPARISON OF FARMERS' CONTRIBUTION TO THE PUBLIC TREASURY AND THEIR BENEFITS FROM IT, 1872–3

Revenue and Expenditure Groups	Amounts (1,000 kese)	Per cent of Total
Revenue contributed mostly by the farmers	2,198	52.0
Expenditures which benefit mostly the farmers	13	0.3
Revenue proportionally paid by the farmers	1,080	25.0
Expenditures from which farmers benefit proportionally . . .	1,952	45.6
Revenue derived mostly from non-farm sources	711	16.0
Expenditures which benefit mostly non-farm people	2,316	54.1

SOURCE: Tables 3 and 5, above.

and 5 as Class 3; tax group 3 of Table 3 corresponds to Class 2 here. The results are summarized in Tables 5 and 6.

These two tables indicate very clearly the adverse circumstance of the farmers under the Ottoman Empire. In conclusion we may say that although the government collected a majority of its revenue from the peasant class, it gave them very little service in return.

CHAPTER I3

Ethnic Division of Labor

What has been so aptly called ethnic division of labor has characterized the Middle East for centuries, and even millenniums. The following selection describes conditions in the Ottoman Empire on the eve of the First World War. A more detailed analysis would give examples of even narrower specialization; for example, a Christian village in northern Iraq supplies a very large proportion of the hotel owners and staff in that country; in the Syrian and Arabian deserts the Solubah tribe provides the smiths, tinkers, and carpenters and their women are dancers, singers, and prostitutes.

The reasons for this development are to be found in geography, history, and religion. The nature of the habitat of certain groups—the desert steppes of the Arabs, the highlands of the Yuruk in Turkey, the cities of the Dönme—excluded them from certain occupations and imposed others on them. The frequent invasions to which the region has been subject brought in conquerors who left the existing population undisturbed in its original activities. And the exigencies of certain religions have influenced the choice of occupation of their members: thus the Mandeans of Iraq, who practice frequent baptism as a purification, have to live near water, and the prohibition of interest by Islam has tended to exclude its adherents from finance.

In the nineteenth century a new, and very important, element was added to this complex picture. The modernization of some sectors of the economy and the massive influx of foreign capital led to the immigration of tens of thousands of Europeans and to the movement of almost as many members of some minority groups, mostly Christians from Lebanon and Syria and Armenians from Turkey. In the oil countries of the Persian Gulf the corresponding process, in this century, led to the influx of Europeans, Americans, Indians, Jordanians, and Lebanese. As a result in several countries, notably Egypt, some of the most important sectors of the economy passed under foreign control. Even some minor branches suffered the same fate. Thus in Egypt: "Boot-mending, as well as boot-making, is almost entirely in the hands of Greeks and Armenians. The drapery trade is controlled by Jews, Syrians, and Europeans, the tailoring trade by Jews." [1]

[1] *Annual Report of H.M. Agent, 1905.*

The following selection also indicates the changes that were being brought about by the First World War. In Turkey the Armenian massacres, the massive exchange of population with Greece, and the exodus of many Jews left a void which was filled by Muslim Turks. In Egypt the process was more gradual, but was greatly accelerated by the Second World War, the Arab-Israeli War, and the Suez attack of 1956, which also had repercussions on other Arab countries. This subject is discussed at more length in the Epilogue.

(See also works by Mears, Hourani [*Minorities*], Cromer, Issawi [*Egypt: An Economic and Social Analysis*], Galante, Sanjian and Polites listed in the Bibliography.)

[A. J. Sussnitzki, "Zur Gliederung wirtschaftslicher Arbeit nach Nationalitäten in der Türkei," *Archiv für Wirtschaftsforschung im Orient*, II (1917), 382-407. Some footnotes have been omitted and others summarized.]

In his valuable study "The Economic Significance of the Language Question in Turkey," [1] Eugen Mittwoch was the first, to my knowledge, to attempt to relate the differences in language in the Ottoman Empire to the occupational structure of the population. The following description of the production activities of the individual nationalities in the Turkish state is, in a way, given as a supplement to his article. For in fact the occupational structure in Turkey coincides in many respects with the racial differentiation. [2] The social stratification which is thus determined can be traced, without difficulty, in the manifold gradations of the national structure. Each single ethnic community is, as it were, a mesh in the greater economic web of the Empire, and its removal would leave in the general economic life a gap which could not readily be filled up. I shall confine myself principally to an exposition of the existing state of affairs. An explanation of why it is so, as well as a substantiation of the problem, would greatly exceed the space at my dis-

posal and I must reserve such considerations for another occasion. [3]

It should finally be noted that our remarks apply chiefly to relations prevailing up to the outbreak of the war. Since then deep changes have occurred in the economic life of Turkey. These changes are not only quantitative, such as greatly increased production, but also, and perhaps even more, qualitative in that the inner life of the population in its relation to the economic organization has experienced a revolution. Especially among the Turks themselves, a change in values regarding economic matters seems to be taking place. What the consequences of this process will be it is hardly possible to say at the moment. The war will bring about great changes everywhere, but especially in Turkey where everything is now in flux. It is therefore appropriate for us to get acquainted with the immediate situation, for through an exact knowledge of the present and recent past one can most easily draw conclusions regarding the shape of things to come in the near future.

If we wish to study the position of nationalities in the individual branches of the economy we must consider the regional distribution of the various ethnic groups. . . . Of the important races, the Turks (about 9 million) [4] are concentrated in a compact

[1] Published in *Archiv für Wirtschaftsforschung im Orient* [*AWO*], 1st year, No. 3/4, pp. 317-43.
[2] Typical parallelisms concerning the Caucasus may be found in Ischanian, "Nationaler Bestand, berufsmässige Gruppierung und soziale Gliederung der Kaukasischen Völker," *Osteuropäische Forschungen*, No. 1 (Berlin-Leipzig, 1914).

[3] The author refers to a forthcoming study on the psychology of the Turks from the standpoint of their economic activity, to be published in *Hamburgischen Forschungen*, edited by Rathgen and Stuhlmann.—Translator.
[4] Most of the figures are taken from Philippson, *Das türkische Reich, eine geographische Übersicht*, Deutsche Orientbücherei No. 12 (Weimar, 1915), p. 92, and Mittwoch, *op. cit.*, pp. 320, 322.

mass in Asia Minor, with the exception of the western regions and Armenia. In these last two regions there is a greater or lesser Turkish Diaspora; there are local, closed, purely Turkish enclaves which are sharply separated from their ethnically different neighbors. The Arabs (about 6 million) also live in a compact group in Syria, Mesopotamia, Palestine, and Arabia; their Diaspora in other regions is small. The Greeks (about 1.5 million) dominate the western and part of the northern coasts of Asia Minor and are also scattered in other localities. The Armenians (about 1.5 million) live in a compact group in Armenia and there is also a significant Diaspora in most other parts of the Empire, especially in the most easterly, but also in considerable numbers in western Asia Minor. A large part of the Kurds (about 1.5 million) also dwell in the areas in which Armenians are concentrated[5] while the numerically insignificant Lazes inhabit the northeastern coasts of Asia Minor. The Jews (about 600,000) are mostly scattered throughout the Empire, forming compact groups only in Palestine and, to a certain extent, in Mesopotamia; a significant characteristic of theirs is that, except in Palestine, they are almost all city dwellers. Also scattered in a Diaspora in every important city are some Persians.

AGRICULTURE

Even in the cultivation of the soil the various ethnic groups show significant differences. Thus the Turks devote themselves mainly to cereal planting and to small-scale gardening—most commonly to the growing of flowers but also to vineyards. Only slowly can they break away from their old-established habit of planting only what is needed for their own consumption. Hence they do not plant those cash crops which are most sought after by Europe. And they accustom themselves only with difficulty to a mode of work which

implies continuous stooping and are therefore averse to root crops [Rubenbau] and plants that need hoeing [Hackfruchten]. The Kurds, Druzes (who are renowned as growers of wheat), Lazes (who are skilled in the cultivation of flax), and also the Arabs are in many respects similar. The Arabs, however, have a particular occupation unknown to the Turks—fruit culture. For the Turkish peasant, who is little concerned with the future and is relatively remote from a sense of acquisitiveness [Erwerbssinne], does not readily devote himself to crops which yield returns only after several years of waiting.[6] In this respect the Arab is more provident. Still less do we find this restriction to cereal cultivation among the Bulgarians, who are to be found scattered here and there in Asia Minor, who are particularly skillful in the cultivation of root crops, and who formerly, in the old European Turkey, represented the most progressive element. The Bulgarians are recognized, together with the Turks, as a really permanent agricultural element. "The Bulgarian tills the soil, the Greek owns the plow" says a proverb, an allusion to the well-known fact that tax farming is, in European Turkey, predominantly in Greek hands just as in Asia Minor it is mainly in Armenian.

This leads us to a consideration of the two other important ethnic groups of Turkey, the Armenians and the Greeks. These two groups, wherever they have been long resident in large numbers, also play a significant part in agricultural activity. But they represent the opposite extreme to the Turks. It is true that cereal cultivation is not entirely unknown to them, especially to the Armenians. However, the inner relation with the soil, the sense of growing together with it, which particularly distinguishes the Turkish peasant, is generally absent. And their broader [ganzer] mind, which is more oriented toward gain, leads them in mass to the cultivation of cash crops and also fruits.

---

[5] In the *vilayet*'s of Van, Bitlis, Erzurum, and Diyabakir; but the Kurds are also found more to the south, e.g., in the *vilayet*'s of Ma'muret al-Aziz, Aleppo, and Mosul.

[6] See Jung, *Das Problem der Europäisierung orientalischer Wirtschaft* (Weimar, 1915), I, 418 ff., and Von der Goltz, *Anatolische Ausflüge* (Berlin, n.d.), p. 235.

Thus they frequently prefer the cultivation of vegetables, tobacco, mulberries, and other fruit to that of cereals,[7] because the former present greater prospects of gain. And through this greater sense of profit they usually push out of agriculture those Turks whom they find in their way.[8] Another fundamental difference between the Greeks and Armenians and the Turks, in the planting of trees, is even more marked than that between the Arabs and the Turks. "The Turks," observes a French writer, "plant trees for shade while the Greeks do so for profit. Hence we see on the one side cypresses and planes and on the other fruit orchards and vineyards." Vine cultivation has for the Greeks a particular meaning, connected with wine-making—probably resting on ancient Byzantine traditions—while among the Arabs and Turks the cultivation of grapes serves other ends,[9] because of religious injunctions.

The particular part played by the Jews in agriculture is similar to that of the Greeks and Armenians. In their case, too, and in so far as they are engaged in agriculture, there is a tendency to grow high-value specialized crops such as vines, almonds, and oranges; they have taken much less interest in cereals and have generally shown little capacity for that branch of agriculture. Lastly, the Persians living in Turkey either do not work in agriculture or so little as not to warrant discussion here.

From this brief sketch we can see how the various ethnic groups in Turkey show distinct differences in the choice of the crops they grow. These differences are traceable to psychological, historical, political, and religious bases which can only be hinted at

here. The contrast between the Turks on the one hand and the Greeks, Armenians, and Jews on the other in the cultivation of cereals and fruits is particularly striking. If, however, we wish to determine the absolute significance of the part played by each nationality in the individual branches of agriculture we must bear in mind the above-mentioned diversity of the regions they occupy. Thus cereal cultivation in western Asia Minor is in large measure in Greek hands, in central Anatolia almost exclusively in Turkish, in Armenia predominantly in Armenian, and in other parts in Arab hands. In fruits and cash crops, the leading role in western Asia Minor is played by the Greeks, further east by the Armenians, and to a small extent in Palestine by the Jews.[10] In the growing of mulberries [for silkworm breeding] the leading groups in western Asia Minor are the Armenians and the Greeks, in Syria the Christian Arabs.

Passing from cultivation to livestock raising, fishing, and hunting, we find that the first and last are in the hands of nomadic tribes. Indeed one can say that as the peoples of the Orient become increasingly sedentary their capability for livestock breeding retrogresses. The particular climatic conditions relating to the need for irrigation, the costs, and the unsuitability of village land as pasture grounds are responsible for this. Thus it is above all the Turkomans, and the ethnically affiliated Yuruks, as well as the Kurds, Lazes, Cherkess, and Arab beduins who devote themselves to livestock raising. But here too differences may be observed, differences due less to ethnic particularities than to the geographical relations imposed by the habitat of the various groups. Thus in the Cherkess economy the breeding of horses and mules plays the leading part. The Kurd has a predilection for sheep and goats, the Yuruk for goats, cows, and camels, while the Arab

---

[7] Of course that does not prevent the Greeks or the Armenians from stepping in after the harvest, buying the Turkish peasants' crops, and conveying them to the towns.

[8] See Von Scherzer, *Smyrna* (Vienna, 1873), p. 48. Since then this process has been accelerated in western Asia Minor.

[9] On this subject see B. Dutemple, *En Turquie d'Asie* (Paris, 1883), p. 187. Moslems eat fresh grapes, make raisins of them, or stew them. In the vine zones of Turkey, bread with white cheese and grapes constitutes, in season, an accepted meal and one that is highly favored by the poor.

[10] The Jews formerly played a very different part in agriculture. On the ancient significance of the Jews as the most important farmers in Mesopotamia, see Krauss, "Die Juden Mesopotamiens in Handel und Wandel," *Oc. M. O.*, 1916, No. 1-6, pp. 71, 84; on the decline of Jewish agriculture, *ibid.*, p. 87.

breeds with equal zeal sheep, goats, camels, and horses.[11]

The settled Christian Arabs, devoting themselves to a branch of animal husbandry which nomads cannot pursue, engage particularly in silkworm breeding. Here the Maronites, inhabiting Mount Lebanon, should be mentioned first. Their extensive silk cultivation annually supplies large amounts of cocoons and raw silk to France and Italy; and their wares, known as Damascene silk embroidery, enjoy great popularity among travelers to the Orient and constitute a not insignificant item among Syria's exports. Finally, mention must be made of the Greeks and Armenians, who are also engaged in silkworm breeding.

Thus in animal husbandry, also, we may discern differences between ethnic groups in the kind of animal breeding they choose. Here too the preponderance of one or another group in any given branch of the economy is the result of regional diversity. For example, in western Asia Minor the Armenians and Greeks dominate silk culture and in Syria the Arabs.

Finally, in regard to hunting and fishing, the Greeks above all others are fishermen, as are the Lazes. The latter are also huntsmen, as are the Arab beduins.

INDUSTRY

The individual national groups also show many differences in their participation in industry. To be sure, all of them engage in some form of industrial activity. But differentiations exist, although they are not always very great and certainly not fundamental, since the external conditions determining industrial activities often repeat themselves in the various national units [Nationalgebilden]. In general the observation may be made that the handicraftsman seeks customers preferably in his own ethnic community.[12] And therefore the more concentrated a national group is in a region and the greater its numbers, the larger will be the number of industrial occupations pursued by its members.

In the non-artistic crafts the Turks show most preference and skill as tanners, saddlers, shoemakers, turners, joiners, potters, wool- and silk-weavers, dyers, soap-boilers, iron- and coppersmiths, and armorers. They are also specialized in the making of numerous varieties of sweetmeats, which are enjoyed all over the Orient. And the Turks have not confined themselves to the crafts serving the needs of the lower strata of the Turkish population but have with great speed taken up the production of European-type goods.[13] The Armenians work as tinsmiths, locksmiths, joiners, silk-spinners, furriers, and also as tanners, bakers, butchers, and silver- and goldsmiths.[14] Among the Greeks the most prevalent handicraftsmen are bricklayers, smiths, mechanics,[15] joiners, cobblers, tailors, furriers, wagon-makers, barbers, bakers, confectioners, butchers, and, especially, winemakers. They also show preference for European-type crafts: thus they have gone in energetically for the production of articles for tourists and souvenirs for pilgrims. The last-named activity is also pursued by Christian Arabs, who are also engaged in the silk textile industry—as are Arabs, more generally, in the textile industry. Finally, the Jews also make the above-mentioned tourist articles and work in much larger numbers as tinsmiths, ropemakers, saddlers, tailors, dyers, weavers, upholsterers, quilters, watchmakers, and gold- and silversmiths. In several large cities they have recently obtained a leading place in modern ready-made clothing, for which they have abandoned custom-tailoring. Mention may also be made of scattered Albanians working as builders, wood-

---

[11] Sometimes beduins also raise cows, as around Acre, where their wealth is expressed in cows.

[12] Quite different, as we shall see, is the small trader, who does not carry articles adapted to special ethnic tastes but rather foreign wares.

[13] For example, during the Crimean War Turkish soldiers learned to imitate coffee grinders and also to repair bicycles and to make new ones out of old parts. Turkish harness-makers also made trunks, traveling bags, and rucksacks on English models. The same is true of shoemakers.

[14] On Armenians as very able dyers (modern dyers) in Aleppo, see Austro-Hungarian Consular Report on Aleppo for 1907, p. 5.

[15] Sometimes also watchmakers.

cutters, gardeners, and irrigation-canal diggers [*Erd- und Wasserarbeiter*], and of the Gypsies who in the cities often work in forges and in general as tinkers and diggers. The members of the interesting, small, nomadic tribe of Kizilbash (Redheads) are occupied in felling trees and cutting them up into boards and have attained such a mastery of this branch that they are often simply referred to as *tahtaci* (board-cutters). Lastly the Lazes who live in the plains have proved their great skill in the production of fine linens.

If we glance finally at the applied arts, we can again observe national peculiarities, and indeed in a sharper degree. Artistic spinning and weaving are practiced at home by all national groups. But the Turks occupy a particularly high place in carpet-knotting. However, if carpet-knotting is a cultural acquisition bestowed on us by the Turkish peoples, today other races, e.g., the Kurds, Armenians, and Greeks, practice it. Apart from this particular capacity one can say, in general, that the Turks play a special part in the applied arts, in so far as these still survive. Their psychological apprehension of economic life and their interlacing of feeling with logical understanding in everything they do allow the Turks to apply themselves in large numbers to the industrial arts—carpet making, earthenware production, metalwork, woodwork, and other branches. In certain respects the Arabs, and to some extent the Armenians, are in the same category as the Turks. The Greeks, Jews, and most Armenians are less given to the highest industrial arts.[16]

Thus in industry, in spite of the prevailing similarity, we can discern distinct differences among nationalities with respect to their choice of occupation, particularly in the industrial arts. If we then ask ourselves what is the absolute significance of each ethnic group in Turkish industry we find that in industrial arts the Turks and Arabs

excel. In other industries Turks, Arabs, Greeks,[17] Armenians, and, to a certain extent, Jews prevail in different localities. Only in a few branches are one or two ethnic groups dominant, e.g., Greeks and Armenians as furriers, Armenians and Jews as goldsmiths, Jews and Turks as dyers.[18]

In urban industries, however, we do not find any far-reaching regional division, since the diaspora of most ethnic groups has thoroughly mixed them in the bigger towns.

Finally, another difference may be noted in industry, regarding the form of industrial organization. Leaving aside the domestic activities practiced by all peasants, we note that Jews, Bulgarians, Gypsies, and also Albanians are more often wandering wage-workers than handicraftsmen. One may, not infrequently, see Jewish tinkers, a small coal oven in one hand and a few tools in the other, wandering from house to house in search of work. In many cases the Jews have not succeeded in following their industrial professions. Turks do not like this kind of wandering work for piece wages, probably because of pride. Greeks and Armenians also practice it only on a small scale, mostly under specific circumstances, except in cases of necessity. On the other hand, Bulgarians, and often Albanians—combining in one person the functions of bricklayer, carpenter, and architect—wander around in small bands, seeking house-repair work here and there and even putting up whole buildings. They also travel extensively, offering their services as gardeners, woodcutters, and, like the Gypsies, diggers.

The same aversion shown by certain groups for wage-work manifested itself—at least until the outbreak of the war—toward factory work. Under the Ottomans, mainly Greeks and Armenians were active in factories, partly as engineers and technicians and partly as entrepreneurs. The conservative Turks, on the other hand, kept away

---

[16] In Jerusalem (Bezalel) some success has been obtained in establishing Jewish industrial arts. On Jewish applied artists of lesser degree see Junge, "Bemerkungen zum Metallkunstgewerbe in Damaskus," *AWO* I, No. 3/4, pp. 509 ff.

[17] These are increasing their industrial role in western Asia Minor.
[18] On indigo-dyeing in Aleppo as an Islamic domain see *Handelsberichte über das Ausland* (Aleppo, 1910), p. 7.

from factory employment, even as workmen, in spite of their capacities as craftsmen and the position they occupied in industrial arts. However, things have now changed. In the factories operating in Turkey today, Turks predominate and by their carefulness and reliability have proved themselves truly fit factory workers.

In factory work another contrast between ethnic groups is that regarding the participation of the sexes. Until the [First] World War, Muslim races sent only men to factories whereas Christian Arab (e.g., in the Syrian silk-reeling plants), Armenian, and Greek women worked in factories. But this distinction too has been effaced by the war; Turkish women have learned to work in factories and have proved themselves excellent.

TRADE

We encounter the sharpest and also most significant distinction between the various nationalities in Turkey when we come to trade. For, taking the occupational fields considered so far, we find that each of the large ethnic groups participates more or less and shows capability as an economic worker. But trade is characterized by a very significant absence of the largest of the Turkish ethnic groups.

Greeks and Armenians work in all branches of trade. But, broadly speaking, the following distinction may be made: goods which serve the immediate necessities of life lie more in the domain of the Greeks whereas those which, so to speak, serve predominantly the needs of civilization belong rather to Armenians. Thus the Greeks trade, both wholesale and retail, in cereals, wine, strong liquor, spices, vegetables, fish, and olives. The Armenians, on the other hand, own large shops dealing in manufactured goods: carpets, iron, zinc and other metals, as well as construction materials.

The Jews are occupied in retail trade, or own shops dealing in fancy goods, haberdashery [Kurzwaren], colonial goods, textiles, and millinery; they have always been peddlers and second-hand dealers, trades from which sprang up, eventually, an active business in antiques and modern carpets. The Jews are, furthermore, small bankers and money changers. The so-called Dönme Jews, who passed over to Islam 250 years ago, and who live mainly in Salonica but are also to be found in small numbers in other Turkish towns, trade in knitted goods and own department stores. Syrian and Mesopotamian Arabs are also engaged in various branches of trade; they undoubtedly distinguish themselves by their intelligence, their intellectual activity, and their commercial talents. The Persians trade predominantly in carpets,[19] precious stones, and drugs; the Albanians and Macedonians are traders in milk products [yurtci] and the Tunisians in fezzes. The Kurds also show up as able traders.

Thus we may discern differences in the choice of branches of trade by the various national groups. The proper importance of the phenomenon becomes clear, however, only when we study the absolute importance of each ethnic group in trade. We first note the fact that in nearly every form of trade Armenians and Greeks dominate the field. Both because they are native to the land and, perhaps more, because of their fortunate distribution in cities and country, these two groups have succeeded, in the course of time, in securing an extraordinarily strong position in commerce. They hardly allow other national groups the possibility of developing their own economic powers. And they often proceed as though their objective were so to divide up the market that the two rival groups might be spared mutual competition. This occurs sometimes because of the above-mentioned division by branches. Sometimes there is also a regional separation, under which Greeks and Armenians pursue the same activity but in different localities; thus there is also a partial division of labor, with the Greeks in western Asia

[19] Especially in trade in Oriental rugs. However, the mercantile importance of the Persians, who at all times were renowned as traders and formerly held with the utmost tenacity the monopoly of Chinese silk trade, has greatly diminished in the course of time.

Minor and the Armenians in eastern.[20] This is particularly striking in the countryside where almost everywhere the *hanci*, the innkeeper, is either a Greek or an Armenian and where there is hardly a large village in which there is not at least one Greek or Armenian *bakal*, a small shopkeeper,[21] who supplies the peasants with the goods they need, buys their produce and takes it to market, or advances them credit at rates which are mostly usurious.

The fact that Greeks and Armenians live in the countryside as well as in the cities and have permanent relations with one another as city and country dwellers has been of decisive significance for their powerful position in trade. The numerous Greeks and Armenians inhabiting the coastal or interior areas constitute, as retailers, a broad foundation for the wholesale trade of the cities. Precisely because, until now, the economic life of many races in Turkey was based on the national community, the result was not only the elimination of foreign elements but also the cohesion of the members of the group [*eignen Genossen*]. A final cause of the standing of the Greeks and Armenians in Turkey should be considered: the protection they enjoyed from foreign powers, whose subjects they sometimes were, thus becoming, thanks to the former Capitulations, exempt from taxation.

All these factors explain the fact that, in petty trade and petty credit activities, but also in wholesale internal trade, import and external trade, and in the high finance of Turkey, the Greeks and Armenians—who for a long time have had their own buying and selling branches in the commercial centers of Europe[22]—have played the decisive role.

[20] For instance the fur trade in Constantinople is in Greek hands, and in inner Anatolia in Armenian.
[21] And even in pure, isolated Turkish villages—contrary to what occurs in handicrafts.
[22] For several centuries Armenians and Greeks dominated the European-Oriental trade, in pursuit of which they formerly went over to the larger European cities much more frequently than they do now; see, e.g., on Armenians in Lemberg in the fourteenth and fifteenth centuries, Wendt, *Schlesien und der Orient* (Breslau, 1916), pp. 23, 25; on Armenians in the sixteenth and seventeenth century in Breslau and Cracow, *ibid.*, p. 122.

Thus we find two nationalities, which neither in agriculture nor in industry have such a great importance, exercising in trade a preponderant influence. Here we do not see the otherwise noticeable division of labor and co-operation based on regions and related to the numerical size of the various peoples which we noted earlier. Rather, two of these peoples are preponderant almost everywhere. Neither the Arabs and Persians, who are able traders, nor by and large the Jews can compete with them. The commercial activity of Muslim Arabs has always been confined within narrow bounds, while Christian Syrians have succeeded in securing for themselves a certain position in wholesale trade in some localities. The Persians have carved for themselves a domain only in wholesale trade in carpets (old rugs), the Albanians and Macedonians in trade in milk products in Constantinople, and the Tunisians in retail trade in fezzes there. The Jews were in partial competition with the Greeks[23] and Armenians, competition which, since in contrast to their opponents they seldom enjoyed [foreign] protection, was seldom crowned with success.[24] Although, except in Palestine, the Jews live in cities and devote themselves fully to business activities, they are—when they have not remained handicraftsmen—at most petty traders whose great concern is to secure their existence, without exerting a great influence on the country's economy. Even the ancient and particular field of the Jews, the financial, is seldom touched by them in Turkey. They seldom go beyond small business activities. However, this general insignificance of Jews in trade is offset by three considerations: First, they have often developed the trade in carpets and antiques to a significant extent, even though they have not succeeded in effacing its origins,

[23] Between these and the Jews there is generally a great tension so that they cannot endure each other's presence in the same locality. Hence the appreciable deterioration of the situation of the Jews (and the Dönme) in Salonica since this city passed under Greek domination.
[24] See my study "Die wirtschaftliche Lage der Juden in Konstantinopel," *Allgemeine Zeitung des Judentums*, 1912, No. 3.

viz., peddling. It should also be remembered that in places where Greek and Armenian competition is not so overwhelming, as in Mesopotamia, thanks to a long historical tradition, a tiny fraction of the Jewish population has great influence over trade and finance.[25] Second, the East European Jews who have fairly recently migrated to Turkey, the so-called Ashkenazim, exercise a greater influence on trade and undoubtedly constitute a new commercial element, especially in textiles and millinery. And, third, the Dönmes have succeeded in certain places in achieving a noteworthy position in wholesale trade. These Dönmes were, thanks to their ability and to their membership in Islam, the most successful competitors of the Armenians and Greeks, but their numbers were too small for them to gain a decisive influence.

However, this partly old and partly newly developed influence of the Jews and Dönmes, as well as the above-mentioned position of the Arabs, until the war constituted essentially reserve forces in trade, insignificant in comparison to the dominance of the Armenians and Greeks. But the real importance of the Jews and Arabs in trade is certainly great compared to that of the largest nationality in Turkey—the Turks themselves—when we consider the number of the latter who are engaged in commercial activities, disregarding the numerous foreigners and Levantines. And here we come up against the most important difference in trade and also against a significant difference between trade and other branches of the economy: *until the outbreak of the World War the Ottoman Turks could not be counted among the mercantile elements of Turkey.* The well-known Oriental proverb, "A Greek can cheat two Jews, an Armenian two Greeks," shows the complete absence of the Turks

from trade. Whenever mention is made of the commercial part of the population, the Turk is ignored, as though he stood entirely outside the ranks. He hardly figures among the disciples of Mercury, from whom he differs not only in degree but in essence.

One of the reasons for this phenomenon is the following: the Turk is a squire, a nobleman or, to be more precise, a landed nobleman. "Eat little, but keep a servant," says a Turkish proverb. The Turkish race [*Rasse*] constitutes the knightly caste in the state, from which warriors and officials are recruited. And through tradition and their natural inclination toward agriculture, the Turks supply skilled peasant farmers as well as large landowners. But they keep away from all activities which presuppose the speculative thinking of the capitalist entrepreneur. It is not that they do not understand what speculative thought is—on the contrary, a theoretical bent of mind and capacity for [intellectual] construction is perhaps a particular characteristic of this people. But the special kind of purely commercial thinking and any inherent inclination toward trade are almost completely absent; and in practical competition, especially with the Armenians and Greeks, the Turk was as a rule worsted until the war. Even when the Turk does devote himself steadily to some commercial activity, it is more often due to a concatenation of circumstances than to a deep inclination, or else to the special conditions prevailing in the trade.[26] However, it would be wrong to attribute the minor significance of the Turks in trade to these internal considerations. Aside from Constantinople, where the Turks are almost exclusively brought up to be government officials, there are in the interior many Turkish merchants. But these can never easily achieve importance, because they have to carry on a difficult struggle against the Greeks and Armenians. Formerly, they were not exempt from taxes, as were the latter when they were foreign protégés. Again,

[25] In the trade of Aleppo and Mesopotamia Jews played for long an important part. This is still true of Jewish traders in Baghdad. But there too a stark contrast between the relatively few rich and the great mass of Jews living in deepest poverty may be observed, a condition which came about through the decline of the agriculture formerly energetically pursued by Jews. See Krauss, *op. cit.*, pp. 86 ff.

[26] For instance in the rose-oil and drug trade in Constantinople which are dominated by Turks and which consist of purely Muslim guilds.

the Turks were burdened by universal conscription. Lastly, no foreign power protected the Turks. On them, as on the Jews, lay the whole pressure of the Hamidian epoch [1876–1909], with its insecurity of property. These external circumstances, together with the above-mentioned preponderant ethnic characteristics, fully explain the insignificance of the Turks in trade, as we find it in practice.

It may be concluded that the *most significant ethnic differentiation up to the outbreak of the war showed itself in trade*, and precisely with reference to the Turks. All other differences in the choice of particular vocations, in regional patterns, and in absolute importance in any given sector of the economy— whether in the whole of Turkey or in part of the country—are eclipsed by that fact.

A few words concerning transport may be introduced, as a kind of appendix, in conclusion of this section. In so far as transport takes place by land, along the old traditional paths, the various ethnic groups participate in it, each according to its location. But the Turkish and Arab *nomadic tribes* stand out particularly as excellent leaders of caravans, and they often hire out their donkeys and camels for riding or as beasts of burden. *City* Turks also often work as porters, as do some Armenians, Jews, and Albanians. The various elements are also found in railway transport, not least among them being the Turks. However, the latter are less frequently employed in occupations which require a pliant attitude to the public, e.g., guards in streetcars, than in those which demand exact and decisive handling of the means of transport, e.g., motormen.

In water transport we find much sharper differences between nationalities. The Greeks above all others devote themselves to this occupation; being bold sailors and daring entrepreneurs they dominate large-scale merchant shipping. Equally skilled as seafarers are the Lazes, and since long ago the Turkish government has recruited men for the imperial navy as much as possible from the Laz coastal region. The Turks, Arabs, and Albanians go in for navigation to a

much lesser extent, and carry only local traffic [*Kleindienst*], although the Turks also produce able sailors. The Armenians and Jews present a complete contrast to the Greeks and Lazes and seem to lack any kind of maritime aptitude; the Armenians, above all, have for a long time completely abstained from seafaring.[27]

CONCLUDING REMARKS

A brief review of our investigation, supplemented by a few remarks regarding the branches of the economy to which the different nationalities direct their main attention, shows that, until now, the Turks have been preponderant in agriculture and have also played a part in industry. The obvious result of the careful and contemplative manner in which they practice industry has been that they have become mainly artistic handicraftsmen. But they have also proved that they can be trained as skilled factory workers and even as manufacturers. And the occupational distribution of the Turkish people corresponds to the above considerations: the talents of the Turks suit them for all kinds of work which demand strength and dexterity, and thus in particular agriculture. The Turkish people is, generally speaking, engaged in agriculture and bureaucracy, and does not have a significant middle class: from the very beginning—and this is the basis of its success —it has been a warrior caste, with all the occupations that go with the nature of the warrior. The straightforward mind of the Turk, immediately directed toward its goal, is relatively far removed from the spirit of capitalism with its subtle profit-speculations and its practical method of observation, feeling out everything; however, other, external circumstances must also be held responsible for the fact that Turks have been engaged to only a slight extent in certain occupations, as we have seen.

The Armenians and Greeks are completely different from the Turks. We find both, so to speak, upright in every saddle. Both play

[27] See also von Scherzer, *op. cit.*, p. 51.

a part in every branch of the economy, especially the agile, never-resting Armenians, bursting with activity.[28] In agriculture, in small- and large-scale industry, in wholesale and retail trade, as in every kind of financial activity, Armenians and Greeks are heavily represented. And particularly in trade we find that they occupy an uncommonly important place, in which the dexterity, frugality,[29] and foresight of the Armenians ensure them pre-eminence over the Greeks. Add to this that the Armenians—who, thanks to the liberality of the Turkish government, occupied all kinds of government posts—often played a very significant intermediary role between the government and the people in which they exhibited a shrewdness which is hardly to be praised. Thus before the war taxes were, to a large extent, farmed out to them; and, not infrequently, they were the financiers of the state. The economic significance of the Armenians took an infinity of forms, although trade probably retained the primary importance. The Arabs, on the other hand, played their part especially in agriculture and animal husbandry, and these two were also the fields of activity of the overwhelming mass of that people. But wherever an opportunity offered itself the mental mobility and the sense of money-making of the Arabs, particularly the Syrians, led them to enter the field of trade. The Jews, lastly, did not occupy a really leading position in any branch of the economy, not even in trade, although they were primarily engaged in that activity, in addition to handicrafts. It is true that we do find purely Jewish elements, or people of Jewish descent such as the Dönmes, playing a part as important trade-entrepreneurs; but no link binds them with the mass of Jews or with the still unformed Turkish middle class.

The position which the individual national groups have hitherto occupied in the economy and the activity to which they have primarily dedicated themselves tell us something of what might be expected in the future. For the various differences we have noted cannot be resolved overnight. In large measure they rest on deep, natural causes which cannot be removed from the outside. This question is gaining in practical importance because of the ever growing efforts of the Turks to "turkify" the economy as far as possible or to grant concessions to politically reliable national groups. The changes will be carried through most speedily in agriculture and the handicrafts; in these fields the Turks have hitherto worked with both inclination and success and the differences [between them and other groups] existing at present are not very great, and are often only regional. The question is quite different in the area of trade. The Armenians and Greeks enjoy not only an actual preponderance in that field but also a particularly strong ethnic capacity for it; these circumstances fully explain the qualification of these groups for this branch of the economy, even had they not enjoyed the protection of foreign powers.

The Dönmes, the Jews, and the Arabs may be regarded as, so to speak, reserve units for trade. According to their particular talents, these can be called upon to enter into the economic heritage of the above-mentioned national groups, when this appears desirable.[30] Until now, the Ottoman Turks have neither played a leading part in trade nor in general engaged in it on a large scale. It is true that external circumstances are partly responsible for this; and it is also true that during the war important changes have taken place.[31] But—except when we are dealing with the Dönmes or with

[28] "The Armenian does not sit down until he is weary," says a striking Oriental proverb.
[29] By contrast with the Greeks.

[30] The Greeks and Armenians, who are brought up in French culture, not only have served to spread French influence in the Orient but have also been the pace-setters of the Western Powers in trade and industry. If the Turkish government can no longer tolerate this state of affairs, it will be the task of the Central Powers to seek to alter existing relations. One of the most effective means for this would be to utilize the hitherto untapped power of the other national groups and make them serviceable.
[31] Trade and production monopolies, mainly in Turkish hands, have been formed and are eliminating all competition by means of their capital, monopoly of transport, etc.

Cretan Turks of Greek origin—these new opportunities are not sufficiently compatible with the national aptitudes and personal inclinations required for a commercial class, as they are in agriculture and industry.

This raises the question of the commercialization of Turkey after the war. A powerful nationalist current has been making itself felt among the Turks for some time, which seeks to wash away not only the activity of foreigners but also that of the other national groups. This should hardly surprise us, for we are dealing with a phenomenon of national psychology which is spreading everywhere, although the movement has unmistakably struck deep roots in Turkey in recent times and exercised its spell on broad circles of the population. However, the dominant elements in the Empire of the Crescent seem to give their allegiance rather to a moderate nationalism. Thus Cavid, the minister of finance, declared in his noteworthy speech of March 3, 1917:[32]

We desire that the Turks, who until now have been kept away from all enterprises established in our midst by foreigners, should henceforth participate, with their labor and their capital, to a determined extent, in all newly founded enterprises. We desire that every time foreigners take the initiative of founding an economic enterprise in any of our provinces they should make sure of the co-operation of the indigenous population and also of those citizens who are particularly fit for this kind of work, either because of their knowledge or because of their capital.

And as though he wished to underline his words, as though to stress that he had made his declaration not only on his own behalf but in execution of the program of the cabinet—and in a certain sense the program of the [Union and Progress] party in whose hands the fate of the country lies—he went on to say: "Let us unite our labor and our capital with the knowledge, science, industry, and capital of the foreigner."

This seems to be, in the present circumstances, the only way open before a wise government if its efforts are to be crowned with success. A people which has until now shown little activity in trade—partly because of external circumstances—can only with difficulty start competing overnight. Only slow, tenacious work, proceeding step by step, can gradually lead to a salutary result. . . .

This seems to be the point of view adopted by the Union and Progress party, the only party which effectively sets the tone in the political life of Turkey.

[32] Cavid Bey, "Türkische Kriegfinanzwirtschaft," *Der deutsche Krieg, politische Flugschriften*, No. 94 (Stuttgart and Berlin, 1917).

PART III

Iraq

IRAQ
Introduction

In perhaps no other country in the world is prosperity so directly dependent on
an intricate system of irrigation, demanding the constant attention of the government, as it is in Iraq. In the northeastern corner of the country, beyond the Tigris—
the classical Assyria and medieval Arab al-Jazira—rainfall is adequate for cultivation. But in the core of the country, in the vast, immensely fertile, alluvial plain
between the twin rivers, known in ancient times as Babylonia and to the Arabs as
al-Sawad, rain is both insufficient in quantity and untimely, since it falls mainly
from December through March, too late for the winter sowing season.

This inadequacy of rainfall cannot be remedied by a simple system of flood
irrigation, such as the one practiced in Egypt for thousands of years. For, as was
pointed out by Sir William Willcocks, probably the greatest engineer who worked
in both countries (see Part III, chap. 8):

The problems whose successful solution will restore Babylonia to its ancient prosperity
are far more difficult than those which faced the irrigation engineers in the Nile Valley.
Of all the rivers in the world, the Nile is the most gentlemanly. It gives ample warning
of its rise and fall; is never abrupt; carries enough of sediment in flood to enrich the land
without choking the canals; is itself free of salt; has its annual flood in August, September
and October, securing both summer and winter crops; traverses a valley with a climate
mild enough to allow of Egyptian clover in winter and Egyptian cotton in summer; and
flows between sandstone and limestone hills, which provide an abundance of building
materials. The Tigris and Euphrates rise without warning; are always abrupt; carry five
times the sediment of the Nile; have their annual flood in March, April and May, too
late for the winter and too early for the summer crops; traverse a country where the
temperature rises to 120 degrees in summer and falls to 20 degrees in winter, and where
both Egyptian cotton and Egyptian clover are out of the question; and flow between
degraded deserts of gypsum and salted mud.

To which may be added the fact that the seasonal and annual variations of the
Tigris and Euphrates are much greater than those of the Nile.

An elaborate system of perennial irrigation has therefore always been necessary
in Mesopotamia. This consists of barrages to raise the level of the river and feed

canals on either bank; irrigation canals; dikes to protect the ripening crops against flood from March through June; and drainage canals to prevent the salination which constantly threatens the soil. Such a system requires constant care, and therefore the country has known prosperity only when it had a strong, stable government, prepared to keep up the irrigation works. The millennial history of Mesopotamia contains long intervals in which the government broke down and agriculture decayed.

The latest of these breakdowns started with the weakening of the Abbasid state and was precipitated by the Mongol invasion, in 1258, which resulted in the ruin of many irrigation works. During the next five centuries Iraq never had a government strong enough to restore its irrigation, and from the sixteenth to the end of the eighteenth century it was a battlefield for the warring Ottoman and Persian armies. The result was that a large part of the land was ruined by salination and that the nomads took possession of the desolated countryside. By the eighteenth century systematic cultivation was restricted to the area around Basra, where an ingenious irrigation system operated by the tide watered the palm groves and other fields; to Diyala, where the canals had survived; and to the rain-fed zone between Arbil, Kirkuk, Mosul, and Diyarbakir, which was protected by Turkish garrisons.[1] The rest of the country was occupied by tribal confederations, uncontrolled by the governors of Baghdad. Each tribe practiced a system of shifting cultivation within the large areas claimed and held in common by its members.

The consequent decline of the population may be judged from the following statement: "Irrigation from the Didjla [Tigris]—and rain cultivation in the north—undoubtedly supported [in medieval times] a population perhaps three times more numerous than that of today," i.e., after a century of rapid growth.[2]

The decline of the towns was not quite so great as that of the countryside, but they too had sunk very low. The population of Baghdad, which in the eleventh century may have been as high as 1,500,000,[3] had shrunk to 50,000–100,000; the three other main towns, Basra, Al-Hillah, and Mosul had 50,000 inhabitants, or fewer, each. The superb handicrafts of medieval Iraq had been greatly reduced in both quantity and quality. By the seventeenth century "the famous 'muslin' had almost ceased to be made" in Mosul,[4] and in both that town and Basra industrial activity had fallen to a minimum. Only in Baghdad did many different handicrafts survive, but here too quality had deteriorated.

However, the chief economic activity of Iraqi towns was not industry but trade. As has been pointed out: "Remarkable uniformity of inter-space [between the main towns] shows the birth of many as caravan-stages."[5] In addition to handling the produce of the surrounding region—grain, wool, hides, and so on—the towns

[1] Haider, "Land Problems of Iraq," p. 223.
[2] *Encyclopedia of Islam*, new ed., *s.v.* "Didjla."
[3] *Ibid.*, *s.v.* "Baghdad."
[4] Longrigg, *Four Centuries*, p. 96.
[5] *Ibid.*, p. 9.

served as stopping points on the route between the Mediterranean and the Persian Gulf. From Europe came woolens, silks, metal goods, and other commodities; from Persia raw silk, wool, rugs, and other goods; and from India and the East Indies indigo, spices, fine cloths, and so on.

This transit trade declined sharply after the Portuguese seized the Persian Gulf, early in the sixteenth century, and diverted much of its trade and that of India round the Cape of Good Hope. By the middle of the seventeenth century a resurgent Iran, helped by the Dutch and British, had succeeded in expelling the Portuguese and this had a favorable effect on transit trade through Iraq. However, in the following century the decline in Iran's economy, the series of wars between Britain and France, the increasing weakness of the Ottoman government, and the growing insecurity combined once more to reduce trade. The process was accelerated by the general breakdown of the Ottoman Empire in the last decades of the eighteenth century and by the devastating Wahhabi invasions at the turn of the century (see Part III, chap. 1).

In the course of the nineteenth century, after sinking even lower during the famine and plague of 1830, Iraq began slowly to move out of this morass of stagnation and decay. The first landmark was the reconquest of the country, in 1831, by the Ottoman government from the Caucasian Mamluks, who had ruled it, practically independently of the Porte, since 1747. It is true that, except for opening a few schools, the government did very little to promote the economic and social development of Iraq until the beginning of the present century, and some of its attempts to do so had very unfortunate consequences, for example, in land-tenure relations. But it did give the country, increasingly until 1914, what it needed most—a greater measure of security; the power of the Kurdish and other semi-independent chieftains was reduced and the hostility of the tribal leaders was diminished by a mixture of force and conciliation. This made it possible for some of the world-wide forces making for expansion to operate on the economy of Iraq.

The first of these forces was the development of modern transport. The ever stronger links binding Britain and India pressed the need for improved communications. Since the shortest route between the Mediterranean and the Indian Ocean ran through Iraq, and since this route had long been used for mail, it was natural that numerous railway and river-navigation schemes should be put forward (see Part III, chap. 2). None of these projects was implemented, and the first railway in Iraq—an isolated stretch of the Berlin–Baghdad line connecting Baghdad with Samarra, 130 kilometers away—was not completed until 1914. Similarly, no modern roads were built, and the total number of automobiles in Iraq in 1914 was "less than a dozen."[6] And, until the First World War, Basra lacked almost every facility found in modern ports. But in the 1860's telegraph lines were laid down connecting Iraq with Turkey, Iran, and India, and by the end of the century all the principal towns had telegraphic communications. Another important by-

[6] Longrigg, *Iraq, 1900 to 1950*, p. 64.

product of the projects of the 1830's was the establishment of a steam navigation service on the Tigris (see Part III, chap. 3). River steamers greatly reduced the duration of the journey to and from the Persian Gulf, cut down freight rates, and made it possible to move the country's rapidly growing volume of foreign trade.

Foreign trade had already begun to show some increase in the 1850's, and it was further accelerated by the establishment of a steam navigation line between Bombay and Basra, starting in 1862 at six-week intervals and becoming fortnightly by 1866. But the greatest stimulus came from the opening, in 1869, of the Suez Canal, which greatly reduced sailing time between the Persian Gulf and Europe. The effect on Iraq's sea-borne trade may be judged from Table 1. The

TABLE 1*
(Annual averages in thousands of pounds)

	Exports	Imports	Total
1864–1871	147	291	438
1880–1887	1,035	725	1,760
1896–1903	1,390	1,257	2,647
1912–1913	2,960	3,468	6,428

* From Hasan, "Foreign Trade in the Economic Development of Iraq, 1869–1939," pp. 42, 130.

money value of sea-borne trade thus increased fifteen-fold in less than fifty years and, since the level of international prices in the 1860's was not very different from that of 1913, it may be taken that the real value rose in much the same proportion. However, overland trade to Iran, Syria, and Anatolia, which until the mid-1860's may have exceeded sea trade,[7] probably declined thereafter. It may therefore be conjectured that the total volume of Iraqi trade increased eightfold between 1870 and 1914.

The rise in exports was almost entirely accounted for by three crops—dates, wheat, and barley—and such products of animal husbandry as wool, hides and skins, and live animals. Thus, whereas in the first half of the century Iraq was generally an importer of grain, by the end of the century it exported some 100,000 tons a year. Between them these items constituted two-thirds to four-fifths of Iraq's exports until oil began to flow out in 1934. On the import side the principal item was textiles, mainly cotton; until 1914 textiles increased both absolutely and as a share of imports, accounting for over 40 per cent of the total. Capital equipment also increased, but still amounted to less than 10 per cent of total imports by 1914.

The direction of Iraq's trade shifted sharply during the nineteenth century. Until the opening of the Suez Canal, Iran was the main partner, accounting for almost two-thirds of the total, followed by India and Britain. In the next fifty years, however, trade with Iran seems to have declined in volume while that with Britain and India rose greatly; by the outbreak of the First World War those two

[7] Hasan, "Foreign Trade in the Economic Development of Iraq, 1869–1939," pp. 39–40.

countries absorbed half of Iraq's exports and supplied over two-thirds of its imports.[8] Germany entered the Iraqi market at the turn of the century and rapidly increased its trade, but by 1914 had not obtained a significant share of the total.[9]

The effect on population of this expansion in foreign trade and the consequent increase in production is discussed in Part III, chap. 4. Briefly, it stimulated population growth; promoted the settling-down of the beduins, since markets for agricultural produce were expanding much more rapidly than those for pastoral produce; and slowed down urbanization by subjecting the handicrafts to more intense foreign competition. The impact on land tenure and on relations within the tribe was equally great, and more complex. Hitherto the tribesman had been valued chiefly as a warrior; now, with the growth of a market for his surplus produce, he came to be regarded as a potential producer and source of wealth. By the same token, land, which had been considered a commonly owned property assuring the subsistence of the whole tribe, began to be coveted as a potential source of private wealth. The forces set in motion by this, and the confusion created by the government's attempt to apply the Land Code of 1858, are described in Part III, chap. 5. Two disastrous consequences followed, which were to plague Iraq until well after the Second World War: a confusion of land titles that greatly impeded land improvement and held up agricultural development; and the alienation to landlords of a great portion of land owned by the state or by tribes.

A comparison .of conditions in Iraq in 1900 (see Part III, chap. 6) with those prevailing in 1800 shows that a considerable progress, both quantitative and qualitative, had been made. Foreign trade had grown; transport had improved; the fiscal system had become somewhat more rational (see Part III, chap. 7); a few foreign banks and business houses had been established; and, thanks to the opening of government, foreign missionary, and local religious schools serving the minority groups, literacy in the towns rose from perhaps 0.5 per cent in 1850 to some 5 to 10 per cent by 1900.[10] But Iraq still lagged far behind such regions as Egypt, western Anatolia, and Syria.

In the period 1900–1914 progress was greatly accelerated. British and German interest in Iraq had risen sharply; the Germans saw in the country, among other things, a potential producer of cotton, comparable to Egypt, which could free them from dependence on American and Indian supplies. The Berlin–Baghdad railway project, held up for many years by international rivalries, was making rapid progress when war broke out. Another scheme that was approaching fruition was the exploitation of the oil fields of northern Iraq (see Part III, chap. 9). Still more important was the new interest being taken in irrigation by the Ottoman government. Apart from some clearing of canals by Gozlikli pasha in the 1850's

---

[8] *Ibid.*, pp. 63–65.
[9] Saleh, *Mesopotamia (Iraq) 1600–1914*, p. 233.
[10] Longrigg, *Four Centuries*, p. 316.

and the abortive schemes of Midhat pasha,[11] almost nothing had been done in the field of irrigation, and conditions actually deteriorated in the second half of the century. But in 1891 the first modern barrage was built, at Hindiyya. It collapsed a few years later but was replaced by one built by Willcocks, who drew up a master plan for the irrigation of Iraq (see Part III, chap. 8). Pump irrigation was also beginning to prove its worth.

In the interwar period, transport by rail and road, the spread of small-scale irrigation works, improved financial and fiscal institutions, and the beginning of oil production combined to set Iraq on the road to rapid economic growth. But it was only after the Second World War that, thanks to a spectacular increase in oil production and the revenues derived therefrom—which were used mainly for the development of agriculture, industry, transport, and social services—the country began to attain a rate of economic and social progress commensurate with its immense potential.

[11] *Ibid.*, pp. 283, 291, 318.

CHAPTER I

Trade in 1800

The author of the following selection, a distant cousin of Jean-Jacques, was French consul between about 1780 and 1798, first at Basra and then at Baghdad. The rapid deterioration of the economy of Iraq in the first decade of the nineteenth century made him look back to the earlier period as a kind of golden age. Among the factors responsible for the better conditions prevailing in the eighteenth century were the relative prosperity of Iran; the diversion of some of its trade from Bushire and Bandar Abbas to Basra;[1] the end of Portuguese domination in the Persian Gulf and increasing trade contacts with the Dutch, French, and British —particularly with the East India Company;[2] and, above all, a greater degree of law and order. To the causes of decline mentioned in the selection must be added the plague of 1801.

The selection conveys a picture of commercial activity and prosperity. However, the very poor condition of the country's agriculture and industry is revealed by the statement that "except for dates, tobacco, and a few woolen manufactures, Baghdad has no indigenous products for export." Commercial activity was concentrated largely on transit trade, Baghdad being one of the main centers on the caravan route from the Mediterranean to the Persian Gulf and Iran.

(See also works by Rousseau [*Voyage*], Longrigg [*Four Centuries*], Wilson, Haider, Niebuhr, Olivier, Buckingham [*Mesopotamia* and *Assyria*] listed in the Bibliography.)

[1] Longrigg, *Four Centuries*, p. 178.
[2] *Ibid.*, p. 254.

[From J.-B. Rousseau, *Description du Pachalik de Baghdad* (Paris, 1809), pp. 117-22.]

... During the reign of the celebrated Sulaiman pasha [1780-1802] Baghdad was the center of a prosperous and extensive trade. Products of Asia and Europe, flowing in from all sides, not only created abundance but also, by their multiplicity, provided merchants with great openings for speculation and the assurance of speedy and brilliant wealth. This trade, formerly so rich and lucrative, has today lost much of its activity, especially since the conjunction of various unfortunate circumstances has changed the shape of things over a large part of the old Continent. The wars between France and England, which make navigation in the Mediterranean dangerous; the usurpations of Russia in Persia and the internal troubles of the latter empire; the disturbances in Kandahar and India; the onerous monopoly held by the British in the products of the latter country; the raids and brigandage of the Wahhabis; the continual disorders prevailing in Turkey; the lack of safety on the highways; the appreciable changes in the currency; and the thoughtlessness of the Ottoman government, which protects neither agriculture nor industry—these are the main factors that have considerably disturbed commercial business in Baghdad. Here, nevertheless, is a succinct account of the commercial operations that take place today.

The products of Arabia, India, and Persia converge on Basra, whence they are carried to Baghdad on large boats that sail up the Tigris or the Euphrates; there they find easy outlets and spread to other cities of Turkey.

Europe supplies Baghdad with all sorts of goods, such as woolens, silks, braids, coral, jewelry, gold and silver cloth, hardware, and other merchandise. Among the items sent by Europe to Baghdad must be included American products such as cochineal and indigo. These goods are first stored in Constantinople, Smyrna, Aleppo, and Damascus. Local consumption is limited and the greater part is sent on to Persia and India.

Coffee, incense, myrrh, galbanum, resins, gums, and various other precious and industrially useful drugs are brought over from Arabia; indigo comes from Gujarat, Bengal, and Lahore; shawls and aromatics from Kashmir; cinnamon from the island of Ceylon, sugar from Java, cloves and nutmegs from the Moluccas, cardamon and pepper from the Malabar coast, and muslins and rich silk and cotton fabrics from the coast of Coromandel. India also supplies Baghdad with aloes, camphor, gum benzoin, ambergris, sal ammoniac, and several other important items.

Persia is also an important supplier of such goods as silk, wool, lamb skins, pipe-wood, shawls from Kerman, saffron, tobacco, sulphur, saltpeter, more or less rich cloths,

dried fruits, fine rugs, occasionally cotton, copper, and iron, and finally the best and choicest drugs. All these goods are sent directly by caravan, or else shipped to Basra from where, as we have seen, they are transshipped to Baghdad up the Tigris or the Euphrates.

Except for dates, tobacco, and a few woolen manufactures, Baghdad has no indigenous products for export; its external commercial relations are maintained exclusively by the circulation and exchange of the foreign goods it receives. Thus, in return for its imports from that city, it supplies Constantinople with shawls from Kashmir, aloes, ambergris, musk, pearls, coffee, tobacco, spices, pipe-wood, muslins from India, and even cotton yarn. It exports to the cities of Syria and Anatolia silk, tobacco, shawls, gall nuts, coffee, cloth, and drugs; to Persia diamonds, rubies, emeralds, pearls, European cloth, woolens, coral, paper, hardware, and cochineal; and to Arabia and India silver, gold, copper, dates, and horses.

I shall conclude this memoir by a brief remark. It would surely be a distortion of truth to claim that Ali pasha gives trade the kind of protection it enjoys in European states. In Europe this profession is regarded as the secondary source from which abundance and public welfare flow and is therefore protected and encouraged by enlightened sovereigns. Here, on the other hand, it is perverted by the introduction of practices which must be condemned in the light of both honesty and common sense, and yet it would not occur to the head of the government to purge it of the host of abuses which dishonor it. All one can say is that if Ali pasha has neither the will nor the skill to encourage trade, at least he does not impede its operations. For that matter, he is not more vigilant in matters concerning the arts and crafts, which languish in contempt. The labor of the workman is not rewarded and it would seem that in Baghdad they ignore the fact that necessity gives birth to industry and that encouragement nourishes it, helps it to develop, and vivifies it in all its branches. . . .

CHAPTER 2

Projected Railway to the Mediterranean, 1850's

From the early seventeenth century, with an interruption in 1673–1745, the East India Company used the Basra–Aleppo route for the dispatch of mail between India, Iran, and England. This practice, and the fact that the Mesopotamian route was the shortest to India, drew attention in the 1830's to the possibility of laying a railway line from the Mediterranean to the Persian Gulf—or at least to the Euphrates, which could be navigated by steamships. The only tangible result of the projects that ensued was the establishment of the Euphrates and Tigris Steam Navigation Company (see Part III, chap. 3).

The first of these schemes, drawn up in 1856 by the Association for the Promotion of the Euphrates Valley, is described in the following selection. Its moving spirit was W. P. Andrew, chairman of the Scinde Railway Company and the European and India Junction Telegraph Company. The scheme failed because the company demanded financial guarantees from both the Ottoman and British governments. The Ottoman government was neither willing nor able to offer such guarantees and the British government did not wish to press the matter against the opposition of Napoleon III, who was blocking the British railway scheme for much the same reasons as Britain was obstructing the French-sponsored Suez Canal. The optimism, or even recklessness, of the promoters is clearly revealed by the wildness of some of the estimates in the following selection, regarding potential production, traffic, and costs.

Interest in the project revived in 1862, and again in 1871 when a select committee of the House of Commons suggested alternative routes for a railway between Alexandretta and Kuwait, at an estimated maximum cost of £10 million. But once more the British government failed to back the scheme, this time largely because the Suez Canal was already functioning successfully.

Britain's annexation of Cyprus in 1878, providing a base that could protect the Mediterranean terminus of the projected railway, led to a further flurry of projects in the 1880's, and at the very end of the century various schemes were put forward by Austro-Russian, French, and British groups. By then, however, interest had

137

shifted to the alternative proposed by the German syndicate headed by the Deutsche Bank—the Berlin–Baghdad railway. A line connecting Anatolia with the Persian Gulf clearly would serve the interests of the Ottoman government better than one between the Mediterranean and the Persian Gulf. For the same reason it was opposed by the British and French, who offered alternatives such as a Port Said–Aqaba–Jauf–Basra railway and a Tripoli–Homs–Palmyra–Dayr al-Zur–Baghdad railway. By 1914, however, "bargains were struck" and work proceeded very rapidly on the railway, including a small stretch in northern Iraq (see Part IV, chap. 4). But it was not until 1939 that the Iraqi railways were connected with the Syrian, thus finally providing a connection with Istanbul and Berlin. By then the Iraqi lines, the first of which was a railway constructed in 1916 by the British armies advancing northward from Basra, crossed the entire length of the country.

In 1929 the British Oil Development Company, a British concern initially which later acquired Italian, German, French-Swiss, and other shareholders, offered to build a railway to the Mediterranean if given an oil concession in Iraq, and in 1935, after receiving a concession, again considered the project. The company, however, ran into financial difficulties, its shares were acquired by Iraq Petroleum Company, and the scheme fell through. Various projects, sponsored by the Iraqi and Syrian governments, or by the Arab League, connecting Baghdad with Damascus or some other Syrian town also failed to materialize because the anticipated volume of traffic across the Syrian desert was deemed to be too small.

(See also works by Hoskins, Grant, Earle, Hüber, Himadeh [*Iraq*], Longrigg [*Four Centuries* and *Iraq*] listed in the Bibliography.)

[From Count Edward de Warren, *European Interests in Railways in the Valley of the Euphrates* (London, 1857); reprinted from articles in the London *Morning Herald*. The footnotes were presumably added by the editor of the pamphlet from which this selection was taken.]

This is an enterprise which at first sight appears gigantic, but its accomplishment, in the opinion of those who are acquainted with the localities, and have examined its capabilities, is considered comparatively easy. An Imperial firman has lately been granted to an English Company, of which General Chesney was the representative at the Porte, for the construction of a railway to cross Turkey in Asia, from the Mediterranean, by the Valley of the Euphrates. It is true, that notwithstanding the representa-

tions of General Chesney and Lord Stratford de Redcliffe, the English ambassador at Constantinople, the Sultan has granted a concession of the first section of the line only, although the whole line may be said to be conceded, for on the carrying out of the first section, the present Company is not only guaranteed the right of extension, but an assurance against any competition. It has also the power of working, in conjunction with the railway, the navigation of the river itself, from that point of the section abutting on the river to the Persian Gulf. . . .

The Euphrates Valley Railway takes for its starting point Souedia (Seleucia-Pieria, the ancient port of Antioch), near the mouth of the Orontes.[1] It follows the valley

[1] The new port and the terminus of the railway are to be at the opposite or southern extremity of the Bay of Antioch.

of this river, passing by Antioch, and going through a tunnel of about a quarter of a mile under a range of hills, named Halakas. Thence it takes its course along an almost insensible incline, and ascends the table-land where the important town of Aleppo is situated. It then descends by an easy incline to the plain of Beles, near the town of that name, where it joins the river Euphrates, opposite the Castle of Giaber (Kalat-Jaber).

The distances in direct line are—	Miles
From Souedia to Antioch . . .	18
From Antioch to Aleppo . . .	42
From Aleppo to the Euphrates, opposite Jaber	39
	99

But in consequence of the curves necessary for the formation of the line, Sir John Macneill, chief engineer of the company, calculates the length of the section at about 125 (150) miles.

This section, once constructed, will be continued by further sections, along the right bank of the Euphrates to Phumsah, the ancient Thapsacus; there it will cross the river Euphrates to enter Mesopotamia, and again descend by a declivity so gentle that the celebrated engineer, Mr. J. Falkowsky (who has devoted himself most especially to the study of this country, and who has kindly communicated to us the result of his investigations), estimates it at about 80 inches per mile[2] from Beles to the Persian Gulf. After touching the two considerable places of Annah and Hit, it proceeds to Baghdad; then, passing at some distance from the ruins of Babylon, runs to the city of Kurnah, situated at the confluence of the Euphrates and the Tigris. These two rivers, uniting at Kurnah, form an important river, named Shatt-el-Arab, so large and deep as to be navigable at all times for steamers of very large tonnage. From Kurnah a branch line of 27 miles[3] will be continued to

Bassora [Basra], where there is a considerable entrepot for merchandise, and a port capable of receiving vessels of the first magnitude. The whole line, according to the prospectus of the company, will not exceed 900 miles in length.[4]

The history of this railway, although it may be at this moment only in project, is far in advance of us and our time, and is one of the most curious examples of the perseverance with which the English, either as individuals or as a nation, appreciate and seize an idea when great or patriotic, and carry it out in triumph over every difficulty. . . .

Under all these circumstances, the result has been in England a conviction that the cherished project of General Chesney, to unite the Mediterranean to the Persian Gulf by means of a canal from the Euphrates to Souedia, would not be advisable[5]—the profits of such an undertaking being something more than doubtful, and the expenses enormous. The case of a railway would be materially different, as its construction will not meet with any serious obstacle in the country, and will have the effect of placing the Persian Gulf at a distance of 42 hours[6] from the Mediterranean. . . .

It is difficult to make a strict calculation of the expense of constructing the Euphrates Valley Railway, but one important point is already ascertained, the existence of a prodigious abundance of necessary materials of all descriptions, as stone, chalk, iron, wood, etc., the two former found immediately on the spot; the neighbouring mountains will furnish all the wood, the sides of the Amanus and Taurus having been renowned for ages for the excellence of the timber for building purposes, besides which there are immense forests close to the old port of Seleucia and Alexandretta; the

---

[2] As Aleppo is only 1,147 feet above the level of the sea, this elevation would give, in the 680 miles from thence to Kurnah, only 20¼ inches per mile.

[3] This distance is in reality 38 miles; but as Kurnah can be reached by the largest steamers, it is proposed to make it the terminus for the Euphrates Valley Railway.

[4] The distance from the Mediterranean to Kurnah, including the curves, will not exceed 771 miles.

[5] Although a line of levels had been carried across Northern Syria for this purpose, the question of the Canal was never examined either by Government or the public.

[6] The distance of 771 miles may easily be accomplished in 36 hours, including stoppages.

mines of Marash, not far distant, produce a large quantity of iron, which will supply all the rails required, and on many parts of the line bitumen is found in abundance. Aleppo is 42 miles from Antioch, and contains a population of 90,000 souls, of which 7,000 are Christians. It is a city of every possible resource, and one of the richest and best built in Syria. Antioch has 7,000 inhabitants, of which 1,000 are Christians. Beles[7] contains 3,000 inhabitants.

The Ottoman Government has made a gratuitous grant to the Euphrates Valley Railway Company of all the lands belonging to the state which lie immediately along that portion of the line; and, further, the use and gratuitous working of land, wood, forests, mines, and quarries within a certain distance of either side of it. It has also undertaken to pass a law, at its own expense, to give possession to the Company of all private property that may be on the line.[8] Notwithstanding all these advantages, and keeping in view the construction of the first section of the line only, the Company is constituted with a nominal capital of £1,000,000, divided into 50,000 shares of £20 each, with power to increase its capital by an issue of new shares, should it be required. Mr. Falkowsky has calculated the cost of the first section of the line at the average price of the German lines—say £10,000 per mile; but this calculation will be found to be above rather than under the fact.[9]

[7] Beles is uninhabited.

[8] The property is to be made good by the railway company in conformity with the law of ex-propriation, which was passed in 1853.

[9] The lines selected by Sir John Macneill and the assistant engineers, during the recent survey for the Euphrates Valley Railway Company, and their estimate of the expense of execution are as follows:

	Miles	£ per mile
From the Harbour to Antioch	20 at	13,484
From Antioch to Sansarin	30 at	4,693
From Sansarin to Dana	7 at	12,754
From Dana to Terrib	8 at	11,070
From Terrib to Chan Teeman	13 at	7,902
From Teeman to Aleppo	12 at	8,847

Being an average of £8,858 per mile as far as Aleppo. It is expected that the remainder of the line will be executed for £6,000 per mile.

Although this section may be said to be the first portion of a great line destined ultimately to extend to the Persian Gulf, it may in itself be considered as a line completed, being at least more important than that of the Mediterranean to the Red Sea. At the point where it joins the Euphrates, 715 miles[10] in direct line above Bussora, the river equals in expanse any of the largest streams of the old world, and may be compared to the Thames at London, the Rhone near Lyons, or the Nile above the upper cataract; its course is obstructed from time to time by shelves of rocks, which serve during the winter months as fords for camels, yet it is navigable all the year from the castle at Giaber, for vessels of small draught of water, such as are used on the Thames, and which would be sufficient for all commercial purposes. On the completion of the first section, a regular and direct traffic would be established, the Company being now engaged in organising steamers and Arab boats for continuing the conveyance of passengers and merchandise. . . .

Let us consider, first, then, the great advantages that this projected railway will find in the localities through which it has to pass, by beginning from its extremity in the Persian Gulf. Babylonia is no longer the Babylonia of past ages; its superb cities have for the greater part disappeared, those that remain being but their shadows; its neglected canals, partly filled up, have allowed the waters to overspread its plains and form innumerable marshes, whose deleterious emanations create a periodical pestilence in the midst of the degenerated populations of these unhappy countries. The soil is in great measure uncultivated, and covered with rushes, large trunks of the tamarind, palm, etc.[11]

[10] From Beles, where the railroad would first touch the Euphrates to Kurnah the correct distance is 631 miles.

[11] These remarks show a decided want of knowledge of the country on the part of the writer. It is true that owing to neglect of the embankments of late years many parts of the country bordering on the lower Euphrates suffer from periodical inundations but still extensive cultivation exists. The tract called El Neil around Babylon is wonderfully productive. The marshes

In the present day, however, the palm trees form the principal riches of the country. They attain a colossal growth, and yield dates of great beauty. During their harvest the waters of the Euphrates literally disappear, being covered by the numerous vessels, which come to be laden with this favourite fruit of the Eastern people. The annual export under the British flag for Bombay alone amounts to 9,000 tons, and is valued at £80,000. The banks of the Euphrates, too, are well cultivated, and numerously populated. At certain parts, cities and villages succeed each other almost without interruption—the wandering tribes confining themselves to that portion of Babylonia situated on the Tigris. There are, also, two considerable cities which may be ranked amongst the most important of those in Turkey in Asia—Bagdad and Bassora.

The city of Bagdad is no longer the fairy city of the "Arabian Nights." It has, however, 80,000 inhabitants, and can boast of the most magnificent bazaar in the East, containing 1,200 shops, where the manufactures of the country are exposed for sale, amongst which are found green and red morocco leather of exquisite workmanship, ordinary muslins, turbans, silk and cotton stuffs, lustring, shawls, carpets in wool and fur, abas, a sort of woollen Arab cloak, etc. The environs are well cultivated, and produce rice, corn, cotton, tobacco, and henna. The silkworm is also highly cultivated; to these various productions are added camels' hair, buffalo skins, common bitumen and naphtha, saltpetre, soda, sal ammonia, and borax, all of which are exported either to Aleppo, Persia, or Bombay.

The city of Bassora contains 50,000 inhabitants; but from its favoured position, being in the centre of the Babylonian Delta, and its proximity to the Euphrates, which is navigable in that part for vessels of large tonnage, still retains its commercial importance, and is the outlet for all Babylonian produce, dates, grain, rice, cotton, buffalo skins, wools, and Arab horses. It may be remembered that the great Kings of Persia had their breeding studs in Babylonia, and the race of these noble animals seems to be perpetuated to this day, for the pachalik of Bagdad has the reputation of producing the finest horses in the world. An annual horse fair is held at Bassora, which is supplied by the Arabs of Bagdad and Zobeir; the English merchants of India, on whose account the largest purchases are made, never pay more than £100 for the finest animal, which often realizes double that sum in Bombay, to which place alone they on an average export 2,500 annually.

In exchange for these exportations, Bassora receives tobacco, sugar, wrought iron, indigo, furnished by English merchants in India, and coffee, which is its principal article of importation, for it is estimated that at least 50[12] vessels laden with this commodity enter the port annually.

The traffic between Bagdad and Bassora may be computed at about 30,000[13] per annum, of which coffee alone, sent between Bassora and Bagdad would be 25,000 or 30,000 tons. There can be no doubt that as soon as the railway is established, this traffic would be increased, but a margin is left for that portion which may be continued to be sent by water carriage. Babylonia, moderately cultivated, would yield more grain than the entire of France. It consists of a superficies of about 16,000 square miles, including the fertile land, which extends on the right bank of the Euphrates to Djarri Zahad. Supposing one-half of this superficies to be arable, and one-quarter only

---

of Lamlum and other places lower down the river are so also. When Mr. Barker (H.M. Vice-Consul at Suedia) sent his last report to the Foreign Office in 1856, there were 50,000 quarters of wheat lying at various places eastward of Aleppo, for which means of transport could not be found.

[12] At the time of the Euphrates Expedition in 1837, the Custom House returns from India showed an annual traffic of 67 English vessels, amounting in tonnage to 14,118 tons, between India and the Persian Gulf, Arabia, etc. 3 Portuguese vessels of 645 tons, and 180 Arab vessels of 28,812 tons, amounting in all to 43,575 tons, value £1,427,012 sterling. No returns of this traffic appear to have been published since those of 1837.

[13] 30,000 tons. Including Guait, [Kuwait], Bushire, and Mohammrah, it is probably about 54,000 tons.

under annual cultivation, these 4000 square miles would produce about 23,000,000 quarters of grain of all descriptions, if it be true that this soil will yield an hundred-fold, as testified by ancient witnesses—witnesses whom we have no reason to question, seeing that lands of the first quality in the East Indies yield in that proportion—that is to say, from 100 to 114 to 1. Whatever the actual state of the case may be, it is certain that the present population of Babylonia, without very much effort, could grow 500,000 quarters of wheat for exportation—that is to say, above what is necessary for their own consumption. This would afford about 140,000 tons for conveyance by the railway towards the Mediterranean. The traffic of Babylonian produce, besides grain—as rice, cotton, tobacco, saltpetre, soda, sal ammonia, borax, wool, and morocco leather, would be about 30,000 tons.[14]

We mention, from memory only, the exportations of Seleucide, Mesopotamia, Taurus, and of Arabia, towards the Mediterranean, and the importations of merchandise from Europe into these countries, although the traffic is not insignificant. The little town of Antioch alone, from the information of the English consul, imports to the Mediterranean 15,000 tons, and exports 8000. Aleppo imports 34,000 tons, and exports 20,000.

We simply mention the traffic of Babylonia with Persia, although the manufactures of this country, notwithstanding its present state of decadence, produce articles for exportation—such as shawls, carpets of Irak, skins, saddlery of Ispahan, and swords and cutlery of Shiraz—all of which are highly esteemed and sought after by the Turks, nor are they despised amongst ourselves. The traffic between Europe and Asia must produce a large revenue to the projected Euphrates Valley Railway, as indeed, it must become the direct route of communication between Europe and India.

The traffic between Europe, various parts

of India, and the extreme East, is principally confined to England, France, and Holland, who may be said to monopolise the commerce of these far-distant countries, and by whom the greater part of the nations of our continent are supplied with the precious commodities of this part of Asia. Merchandise from India comes round by Africa to England, France, and Holland, from whence it is exported to all parts of the continent, as far even as the shores of the Mediterranean. If, on the completion of the Euphrates Valley Railway the port of Souedia, situated on the Mediterranean, and its neighbouring town of Antioch, is brought within ten days' distance of Bombay, it must be admitted that a great advantage will be gained by the ports of Marseilles, Algiers, Genoa, Leghorn, Naples, Palermo, Trieste, Constantinople, and Odessa, in being enabled to seek the productions of India and the extremity of Asia at the *entrepôt* which would be established at Antioch.

It is indeed more than probable that France and England herself would prefer to receive by this route all commodities of Asia which deteriorate by a sea voyage, or of which the prices are subject to sudden fluctuations, such as indigo, tea, coffee, pepper, resin, oleaginous seeds, oils, cinnamon, mace, nutmegs, cloves, and delicate roots and flowers. The carriage may be somewhat more expensive, but the difference will be largely compensated for by the greater certainty of the transactions, in shortening the sea passage, securing prompt arrival, and the perfect state of preservation of the articles. . . .

The following tables are taken from French, English, and Dutch official documents, comparing the actual importation by the Cape of Good Hope, with the presumable importation of the projected railway [p. 143].

The 123,000 tons, importable into Europe by the Euphrates Valley Railway according to this calculation, will be seen to be less than one-fifth of the general importation of Meridional Asia into Europe, and about one-tenth of the total amount of merchan-

[14] The returns show about 45,000 tons for Babylonia at present.

	By the Cape of Good Hope Tons	By Railway Tons
Coffee	86,933	28,977
Pepper	3,936	1,312
Indigo	3,154	1,051
Sugar.	183,351	61,117
Tea	27,767	13,888
Various articles intended for the countries on the Mediterranean .	386,839	16,839
Total	691,980	123,184

dise exchanged between Europe and those regions. Nevertheless, this small part, taken from the actual traffic round Africa, will yield to the railway Company 5½ per cent.[15] on the capital necessary for the construction of the line.

The Euphrates Valley Railway will not merely be confined to the conveyance of merchandise between Europe and the extreme East; it will serve for other and important interests, which may easily be defined. It may serve as the bond of union between Persia and Europe. The traffic passing by Trebizonde, intended for Persia, and by that port for Europe, amounts annually, according to the *Annales du Commerce Extérieur*, to upwards 3,106,720 tons, which could be conveyed by the Euphrates Valley Railway in 36 hours from Souedia to Bagdad,[16] on the confines of Persia. It is impossible to estimate the effects that may result from this projected railway, not merely in a commercial point of view on the immediate countries through which it will pass, but in regard to its future influence on its resources—resources which the railway will itself inevitably create, as its rapid means of communication will bring forth new life and promote civilisation in a region

at once blessed with climate and soil. If the railway had no other object than to unite Mesopotamia and Babylonia to the Mediterranean, its utility, not only commercially but socially, would be unhesitatingly acknowledged; but as it affects the means of subsistence, it rises to be of still greater importance.

Europe has been for a long time past under the necessity of seeking from America and Africa a portion of wheat necessary for the subsistence of its mass of populations. England, Italy, the Germanic States, and Scandinavia, even France herself, during the last ten years, have made large annual importations of grain. . . .

. . . It is then clear how useful, nay urgent, it is for Europe to connect itself by means of a railway to such a country as Babylonia, which was in ancient times the granary of Asia, and which, supposing that the one-half only of its superficies was put into cultivation, would produce grain equal to the production of the whole of France, with less than a twentieth part of its population. Europe could then receive ample supplies from this fine country, where the railway would soon revive cultivation, now neglected. Thus the grain of Babylonia would be sent by railway to Souedia, and by sea to Trieste, Leghorn, Genoa, Marseilles, and London, where it could be purchased at the same price, if not cheaper, than that brought from Odessa, with the advantage of its arriving periodically at the commencement of the spring, a season of the year when the price of wheat is usually on the advance in our markets. We will not, however, anticipate these riches, but confine ourselves to the question of commerce and finance.

The traffic of passengers on the Euphrates Valley Railway may be computed at 125,000 per annum between Souedia and Feludja, and between Feludja and Bassora at 250,000. The Euphrates Valley Railway being the most direct and convenient route from Europe to India, and *vice versa*, would most certainly be chosen by travellers who now take the mail by way of the Red Sea and Lower Egypt; and, as it would connect

[15] Estimating the existing local commerce only, and without taking into account either passenger traffic or the Asiatic commerce, the gross annual receipts on the first and most expensive portion of the line are calculated at £225,000. Deducting 50 per cent or £112,000 for working expenses, there would be a balance of £113,000 or about eight per cent on the outlay of £1,400,000.

[16] Not only to Bagdad but likewise by Mohammerah and the river Karun into Central and Southern Persia, at a much less expense and in about a fourth part of the time now consumed in going thither by way of Trebizonde.

the towns of Aleppo, Bagdad, and Bassora, whose fairs are renowned in the East, and numerously attended by the wandering tribes of the country, they would prefer this mode of conveyance to a long journey on the back of a camel.

At the fair held at Bassora as many as 80,000 or 100,000 persons arrive from different parts of Turkey in Asia and Persia, most of whom come by way of the Euphrates. The pious pilgrims of the two principal sects of Mussulmans will find that the easiest and most ready means of visiting the saints which they venerate will be the Euphrates Valley Railway, as it will pass at its eastern extremity near the tombs of Ali, of his son Hoshein, and other places of pilgrimage much visited by the Shiites, a sect to which all the Persian population, as well as a part of that of Mesopotamia and Kourdistan, belong; whilst at its western extremity it will join many places, and meet the caravans going from almost all parts of Turkey to Mecca; the town of Aleppo being the place where all these pilgrims congregate. Many other sources which we have not named would furnish considerable traffic between Europe, India, and the extreme East, and produce a revenue far beyond our calculation, and which we truly believe will amount to 28 per cent. per annum net on the amount of capital.

A question may arise as to a competition with the projected maritime canal from the Bay of Pelusium to Suez and the Euphrates Valley Railway. A little reflection will make it perfectly clear that there can be no collision between the railway and the canal, as each will have its distinct and immediate line of business. The railway will save about 12 days, compared with the steam navigation by the Red Sea and the canal, in the accomplishment of the journey from Europe to India. The canal, on its part, will be an economy in the expense of carriage, as the trans-shipment of all bulky goods will be avoided.

The Euphrates Valley Railway will be the means of conveyance chosen by travellers, and for letters, dispatches, and light goods; and the canal for all merchandise in large bulk, which would not be sent by railway even if the canal were not in existence, but as it is at present, by long sea-voyage. Thus the canal will not be prejudical to the interests of the railway; and, on the other hand, the railway would leave a considerable traffic to the canal, as upon 692,000 tons of importation from Europe to India we have calculated that by railway at 123,000 tons only, or about one-fifth.

The two undertakings will, therefore, be equally important—the one assuring economy, the other rapidity of communication.

It has been mooted that the canal of Suez would give rise to a coasting trade between the Mediterranean and the Indian seas, which might in some measure supersede the navigation by the Cape of Good Hope, as it would more especially tend to benefit those parts situated on the Mediterranean, and consequently injure the navigation round by Africa, which is almost exclusively English. Admitting to a certain extent that this coasting trade would cause a loss to English merchant vessels of 30 or 40 per cent. upon the importations of Indian colonial produce intended for ports in the Mediterranean, it can easily be proved that the canal would not only be the means of compensating for this trifling loss, but in a few years augmenting the profit of the English merchantmen, more than 300 per cent., in the carriage of one colonial production alone—that of cotton—whose importation to England is constantly on the increase. The quantity of raw cotton imported annually into the United Kingdom—take for example, the year 1854—amounted to, at least, 887,335,904 lbs., of which the United States supplied 722,154,101 lbs. that is to say seven-eighths, whilst the English possessions in the East Indies exported to the mother country only 119,836,000 lbs., or about one-eighth. Now we are well aware how much the English have striven for some years to be relieved from the intolerable duty imposed by the American republic. The desire to be released from this duty has of late years been increased by the affronts on the part of this turbulent democracy, which the English government, so proud, so energetic, so jealous of its honour in face of other nations, has been obliged silently to submit to—its *amour propre* bending to the necessity of obtaining a constant supply of cotton indispensable to the numerous manufactures of Great Britain. But England has resolved, at no very distant period, to draw all her supplies of cotton from her Indian colonies. It is well known that in many parts of India, more particularly in the dominions of the Nizam of Hyderabad, the tree in the cotton district attains its highest perfection, and its productions are equal to any of the finest of America. *The cotton fields of Berar would alone produce three or four times the quantity of cotton necessary for the consumption of the whole world.*

The *means of conveyance* alone are wanting, for at the principal market of Oumrawaty, scarcely 400 miles from Bombay, cotton of the finest quality can be purchased at 1½d. per lb., whilst in the United States the price is at least 2½d. The Railways now in the course of construction in India, and whose works proceed with wonderful rapidity, will be the instrument to remedy this state of things; and the time will soon come when England will supply herself from her own

sources with this necessary commodity.[17] But without the canal of Suez the conveyance of such a prodigious quantity as we have mentioned would involve difficulty and danger, from the length and uncertainty of, and the multitude of vessels of large tonnage required for, the long sea voyage; whilst with the canal all is simplified. The same vessels would in the same space of time, make three voyages instead of one, and at an increased profit of 500 or 600 per cent.

Viewed as a commercial speculation, as a financial operation, as a measure of general interest to the whole human race—for the relief of the miseries of Europe in particular, as assurance against famines and periodical dearths,—and as a social and sound philanthropic work, the undertaking of the Euphrates Valley Railway is one of the most noble concepts of the present day. . . .

[The author concludes with the plea that the projected enterprise be run by "a great international Company," since a purely British concern would give Britain a predominant influence in the region and constitute a threat to other countries.]

[17] Count de Warren has overlooked the fact that cotton is extensively cultivated both in Syria and Mesopotamia, and the quantity grown will increase largely whenever a cheap means of transport is found for it.

CHAPTER 3

Steam Navigation on the Tigris and Euphrates, 1861–1932

The first survey of an Iraqi river for the purpose of steam navigation was made in 1830 by James Taylor, who took a concession for a service on the Tigris from the still independent pasha of Baghdad. Taylor was killed by beduins and his project failed, but in 1831 Francis Chesney surveyed the Euphrates down to Basra. In 1834 a select committee of the House of Commons examined the alternative routes to India (see Part III, chap. 2) and decided in favor of the Mesopotamian rivers. In 1836 an expedition under Chesney sailed down the Euphrates; however, one of the two steamers of the expedition was lost on the way and the high costs of the attempt did not seem to be justified by the results achieved or by the anticipated volume of traffic; hence, the following year, another select committee pronounced itself in favor of the Red Sea route, which had by then become accessible to steamers [see Part VI, chap. 7].

Nevertheless, between 1839 and 1842 four British steamers, belonging to the East India Company, sailed up and down the Tigris, the Euphrates, and the Karun, surveying the rivers and carrying passengers and mails. In 1841 the Ottoman government authorized Captain Lynch, who had been in command of the above-mentioned flotilla, to operate two steamers. The subsequent history of the Lynch firm is told in the following selection. Until the First World War its only competitor—apart from one or two very small concerns—was an Ottoman line, founded in 1855 as a mixed government-private enterprise, reorganized in 1869 as the publicly owned Oman-Ottoman Administration, bought in 1900 by Sultan Abd al-Hamid's Saniya Administration and renamed Hamidiya, and restored as a government department under its former name after the fall of the sultan in 1909. During this period profits were high, not falling below 20 per cent of paid-up capital.[1] After the war, competition from both rival firms and other means of transport increased greatly, as is described in the selection. Lynch met it partly by modernizing their fleet and partly by merging with the trading firm of

[1] Hasan, "Foreign Trade in the Economic Development of Iraq, 1869–1939," p. 196.

Gray, Mackenzie and Company; however this merger was dissolved in 1936. The Second World War gave the firm a renewed stimulus, but the return of peace and new competition forced it into voluntary liquidation, its ships being sold to its principal rival, Hanna al-Shaykh.[2]

Until railways were built in Iraq during and after the First World War, river navigation constituted the only modern means of transport. By the 1860's sailing time from Baghdad to Basra had been reduced to 52–60 hours by steamer, compared to 5–8 days by sailing ship, and the return journey upstream to 4–5 days, compared to 40–60 days.[3] Costs were also reduced; thus the freight from Basra to Baghdad up the Tigris, by steamship, was 150 piastres per *taghar* (2,690 pounds), but up the Euphrates, by sailing ship, it was 200 piastres.[4] Nevertheless costs remained high, and in the late 1870's it was estimated that "it costs about as much to send goods from Basra to Baghdad as to get them from London to Basra."[5]

Among the indirect effects of river navigation were: "The rise of 'Amarah and Kut, a perceptible educational effect on riverain tribes, and the denudation of the banks of willow and tamarisk, with increased degeneracy in the regime of the river."[6]

(See also works by Chesney [*The Expedition* and *Narrative*], Longrigg (*Four Centuries* and *Iraq*], Hoskins, and Hall listed in the Bibliography.)

[2] Longrigg, *Iraq*, p. 378.
[3] H. L. Hoskins, *British Routes to India* (London, 1928), p. 427.
[4] Haider, "Land Problems of Iraq," p. 266.
[5] Geary, quoted in Hasan, *loc. cit.*
[6] Longrigg, *Four Centuries*, p. 294.

["The Story of the Euphrates Company," *The Near East and India*, XLI (1935), 948–54; reproduced by kind permission of the editors of *Achievement*.]

... Messrs. Lynch Bros. for some time [i.e., after the foundation of the firm, in Baghdad in 1841] had the field largely to themselves; they combined trade and transport in what, in a modern sense, was a new country; they owned a fleet of river craft, and they established a line of sailing ships between the United Kingdom and Busreh [Basra]; later on, they established the London and Baghdad Banking Company, thereby adding an important, and indeed, an indispensable facility to the trade which was steadily increasing under their guidance and control. The need for increased transport facilities on the Tigris had been growing for some years, very largely as the result of the expansion of trade following upon the activities, not only of the brothers Lynch in Baghdad, but also those of Messrs. Gray, Mackenzie and Co., Agents of the British India Steam Navigation Company, Limited, in Busreh; and in fact, the time was ripe for the introduction of more up-to-date methods of navigation in Mesopotamia.

In 1860, the brothers Lynch commenced negotiations with Her Majesty's Government for the acquisition of navigation rights on the two rivers, and they at the same time included a proposal for a mail service between Busreh and Baghdad. The navigation rights were granted by the Sublime Porte, subject to certain minor conditions, such as the payments of river dues, the flying of flags, etc., and the Euphrates and Tigris Steam Navigation Company, Limited, came into being. The company was incorporated on April 25,

1861. The initial capital was no more than £15,000, divided into 300 shares of £50. It was, however, increased as time went on, and as circumstances demanded, to £300,000 in 1919. The first Directors were Captain H. B. Lynch, of Chesney fame, and his brothers Tom and Stephen. At the first meeting of the Company, it was decided to call for tenders for the first steamer—the City of London—the material for which was despatched by sea to Busreh, and there assembled. The vessel was commissioned early in the following year, viz., 1862. Very meagre records appear to have been kept of the Company's activities during the early years of its existence, but it was not long before we come to references of Ottoman hostility and obstruction, which abated little at any time until Turkey was eventually driven out of Mesopotamia in the Great War. Still, in spite of this repressive policy, trade continued to expand, thereby necessitating an increase in the Company's fleet and, on June 24, 1865, a new vessel, the Dijla, was put into commission for river service. It was during this year that the Company, with a view to increasing the productivity of the rich Mesopotamia soil, and particularly with a view to encouraging the cultivation of cotton and rice, imported a number of steam pumping sets. The Turkish authorities, in keeping with their shortsighted and obstructive policy, strongly opposed the action of the Company, and after protracted negotiations, the machinery was eventually taken over by the Pashalik, at a price, though there is no record of the machinery ever having been erected. The directors seemed hopeful of succeeding later on, but the attempt does not appear to have been repeated.

No striking incident took place during the next few years. The service continued to yield good results. The demand for cargo space increased, and, as a result, we find the Turkish Government considering the desirability of entering the field as a competitor for the Tigris traffic. Their eyes had been opened to the advantages of steam navigation; moreover, they were desirous of restricting as much as possible the operations of the English steamers, and so, in the early seventies the Turks introduced four steamers on the Baghdad-Busreh service. In the year 1873, the Company's position was becoming increasingly difficult, as their diminutive fleet was hopelessly inadequate to cope with the expansion of trade. It is true that the Turks had entered the freight market with a number of steamers, but their service was very inefficient, and inspired little or no confidence with the shippers, particularly with the English shippers. In 1876, the Dijla was lost in a storm. Fortunately no lives were lost, and with the aid of divers, some of the cargo and stores was salvaged, though a good deal had to be abandoned owing to a sudden rise in the river. The vessel was not replaced until 1878, when the Company sent out the Blosse Lynch, a powerful two-funnel vessel 220 feet in length and 46 feet in beam. This vessel was of a much improved design as the result of sixteen years' experience of river conditions.

An important event now took place in the history of the Company, for in 1879, it became more closely associated with the great British India Steam Navigation Company. Both Companies had been mutually interested in the encouragement of through cargo from the United Kingdom and India to Baghdad, and it was appropriate that they should work in close association for their mutual benefit. The Euphrates Company at the same time increased their share issue by 400 shares of £50 each, and Mr. (afterwards Sir) Edwin Dawes—a partner of the firm of Gray, Dawes and Co.—was given a seat on the Euphrates Company's Board. It was in this same year too, that the Turkish Administration, having failed to make a success of their four steamers, decided to withdraw from the service, and the whole fleet was offered for sale. No buyers came forward, however, and in consequence, they reluctantly decided to carry on. The decision on the part of the Turks to withdraw their service was, doubtless, influenced by the fact that the river, owing to a prolonged drought throughout

Armenia and Turkish Arabia, fell to an exceptionally low level, rendering navigation extremely difficult. The shortage of water was so great that much distress was felt among the inhabitants of the rice-growing districts round Amara, and the position became so serious that the Turkish Authorities, disregarding the interests of navigation, constructed a barrage across the river in the Narrows, but it was so inefficiently carried out that the construction turned out to be injurious alike both to cultivation as well as to navigation! Direct navigation between Busreh and Baghdad was thus suspended from July to November; during the latter month an early freshet swept the obstruction away. During this period, the process of getting cargo over the barrage was so slow that through cargo from Europe and India had accumulated to such an extent that bookings had to be suspended.

At this time the Company proposed once more to go into the question of navigating the Euphrates, and Mr. Tartt, the Company's Superintendent Engineer, was deputed to survey the river as far as the Belis—Chesney's up-river port. The report, though interesting, was not sufficiently favourable to warrant a further exploitation of the project. In the following year, i.e., 1880, the Company placed a new steamer on the river— the Khalifah—a modern vessel even more adaptable to Tigris conditions than the Blosse Lynch. Though the Khalifah is now more than half a century old, she is still capable of doing good service at the present day. The first voyage of the new steamer was devoted to the carriage of foodstuffs which were being hurried up to Baghdad for the relief of the famine which devastated the whole of Northern Mesopotamia. Throughout the whole of 1881 fruitless endeavours were made by the Company, aided by the Foreign Office, to persuade the Turkish Authorities to permit the towing of barges, to enable the Company to deal with the ever-increasing demands for cargo space in respect of both import and local cargo. The Chairman himself went to Constan-

tinople, and, after several months of negotiations, he secured a favourable decision from the Council of Ministers. The Sultan, however, refused to seal the order addressed to the Governor-General of Turkish Arabia. Unfortunately for the Company, this unfavourable decision was followed by the loss of the City of London, the first vessel of the Company's diminutive fleet, which foundered off Gurnah, at the junction of the two rivers, whilst she was under charter to the Government of India. This loss reduced the fleet once more to two vessels; a third steamer was, therefore, put in hand—the Mejidieh, a vessel of the same build and dimensions as those of the Khalifah, excepting that she had three feet more beam than the older vessel. Neither the Euphrates Company, nor any English concern for that matter, was particularly popular in Turkish official circles at this time, and the feeling was undoubtedly intensified by the British invasion of Egypt in 1882. This move on the part of Great Britain, with the subsequent defeat of Araby Pasha, occasioned universal distrust of Great Britain in all Muhammadan countries, and it had its repercussion in Turkish Arabia, resulting in severe trade depression; several failures among the more influential native merchants occurred in Baghdad about this time. The unpopularity of the British evidently continued well into 1883, in the early part of which year an order was received from Constantinople by the Governor-General in Baghdad, to the effect that henceforward no foreign shipping would be allowed to ply on the Mesopotamian rivers. The order was put into execution on June 28, and the Company's vessels were laid up. The interdict was removed, however, on August 5, under pressure from the British Foreign Office, but the cargo service had been completely dislocated and through cargo engagements from Europe and the East had once more to be suspended. The Company submitted a claim for the heavy losses sustained as the result of this petulant order by the Porte, but it was withdrawn under the advice of Lord Granville.

In 1885 the British India Company

appeared anxious to become more closely associated with the navigation of the River Tigris. The subject was discussed at a Board Meeting of the Euphrates Company, held on April 20, at which Mr. (afterwards Sir) George Mackenzie was invited to be present. Mr. Mackenzie said he had proposed that his firm—Messrs. Gray, Mackenzie and Co.—the Agents of the British India Company in Busreh and the Persian Gulf, should apply to the Turkish Government for a concession to run a line of steamers between Busreh and Baghdad. In the discussion which followed this announcement, the Chairman—Mr. T. K. Lynch—stated that the Euphrates Company had been endeavouring for some years to obtain, not a new concession, but additional facilities for his Company's service; so far, he said, the required facilities had been withheld, the idea being unacceptable to Turkey. Mr. Mackenzie went on to say that in the event of his firm being successful in obtaining the proposed concession, he would place it absolutely at the disposal of the Euphrates Company, to be organized and carried out in such a manner as the Directors might think fit. In commenting on this decision Sir Edwin Dawes, partner of Messrs. Gray, Dawes and Co., said he would never consent to his firm, either directly or indirectly, encouraging any opposition to the Euphrates Company. From this time onwards the Euphrates Company has worked in close association with the British India Company, doubtless to the benefit of both concerns. Mr. Mackenzie's proposal did not materialize, but in 1886 the Euphrates Company decided to enter the field with a similar object, namely, to sue for a concession to form an Ottoman Company for the purpose of navigating the Tigris under the Turkish flag. The Chairman himself went to Constantinople to conduct the negotiations, but after wasting months of valuable time the mission proved abortive, and Mr. Lynch returned to London. Still, the mission was not entirely fruitless, for the Turkish Authorities, although they would not grant the new concession, were persuaded to

despatch orders to their officials in Baghdad authorizing the Company to use barges. This facility, however, was withdrawn without notice at the end of three months. One, of course, sees the spectre of Russia at the back of this intransigent attitude on the part of Turkey, for that Power was at this time ever on the alert to forestall any advantage sought by an English Company on the Tigris. The position was most trying, and it is only fair to record that throughout all their difficulties with the Turks the Company did everything possible to conciliate them; all sorts of privileges were given them, and such services as the Company were able to give were freely rendered. Moreover, every effort was made by the Company's Agents to carry on their business in Mesopotamia in a manner least likely to cause umbrage, or offend the susceptibilities of the Turkish officials.

During the next two or three years the Company devoted a good deal of attention to the possibilities of trade development on the Karun, the only navigable river in Persia. . . .

Throughout this decade, the traffic demand was increasing. The service, such as it was, was well and efficiently run, but it was inadequate, and it became frequently necessary to suspend bookings from Europe and India in order to work off accumulations of cargo at Busreh. It was not until August, 1899, that, after much negotiation, the Turkish Government was prevailed upon to permit the Company to tow barges between Busreh and Baghdad, a right it has retained to the present day. Almost immediately afterwards, the Turkish Government ordered two new and powerful steamers for the Tigris service, in competition with the Company. The vessels were not, however, commissioned until 1904, and it was during this year that the administration of the Turkish River Service on the Tigris was transferred to the Sinieh (i.e., the Privy Purse Administration). From this it is evident that the Company was, during its pre-War existence, competing against the Turkish Government, and this, in addition to all the restrictions which that Government found it possible to impose; all of which goes to show that the English Company never at any time enjoyed anything like settled conditions; it carried on its work continually in an atmosphere of apprehension, from which it did not emerge until the end of the Great War; its main strength lay in its efficiency, and in the confidence which it enjoyed at the hands of its shippers both at home and abroad.

The year 1902 saw the birth of a new enterprise. Following upon the success of the Karun venture and the construction of the Bakhtiari Road from Ahwaz to Ispahan, the Company was induced by the Foreign Office to consider the acquisition from the Imperial Bank of Persia of a concession granted by the Shah to construct a metalled road from Teheran to Ahwaz, and to instal thereon a traffic service. . . .

To revert to the Tigris, the Company during the earlier years of the present century experienced a good deal of trouble from the riverain Arabs. The Turkish yoke was none of the lightest, and the tribesmen, doubtless, had much to put up with. Small wonder, then, if, in attacking the Company's vessels, these tribes found a successful means of coercing the local Government, they did not hesitate to do so. In consequence, it became necessary to arm the vessels and to protect the passengers and crew with sandbags. The nuisance became so serious that during 1909 the traffic was interrupted for a month, while the Sublime Porte was being brought to book. The experience was as nothing, of course, in comparison with what the Company's vessels and their personnel had to face during the War, but one does not expect to have to fight one's way from port to port, with a fair chance of being holed, in times when we are supposed to be at peace. It was about this time that Middle Eastern affairs generally attracted an increasing amount of attention in Europe. The Hindiyah Barrage, nearing completion, was expected to add considerably to the wealth of the country. Again, there was talk of considerable oil "shows"

in the Mosul districts. Persia, too, was coming more to the fore; it had adopted representative institutions, and the Swedish advisers were doing splendid work with the raising of a new Gendarmerie Establishment. Attention was given by the Central Government to better and safer communications, and the time seemed ripe for the construction of a railway connecting the Capital with the Persian Gulf. In 1911, the Euphrates Company's Board associated itself with a group of important interests, to acquire a concession for the construction of this line. Great progress was made with the negotiations in Teheran, but, unfortunately for the Group, and also for Persia, the scheme fell a victim to Russian intrigue. But the most striking event of all, in what was intended to be the renaissance of the Middle East, was the conclusion of the negotiations which resulted in a convention between the Sublime Porte and the Deutsche Bank (the latter representing a German Railway Group), for the construction of what was to be known as the Baghdad Railway—a scheme which, if completed, would have placed Berlin in direct rail communication with the Persian Gulf. The War sealed the fate of the Baghdad Railway, but for such time as the Eastern Section of the line was under construction it provided work for a new River Navigation Company called the Société de Transports Fluviaux en Orient, floated for that specific purpose in 1912. The local administration of the new Company was in the hands of the Euphrates Company, which held 50 per cent of the shares, the remaining 50 per cent being held by the Deutsche Bank. The Anglo-German Company operated for two years until war broke out, and then, after the Armistice, went into liquidation. Another great scheme in which the Company was vitally interested, and which was killed by the war, was the proposed fusion of the Company's navigation interests with those of the Turkish Company. Negotiations had been going [on] for some years, and agreement was actually in sight. The result was to combine all the navigation interests on the Tigris, and also the new

Anglo-German Company which had already been formed for carriage of the German Railway material. This was in 1914, and then came the War. . . .

When the year 1918 opened, the Company's fleet returned to civil life, but it was a lame fleet; for not only was it much reduced in numbers, but the vessels which remained were in need of thorough overhaul, and, therefore, wholly inadequate to meet the traffic needs of a trade centre like Baghdad, which had been starved since the autumn of 1914. The Turkish river fleet as a competitor was no more, but as navigation was now free to all and sundry, a number of river craft, native owned, appeared on the scene to meet the demand. The local population, having grown wealthy in the process of supplying the needs of the British Army of Occupation, were longing to spend their money, and they created a demand, which, even when transport increased in volume, took many months to satisfy. But in addition to this, a totally wrong impression of the future seemed to seize everyone—not only in Iraq, but everywhere—and a natural, though quite unjustifiable optimism prevailed, with the further result that in Iraq, at any rate, a number of businesses sprang up, seeking to benefit by the arrival of what so many judged to be a new era of prosperity—a super-boom after a super-War. So the demand for cargo space in the odd collection of steamers which now appeared on the river was so unprecedented that freights offered for the carriage of goods from Busreh to Baghdad rose from the pre-war average of 30s to, in some cases, £40 per ton. As soon, however, as the Company's vessels were able to resume their normal routine, freight fell to reasonable limits.

Long before the crest of the demand was anywhere near in sight, or even suspected, the Company considered it to be in its best interest to meet the situation whilst it lasted and also in the firm opinion, shared by most people, that under British tutelage Iraq would develop rapidly in all departments, just in the same way as Egypt had developed

after it was severed from Turkey. So it promptly laid out £200,000 in new vessels —or, rather, comparatively new vessels, which had been withdrawn from the service of the Inland Water Transport, and offered for sale. In order to do this, it was necessary to increase the Company's authorized capital from £100,000 to £300,000. The Company now possessed a fleet of entirely up-to-date vessels, and very shortly after the peak of the demand for space had passed, and freights reduced to normal, the odd collection of craft which had appeared on the scene directly the river was free for civil traffic for the most part disappeared rapidly. Two or three of the more well-to-do local ship owners, however, remained, whilst the most important of these, viz., the Khedery Line, was absorbed by the Company in 1924. There still were two or three local companies competing for the Busreh-Baghdad trade.

The competition against the Company, however, is not limited to its rivals on the river, for a new and powerful competitor has arisen in the shape of the new railway line which connects Baghdad with Busreh. This line, which represents one—and the most important—section of the Iraq Railway system, might well be known as the Euphrates Valley Line, for it follows very largely the course of that river from Babylon southwards. Built with British public funds for military purposes during the War, this railway was handed over for civil use in 1920. It is now mainly the property of the British Government, but, as is known, it is to be granted an administration under terms with the Iraq Government, as a result of the termination of the Mandate. In 1923 and 1924, times were extremely difficult. Trade was contracting, and competition both by rail and by river was severe. Drastic economies were made, and, although the results of the year following, that is, 1926, were somewhat more encouraging, it was evident that nothing short of a reconstruction would meet the situation. . . .

As soon, therefore, as Colonel Picot had assumed control, his first attentions were devoted to the Company's financial position, and after the prescribed preliminaries, the Company wrote down their £50 shares to £30, and subdivided the reduced shares to 30 shares of £1 each. This was a substantial reduction, but there was no help for it; the Company's assets had depreciated in value, and recovery would naturally be a slow process until world trade generally resumed normal conditions. Among other improvements should be recorded the installation of Diesel, in place of steam, engines, on several of the Company's towing units, an important economy measure in itself, and also a drastic cutting down of expenditure generally....

CHAPTER 4

Population Movements, 1867–1947

The demographic evolution of Iraq, described in the following selection, has paralleled that of the other Arab countries. Population began to grow quite rapidly—at roughly 1 per cent—upon the establishment of order and security, the introduction of enough modern hygiene to reduce the toll taken by epidemics, and the provision of more adequate food supplies; in the more advanced countries, such as Egypt (see Part VI, chap. 1), Syria (see Part IV, Introduction), and Iraq, this growth started in the nineteenth century and in Arabia (see Part V, Introduction) and in the Sudan (see Part VII, Introduction) in the twentieth. The rate of increase went up sharply when modern drugs and pesticides began to be used in the 1940's and 1950's; in Iraq, the annual rate of growth between 1947 and 1957 was 3.1 per cent, and in 1957 the population stood at 6,538,000. The proportion of the nomadic to the total population declined considerably, and for some tribes there was an absolute decrease. As the government grew increasingly stronger it became possible to check the beduins and reclaim for agriculture lands previously used as pastures; this in turn reinforced the pressure on nomads to settle down.

The rate of growth of the urban population at first barely kept pace with that of the total population, or only slightly exceeded it, and the proportion of the urban to the total remained constant or rose very little; this was because the increase in urbanization due to greater commercial, transport, and other activities was offset by the decline of the handicrafts. However, in the last forty years or so, urbanization has rapidly accelerated, and the percentage of the population living in towns has sharply risen. Industrialization and, still more, the development of the state apparatus have "pulled" countrymen to the towns; and the growing population pressure, coupled with the form of land tenure, has "pushed" landless peasants off the land.

Lastly, although in most countries there has been a shift in population from the interior to the coastal areas, owing to the rapid growth of foreign trade and the consequent emergence of large seaports, in this regard Iraq has been an exception, because of its very narrow sea frontage, the marshy land surrounding Basra, and the extensive overland trade. In recent years, however, the development of the oil fields around Basra has increased the relative population and economic importance of the southern area.

(See also works by Kemball; Cuinet; Great Britain, Admiralty [*Handbook of Mesopotamia*]; Longrigg [*Iraq*]; I.B.R.D.; Himadeh [*Iraq*]; and Adams [*Iraq's People*] listed in the Bibliography.)

[M. S. Hasan, "Growth and Structure of Iraq's Population, 1867–1947," *Bulletin of the Oxford University Institute of Statistics*, XX (1958), 339–52; reproduced with omissions, by kind permission of the author and the Institute.]

. . . Although the first Official Census of Iraq's population was taken in 1947, there are some population figures in the British Consular Reports, particularly around 1866–67; some estimates derived from a partial census of population of the Ottoman Empire in 1890; other British population estimates for 1900–1908 and 1919; finally there is the information based on the Iraq Government's general enumeration of population originally made for purposes of National Service and Elections in 1934. Despite the margins of error involved in these "guesstimates," estimates and Census results, and also in the adjustment for boundary changes and gap-filling, they can nevertheless indicate the general trend of population growth in modern Iraq.

Table I shows the total and regional population from 1867 to the 1947 Census of population. In the course of these three generations, Iraq seems to have almost quadrupled its population. In the last one and a half generations, the period 1905–1947, Iraq's population slightly more than doubled.

This general trend of population growth has not been uniform among the various regions. Thus regional population has risen about five-fold in the North, over four-fold in the Centre, and well under three-fold in the South over the period 1867–1947. It may also be observed that this differential growth in the regional population of Iraq tends to increase over time. Thus, during the more recent period of 1919–47, the population of the Northern region almost doubled, that of the Central region more than doubled, whereas that of the Southern region increased by under a quarter.

In order to throw into clear relief this total and regional growth of population, the absolute increases and the rate of population increase have been calculated in Table II. Generally speaking, Table II shows that the rate of population increase rose up to 1905, then dropped slightly till 1935, since when it has considerably increased. In the early period of 1867–90, Iraq's population rose at an average rate of 1.3 per cent per annum, but this rate of population increase rose to 1.8 per cent per annum between 1890 and 1905. This acceleration in the rate of population increase was not only checked, but slightly reversed during the period 1905–35, when the rate first fell to 1.7 and later to 1.5 per cent per annum. It is therefore clear that it was only during

TABLE I

TOTAL AND REGIONAL GROWTH OF IRAQ'S POPULATION, 1867–1947
(Thousands)

Division	1867	1890	1905	1919	1935	1947
Northern region	265	401	540	703	1,041	1,347
Central region	491	575	855	966	1,319	2,043
Southern region	524	750	855	1,179	1,245	1,426
Iraq	1,280	1,726	2,250	2,848	3,605	4,816

the period since 1935 that Iraq's population began to grow at a rate markedly higher than at any other time from the middle of the nineteenth century onwards, 2.4 per cent per annum.

Just as the total growth of population was not uniform throughout the country, so the annual rate of increase was not uniform among the various regions. It is significant to note that, although the differences in the rates of regional population increase were not negligible even during the early period of 1867–90, they increased appreciably since. The regional rates of population increase were 1.8 in the North,

The vital statistics that are available do not admit of an accurate answer to this question. . . .

But even so, one point of comparison may be of some, if limited, consequence: namely, that between the annual rate of regional growth of population and the rate of natural increase of these three larger cities, between 1935 and 1947. Thus, while the rate of natural increase of the Northern City of Mosul was 1.6 per cent, that of the Central city of Baghdad 1.3 per cent, and that of the Southern city of Basra was 0.4 per cent, the annual growth of their respective regions had been 2.2, 3.7, and 1.1

TABLE II

ABSOLUTE INCREASES AND ANNUAL RATES OF INCREASE IN IRAQ'S POPULATION, 1867–1947
(Thousands)

Region	1867–90		1890–1905		1905–19		1919–35		1935–47	
	Absolute	Per Cent	Absolute	Per Cent	Absolute	Per Cent	Absolute	Per Cent	Absolute	Per Cent
Northern	136	1.8	139	2.0	163	1.9	339	2.4	306	2.2
Central	84	0.7	280	2.7	110	0.9	354	2.0	724	3.7
Southern	226	1.6	105	0.9	325	2.3	65	0.3	181	1.1
Iraq	446	1.3	524	1.8	598	1.7	758	1.5	1,211	2.4

0.7 in the Centre and 1.6 per cent per annum in the South during 1867–90; and 2.2, 3.7, and 1.1 per cent per annum during 1935–47. Further, it is not only the magnitude of the differentials in the regional population growth that have increased over time, but also their geographical direction, showing a relatively increasing decline in the Southern region and an accelerating rise, mainly in the Central but also in the Northern regions. Thus, in the period between 1935 and 1947, the annual rates of population increase in the Central and Northern regions were as high as 3.7 and 2.2 per cent per annum respectively, while their counterpart in the Southern region was as low as 1.1 per cent per annum.

How far can these differences between the regions in the absolute growth and the rates of increase of population be explained by differences in the regional birth and mortality rates?

per cent during the same period. Bearing in mind the locational incomparability of these figures alone, one could only tentatively suggest that differences in rates of regional growth of population, particularly in the Central region, cannot be wholly accounted for by regional differences in birth and mortality rates. In the absence of any significant international emigration and migration, these regional differences between rates of natural increase and regional population growth must be due to internal migration between the regions, particularly towards the more urbanised Centre, and away from the more backward South, a conclusion which also seems to be borne out by the structural changes in the regional population of Iraq.

While long-term growth of population normally indicates the general level of economic activity, the long-run movements in the composition of population show the relative changes in the structure of production and pattern of consumption. Table IV [Table III omitted in this excerpt] purports to throw some light on both the national and regional changes in the nomadic-rural-urban composition of Iraq's population since 1867.

The figures in this Table are not strictly comparable; they are derived from different sources, with different margins of error, and are classified on the basis of somewhat diverse criteria. They are, however, reliable enough to bring out the general trend of the change in the nomadic-rural-urban composition of population. Thus, around the middle of the nineteenth century, Iraq's population of just over one and a quarter million was made up of nearly half a million nomadic people who lived largely on the transport of the "mediaeval"

caravan trade; slightly over half a million "rural" (agricultural and pastoral) population who depended on the land for cultivation or grazing; and just under a third of a million people who earned their living in larger or smaller towns, through handicraft industries, internal or Middle Eastern trade, and administration. But towards the middle of the present century, Iraq's population has grown to about five millions, of whom only a quarter of a million are strictly nomadic; 2.7 million are rural, while about 1.8 million are urban people, who earn their living either in the larger commercial and industrial towns or in the marketing towns which occupy a position intermediate between rural and urban life.

The trend of the change in the nomadic-rural-urban population structure, as shown in Table IV, is quite unmistakable; in the

TABLE IV

Changes in the Nomadic-Urban Composition of Population, 1867–1947
(Thousands)

Date	Region	Nomadic	Per Cent of Total	Rural	Per Cent of Total	Urban	Per Cent of Total	Total
1867	Northern	70	26	140	52	55	22	265
	Central	115	23	170	39	206	41	491
	Southern.	260	50	215	41	49	9	524
	Iraq	450	35	525	41	310	24	1,280
1890	Northern	93	23	223	55	85	22	401
	Central	65	13	340	59	270	28	675
	Southern.	275	37	400	53	75	10	750
	Iraq	433	25	963	50	430	25	1,826
1905	Northern	153	28	254	47	133	25	540
	Central	70	7	468	78	317	15	855
	Southern.	170	19	602	72	83	9	855
	Iraq	393	17	1,324	59	533	24	2,250
1930	Northern	82	11	519	66	174	23	765
	Central	64	4	855	56	531	36	1,460
	Southern	88	8	872	83	103	9	1,063
	Iraq	234	7	2,246	68	808	25	3,288
1947	Northern	70	5	795	59	482	36	1,347
	Central	25	1	1,074	53	944	46	2,043
	Southern.	155	10	833	59	438	31	1,426
	Iraq	250	5	2,702	57	1,864	38	4,816

first place, there had been an absolute as well as relative decline in the nomadic component of Iraq's population, falling absolutely from about half a million in 1867 to a quarter in 1947, and relatively from 35 per cent to 5 per cent of the total population.

Secondly, there had been, until 1930, at any rate, an absolute as well as relative increase in the rural population, which rose absolutely from just over half a million in 1867 to nearly two and a quarter million in 1930, and relatively from 41 per cent to 68 per cent of the total population respectively. Since 1930, however, while the absolute level of Iraq's rural population continued to rise up to 2.7 million in 1947, its relative magnitude declined to 57 per cent of the total population, owing to the rise of the urban population.

Finally, although the absolute level of the urban population rose from about a third of a million in 1867 to over one and three quarters in 1947, its relative position remained virtually constant at 24–25 per cent of the total population, until the period 1930–47, during which it rose to 38 per cent of the total population.

These three trends in the composition of Iraq's population are not uniform among its various regions. The absolute and relative decline of the tribal population is much more marked in the Central than in the Southern and Northern regions. While the Central region's tribal population fell from about 115,000 in 1867 to about 25,000 in 1947, that of the Southern region declined from about 260,000 to 155,000, but that of the Northern region, with some upward and then downward fluctuations, remained absolutely constant over the same period. The same can be said of the decline in the relative position of the nomadic components of the various regional populations. Thus, while the fall in the nomadic proportion of the Central region was from 23 per cent of the regional population in 1867 to 1 per cent in 1947, the Southern counterpart fell from 50 per cent to 10 per cent and the Northern equivalent from 26 per cent to 5 per cent.

This proportional decline in the tribal population corresponds to a proportional rise in the rural population in each region. Thus, while the Central region's rural population rose from about 170,000 in 1867 to 855,000 in 1930, the Southern and Northern counterparts went up from 215,000 and 140,000 to only 872,000 and 519,000, respectively. But the relative rise in the rural population was much more pronounced in the Southern region, rising from 41 per cent of the regional population in 1867 to 83 per cent in 1930, while the Northern and Central counterparts of this constituted a much smaller rise, from 52 per cent to 66 per cent in the former and from 36 per cent to 56 per cent in the latter.

After 1930, while the absolute level of rural regional population increased, however, the relative importance of the rural population declined in all the regions, because of the relatively sharp rise of the urban population. The early and more rapid beginning of the decline in the tribal and rise in the rural population, particularly in the Central region, and the later and slower fall in the tribal and rise in the rural population, particularly in the Southern region, explain the relatively greater fall in the rural population of the latter from 83 per cent in 1930 to 59 per cent in 1947, than in the former from 56 per cent to 52 per cent respectively.

As for the regional diversity of the absolute and relative change in the urban component of population, it is sufficient to point out that, up to 1930, the Northern region more than tripled and the Southern region slightly more than doubled the absolute level of their urban population, largely due to the rise of the marketing towns, while the equivalent change in the Central region was half way between. But the relative position of the urban population in the Northern and Southern regions remained almost constant over the same period, 1867–1947, while that of the Central region declined sharply from 41 per cent in 1867 to 15 per cent in 1905, mainly because of the sharp decline of the Baghdad handicraft industries under the competitive pressure of cheaper machine-made imports, and rose to 36 per cent by 1930. During the period 1930–47 the urban component of population rose to almost a third of the Northern and Southern regional population, while that of the Central region rose to just under half of its population.

Another equally important aspect of population composition is the sex-age distribution, as it shows, or should show, the size and the nature of the labour force. In the absence of any reliable statistics of age-sex distribution prior to the first and only Census of population, the present discussion is confined to the structure of the economically active population, and its occupational distribution in 1947. . . .

Iraq, like most underdeveloped countries, has a very young population, about half of it being under the age of 20. The relative proportion of active (producers/consumers) and inactive (consumers/non-producers) population is of paramount importance in economic development. Table V [omitted in this excerpt] shows that out of a total non-nomadic population of 4.5 millions, 2.2 million are active and 2.3 million are inactive. The economic burden of the inactive or dependent population becomes even heavier when the sex distribution of the active population is considered in relation to differences in duration and type of economic activity of the sexes. Thus, the economically active population, which amounts to only 49.5 per cent of the total, consists of 22.5 per cent male-active and 27 per cent female-active. The remainder of 50.5 per cent, which represents the inactive population, is divided into 24.2 male-inactive and 26.4 per cent female-inactive. This, in effect, means that the number of women who are actually active is much less than the total female population of working age. . . .

It is clear from Table VI [omitted in this excerpt], that the primary sector of the Iraqi economy, which consists of agriculture and livestock, fishing and hunting, accounted for 748,455 workers, 57 per cent of the total

occupied population according to the 1947 Census. These figures, though they adequately reflect the number of men occupied, underestimate the proportion of women engaged in this sector. Thus, while men employed in the primary sector account for 52.2 per cent of the total occupied labour force, women in the primary sector account for only 4.8 per cent. The downward bias in the figures of the employment of women is largely due, I think, to a social attitude which considers the household to be the only honourable place for them.

The smallest sector of the economy, the secondary, contained only 95,923 or 7.3 per cent of all occupied persons. Of this, textile and tailoring employees represented about one third; oil and light manufactures accounted for a quarter; the rest was mainly in building and construction, carpentry, leather and leather goods, public utilities and some light chemicals, etc. The relative importance of women engaged in industry was even less than in agriculture. This is partly due to the prevailing social attitude, but also partly due to the nature and demand for tertiary occupations.

The tertiary sector occupies in the economy of Iraq, as it does in all countries developing from primary to secondary stage of production, the second largest proportion of active population. The tertiary sector, which consists of commerce, public and domestic services, transport and all other administrative and professional services, in that order of importance, represents 470,979, or 35 per cent of all registered occupied population. The proportion of women engaged in this sector is 1.9 per cent of the total national labour force. This is greater than its counterpart in the secondary, but smaller than that of the primary, sector.

Table VI, therefore, shows that the primary or agricultural sector of the Iraqi economy is the largest, the secondary or industrial sector is the smallest, while the tertiary or commercial sector is in between.

This conclusion holds good for all the regions. But it is important, nevertheless, to note the regional variations in the occupational distribution. While the Southern and Northern regions account for 29.6 per cent and 28.3 per cent of all occupations, the Central region is responsible for as much as 42.1 per cent. Further, the tertiary (or commercial) and secondary (or industrial) employment in the Central region is almost as much as the total in both the Southern and Northern regions. In other words, while the secondary and tertiary sectors represent about one half to two thirds of the primary sector in the Southern and Northern regions, other sectors combined are greater than the primary sector in the Central region.

It is interesting to compare the results of Tables V and VI, which were calculated from the 1947 Census of Population. According to Table V, the number of people of working age amounted to 2.2 millions; while the occupied population, as shown by Table VI, did not exceed 1.3 million. Before drawing any conclusion from these figures, they must be qualified in several respects. In general, not all the active population is actually available for employment, as it includes the sick and the disabled, the students and the Armed Forces, and a substantial proportion of women. Nor is all the occupied population actually employed, as the definition of "occupation" adopted in the 1947 Census is so loose as to include all those belonging to an industry. More specifically, while child labour below the age of 10 and the labour of those aged 50 and above is included in the figure of occupied population, they are excluded by definition from the active population. Bearing these qualifications in mind, one could only suggest, rather tentatively, that the gross ratio of occupied to active population is very low.

Before drawing the main conclusions, I should like to state my opinion that the sources I have used can, of their nature, only yield estimates which are capable of showing the broad generation-by-generation changes in the size and structure of Iraq's population. On the whole, my estimates of absolute

growth are more reliable than my estimates of differences in rates of increase. The weakest estimates are, of course, those of the nomadic population.

In general, one may observe that the growth and structure of Iraq's population during the period 1867–1947 seem to reflect the trend and stages in its course of economic development. The introduction of European sea and river transport ushered in the decline of tribal population and the fall of the "mediaeval" Middle Eastern caravan trade. This contributed to the rise of the rural population, and the expansion of Iraqi-European-cum-Indian export trade. While this increase in foreign trade added to the commercial part of the urban population, the consequent rise in the European imports destroyed the local handicraft industries and thus helped to keep the urban population relatively constant till the early 1930's. The more recent growth of foreign oil investment and the rise of some consumers' goods industries is accompanied by the relative rise of urban and fall of rural population.

More specifically, however, one may point out four major conclusions:

1. The general growth of Iraq's population seems to have passed through three phases of development: one phase of rapid growth, 1867–1905, during which population rose from 1.25 to 2.25 millions, growing at an average rate of between 1.3–1.8 per cent per annum; another phase of slackening growth, 1905–35, during which population increased to 3.6 millions, at an average rate of between 1.7–1.5 per cent per annum; and finally a phase of more rapid growth, 1935–47, during which population rose to 4.8 millions, at an average rate of 2.4 per cent per annum. At this more rapid rate of growth, Iraq may double its present population by 1980.

2. The long-term change in the social composition of Iraq's population tends to fall into two stages: in the first stage, 1867–1930, the absolute and relative decline of the tribal population, from under half to under a quarter of a million, or from 35 per cent to

7 per cent of Iraq's population, was accompanied by an equally sharp rise in the absolute level and relative magnitude of the rural population, from just over half a million to nearly two and a quarter millions, or from 41 to 68 per cent of total population, while the urban component of the population remained virtually constant at 25 per cent of total population. The second stage, 1930–47, shows that the urban population (which originally was about one-third of a million in 1867), rose absolutely from just over three-quarters of a million in 1930 to over a million and three quarters, and relatively from the original 25 per cent to 38 per cent in 1947, while the relative importance of the rural population declined to 57 per cent. This difference is no doubt largely due to rural exodus.

3. The most striking feature of the present structure of Iraq's population is, perhaps, the high ratio of dependent to active population: 2.3 to 2.2 millions. On the average, therefore, each person of working age has another who is economically inactive either because he is too young or too old to contribute to production. Iraq's active population constitutes only 49.5 per cent of the total. It is lower than that of Egypt, where it is 61 per cent according to the 1947 Egyptian Census of population. The high ratio of the dependent population requires the fullest and most productive employment of the economically active population.

4. But, as it appears from comparing Tables V and VI, the ratio of the occupied to active population is very low: 1.3 to 2.2 millions. Thus, the gross estimate of the unemployed and underemployed population constitutes about 40 per cent of the total active population. The employment of this large supply of potential labour force is an essential factor in the process of economic development in Iraq.

Appendix on Statistical Sources and Methods

1. Iraq's boundaries, as established after the First World War, are considered in this paper to be the standard in accordance with which earlier boundaries were adjusted. The whole of the Wilayets (provinces) of Baghdad and Mosul have been included; the Najd part of the Wilayet of Basra has been excluded.

2. The present regional divisions are also taken as the standard, i.e. the Northern region or the former Wilayet of Mosul includes the Liwas of Arbil, Kirkuk, Mosul and Sulaimaniyah. The Central region, or the former Wilayet of Baghdad, includes the Liwas of Baghdad, Diyala, Dulaim, Hillah, Kerbella and Kut. The Southern region or the former Wilayet of Basra includes the Liwas of Amarah, Basra, Diwaniyah and Muntafiq. It must be noted, however, that in 1890 Hillah included Diwaniyah, and so the latter was excluded from the Central and included in the Southern region.

3. The term "nomadic population" is used here to cover that part of the population which roams about in an almost unlimited area, depending almost entirely on the camel for its livelihood, and thus remaining virtually wholly outside the main sectors of the national economy. On the other hand, all those who have been engaged in pasture or agriculture are included in the rural population. Urban population is defined to include all those living in towns with more than 5,000 inhabitants.

4. The estimate of the population of Iraq in 1866–67 is based, in the main, on the information available in the British Consular Reports on the Trade of Baghdad and Basrah, as published in the British Parliamentary Papers, 1867, LXVII, 266–67. These estimates were prepared by the exceptionally able Consul-General, Sir A. B. Kambell, [*sic*—Kemball] during his thirteen years of residence in the country. He probably had access to the earlier but incomplete estimates of the population of the tribes made by M. B. Al Tamimi for the British Resident at Baghdad, Mr. C. J. Rich, about 1818, and also to Captain Chesney's estimates published in the Euphrates Expedition of the 1830's.

Kambell's estimates of Iraq's population explicitly exclude the eyalets (districts) of Mosul and Sulaimaniyah, but include that of Kirkuk. In order to fill in this gap the present writer calculated the population of the eyalets of Mosul and Sulaimaniyah thus: the population of these two eyalets for 1890 is known, while that of Kirkuk (the other district in the Northern region) is known for both 1867 and 1890. The average annual rate of growth of Kirkuk's population between 1867 and 1890 was calculated. As there is no reason why the population of the eyalets of Mosul and Sulaimaniyah should grow at an average rate significantly different from that of Kirkuk, the population of the two eyalets for 1867 was derived from their known population in 1890 minus their estimated growth since 1867.

Moreover, although Sir A. B. Kambell gives the urban population and the agricultural population separately, he combines the nomadic and pastoral population. In order to obtain the rural (agricultural plus pastoral) population, we must separate the nomadic from the pastoral population. A rough estimate of the pastoral population can be derived from the known settled agricultural population by assuming that the ratio of agricultural to pastoral population was more or less the same as the ratio of agricultural to pastoral exports. Subtraction of this estimate from Kambell's figure of the combined nomadic and pastoral population gives an admittedly precarious estimate of the nomadic population. Addition of this estimated pastoral population to the known agricultural population yields an estimate of the rural population. (It is clear that this method of calculation may underestimate the agricultural and overestimate the pastoral population, as agriculture requires relatively more peasants than pasture requires shepherds per unit of exports. On the other hand, a greater share of agricultural produce was exported than of pastoral produce because of the relatively greater accessibility of the agricultural produce to export markets, which implies a bias in the other direction. But of course these two biases need not cancel out.

5. The 1890 population of Iraq was taken with only very slight adjustment (i.e., the exclusion of Najd and the inclusion of Diwaniyah in the Southern instead of the Central region) from M. Vital Cuinet's work *La Turquie d'Asie* (4 volumes), Paris, 1892, particularly vol. II, pp. 764–65, and vol. III, pp. 119–48, p. 151 and p. 221. M. Cuinet says that his information was supplied by the Department of Census, which carried out a census of population for the Ottoman Empire. The present writer has been unable to see the original Census.

6. The estimate of the population of Iraq in 1905 is based on the British Consular estimates as given in the *Handbook of Mesopotamia*, published by the Admiralty Naval Intelligence Service (London, 1918), which covers the period 1900–1908. See in particular vol. I, pp. 87–94. The nomadic population was there stated to be

between 15 and 20 per cent: the present writer has put it at 17 per cent.

7. The estimate of the population of Iraq in 1919 is based on the British Political Officers' estimates given in their district reports on the *Administration of Mesopotamia*, 1918–23. These estimates are more detailed as the country was divided into a relatively large number of divisions. Urban population was estimated from an enumeration of households; rural population was estimated from the collection of taxes on agricultural produce and animals; nomadic population is thus estimated as a residual item.

8. The estimate of the population of Iraq in 1934–35 is that made by the Government of Iraq as a result of enumeration of households and published in the Iraq Directory of 1936. The estimate for 1930 is taken from E. Dowson, *Land Tenure in Iraq*, p. 12. . . .

9. Table III [omitted in this except] was derived from the Iraqi Ministry of Economics, *Abstract of Statistics*, 1939, p. 7, and from the Public Health Directorate, *Vital Statistics*, 1935, p. 54.

10. The estimate of the population of Iraq in 1947 is taken from the *Report on the Census* of Population of that year (the first census of a modern type), published in three volumes in 1955, one for each of the three regions. The Census excluded the nomadic population, though an estimate of the latter was made by the Department of Census. But it is nevertheless the best source so far available: the estimates in the United Nations Demographic Year Books for the period 1948–55 are bound to be less reliable. For an excellent appraisal of the census, see Dr. Doris Adams, "Current Population Problems of Iraq," in the *Middle East Journal*, Spring, 1956.

11. Tables V and VI [omitted in this excerpt] were derived from the *Report on the Census of 1947*. It is worth noticing that while the number of active males is put at 1.0 million, occupied males are estimated to number 1.2 million. The discrepancy is due in part to the exclusion of both child labour and workers more than 49 years old, and in part to the downward bias in the census returns for the age groups between 15 and 30 years of age springing from the fear of conscription. But the high level of underemployment, particularly among the active female population, remains valid.

12. The annual rates of population increase of Table II were calculated by applying a compound rate of growth. Differences in the number of years in the periods of comparison were ignored as insignificant given the nature of the data.

CHAPTER 5

Land Tenure in the Nineteenth Century

At the beginning of the nineteenth century the greater part of the cultivated area of Iraq—the land lying outside the rain-fed northern zone—was held under a system of communal ownership. The *dira*, the area claimed by the tribe, was regarded as belonging jointly to all its members. It is true that a large portion, sometimes as much as a third or a half of the area actually cultivated, was ear-marked for the tribal *shaikh*, but he was supposed to use the revenues accruing from it mainly for such communal purposes as the upkeep of the tribal militia, the maintenance of order, and the entertainment of guests. The rest of the cultivated land was held either by subtribal chiefs (*sirkal*, from the Persian *sirkar*), on much the same conditions, or by sections of the tribe or households. The actual unit of farming, the *qit'a*, was large; it was supervised by the *sirkal*, who subdivided it into plots, *faddan*, worked by a group of farmers, known as *jauq* and usually consisting of four to eight men. These men divided the labor of cultivation but harvested in common and shared the crop. The *sirkal* divided the plots, fixed the dates of sowing and harvesting, supervised the irrigation works, and sometimes advanced seed or money. Although the area of the *dira* was fixed, the *qit'a* and *faddan* shifted constantly, because of the salination or exhaustion of the soil.

Following the establishment of steam navigation on the Tigris (see Part III, chap. 3) and the opening of the Suez Canal, foreign demand for Iraqi produce increased greatly (see Part III, Introduction). This greatly increased the value of land and led to a desire on the part of the tribal chiefs and subchiefs to appropriate it for themselves. At the same time the leading Ottoman reformer, Midhat pasha, who served as Governor of Baghdad in 1869–71, tried to apply to Iraq the Land Code of 1858 (see Part II, chaps. 8 and 9). *Tapu* rights were to be granted to, and land settled in *miri* tenure on, all who could prove that they had cultivated a given piece of land for ten consecutive years. But, given the shifting and communal system of agriculture, the ignorance of the tribesmen, and their fear that registration was a prelude to conscription, the vast majority either could not or did not attempt to prove continuous cultivation. The following selection describes some of the difficulties that ensued.

The government therefore offered title to land against payment of its assessed value, or put it to auction. Some tribal chiefs took advantage of this and registered the tribal lands in their own name, or those of close relatives. A large amount of tribal land was similarly acquired by townsmen. When, however, the new urban owners tried to assert their rights, they were opposed by the tribesmen, who refused to recognize the alienation of their lands. The conflict was usually settled by the relative power of the government and the tribes: near the towns the new owners were upheld and the tribesmen reduced to tenants, while in the more remote regions the new owners were not allowed to take possession. Nor were matters made easier by confused and conflicting tribal claims, the chaotic state of the Ottoman registers, and the ignorance and corruption of the officials.

The government therefore in 1880 and 1892, suspended the granting of title to occupants. By then about a fifth of the cultivable land had been registered as *tapu* land; the remaining four-fifths was set up as a new class of land in which, notwithstanding the fact that it was occupied, the state retained both property (*raqaba*) and usufruct (*tasarruf*) rights; such land was designated as *miri*, or *amiriya*, a new use of the term, very different from the old. Occupants of such land were regarded as tenants-at-will, who could be evicted at any time and from whom the state could demand any rent.

It is impossible to follow here the further developments of land tenure in Iraq. During the First World War the Turks took away or destroyed the land records. Under the mandate the British, who relied heavily on the tribal chiefs and large landowners, by and large maintained the Ottoman system, with slight modifications. The establishment of security and the spread of pump irrigation reinforced the drive to appropriate land and settle titles. An attempt at an over-all policy drafted by Sir Ernest Dowson in 1930 was frustrated by the landlords and *shaikh*'s, who dominated the Iraqi parliament. After the Second World War the government used its large reserves of land to settle tens of thousands of farmers in model settlements—the *miri sirf* scheme. The Land Reform Law of 1958 greatly curtailed the power of the landowners, but in the process disrupted agricultural production, and the problem of land tenure in Iraq is still far from being solved.

(See also works by Warriner [*Land and Poverty*], Dowson, Adams [*Land behind Baghdad*], and Longrigg [*Four Centuries* and *Iraq*] listed in the Bibliography.)

[From Saleh Haider, "Land Problems of Iraq" (unpublished thesis, London University, 1942), pp. 556–660; printed with omissions, by kind permission of the author.]

THE IRRIGATION ZONE

THE POLICY OF MIDHAT PASHA (1869–71)

. . . In the irrigation zone, the tribe rather than the village was the social and economic unit. Only in the vicinity of the main towns and in the areas irrigated by lift or perennial canals where the tribes had disintegrated, could landholding be said to be individualistic. In other parts tribal tenure was predominant. This was based on the conception of the tribal *dira* over which the tribe exercised an exclusive right of occupancy. The *dira* was not limited to parcels of land actually tilled, but extended to other non-cultivated land, and even to marsh lands (as in the rice areas) which were submerged by water and which were reserved for subsequent reclamation. Claims of this nature, over desert, marsh, or cultivated land may be asserted even after the reason on which they were based, i.e., occupancy, is no longer valid because of the emigration of the tribe to another area.

Cultivation in the tribal *dira* shifted annually because of the exhaustion of the land, the variability of the water supply, the timeliness of rain, the level of the marsh, and the extent of the flood, as well as other internal and external disturbances.

The cultivated parts of the tribal *dira* were usually divided into parcels and left, generally in the hands of the heads of the tribal sections and the clans, with the paramount sheikh retaining an additional area to enable him to dispense the duties of sheikhdom and the expenses of the *mudhif*. But these holdings, including that of the sheikh, were not personal and individual, but communal, belonging to the tribe as a whole or to that section of it which the head represented. In some cases the division of the land goes so far as to be almost individualistic or familial. In other cases large estates are held by a few leading tribesmen.

Inside these holdings one sometimes finds distinctive prescriptive rights pertaining to individual tribesmen or families. These originated from partition, first revival, and development—as, for instance, the planting of trees or the erection of a water lift—or simply by a grant from forefathers who acquired it by some such ways. These rights have various names, for instance, *naqsha*, *saham*, *jisim*, *hussa*, but these constitute only a small part of the land. In any case they could not truly be considered the absolute individual property of their holders as they are a part of the tribal *dira* and subject to tribal custom. The large holdings of the tribal sheikhs or subtribal chiefs which are more communal than individual are more commonly called *lazma* especially on the Tigris, and defined as "the right of occupa-tion and cultivation" (*Haq el sukna wal zira'a*).

As cultivation was shifting, the *lazma* included cultivated as well as uncultivated land. The cultivated part was actually tilled by the *fellahin* or the *afrad* (tribesmen) under the management of the *lazma* holder, generally according to the crop-sharing system. Nominally the *fellahin* were mere agricultural laborers or lessees from the *lazma* holder; actually most of them were related in blood and were kin to him and could be considered partners not only in the crop but also in the *lazma* itself. The difference between the conception of lease and the conception of partnership as applied to the relation between the *fellah* and the *lazma* holder is not very well defined and varied from area to area. In general it can, however, be stated that where tribal solidarity was weakened there was a tendency for the *lazma* holder to be the lessor and the *fellah* the lessee of the land, and thereby the conception of partnership other than in the crop weakened. This can clearly be seen in the well-developed areas in the vicinity of the towns, as for instance in Diyala, Basra, and parts of Hilla, where individual ownership has replaced communal ownership in the cultivated land. On the other hand, where tribal solidarity was still strong as in Muntafiq, Diwaniya, Amara, and Kut, "there was no personal lazma rights; allotments to individual tribesmen could be and frequently were resumed by the sheikh."[1]

Hence two principles can be deduced from the tribal system. Firstly the tribal land was in general communal property, and the chiefs, though in name and in relation to the government they were the lessees of the land and the tribesmen were the sublessees, according to local practice they were the representatives of the tribe and trustees of the land, and not the land-owners.

Secondly, cultivation was mostly shifting and not stable in one particular spot. It

[1] Sir Ernest Dowson, *Enquiry into Land Tenure* (Letchworth, 1931), p. 26.

follows that the *fellahin* rarely had a chance to develop a prescriptive right to any particular plot.

These two features of the tribal system were in direct conflict with the principles of the Land Code [of 1858, see Part II, chaps. 8 and 9] which forbade communal ownership of the land (except as *metrouke*) and recognized a prescriptive right of the land only to individual cultivators who could prove actual possession and cultivation of a particular plot of land for at least ten years.

Hence, it is clear that the first provision of Article 78 of the Land Code, i.e., the grant of *tasarruf* gratuitously under *haq-el-qarar*, could apply to hardly any part of the irrigation zone, because neither the peasant nor the *lazma* holder nor the sheikh fulfilled the conditions of *haq-el-qarar*. The peasant's claim was invalid because he could rarely prove ten years' possession in any plot of land, and he almost always surrendered a share of the produce of the land to the *lazma* holder, and sometimes directly to the legal holder which legally proved a right to other parties in his land; the *lazma* holder could not substantiate his claim under the Land Code because he did not cultivate the land himself and he was considered legally to hold his land by a contract of lease either directly from the government or from his sheikh. The sheikh was not entitled to the land because he did not cultivate it himself and because he was a representative of the tribe rather than the owner of the land. In no case, as the origin of landholding in the tribal areas was by squatting, could any one of these classes normally prove that the origin of his claim was derived from one of the three roots of title recognized in Turkish law, namely, devolution by inheritance, purchase from the previous possessor, or grant by competent authority.

Hence *haq-el-qarar* in the irrigation zone came almost universally to mean the grant of land in the *tapu* against *bedel mithl*, and the application of the Land Code had to be based on the second and third provisions of Article 78, i.e., the grant of title against *bedel tapu* or, if the apparent claimant refused it, the sale of land by auction.

Furthermore even according to the second provision of Article 78 it was by no means clear who among the various classes of the rural population was entitled to the *tasarruf* by payment of *bedel mithl*. In the vicinity of the towns where the tribes had mostly disintegrated and where individual proprietorship was more marked, whether in the form of landlord and tenant as in the estates near Baghdad and Diyala, or in the form of a cultivating proprietor as in the case of a *charid* owner or a tree planter in the riverain and some canal areas, the apparent beneficiary to this right could perhaps be easily pointed out. Similarly, those comparatively few who held the land under the feudal *tasarruf* and possessed documents to support their claims could now register their right in the *tapu*.

But in most of the land which was occupied by the tribes, all classes of the tribal population can be said to have some sort of title to the land of the tribe; but the alienation of the tribal land in favor of one class, e.g., the sheikhs, the *lazma* holders, or even the peasants, would do a great injustice to the other classes apart from the fact that it might be entirely impossible from the practical point of view. . . .

As will be seen later, the reduction of the share of the state in alienated land and in land that needed development also shows that the real purpose of the land policy of Midhat pasha was to encourage cultivation in Iraq and to induce the tribes to settle into peaceful pursuits for gaining their livelihood. His attempts to introduce irrigation and railway schemes into the country, to improve river transport, and to establish strong centralized administration tended in the same direction. Hence his land policy must be seen in this light. On payment of *the tapu* value which was arranged on easy instalments, the *miri* land was to be alienated in small and large tracts to holders of *ferman*'s and other documents of the previous age, to villagers who had cleaned a canal or planted a garden, and most important of all to sheikhs and subtribal chiefs of the tribes in their respective tribal areas. The *tapu* holders would then enjoy a security of tenure which was denied to them by the policy of the state ownership of the land pursued in the Régime of Coercion. The revenue demand would be considerably reduced and the cause of cultivation and settlement would correspondingly be enhanced. Furthermore landholding. which has been a ripe source of dispute and rivalry among the various tribal sheikhs and a weapon often used by the central administration to sow dissension within the leading families of the various tribes, would once and for all be settled, and with the development of transport, irrigation, security of tenure, and reduction of the revenue demands, the tribes would be occupied with peaceful means of gaining their livelihood and tribal disintegration would inevitably follow as a new age of prosperity swept away the old conditions of insufficiency which nursed and maintained the tribal system.

Unfortunately, like others of his major schemes, his land policy was launched without a preliminary study of the local conditions and investigation of the multifarious claims to the land by the various occupants of it. For he appears to have singled out tribal sheikhs and townsmen to be the most favored recipients of his *tapu* grant of the land over the head of the *lazma* holders and the peasants. Thus Ibn Hadhdhal of the Anizah beduin tribe acquired gardens and land on the Upper Euphrates, Farhan of the Shammar Jarba was granted a *tapu sanad* on part of the tribal *dira* of Shammar at Shirgat, the Sheikh of Chaab was granted land on the Shatt al Arab, but the most glaring example was the manner in which he alienated the land in the Muntafiq area. Here he authorized Nasir pasha al-Sadun, his nominee chieftain of the tribal confederation of the Muntafiq, whom he had appointed a *liwa* governor (*mutasarrif*) of the district, to have the major part of the tribal land of the Muntafiq Confederation registered in his name and in the name of

various members of his family; and granted large estates to his Christian clerk, Naoum Serkis, to his Jewish banker, Mr. Danial, as well as to some townsmen in Shatra and Nasiriya. Few of the subtribal chiefs and *lazma* holders of the Muntafiq Confederation and hardly any members of the cultivating peasants secured registration of their holdings in the *tapu*.

Nevertheless the majority of the tribal sheikhs did not look with favor on this scheme and declined Midhat's offer to have the tribal land registered in their name, mainly because they were mistrustful of all Turkish schemes after centuries of Turkish misrule and oppression. They also feared that adherence to such a policy would bring them under the direct control of the government and would involve the much dreaded enforcement of the compulsory military service which Midhat pasha had been simultaneously trying to apply more rigorously in Iraq, and from which the tribes had been, hitherto, for the most part exempt. The attitude of the tribal sheikhs to Midhat's land policy is explained by Mr. Longrigg as follows[2]

... Many saw the clear purpose of detribalizing; more suspected any blessing that issued from the Serai; and more again were still too well content with their own remoteness to accept a change. Vivid fear of conscription kept the tribes from accepting the obligation of settlement, which had other evils enough in accessibility, toil, dependence on canals and markets. There was in any case, money to be paid. The majority of tribal leaders feared and shunned the new status; some were forestalled as purchasers by a town-dwelling speculator friendly with the tapu officials; some gladly acquired rights, but in land far from their own people; others paid a first instalment and withheld the rest. Thus if the aim of Tapu settlement was fixity of tribal cultivating tenure which should transform sheikh into landlord, it was an aim largely frustrated by the hesitancy of the sheikhs.

Townsmen on the whole were much more attracted to the new policy than

[2] S. H. Longrigg, *Four Centuries of Modern Iraq* (Oxford, 1925), p. 307.

tribesmen. Apart from those absentee landlords who held *hujja*'s for *mulk* land and *ferman*'s for life grants under the old regime, and who had duly registered their title to the land in the *tapu*, a considerable number hastened to acquire land over the heads of the cultivators, particularly in settled and semisettled areas where the control of the government was strong enough to permit the effective possession of the land and the due payment of rent from the cultivator. Thus in some parts of the more settled districts of Diyala, Hilla, and Baghdad the land was in effect sold to large landowners the majority of whom were townsmen. Thus a considerable number of the leading families in Baghdad came to possess land in Diyala, Karradi, Salman Pak, Ridhwaniya, Kut, and Samarra. Similarly some of the leading families of Hilla had purchased canals in that *liwa*. Cuinet specifically mentions the name of M. Zarifi, a retired Turkish banker who, he asserts, acquired about 45,000 hectares of land in Beledruz in the Diyala *liwa*.[3]

The greatest single landowner, however, who had benefited from the application of the *tapu* system in Iraq was Sultan Abdul Hamid himself. He acquired most of his estates in Iraq in the late eighties, i.e., subsequent to the governorship of Midhat pasha, and the manner of his acquisition was like that of any *tapu* holder who had purchased land from the state over the heads of the cultivators. The extent of his estates has been mentioned elsewhere; it is sufficient here to say that they included some 30 per cent of the total cultivated land in the *Vilayet* of Baghdad and correspondingly large estates in the *Vilayet*'s of Basra and Mosul.

Even including the lands which were acquired by the sultan and became *saniyya*, alienation of *miri* land in the *tapu* was not complete and a large portion of the total cultivable and cultivated land in the irrigation zone remained throughout this period legally in the hands of the state as crown lands. According to Cuinet, of the total cultivated area in the *Vilayet* of Baghdad, about 30 per cent belonged to the civil list, 20 per cent was *waqf*, 20 per cent belonged to private individuals, and the remaining 30 per cent "belonged to the government directly."[4] Thus if these proportions could be relied upon, and excluding the *saniyya* lands which were acquired after Midhat pasha, and *waqf* lands which it is safe to assume were mostly *waqf* before he came, only 20 per cent of the cultivated land was held by private individuals in the *Vilayet* of Baghdad and that included some *mulk* plantations particularly in Diyala, Hilla, and Karbala and the vicinity of Baghdad and Salman Pak, which are mostly non-tribal and the title for which is rarely disputed. It also included land of the *tamlik* or life-grant category of the previous period, the title for which was supported by *ferman*'s and other documents which were not replaced by a *tapu sanad*. While the fertile area between the Tigris and Euphrates west of Baghdad, most of the area lying on both sides of the Hindiyya branch of the Euphrates, and by far the greater part of the Kut and Diwaniya *liwas* were not alienated in the *tapu* to private individuals, although some of the best parts of these lands were later acquired by the *saniyya*.

In the *Vilayet* of Basra registration in the *tapu* seems to have been more extensive. It included nearly all the area of Shatt al Arab from Fao to Qurna and the whole of the cultivable area of the Muntafiq *liwa* with a great portion of the *qadha*'s of Kut and Hai. In the *liwa* of Amara there was comparatively little land alienated in the *tapu* until the civil list acquired its large estates there.

Hence, as in the rainfall zone, registration in the *tapu* was incomplete. But in the irrigation zone the reason was not only the antipathy felt toward registration by the tribes. Unlike the rainfall zone, where registration had continued throughout this period, in the irrigation zone two *irada*'s

[3] Vital Cuinet, *Turquie en Asie* (Paris, 1896), III, 109, 121.

[4] *Ibid.*, p. 44.

were subsequently issued which in effect abrogated all the provisions of Article 78 of the Land Code as far as it applied to land in this zone, and thus prohibited alienation of state lands to private claimants and put the policy of Midhat pasha at an end. The causes and results of these two *irada*'s will be considered later. It is sufficient here to say that the policy of Midhat pasha did not last more than ten years. During this period it not only failed to accomplish its purpose, but it also introduced new problems and additional confusion in that part of the land which was already alienated and generally called *tapu* land in Iraq. . . .

Thus the *tapu* system in the manner it was applied by Midhat pasha had failed. Sir Ernest Dowson summarily puts the reasons for its failure in the following terms:

It failed for two reasons, either of which would have been decisive. It was foredoomed to fail as it failed generally throughout the Ottoman Dominions because the administrative experience and machinery, the technical knowledge and the qualified staff needed to accomplish so formidable a task were lacking. It was also foredoomed to fail because it attempted immaturely to cast in a rigid (and an alien) mould the fluid practices of a still predominantly primitive society.

These reasons are borne out by the facts stated above. But it must be added that the experiment left a legacy of confusion and acute agrarian problem wherever the *tapu* system was applied and more particularly in the tribal areas.

MIRI LAND

The *tapu* experiment did not die a natural death in the irrigation zone of Iraq. It was abandoned by the Turks and Article 78 of the Land Code was in effect repealed, as far as it applied to the still unalienated land of the irrigation zone, by two *irada*'s issued during this period subsequent to the governorship of Midhat pasha. The first *irada* repealed the last two paragraphs of Article 78 by forbidding the sale of *miri* land against *bedel mithl* or in auction. The second so interpreted the first part of Article 78 as to deprive of the right of *haq-*

el-qarar all holders of *miri* land from the state, if such holding was made according to the contract of *muzara'a*. . . .

These facts lead to the conclusion that there were other motives for the two *irada*'s. There could have been two other motives:

In the first place, the Turks subsequent to Midhat pasha saw that in the alienation of land to the tribes and particularly to tribal sheikhs, the government would forfeit a weapon which if retained would still be of great value for the control of the tribes and their chiefs. Hence in subsequent years they lost no opportunity to exploit the principle of state landownership and to appoint as lessees those of the tribal chiefs who showed loyalty to them, and to sow disaffection within the tribes by buying off a subtribal leader or a rival to the sheikh through the grant of lease of a part or the whole of the land that is held by another who had shown a sign of disobedience to their orders or provoked their displeasure.

Secondly, unlike other parts of the Ottoman Empire, the land in the irrigation zone of Iraq was nominally paying a much higher rate than the *'ushr* [tithe] that is due on *tapu* land. Hence the alienation of the land in the *tapu* would involve the abdication by the state of its additional share of the produce over and above the *'ushr*, while payment in lieu of the *tapu* value and in registration fees proved disappointing.

If these reasons were not the motives for the issue of the two *irada*'s, and more particularly the first one, they were certainly the results of them. For their issue marked a direct reversal of the policy of Midhat pasha of alienating state lands in favor of the policy of state landlordism followed by the governors of the Régime of Coercion in the generation previous to Midhat's governorship. It suspended the operation of the Land Code in the unalienated lands of the irrigation zone and made the state an absentee landlord just as the application of the Land Code had created absentee landlords in the lands which were already granted in the *tapu*. It indeed caused the creation of an extra-legal class of land that was neither intended nor provided for by the Land Code; nor have the *irada*'s been supplemented by legislation to regulate this class. This is the class of land which may or may not be actually cultivated but was invariably subject to a prescriptive tribal claim as a result of long occupation. It was clearly neither *mulk* nor *waqf* nor *metrouke*; it was not *tapu* or subject to a *tapu* right that awaits registration; it does not fall within the definition of *mewat*, as it is more often occupied or even cultivated. It is generally called *amiriya* or simply *miri* in Iraq, while state land, the *tasarruf* of which had been alienated and a *tapu sanad* issued for it, is called *tapu* land. This class reveals still more clearly the conflict between the law and the practice in the irrigation zone. Indeed, so divergent had the legal and customary systems become that in the "*miri*" the inhabitants of the irrigation zone also included the *mewat* land and often also the *metrouke*. These latter terms were seldom used outside legal and departmental circles.

From the point of view of the state, the *miri* land was considered simply a part of the public domains, the *tasarruf* as well as the *raqaba* of which belonged to the crown. It was leased to the cultivators nominally by annual contracts and generally according to the *muzara'a* or crop-sharing system. From the point of view of the cultivator, it was considered his own land just as the *lazma* holder in tribal land which was alienated in the *tapu* to other than himself considers the land his own. There is, however, one important difference. From the purely legal point of view, it can be said that the position of the *lazma* holder in *tapu*, *mulk*, or *waqf* lands is governed by a contract which could be upheld by the courts and by the Islamic laws of tenancy as well as by the Land Code and other Ottoman legislation. The *lazma* holder or tenant in *miri* land is not so protected, as the courts were forbidden from hearing cases relating to land which was not registered in the *tapu* and supported by a *sanad*. Indeed, the *miri* holder had no legal remedy even against encroachments made by a neighboring *tapu* holder on his land unless the state was willing to take his side as a third party to the suit.

Hence the *miri* land was dealt with outside the framework of the legal system and was administered and managed according to the discretion and arbitrary wil of the provincial administration. How did the provincial administration dispose of the *miri* land and what were their relations with the *miri* holders?

As the provincial administration treated land revenue and rent in the same way and collected them together in this class of land, these questions will be considered in the next section, which deals with land revenue in the irrigation zone both in *miri* and other classes of land. . . .

It appears that the actual receipts by the Turkish government in tithes constituted a great proportion of the produce of the land and the income of the cultivator. The total receipts from the tithes in the three *Vilayet*'s of Baghdad, Mosul, and Basra, on all agricultural produce (including receipts in lieu of the *mellakiyyah* and in the form of *maqtu'* or *iltizam*) amounted to £311,929 in 1890 and £527,175 in 1911. Unfortunately we cannot correlate these figures with the total cultivated area to find land taxation per acre, nor can we correlate them with the total agricultural produce in order to find the percentage of the government share to the total produce. Table 1, however, compares these figures with the estimated population and the value of the export of the dates and grain, which are by far the most important crops in the country. The corresponding figures for the year 1937 are also stated for comparison.

The total receipts from revenue on agricultural produce were proportionately much smaller than the value of date and grain exports in 1937 as compared to 1911 and still smaller as compared to 1890. This is despite the fact that the population, and therefore local consumption of these products, increased steadily from 1890 to 1937. In 1937, the rates of revenue demand ranged

TABLE I

	1890	1911	1937
Population	1,850,000	2,849,000*	3,560,000
Date export	£250,955	£456,795	£974,216
Grain export	£278,540	£1,198,119	£2,156,867†
Total government revenue from agricultural produce.	£311,929	£527,175	£624,220‡

* This number of population is an estimate for 1919.
† Including seeds.
‡ The financial year ending in March of the following year.

from 10 per cent of the gross produce (or the produce sold in the market) to a maximum of 30 per cent of that produce. It must therefore be concluded that the actual receipts by the Turkish government from the tithes constituted even larger proportions of the gross produce. Indeed, the Ottoman Bank estimated the share of the state in the receipts from the grain exported in 1911 to be 30 per cent of those receipts, while the agriculturalists received only 54 per cent of them, leaving 16 per cent for the cost of internal transport and storage and dealers' profits.[5] Thus it can be said that perhaps nowhere in any part of the world was agricultural production taxed so heavily as it was taxed in the irrigation zone of Iraq during this period. . . .

CUSTOMARY SYSTEM OF LAND TENURE AND POSITION OF THE CULTIVATOR

The cultivated land of the irrigation zone of Iraq was divided into *muqata'a*'s (estates): these *muqata'a*'s were divided into *qit'a*'s (pieces) which were in their turn split up into plots variously called *faddan, khait, jerib, shigga, wusla, juft jisim, saham, hussa, nagah, tali'a, shkara,* etc., according to the area of the plot, the kind of crop grown, and the manner of its tenure.

Generally speaking these divisions would correspond with the social division of the tribe and the system of tribal tenure. The tribal *dira* usually consisted of one or more *muqata'a*'s leased by the sheikh from the legal owner of the land whether that legal owner was the state, the *saniyya*, the *waqf*

[5] *Consular Reports, Trade Series* (1912), No. 4890.

or the *tapu* holder. Some *muqata'a*'s ran to thousands of acres and even to tens of thousands in the winter-crop areas, where some are known to have exceeded a hundred thousand acres. In the rice areas, few *muqata's*'s exceeded a few thousand acres and most were less than a thousand acres. In date plantations they were naturally still smaller.

The *qit'a*'s were generally held by a sub-tribal chief variously called *sahib al-lazma, mellak, musaggim,* or *sarkal*. The *qita'a* ran to a few hundred acres in the winter-crop areas and was commonly under a hundred acres in the rice areas and in date plantations.

The plots in every *qit'a* would correspond to the holding of the peasant or *fellah* and ranged from ten to fifty acres in the winter-crop areas and from three or four to ten acres in rice areas and in date plantations.

The relation of these agrarian classes to each other and to the legal holder varied from area to area according to the nature of the crop grown, the method of cultivation, and above all the solidarity of the tribe. In general the irrigation zone could be divided into three areas: (a) The purely tribal areas where the tribal bond was very strong as in Muntafiq, Diwaniya, Amara, Dulaim, and among the tribe of Rabi'a in Kut and the Zubeid in Hilla. (b) In areas which were still tribal but the solidarity of the tribe had weakened but the solidarity was broken up into their component sections down to the *qit'a* holder or sarkal as in some parts of Hilla, in Samarra and the Dujail area, in Mahmudiya and the area west of Baghdad, and also along the Tigris below Baghdad to Bughaila. (c) The areas where the tribes had completely disintegrated down to the individual tribesman and for all purposes did not exist or existed only in name and social affiliation but had no economic significance; such for instance were the areas in the gardens and date plantations of Basra, Karbala, Diyala, and Baghdad and also in the grain lands neighboring or attached to them.

a) Where the tribal organization was still strong, the tribal dira, composed of one or more muqata'a's, was farmed by the tribal sheikhs from the legal holder according to a contract called the shartnamah or sanad-el-tisgam, whereby the sheikh undertook, against the lease of the land, to pay to the legal owner a share of the produce or (much less frequently) a fixed amount of rent in kind or in money every year. Sometimes the tribal sheikh could actually move sections of the tribes from one qit'a to another as he sublet the land against a share of the produce (or as in Amara, against a fixed sum) to the subtribal chiefs. Thus in Amara, a few tribal sheikhs farmed the muqata'a's of the whole of the land of that liwa, each in his own tribal dira. These sheikhs then sublet the qita'a's to the sarkal's or the subtribal chiefs, whom they actually could move from one qit'a to another and even from one muqata'a to another, together with the whole of the tribal section under their leadership. This is more or less the case among the tribe of Rabi'a in Kut and the Zubeid in Hilla, and some tribal sections of the Muntafiq confederation.

More generally, however, the triba sheikh had no such power over the movement and holding of the subtribal chiefs. Each muqata'a was divided into qita'a's held traditionally by one or another subtribal chief whom the tribal chief could not move without incurring the enmity and disloyalty of that particular section to which the land belonged. The sheikh also had his own land which belonged partly to him as the leader of his own tribal section and partly to his office as the paramount tribal sheikh, and was therefore called the share of the mudhif. He either managed his holding by himself

or engaged a sarkal for the tisgam (cultivation and management) of the land. When the qit'a holder also claimed a prescriptive right to the land and could not be moved by the tribal sheikh, the latter was a tax farmer of the government share and the collector of rent due to the legal holder of the muqata'a's under his farm. This is mostly the case in Diwaniya. In Dulaim, Kut, and Muntafiq, the tribal sheikh was more than a farmer of the government share; he had a share in the produce of the land of the sarkal's and could sometimes move them from their holdings.

In both these cases the sheikh had several other important duties to perform, such as the maintenance of order and security in the tribal dira and the arbitration in disputes among his tribesmen; he represented the tribe vis-à-vis the government, the legal holder, and the neighboring tribes, and he organized the defense of the locality against outside aggression; he organized the hashir or forced labor contributed by the qit'a holders for the clearing of canals, the strengthening of the river banks, the building of temporary and permanent weirs over the rivers and canals, and other general communal work that was needed in the tribal dira; finally he supervised the distribution of the canal water among the qit'a holders and prevented any trespassing or damaging of the crop of one qit'a by the alignment of the drainage lines of another.

Apart from his share of the produce in his own qit'a's, the sheikh sometimes claimed certain dues from the subtribal chiefs. These took the form of either a share of the produce of the land as in Kut, or a fixed amount from every faddan or bakra as in Dulaim, or the crop of small plots of land (called tali'a) to be cultivated by the fellahin for his benefit as in some parts of Muntafiq.

He also received considerable revenue from the lease of uncultivated land to shepherds who visited the tribal dira from another area and did not belong to the same tribe and often also levied taxes on river craft and caravans passing through the tribal dira.

But his most important remuneration

accrued to him from his capacity as the farmer of the government revenue and the lessee of the land from the legal holder. In most cases the government allowed him a rebate of a part of its share up to about 6 per rent of the gross crop. In addition, he retained a good portion of the land revenue and the *mellakiyyah* (rent) which was never paid in full, whereas he often collected it in full from the *qit'a* holders. This rule, however, is not universal. In Diwaniya, for instance, whatever the sheikh paid to the government was actually divided among the various holders of the land according to their holdings.

b) Where the tribe had partially disintegrated, the *qit'a* holders were more or less completely independent of the paramount sheikh to whom they owed only nominal allegiance. They held the *qit'a*'s directly from the legal holder under a contract of *tisgam* and performed all the duties regarding canal clearance and arbitration of disputes. Thus, for instance, the *muqata'a*'s situated on the left bank of the Hilla River were divided into independent *qit'a*'s each held by a separate holder of the Jubur tribes. This is also true of most of the *muqata'a*'s in the area enclosed by Felluja, Musaiyib, and Baghdad. Here also the tribes have disintegrated into sections each holding a *qit'a* independently of his neighbor. Similarly in the Dujail area above Baghdad and on the left bank of the Tigris below Baghdad down to Bughaila, the land was leased mostly by the *qit'a* rather than by the *muqata'a* from the legal holder. It appears that wherever the *saniyya* had land, the tribes seem to have disintegrated into their component sections and the land was leased by the *qit'a*. The only exception to this rule seems to have been in Amara, where the land was farmed in *muqata'a*'s to the tribal sheikhs. This may have been the result of a deliberate policy followed by the *saniyya* to go beyond the sheikh to the subtribal leaders and deal with the latter directly. The success of this method is undoubtedly due not so much to the power at the disposal of the *saniyya* administration

as to the fact that that administration took over duties of the tribal sheikhs such as the maintenance of order, protection from external aggression, and the organization for canal clearance; therefore, the duties of the paramount sheikh having more or less disappeared, his office became redundant and he gradually sank into the ranks of *qit'a* holders.

c) In the settled areas, in the vicinity of Baghdad, in the *liwa* of Diyala, in Karbala and, above all, in Basra, the tribe having disappeared or disintegrated, the legal holder generally had the effective possession and management of the land. Here the legal holder or his agent replaced the tribal sheikh in the *muqata'a*'s while the *qit'a*'s were managed by *sarkal*'s who acted as mere tenants, both in practice and in law, to the legal holder. In some cases the legal holder managed the *qit'a*'s by himself by employing the *fellahin* mostly on the crop-sharing system and had a paid *wakil* to look after his interests.

Hence as a rule the *qit'a* was the unit of cultivation in the irrigation zone of Iraq, and there was generally an intermediary between the legal holder of the land and the actual cultivators (the *fellahin*) of it. This is true in the purely tribal areas, as well as in the semi-disintegrated tribal areas and the nontribal or settled areas. His agricultural functions were generally called the *tisgam*. Under this term fell such work as the employment of the *fellahin* on the land and lending them "assistance" (*musa'adah*) or "advance" (*silfeh*) in the form of seeds and sustenance until the harvest. He decided which part of the *qit'a* should be plowed and which should be left fallow. He allotted the plots to the cultivators and organized the distribution of water in his *qit'a* and chose some members of his *fellahin* or all of them for the *hashir* for canal clearance or other duties inside his *qit'a* or outside it.

In the purely tribal areas the *qit'a* holder generally held his land in his capacity as the representative of his own tribal section. The holding in this case was heritable and passed to his direct male descendants. Females did not as a rule inherit land in the tribal areas. The holding was generally not partitioned among the heirs, but passed as the sheikhdom itself to the most promising and influential member of the family of the deceased. Although the elder son was the apparent successor, a younger son, a brother, or a nephew might be the succeeding holder of the *lazma*. Other members of the family either worked under him or were joint partners in the proceeds or were allowed plots of land free of the share of the *mellak*. Sometimes the *lazma* holder allotted parts of the land to his relatives before his death, and they retained possession of them after his death so that the land was in practice partitioned. In other cases where the *lazma* holding was large and there was a cleavage within the family of the deceased *lazma* holder, partition actually took place, but such partition was usually accompanied or followed by much ill feeling and feuding. These problems of inheritance also related to the holdings of the sheikh and to his office and were often exploited; and disaffection was frequently encouraged by the Turks in their effort to break the solidarity of the tribe.

The *lazma* holding originated in various ways. Sometimes it was a result of the partition of the tribal *dira* among the ruling family or among the subtribal chiefs, after the death of a powerful paramount sheikh who held the whole area under his sway. Sometimes it was a result of partition among the tribal sections after the conquest of the land in battle and according to the number of fighters in each tribal section who participated in the battle. Often it was originally a grant to a subtribal chief for services rendered or as an inducement to make him contribute his forces in case of need. Sometimes it was as a result of development carried out by the tribal section of which the *lazma* holder was the leader. It will be seen that in all these cases ownership of the land was not individual but accrued to the whole of the tribal section of which the *lazma* holder was the leader.

Nevertheless, individual holdings were not entirely absent in the tribal areas. Within the *qit'a*'s we sometimes find individual prescriptive rights to plots of land pertaining to the rank and file of the tribe (the *afrad*). These individual rights were variously called *nagsha, hussa, saham, jisim, shigga, khait, skhara,* etc. These rights arose either by subdivision of the *lazma*, which led to the creation of a peasant-proprietor type of holding, or by original partition of the land among the individual *taffagah* (riflemen). More often it originated from first development or by a grant from the *lazma* holder or the sheikh for services rendered. Thus the installation of a *charid* in a riverain plot or the planting of trees may be the origin of such individual prescriptive rights. In other cases, the grant by the *lazma* holder or the sheikh of a plot of land to a tribesman in what is called *flahah mlachah*, i.e., "with the right of the *fellah* as well as the right of the *mellak* in the crop," may be the origin of it. The recipients of such favors were sometimes the relatives of the sheikh or the *lazma* holder, the *sayyid*'s, who were the ambassadors and the priests and the arbiters of dispute in the area, or influential tribesmen who immigrated to the area from another section, and ordinary tribesmen who had distinguished themselves in battle or on other occasions.

These peasant-proprietor holdings sometimes constituted a great proportion of the cultivable land particularly in rice areas and date plantations. . . .

The most typical holding in the irrigation zone was that of a *qit'a* held by an intermediary between the legal holder and the *fellah* who employed the *fellahin* on the crop-sharing system. The great majority of the actual cultivators of the soil held the land under this tenure.

LAND HOLDING

The system of crop-sharing tenure has been known in Iraq since the First Babylonian period or perhaps earlier. . . .

This form of tenure was followed not only between the peasant and the *lazma* holder, but also between the latter and the legal holder or the state. As we have seen in the relation between the legal holder and the *lazma* holder or the sheikh, the form of *muzara'a* (outside the settled areas) was merely a legal fiction and the legal holder had no power to evict the cultivating partner from the land at the end of the harvest. This is also true of the relation of the *lazma* holder with most of the cultivating peasants or the *fellahin*. The sanction against eviction of the *fellah* in this case was tribal custom rather than laxity of administration.

There were two classes of *fellahin* or *afrad*: those who belonged to the same tribe as the *lazma* holder and were therefore related to him in blood and kinship, and those who were of different tribes and took refuge in the areas with the permission of the tribal sheikh or the *lazma* holder. They were both in theory tenants-at-will and their contracts, written or oral, lasted for one season and were renewed if the *lazma* holder thought it desirable. But practice diverged from theory and the latter was more true with regard to the "alien tribesmen" than with regard to the native. It was also nearer the truth in the settled areas. In the purely tribal areas, and especially with the native tribesman, the *fellah* could not be called an agricultural laborer or a tenant-at-will. His economic position was inescapably governed by his social position. His duties and rights arose more out of his tribal affiliation than out of his economic function as a tiller of the soil. In these turbulent areas fighting was as much a function of the *fellah* and other members of the tribe as the tilling of the soil. Indeed, he was first a fighter and then a cultivator of the soil. Those who came from another tribe were employed on condition that they too accepted tribal law and carried arms and defended the honor and possessions of the tribe whenever they were called upon to do so. If a *fellah* was ejected from his holding or left it voluntarily, he was readily welcomed by another *musaggim* or tribal leader, unless he was known to have committed a dishonorable act. Hence the

lazma holder was loath to part with his *fellahin* and risk the waning of his tribal influence, while the influence of his rivals grew.

Moreover, whatever development had taken place, such as the opening of a new canal, the draining of a marsh area, the constant clearing of the existing canals, and the building of weirs and embankments, was done by the aid of the *fellah*, not in his capacity as a laborer who was paid for the job, but in his capacity as a tribesman called upon by his chief to give a hand in this and many other communal duties. Hence in purely tribal areas the *fellah* can be said to have a share in the land as well as in the crop which he raised. He could not be evicted from the tribal area by the *musaggim* or by the sheikh except for a serious breach of the tribal law. Indeed this partnership is sometimes implicitly acknowledged by the sheikh or the *lazma* holder, as for instance when the tribesmen were closely related to him in blood or when reallotment took place as in some parts of Shatra, Afaq, and Diwaniya.

This was not exactly the case with that class of tribesmen (generally very small in the purely tribal areas) who belonged to a different tribe and took refuge or sought employment with the lazma holder. These could usually be called tenants-at-will, and their relation to the land was more economic than social. They could be evicted at the end of the harvest and indeed they constituted a more or less floating population who sought employment with this or that *musaggim*. But even here some of them were assimilated into the tribe as time went on. When they stayed with the same *musaggim* for a long period, they too developed a moral right of employment in the land, and it was considered a breach of good tribal morality to evict them from the land. All these tribesmen participated in battle and in the communal labor and accepted the tribal code and custom; hence their relation too was not entirely economic, but gradually took on a social nature the longer they stayed in the tribal *dira*.

Where the tribe had disintegrated or was

undergoing disintegration, the reverse tendency took place, i.e., the position of the *fellah* tended to change from a social to an economic relation, and the *qit'a* tended to be held by the *lazma* holder or *mellak* more as a private holding, with individual ownership, than as a communal property with the holder as the trustee or representative of the tribal section occupying the *qit'a*. It follows that the tenure of the *afrad* in these areas tended to be based more on their contracts and less on their social status as members of the tribe. Wherever tribal disintegration had set in, the tribal sheikh too tended to consider his *qit'a*'s and the share of the *mudhif* as his private property. These tendencies were induced by the rise of a commercial spirit in the rural areas, and by the increase of security in some parts of the country which was within the reach and control of the central administration. Here the function of the *fellah* as a soldier began gradually to lose its significance and reality, and the sheikh could dispense with his services without undue loss of power or prestige as these began to be derived more from ownership of the land and less from tribal chieftainship. The legal conception of land tenure of *muzara'a* and *musaqat* based on private holding and tenancy exerted its influence in the same direction. The Turkish and above all the *saniyya* policy of dealing with the sheikh or subtribal sheikh as the lessee of the land was also another factor. Hence *lazma* holdings began to be sold or bequeathed by their holders in these disintegrated tribal areas, often with the full recognition of the Turkish administrative officials who were included as witnesses in the body of the contract.

But this was not a large-scale movement in the irrigation zone even by the end of the period. By far the greater part of the tribal land was still held under tribal tenure and communal ownership. The *fellah* was mostly a partner in the land and in the produce. The land was usually not sold or bought by tribesmen, except perhaps in those holdings which were of the peasant-proprietor type, such as the holdings of the

afrad in the rice areas of the lower Hindiyya and the *nagsha*'s in Suq al Shuyukh. The holding of the *lazma* and the share of the *mudhif* were communal. Even the *sarkal*'s employed by the sheikh and the larger tribal chiefs would not be considered tenants-at-will or employees of the sheikh, but had a share together with their followers in the holding under their cultivation. Only in the postwar period did the tendency of communal ownership to become private ownership by the larger tribal holders assume the proportions of a real and definite large-scale movement and begin to transform tribalism into feudalism or capitalistic cultivation.

In the vicinity of the towns and in the settled areas, the relation of the agrarian classes to the legal holder was more contractual and economic than social. There the *lazma* holder himself became a mere *sarkal* or a tenant of the legal holder bound by a contract of lease, paying a share of the produce or a fixed sum as a rent to the legal holder. Sometimes he was not even a lessee but a mere wage earner paid by the legal holder to look after the interests of the latter, while the *fellahin* were employed directly by the *tapu* holder. The status of the *fellahin* too was based on a contract and they often could be dismissed at will. Some of them were paid monthly wages in money or in kind, while the majority of them were crop-sharing tenants. . . .

Thus, broadly speaking, the share of the *fellah* varied from one-third to a half of the produce in summer and winter crops, and he had to provide his own seeds, cattle, and implements for cultivation. If he had none of these, he had to surrender up to a half of his share to the one who supplied him with them. Seeds alone were often lent by the *musaggim* to be recovered at harvest time either at interest as in the settled areas or free of charge as in the tribal areas. Another 20 per cent of the produce went to the government as revenue and was collected by the sheikh or *sarkal*, while the remainder of the crop was disputed between the legal owner of the land and the sheikh and the *sarkal.* Generally 20 per cent of the gross produce was the share of the legal owner of the land whether it was the state, the *saniyya*, the *tapu* holder, or the *waqf* authority (or their lessees). Actually this share was never paid in full and a big or small slice of it was retained by the sheikh or the *lazma* holder (if he was independent from the sheikh) or divided between them. The remaining part of the produce, between 10 and 30 per cent, was the share of the intermediary between the *fellah* and the legal holder. He might be at once the sheikh of the tribe, the holder of the *qit'a*, and the *musaggim* for the cultivation. This was true of a tribal *qit'a* under the direct holding and management of the tribal sheikh. It was also true of the independent *lazma* holders who were also the *musaggims* of the land. Sometimes, however, the *sarkal* was, in name or in practice, a tenant of the sheikh and his share of the produce depended on agreement with the sheikh. In this case the sheikh sometimes, as in Kut, received a portion of the *mellak*'s share with the *sarkal*. In other cases, as in Dulaim, he received a fixed amount of the produce. In still other cases, as in the settled areas, the *sarkal* himself was paid a fixed amount and the remainder of the crop went either to the sheikh or the townsman.

THE POSITION OF THE CULTIVATOR

The economic position of the cultivator during this period and particularly in the irrigation zone was unenviable. In the first place, the share of the produce that he got was not net income. He had to bear the entire cost of production in his plot in the form of seeds, cattle, and implements. If outside labor was employed for the harvesting, threshing, and winnowing of the crop, as was usually the case, the remuneration of this labor came out of the crop before its division, and he therefore had to bear his share of the cost. Furthermore he had to contribute to the maintenance of certain officials in the tribal area, such as the *qahwachi* or the attendant of the *mudhif*, the *sayyid*, the guard, or in some cases even

the agent of the sheikh or *sarkal* in the land. Some even had to bear the cost of transporting the share of the sheikh, the townsman, or the *lazma* holder to the stores or the village.

In addition, the share itself or what remained of it after these deductions did not amount to a great deal owing to the very low yields per acre obtainable in the irrigation zone. According to estimates made by the assistant political officers in 1919, the average yield per donum for the winter crops was found to be about 200 kilos (320 kilos per acre) in Baghdad,[6] 180 kilos per donum in Nasiriya, 160 in Shamiya, 134 in Dulaim, 105 in Kut, and 86 in Baquba. But the harvest seems to have been an exceptionally poor one in that year.[7] The average yield per donum is about 200 kilos for wheat and 250 for barley.[8]

The average size of a holding of the *fellah* in the irrigation zone is about 40 donums, of which half is cultivated and the other half left fallow. The gross produce would therefore be about one and a half short tons of wheat and three and a quarter tons of barley, of which the share of the *fellah* (say at 40 per cent of the gross produce) would be about 600 kilos of wheat and

[6] *Revenue Report for Baghdad, 1919,* Appendix D, p. 50. The assistant political officer also mentions 50 to 150 kilos per donum in some parts of Baghdad (*ibid.*).
[7] *Ibid.*, p. 8.
[8] In 1923 M. Sellier, the director general of irrigation, in a report on the development of the Euphrates estimated the average yield on canal land on the Euphrates to be about half a ton per acre of wheat (317 kilos per donum) and three-quarters of a ton of barley (476 kilos per donum), but this would apply only to well-watered land supplied with scientifically constructed perennial canals, whereas the larger part of the area in the irrigation zone was supplied in this period with inundation canals. In 1928, the average produce per donum was estimated by the government for the purpose of revenue collection to be 400 kilos per donum for first-class land, and 300, 200, 100, and 75 kilos for the other classes (*Annual Report of the Revenue Department* [Baghdad, 1929], Appendix M, p. 47). Although the areas in which these methods were applied were mostly in Baghdad, Diyala, and Hilla, where canal water is better served, most of the land was assessed at classes 2, 3, and 4, where the average yield was estimated between 300 and 100 kilos (*ibid.*). The figures of 200 kilos for wheat and 250 for barley per donum represent an estimate made by an official of the Department of Agriculture, well versed in these matters, and they seem to be reasonable estimates.

about 1,300 kilos of barley; or about two tons of grain in all. At the prices ruling in July, 1911 (i.e., about £4 per ton of barley and £6/10 for wheat),[9] the share of the *fellah* would represent a gross income of about £9 per annum. If he had to borrow his seeds and implements, etc., his income would be about £4/10/0. Sometimes this holding of 40 donums is shared between two *fellahin* and in all cases the *fellah* worked on the land with his children. Hence this income represents the gross earnings of the family. A large family of three or more adult males usually held larger areas.

In the rice areas the average holding of the *fellah* was from four to five donums, and his gross receipt was estimated by Mr. Ahmed Fahmi in 1925[10] to be 1,268 kilos per *fellah* in the lower Hindiyya area. At the prices prevailing at the end of 1911 (viz., about £6 per ton),[11] the income of the *fellah* would amount to a little more than £7/10/0 per annum.

In the date gardens the normal holding of a *fellah* was about five jeribs (4.75 acres), the gross crop of which would probably be roughly ten tons, of which the *fellah* received half or a quarter of the produce. At the price of about £5 per ton, the share of the *fellah* would be from £25 to £12/10/0 per annum.

These figures are by no means underestimates of the income of the *fellah* in the irrigation zone. They are verified by the monthly wages taken by gardeners in the towns during this period. According to a consular report for the year 1907, a gardener in Baghdad took a monthly wage of 13/4 (£8 per annum) to 18/0 (£10/16/0 per annum).[12] These wages rose in 1911 according to another consular report[13] to between 17/- per month (£10/4/0 per annum), and 20/4 per month (£12/4/0 per annum). Taking into consideration that the gardener was more or less a skilled laborer who had been attracted to the town by the

higher wages, it will appear that the returns of the *fellah*, particularly in the *shitwi* crop areas cultivated by the precarious inundation canals, were if anything overrated. The latter sometimes supplemented his earnings by such subsidiary occupations as the rearing of livestock and helping in the harvest in another area. Some *fellahin* could also supplement their earnings by growing small plots of the more valuable summer crops (other than rice) whenever water could be commanded in their land. Further, the *fellah* generally lived on the harvest for over two months from the time it ripened till the time it was divided.

In the rainfall zone, both the average produce per donum and the share of the *fellah* were much higher; hence the economic position of the *fellah* was much better than that of his counterpart in the irrigation zone. This is particularly the case with the peasant-proprietor and the *fellah* with the prescriptive right to the land. The position of the *murabi'ji* [share cropper], however, does not seem to have been any better than the position of the *fellah* in the irrigation zone. The holding of the peasant varied in the north from place to place according to fertility and ownership of the land. The peasant usually cultivated from one to four faddans. The faddan in this zone was defined as the area that could be plowed by the animal of the *fellah* and varied according to whether the animal was a donkey, an ox, or a mule. Generally it was from fifteen to about forty donums. The average produce per donum in Kirkuk in 1919 was 714 kilos as against 200 kilos in Baghdad. In Arbil Plain the normal yield is ten times the amount of the seeds sown. As the *fellah* sows from one to four tons in his holding, the gross crop would be from ten to forty tons of grain, of which from two-thirds to four-fifths are wheat and the remainder barley. As he paid almost a fifth of the produce in land revenue and as a share of the *tapu* holder, his share amounted to from eight to thirty-six tons of grain. And his income was several times greater than the income of the *fellah* in the irrigation zone. . . .

[9] *Consular Reports, 1912*, No. 4980.
[10] *Taqrir*, p. 87.
[11] *Consular Reports, 1911*, No. 4980.
[12] *Consular Reports, 1908*, No. 4073.
[13] *Consular Reports, 1912*, No. 4999.

CHAPTER 6

Production, Transport, and Foreign Trade in the 1900's

The dominant note of the following selection is the contrast between the immense potential of Iraq and the existing state of "lethargy." A comparison of conditions in the 1900's with those in the 1800's (see Part III, chap. 1) shows how little progress had been achieved in the previous hundred years. Agricultural techniques had not changed, though the cultivated area had been greatly extended and output had risen correspondingly. The handicrafts had retrogressed, and the number of steam-driven plants was exactly five. Methods of land transport showed no improvement whatsoever and costs of such transport remained high.

The main changes were in the sphere of international trade and transport. Steam navigation on the Tigris (see Part III, chap. 3) had made it possible greatly to increase the quantity of the country's exports and imports and to reduce freight rates. The volume of foreign shipping calling at Basra had risen several-fold, in spite of the almost complete lack of facilities in the port. The quantum of foreign trade had also multiplied, but the combined value of exports and imports still amounted to under $15 per head of population, and the number of foreign merchants and financial and transport agents handling foreign trade had also increased appreciably, though here too the total amounted to only a few dozen. Clearly, the realization of Iraq's potentialities still lay in the future.

(See also works by Cuinet, Himadeh [Iraq], and Longrigg [Iraq and Four Centuries] listed in the Bibliography.)

[Adriano Lanzoni, "La Mesopotamia economica," Bolletino della Società Geografica Italiana (Rome), XLVII (1910), 23–37; reproduced by kind permission of the Society.]

From the general account of the physical and social conditions of Mesopotamia previously given,[1] it seems quite clear that this region is eminently suited to agriculture, being favored by the quality and quantity of the existing silt and humus; by irrigation by a great mass of water coming from the mountains of Persian and Turkish

[1] See this Bulletin [Bolletino della Società Geografica Italiana], 1909, fasc. 7, pp. 740–53 and fasc. 8, pp. 883–87.

Kurdistan and Armenia, which crosses it in all directions; and by the possession of underground water that can serve for irrigation by means of artesian wells. Its geographic location facilitates a large trade with Persia, the Persian Gulf, India, Africa, the Far East, Anatolia, Syria, Egypt, Europe, Russia, and America.

At present the productive energy of Mesopotamia is dozing off in a lethargy that goes back to the glorious days of the Abbasid caliphs, Ottoman rule having doomed the population to a life of ignorance and barbarism. Agriculture and industry are very limited, whether compared to the vastness and fertility of the land, or to their scope in ancient times. Nowadays industry is confined to certain localities, because of the obstacles that the government continually puts in the way of every attempt at greater expansion, and also because of the hostility of the indigenous population. Agriculture is limited to the areas along the water courses, since the old canals have long ago been filled with debris and abandoned. Thus industry just meets the needs of the country, and only in certain years of abundance does agricultural production exceed local needs and provide a surplus for export.

The poor social conditions of the peoples inhabiting Mesopotamia have adverse effects on the economy and the legislative and political organization, which are vital factors of trade, hence commercial activity, lacking sufficient production, is not intensive. However, one can already anticipate that it will increase with the growing inducement to work evident during the last few years.

Statistics on agricultural production in the *vilayet* of Baghdad alone, which I have taken from Cuinet, give an idea of the production of the soil, which is both under-cultivated and poorly cultivated.

In this part, I will deal only with the *vilayet* of Baghdad, since it is the most important one, being the center of agriculture, industry, and commerce of all Mesopotamia. The main agricultural crops

are grains: wheat, barley, rice, sesame, maize, millet, etc.; leguminous crops: beans, kidney beans, lentils, etc.; and dates. In the *vilayet* of Baghdad, according to Cuinet, average annual agricultural production is as follows: [2]

	Tons
Wheat.	173,907
Barley.	409,374
Millet.	61,560
Maize.	49,248
Rice.	126,198
Sesame	13,851
Mash (a kind of lentil)	23,085
Kidney beans.	50,865
Potatoes	5,100
Cotton	385
Melons and water-melons	94,700
Oranges and lemons.	540,500
Grapes.	150,000
Pot herbs and fruits.	1,191,221
	2,890,053

Animals	Heads
Cattle.	235,000
Horses.	85,000
Asses and mules.	104,000
Camels.	95,000
Sheep.	2,140,000

The handicrafts have lost much of the importance they had in the days of the Abbasid caliphs, but still play a valuable and useful part in the economic life of the country.

Baghdad is the industrial center of the *vilayet*. Here are manufactured the *'aba* of wool or silk (a kind of peplos) embroidered with gold or silver and worn by men and women; the *kufiya* (big kerchiefs) made of silk or cotton embroidered with gold and silver and bordered with fringes of small cords at the ends, used by the Arabs to cover their heads; the *awtar* made of cotton (a kind of long gown); the *charchaf* and the *izar* of silk or cotton, embroidered with gold or silver, that women use to cover themselves when they go out.

There are many tanneries, and numerous shoemakers, for both the indigenous inhabitants and the Europeans. There are also coarse gold and silver handicrafts. Copper work is very good and highly valued. The

---

[2] Several of these figures seem highly exaggerated.— Translator.

manufacture of bricks and the art of ceramics, which go back to ancient days, are also developed and flourishing.

All the industrial output of al-Iraq al-Arabi is produced by means of a primitive system of handicrafts, helped by horses and cattle when human strength is not enough to put into motion one primitive instrument or another. Modern industrial installations consist of: a state-owned steam factory, whose machinery was imported from Europe, for the manufacture of clothing used by the troops, two steam mills and two ice plants.

In the *vilayet* of Basra are found the same industries as those mentioned above as well as the manufacturing of matting. The sailboats built in the region for sea and river navigation are renowned, as are also special types of boats for navigation in the marshes of the Basra *vilayet*.

In Mosul everything is in a state of decadence; some silk and cotton industries are still to be found, however, as well as the ones enumerated for Baghdad, although to a minor degree.

Internal communications are by land and river; the main flow of international trade is by river and sea. In the *vilayet* of Basra there are a few caravan routes leading to Najd and the Arabian coast of Kuwait and Qatif. Others, of minor importance, follow the course of the Shatt al Arab, and then ascend the courses of the Tigris and the Euphrates. The rivers connect them with Baghdad, Muhammerah, the interior of Persia and the sea. In the *vilayet* of Baghdad the river system facilitates direct communication with Basra, the Persian Coast, and India, and the desert routes with Syria to the west, Persia to the east, and the *vilayet* of Mosul and Asia Minor to the north. The *vilayet* of Mosul is in direct communication by river with Baghdad and by land with Persia, Syria, and Anatolia.

In Baghdad there are two companies for river navigation, one Ottoman (the Hamidieh Imperial Company) the other English (the Euphrates and Tigris Steam Navigation Company). The Hamidieh has eight steamships, and the English company has five. These steamships can transport passengers and merchandise and, the space available on board for freight being limited, they often tow a barge carrying up to 150 tons of cargo. [See Part III, chap. 3.]

The English steamships also carry the English mail, and their service coincides with the weekly mail service to India of the British India Steam Navigation Company. At Basra steamships of the Bombay and Persian company also call twice a month; those of the Persian Gulf Trading Company and the Persian Gulf Steamships; a steamship of the Russian Company calls every three months, and one of the Hamburg-Amerika of Hamburg calls each month. Other steamships of various companies also arrive during the date season (September–October). [See Part V, chap. 10.]

The land routes of communication are:

1. From Baghdad, through Persia, to Kermanshah the mail takes from six to eight days.

> Baghdad–Khan Bani Said (4 hours)
> Baghdad–Baquba (4 hours)
> Baghdad–Sheraban (8 hours)
> Baghdad–Kezrabat (4 hours)
> Baghdad–Khanaqin (4 hours)

From Khanaqin in one hour and a half the Turkish-Persian frontier is crossed, and one arrives in Qasr-i-Shirin, four hours after leaving Khanaqin; from there it takes three days to Kermanshah. This route is followed by caravans, and carriages can run from Baghdad to Qasr-i-Shirin.

2. From Baghdad to Constantinople the mail takes twenty-two days following the route: Baghdad–Khan Bani Said–Salahiya or Kifri–Mosul–Diyarbakir and Constantinople. By land from Baghdad to Mosul it takes seven days; by river from eight to three days.

3. From Baghdad to Damascus it takes twelve days, crossing the desert and the region inhabited by the Anazah tribesmen, 450 kilometers.

4. From Baghdad to Aleppo the time required varies according to speed, from a

maximum of twenty-two days to a minimum of sixteen by caravan; carriages take from twelve to eight days.

5. From Baghdad to Musa Yab there is a road for caravans and carriages (eight hours). From Musa Yab to Karbala four hours are required by carriage and from Karbala to Najaf eight hours.

This route to Najaf (center of the Shiite pilgrimage), passing through Karbala, Musa Yab, Baghdad, Baquba, Khanaqin, Qasr-i-Shirin, and Kermanshah, is the usual route taken by Shiite pilgrims from Persia, from parts of Afghanistan, and from Caucasian Russia, to visit every year the tombs of Imam Ali in Najaf, of Imam Husain and Imam Abbas in Karbala, and of Imam Kazim in Kazimia, near Baghdad.

Rates for transport of merchandise on river steamships are as follows: From Basra to Baghdad: for each ton of general cargo, £1/7/0; for each ton of sugar, £1/5/0. From Baghdad to Basra: for each ton of cargo, £1/5/0.

RATES OF TRANSPORT BY LAND FROM BAGHDAD TO KERMANSHAH

Merchandise	Per Ton of Cargo by		
	Mule	Ass	Camel
Cotton goods . . .	£7/5/10	...	£5/16/9
Coffee	8/1/6	£7/5/9	7/10/0
Spices (droghe) . . .	8/1/6	7/5/4	...
Sugar in bags . . .	...	8/5/9	
Sugar in cases . . .	8/1/6	...	7/10/9
Tea	8/15/9	....	7/1/3
Cassia	9/0/9	...	6/6/6
Candles	8/1/6	7/5/3	5/13/0
Cotton yarn	...	8/5/9	...
Iron	...	7/10/9	...
Other merchandise by crates or bundles . .	...	8/4/3	...

The approximate duration of the journey from Baghdad to Kermanshah by mule is thirteen days, by ass fifteen days, and by camel twenty days.

From Baghdad to Hamadan the cost of merchandise transport per ton ranges from £3 to £4; the approximate time by mule is twenty-one days, by ass twenty-five days, and by camel thirty-two days.

From Baghdad to	Per Ton of Cargo by		
	Mule	Ass	Camel
Kirkuk . . .	...	£3/9/6	£3/19/0
Arbil	...	5/4/3	4/2/3
Sulaimaniya . .	...	6/19/0	5/13/0
Mosul . . .	£5/13/0	5/13/0	5/0/6
Karbala . . .	1/14/9	1/6/0	0/12/0
Najaf	...	2/3/6	...

There is a carriage service at the following rates per person: from Baghdad to Karbala, 1 to 2.5 mejidieh; from Baghdad to Najaf, 2 to 5 mejidieh; from Baghdad to Hilla, 1 to 2 mejidieh. Each carriage can transport eight persons.

From Aleppo to Baghdad, and vice versa, the rates for merchandise transport are £13 to £15 per ton, the journey taking from twenty-four to thirty days.

Roads in the real sense do not exist, since the Ottoman government has not built any; the paths beaten out by caravans and followed by carriages are good enough the year around, except during the rainy season.

International exchange is relatively intensive in view of the insufficiency of existing communications and of the means of transport by land and sea; the very high freight rates on the river steamships going from Basra to Baghdad and Mosul, and on the internal system of communications, is one of the principal causes that slow down its growth. The customs tariff and port dues are similar to those in effect throughout the Ottoman Empire.

Mesopotamia imports primarily from India and Persia. I have been able to assemble a table showing imports from these countries by sea. Commercial exchange by land, up to the present is not controlled, the Ottoman customs in Mesopotamia being insufficient to compile statistics on the whole commercial exchange. The new system of operation adopted by the customs in 1908 may in the future offer more exact information on the state of imports and exports of merchandise between the Ottoman Empire and neighboring nations.

The merchandise imported from India is commonly of British origin; following India in importance come England, France, Belgium, Russia, Austria, Germany, America (North and South), and Italy.

Tables 1 and 3, below, show the quality and quantity of the merchandise imported and the place of origin. The preparation and packing of the merchandise is generally made with great care. The merchandise that has to be transported by caravans is prepared in a special fashion suitable for carriage by beasts of burden, and must not be over 140 English pounds in weight. Alcohol and spirits are imported in double barrels [*doppio fusto*]. The value of merchandise

TABLE 1

IMPORTS OF BAGHDAD FROM EUROPE AND AMERICA, 1907

Merchandise	England	France	Hamburg	Antwerp	Other	Total*
Books (crates)	...	...	7	...	19	26
Candles (crates)	419	...	...	3,150	...	3,569
Cement (barrels)	10	...	...	...	...	10
Coal (tons)	1,308	...	...	...	...	1,308
Cochineal (bags)	...	209	...	...	...	209
Coffee (bags)	6,378	292	262	501	430	7,863
Dyes (crates)	16	...	11	214	1,662	1,903
Cotton fabrics (bags and crates)	32,390	599	589	350	1,254	35,182
Cotton yarn (bags and crates)	59	...	...	...	...	59
Sugar (bags)	...	...	7,203	2,097	99	9,399
Pottery (crates)	...	...	74	12	35	121
Glassware (crates)	69	41	...	...	1,052	1,162
Gold thread (crates)	1	...	1	...	12	14
Furniture (crates)	450	...	99	...	191	758
Iron (bales)†	12,530	...	...	8,430	124	21,066
Iron nails (crates)	121	...	...	2,469	...	2,590
Iron bars (bales)	...	...	69	1,240	...	1,309
Jewelry (crates)	16	...	...	9	...	25
Hides and skins (crates)	109	106	36	43	56	350
Flax (crates)	15	...	25	...	197	237
Sugar loaves (bags and crates)	530	64,666	779	22,253	3,913	92,141
Machinery (bales)	247	73	...	...	...	320
Copper	182	...	...	...	...	182
Sewing machines (crates)	...	...	...	...	224	224
Matches (crates)	412	...	2,376	2	...	2,790
Medicines (crates)	115	2,146	...	...	...	2,261
Sundry goods (bales)	216	612	...	102	2,657	3,587
Spirits (crates)	909	1,892	676	65	98	3,641
Paints and oil (crates)	1,424	...	...	...	...	1,424
Paper (bales)	...	41	20	...	5,876	5,938
Petroleum (crates)	...	...	...	...	29,920	29,920
Wood (pieces)	...	...	...	...	140	140
Canned food (crates)	808	10	1	5	885	1,709
Seeds (bags)	...	...	...	...	84	84
Silk (crates)	...	15	8	8	34	65
Soap (bags and crates)	306	...	...	...	1,411	1,711
Office supplies (crates)	50	...	...	...	10	60
Steel (bales)	...	...	...	282	...	282
Window glass (crates)	1,574	...	...	200	...	1,774
Woolens (bags and crates)	229	25	60	97	7	418
Total	60,893	70,727	12,296	41,530	50,391	235,837

* The original table gives the following breakdown: Austria, Port Said, Santos, Rotterdam, Genoa, Odessa, Italy, Moscow, Russia, and Constantinople; except for petroleum, which was wholly provided by Russia, the bulk of the merchandise under this heading came from Austria, its total being 15,667.—Translator.
† I have translated *collo* throughout as "bale"; alternatives are "package," "piece."—Translator.

imports from Europe in the last few years is shown by the following figures (in pounds sterling):

1905	1,093,150
1906	1,520,707
1907	1,781,166
	4,395,023

this gives an average of £1,465,007 per year.

Commercial usages.—For all kinds of goods, sales are on a cash basis, or by documentary bills which the sender consigns to the Ottoman Bank, where they are claimed by the addressee. The Imperial Ottoman Bank has established branches in Baghdad, Basra, and Mosul.

The main commercial establishments are foreign, and among these are the following:

1. Stephens Lynch and Company (English), which is moreover a river-navigation company with three steamships (import, export).

2. Blockey, Cree, and Company (English), for a long time established in Mesopotamia, deals mainly with the import of cotton fabrics from Manchester (import, export).

3. Berg, Puttman, and Company (German; import, export).

4. The Società Anonima di Commercio (Austrian-Oriental), founded by the Imperial Royal Credit Bank with a share capital of three million crowns; it therefore has a sound basis and enjoys excellent credit (import, export). The main purpose of this company is the development of trade between Austria and the Orient; for this purpose, it has opened branches in all the

TABLE 2

EXPORTS OF BAGHDAD TO INDIA, EUROPE, AND AMERICA, 1907

Merchandise	INDIA		EUROPE	
	Quantity	Value £ (Pounds)	Quantity	Value £ (Pounds)
Grains (bags)	61,183	45,887	95,206	71,404*
Barley (bags)	...	...	Large quantities	
Millet (bags)	1,705	852	2,389	2,986
Pulse	...	...	...	...
Seeds† (bags)	1,723	1,483	9,090	9,043
Almonds (bags)	601	3,606	368	2,208
Rugs (bales)	3	60	695	31,800*
Colocynth (bales)	...	...	681	2,385
Dates (bags)	6,612	4,959	4,032	3,024
Skins (bags)	1,806	1,174	19,141	12,442
Skins (crates)	...	...	13,981	4,893
Skins (bales)	16	320	6,813	102,195
Nutmegs (bags)	1,110	6,660	6,082	36,492
Gum (bags)	27	216	3,926	29,133
Opium‡ (crates)	1,180	82,600	15	1,050
Butter (crates)	...	...	640	1,440
Salted guts (casings) (crates)	...	...	329	6,580
Liquorice roots (bales) §	...	...	1,525	915§
Goat hair (bales)	...	...	1,100	17,600
Dung (bags)	...	...,	4,180	2,090
Wool (bales)	289	2,890	21,160	211,600
Other‖	1,437	2,597	1,342	4,223
Total	77,695	153,304	192,706	548,668

* Considerable re-exports to America from Europe.
† Broken down in original.—Translator.
‡ From Persia to China.
§ Considerable exports to America from Basra.
‖ All items under £1,000 in value; broken down in original.—Translator.

TABLE 3

IMPORTS OF BAGHDAD FROM INDIA, PERSIAN GULF, AND CHINA, 1907

Merchandise	Quantity	Value £ (Pounds)
Rugs (bales)	77	2,310
Cassia (crates)	3,104	9,312
Dyes (crates)	76	2,660
Copper (bales)	120	1,200
Cotton yarn (crates)	189	5,670
Drugs and Medicines (packages)	6,362	25,448
Dry lemons (baskets)	345	2,070
Chinaware (crates)	250	1,500
Ebony wood (pieces)	1,326	5,304
Ginger (bags)	202	1,212
Glass (crates)	508	2,032
Gunnies (bales)	2,467	24,670
Metal furniture (crates)	791	7,910
Henna (baskets)	948	1,896
Indigo (crates)	925	34,225
Wrought iron (bales)	4,312	4,312
Pepper (bags)	3,616	10,848
Cotton fabrics (bales)	7,665	114,975
Wood (pieces)	82,812	8,281
Soap (crates)	499	1,996
Sugar (bags)	5,142	6,427
Sugar candy (bags)	992	1,488
Tamarind (bales)	4,988	2,743
Tea (crates)	19,423	72,836
Tin (sheets)	2,059	14,803
Tobacco (bales)	8,439	16,878
Turmeric (bales)	1,744	2,616
Cotton yarn (bales)	5,129	102,580
Other*	5,098	19,387
Total	169,608	507,581

* All items under £1,000 in value; broken down in original.—Translator.

main Oriental cities; in the Balkans: Constantinople, Bucharest, Sofia, Salonika, Scutari, Yannina, etc.; in Anatolia: Smyrna, Trebizond, Beirut; in Egypt: Alexandria, Cairo, etc.; and also in Persia (Tabriz and Teheran); and it deals with imports in general. Such organization puts it in a position to compete successfully in all the Oriental markets, thus providing Austrian industry with a profitable outlet; hence the government looks at it favorably, supporting its activity and development. (For example, it was entrusted with the official representation of the Imperial Handelsmuseum of Vienna.) Naturally, the company exports German, French, English, and other goods, devoting itself to the exchange of merchandise in general (import, export).

5. F. T. Langridge (English; import, export).

6. Rençon (French; import, export).

7. Simon (Hungarian), representing the Handelsmuseum of Budapest (import, export).

8. Ezra Ashair Salem (Ottoman), representing E. D. Sassoun and Company (import, export).

9. Ezkiel Yahoudi (Ottoman; import).

10. Abdul Kader Pasha Kaderi (Ottoman; export).

11. Eliao Dangouar (Ottoman; import).

12. Ezrah Sassoun–Ezrah Sassoun (Ottoman; export).

13. Meneki Shohet (Ottoman; import).

CHAPTER 7

Taxation in the 1900's

As the following selection points out, until the First World War the fiscal system of Iraq was the same as that of other Ottoman provinces. In the course of the nineteenth century the Ottoman fiscal structure changed considerably. For many centuries, as is characteristic of "feudal" states, the bulk of the revenue raised from the cultivators remained in the hands of the *sipahi* fief-holders (see Part II, chaps. 8 and 9), who used it to meet the costs of defense, security, and other objects of local interest. The sultans, like medieval European monarchs, derived some revenue from the imperial domains and in addition drew on such sources as war spoils, tribute, the poll tax on non-Muslims, customs duties, and the produce of mines and salt works. At first these *shar'i* (i.e., sanctioned by Muslim sacred law) revenues sufficed to defray the expenses of the sultan's janissaries and other dependents, but in time they were increasingly supplemented by various dues regarded as not *shar'i*.[1] More important, the transformation of "feudal" *timar* into tax farms (*iltizam*) greatly increased the cash revenues of the crown. The repeated raising of customs duties in the course of the nineteenth century provided a further growing source of revenue (see Part II, chap. 3).

The first Ottoman budget drawn up on modern lines was that of 1863–64. Revenue was estimated at the equivalent of 346.2 million francs, of which tithes accounted for 94.9 million, the personal tax (*vergi*) for 78.2 million, and customs duties for 57.5 million. Expenditures were put at 327.2 million francs, of which no less than 78.5 million were for debt servicing, and moreover this figure does not include charges on the internal floating debt. Other important items of expenditure were the armed services, which absorbed 123.8 million francs, the ministry of interior and the police, 44.9 million, and the civil list, 27.7 million; allocations to the ministry of instruction and public works, the sole heading showing expenditure on development, amounted to only 1.1 million francs, and the ministry of commerce received 0.5 million.[2]

By way of comparison, the 1911–12 estimates put revenue at £T31,109,000;

[1] Gibb and Bowen, *Islamic Society and the West*, Part II, pp. 1–37.
[2] Velay, *Essai sur l'histoire financière de la Turquie*, pp. 176–88.

of this, taxes on land, livestock, and real estate totaled £T13,429,000, showing how heavy the burden on the peasants had remained (see Part II, chap. 12); customs duties amounted to £T4,556,000; and state monopolies brought in £T2,745,000. On the expenditure side the public debt absorbed £T11,288,000, the armed services £T13,535,000, and the ministry of interior, police, and gendarmerie £T3,228,000; however, appropriations for public works had risen to £T1,186,000, for public instruction to £T851,000, and for commerce and agriculture to £T374,000, amounting in all to about 6.6 per cent of total expenditure.[3]

(See also works by Gibb and Bowen, Ubicini [*Etat présent*], Moravitz, Velay, Mears, Hershlag, and Azzawi [*Al-daraib*] listed in the Bibliography.)

[3] Mears (ed.), *Modern Turkey*, p. 399.

[From Sa'id Himadeh, *Al-nizam al-iqtisadi fi al-'Iraq* (*The Economic System of Iraq*) (Beirut, 1938), pp. 461-69; reproduced by kind permission of the author.]

MAIN SOURCES OF REVENUE

The fiscal system of Iraq before the [First World] War was the one prevailing in the Ottoman Empire, of which Iraq formed a part. At that time the country consisted of three *vilayet's*—Mosul, Baghdad, and Basra; their total public revenue in 1911 was 1,653,000 Iraqi dinars, which may be compared with 6,027,000 dinars for the country in 1936–37. Table 1 shows the amounts derived from the principal sources in the three provinces. . . .

TABLE 1

PUBLIC REVENUE OF IRAQ IN 1911

Source	Revenue in 1911 (Iraqi dinars)	Proportion of Total Revenue (Per Cent)
Agricultural tithes . .	527,175	31.89
Customs duties . . .	380,625	23.02
Sale of public property, movable and immovable	180,450	10.91
Animal tax	179,475	10.85
Pension contributions .	56,850	3.43
Military exemption fees .	52,125	3.15
Land and buildings tax .	44,850	2.71
Posts, telegraphs, telephones	39,900	2.43
Tamattu'	29,625	1.79
Total	1,491,075	90.17

The most important direct taxes were agricultural tithes (*'ushr*), animal tax [*kuda*], land and buildings tax [*werko, vergi*] and *tamattu'*; the leading indirect taxes were customs duties, excise duties on alcoholic drinks, tobacco, and salt; and stamp duties. The Ottoman Public Debts Administration was allocated all, or part of, the revenue from duties on drinks, tobacco, and salt, from stamp duties and from other minor taxes, as well as an additional tax of 3 per cent on imported goods.

AGRICULTURAL TITHES: TAXES ON AGRICULTURAL PRODUCE

As its name indicates, the tithe originally equaled 10 per cent of the gross produce of the soil. But the proportion of the tax changed greatly, and its history is difficult to trace because of the many radical transformations it underwent during the Ottoman period. Some of these changes were reasonable, others were arbitrary, and some had no connection whatsoever with the principle of the tithe.[1] Thus the Turks had ceased to consider the basis of the tax as 10 per cent, and long before 1917 it had been levied at a higher rate, determined by law and custom.[2] The other changes, which

[1] [United Kingdom Government], *Special Report on the Progress of Iraq*, p. 110. [Hereafter cited as *Special Report*.]
[2] In 1883 the tax rate was raised by 1.5 per cent, 1 per cent being allocated to the Agricultural Bank and 0.5 to public education; in 1897 a further addition of 0.5 per

are not connected with the principle of the tithe but which affected the share of the government, were: the imposition of a supplementary tithe on land which could be watered by flow irrigation; the distinction between land to which *tapu* rights had been granted [see part III, chap. 5] and other land; and the imposition of a rent on the latter kind, in the form of a tithe or a fraction of a tithe; and the transfer of part of the tithe or tithes to persons who the government believed could help it and facilitate the imposition and levying of these taxes.[3] Another fundamental departure from the original basis was that the tithe was no longer levied in kind; the general practice in Iraq had become the conversion of the government's share of this tax into a cash sum payable by the taxpayer.[4] The methods used by the Turks for estimating the government's share of the tax were not based on direct estimates of the crops. Among these methods were, first, the carrying-out of the estimate in government departments for such crops as were subject to excise duties; second, the imposition of a fixed rate per unit area [*jarib*] planted to palm trees in Basra and Qurna; third, the imposition of a fixed rate per unit area [*faddan*] for land under winter grains; fourth, the imposition of a fixed rate per unit of machinery used in irrigation. Most of these methods were based on custom, not law, and the public was not aware of the relation between these taxes and the original tithe basis. Usually, the levying and collection of these taxes was farmed out to individuals, against payment of a fixed sum.

This brief account of the old tithe system has brought out serious defects, both theoretical and practical. Thus the principle of calculating the tax as a share of the gross output of the soil implies the inclusion of the additional expenditures for cultivation incurred by the farmer, who is the taxpayer; it therefore discourages the advance of intensive cultivation, without which no real agricultural progress can be made. In addition, the government's revenues from this tax were much less than the amount raised from the farmers and peasants.[5]

If to agricultural tithes are added revenues from other agricultural and natural resources, such as the *werko* on land, tobacco and silk tithes, and taxes on privately owned forests, total proceeds from agricultural and natural resources amounted in 1911 to about 550,950 Iraqi dinars, or 33.33 per cent of the public revenue. This may be compared with present revenues from *istihlak* taxes, payments in lieu of rent, and water dues based on agricultural and natural produce; these revenues amounted in 1936–37 to 636,373 dinars or 10.5 per cent of the total public revenues.[6]

CUSTOMS DUTIES

Until 1838 Turkey adhered to a policy which made foreign trade prohibitive because of very high octroi duties.[7] But in that year the policy was abandoned and a trade convention was concluded with Great Britain [see Part II, chap. 3], and subsequently similar conventions with the other European states. Under these conventions import duties of 5 per cent and export duties of 12 per cent were levied; the high level of the latter contributed to paralyze export trade. The collection of customs duties was farmed out. In 1861 and 1862, the 1838 conventions were replaced by similar ones with all European countries and the United States, raising import duties

---

cent was made and in 1900 one of 0.63, for military purposes; as a result the rate had risen to 12.63 per cent (Kurt Grunwald, *The Government Finances of the Mandated Territories in the Near East* [Tel Aviv, 1932], p. 16, and *Special Report*, p. 110).

[3] *Special Report*, p. 110.

[4] *Ibid.*

[5] This observation regarding the tithe system, which at that time was still the Ottoman system, was made by the special mission appointed in 1925 to study financial conditions in Iraq (*Report of the Financial Mission Appointed by the Secretary of State for the Colonies to Enquire into the Financial Position and Prospects of the Government of Iraq* [London, 1925], p. 12).

[6] *Annual Report of Accounts Department on Iraqi Government Accounts* for fiscal 1936 (in Arabic). [Hereafter cited as *Annual Report.*]

[7] A. Granovsky, *The Fiscal System of Palestine* (Jerusalem, 1935), pp. 23–27.

from 5 to 8 per cent, lowering export duties from 12 to 8 per cent, and making the latter subject to an annual reduction of 1 per cent per annum until such time as they should fall to 1 per cent, which took place in 1869. The Ottoman government insistently demanded the modification of the 1861 and 1862 conventions to permit the raising of import duties, but this was met by strong opposition from the foreign states, even after the treaties had lapsed, in 1890. Things remained unchanged until 1907, when Turkey was permitted to raise its duties by 3 per cent ad valorem, the proceeds to be allocated to the Ottoman Public Debts Administration. Import duties were thus raised to 11 per cent, at which level they remained until the outbreak of the Great War; this rate was levied on all imports except for some exempted goods.[8] The duty was levied on the value of the goods, as estimated by customs officials, which put the importers at the mercy of these evaluators. The only protection available to importers was to pay duties in kind, a procedure which could not be followed for all imported goods. After 1908, duties were levied on the basis of invoices which had to be forwarded together with the goods; payment in kind was replaced by cash payment, and the farming-out of customs duties was abolished, the government itself collecting the dues.

The essential aim of the Ottoman tariff was the raising of revenue for the treasury, not the stimulation of local production by protection and exemption. Thus the uniform 11 per cent duty was insufficient to protect local industry, or local agriculture, which was subject to the crushing tithes. In addition, the impact of the duty on imported industrial raw materials was equal to its impact on manufactured goods. And

an examination of the incidence of customs duties shows that it was relatively heavier on the poor and the middle class than on the rich.

Before the war, revenue from customs duties was much smaller, both absolutely and relatively, than it is today; thus in 1911 the total was 380,625 dinars, or 23.02 per cent of total public revenue, compared to 2,083,225, or 38.9 per cent, in 1935–36 and 2,278,504, or 37.8 per cent, in 1936–37.[9] This increase is due to the rise in the level of duties, the increase in foreign trade, and the reorganization of the administration. Thus the uniform prewar import duty of 11 per cent had given way, by 1934–35, to a tariff wall of about 32 per cent of the value of dutiable imports. Government imports rose from about 2,985,000 dinars in 1912[10]—of which a large part was in transit through Iraq—to 9,331,964 in 1935–36, of which 7,148,161 was declared to be for local consumption and 2,183,803 in transit.

ANIMAL TAX

The animal tax [kuda] was levied on goats, sheep, camels, and water buffaloes, while bulls, donkeys, and mules were exempt. Receipts in 1911 amounted to 179,475 dinars, or 10.85 per cent of public revenue, compared to 227,732, or 3.77 per cent, in 1936–37.

WERKO [VERGI] TAX

The werko, a tax on land and buildings, was imposed in the province of Mosul.[11] Under the decree [iradeh] of April 13, 1887, the rate of the werko was fixed at 0.4 per cent of the value of land subject to tithes and 1.0 per cent of the value of land not subject to tithes.[12] The value that was actually taken as a basis was the sale value, as determined by the estimating committees. New estimates were supposed to be made every five years, but this did not take place

---

[8] Exemption was applied to basic industrial machinery and equipment, agricultural machinery and implements, and materials for construction of railways, roads, and other public and municipal works. Diplomatic and consular representatives of foreign states enjoyed total exemption, and schools, monasteries, hospitals, orphanages, and other religious or charitable institutions partial exemption.

[9] Annual Report.
[10] Special Report, p. 207.
[11] Report by His Majesty's Government on the Administration of Iraq for 1923–24 (London, 1925), pp. 123, 142.
[12] George Young, Corps de Droit Ottoman (Oxford, 1906), p. 119.

and the tax continued to be levied on the basis of the estimate carried out in 1303 A.H. (1887).[13] The *werko* on buildings ranged from 0.5 to 0.8 per cent of the value of buildings occupied by their owners and was 1.0 per cent for rented buildings.[14] Various additions were made to the *werko* from time to time, totaling at times up to 60 per cent of the amount of the *werko* on land and 41 per cent of that on buildings.[15] Receipts from the *werko* on land in Mosul province totaled 20,625 dinars in 1911, and those from that on buildings, 24,225.[16] During the British occupation of Iraq, the *werko* on land was abolished and that on buildings was replaced by a tax on buildings applicable to the whole country.

TAMATTU' TAX

The *tamattu'* tax, which was more of an occupational than an income tax, was of little fiscal importance. In the majority of cases it was based on convenient indices which are presumed to indicate the size of income, and only in a few cases directly on income itself; where such bases were not available the law itself fixed the amount of tax.[17] This tax was abolished at the beginning of the British occupation, since its receipts were incommensurate with the administrative costs of levying it.[18] In its place Iraq now has a tax on income.

OTTOMAN PUBLIC DEBTS ADMINISTRATION

The administration and collection of some items of public revenue were entrusted, before the war, to the Ottoman Public Debts Administration. Among the causes directly responsible for the establishment of this Administration were the large size of the sums borrowed and the difficulties encountered by the Ottoman government in meeting interest payments on the huge debt. Thus the nominal amount of foreign debts in 1875 was 227 million Turkish gold pounds[19] [see Part II, chap. 11]. . . . For its part, the Ottoman government consented to the establishment of the Ottoman Public Debts Administration as an independent international body, and the allocation to it of various items of government revenue. The revenues assigned under the Moharram Decree were of three kinds. First, there were resources directly managed by the Administration, namely, the salt monopoly, stamp duties, duties on alcoholic drinks, duties on fisheries, the silk tithe, duties on hides, and licenses for fishing, shooting of birds, and sale of tobacco. Second, there were revenues that were farmed out, such as the tithe on grains in certain localities and that on the tobacco monopoly. Third, there was the supplementary duty of 3 per cent on customs, which was collected by the government.[20]

The Administration was a large enterprise; in 1914 it had 698 offices, with a staff of 8,931, and its activities extended all over the Ottoman Empire.[21] It managed its resources very efficiently and its revenues rose steadily until the war.[22] In Iraq, the Administration continued to function as an independent entity until 1917.[23] In that same year the tobacco monopoly, the Société de la Régie Co-intéressée des Tabacs de l'Empire Ottoman, was also abolished.

[13] Faris al-Khury, *Mujaz fi 'ilm al-malia* (Damascus, 1924), p. 236.
[14] Grunwald, *op. cit.*, p. 20.
[15] *Ibid.*
[16] *Report by His Majesty's Government*, p. 133.
[17] Said Himadeh, *The Economic Organization of Syria and Lebanon* (Beirut, 1936), p. 398.
[18] Grunwald, *op. cit.*, pp. 22–23.

[19] G. Bie Ravndall, *Turkey: A Commercial and Industrial Handbook* (Washington, 1926), p. 212.
[20] Himadeh, *op. cit.*, p. 434.
[21] *Ibid.*
[22] *Ibid.*
[23] *Review of the Civil Administration of Mesopotamia* (London, 1920), p. 7.

CHAPTER 8

Irrigation Projects in the 1900's

By the end of the nineteenth century a realization of the agricultural potentialities of Iraq and an actual deterioration of the irrigation system, because of flooding, silting, and the consequent diversion of some river branches, as well as continued salination, combined to move the Turkish government to plan some irrigation works. In 1891 a barrage was built at Hindiyya, on the middle Euphrates, but it collapsed ten years later. Attempts to repair it proved fruitless, and in the meantime attention shifted to the over-all irrigation plan for Iraq drawn up by Sir William Willcocks, who had served with great distinction in India and Egypt. This plan, designed to prevent floods, provide irrigation water, and improve navigation, has formed the basis of the irrigation works built by the Iraqi government in the last fifty years; it was elaborated and brought up to date by the Haigh Commission, which drew up its report in 1946–49.

Flood control on the Euphrates was to be ensured by opening an escape near Ramadi into Lake Habbaniya and the Abu Dibis depression; on the Tigris the escape was to be opened from Samarra, into the Tharthar depression. Barrages, designed to raise the water level during the low season, were to be built near Balad and at Kut al-Amarah. And some of the ancient branches and canals were to be cleared.

The only part of this program actually implemented by Willcocks was a new Hindiyya barrage, completed in 1913 at a cost of £500,000, but other works were begun under his supervision. In the interwar period several channels and canals were cleared and some minor barrages were built. It was only after the Second World War, with the great increase in oil revenues accruing to the government (see Part III, chap. 9) that the Willcocks plan was finally carried out and surpassed.

But the progress achieved in the meantime, with the minor works mentioned above and the rapid spread of pump irrigation, should not be underrated. A few pumps were installed in the nineteenth century, and as late as 1921 there were only 143 in the whole country, irrigating 19,000 hectares. By 1929 the number had risen to 2,031 and the area irrigated to 738,000 hectares, and after the end of the Second World War the area thus irrigated exceeded a million hectares.

(See also works by Willcocks, Buckley, Ionides, Sousa, Longrigg [*Four Centuries and Iraq*], and Salter listed in the Bibliography.)

[Sir W(illiam). Willcocks, "Mesopotamia: Past, Present, and Future," *Geographical Journal* (London), XXXV (1910), 1–18; reproduced by kind permission of the Royal Geographical Society.]

. . . In the time of the Sassanian kings of Persia, in the early centuries of the Christian era, the delta probably saw its greatest prosperity. The gigantic Nahrwan canal, 400 feet wide and 15 feet deep, irrigated all the country to the east of the Tigris, and the Dijail irrigated that to the west. The Euphrates gave off the four canals already mentioned by Xenophon, and canals fed by the Babylonian branch from near Babylon irrigated the country right up to the ancient Tigris, or the modern Hai branch. Ammianus Marcellinus, who traversed the whole length of the delta in the fifth century of our era, describes the country as a forest of verdure from end to end.

The centres of development varied from period to period. While during the earliest times, Tel Lo, Senkere, and Ur of the Chaldees were the heart of the country, Sippara and Babylon took their place in Babylonian times, and Opis and Ctesiphon in that of the Persians.

In the seventh century of our era, the Arabs overthrew the Persian Government, and substituted Kufa, Wasit, and Basra, as capitals in place of the earlier cities. These soon gave place to Baghdad, which till to-day has remained the most important town in the delta. Baghdad saw its greatest days about A.D. 800, in the reign of Haroun-el-Rashid. Under the Arabs, the prosperity of the country steadily declined, but the final blow was given by the Mongols under Zengis Khan and the Tartars under Timur in the thirteenth and fourteenth centuries. Previous disasters had drenched the country

in water; it was now drenched in blood. In the anarchy and confusion which ensued, all the great works of antiquity were swept away one after another, until not a single one remains to-day. Nimrod's earthen dam on the Tigris was breached, and the level of the water in the river fell some 25 feet, leaving the great Nahrwan and Dijail canals dry and waterless. Both banks of the Tigris in the upper part of the delta became a desert. The Tigris, lower down its course, fared no better. Near Kut, the river breached its left bank and wasted itself in the marshes on the Persian frontier, while the ancient channel past Wasit and Tel Lo received a limited supply of water only in flood-time. The ancient dyke across the Sakhlawia branch of the Euphrates was breached, and Western Baghdad with its irrigation system was wiped out. All the canals taking water from the Euphrates which had come down from a remote antiquity, the Issa, Sarsar, Melcha, Kutha, Araktu, Surat, Nil, and Nars, silted up and ceased running; and finally in our day the Euphrates of Babylon has dwindled into an insignificant stream, and the whole of the waters of the river are flowing through the Nejef marshes. The Tigris and Euphrates, left to themselves, have deserted the high lands which they irrigated in old days, and are now traversing the lowlands and marshes along the extreme east and west of the delta.

Things would have been far more desperate than they actually are had not a new crop been introduced into the country, which has permitted of large areas of swamp being turned into valuable fields. When rice first appeared in the delta no one can tell, but it is the most valuable crop in the country to-day after the date crop.

The delta of the two rivers has an area of some 12,000,000 acres, of which about 9,000,000 are desert, and 2,500,000 acres freshwater swamp. In the upper parts of the delta there are stretches of cultivation along the river-banks in places, and along a number of small canals; but in the lower part of the delta there are magnificent reaches of date groves and gardens interspersed with clover and cereals, and large areas under rice in flood.

We have seen that the earliest settlers in the delta clustered round the reaches of the rivers where the water was free of silt. It is the same to-day. This water, though free of sand, is opaque in colour, and retains the rich chemical ingredients so necessary for agriculture. It is totally different from the dark-looking, transparent water which has stagnated in the marshes.

The rainfall is on the average about 8 inches per annum. The whole of the rain falls in winter, and there have been years in succession when the total fall has not exceeded 4 inches. Of such tracts, President Roosevelt, in his first message to Congress, has well said, "In the arid region it is water, not land, which measures production." We therefore turn to the amount of water in the two rivers. The Euphrates has a high flood of 120,000 cubic feet per second, and a low supply of 10,000 cubic feet. The corresponding figures for the Tigris are 180,000 and 10,000.

The rivers are in flood in March, April, and May, while August and September are the months of low supply. We may, without the aid of reservoirs, count on 6,000,000 acres of winter crops, and 3,000,000 acres of summer crops. We shall have wheat, barley, and beans in winter, and cotton, Indian corn, and rice in summer. To-day, if the winter rains are above the average, large areas of land are put under barley, for the deserts of Mesopotamia are not deserts like those of Egypt, but in great part steppes capable of supporting millions of sheep. The date palm is at home everywhere in the delta, while the Basra groves are credited with ten million trees. Dates and wheat are considered as growing wild at Anah.

The winter is severe, and the summer is very hot and prolonged. Live stock of every kind is abundant, and of superb quality. Old Mahomed Pasha il Daghistani has two hundred Arab mares in his studs at Azazia, on the Tigris. Live stock will always be one of the principal exports of the country.

The delta is strangely flat. Baghdad, removed some 500 miles from the sea, is only 115 feet above sea-level. Opposite Baghdad the Euphrates is 25 feet higher than the Tigris. Between the two rivers runs a regular valley, across which are carried the giant banks of the ancient canals like miniature hills.

The waters of the two rivers and the soil of the country are yellow in colour, and very different from the black soil of Egypt. The percentage of lime in water and soil is as high as fifteen, and consequently the soil is far more friable than the stiff clay of the Nile Valley. The chemical analyses of soil and water testify to their richness.

Beginning at Beled, the delta first consists of bare plains of clay with the silt banks of countless canals, showing what a desperate fight the wretched agriculturists made for existence when the dams were carried away and the level of the water fell. We then have alternate stretches of level country covered with a thorny leguminous plant which dies down in winter, and the same bare plains which we met in the north. Near the river are jungles of liquorice plant and the same leguminous thorn. On the rivers themselves, but especially on the Euphrates, wherever there is a foreshore there is a luxuriant growth of poplars and sometimes of willows. On the upper Euphrates, and as one approaches Babylon, we have great stretches of salted land interspersed with bare plains and low sanddrifts. All this land is capable of easy levelling and reclamation. The presence of 15 per cent. lime in the soil renders reclamation very easy compared with similar work in the dense clays of Egypt. One is never far away from the giant banks of old canals and ruins of ancient towns. As one goes south the salted land increases in area, and then the marshes begin with their stretches of rice. On the lower Euphrates and on the Basra river are luxuriant date groves and gardens mingled with wheat and clover. The lower Euphrates, past Nasrie and Suk es Shayuk, is a veritable garden surrounded with water.

The junction of the Tigris and Euphrates is no longer at Kurna, where it had been for 500 or 600 years, but at Garmat Ali, near Basra.

Such is Mesopotamia to-day. From what has been already said it will not be difficult to gather that the first works before the hydraulic engineer are the protection of the country from floods and the provision of water as free of silt as possible. The levels and surveys of the twelve engineers who are working for me in Baghdad, with a devotion worthy of the task they have undertaken, have shown that we can do both. We have already submitted to the Government a project for escaping the excess waters of the Euphrates down the depressions of the ancient Pison,[1] the first of the four rivers of Genesis. An expenditure of £350,000 should suffice for the work, and it should take three years to carry out. I am under and not over the mark when I say that the cultivated area will be doubled and the yield of wheat trebled along the Euphrates the day this work is completed. The cultivators to-day are afraid to sow anything like the crop they could put in; and, moreover, they count on losing everything every third year. If Noah had been an hydraulic engineer, he would have constructed the Pison river escape instead of an ark, and saved not only his family but his country as well, This escape has been approved of by the Turkish Government, and the necessary funds have been assigned for beginning it immediately. Its effect will be far-reaching.

The surveys and levels are now in hand for a project for the great canal of the delta, which will irrigate 3,000,000 acres of the best land in Mesopotamia, and carry water free of silt. North-west of Baghdad, between the Tigris and the Euphrates, lies a strange depression known as the Akkar Kuf

[1] The Habbania-Abu Dibbis depression.—Editor.

lake. It has an area of 40 square miles at extreme low water, and 300 square miles when full. Its level is 35 feet below that of the Euphrates, and 10 below that of the Tigris. Into this depression runs the Sakhlawia branch of the Euphrates, the ancient Hiddekel, or the third of the rivers of Genesis, with a channel 250 feet wide and 25 feet deep at the head, which splits up into some twenty small channels as it enters the western side of the lake. The head of the Sakhlawia branch will be provided with two powerful regulators to control the supply leaving the Euphrates. On the Euphrates downstream of the branch will be a barrage to control the river itself. These works will ensure our supply from the side of the Euphrates.

On the Tigris, we propose to construct at Beled, near the site of Nimrod's dam, a weir for controlling the river. This work will be above the Tigris rapids, where the water is 60 feet higher than that of Lake Akkar Kuf. From the upstream side of this weir we shall construct a canal to irrigate the rich lands north of Baghdad, with an escape into the lake. The escape will keep the canal free of silt, and feed the lake with Tigris water. We shall thus have all the water we need from both rivers, entering the lake at its western and northern sides.

From the south-eastern end of the lake, near Baghdad, will start a canal which will run along the right bank of the Tigris and finally tail into the Hai branch or ancient Tigris near its head. In the days to come, this canal will irrigate 6 million acres, but not now. The excessive silt of some fifteen days per annum, which does all the mischief, will be decanted in the lake, and so will all the silt we do not need. At certain stages of the flood when the river-water is not heavily charged with silt, it will be possible to take in supplies at different points of the canal. All these details will come later. We are now concerned with broad issues.

The left bank of this canal, which I shall submit to the authorities to be called after the name of the first constitutional sovereign of Turkey, will act as a dyke for protecting the country from the Tigris floods, and will, moreover, carry a railway to transport the abundant harvests of the country. We shall again see Sippara, Kutha, Jil, Niffur, Erech, Tel Senkere, and Tel Lo important centres of life and prosperity.

Dealing with water free of silt, it will not be necessary to complete the whole length of the canal before we can begin sending down our supplies, as we should have had to do with muddy water. We shall first complete some 30 miles, and immediately use the water for irrigation in this reach while we are digging the second reach of 30 miles. In this way we shall waste no time.

The works should, I think, be carried out on the following principles. The Government should undertake the construction and maintenance of the barrages on the rivers, the main feeder canals, the main drains, the navigation works if any, the flood escapes, and the flood embankments. In this way the control of the rivers and their supplies would be in the hands of the authorities. All minor canals, drains, and masonry works of every kind should be left to the agricultural community and to interested parties. In return for constructing and maintaining these works they would receive title-deeds for the lands they irrigated. I had at first thought of recommending the Chenab system of irrigation works, but acquaintance with the people has taught me that all details should be left to the agriculturists themselves. They have their own ideas, and will be far happier working on their own lines, many of which have come down from the remotest antiquity, and are well worthy of preservation.

I have shown how the country can be protected from floods, and how a beginning can be made with the irrigation of 3,000,000 acres of land capable of producing annually 1,000,000 tons of wheat, and 2,000,000 cwt. of cotton. It now remains to consider how we are going to get this produce to the markets, where it will be sold, and how we are going to dispose of the millions of sheep and hundreds of thousands of cattle which the delta will contain.

Every merchant and man of business I have talked with in Baghdad is convinced of one thing, and that is that the backward state of the country is due in great part to the fact that while communication is open by river with the east, it is to the west that the whole produce of the country wants to find a way. In this direction there is no outlet. The principal products of Mesopotamia to-day—sheep, cows, buffaloes, wool, liquorice, wheat, barley, and rice— have their market in the Eastern Mediterranean and in Europe, and all the imports the country stands in need of could come most readily from Europe. What is wanted, therefore, is a cheap railway connecting Baghdad with the Mediterranean by the shortest and cheapest line possible. Such a railway would have its outlet on the Mediterranean coast near Tyre and Sidon. These centres of commerce did not place themselves by accident where we find them to-day. They fulfilled the requirements of the trade of Western Asia. Haifa and Beirut, to the immediate south and north of Tyre and Sidon, are the modern representatives of these old Phoenician cities. They are connected by railway with Damascus. Very shortly Tripoli, to the north of Beirut, will be connected by railway with Homs, on the Damascus-Aleppo railway.

Any railway going east from Damascus or Homs must pass through Palmyra, founded by Solomon in Israel's great days, and the capital of Zenobia in later times. From Palmyra will diverge the railways of the future, which will either go north to Thapsacus on the Euphrates, another creation of King Solomon, or to Der Zor of the Khalifs, or east-wards to Abu Kimal near Salahia, a creation of Saladin's. The Damascus–Baghdad railway will pass through Palmyra, Abu-Kimal, Hit, and Baghdad. At Abu Kemal the railway will tap the only part of the upper Euphrates valley capable of great development. In the centre of this tract is situated the rising town of Meyadin, on the site of the ancient Rehoboth. At Hit we have the terminus of free navigation on the Euphrates and the future port of the river. Rivers whose waters are used up in irrigation have their ports where they begin to be navigable.

The Euphrates upstream of Hit, up to El Kaim past Anab, has a narrow valley, but the current is sufficiently strong to turn large water wheels, which irrigate the country up to the edge of the desert. Upstream of Suk-es-Shayuk this is the only tract on either of the rivers which enjoys perennial irrigation without having to lift the water by means of oxen or pumps. For the area cultivated the population is very dense and the crops excellent. We can here form an idea of what the country will be when perennial irrigation with free flow is available over extensive areas.

From El Kaim near Abu Kimal right up to Meskene opposite Aleppo, the current is incapable of turning water-wheels, and the cultivation is confined to the areas flooded by the river or irrigated by lifting machinery. From Abu Kemal to Der Zor past Meyadin the valley is very broad, and, judging from the ruins of towns and villages, must have been at one time well cultivated. To-day the cultivation is confined to the water's edge. From above Der Zor to Meskene past Rakka, the summer residence of Harun-el-Rashid, the valley contracts and the ground is covered with dense jungle, which supports very many buffaloes, sheep, and camels. Occasionally one meets a patch of rich cultivation, as at Meskene, where an Englishman had erected many water-wheels and was preparing to put up a 20 H.P. engine and pump.

The desert at Hit is flat, and only 50 to 100 feet above the level of the Euphrates valley. This height gradually increases until at Meskene it is from 300 to 400 feet. For some miles on either side of the valley the desert is broken up into ravines; but as one leaves the river the desert becomes flat, and was described by Xenophon as being level like the sea. The further north one goes the more undulating becomes the desert, but south of Der Zor the undulations are insignificant. Here and there one meets a wady finding its way to the Euphrates

valley. Gypsum is the ordinary rock, and there are considerable outcrops of limestone, while immense areas are covered with pebbles, and are known as haswa to the Arabs.

During the winter months the deserts are covered with grass and the hollows are sown with barley. This refers to the country past Hit. The rainfall increases as one goes northwards, and by the time one reaches Meskene the whole country is capable of producing barley with the aid of the rainfall.

The total length of the railway from Damascus to Baghdad will be 550 miles which could be constructed for £2,200,000. This allows £4,000 per mile along an easy alignment, while Nigeria is being developed traversing more difficult country at £3,000 per mile. According to the Beduins and the Turkish officers who annually escort the sheep from Abu Kemal to Damascus, water is sufficiently evenly distributed to allow of hundreds of thousands of sheep travelling from the Euphrates delta to Damascus.

In addition to the transport of the exports and imports of the Tigris-Euphrates delta, the railway from Baghdad to Damascus will be the highway for the merchandise of Persia and for all the Moslem pilgrims of Central Asia to the holy cities of Islam. It will carry all the materials and fuel needed for the future irrigation works of the delta, and when continued along the bank of the great central canal to Basra, it will be the shortest route possible between east and west, and will one day be carrying the mails between Europe and India.

Though zealously advocating the direct railway connecting the Tigris-Euphrates delta with the Mediterranean, as without it the development of the country will not be possible, my hopes are centered in the delta itself, where it is my ambition to see the works carried out which we are planning to-day. I know that in these western countries of Europe, where rainfall is timely and abundant, and where ruin and disaster cannot overtake a country in a day, we are apt to imagine that works of restoration must also take long years to bear any fruit. But in the arid regions of the Earth it is not so. There, the withdrawal of water turns a garden into a desert in a few weeks; its restoration touches the country as with a magician's wand. In her long history of many thousands of years Babylonia has again and again been submerged, but she has always risen with an energy and thoroughness rivalling the very completeness and suddenness of her fall. She has never failed to respond to those who have striven to raise her. Again it seems that the time has come for this land, long wasted with misery, to rise from the very dust and take her place by the side of her ancient rival, the land of Egypt. The works we are proposing are drawn on sure and truthful lines, and the day they are carried out, the two great rivers will hasten to respond, and Babylonia will yet once again see her waste places becoming inhabited, and the desert blossoming like the rose.

CHAPTER 9

The Struggle for Oil in Iraq

The discovery of petroleum in Pennsylvania in 1859, and the subsequent development of the oil industry in the United States and Russia, led to a world-wide search for oil by the major American, British, and Dutch companies. In the Middle East the first country to grant an oil concession was Iran, but the two earliest ones, in 1872 and 1889, were canceled, and it was not until 1908 that oil was struck in commercial quantities. In Egypt sporadic attempts to find oil were made, starting in the 1880's, but no discovery was made until 1909; in 1911 the rights of the company that had struck oil were taken over by Anglo-Egyptian Oil Fields, an affiliate of Shell, which has continued to exploit the Red Sea fields. After the First World War other British and American companies joined the search for oil in Egypt, with varying degrees of success.

In the Ottoman Empire the Mining Law of 1886 was amended in 1901 and in 1906 was replaced by a more liberal code, under which some leases were issued to Ottoman subjects. At the same time, several British and American companies took out exploration licenses and started prospecting in various parts of Syria, Palestine, Anatolia, and Arabia, but none of these efforts resulted in any substantial discovery. In the Persian Gulf area the British government, as part of its policy to deny access to that region to other Great Powers, signed agreements in 1913–15 with the rulers of Kuwait, Bahrein, Oman, Qatar, the Trucial Coast, and Najd, by which they undertook not to grant oil concessions without British approval.[1]

The early history of the Turkish Petroleum Company, which eventually obtained a concession in Iraq in 1925 and changed its name to Iraq Petroleum Company in 1929, is described in the following selection. After the First World War two major controversies centered on this company, both of which were resolved by the "Red Line" Agreement of 1928. The first arose from United States pressure for the inclusion of American interests, which were eventually allotted 23.75 per cent of the shares, the French the same, and the British and Anglo-Dutch twice as much. The second concerned the provision of the 1914 agreement, under which the participating groups undertook "on their behalf and

[1] Longrigg, *Oil in the Middle East*, pp. 25–27.

on behalf of companies associated with them not to be interested directly or indirectly in the production or manufacture of crude oil in the Ottoman Empire" except in Egypt, Kuwait, and the transferred territories on the Turkish-Iranian frontier. The "Red Line" Agreement upheld this self-denying clause, which was not formally abolished until 1948 and which greatly complicated the subsequent pattern of concessions in the Middle East.

In the course of the next fifteen years I.P.C. affiliates obtained concessions in the Levant and in several Arabian sheikhdoms as well as in the remaining parts of Iraq. Most of these concessions were subsequently abandoned but some developed major sources of production, e.g., in Qatar and Basra. In the meantime, starting in Bahrein in 1930, American interests (mainly Standard Oil of New Jersey, Standard Oil of California, Socony, The Texas Company, and Gulf Oil Corporation) developed some of the largest fields in the region—Saudi Arabia, the Neutral Zone, and, in partnership with British Petroleum, Kuwait. Recent years have seen the entry of several other companies into the region, including Italian, Japanese, Belgian, and German, and the setting-up of national companies owned and operated by Middle Eastern governments.

As a result of these developments, and of the investment of some $5 billion in the industry, the Middle East has become a major producer of oil. In 1933 the region's output was only 7.5 million tons, or 4 per cent of the world total, but by 1964 this had risen to 384 million, or over 27 per cent; at that date the region was estimated to contain more than 60 per cent of the world's proven oil resources.

(See also works by Longrigg [*Oil in the Middle East*], Shwadran, Issawi and Yeganeh, and Philby listed in the Bibliography.)

[From Karl Hoffmann, *Oelpolitik und angelsächsischer Imperialismus* (Berlin, 1927), pp. 67–72.]

... Just as German Near East policy, with the Baghdad Railway and its extension to the Persian Gulf, cut to pieces the English idea of an overland connection from the eastern basin of the Mediterranean Sea to India, in like manner the Mesopotamian oil interests of the Deutsche-Bank group concerned with the Baghdad Railway came into conflict with British oil strategy. The following time considerations are important: in the year 1903 the Baghdad Railways document was signed, and the next year, 1904, the realization of the English encirclement policy began in a systematic way and Lord Fisher produced his new program of support for an oil-burning fleet.

The Mesopotamian interests of the Deutsche-Bank–Petroleum A.G. group were based partly on the above-mentioned special treaty of 1904 of the Anatolian Railway Company and partly on Article 22, Section I, of the concession document dated March 5, 1903, of the Baghdad Railway Company. There it was stated that "the concessionaire may exploit mineral deposits discovered in a zone 20 kilometers wide on either side of the roadbed, by following the laws and regulations pertaining to [the deposits] but without this constituting a privilege or a monopoly for him."[1] To the extent that the latter limitation might have involved Mesopotamian oil, it was explicitly removed through the agreement of the Anatolian Railway Company,

[1] See Walther Schweer, *Die türkisch-persischen Erdölvorkommen* (Hamburg, 1919), p. 221.

concluded in 1904 with the Turkish civil list, i.e., with Sultan Abdul Hamid. In this agreement, the Deutsche-Bank group was granted special privileges, including, for one, the right to explore the oil fields in the *vilayet*'s of Mosul and Baghdad and, for another, the right to an option for their exploitation. Whether or not this agreement constituted a monopoly, it certainly created the constitutive preconditions for one.

At that time the English had no designs of any kind regarding oil concessions in Mesopotamia. At the outset the English had been satisfied with blocking a possible penetration of the Deutsche-Bank into southern Persia, indirectly at first, through the Board of Admiralty, i.e., through their representations with Lord Strathcona and William Knox D'Arcy. But in 1908 positive countermeasures began. Here also time considerations are important. In the year 1907 the agreement reached between Lord Curzon and Prince Trubetskoy over a division of Persia into north and south, or into English and Russian spheres of influence, had come into being; likewise in the year 1907, according to later testimony of Admiral Kolchak before his Bolshevik trial court, a crucial meeting of the Russian crown council is said to have taken place, in which the decision to leave the German Reich in the lurch for the sake of future policy and to choose the party of the "entente," i.e., Great Britain, was imposed on the tsar's government. With that the system of encirclement in the east—in the Near East as well as in Europe—was essentially complete; and in 1908 the Turkish revolution took place. It created for British policy initially the impression that it might be possible to pry the Young Turk regime away from the German orientation of Abdul Hamid and to induce it to change its course in a way unfriendly to Germany.

Even before the fall of Abdul Hamid, D'Arcy appeared in 1908 as a competitor for Mesopotamian oil, without, however, getting a concession or any sure hope for one, while at the same time in that area the

Burmah Oil Company, on its own account, was having its engineers do experimental drillings. Under the at least "moral" cover of the Admiralty, there followed in 1909 the founding of the Anglo-Persian Oil Company, so that now the cross-blows [*Querstösse*] from the southeast, with powerful support in the Persian Gulf, were considered all the more lasting. D'Arcy then maintained that he had obtained a promise from two Turkish grand vizirs that he would be given the concession for Mesopotamia after 1912. A new company, perhaps for taking on this concession, had been formed under the name "African and Eastern Concessions, Ltd." (capitalized at £50,000). A positive connection between the two [D'Arcy and the new company] was not clearly distinguishable, however.[2] Apparently a Shell enterprise or Sir Ernest Cassel with the "National Bank of Turkey"—or both—had stood behind the new company from the very beginning.

A parallel expansion of the Shell group was generally observable at the same time— approximately from 1907–8 until 1912– 13. . . .

Shell extended its Russian holdings in 1913 with other annexations. During this time the "Anglo-Egyptian Oil Fields" (with a nominal capital of £1,808,000) had been set up in Egypt. In other words, the conscious strategy of production in an oil-encirclement policy corresponded to the political system of encirclement directed against us [Germany].

But the British, in pinning their hope on the Young Turk regime, had been thoroughly mistaken. Instead of separating themselves from us, the Young Turks stuck to the earlier foreign-policy direction of their empire. In the Mesopotamian oil question they seemed to prefer a compromise between the German and English interests to bringing the conflict to a head,

[2] See, in addition to Schweer, *op. cit.*, E. H. Davenport and Sidney R. Cooke, *The Oil Trusts and Anglo-American Relations* (London, 1924), and Wilhelm Mautner-Amsterdam, "Der Kampf um die mesopotamischen Erdölvorkommen," *Petroleum*, 1924, Nos. 22 and 23.

and in the period of 1912 to 1914 there was Bethmann-Hollweg's policy of German-English understanding with its aim for a "Baghdad peace." Under the influence of this policy, or making use of it, Sir Ernest Cassel in particular worked for a unification of English and German interests in the Mesopotamian oil question. Out of this arose the "Turkish Petroleum Company," which was to become world-famous after the war.

According to the agreement of October 23, 1912, the Deutsche-Bank group, by taking and contributing their Mesopotamian oil rights, entered the "African and Eastern Concessions, Ltd.," which, with an increase in capital to £80,000, now took the name "Turkish Petroleum Company." The division of shares was as follows: 50 per cent for the National Bank of Turkey (Cassel), 25 per cent for the Anglo-Saxon Petroleum Company (Royal Dutch Shell), and 25 per cent for the Deutsche-Bank group. Why the latter contented itself with a minority share of 25 per cent is not clear. Allegedly it was compensated through concessions other than commercial oil. In the beginning, the partnership in the Turkish Petroleum Company was conceived and construed as a purely commercial agreement. But it rather quickly lost this meaning, since after a while the British government was able to dominate through the Anglo-Persian Oil Company.

In 1913, when Churchill sent his "research committee" under Sir Edmund Slade to South Persia, the statutory entry of the government into the Anglo-Persian Oil Company seems already to have been a certainty, so that its interest was immediately carried over to the Turkish Petroleum Company. By referring to D'Arcy and the promise of the two Turkish vizirs, i.e., to what it supposed to be valid claims to a concession for the Anglo-Persian Oil Company, the government was able, shortly before its own entry, to effect the entry of the Anglo-Persian Oil Company into the Turkish Petroleum Company. On March 19, 1914, a "re-constitution" of the Turkish Petroleum Company ensued, which mainly involved a withdrawal by the National Bank of Turkey of its 50 per cent share of the total capital, at the once more increased level of £160,000, in favor of the Anglo-Persian Oil Company. The pertinent document was signed not only by representatives of the two companies, but also by representatives of the two governments, Sir Eyre A. Crowe for the government of His Britannic Majesty and Herr von Kühlmann for the imperial German government.

With this the Turkish Petroleum Company, with a 75 per cent majority shared by two British groups, was turned into a tool of British oil policy and, because of its "simple majority" 50 per cent of the Anglo-Persian Oil Company, into a branch of the British government concern. Its concession for the *vilayet's* of Mosul and Baghdad in Mesopotamia, which subsumed the "right of option" of the Anatolian Railway Company of 1904, was confirmed anew, granted once more, or recognized, as a "German-English concession" through an *iradeh* of June 28, 1914, of which the English ambassador, Sir Louis Mallet, handled the distribution to interested European quarters. To the extent that the Germans had a voice in this "reorganization," the transaction was connected in a vague way with the initially secret agreements of the "Baghdad peace" which were reached by Prince Lichnowsky and Sir Edward Grey in July, 1914, and could no longer be ratified. The Deutsche-Bank group was allegedly promised participation in the British shipping monopoly on the Shatt al Arab (mouth of the Tigris-Euphrates), as well as in shipping in the interior on the Tigris and the Euphrates.

That was the Turkish Petroleum Company shortly before the war; the outbreak of war precipitously dissipated the form it then had. After the war the legality of its monopolistic concession for Mesopotamia was disputed. It was claimed that this concession of June 28, 1914, had not been ratified by the Turkish parliament. In addition, it was claimed that on the part of the Turks even the *iradeh* had not stipulated the conditions of the concession exactly and perfectly, so that basically no real "concession" had been awarded. And finally it was claimed that, on the part of the Germans and English, a documentary entry of the old German right in the names of the Turkish Petroleum Company had not taken place and, because of the outbreak of war, could no longer have taken place. In any case, Turkey, after her entry into the war in November, 1914, notified the Anglo-Persian Oil Company that she viewed as void the permission given earlier.

Long before this notification, England had removed the German share of 25 per cent and transferred it to loyal hands, to the administration of Launcelot Grey Hugh Smith, chairman of the Turkish Petroleum Company, so that England, from its own point of view, had obtained full ownership. And in August, 1914, long before the entry of Turkey into the war, the British Empire had already begun military operations in Mesopotamian districts, had continued these operations with tenacity until the conquest of Baghdad in March, 1917, and in November, 1918, after the cessation of hostilities, had occupied Mosul as well. Under her own power Great Britain, even before the signing of the Versailles treaty, discussions with France having become pressing, disposed of the participation relationship and, by taking up Berenger's ideas, gave up or offered to give up 25 per cent to France.

Along with the situation based on military power there was a legal situation which was juridically opaque. For that reason Mesopotamia became the main arena of conflict in this hemisphere, while Mexico remained the main arena of conflict in the Western Hemisphere; and with the objections of North America, the "Mosul question" which arose took on a world-wide political scope and fame. . . .

PART IV

Syria

SYRIA
Introduction

In the early medieval period Syria failed to reach the level of economic prosperity attained by Iraq, but it never sank as low as Iraq did after the thirteenth century. For one thing, whereas Iraq's agriculture was based on an intricate and fragile irrigation system (see Part III, Introduction), Syria's agriculture could rely on rainfall and could therefore more easily survive wars and misgovernment. For another, order never broke down so completely in Syria. Under the Mamluks, and during most of the Ottoman period, the central government retained control over the greater part of the productive areas of Syria. The country was closer to the capital of the Empire than Iraq was and had great strategic significance; and the fact that it was the starting point of the pilgrimage caravans to the Holy Cities of Arabia gave it a certain measure of protection. In addition, the industrial activity of the Syrian towns did not slacken, and urban life continued to flourish. In the fourteenth and early fifteenth centuries both Damascus and Aleppo may have had as many as 100,000 inhabitants—a figure unmatched in Europe at that time, except in Italy—and in the sixteenth and seventeenth centuries the population of Aleppo was probably around 200,000, putting it in the class of Constantinople and Cairo. Lastly, Syria's accessibility to Europe by sea greatly facilitated the establishment of commercial contacts. Even during and after the Crusades trade between Syria and Europe never ceased completely, and in the sixteenth and seventeenth centuries it increased considerably; in addition to exporting its own agricultural and industrial products, Syria had a brisk transit trade, re-exporting goods from Iran and India and European merchandise destined for the Persian Gulf.

Around the middle of the eighteenth century, however, the situation in Syria began to deteriorate drastically. The central government lost its grip on the country and the various pashas and governors came to rule their provinces almost independently of Constantinople; sometimes, as in Damascus and Mount Lebanon, they even succeeded in handing down the reins of government to their sons and grandsons. But most of them failed completely to provide the order and security which Syria needed so badly. Their unruly soldiery, frequently out of control, pillaged and destroyed. The feuds between rival factions, quarters, and villages proceeded unchecked. Worst of all, the beduins raided the countryside with impunity, as far west as the Palestinian coast. Some towns, such as Aleppo and Hama, paid protection money to the neighboring tribes, as did many villages; other villages, unable to meet the combined extortions of the government and the beduins, were deserted by their inhabitants (see Part IV, chaps. 1 and 5).

This internal decay was accelerated by outside forces. The decline of the Persian economy dealt a blow to the transit trade in silk and other goods, which had played an important part in the economic life of Aleppo and Damascus. Still worse was the growing insecurity in the Syrian desert, which led to a suspension of the mail service between India and England and caused a diversion of transit trade from Aleppo to Erzurum (see Part II, chap.2). A comparable deterioration occurred in the Mediterranean, where the long series of wars between England, France, and Spain, as well as the Russo-Ottoman war of 1768–74, frequently interrupted trade.

Further disasters struck Syria in the first half of the nineteenth century: Napoleon's expedition in Palestine and his retreat; the confusion and local wars that followed; Muhammad Ali's invasions and the Ottoman and European counterblows; and the civil strife that flared up in Lebanon from 1840 to 1860, in Aleppo in 1850, and in Damascus in 1860. The establishment of steam navigation in the Black Sea and the opening of the Suez Canal diverted some transit trade away from Syria. But also at work were new forces of regeneration, which made themselves felt increasingly after 1830. The Egyptian occupation (1830–41) introduced order and security, at least for a time, removed many of the restrictions from which the Christian minority had suffered, opened the country to foreigners, and activated its economy.[1] The establishment of Commercial Courts, composed of both foreign merchants and Syrian Muslims, Christians, and Jews, in Beirut and Damascus in 1850 gave merchants a greater sense of security and stimulated trade.[2] The Christian Maronites had been in close touch with Rome since the sixteenth century, and a much looser connection also developed between the Orthodox and the Greek and Russian churches. Thanks to these contacts and to

---

[1] See the reports of the British consul-general in Egypt, Col. Campbell, and other consular agents in MacGregor, *Commercial Statistics*, II, 127–56.

[2] The remarks of the British consul in Beirut on the establishment of a commercial court administering European law are worth quoting. "A comparison of two systems, the one the offspring of a dark age adopted by a people wholly unacquainted with foreign commerce, the other the result of ages of civilization and experience, cannot fail to show the vast superiority of the latter. A people so intelligent as the Syrians will not be slow in perceiving this; and a radical change in the Mahometan system of law must, as already be observed, be the consequence" (Despatch from N. Moore to Lord Palmerston, May 30, 1850, Public Record Office, F.O. 78, no. 836). The court at Damascus was formed as follows: the European consul submitted seven names, two Europeans, the other five "Syrian Christians and Jews enjoying Foreign Protection" to which the Ottoman commissioner added five Muslims (including the president of the court), two Christians, and a Jew (C. Calvert to Palmerston, June 15, 1850, F.O. 78, no. 837). A court was established in Aleppo in 1858 but soon broke down (Skene to Bulwer, March 31, 1859, F.O. 78, no. 1452).

the establishment of religious schools in Lebanon, Christians received a fair measure of western education, attained some understanding of the contemporary world, and were thus able to play an important part as entrepreneurs, civil servants, and professional men in the economic development of Syria. Their position was both supplemented and reinforced by the influx of European and American missionaries, educators, and traders.[3]

Economic relations with Europe were greatly strengthened by the establishment of steam navigation in the Mediterranean. By 1840 two lines, a British and an Austrian, had regular services to Syria, and although the British company soon ceased operation, its place was taken by a French one. The number of steamships calling at Syrian ports increased rapidly thereafter. Writing in 1862, J. L. Farley could say: "Now the mails leave London for Syria every Friday via Marseilles and every Monday via Trieste; while English steamers run regularly between Beirut and Liverpool."[4] By 1914 nine lines had regular services to Syria, at intervals ranging from a week to a month, and the freighters of several companies made irregular calls.[5] And whereas in the 1830's the total shipping entering the port of Beirut—which was already by far the most important of the Levant—averaged well under 50,000 tons a year, by 1886 it had risen to over 600,000 tons.[6] The building of a modern port in Beirut in 1890–95 by a French concessionary company, raised Beirut's tonnage to 1,672,000 by 1910; but traffic to other ports also increased greatly, the corresponding figure for Jaffa being 1,115,000 tons and that for Alexandretta 632,000.[7]

These developments stimulated the production of cash crops for export and the transformation of the economy from a subsistence to a market one, especially in

[3] According to the French consulate in Beirut, in 1826 out of 34 commercial firms dealing with Europe in that town, 15 belonged to local Christians and 6 to "Turks," i.e., Muslims. In 1862, out of 44 silk-reeling firms, 33 belonged to natives, who controlled 1,350 of the 2,200 pans in use; most of these industrialists were also Christians (France, Ministère des Affaires Etrangères, Correspondance commerciale [Beyrouth], I, 398 [1826], and VII, 354 [1862]).

In 1854, the British consul in Beirut reported: "Indeed the British Trade in Syria, which is rapidly increasing has passed, almost entirely, into the hands of Native Merchants, who are the Agents of Levantines [i.e., Greeks] naturalized and domiciled in London" (Moore to Clarendon, June 30, 1854, F.O. 78, no. 1031). The names mentioned in this and other dispatches show that most of these merchants were Christians.

It is also significant that when, in 1854, the local government in Beirut floated—in a single day—a loan of 1,000,000 piastres (over £8,000), the European merchants subscribed 700,000 piastres, "the Rayah Merchants took up a large portion of the remainder; and the Mahomedan Merchants only came forward when there was but little more required" (Calvert to Stratford de Redcliffe, January 7, 1854, F.O. 78, no. 1030).

In 1883, the number of Syrian children attending school was 63,000, about one-half of them in Lebanon (see Gharaybeh, *Tarikh Suriya*, pp. 164–65); these figures probably represent higher ratios to total population than in any other part of the Ottoman Empire inhabited by Arabs or Turks.

[4] Farley, *The Resources of Turkey*, p. 209. In 1859, the British vice-consul at Alexandria listed eight regular monthly services, by French, Austrian, and Russian lines, and six irregular ones, by British, Turkish, and French lines, calling at the Syrian ports (V. C. Sankey, report dated January 10, 1859, F.O. 78, no. 1452). In 1861, 204 French, Austrian, Russian, and British steamers called at Beirut (Report on Trade of Beirut, 1861, F.O. 78, no. 1690).

[5] Ruppin, *Syrien als Wirtschaftsgebiet*, p. 489.

[6] MacGregor, *op. cit.*, pp. 145, 151; Verney and Dambmann, *Les Puissances Étrangères dans le Levant, en Syrie et en Palestine*, p. 343.

[7] Ruppin, *op. cit.*, p. 492.

Lebanon (see Part IV, chap. 3).[8] In the eighteenth century Syria had exported to Europe silk, cotton, cotton yarn and textiles, and a small quantity of tobacco. After the 1830's Syrian handicrafts (see Part IV, chaps. 2 and 3) were badly hit by the competition of European machine-made goods, and imports of textiles—especially cotton—increased enormously; however, Syria continued to export some specialized silk and cotton products to neighboring countries. The decline of local cotton textiles in turn seems to have discouraged the growing of cotton in most parts of the country. But the output of silk rose several-fold, especially in Lebanon, and silk came to account for a quarter of all exports;[9] tobacco cultivation spread in the Latakia district but was checked when a government monopoly was set up (see Part II, chap. 6); Jaffa oranges entered world markets and in 1857 the British consul put the number exported at 6,000,000, worth £9,200; and increasing quantities of Syrian barley and hard wheat, used for beer and dough products, were sold abroad.

It is impossible to estimate with accuracy the value of Syria's foreign trade over the years. Reconstruction of the facts is complicated because the northern boundary of the country was vague until after the First World War, and so foreign trade figures often included what are now parts of Turkey; there was much land trade for which no figures are available; and trade with other Ottoman provinces was not regarded as foreign trade. In the 1780's export plus import trade with Europe may have averaged around 10 million francs or £400,000; by the late 1830's, following a sharp increase under Egyptian rule, total sea-borne trade fluctuated between £1,000,000 and £1,500,000.[10] In the next decade little progress was made, but by the early 1860's total sea trade seems to have been around £4,500,000.[11] By the 1890's the figure may have risen to a little over £9,000,000,[12] and by 1910–11 sea trade was about £10 million and overland trade was estimated at a quarter to a third of that amount.[13] Assuming that in the

---

[8] Under the enlightened rule of the Druze Amir Fakhr al-din (1585–1635) Lebanon established close commercial and cultural relations with Tuscany and took some steps toward economic and social development. However, the deposition of Fakhr al-din and the re-establishment of Ottoman rule wiped out most of the progress that had been made.

[9] Huvelin, "Que vaut la Syrie " *L'Asie Française* (Paris), 1921. The first silk-reeling factory using steam power was established in 1846, at Shimlan, by an Englishman (see letter dated May 24, 1852, F.O. 78, no. 911).

[10] Masson, *Histoire*, pp. 520–36; see also Part II, chap. 2, and Part IV, chap. 1; MacGregor, *op. cit.*, p. 250.

[11] Farley, *Two Years in Syria*, pp. 220–21. In 1855, the British consul-general in Beirut estimated Syria's imports from Britain at £1,200,000—twice the figure for the preceding year; of this one-fifth found its way to Baghdad and Persia (Moore to Clarendon, "Annual Report on Trade in 1855," F.O. 78, no. 1121). Syria's exports to Britain are not given, but were only a small fraction of imports—for example, Beirut imported £455,000 and exported £97,000. Syria's imports from France were put at £370,000 and its exports at £350,000. Imports from Austria were put at £411,000 and exports at £597,000 (Moore to Clarendon, Trade Report for 1856, F.O. 78, no. 1298). Since these three countries between them accounted for almost the whole of Syria's trade with countries other than the Ottoman Empire and Egypt, the total of imports and exports may be put at £3,000,000 to £3,500,000. The figure for 1857 was, however, distinctly lower, because of poor crops in Syria and the financial crisis in Europe—according to Moore the decline was more than 25 per cent (F.O. 78, no. 1387) and the consul in Aleppo also records a sharp fall (F.O. 78, no. 1389). The figures for Beirut in 1858, 1859, and 1860 were also below those of 1855 and 1856 (F.O. 78, no. 1539 and F.O. 78, no. 1608) but those for 1861 showed a recovery (F.O. 78, no. 1690).

[12] Verney and Dambmann, *op. cit.*, p. 482.   [13] Huvelin, *op. cit.*

1820's sea-trade averaged £500,000 a year, one may estimate that its money value rose nine- to tenfold.by the 1860's and doubled again by 1913; since international prices in the 1820's were one and a half to two times higher than those in the 1860's, which in turn were about equal to those of 1913, the increase in volume was still greater, perhaps as much as thirty-fold over the whole period. But the increase in the overland trade was probably smaller.

It may be added that the trade of Syria showed an increasing import surplus, which was covered by the profits on the transit trade, by the disbursements of Christian and Jewish pilgrims in Jerusalem and Muslim pilgrims setting out from Damascus,[14] by remittances sent by Arab emigrants, by remittances to Jewish immigrants (see Part IV, chap. 6), and by capital inflow and gold outflow. As for direction, there was a shift away from Turkey and Egypt, which in the 1830's absorbed over half the total, to France and Britain, which in 1910 accounted for nearly half the total trade, Britain dominating the import field and France the export. By then the combined share of Turkey and Egypt had fallen to under a third.[15] This growth in foreign trade presupposes a large, though unmeasurable, increase in output, made possible by increased inputs of the factors of production, labor, land, and capital.

Since a comprehensive census was not taken in most parts of Syria until the 1930's or later, earlier estimates of population contain a very wide margin of error. It is clear, however, that the usual factors making for growth were also at work in Syria: greater security, a sharp reduction in epidemics, and the virtual elimination of famine—except during such catastrophic periods as the First World War, when a large part of the Lebanese population starved to death. In the 1780's Volney put the population of Syria, using the term in its widest sense, at 2,305,000,[16] but this seems too high. In the 1830's estimates made by British consular agents range from a minimum of 1,000,000 to a maximum of 1,864,000, but most of these estimates, which were based on tax returns, fall between 1,250,000 and 1,450,000.[17] For 1890 Cuinet put the total at 2,693,000, for 1910 Weakley put it at 3,500,000 (see Part IV, chap. 7), and for 1915 Ruppin[18] put it at 3,423,000, which he believes should be raised by 25 per cent to allow for underregistration. The rough censuses taken in Lebanon, Palestine, and Syria in 1921 and 1922 suggest a total population of 3,200,000 (see Part IV, chap. 7), which is not incompatible with the estimates of Ruppin and Weakley, in view of losses incurred during the war and of the transfer of some border zones to Turkey.

[14] Equipping the annual Haj (pilgrimage) caravan from Damascus to Medina and Mecca cost the Ottoman government, in the 1850's, about £70,000 each year (R. Wood to Clarendon, November 25, 1854, F.O. 78, no. 1029 and despatches in previous years).

During the same period the British consul in Jerusalem estimated the usual number of Christian pilgrims at over 5,000 a year (J. Finn to Clarendon, February 27, 1854, F.O. 78, no. 1032). A few months earlier he had noted the arrival of the first commercially organized party of pilgrims and stated that others were on their way (Finn to Clarendon, October 5, 1853, F.O. 78, no. 962).

[15] Huvelin, *op. cit.*.   [16] Volney, *Travels through Syria and Egypt*, II, 214.

[17] Bowring, *Commercial Statistics of Syria*, pp. 3–4.   [18] *Op. cit.*, p. 185.

The population growth was somewhat slowed down by the massive emigration which started in the 1860's and continued at an accelerating rate until 1914. The adverse effects of the consequent loss in manpower, however, were more than off-set by the remittances sent by the emigrants and by the capital and new ideas transmitted by them (see Part IV, chap. 6).

The increase in total population was accompanied by certain shifts. First, there was an increase in urbanization. This was smaller than in some other countries because Syria had been highly urbanized long before the nineteenth century and also because the handicrafts had declined, offsetting the growth due to the development of commerce and services (see Part IV, chap. 2). By 1914, nevertheless, 20–25 per cent of the total population lived in towns of over 10,000 inhabitants.[19] Second, there was a shift from the interior to the coastal regions where, for instance, the population of Beirut increased from 10,000–12,000 in the 1830's to 150,000–200,000 by 1914 and that of Tripoli from 15,000 to 50,000; during the same period the population of Damascus, Aleppo, Homs, and Hama only doubled or, at most, tripled. Lastly, there was a movement into the newly developed areas on the eastern borders of Syria.

The last-mentioned shift was responsible for most of the additional land brought under cultivation during the period under review (see Part IV, chap. 5). Accurate figures are not available, but the map referred to on page 268 gives an idea of the area reclaimed. This extension of cultivation was accompanied by a disintegration of the old communal forms of land tenure, a process that left great complications in its wake (see Part II, chap. 8).

As for capital, the greatest portion of new investment went into transport and other utilities (see Part IV, chap. 4) and into housing; there was also a small amount of investment in trade, banking, and the silk industry. The capital actually invested in the Syrian and Palestinian railways up to 1914 was slightly over 130 million francs, to which should be added 95 million for the Hijaz Railway and perhaps 50 million for the 300 kilometers of the Berlin–Baghdad railway passing through Syria—or a total of slightly less than 300 million francs, i.e., about $60 million. Investment in the port of Beirut, the streetcars and electricity of Beirut and Damascus, and the waterworks of Beirut, Damascus, and Tel Aviv amounted to somewhat under 50 million francs, or about $10 million. It is highly unlikely that foreign investment in all other branches of the economy—industry, trade, and finance—amounted to over $10 million, giving a total of about $80 million.[20] To this should be added the $6 million sent back annually by Syrian emigrants, the $2 million sent to Christian churches, missions, and educational establishments, and the $2 million remitted to Jews in Palestine (see Part IV, chap. 6).

No figures are available regarding domestic capital, but it seems to have been more abundant—or at least more readily available—than in other parts of the

[19] Ruppin, *op. cit.*, pp. 187–88.
[20] See Elefteriades, *Les Chemins de fer en Syrie et au Liban*; Verney and Dambmann, *op. cit.*; Ruppin, *op. cit.*

Middle East. Thus in 1852 the British consul in Damascus reported that "both the native and foreign merchants in this country have been in the habit of making advances to the peasants and agriculturists, either against their produce or to enable them to pay their taxes, at an interest varying from 20 to 24 per cent per annum."[21] These figures are not as exorbitant as they seem, given the difficulty of collection and the fact that the currency was depreciating. As the consul pointed out, such rates compared favorably with the 12 per cent paid on the government's bank notes (*kaimeh*, see Appendix II) and the 20 per cent charged by small bankers in Istanbul. By the beginning of the twentieth century interest rates must have been distinctly lower.[22]

There is no doubt that the building of railways greatly helped Syria to increase its agricultural production and foreign trade. But there is also no doubt that the alignment chosen was far from ideal and that the use of different gauges on the various lines further complicated matters and increased costs of transport. Of course, Syria started with great natural handicaps: the two parallel mountain chains running the length of the country; the lack of gaps to the coast; and the complete absence of navigable waterways. A still more important factor was that, during the period of railway construction, Syria was neither the center of an independent government—as was Egypt in 1850–80 and Iraq after 1920—nor under an efficient colonial administration with access to outside funds, as was the Sudan in 1898–1956; rather it was a province of a backward, disintegrating empire. Most serious of all were the international rivalries which forced the Ottoman government to grant concessions for the projects desired by the various European powers, irrespective of whether or not they furthered the best interests of the Empire. The relations between the powers and the Ottoman government are typified in the reply the minister Javad gave to the French ambassador, who was thanking him for granting a concession for the Damascus–Birejik railway: "Cher Monsieur, la France veut nous prendre la Syrie."[23] Lastly, the political disintegration of the region in 1918–20, and again in 1947–50, further complicated the task of co-ordination.

As a result Syria failed to get the railway network demanded by its topography and location: a line connecting the Anatolian and Egyptian railways, with branches to the main ports and a long extension to the Jezireh and Iraq. Through traffic between Turkey and Egypt was finally established by the construction of the Beirut-Haifa line by the British army in 1942, but has been interrupted since the Arab-Israeli War of 1947. Various projects for a railway from Iraq to the Mediterranean failed to mature (see Part III, chap. 2), but a roundabout connection, through Turkey, was established in 1940. Work has only just started on a railway linking Latakia, Aleppo, and the Jezireh. It should be added that the

---

[21] Richard Wood to Sir Stratford Canning, January 28, 1852, F.O. 78, no. 910.
[22] See statement by Ruppin, on page 272, below.
[23] Samné, *La Syrie*, p. 163.

inadequacy of railroads was partly compensated for by the development of a fairly good system of roads after the First World War.

Syria on the eve of the First World War (see Part IV, chap. 7) was a country which had laid down a considerable part of the foundation required for economic development. The hardships of that war, and the political and economic disruptions of the interwar years, prevented a "take-off" into rapid growth until the outbreak of the Second World War. During that period, however, further progress was made on building the infrastructure, notably the establishment of security, which made it possible to push the margin of cultivation much farther east and north; the building of roads, ports, and airports; the extension of education; and the great improvement of financial and fiscal institutions. After securing their independence in 1943, Syria and Lebanon were thus enabled to enter a period of rapid economic and social progress.

CHAPTER I

Agriculture and Trade in the 1780's

C. F. Volney, from whose work the following selection has been taken, was probably the most perceptive European traveler to visit the Middle East before the nineteenth century. His description of Syria in 1785 shows the country at almost the lowest point it ever reached in modern times (see Part IV, Introduction). The miserable and deteriorating condition of the villages is vividly brought out and the underlying causes clearly analyzed: extortionate taxation, levied collectively on the whole community and therefore becoming increasingly burdensome as more and more peasants fled from the village; the lawlessness of the soldiery; the depredations of the beduins; the usurious rates of interest; and the primitive state of agricultural methods and implements. To this should be added the feuds that divided most villages into Qaysi and Yamani factions.

Conditions in the towns were much better, as Volney clearly saw. But he fails to emphasize sufficiently that this was largely due to the relative prosperity of the handicrafts (see Part IV, chaps. 2, 3, and 7). Syrian industrial products, such as textiles and soap, found markets in Egypt, Anatolia, and Arabia and some, e.g., cotton yarn and cloth, were even sold in Europe. Lack of security, the very poor means of transport, and the shortage of credit described in the selection tended to confine trade to high-value lightweight goods, except for the movement of foodstuffs to the towns. The main trading centers lay in the interior—Aleppo, Damascus, Hama; the ports, which lacked all facilities, had shrunk greatly, and it seems unlikely that any of them had a population exceeding 10,000. Lastly, it may be noted that the minority groups had already established their supremacy in trade, a phenomenon that was to characterize Syria until very recently (see Part II, chap. 13).

(See also works by Gibb and Bowen, Masson, Charles-Roux [Les Echelles], Olivier, Burckhardt, Bowring, and Poliak listed in the Bibliography.)

[From C. F. Volney, Travels through Syria and Egypt (London, 1787), II, 406–31.]

... In Syria, and even throughout the Turkish empire, the peasants, like the other inhabitants, are deemed slaves of the Sultan; but this term only conveys the meaning of our word subjects. Though master of their lives and properties, the Sultan does not sell men; he does not limit them to a certain spot. If he bestows an appanage on some grandee, it is not said, as in Russia and Poland, that he gives five hundred or a thousand peasants; in a word, the peasants are oppressed by the tyranny of the government, but not degraded by the servitude of feodality.

When Sultan Selim had conquered Syria, in order to render the collection of the revenue more easy, he established a single territorial tribute [land tax] called the *miri*. It should seem, that this Sultan, notwithstanding the ferocity of his character, understood the importance of favouring the husbandman, for the miri, compared with the extent of the lands, is an infinitely moderate impost; and it was the more so at the time in which it was fixed, as Syria was then better peopled than at present, and perhaps also possessed a greater trade, as it lay on the most frequented route to India, little use having been yet made of the passage by the Cape of Good Hope. That this tax might be collected regularly, Selim gave orders to prepare a *deftar*, or register, in which the contingent of each village should be set down. In short he established the miri, at an invariable rate, and ordered it should neither be augmented nor diminished. Moderate as it was in its original establishment, it could never be oppressive to the people; but by abuses inherent in the constitution of the Turkish government, the Pachas and their agents have found the secret of rendering it ruinous. Not daring to violate the law established by the Sultan respecting the immutability of the impost, they have introduced a multitude of changes, which, without the name, produce all the effects of an augmentation. Thus, having the greatest part of the land at their disposal, they clog their concessions with burthensome conditions; they exact the half, nay even two-thirds, of the crop; they monopolize the feed and the cattle, so that the cultivators are under the necessity of purchasing from them at their own price. The harvest over, they cavil about losses,

and pretended robberies, and as they have the power in their hands, they carry off what they think proper. If the season fails, they still exact the same sum, and to pay themselves, expose everything the poor peasant possesses to sale. Happily, his person at least remains free, for the Turks are ignorant of the refinement of imprisoning for debt the man who has no longer any property. To these constant oppressions are added a thousand accidental extortions. Sometimes the whole village is laid under contribution for some real or imaginary offence; and sometimes a service of a new kind is introduced. A present is exacted on the accession of each governor; a contribution of grass is demanded for his horses, and barley and straw for his cavaliers: they must provide, likewise, for all the soldiers who pass, or who carry orders, and the governors take care to multiply these commissions which are a saving to them, but inevitable ruin to the peasants. The villages tremble at every *Lawend* who appears; he is a real robber under the name of a soldier; he enters as a conqueror, and commands as a master: *Dogs, Rabble; bread, coffee, tobacco; I must have barley, I must have meat.* If he casts his eyes on any poultry, he kills them; and when he takes his departure, adding insult to tyranny, he demands what is called *kera-el-dars*, the hire of his grinders. In vain do the peasants exclaim against this injustice; the sabre imposes silence. Justice is remote and difficult of access; nay, complaints are even dangerous. What is the consequence of all these depredations? The poorer class of inhabitants ruined, and unable any longer to pay the miri, become a burthen to the village, or fly into the cities: but the miri is unalterable, and the sum to be levied must be found somewhere, their portion falls on the remaining inhabitants, whose burthen, though at first light, now becomes insupportable. If they are visited by a two years drought and famine, the whole village is ruined and abandoned; but the tax it should have paid is levied on the neighbouring lands. They proceed in the same manner with the *Karadji* [*kharaj*] of the Christians. Its amount having been estimated at the time they were first numbered, it must always produce the same, though those who pay should be less numerous. Hence it happens that this capitation is sometimes carried from three, five, and eleven piasters, at which it was first fixed, to thirty-five and forty; which absolutely impoverishes those on whom it is raised and obliges them to leave the country. These burthens are more especially oppressive in the countries bestowed as an appanage, and in those which are exposed to the Arabs [i.e., beduins]. In the former, the Titulary, greedy to augment his revenue, delegates full power to his Lessee to augment the taxes, and he is well seconded by the avidity of the subalterns. These men, refining on the arts of wringing money from the people, have contrived to impose duties on every commodity brought to market, on entries, the conveyance of goods, and even the burthen of an ass. It is remarked that these exactions have made a rapid progress, especially in the past forty years, from which time they date the decline of agriculture and the depopulation of the country, and the diminution in the quantity of specie carried to Constantinople. With respect to the Bedouins, if they are at war, they pillage as enemies; and if at peace, devour every thing they can find as guests; hence the proverb, *Avoid the Bedouin, whether friend or enemy.* The least wretched of the peasants, are those of the countries which raise themselves a certain stipulated sum, as is done by the Druzes, the Kesraouan, Nablous, etc. yet even there they are liable to be oppressed and impoverished by various abuses. But nothing is more destructive to Syria, than the shameful and excessive usury customary in that country. When the peasants are in want of money to purchase grain, cattle, etc. they can find none but by mortgaging the whole, or part of their future crop, greatly under its value. The danger of letting money appear, closes the hands of all by whom it is possessed; and if it is parted with it must be from the hope of a rapid and exorbitant gain; the

most moderate interest is twelve per cent, the usual rate is twenty, and it frequently rises as high even as thirty.

From all these causes we may easily conceive how miserable must be the condition of the peasants. They are everywhere reduced to a little flat cake of barley or dourra, to onions, lentils, and water. They are so little acquainted with dainties that they esteem strong oil and rancid fat as delicacies. Not to lose any part of their corn, they leave in it all sorts of wild grain, even tares,[1] which occasion vertigoes, and dimness of sight for several hours, as I have myself experienced. In the mountains of Lebanon and Nablous, in time of dearth, they gather the acorns from the oaks, which they eat, after boiling or roasting them on the ashes. The truth of this has been authenticated to me among the Druzes, by persons who have themselves made use of them. We must therefore no longer accuse the poets of hyperbole; but it will only be the more difficult to believe that the golden age was the age of abundance.

By a natural consequence of this misery, the art of cultivation is in the most deplorable state; the husbandman is destitute of instruments, or has very bad ones; his plough is frequently no more than the branch of a tree, cut below a bifurcation, and used without wheels. The ground is tilled by asses, and cows, rarely by oxen; they would bespeak too much riches; beef is therefore very scarce in Syria and Egypt, where, besides, it is always lean and bad, like all the meat of hot countries. In the districts exposed to the Arabs, as in Palestine, the countryman must sow with his musket in his hand. Scarcely does the corn turn yellow, before it is reaped, and concealed in *Matmoures*, or subterraneous caverns. As little as possible is employed for seed corn, because they sow no more than is barely necessary for subsistence; in a word, their whole industry is limited to a supply of their immediate wants; and to procure a little bread, a few onions, a wretched blue shirt, and a bit of woollen much labour is

[1] In Arabic Ziwan.

not necessary. The peasant lives therefore in distress; but at least he does not enrich his tyrants, and the avarice of despotism is its own punishment.

OF THE ARTISANS, TRADERS, AND COMMERCE

The class of men who give value to commodities, by manufacturing them, or bringing them into circulation, is not so ill treated in Syria, as that which produces them; the reason of which is, that the property of the artisans and traders, consisting in personal effects, is more concealed from the scrutinizing eye of government than that of the peasants; besides which, the artists and merchants, collected in the towns, escape more easily, in the crowd, from the rapacity of their rulers. This is one of the principal causes of the populousness of the towns in Syria, and even throughout Turkey. While in other countries, the cities are in some measure the overflow of the country, there they are the effect of its desertion. The peasants, expelled from their villages, fly thither for refuge, and find in them tranquillity and even a degree of ease and plenty. The Pachas are more particularly attentive to this last article, as on it depends their personal safety; for besides the immediate effects of a sedition, which might be fatal to them, the Porte would not pardon them for endangering the safety of the empire, for want of supplying the people with bread. They take care therefore to keep provisions cheap in all the considerable towns, and especially in that in which they reside: if there be a dearth, it is always least felt there. In case of a failure in the harvest, they prohibit the exportation of grain, and oblige every person who possesses any, to sell it at the price they fix under pain of death; and if there be none in the province, they send for it to other countries, as was the case at Damascus in November 1784. The Pacha placed guards on all the roads, permitted the Arabs to pillage every carriage going out of the country, and sent orders into the Hauran, to empty all the *Matmoures*,

so that while the peasants were dying with hunger in the villages, the people of Damascus paid for their bread but two paras, or two sols and a half (one penny farthing), the French pound, and thought it dear even at that price; but as in the political machine no part is independent of the rest, it was not possible to give such a mortal wound to agriculture, without its being felt by the arts and commerce. The reader will judge from a few details, whether the government be not as negligent in this as in every other particular.

Commerce in Syria, considered as to the manner in which it is carried on, is still in that state of infancy which characterizes barbarous ages and uncivilized countries. Along the whole coast there is not a harbour capable of admitting a vessel of four hundred tons, nor are the roads secured by forts. The Maltese corsairs formerly availed themselves of this want of vigilance, to make prizes close in with the shore; but as the inhabitants made the European merchants responsible for such accidents, France has obtained from the Order of Malta a prohibition to their corsairs from appearing within sight of land; so that the natives may peaceably carry on their coasting trade, which is tolerably brisk, from Latakia to Yafa [Jaffa]. In the interior parts of the country, there are neither great roads nor canals, nor even bridges over the greatest part of the rivers and torrents, however necessary they may be in winter. Between town and town, there are neither posts nor public conveyance. The only convenience of this kind is the *Tartar* courier, who comes from Constantinople to Damascus, by way of Aleppo. This courier has no relays but in the large towns, at very great distances; but in case of need he may dismount the very first horseman he meets. He leads with him, according to the custom of the Tartars, a second horse in hand, and has frequently a companion for fear of accidents.

The communication between one town and another is maintained by carriers, who have no fixed time of departure. This arises from the absolute necessity of forming troops, or caravans; nobody travels alone, from the insecurity of the roads. One must wait for several travellers who are going to the same place, or take advantage of the passage of some great man, who assumes the office of protector, but is more frequently the oppressor of the caravan. These precautions are, above all, necessary in the countries exposed to the Arabs, such as Palestine, and the whole frontier of the desert, and even on the road from Aleppo to Skandaroon, on account of the Curd robbers. In the mountains, and on the coast, between Latakia and Carmel, we may travel with more safety; but the roads in the mountains are extremely bad, as the inhabitants are so far from levelling them, they endeavour to render them more rugged, in order, as they say, to cure the Turks of their desire to introduce their cavalry.

It is remarkable, that we never see either a waggon or a cart in all Syria; which arises, no doubt, from the apprehension of having them seized by the minions of government, and suffering a great loss at one stroke. Every thing is conveyed on the backs of mules, asses, or camels; all which animals are excellent here. The two former are employed in the mountains, and nothing can equal their address in climbing and sliding over the slopes of the craggy rocks. The camel is more made use of in the plains, because he consumes less and carries more. His usual burthen is about seven hundred and fifty pounds. His food is every thing you choose to give him; straw, brambles, pounded dates, beans, barley, etc. With a single pound of food, and as much water in a day, he will travel for weeks together. In the whole way from Cairo to Suez, which is a journey of forty or forty-six hours, including the time of repose, they neither eat nor drink; but these fastings, repeated, exhaust them as well as other animals. Their breath then becomes foetid. Their ordinary pace is very slow, not exceeding thirty-four or thirty-six hundred yards in an hour. It is needless to press them, they go no quicker; but by

allowing them to rest, they will travel from fifteen to eighteen hours a day . . . .

Our European merchants are not contented with such simple accommodations. Their journeys, therefore, are very expensive, and consequently not frequent; but even the richest natives of the country make no difficulty in passing part of their lives in the manner I have described, on the roads of Baghdad, Bassora, Cairo, and even of Constantinople. Travelling is their education, their science; and to say of any man he is a merchant, is to pronounce him a traveller. They find in it the advantage of purchasing their goods at the first hand, procuring them at a cheaper rate, ensuring their safety by escorting them themselves; preventing many accidents, and obtaining some abatement of the numerous tolls. They learn, in short, to understand weights and measures, the extreme diversity of which renders theirs a very complicated profession. Each town has its peculiar weight, which, under the same denomination, differs from that of another. The *Rotle* of Aleppo weighs about six pounds, Paris weight; that of Damascus five and one-quarter; that of Saide less than five; that of Ramla near seven. The *Derhem* alone, that is the drachm, which is the first element of these weights, is the same every where. The long measures vary less; only two are known, the Egyptian cubit (*Draa Masri*), and the cubit of Constantinople (Draa Stambouli).

Coin is still more fixed; and you may travel over the whole empire from Kotchim to Asouan, without experiencing any change in its denomination or its value. The most simple of these coins is the *Para*, called also a *Medin*, a *Fadda*, a *Kata*, or a *Mesria*. It is the size of an English silver threepence, and is only worth five liards (a little above a halfpenny). After the para, follow successively pieces of five, ten, and twenty paras; then the *Zolata*, or *Islote*, which is worth thirty; the Piastre, called *Kersh-Asadi*, or Piastre of the Lion, worth forty paras, or fifty French sols (two shillings and a penny); and is most generally used in commerce; and, lastly, the *Abou-Kelb*, or Piaster of the Dog, which is worth sixty paras. All these coins are silver, but with such a mixture of copper alloy, that the *Abou-kelb* is as large as a crown of six livres, though its value be only four livres five sols (Three and sixpence half-penny). They bear no image, because of the prohibition of the prophet, but only the cypher of the Sultan on one side, and on the other these words: *Sultan of the two Continents, Kakan,*[2] (i.e. *Lord*) *of the two Seas, the Sultan, Son of the Sultan N. struck at Stamboul,* (Constantinople), or at *Masr* (Cairo); which are the only two cities where there is a mint.

The gold coins are the sequin, called *Dahab,* or piece of gold; and also *Zahr-Mahaboub,* or Well-beloved Flower. It is worth three piastres of forty paras, or seven livres ten sols (six shillings and three-pence); the half sequin is only worth sixty paras. There is likewise a sequin, called *Fondoucli,* which is worth one hundred and seventy paras; but it is very rare. Besides these coins, which are those of the whole Turkish empire, some of the European specie has as much currency; such are the silver dahlers of Germany, and the gold sequins of Venice. The dollars are worth in Syria from ninety to ninety-two paras, the sequins from two hundred and five to two hundred and eight. These two coins are worth from eight to ten paras more in Egypt. The Venetian sequins are in great request from the fineness of their standard, and the practice they have of employing them for women's trinkets. . . . The effect of this luxury on commerce, is the withdrawing considerable sums from circulation, which remain dead; besides, that when any of these pieces return into common use, having lost their weight by being pierced, it becomes necessary to weigh them. The practice of weighing money is general in Syria, Egypt, and all Turkey. No piece, however effaced, is refused there; the merchant draws out his scales and weighs it, as in the days of Abraham, when he purchased his sepulchre. In considerable

payments, an agent of exchange is sent for, who counts paras by thousands, rejects a great many pieces of false money, and weighs all the sequins, either separately or together.

Almost the whole commerce of Syria is in the hands of the Franks, Greeks, and Armenians: formerly it was engrossed by Jews. The Mahometans take little part in it; not that they are prevented from engaging in it by the prejudices of their religion or by indolence, as some political writers have imagined, but from the obstacles thrown in their way by their own government. The Porte, constant to its usual system, instead of giving a decided preference to the Turkish subjects, finds it more lucrative to sell their rights and industry to foreigners. Some of the European states have, by treaties, obtained a diminution of custom-house duties to three *percent.* while the merchandise of the subjects of the Sultan pays strictly ten, or, when favoured, seven per cent. Besides this, the duties once paid in any port, the Frank is not liable to pay a second time in another. But the case is different with the Ottoman subject [see Part II, chap. 3]. The Franks, too, having found it convenient to employ Latin Christians as agents, have procured them in a participation of their privileges, and they are no longer subject to the power of the Pachas, or amenable to Turkish justice. They cannot be plundered; and whoever has a commercial process [law suit] with them, must plead before the European consul. With such disadvantages, is it surprising that the Mahometans should relinquish commerce to their rivals? These agents of the Franks are known in the Levant under the name of *Baratary Drogmans;* that is, privileged Interpreters.[3] The *barat,* or *privilege,* is a patent, of which the Sultan makes a present to the Ambassadors residing at the Porte. Formerly these ambassadors, in their turn, made presents of

[2] Kakan [*Khaqan*] is a Tartarian word.

[3] An interpreter in Arabic is called Terdjeman, of which our old writers have made Truchement. In Egypt it is pronounced Tergoman; of which the Venetians have made Dragomano, and the French converted into Drogman.

them to particular persons in each factory; but within the last twenty years they have been made to understand it is more lucrative to sell them. The present price is from five to six thousand livres (two hundred or two hundred and fifty pounds). Each Ambassador has fifty, which are renewed on the death of the possessor, and form a pretty considerable perquisite.

France has the greatest trade to Syria of any European nation. Her imports consist in five principal articles; 1st, the cloths of Languedoc. 2ndly, Cochineal from Cadiz. 3dly, Indigos. 4thly, Sugars. and, 5thly, West India coffee, which is in great request with the Turks, and which they mix with that of Arabia, more esteemed indeed, but too high priced. To these must be added hardware, cast iron, sheet lead, tin, Lyons laces, soaps, etc.

The returns consist almost wholly in cottons, either spun or raw, or manufactured into coarse stuffs, some silks of Tripoli, the others being prohibited, in gall nuts, in copper and wool, which come from countries out of Syria. The Factories, or as we call them, Echelles,[4] of the French, are seven in number, i.e. Aleppo, Skandaroon, Latakia, Tripoli, Saide, Acre, and Ramla. The sum of their imports amounts to 6,000,000 of livres (250,000 *l*) viz.

For Aleppo and Skandaroon,	3,000,000
Saide and Acre,	2,000,000
Tripoli and Latakia,	400,000
Ramla	600,000
Total	6,000,000

All this commerce passes through the single channel of Marseilles, which possesses the exclusive privilege of sending ships to,

[4] This whimsical name of Echelles (in English ladders) was adopted by the inhabitants of Provence, from the Italian *scala*, a corruption of the Arabic word *Kalla*, which signifies a place proper to receive vessels, a road, a harbour; at present the natives say, as the Italians, *scala, rada*.

and receiving them from, the Levant, notwithstanding the remonstrances of the Province of Languedoc, which furnishes the principal commodities. Strangers, that is, the natives of Turkey, are prohibited from carrying on their commerce, except through the medium of the Marseilles factors, established in their country. This prohibition was abolished in 1777, for several reasons set forth in the ordinance; but the merchants of Marseilles made such representations, that, since the month of April, 1785, matters have again been placed upon their former footing. It is for France to determine how far this trade is to her interest. Considered relatively to the Turkish empire, it may be averred, that the commerce of the Turks with Europe and India, is more detrimental than advantageous. For the articles exported being all raw unwrought materials, the empire deprives itself of all the advantages to be derived from the labour of its own subjects. On the other hand, the commodities imported from Europe and India, being articles of pure luxury, only serve to increase the dissipation of the rich and the servants of government, whilst, perhaps, they aggravate the wretched condition of the people, and the class of cultivators. Under a government which pays no respect to property, the desire of multiplying enjoyments, cannot but irritate cupidity, and increase oppression. In order to procure more clothes, furs, laces, sugars, shawls, and India goods, there must be more money, cotton and silks, and more extortions. A momentary advantage may have accrued to the states which furnish these objects of luxury; but are not the advantages of the present moment borrowed from the wealth of future times? And can we hope long to carry on an advantageous commerce with a country which is precipitately hastening to ruin? . . .

CHAPTER 2

Handicrafts and Trade in the 1830's

For at least two thousand years, Syria has been a highly urbanized country. The proportion of the total population living in towns has been greater than in other parts of the Middle East, and indeed than in most European countries until the latter half of the nineteenth century, when the industrial and transport revolutions caused a sudden rise in urbanization.[1] The reasons for this phenomenon are manifold: the scarcity of water, which prevented scattered settlement and made for concentration in large villages or towns; the insecurity of the countryside, which led many farmers cultivating land in the immediate vicinity of a town to live within its walls; the relatively flourishing condition of the handicrafts; and the active internal and international trade. At the end of the eighteenth century the population of Aleppo was probably around 150,000 and that of Damascus about 100,000,[2] and several other towns such as Tripoli, Hama, Homs, and Jerusalem may have approached the 10,000 mark. In the 1830's the British consul in Beirut gave the following estimates: Damascus, 100,000–110,000; Aleppo, 60,000–85,000 (a rather low figure); Hama, 44,000 (a rather high figure); Tripoli, 15,000; and Beirut, 10,000.[3] The addition of the smaller towns would raise the total to nearly 300,000 or perhaps 20 per cent of the total population. By 1914, according to Ruppin's estimates,[4] 1,600,000 out of a total population of 4,000,000 lived in towns of over 10,000, though this may well be an overstatement.

The relatively small increase in urbanization until the First World War is probably attributable to the decline in the handicrafts. The following selection, which portrays the economic life of the main cities at the very beginning of the nineteenth-century transformation, stresses trade and handicrafts. Trade continued to flourish throughout the period under review; however, the position of the inland cities was adversely affected by both the shift to the ports (see Part IV, Introduction) and the diversion of some transit trade through the Suez Canal. Urbanization was also promoted by the development of modern transport, by

[1] Bonné, *State and Economics in the Middle East*, p. 224.
[2] Gibb and Bowen, *Islamic Society and the West*, I, 281.
[3] MacGregor, *Commercial Statistics*, p. 120.
[4] Ruppin, *Syrien als Wirtschaftsgebiet*, pp. 187–88.

the growth of the bureaucracy, by the rise in the income of landowners, almost all of whom lived in cities, and by the increase in construction and service industries. But the handicrafts were hard hit by the competition of machine-made goods and by the subsequent shift in tastes to European-style clothing and furniture. Thus the number of handicrafts in Damascus is estimated to have declined from 1,966 in 1852 to 1,395 in 1889, and the number of persons occupied in them from 30,000 to 8,000 [5]—but it is not clear how much reliance should be placed on those figures. In 1858 the British consul in Aleppo reported: "The manufactures carried out at Aleppo are much less numerous than formerly, the introduction of English goods having caused many establishments to cease operations from their inability to produce articles as cheap as foreign stuffs. Native manufactures, however, still continue to be produced, and were it not for the pernicious system of monopolies, they might compete more advantageously with those of Europe." [6] (See Part II, chaps. 4 and 5, Part IV, chap. 3.) However, the description of Syrian handicrafts on the eve of the First World War, given in Part IV, chapter 7, shows that the extent of the decline should not be exaggerated and that several industries showed much resilience.

The following selection consists of extracts from British consular and other reports.

(See also works by Charles-Roux [*Les Echelles*], Guys, Urquhart [*Lebanon*], Michaud and Poujoulat, Burckhardt [*Syria*], Houry, Churchill, Rustum and Sauvaget listed in the Bibliography.)

[5] Gharaybeh, *Tarikh Suriya*, pp. 145-46, citing al-Hasani and Qoudsi.
[6] Skene, "General Report on Aleppo," F.O. 78, no. 1389.

[From John MacGregor, *Commercial Statistics* (London, 1847), II, 140-50.]

ALEPPO

... *Manufactures of Aleppo, Soap.*—There were in 1838 in Aleppo 30 soap manufactories, and in Edlip half that number, employing about 1000 men, at wages of from 5 to 10 piasters per day. The quantity produced varied from 500 to 1500 tons annually, according to the crop of oil.

Stuffs.—Aleppo was famous throughout the east for her woven goods. Those which are still manufactured, consist of silk stuffs, with gold and silver thread; silk and cotton, flowered and striped; and the striped cottons, called nankins. Few modern improvements have been introduced into the machinery; the fabrics are, many of them, beautiful, and costly when silver and gold are used. There are in all about 4000 looms employed, and about 4800 persons, men and children, earning from 3 to 12 piasters per day. Of the 4000 looms 300 are employed in producing stuffs of silk and gold

1700 looms are employed in making the stuffs of silk and cotton, producing about 340,000 pieces per annum, of the average value of 40 piasters per piece, giving a total value of	13,600,000
1000 looms are employed in making the cotton stuffs, of which they produce annually about 500,000 pieces, worth 12 piasters per piece, giving a total of	6,000,000
Besides these there are about 1000 looms employed on low muslins, used for printing on; they occupy about 1200 persons, at rather lower wages than the others, and produce annually about 500,000 pieces, worth 10 piasters per piece, giving a total of	5,000,000
Total piasters	25,500,000
Sterling	£250,000

and silver thread, yielding per annum about 6000 pieces; averaging, per piece, 150 piasters each, which gives a total value of 900,000 piasters.

These stuffs are sent east, north and south, and form a large part of the trade of Aleppo. All the British twist imported consumed was in these looms.

The rich stuffs are worn by brides and wealthy women; all other sorts are used for the every day outer garments of men and women.

Dyeing and Print Works.—There are about 100 dyeing and print works in Aleppo, employing about 1500 persons, who earn from 5 to 14 piasters each per day. The dyeing is chiefly that of silk and cotton yarns used for stuffs, and, in fact, all fast colours. The printing is also on fast colours, but in a very rude state. Compared with the other manufactures here, the chief business is printing the handkerchiefs worn by women and lads, tied round the heads, and for veils for the women when they go out of their houses.

Gold and Silver Thread.—There are 15 workshops of gold and silver thread, in each of which about four persons are employed.

The ports of Aleppo are Alexandretta or Scanderoon and Latakia. The conveyance of goods to and from the coast is by mules and camels. The journey to and from the latter is done in winter, by camels, in 7 to 8 days; by mules, 5 to 6 ditto. In summer, by camels, 5 to 9 days; by mules, 4 to 5 days.

The Charge of carriage varies from 60 to 120 piasters per cantar of $187\frac{1}{2}$ okes.

The journey from Latakia occupies from two to three days more, and the charge of carriage is from 30 to 50 per cent higher.

Caravans.—The caravans between these places vary from 10 to 100 mules or camels. There are muleteers who are continually employed on these roads, so that there is always abundance of opportunities for the transmission of goods, except when a seizing by government takes place. The communication with Moussul and Diarbekir, Bagdad, etc., is not so frequent, and the caravans are generally accompanied by the merchants who load them.

TABLE showing the per Centage which the expense of Carriage amounts to on the following Articles by the different Routes [from Aleppo]

Articles	Scanderoon	Latakia	Tarsous and Adana	Marash, Aintab, and Killis	Orfa	Diarbekir and Merdein	Moussoul and Bagdad
				Per Cent			
Twist and heavy cotton	$1–1\frac{1}{2}$	$1\frac{1}{2}–2\frac{1}{2}$	2–3	$\frac{3}{4}–\frac{1}{2}$	$\frac{1}{2}–2\frac{1}{2}$	$2\frac{1}{2}–4$	$3\frac{1}{2}–5$
Other British manufactures, cochineal, indigo, and spices	$\frac{3}{10}–\frac{3}{5}$	$\frac{1}{2}–1$	$\frac{3}{5}–1\frac{1}{4}$	$\frac{1}{5}–1$	$\frac{1}{2}–1$	$1–1\frac{1}{2}$	$1\frac{1}{4}–1\frac{3}{4}$
Sugar, Coffee, Pepper, and metals	4–8	6–10	7–12	7–10	6–10	10–16	20–30
Galls	4–8	6–10	7–12	7–10	6–10	10–16	20–30
Silk	$\frac{1}{4}–\frac{1}{2}$	$\frac{1}{3}–\frac{3}{5}$	$\frac{1}{2}–\frac{3}{4}$	$\frac{1}{2}–\frac{5}{8}$	$\frac{1}{3}–\frac{3}{5}$	$\frac{3}{5}–1$	$1\frac{1}{4}–1\frac{3}{4}$
Cotton	6–12	9–15	11–18	9–15	9–15	15–24	30–45
Wool	9–18	13–22	16–27	16–22	13–22	22–36	45–67

Quarantines.—There was, and we believe there is still, a quarantine established at about two days' journey beyond Adana on the frontiers of Syria. The effect of this quarantine has been to shut out from the markets of Tarsous and Adana all the population of the interior of Asia Minor. The caravans which formerly came from Tarsous and Adana, from the country on the north side of the Taurus, have for some years gone to Smyrna and Constantinople, in order to avoid from 7 to 20 days quarantine on a journey of 4 days.

The same is true on the frontiers towards

the Euphrates. These quarantines are absurd from the fact they can almost always be passed by paying money; a *bakshish*, or a bribe, usually procures an immediate pass.

Posts.—The communication with Europe was during the possession by Ibrahim Pacha carried on by post sent to Beyrout, to meet the steamer from England, once a month, and by Tatars to Constantinople about once every six weeks, but there was no regularity in their time of starting. The post used to go to Constantinople in 7 days in winter, and 5 days in summer; the postage was about 4*d.* for a single letter. The Tatar went to Constantinople in 12 days in good weather, and in bad weather he was frequently 20 days on his journey; the postage, by him, for a single letter was about 9*d.* He carried money at the rate of one-half per cent for gold, and one-third for silver. There were also two opportunities per month by horse post, for the conveyance of money to Beyrout; one was in the hands of the British merchants, and its rates of carriage were three-eighths per cent for gold, and one-eighth for silver. Since the evacuation of Syria by Mehemet Ali, the same system was presumed to continue; but there is less security and regularity.

Aleppo, as an entrepot, supplies not only the surrounding country, but also parts of Armenia, south from Arabkir. To the north it supplies Marash and its neighbourhood; to the east and south-east, Orfa, Diarbekir, Merdin, and Moussul are supplied from Aleppo and it sends a caravan, once a year, to Bagdad . . ..

DAMASCUS

Mahomedan Merchants.—There are in Damascus 66 Mahomedan commercial establishments which trade with Europe. The whole amount of their capital is estimated at from 20 to 25,000,000 of piasters—200,000 *l.* to 250,000 *l.* sterling. Of these houses, eight are believed to possess a capital exceeding 1,000,000 of piasters. There are two (Abderachman Ashim and Mahomed Said Aga Bagdadi) who trade with Bagdad, whose capital is estimated at from 1½ to 2,000,000 piasters; and one house (Hadji Hussein Chertifchi) which is supposed to have from 2 to 2,500,000 piasters in trade. The larger houses generally trade with Europe and Bagdad; those of smaller capitals with Constantinople and Smyrna. There are about a dozen engaged in the Egyptian trade with Cairo and Alexandria, one or two with the holy cities of Mecca and Medina, and a few with Jerusalem, Nablous, and other parts of Palestine. There is one of the principal houses whose commercial relations extend as far as the East Indies.

Christian Merchants.—There are 29 Christian merchants at Damascus engaged in foreign trade, the whole of whose capital is estimated at 4½ to 5,500,000 of piasters. By far the wealthiest of these establishments is that of Hanah Hanouri, having a capital of from 1½ to 2,000,000 of piasters, and carrying on a trade with England, France, and Italy, besides being a considerable manufacturer of Damascus stuffs. Several others of the Hanouri family are engaged in foreign commerce, and are among the most opulent of the Christian merchants. A great proportion of the Christian commercial houses have connexions with Great Britain. They are less opulent than the Mussulmans or the Jews.

Hebrew Merchants.—As a class the Jewish foreign merchants of Damascus are the most wealthy. There are 24 Hebrew houses engaged in foreign trade, and their capital is estimated at from 16,000,000 to 18,000,000 piasters; making an average of 6,000 *l* to 7,000 *l* sterling each. Among them there are no less than nine houses whose capitals vary from 1,000,000 to 1,500,000 of piasters. The two most opulent are believed to be Mourad Farhi and Nassim Farhi, whose wealth in trade exceeds 1,500,000 each. Most of the Jewish foreign houses trade with Great Britain.

Retailers of British goods.—There are 107 shopkeepers who retail British goods in Damascus. The whole amount of their supposed capital is from 1,600,000 to 2,100,000 piasters, so that the average capital possessed by each is only from 150 *l.* to 180 £ sterling. Their bazaars are kept up to a great extent by of those [*sic.*] who sell them goods on credit.

Woollen Shopkeepers.—There are 15 sellers of woollen cloths by retail. They are the most affluent body of the shop-keepers, and are deemed to have from 650,000 to 800,000 piasters employed in all; making the average of their capitals from 400 £ to 500 £ sterling; the wealthiest of them, having about double that amount, and the lowest among them being supposed to possess from 200 £ to 300 £.

Stuff Manufacturers.—There are 14 Mahomedans engaged in the stuff manufactures of Damascus; their capital varies from 200 £ to 1200 £ sterling, and the whole amount engaged is from 600,000 to 750,000 piasters, giving on an average from 400 £ to 500 £ sterling. The two most opulent of these manufacturers are dervishes.

There are 45 Christian establishments for manufacturing Damascus stuffs. Their total capital is from 1,100,000 to 1,500,000 piasters, or an average from 220 £ to 335 £.

The number of looms for silk and cotton stuffs in Damascus is about 4000; each of which produces weekly from 4 to 5 pieces, of 11 pikes in length by 1 in width, containing about 100 drachms of silk, and 100 drachms of cotton twist of Nos. 16 to 24. The price of the piece varies from 80 to 95 piasters. The price of labour is from 8 to 10 piasters per piece.

The number of looms for cotton stuffs is about 400, which make each about 7 to 8 pieces per week, requiring about 200 drachms of cotton twist, Nos. 16 to 24; each piece is 11 pikes long and one broad. The price is 20 to 21 piasters; the labour, 6 piasters per piece.

Grocers and Druggists.—Grocers and druggists are numerous, and are computed to be about 80, having one with another, on an average, a capital of about 10,000 piasters each. . . .

BEIRUT

Beyrout is the seaport of Damascus, from which it is distant about 70 miles. It is little more than a deep roadstead, with good anchorage, the mole being neglected. Its population is estimated at about 15,000, and its bazaars are large, and generally well supplied with merchandize. The consul states in his report, written before the retreat of Ibrahim Pacha,—

The internal trade of the country has increased within the same period, as native capitalists now venture to embark their fortunes in commercial speculations, which formerly they did not venture to do. It would, however, be an error to suppose that the *international consumption* of European goods in Syria has materially augmented. No direct commerce is carried on betwixt Tyre, Sidon, or Acre, with England or other British ports, as no British subject with a capital adequate to important commercial operations, resides in those places; but an internal, and I have reason to believe an increasing trade exists between those places and Beyrout for articles of British produce.

The importations in transit, forwarded to Damascus, not being for the consumption of that city only, go by the caravans to Bagdad, whence they are distributed in the adjacent countries. Those, again, destined for Aleppo find their way into Asia Minor, especially to the towns of Orfa, Diarbekir, Malatiah, Sivas, etc.

Beyrout is certainly, at present, the most flourishing commercial city in Syria in proportion to its size; and, as my personal observations have hitherto been confined to this place, I may be inclined to overrate the general commercial prosperity of the country. A wealthy class of Christians reside here, whose habits, both as regards dress and the consumption of other luxuries of civilized society, exceed those of the generality of their countrymen. This body of Christians were, under the former government, refugees to Mount Lebanon, and have now returned to Beyrout since the Egyptian invasion. If any Christians feel a leaning to the present government, it is those who have found a security to their property under it, which they did not previously enjoy; even these feel that they possess, by a most precarious tenure, their advantage.

According to all the information which we have since received, misrule, corruption, and insecurity, have succeeded the security of the military despotism, and severity of Ibrahim Pacha's government; and this is confirmed by the consul, who states that the articles imported, have, in 1842, increased in quantity, but being of a coarse kind, not in value; that there is no safety or security in the interior, and that the system of selling on credit has been greatly limited; a proof of commercial insecurity.

With respect to the moral state of Syria, Mr. Moore, the consul, states it must be considered as one of degradation—where man is no longer looked upon as a free agent, and treated accordingly; it cannot be otherwise; and we need not be surprised if we meet with little of either rectitude of principle, or dignity of conduct in the native Syrian; whilst the reverse of this is too frequently found—intrigue, pusillanimity, and falsehood, forming the component parts of his character. In a commercial point of view, the position of Syria is highly favourable: its coasts afford facilities for the external supply of its wants, whilst its topographical position, as respects part of Asia Minor, Mesopotamia, Bagdad, Persia, and Arabia, is equally advantageous for furnishing these countries with our produce.

In a manufacturing point of view, Syria has lost, in proportion to her importation of foreign goods, as well as on account of her diminished population, and the gradual impoverishment of the country. Agriculture has equally declined for the two latter causes . . . .

Mr. Moore, consul at Beyrout, gives the following rates of wages in the Beyrout districts: Field labour 5 to 6½ piasters = 12*d.* to 15*d*; artisans, masons, and carpenters, 14 to 15 piasters = 2*s.* 10*d.* to 3*s.* 10*d.*

The annual cost of clothing for one of the labouring classes is 3 *l.* to 4 *l*; food, 7 *l.* to 8 *l.*; lodging, in town, 2 *l.* to 4 *l.*; lodging, in country, 1 *l.* to 2 *l.* The habitation generally consists of two rooms.

Ports of Syria.—Exclusive of Alexandretta and Beyrout.

Mersin, the port of Tarsous, is safe for a limited number of small vessels.

The port of *Latakia* (anciently *Laodicea*) is small, the entrance to it very dangerous and intricate, with ruins falling into it; not more than two or three vessels can now anchor in it, and, except in the summer months, it is always considered unsafe.

The port of *Tripoli* is very small, and cannot be considered an harbour, except for vessels of a moderate tonnage. The anchorage in the roadstead can only be made use of in summer.

The bay of *Akka* or St. Jean d'Acre is large, but much exposed. It is frequented chiefly by French, Italian, and Austrian vessels. British vessels seldom touch there. The anchorage at Hypka, under the southernmost point, affords some little shelter.

The ancient ports of *Jaffa*, *Tour* (Tyre), and *Sayda* (Sidon) are now all choked up, and offer no security to shipping.

The harbours on the coast of Syria are many of them susceptible of being sufficiently improved for the safety of trading vessels; but no undertaking requiring permanent security for capital and enterprise can be entered upon, while the condition of the country in regard to its administration remains under the Turkish pachas.

In a recent report of the consul at Beyrout, he states that internal disorder, and insecurity in respect to person and property, still prevail in Syria. . . .

CHAPTER 3

From Subsistence to Market Economy, 1850's

The following selection is an outstanding example of the work being done by the younger Soviet scholars on the history of the Middle East during its last two hundred years. It deals with a subject to which Marx devoted much attention and analyzed with great depth and perception in many of his writings. This was the transformation of the age-old subsistence economy into a market economy under the impact of European capitalism, a process that occurred in most under-developed countries in the course of the nineteenth century. Among the common features marking this change are: the growing of cash crops for export or to supply the cities; the disintegration of the communal system of land tenure and its replacement by private property (see Part II, chaps. 8 and 9), a process that leads to increasing inequality of wealth; the breaking of the ties binding peasants to the soil or to the village; the growth of a large body of traders, brokers, and financial agents engaged in foreign and domestic trade; improved methods of transport; increasing urbanization; and the ruin of the handicrafts by foreign competition.

Like other Marxist accounts of social change, the following selection tends to point out the darker parts of the picture. Thus it gives the impression that the decline of the handicrafts was much swifter than it actually was (see Part IV, chap. 7). It also suggests that the lot of the workers and peasants deteriorated markedly. Although this may well be true of some skilled workers, whose products could no longer sustain the competition of machine-made goods, it does not seem to apply to the mass of the people; indeed the available evidence seems to indicate a rise in the general level of living, as evidenced by greater consumption of staple articles and improved health conditions.

Four additional points may be noted. First, in many important respects the transition to a cash economy in Lebanon may be traced back to the seventeenth century. The planting of mulberries and export of silk to Europe started in that period and developed rapidly until the middle of the eighteenth, when it was hit by Italian competition and the effect of the European wars. This trade was accompanied by two features of a cash economy: sharp fluctuations in silk prices and the emergence of an active class of merchants and money lenders.[1]

[1] Chevallier, "Aux origines des troubles agraires libanais en 1858," *Annales*, January, 1956.

Second, the main impetus to the expansion of production and marketing of grain and other crops seems to have come from greater foreign demand in the late 1840's. Thus the British consul in Aleppo pointed out that the sum for which the tithes of the Pashalik of Aleppo were farmed out had steadily risen from 6,000,000 piastres in 1846 to 14,000,000 in 1856. "This increase commenced with the exportation of grain in 1844," following the arrival of European ships in ballast returning home after discharging their cargoes of manufactured goods in Constantinople or Smyrna. "Cultivation extended in proportion to the rise in prices. A new demand created a new supply and even new articles of produce soon sprang up," for example, sesame, while others, such as cotton, were given up. Similarly the British consul in Jerusalem noted in 1850: "As this country has been drained of corn by an extensive exportation from the Seaports for Europe and especially for England—a scarcity would have been felt had not the Arabs beyond Jordan cultivated grain to an unusual degree—which produce they have lately brought to Jerusalem in large quantities."[2] The Crimean War, naturally, gave a further impetus to the export trade.

Third, in the nineteenth century population growth, largely due to improved hygiene, was a major cause of the great increase in the number of landless peasants. Offsetting this increase was the breakup of large estates under the system of *mugharasa*, by which peasants were allotted plots of uncultivated land in which they planted olives or mulberries and, when the trees matured, divided the plot with the landlord.

Fourth, the Egyptian occupation of 1831–41 was of crucial importance. It was during this period that security was first introduced and that the country was opened to Europeans. As a result, some years later, settlement of deserted areas began (see Part IV, chap. 5), city people began to invest in land, the silk industry was modernized by the introduction of European reeling machinery, internal and foreign trade expanded greatly, and European machine-made goods began to flood the local market. No less important for the subsequent economic, as well as political, history of the country was the dislocation of the prevailing feudal relationships and the change in the balance of forces between the various religious communities.[3]

(See also works by Polk, Chevallier, Kerr, Ismail, Rustum [*Materials* and *Calendar*], Burckhardt [*Syria*], Churchill, Guys, and Farley, listed in the Bibliography.)

[2] Skene to Lord Stratford de Redcliffe, July 15, 1857, F.O. 78, no. 1297, and Finn to Lord Palmerston, February 15, 1850, F.O. 78, no. 839.

[3] See Polk, *The Opening of South Lebanon.*

[I. M. Smilianskaya, "Razlozhenie feodal-nikh otnoshenii v Sirii i Livane v seredine XIX v." ("The Disintegration of Feudal Relations in Syria and Lebanon in the Middle of the Nineteenth Century"),

Peredneaziatskii Etnograficheskii Sbornik (Moscow), I (1958), 156–79.]

In the mid-nineteenth century when Syria, Lebanon, and Palestine fell prey to the expansion of foreign capital, primarily English and French, feudal relations of production disintegrated in these countries. The commodity-monetary nexus was relatively well developed. But the barter economy, where capitalist exploitation cropped up, although sporadically, in agriculture (seasonal migratory work) and in industrial production (manufacture), was subject to dislocation. The precondition for this process was the growth of productive forces caused by the increasing division of labor between city and village in both the industrial and agricultural sectors.

Farm specialization in various cash crops and the increase of a marketable surplus in agriculture was observed in the first half of the nineteenth century, when social division of labor in agriculture became apparent in Syria, Lebanon, and Palestine. V. I. Lenin, in pointing out a specific means of converting agriculture to commodity production wrote:

From the very nature of agriculture its conversion into commodity production occurs in a particular manner, unlike the corresponding process in industry. Manufacturing industry splits into separate, completely independent branches, each devoted exclusively to the manufacture of one product or part of a product. Agriculture on the other hand does not split into completely separate branches, but merely specializes in producing, in one instance, one market product, in another, another market product, the other agricultural aspects being adapted to this principal (i.e., market) product.[1]

Available sources clearly outline the regions of agricultural specialization in Syria, Lebanon, and Palestine in the first half of the nineteenth century: in Mount Lebanon, sericulture; in the region of Latakia and in the mountains of Ansaria, tobacco growing; in the Biqa' valley and Hawran, wheat cultivation; the region of Saida was already known at the end of the eighteenth century for its cotton cultivation. Large quantities of cotton were also grown in the northern part of Syria during this period; the oasis of Damascus and the region

of Tripoli were famous for export-oriented horticulture. Truck farming had long since been practiced near large towns, such as Aleppo and Damascus.[2] Over-all specialization never excluded diversification within each major region, or even village, nor did it reduce the significance of secondary crops.[3]

Every peasant farm generally cultivated the various crops required to meet the personal needs of the peasant family, but in regions where specialization had developed, as a rule, one or two cash crops prevailed. Information exists on the management of a peasant farm in Mount Lebanon in the late 1840's.[4] On a strip of land owned by a peasant family, 200 mulberry trees and 200 grapevines were grown, between which a relatively small amount of grain was sown and vegetables were planted. Grain and vegetables were consumed by the family, whereas wine and floss were almost entirely marketed. The earned income was used to pay taxes and to buy clothing, bread, and foodstuffs (the harvest from the plot did not cover the food requirements). It is quite clear that this farm specialized in two cash crops—mulberry trees and grapes—whereas grain and vegetables were only subsidiary crops. This farm, having lost its barter characteristics, was closely tied to the market.

[2] In some regions such specialization had long existed, based on the division of labor developed among the population of regions with differing natural conditions.
[3] Lebanon can be cited as an example. In the north (in the region of sericulture), there was enough local bread [grains] for only three months of the year, a fact which is indicative of the substantial development of the commodity-monetary nexus; the rest of the bread [grains] was bought in coastal towns or in the villages of Zahleh or Dair al-Qamar. The exception was the village of Ehden, where wheat and barley were processed for sale. "Traffic in bread . . .," wrote Artemii Rafalovich, a Russian researcher, "is the major business of the inhabitants of Ehden who have more than enough to spare" (S. A. Rafalovich, "Zapiski russkogo vracha, otpravlennogo na Vostok" ("Notes of a Russian Doctor Sent to the East") Zhurnal Ministerstva vnutrennikh del, 1848, part 22, p. 435. At the same time tobacco growing was developed in the southern regions of Lebanon, and olive trees and vineyards played an important part throughout Lebanon.
[4] D. Urquhart, The Lebanon (Mount Souria). A History and a Diary (London, 1860), I, 390–91.

[1] V. I. Lenin, Works, III, 267.

During the first half of the nineteenth century, specialization in different areas often changed over short periods of time. In the 1830's in Palestine and northern Syria increased emphasis was placed on the cotton plant.[5] According to an account in 1841 by K. M. Bazili, the Russian consul general in Beirut, until Muhammad Ali's conquest of Syria the annual cotton yield did not exceed 4,000 qantar,[6] barely a third of which was exported. By 1840 the cotton harvest had doubled, while exports quadrupled.[7] But cotton growing declined sharply after 1840, owing to a disastrous falling-off in local textile production (under the impact of competitive European manufactured goods), the displacement of Syrian cotton by Egyptian on the external markets[8] and imports of English yarn into an already greatly shrunken domestic market.[9] Instead of raising cotton, the Palestinian peasant began growing sesame and wheat. Tobacco growing was expanded in the region of Saida. Northern Syria began

exporting grain. In the 1850's, when grain exports from the Black Sea region ceased because of the Crimean War and demand for Syrian grain rose, northern Syria and Palestine increased their wheat crop.[10]

The above-mentioned changes in specialization resulted from the response of the Syrian economy to the requirements of the foreign market. They testify to the rapid reorientation of agriculture to market production. At the same time all these changes pointed to the growing dependence of Syrian, Lebanese, and Palestinian agriculture on the external market, as well as to that of the peasant economy on foreign capital.

The extent to which the commodity-monetary nexus penetrated Lebanese agriculture and the degree to which it depended on the world market can be gauged by the development of sericulture in the first half of the nineteenth century. Specialization in raw-silk production in Lebanon had existed for more than a century. It is probable that, in the seventeenth century, the prosperous silk manufacturers of Damascus had used Lebanese raw silk. By the beginning of the eighteenth century raw silk was already being exported from Lebanon to France.[11] In 1840 Syria produced 3,000 qantar of raw silk, of which only half was locally processed (primarily on farms), one-fourth exported to Europe (primarily to France), and one-fourth delivered to silk-spinning workshops in Aleppo, Damascus, and Cairo. The French consul Guys gives data on the distribution of raw silk produced in the province of Beirut in the 1840's.[12] Out of 1,800 bales, 920 were shipped to Egypt, 130 to North Africa, 350 to Marseilles, 100 to Damascus, and 100 to Aleppo; 200 were consumed locally, i.e., the peasants themselves processed only slightly over 10 per cent of the silk. Hence in the regions adjacent to Beirut nearly all raw silk, which

[5] The growing of cotton, used by the Aleppo and Damascus textile industries, was considerably developed in northern Syria and Palestine at the end of the eighteenth century. The major export of Acre, Saida, Lydda, and Ramla was cotton, and most was exported as yarn. The peasants prepared cotton wool for spinning and spun it on their farms, and a considerable part of the cotton was consumed on the farm (C. F. Volney, *Voyage en Egypte et en Syrie, pendant les années 1783, 1784, et 1785* [Paris], II, 332, 350–51; III, 53).

[6] K. M. Bazili's calculation was based on a rate of 1 qantar being equal to approximately 13 poods (213 kilograms).

[7] Arkhiv vneshnei politiki Rossii, fond "Posolstvo v Konstantinopole" (Russian Foreign Policy Archives, "Embassy in Constantinople" Fund), case 718, l. 112 (cited hereafter as AVPR).

[8] See F. Charles-Roux, *Les Echelles de Syrie et de la Palestine au XVIIIᵉ siècle* (Paris, 1928), p. 8. The author of the book finds that Muhammad Ali's policy of promoting Egyptian cotton growing had a direct bearing on the falling-off of demand for Syrian cotton on foreign markets. It seems more correct to link this fact not only with the expansion of cotton growing in Egypt but also with the elimination of trade monopoly and the inclusion of Egypt, in 1841, in the 1838 Anglo-Turkish Trade Convention. [See Part II, chap. 3.]

[9] In 1857 Skin [Skene], the English consul in Aleppo, wrote: "Twenty years ago three times as much cotton was cultivated here, primarily for local consumption, but English imported yarn ruined the cotton industry since local plant owners found it cheaper to use imported raw material for their weaving" (*Abstract of Reports on the Trade of Various Countries* [London, 1860], p. 433).

[10] *Ibid.*, p. 426.

[11] *Voyages de Richard Pockocke ... en Orient, dans l'Egypte, l'Arabie, la Palestine, la Syrie, la Grèce, la Thrace, etc.* (Neuchâtel, 1773), III, 306.

[12] H. Guys, *Relation d'un séjour de plusieurs années à Beyrout et dans le Liban* (Paris, 1847), I, 55.

was the primary product of local farms, was for sale. This testifies to the relatively advanced stage of commodity economy.

The following facts attest to the rapidly growing export of raw silk from Lebanon in the nineteenth century: in the early 1840's Beirut's outgoing seaborne trade in raw silk was estimated at approximately 3 million piastres[13] (the total production of silk in the region of Beirut averaging 9 million),[14] and in 1857, exports rose to almost 34 million.[15] These facts, although rough estimates at best, indicate both the tremendous increase in export of raw silk from the country in a relatively short period of time (less than two decades) and the significant growth of the market share of silk culture. They also reveal the parallel ruin of the domestic production of silk fabrics and the reduction of silk weaving in Damascus and Aleppo. In other words, Syria was becoming a supplier of silk for European industry.

The increase of regional specialization in various products was inseparably linked with the strengthening of trade ties between various regions· in Syria, Lebanon, and Palestine and the growth of the domestic market. Mount Lebanon depended on the Biqa' valley, northern Syria, and the coast of Lebanon for its supplies. Lebanese farmers bought grain and livestock in the markets of Zahleh, Dair al-Qamar, Beirut, and Tripoli. During periods when food supplies ran low, food was brought into Lebanon from Nablus. Fish caught near Antioch was consumed throughout Syria (Orthodox Christians ate fish during fasting periods).[16]

Close commercial ties sprang up between towns and neighboring farming regions. European observers described how peasants in neighboring villages daily supplied Damascus markets with foodstuffs (beans and other vegetables, fruits, including

melons, also groats, etc.), for consumption in the populous town. Various villages and districts specialized in one specific product marketed in town: villagers from Duraijeh cultivated fine grapes,[17] the inhabitants of another village prepared cheese for the Damascus markets,[18] Hawranis provided grain and charcoal. The same practice could be observed in the suburban farms of Aleppo, Jerusalem, Alexandretta, etc.

Regular ties were common between remote territories. Letters from the French historian Michaud and the journalist Poujoulat provide information on Beirut markets in the middle 1830's. "Victuals," they reported, "abound in markets, but nearly all provisions come from the outside, there is no town on the sea-coast where edibles are cheaper than in Beirut."[19] Grain, vegetables, and oil came to Beirut from Palestine. Villages in the neighborhood of Jaffa sent their watermelons to the town,[20] and the fishermen of Saida supplied the town with fish.[21]

Equally close and extensive ties sprang up between artisan centers and farm regions which provided them with raw material. Damascus weavers received raw silk from Lebanon and Anti-Lebanon; Lebanon also supplied raw silk to the Aleppo silk-spinning filatures; hemp for the production of rope came to Damascus from nearby villages.[22] The Nablus district supplied cotton to the Anti-Lebanon village of Hasbaya for weaving, etc.

With the expansion of domestic trade, new trading centers arose. In Lebanon during the first half of the nineteenth century two towns sprang up on the site of small villages: Dair al-Qamar and Zahleh.

[13] Calculations according to Guys (Ibid., pp. 55, 58).
[14] Ibid.
[15] J. L. Farley, Two Years in Syria (London, 1858), p. 372 (the conversion of pounds sterling to piastres was done at the rate of 110 piastres to 1 pound).
[16] Volney, op. cit., II, 279.
[17] J. G. Wetzstein, "Der Markt in Damaskus," Zeitschrift der Deutschen morgenlandischen Gesellschaft, XI, (1857), 478–79.
[18] J. L. Burckhardt, Travels in Syria and the Holy Land (London, 1822), p. 44.
[19] M. Michaud and M. Poujoulat, Correspondance d'Orient 1830–1831 (Paris, 1833), VI, 125.
[20] P. Uspenskii, Kniga bytiia moego: Dnevniki i avtobiograficheskie zapiski (Book on my Life: Diaries and Autobiographical Notes) (St. Petersburg, 1896), III, 266.
[21] F. A. Neale, Eight Years in Syria, Palestine, and Asia Minor from 1842–1850 (London, 1851), I, 205.
[22] Wetzstein, op. cit., p. 480.

The speed with which these towns grew is noteworthy, for it is indicative of the development of trade activities in Lebanon. Toward the end of the eighteenth century, Zahleh, a small village in the Biqa' valley, had only 200 houses; by the 1820's it had 800–900, while the population numbered nearly 5,000.[23] In the 1850's the town population increased to 7,000–8,000.[24] Zahleh was located at the intersection of trade routes and served as a depot for grain gathered in the Biqa' valley. The town supplied Beirut and Lebanese silkworm breeders with grain. Nomads from Arabia and Kurdistan drove their livestock there and bartered their goods for Lebanese and European manufactures. Production of handicrafts (leather, woven and dyed goods) played some part in the town. A stratum of tradesmen was formed in Zahleh in the mid-1800's, about which the Russian consul in Beirut, K. D. Petkovich, reported: "There are rich merchants among the (Zahleh) townspeople who run a large grain business of their own and serve as brokers for commercial houses of Beirut.[25] By then, merchants were not merely engaged in buying nomadic live-stock and leather in the Aleppo and Damascus *vilayet*'s. Leatherworks and dyeworks in the town were owned by Zahleh merchants;[26] some of them owned fields in the Biqa' and employed hired labor.

The information given above (and it could be augmented) shows the effect of growing agricultural specialization on domestic trade relations, which were relatively extensive and well established by the middle of the nineteenth century. Towns played the role of regional commercial centers (as may be observed, for example, in Damascus, Beirut, and Zahleh). The development of commercial relations (information given below attests to the impact of growing industrial production on the development of the domestic market) suggests the evolution toward a common market which for the time being was confined to Syria, Lebanon, and Palestine. The "guiding spirit" of this movement was the emerging national commercial bourgeoisie, which in certain places (as for instance in Zahleh) invested part of its capital in industrial production. Dependence on comprador capital, clearly observable in the transactions of the Zahleh merchants, was a characteristic feature of this bourgeoisie even in its earlier stages of development. The Zahleh merchants and entrepreneurs in the 1860's and 1870's depended for credit on the merchants of Beirut. According to K. D. Petkovich's brief description of this dependence, Zahleh's commercial transactions were realized "by money received on credit from Beirut merchants."[27] Beirut merchants on the other hand were typical compradors, having amassed immense fortunes as commercial middlemen.

Trade, combining export of agricultural produce and import of manufactures, determined the drift of major commercial operations in the mid-nineteenth century. Developments in foreign trade resulted in increased dependence of the economies of Syria, Lebanon, and Palestine on foreign capital. It is noteworthy that the growth in the volume of foreign trade at that time entailed a reduction of, and sometimes severed, those domestic ties existing in the 1830's to 1840's, thereby delaying the creation of a common market. Thus, for example, export of Lebanese raw silk through Beirut increased each decade. In the years when world prices were high, raw silk, normally consumed in local industries, was pumped out of the country *in toto*.[28] Aleppo cotton-weaving manufactories in the 1840's used English imported yarn while local cotton production suffered a

[23] Burckhardt, *op. cit.*, p. 5.
[24] I. Abkarius, *The Lebanon in Turmoil: Syria and the Powers in 1860*, p. 89.
[25] K. Petkovich, "Livan i livantsy," *Sbornik geograficheskikh, topograficheskikh i statisticheskikh materialov po Azii*, (St. Petersburg, 1885), 175.
[26] *Ibid.*

[27] *Ibid.*
[28] Some years owners of Lebanese silkweaving shops were forced to buy Smyrna silk at higher costs because the local thread was bought up by agents of foreign capital trade.

decline, owing to a lack of demand for cotton. English, French, and Swiss calico and broadcloth, which flooded the Syrian, Lebanese, and Palestine markets, displaced the fabrics of the Damascus and Aleppo textile industries.

An obvious indicator of the development of foreign trade was the rapid growth of coastal towns which exported foodstuffs. The following figures depict Beirut's population growth over a century.[29]

	Inhabitants
1782.	6,000
1830–31.	9,000
1846–47.	10,000–12,000
1860's	40,000
1885.	100,000

In the mid-nineteenth century, most of the seaport trade centered in Beirut. The town of Saida, which at one time had been an important provincial center, dwindled in size, and its population of 6,000–7,000 depended entirely on Beirut. In Palestine, the town of Haifa became a rapidly growing port exporting grain, sesame, olive oil, and soap to Europe. In the early 1840's Haifa was an insignificant fishing village with a population of 200, in whose bay Arab feluccas sought shelter from storms. In 1850 the population rose to 3,000 and housing facilities could not absorb the daily influx of settlers, who failed to meet the growing demand for labor. In two autumn months of 1850 alone, eight English vessels transporting wheat anchored at Haifa, not counting a large number of Greek vessels carrying wheat to Bristol and northern Ireland.[30]

Industrial production did not develop in either Beirut or Haifa. These were market towns. Beirut had only a few dyeworks, pottery workshops, and a small shipyard which built feluccas.[31] However, Beirut

had dozens of foreign commercial offices and offices of local compradors and usurers. In the 1850's a branch of the Ottoman bank (with English capital) was opened in the city, a commercial court was established, and the first hotels, owned by local compradors, were built in the European style.[32] In 1858 French capital built the first roadway linking Beirut to Damascus. This road facilitated the import of European manufactures into Syria and the export of food products from Lebanon, which it crossed. A comparison of data on the population growth of Zahleh and Beirut gives a clear indication of the predominating processes in the growth of trade. Foreign capital took roots in Syria, Lebanon, and Palestine and exploited the level of commodity-monetary nexus and agricultural specialization attained in the first decade of the nineteenth century in these countries in order to subject them to the interests of western capitalist industry. The results were already visible by the 1840's.

Trade relations do not reveal those internal processes which were developing in the village under the impact of the commodity-monetary nexus. They do not give a clear-cut reply to the question of how close a link existed between Syrian and Lebanese farming and the market. One can only surmise the degree to which this nexus dominated agriculture and the degree to which farming was subject to foreign capital.

While the growing commercialization of peasant farming must be noted, it must not be overrated. One should bear in mind that in the first place rent was paid in kind in the market. This rent was collected from peasants by landowners and tax farmers and, hence, peasant farming was not directly linked to the market in this instance.[33]

One can judge the enormous size of the rent realized by feudal lords in the market from the following data. The annual

[29] For data on 1782, see Volney, op. cit., II, 309; 1830–31, Michaud and Poujoulat, op. cit., VI, 123; 1846–47, Rafalovich, op. cit., p. 427; 1860's R. Thompson, The Land and the Book (London, 1886), p. 37; 1855, N. Verney and G. Dambmann, Les Puissances étrangères dans le Levant, en Syrie et en Palestine (Paris-Lyon, 1900), p. 339.
[30] Neale, op. cit., p. 115.
[31] Farley, op. cit., pp. 109, 111.

[32] Ibid., p. 54.
[33] While not directly linked to the market, the peasant nevertheless felt its impact, if only by being frequently ordered by the landlord to raise crops which were in great demand on the market and to supply rent in kind.

income of one of the most powerful sheikhs in Lebanon, Bashir Jumblat, amounted to 50,000 pounds sterling in the 1820's, according to Burckhardt.[34] Another wealthy Lebanese feudal lord received, at the turn of the 1850's, a rent of £15,000 from his olive "plantations" alone,[35] as did Mas'ud-Effendi, a feudal lord from Antioch who had a similar revenue from silk "plantations."[36] Bearing in mind the conditions of production in Syria at that time, one can state with assurance that the so-called "plantations" were cultivated by *métayers* while the money income of feudal lords represented a feudal rent in kind realized in the market. As a rule wealthy landowners sold their agricultural produce to merchants in neighboring towns. Thus, during the Druze–Maronite conflict in 1860, close economic ties between Maronite merchants of Dair al-Qamar and Druze feudal lords in southern Lebanon were disclosed.[37]

However, not only the share of peasant products supplied to the feudal lord as rent in kind was marketed (and this was the predominant type of rent), but also a significant share of the produce retained on the farm. Farmers' reliance on the market was particularly apparent in Lebanon. Urquhart notes that in the late 1840's Lebanese silk farmers sold their entire silk yield. Close ties between farmers and markets were observed in other regions as well.[38]

Disruption of domestic industry was the inevitable precondition which made possible the disintegration of the barter economy and increased commercialization of peasant farming.

In his study on Syria[39] Volney describes Lebanon's barter peasant economy in the last quarter of the eighteenth century. Primitive agricultural tools as well as clothing were made in the peasant household. Even in the late eighteenth century, however, the peasant economy was not an entirely closed one. Peasants even then brought crude linen, silk, and cotton thread, i.e., home-industry products, to market. Half a century later however, in the 1840's, the English traveler Urquhart noted that home industries had been ruined everywhere in Lebanon. Peasants not only ceased weaving,[40] replacing homemade fabrics with cheap English cottons, but at times even stopped reeling silk filaments from cocoons, this work having been taken over by silk-spinners who sprang up in Lebanon.

Home industries continued to prevail in remote regions of Syria, hardly touched by foreign capital. Even in Lebanon vestiges of home industries were retained for a long time. Peasants wove garments from silk tufts or tow, because the reeling of silk filaments from cocoons was for the most part done by the peasant families.

As the dependence of the peasant household on the market grew, the nature of this relationship changed. According to Volney, the Lebanese peasant in the latter part of the eighteenth century marketed his produce, unassisted, in coastal town bazaars. The Hawrani peasants, even in the mid-nineteenth century, were still actively engaged in supplying grain to the Damascus market.[41] But charcoal, with which they also supplied the city, was purchased as a rule at the city wall by dealers (*perekupsh-chiki*) who greatly enriched themselves from these transactions. The Lebanese

[34] Burckhardt, *op. cit.*, pp. 196–97.
[35] Urquhart, *op. cit.*, p. 183.
[36] Neale, *op. cit.*, II, 30.
[37] At the time of the Dair al-Qamar raids by Druze detachments in 1860, their leader, Shaikh Said Jumblat, saw to the safety of those Christian merchants with whom he had close commercial ties.
[38] Inhabitants of Hawran, one of the backward regions in Syria, supplied Damascus with wheat. Caravans loaded with grain, escorted by entire peasant families, arrived in Damascus from Hawran. The Hawranis increased or curtailed their wheat crop in accordance with market demand. The Russian Orientalist Porfirii Uspenskii reported that the Hawran Druze who raised arms against conscription decided to reduce their wheat crop in order to compel the Turkish authorities in Damascus, by means of famine or high prices of grain, to exempt them from service.
[39] Volney, *op. cit.*, III, 149.
[40] Urquhart, *op. cit.*, pp. 321–22.
[41] This conclusion can be drawn from Lortet's description (Lortet, *La Syrie d'aujourd' hui: Voyages dans la Phénicie, le Liban et la Judée*, 1875–1880 [Paris, 1884], pp. 599–600).

peasant, on the other hand, was already completely cut off from the market in the mid-nineteenth century. The buyer and the middleman had entrenched themselves between him and the market. What was novel, however, was not so much the distance separating the *fellah* from the market, but rather the altered nature of the transaction, which became entangled in usurious deals. This state of affairs was made possible by the *fellahin's* misery and lack of rights, which were the result of the high degree of feudal exploitation in villages. K. M. Bazili drew the following picture: once a year, when taxes were collected (i.e., when peasants were in particularly dire straits) a swarm of buyers headed for Lebanese and Syrian villages. Taking advantage of the peasants' financial need, these buyers extended loans to the *fellahin* against their future harvest at 3–5 per cent per month, or bought up the standing harvest at two-thirds or half its price. The interest rate varied with each crop and, characteristically, with the degree of feudal exploitation in a given region (in the latter case dependence was direct). Deals were even more crushing in the valleys directly under Turkish authority, where exploitation of the peasantry by Arab and Turkish feudal lords was more oppressive.[42]

Buyers operating in Syrian villages were usually agents of foreign merchants. Foreign capital found a fertile soil for its commercial and usurious activities in villages pressed beneath the feudal yoke. European commercial houses in Beirut often sent their salesmen to the villages to purchase raw materials. Most of the salesmen, however, were in the service of local compradors. Similar deals were transacted by the agents of local or foreign silk-spinners. Hence, commercial and usurious capital penetrated the villages from outside, except where the usurer or merchant was himself the feudal lord of the village; this was the case in commercially developed parts of the country. But the feudal lord was often supplanted by the representative of com-

mercial and usurious capital. According to an account by the English consul, Neale,[43] feudal lords—owners of land around Antioch who extended loans to *métayers*—often borrowed money from European and local Aleppo and Antioch merchants. Such was the intricate intermeshing and interaction of feudal exploitation and usury.

The reasons for the highly developed practices of commercial and usurious exploitation in Syria and Lebanon in the mid-nineteenth century were hidden not only in the high degree of feudal exploitation, which hampered free development of a commodity-monetary nexus in the villages, but also in the very trend of economic development in these countries, which had already been determined in the 1850's. The impoverished peasant could not leave the village to seek a living in town for, by the 1840's, industrial production was sharply declining and the peasant was therefore forced to hang on to his farm, thus falling prey to the usurer.

Feudal and usurious exploitation drained peasant farms, creating conditions in which the inception and development of capitalistic relations was extremely slow despite the relatively highly developed commodity-monetary nexus. Nevertheless, new types of exploitation began to appear in Syria, Lebanon, and Palestine.

As far back as the latter part of the eighteenth century Volney wrote of the Lebanese peasants' migration in search of work. Having collected silk-worm cocoons, mountaineers descended into the valleys to garner the crop like "the Limousins."[44] K. D. Petkovich reports a similar practice, namely, the Lebanese peasants' migration to Biqa' and other regions in the 1870's. Uspenskii encountered an analogous phenomenon in Palestine in the 1840's, where peasants from remote villages came to harvest in grain cultivation areas;[45] he struck up an acquaintance in the region of

[42] AVPR, *loc. cit.*

[43] Neale, *op. cit.*, II, 33–34.
[44] Volney, *op. cit.*, III, 198. (Limousin is an ancient French province.)
[45] Uspenskii, *op. cit.*, II, 58.

Hebron with a peasant from the village of Bait Jala, who came to the region each year to work in the fields.[46]

Reports from Volney, Petkovich, and Uspenskii of peasants migrating in search of a living were substantiated by Urquhart. He gives a family budget for one such family from a Lebanese village, the owner of a plot of land. The family consisted of four persons (two men and two women). Their expenses, including taxes of 115 piastres a year, amounted to 1,575 piastres in monetary terms. The family income amounted to 500 piastres from the sale of silk and whatever sum they received from the sale of wine, but half of the expenses was covered by earnings from farm labor. Every year both men spent two-thirds of the farming season (over four months) working as farmhands, thus earning 3 piastres daily, which totaled approximately 800 piastres. In this manner the family was able to make ends meet.[47] It can safely be stated that the foregoing conveys a picture of an allotment-holding farm worker. The allotment consisted of a plot of land, the revenue from which covered only half of the family's expenses. For this family farm labor was the most important and permanent source of income. The members of this family divided their time "between seeking various employments and their own farm" (V. I. Lenin).

It is noteworthy that there already existed in the mid-nineteenth century a standard rate for hired labor in the various regions of Syria and Lebanon. Skin reported in the late 1850's (apparently in 1859) that the wages of hired field hands in the Aleppo region was 7 pence a day, i.e., approximately 3.5 piastres. He pointed out, however, that wages were 30 per cent higher that year.[48] Thus, the normal wage of a hired hand in

the Aleppo region was 2.5–3 piastres a day, which equals the amount earned by a hired hand in Lebanon. An unskilled worker in Aleppo and Damascus manufactories earned approximately the same wage. Therefore, in various regions of Syria and Lebanon (in both towns and in rural areas) similar conditions prevailed for hiring manpower. This already indicates that a common Syrian–Lebanese market of hired labor was being formed, which was a constituent part of the over-all development of a national market. But this process was still in its earliest stages.

A number of sources attest to the existing differentiation among the peasantry in Syrian villages in the nineteenth century. Guys wrote of "the poor day-laborers" in Lebanon, who, three-fourths of the time, lived in anticipation of the season when they would be needed.[49] Moreover Guys, in listing various strata of the population, placed particular emphasis on the most numerous one (and this undoubtedly is an exaggeration) which, in his opinion "were the most miserable people" and from whom were recruited artisans, shepherds, journeymen, muleteers, wood-cutters, etc.[50] It is known that peasants who migrated in search of a living worked in silk-reeling filatures in Syria and Lebanon, on the construction of the Beirut-Damascus road, etc.

The Lebanese peasants' state of impoverishment and dispossession became particularly acute in the last third of the nineteenth century, when the mass overseas emigration of surplus peasants became widespread.

At the other extreme, already in the earlier part of the nineteenth century a much less numerous [than the peasants] group of prosperous farmers began to appear in the villages. They had acquired private property as a means of production and tended to become the rural bourgeoisie. Guys writes of the stratum of landed "proprietors consisting of affluent peasants," who hired

---

[46] As a result of an increase in grain export from Palestine, demand for manpower in the mid-nineteenth century was relatively high. Thus, 150 Trans Jordanian peasants who left their villages in 1847 owing to famine found work in various villages near Hebron (AVPR, case 915, l. 174).

[47] Urquhart, *op. cit.*, pp. 389–91.

[48] *Abstract of Reports* . . .

[49] Guys, *op. cit.*, II, 145.

[50] *Ibid.*, pp. 145–46.

"poor journeymen to collect silk-worm cocoons."[51] However, aside from this brief description, the French consul gives no information on the wealthy peasantry. We have no specific information on farms employing hired help. Only indirect data indicate that a certain portion of farms in the Biqa' valley belonged to this type. Some of the rich Lebanese peasants engaged in trade. Among the witnesses to a feudal Druze trial in 1861 was a certain Shahin Milhidi from the village of Ain Bal, who lived in Mukhtara, a large village in southern Lebanon, and engaged in trade.[52] The inhabitants of the Lebanese village of Bikfayya traded in tobacco, tar, horses, and various livestock with different regions in Syria and even Egypt. At the same time this village served as a summer resort for well-to-do Beirutis, and its residents consequently earned money by renting their homes and serving the town dwellers in the summer season.[53] In artisan villages which will be discussed below, an upper crust was formed which employed hired labor in handicraft.

The new socioeconomic structure in Syria in the first half of the nineteenth century was, however, extremely rudimentary and underdeveloped. Capitalist production made only a sporadic appearance here.

The nineteenth-century Syrian peasantry retained the basic class-estate characteristics of a feudal society. It fell into categories and groups according to the form and size of landownership and the nature of personal dependence. The socioeconomic differentiation of the peasantry and the emergence of new types of rural population (kulaks and proletarians) were barely noticeable. The evolution of the Syrian peasantry, the disintegration of feudal relations, and the crumbling of the barter economy were manifested primarily in the dispossession of peasants and their transformation from owners of allotments and small proprietors

to métayers. This phenomenon gained considerably in scope.

The transformation of peasant-proprietors to métayers in the first half of the nineteenth century was largely due to the acute deterioration of their economic and legal situation. The métayers were expected to pay their feudal landlord a specific, traditional share of the harvest, the size of which depended on the crop raised on the plot of land, on whether the métayer owned tools, draught animals and seeds, on irrigation conditions, etc. This portion of the harvest yield was considerably higher than the land tax paid by the peasant-owner of an allotment.

Besides the payment of a portion of the harvest yield to the land proprietor, métayers were required to pay other requisitions in kind, e.g., fowls, eggs, cheese, oil, milk, and other products, and were required to supply the house of the feudal lord with charcoal and firewood. Métayers were required to perform corvée by building houses, palaces, and forts for the chief amir (in Lebanon) and for their landlords. These requirements and obligations are reminiscent of the duties fulfilled in Western Europe (in particular in southwest Germany on the eve of the Peasant War) by peasants to their seigneurs by virtue of personal dependence. There is clear indication that the métayer was personally dependent on the feudal lord: the former did not have the right to marry without the landlord's permission; upon his marriage the métayer paid a fee ("kartak"), and, according to some sources, the métayer could not leave his feudal lord at will, whereas the latter could forcibly transfer a métayer to another estate.[54]

The new economic conditions left their mark on the feudal economy. In seeking to meet the growing need for money, the feudal class intensified its exploitation of the peasantry.[55] Attempts were made to sub-

51 Ibid., p. 145.
52 AVPR, case 1308, l. 185.
53 Dar al-Ma'arif Encyclopedia, V, 526 (article on Bikfayya).

54 Aouad, Le droit privé des Maronites du temps des émires Chihab (1697–1841) (Paris, 1933), pp. 131–32. Churchill, The Druzes and the Maronites under Turkish Rule from 1840–1860 (London, 1862).
55 The intensification of feudal exploitation—a development typical of this period in the history of

stitute money for rents in kind. As reported by Urquhart,[56] monks of the Mar-Hanna monastery (in the village of Shwair) used to clothe themselves in homemade cotton and woolen fabrics provided to the monastery by peasants as feudal rent. Volney still found a developed manorial handicraft in that monastery. The monks, wrote the French traveler, "engaged in a type of handicraft, indispensable or useful to the monastery. One monk is a weaver and makes fabrics; another a tailor and sews clothes; a third a shoemaker." He then mentions a mason, baker, binder, etc.[57] However, by the 1840's the monastery bought clothes made of American cotton and all that was left for the monks to do was to dye them the appropriate color. In order to replace the abandoned manorial handicraft, one of the pillars of the barter economy, the monastery imposed a money rent on its peasants. Urquhart indicates that "the peasants would have been glad to bring cotton or wool, but they (monks) preferred piastres."[58] The commutation of rent-in-kind, however, did not become widespread; as of old, *métayage* was based on rent-in-kind.

The growing demand for agricultural produce on the foreign market, and the economic depletion of the peasant farm, prompted separate feudal lords to set up their own commodity economy by using *corvée* labor and that of hired workers. Bazili repeatedly reported the growing practice of the *corvée*. The plantations of sheikhs, amirs, and monasteries were generally tended by peasants, who turned over half of their produce (as rent) to the owner. He writes, "but many nobles, who had inherited from preceding generations the practice of patriarchal authority, introduced the practice of employing unpaid peasants

for this type of work."[59] In another place, he notes that "peasants were required to work on seignorial lands almost for nothing."[60]

Large estate farming, however, did not become widespread in Syria. The exploitation of the peasant *métayer* remained the basic form of farm management, this practice apparently being more profitable. Preference for the *métayage* system of land cultivation in the above-mentioned Mar-Hanna monastery, as reported by Volney, is of some interest. In the latter part of the eighteenth century the monastery leased considerable tracts of land from two amirs, for which it paid a rent of 400 piastres. "These lands were formerly plowed by monks but now they prefer to have them cultivated by peasants, who turn over to them half of the total yield."[61]

Uspenskii furnishes interesting information on the use of hired labor in monasteries. The Orthodox monastery of St. George in Lebanon, located on the main road between Aleppo and Tripoli, served as a resting place for traveling merchants. It housed entire caravans within its walls and used great quantities of grain, rice, oil, wine, etc., to feed its guests. The monastery's expenses were more than covered by voluntary contributions from travelers. Increasingly in the nineteenth century, the monastery began to acquire land. It owned vineyards, silkworm plantations, and arable lands in varying degrees of proximity to the monastery. Besides this, the monastery had 700–800 sheep, as many goats, 25 cows, 10 mules, 3 horses, and 10 pairs of oxen. The monastery's annual revenue was 120–130 thousand piastres, one-sixth of which was used for the needs of the twenty-two monks and the rest sent to the prelates. The patriarch alone demanded 20 thousand piastres from the monastery. Forty servants, who received board and wages, were employed to care for lodgers and manage the monastic household. Part of the arable

---

Syria, Lebanon, and Palestine—was the basic reason for the heightened class struggle in villages. See I. M. Smilianskaia, "Krestianskoe vosstanie v Kesruane (Livan, 1859–1860)," *Kratkie soobshcheniia Instituta vostokovedeniia AM SSSR* (USSR), XIV issue, 1955.

[56] Urquhart, *op. cit.*, II, 7.
[57] Volney, *op. cit.*, p. 326.
[58] Urquhart, *loc. cit.*

[59] AVPR, case 718, l. 114.
[60] *Ibid.*, l. 155.
[61] Volney, *op. cit.*, p. 327.

land was likewise cultivated by hired wage laborers. Workers were also hired to mind the livestock. Forty other persons worked outside the precincts of the monastery. In all, the monastery employed over 80 persons. Most of the land was farmed, on various *métayage* terms, by peasants drawn from neighboring villages dependent on the monastery. These peasants, Uspenskii pointed out, "feed, clothe themselves and build houses" unlike wage workers.[62]

Thus the monastery employed a considerable number of workers for domestic purposes and for tending livestock, while most of the arable land was cultivated by *métayers*. The monastery did not engage in large-scale farming. There is indication that monasteries employed many workers on a short-term basis, but here again in work unrelated to land cultivation.[63]

The routine technology prevalent in Syrian farming prevented the emergence of large-scale farming based on hired labor. V. I. Lenin pointed out the incompatibility of backward feudal technology with large-scale farming.[64] A typical fact vividly confirms this. Monks in Syrian monasteries sometimes received allotments from the monastery to cultivate on their own. Hence, even with unpaid labor power collected under one roof, there was no wide-scale farming inasmuch as land was traditionally cultivated by plots.[65]

Large-scale farming would have required considerable sums to purchase agricultural implements, the use of more advanced agricultural technology, etc. With the limited internal market for agricultural produce and an unstable foreign market, however, wide-scale farming entailed risks which Syrian feudal lords, who in the past by and large had no farms of their own [i.e.,

managed directly by them], were not ready to incur. It is noteworthy that information on the emergence of farms employing *corvée* or hired labor pertains to the 1850's. At that time, particularly during the Crimean War, the great demand for Syrian agricultural produce on the foreign market stimulated farming.[66] Attempts to introduce winnowing machines and cotton gins in the country were made in the 1850's, but these were not widely used. Hired labor was more frequently employed in grain-cultivating regions (the Biqa' valley, Palestine); this phenomenon was apparently related to the existence of a more stable internal grain market. This market developed in response to specialization in industrial crop production in various areas of the country. Large urban populations also consumed great quantities of grain. But even in grain-cultivating areas hired labor was not widely adopted.

The catastrophic decline of handicraft and manufactorial industry starting in the 1820's led to a sharp fall in the population of such urban handicraft centers as Damascus and Aleppo[67] and hence to a contraction of the internal grain market. A large number of city dwellers returned to the villages, thus creating a surplus population by the first half of the nineteenth century. (We have no information of any noticeable parallel expansion of sown areas at that time.) Statements by the French consul with regard to this surplus population have already been cited; in the 1840's there resided in Lebanon a large number of exceedingly poor inhabitants who lived three-fourths of the year in anticipation of the season when silkworms were collected and when their labor would be needed.[68] The appearance of a surplus population in villages forced peasants to do everything possible to retain leased plots of land, while

[62] Tsentralnyi gosudarstvennyi istoricheskii arkhiv v Leningrade (The Central Historical State Archive in Leningrad), fd. 797, op. 87, ed. khr. 57, 1847; Uspenskii, *op. cit.*, I, 284.

[63] *Ibid.*, p. 310.

[64] See Lenin, *op. cit.*, IV, 99.

[65] Uspenskii, *op. cit.*, p. 283. (Uspenskii reports the fact that St. George monastery, having purchased land, turned it over to a monk to farm. Upon his death the land reverted to the monastery.)

[66] *Abstracts of Reports . . .*, pp. 442–43.

[67] According to Bazili, the population of Damascus and Aleppo decreased by more than 100,000 over 20 years (1820–40) (AVPR, ll. 99, 100). An appreciable growth of coastal towns began only in the second half of the nineteenth century.

[68] Guys, *loc. cit.*

feudal lords used this opportunity for unconstrained and increased exploitation of such a peasantry. (Note was made earlier how this affected usurious exploitation.)

Exploitation of the *métayer* turned out to be profitable; it did not entail risks, trouble, or capital. But *métayage*, per se, under new economic conditions, slowly acquired a new social significance. From a serf, the *métayer* evolved into a farmhand; this process, however, was extremely slow and painful and progressed through many stages. Unfortunately material at our disposal on *métayage* is inadequate to retrace this evolution. One can only outline some of its characteristics.

In the nineteenth century, according to Guys, Petkovich, and Berkenheim,[69] of the various forms of *métayage*, a nominally short-term lease was most widespread, under which the *métayer* had no landholding rights and could be arbitrarily driven off the land by the landowner. (As a matter of fact, the *métayer* was usually in oppressive dependence on the feudal lord and could not leave the land without his permission.) The ruin and impoverishment of the Syrian peasantry in the nineteenth century was accompanied not only by the loss of rights to land but also by the forfeiture of agricultural implements and draft animals. It is common knowledge that "the landless, horseless, propertyless peasant was an unsuitable object for feudal exploitation."[70] For this reason the Syrian feudal lord provided such a peasant with land, implements, often livestock and seeds. Moreover, he frequently put living quarters at his disposal and lent him money. In return, the peasant was required to content himself with only a minimal share of the harvest. A complex combination of feudal exploitation and capitalistic elements resulted.

The abrogation of the feudal lord's judicial power and the introduction of equal tax obligations for all classes of the popula-

tion, which took place in Lebanon in 1861, undermined the peasants' personal dependence. There is no doubt that the relationship between the peasant and the landowner changed also in cases when a merchant or a usurer, i.e., a representative of the stratum with limited political rights as compared with the feudal class, became a landowner. It can thus be concluded that (at least in Lebanon) noneconomic coercion applied to peasants by feudal landowners began to weaken in the second half of the nineteenth century. Instead of a personal dependence, however, the peasant *métayer* was economically enslaved by the landowner. While feudal relations of production disintegrated, they survived in semifeudal forms. The stability of feudal and semifeudal forms of exploitation in the village was determined not merely by the nature of agrarian development but also by the absence of widespread capitalistic relations in industry. Both these factors were the outcome of the transformation of Syria, Lebanon, and Palestine into semi-colonies of the European bourgeoisie.

Before turning to an analysis of the industrial situation in these countries, mention should be made of how representatives of the feudal class used the capital they accumulated by the exploitation of peasants. This capital was not invested in agriculture as a rule, but in trade and usurious operations, in building and buying urban buildings to rent as shops, warehouses, stores and apartments; it was much less frequently invested in industry, to set up spinning mills and manufactories. During the rapid growth of trade, primarily the export of raw materials and the import of European manufactures, investment of capital in trade provided the highest returns. One branch of the ancient feudal family of Dahdah, owners of a *muqata'a* in northern Lebanon, had commercial offices in Marseilles, Paris, and London.[71] A bishop of the Maronite church, Tobia, was co-owner of the Beirut commercial firm of "Tobia and Asfar."[72]

[69] *Ibid.*; Petkovich, *op. cit.*; A. M. Berkenheim, *Sovremennoe ekonomicheskoe polozhenie Sirii i Palestiny* (*Contemporary Economic Conditions in Syria and Palestine*) (Moscow, 1897).

[70] Lenin, *op. cit.*, XV, 66.

[71] Yusuf al-Dibs, *Al jami' al-mufassal fi tarikh al Mawarina al-muassal* (Beirut, 1859), p. 538.

[72] Farley, *op. cit.*, p. 385.

The Lebanese feudal lords Talhuq, Djumblat, and Arslan dealt in trade. Large revenues from the lease of urban buildings were earned by Syrian monasteries and feudal families. Amir Milhim Shihab earned an annual rent of £400 (approximately 44,000 piastres) from his urban buildings and shops.[73] The wealthy monastery of Sinai alone owned twenty-seven houses and shops in Cairo and a three-storey stone house in Alexandria which "it rented."[74] Sheikh 'Abd al-Malik invested his capital in a medium-size silk mill built in Lebanon in the 1840's by European merchants.[75]

Thus there stood out within the feudal class a landed gentry which was associated with the bourgeoisie through its economic interests. Affiliated with these were tradesmen and usurers who had acquired land and exploited peasants through feudal and semifeudal methods. However, only an insignificant portion of the feudal class managed to adapt to the new conditions; the majority of Syrian feudal lords were ruined and impoverished, one of the manifestations of the crisis of the feudal economy. Sources often refer to the large indebtedness of feudal lords. Lands of ruined Lebanese feudal lords passed into the hands of Beirut merchants, who constituted a new feudal layer. Ancient Lebanese feudal families met particularly quick ruin after 1861. The peasant uprising of 1859–60 dealt a harsh blow to Lebanese feudal lords. The transfer of lands to representatives of commercial and usurious capital was not accompanied by a basic change in exploitation of peasants who cultivated this land.

The inception of capitalist elements in industry preceded their development in agriculture. Manufactories already existed in Syria in the late eighteenth century. But at the beginning of the nineteenth century the country's industrial development was dealt a fatal blow. Under the competitive impact of European manufactured goods, handicraft and manufactory industry began to disintegrate rapidly. Aleppo and Damascus, ancient handicraft centers, were hit particularly hard. However, the ruin of handicraft workshops and of manufactories did not mean that industry came to a complete standstill. Industrial production continued, though on a very limited scale, and the rudiments of capitalistic elements in it developed very slowly.

Production of traditional household articles, utensils, and cloths and fabrics in national style, was in a much more favorable position.[76] This type of production in Lebanon, in the mid-nineteenth century, even underwent a certain upsurge. It developed on the basis of village industry; it could contract and expand according to demand and, in the final analysis, was geared to a relatively restricted market.

The development of village industry was part of the process by which industry became disassociated from agriculture. "The first type of industry to sever from patriarchal agriculture was handicraft, i.e., production of articles made to order."[77] "For purposes of local consumption," writes K. D. Petkovich, "inhabitants of villages and small towns engage in various types of handicraft, and among Lebanese one finds masons, carpenters, locksmiths, tailors, shoemakers, dyers, weavers and others, working with the most rudimentary tools."[78] These craftsmen, as a rule, purchased their own raw materials in Damascus, Tripoli, and Beirut. Most of the artisans worked continuously in one sort of trade or another, but had farms of their own as well. Work was nearly always done to order, and craftsmen supplied their output only in their immediate neighborhoods and usually handed down their craft from father to son. Such a craftsman was the father of one of the active participants of the Druze-Maronite clash,

[73] Urquhart, op. cit., p. 285.
[74] P. Uspenskii, "Sinaiskii obitel," Zhurnal Ministersva narodnogo prosveshcheniia, 1848, No. 12, p. 198.
[75] AVPR, case 736, l. 264.
[76] K. M. Bazili termed them "articles of a capricious fashion." Such were scarves, kerchieves, runners, etc., of silk with gold, adorned with the most fantastic designs in the eastern style (ibid., case 833, l. 203).
[77] Lenin, op. cit., III, 285–86.
[78] Petkovich, op. cit., p. 169.

Abu Samra Ghanim. He was a professional mason, filling various jobs in nearby villages, whose family permanently resided in its native village. When Abu Samra grew up, his father began taking him along on jobs. Remuneration was in the form of money: the master builder (at the beginning of the nineteenth century) received 2.5 piastres daily, an ordinary mason, 1 piastre, youths, 10 para.[79]

The transformation of village artisans into small-commodity producers was typical of a series of branches of Syrian (and especially Lebanese) handicraft in the first half of the nineteenth century. Moreover, entire villages took up a specific trade. Permanent handicraft centers sprouted. A large village in northern Lebanon, Zuq Mikhail, was famous for its weaving as far back as the beginning of the nineteenth century. According to Burckhardt the majority of the inhabitants of Zuq were shop owners and craftsmen who supplied Kisrwan with clothing and luxury items.[80] The shoemakers of this village were also famous. The villagers of Bait al-Din (the residence of the amir Bashir Shihab) produced various articles of clothing for the mountaineers during the same period. The townspeople of Zahleh manufactured cotton garments for the beduins,[81] who bartered their nomadic items for grain and manufactured goods in that town.

At the beginning of the nineteenth century a substantial part of handicraft was still geared to a limited market, essentially to satisfy the needs of the feudal stratum. According to Burckhardt, craftsmen of Dair al-Qamar skillfully produced 'aba's (woolen fabrics) woven with gold and silver for sheikhs. The value of one 'aba amounted to 800 piastres.[82] The product was generally sold in small local markets. Such a market, for example, existed in the town of Lydda, where, once a week, peasants from nearby villages sold cotton yarn;[83] similar bazaars were found in the large village of Riha,[84] in an ancient dilapidated khan not far from Hasbaya, where "villagers who lived a day's journey away converged on Tuesdays."[85] However, in the 1850's— and for some branches of handicraft in the early part of the nineteenth century—mass production for a widespread stratum of consumers was already well known and handicraft wares were spread over a large area. The village of Rashaya (Anti-Lebanon) specialized in earthenware crockery, which was marketed at a distance of a four to five days' journey in Hawran and Jaulan in particular.[86] Nearly every house in the village, reports Burckhardt, had its own pottery. Villages located near Damascus fashioned their wares for the Damascus market.[87] Peasants from villages in the valley of Halbun made lamp wicks and sold them at Damascus bazaars. The villagers of Bethlehem, as far back as the latter part of the eighteenth century, cut rosaries for pilgrims.[88]

Handicraft production, which had sprung up in villages, developed successfully in the nineteenth century. Hawrani peasants made millstones which were widely distributed in Syria and exported to Egypt.[89] Cotton materials made by Safadi artisans were marketed in Anti-Lebanon and Damascus.[90] At the beginning of the nineteenth century the village of Zuq supplied only Kisrwan with clothing articles, but by the second half of the century Zuq silks were well known throughout Syria, and even outside the country. They were exported to Egypt, to other provinces of the Ottoman Empire, and to Europe. The relatively extensive market for village handicraft wares is an indicator of the correspondingly high degree of development of small-scale commodity

[79] Kh. Kh. Faiz, *Abu Samra Ghanim, or the Lebanese Hero* (Cairo, 1905), p. 16 (in Arabic).
[80] Burckhardt, *op. cit.*, p. 183.
[81] *Ibid.*, pp. 6–7.
[82] *Ibid.*, p. 193.

[83] Volney, *op. cit.*, III, 53.
[84] Burckhardt, *op. cit.*, p. 125.
[85] *Ibid.*, p. 34.
[86] *Ibid.*, p. 36.
[87] Wetzstein, *op. cit.*, p. 490.
[88] Volney, *op. cit.*, p. 45.
[89] Burckhardt, *op. cit.*, p. 57.
[90] Rafalovich, *op. cit.*, 1847, No. 20.

production in the above-mentioned trading villages. The inhabitants, of these villages, however, continued to farm. For example, the village of Zuq was famed for both its sericulture and viticulture. The men of Hawran and Zahleh tilled the soil, etc. V. I. Lenin noted that "commodity production on the smallest scale in peasant industries already begins to separate industry from agriculture, although at this stage of development the industrialist is not in most cases distinct from the agriculturist".[91]

Unfortunately the material at our disposal throws hardly any light on the economic organization of handicrafts. The size of markets, upon which handicraft production depended, suggests that wares were marketed by merchants and that artisans were therefore already subordinated to commercial capital. Differentiation among handicraftsmen, which was an inevitable result of the development of small-commodity economy, can be observed in Lebanese village industry from data for the 1860's and 1870's. K. D. Petkovich describes the weaving industry of Zuq half a century after Burckhardt.[92] This production no longer relied exclusively upon local raw materials. Cotton yarn, silk, and wool were purchased in Beirut, and Austrian and German gold thread in Aleppo and Beirut. The village numbered 125 looms which wove material worth 10,000–15,000 Turkish liras a year; burnooses ('*aba*'s) were made, worth 5,000–6,000, etc. Zuq manufacturers, reported K. D. Petkovich, did not need a large amount of capital for their production; they worked on a day-to-day basis selling their goods on the spot, expanding and contracting production in accordance with demand. "Workers weaving silks and gold materials earn a daily wage of 10 piastres, and those who made burnooses, cotton, and woolen fabrics in general

content themselves with 5 piastres a day."[93] The workers referred to by Petkovich were people who sold their labor, in all probability to the so-called "factory owners"— workshop proprietors. But even these "factory owners" were no longer independent but depended on "the tradesmen who bought up their wares on the spot."

In the 1860's and 1870's the nature of production in the villages of Bikfayya, Shuwayfat, and Brummana increasingly resembled that of Zuq. K. D. Petkovich counted up to 1,500 looms in Bikfayya and neighboring villages, which turned out fabrics worth 100–110 thousand Turkish liras a year.[94]

In the mid-nineteenth century the weaving production of Dair al-Qamar, which developed on the basis of village crafts, was represented by small workshops. The extent of hired labor employed in these shops can be judged only by incidental, tentative information. Following the Druze-Maronite carnage of 1860, as a result of which the town was destroyed, workshop proprietors received a loan of 30,000 francs (750,000 piastres) from the French government to rehabilitate 42 workshops in which over 400 workers—men and women—were employed.[95] In all likelihood, these workshops basically reproduced the types and perhaps even the size of former workshops and hence had an average of 10 workers each.

Besides textile workshops, there were soap, gunpowder, and metal shops in Lebanon which also apparently employed hired labor. Thus, the village of Bait Shabab (central Lebanon) had a bell-casting plant (up to 20–30 per year) which also made various iron tools and articles: plows, horseshoes, silk-reeling pans, etc. The scope of such production presupposes hired labor. A small amount of metal was actually smelted in Lebanon (Kisrwan) but most

---

91 Lenin, *op. cit.*, p. 289.

92 During this time the variety of goods substantially increased and trade relations expanded. Woolens and silks woven with gold thread and articles made of these, i.e., pillows, table cloths, tobacco pouches, slippers (*tufli*), shawls, portraits, upholstery fabrics were made in Zuq. Zuq fabrics were noted for their sturdiness and beautiful designs and were widely esteemed in Syria, Egypt, and other provinces of the Ottoman Empire.

93 Petkovich, *op. cit.*, p. 171.

94 *Ibid.*, p. 172.

95 E. Louet, *Expédition de Syrie: Beyrouth le Liban, Jerusalem, 1860–1861* (Paris, 1862), pp. 345–46; 30,000 francs was equal to only about 130,000 piastres.— Translator.

of it was imported from Sweden and Germany.

K. D. Petkovich counted 14 soap works in Lebanon, which produced 500–600 qantars of soap a year, worth 480–600 thousand piastres. Soap was marketed in Lebanon and exported to Beirut and Egypt. Many soap plants were located in Palestine, which exported soap. In the 1840's up to 200,000 poods (3,276 metric tons) of soap were exported from Syria. [See Part IV, chap. 2.] Glass shops existed in Hebron, which in Volney's day already made artistic glassware for export to Constantinople.[96] Uspenskii, visiting Hebron some seventy years later, found several glass shops there. He saw "several large and small ovens installed in sooty and dirty cellars. Several black, emaciated Arabs sit near these ovens fashioning glassware." "I was in two works," writes Uspenskii, "one produces only glasses and jugs of a dark-blue shade, the other bracelets. All articles are very crude; it would be useless for anyone to look for cut glass or gilded glass or a glass store in Hebron. Besides, Hebron works market quite a bit of wares and they make up the major stock of trade and hence set the wages of the lowest, poorest stratum of Arabs."[97] The number of workers in workshops of this kind probably did not exceed five to ten. K. M. Bazili mentions gunpowder workshops which employed five workers. Lebanese village industry did not attain, and could not attain, a higher level of simple capitalistic co-operation and a rudimentary form of manufactory owing to mass imports of European industrial goods. It is noteworthy that, at the beginning of the twentieth century, researchers also mention the same Lebanese craft centers with the same assortment of wares and volume of production.[98]

A fully developed manufactory, and even some small factories, sprang up in the country only in those industrial areas where raw materials were processed for export. Silk-reeling manufactories, and some small factories using steam engines, appeared in Syria in the 1840's. These enterprises usually developed in rural areas close to sources of raw materials and were owned by foreign capitalists and local tradesmen. The first proprietors of factories were European (French and English) tradesmen living in Syrian coastal towns.[99] Thus, Sheikh Yusuf 'Abd al-Malik invested his capital in a silk mill founded by the French tradesman Portalis, who lived in Beirut. K. D. Petkovich names the proprietors of similar enterprises (among the local inhabitants the Asfar brothers, the usurer Sursuq brothers, and others). The stability of silk-reeling enterprises and their high earnings, secured by a cheap labor force as well as high demand for silk, attracted commercial capital. Until the 1860's there were only five or six such mills "with 100 reels each" in Lebanon, but then their number began to grow. By the eighties there existed in Lebanon sixty steam-operated silk mills with 3,850 reels.[100]

Employment in mills was seasonal, approximating 200 days a year. Up to 5,200 persons worked in 60 mills, i.e., an average of 80–100 per mill. Wages amounted to 5 piastres a day,[101] i.e., on a par with the earnings of the least skilled weaver. Along with the use of machines in silk-reeling mills, cheap female labor was employed and was even favored. Uspenskii mentions an English employer, proprietor of a silk-reeling factory in the region of Latakia, who preferred employing female labor.[102]

The condition of industry in old trade-craft centres, such as Aleppo and Damascus, was characterized by certain peculiarities. The industrial production of these towns was known far beyond Syrian borders. Aleppo gold brocades, Damascus and Aleppo semi-silks known in Russia as "*alaja, kubny, and cheremshuta*" were particularly

[96] Volney, *op. cit.*, pp. 46–47.
[97] Uspenskii, *op. cit.*, II, 40.
[98] See A. Ruppin, *Sovremennaia Siriia (Contemporary Syria)* (Petrograd, 1915).

[99] Petkovich, *op. cit.*, pp. 169, 179–80.
[100] *Ibid.*, p. 169.
[101] *Ibid.*, p. 170.
[102] Uspenskii, *op. cit.*, III, 600; IV, 85.

in vogue.[103] They were marketed not only throughout the Ottoman Empire but in Russia and Western Europe as well. In the eighteenth century this production was in a phase of capitalist manufactory. By then, the social composition of these cities had markedly changed: the role of the commercial-industrial bourgeoisie had gained in importance, hired labor appeared, and the process of differentiation among artisans developed extensively.

By the second quarter of the nineteenth century, however, the growth of commercial-industrial Syrian towns reached a turning point. A sharp population decline is indicative of this. According to K. M. Bazili, Aleppo numbered 150,000 in the 1820's, but only 80,000 in the forties. During that same period, the population of Damascus dwindled from 120,000 to 80,000.[104] The decline in urban population was due to the ruin of weaving and manufactorial and craft industry under the impact of competitive English fabrics.

Scant but interesting information exists on the organizational aspects of Aleppo handicrafts. There is hardly any mention of guilds for the end of the eighteenth century, even less for the beginning of the nineteenth. Apparently the guild system was in a state of disintegration and did not extend to the more developed crafts. This deduction is based on the fact that simple capitalistic co-operation had already arisen in urban crafts.

In reports for 1857–59, the English consul Skin in Aleppo cites a table illustrating the state of the town's crafts.[105] This table does not include those lines of production which had attained the level of manufactories. It does not include weaving, soap boiling, or rope production. The table has three charts: (1) branches of crafts and trade; (2) the number of shops and workshops in each branch; (3) the number of workers. The table includes both tradesmen and artisans and it is often impossible to determine whether reference is being made to a craft workshop at a bazaar which also sells the wares of the workshop, or to an ordinary commercial shop. According to the table, on the average, fifteen persons were employed per spinning workshop (400 workshops—6,000 workers); per bakery, 6 persons; per dyer's workshop, 9; per carpenter's, 4; gunsmith's, 4; tinsmith's, 4; turner's, 5; saddler's, 4; tinner's and coppersmith's, 3 each; shoemaker's, upholsterer's, perfumer's, and furrier, 2 persons each. If workshops averaging 2–3 persons used apprentices, members of the family and hired labor occasionally, then workshops which engaged 5–6 or more workers must have permanently employed hired labor, sometimes in large numbers. Thus, simple capitalistic co-operation had already come into being in these branches. It is noteworthy that besides spinning and baking the greatest incidence of hired labor was found in the construction trade (masons, carpenters, painters). Work in metal trades was insignificant. Skin counted only 40 blacksmiths in Aleppo[106]; in Damascus, there were only 54, and 50 tradesmen in iron.[107] The insignificant consumption of iron attests to the extreme backwardness of production.

To all appearances, manufactorial production began toward the end of the eighteenth century in Damascus and Aleppo. "Weaving was first among manufactories and remained the most important."[108]

The Lebanese writer Houry reported that Aleppo weaving manufactories operated 4,000 looms on which 4,800 men and children worked. All received wages, ranging from 3 to 12 piastres a day. Labor in this production generally followed the kind of commodity produced: 300 looms produced silks with gold and silver thread, 1,700 looms produced silks and cottons, 1,000 cottons, and finally 1,200 persons

103 AVPR, case 833, l. 203.
104 Ibid., case 718, l. 99. Rafalovich in referring to "the most reliable" sources estimated Aleppo's population in the 1840's at 77,500 (Rafalovich, op. cit., 1848, No. 23, p. 543).
105 Abstract of Reports . . ., p. 430.
106 Ibid.
107 Michaud and Poujoulat, op. cit., p. 168.
108 K. Marx and F. Engels, Works, 2d ed., III, 55.

working on 1,000 looms turned out coarse muslin prints. Wages in the latter case were the lowest. According to Houry's calculations, Aleppo's total output of fabrics was worth 25.5 million piastres a year.[109] Gold and silver thread was produced separately, in 15 work places employing 60 workers who earned 5–20 piastres a day.[110]

Printing and coloring of fabrics was executed in the town's dyeworks, which numbered 100; 1,500–1,600 workers were employed and earned 5–14 piastres a day. Thus, in the town's textile production there was a division of labor between spinning, weaving, manufacture of gold and silver thread, coloring and printing of fabrics. Moreover, division of labor existed according to the kind of commodity produced within each of these branches.

The size of Aleppo and Damascus manufactories was not big. In the 1830's, the Muslims of Damascus owned fourteen weaving manufactories whose capital amounted to only 700,000 piastres. Forty-five manufactories were owned by Christians; the capital of each of these ranged from 35,000 to 100,000 piastres,[111] i.e., was roughly equivalent to 2,000–6,000 silver rubles [See Part IV, chap. 2]. Among the proprietors were wealthy tradesmen and clergymen. Two particularly prosperous Damascus manufactories were owned by a Dervish Order. One of the most prosperous Damascus manufacturers was M. Hanuri, a joint owner of a commercial house with a capital of 2 million piastres.[112] Thus in both rural and urban trade the organizer of production was commercial capital, and the transition from rudimentary craft production to manufactory in the country came about by subordinating the immediate producer to commercial capital. This deduction, however, can be accepted only as a hypothesis, inasmuch as the dearth of material does not permit tracing this development in any detail.

According to Houry, soap-boiling production was also in the manufactorial phase. Toward the end of the 1830's Aleppo had thirty establishments of a manufactorial type in this branch; the town of Idlib, 15; 1,000 workers were employed in them whose [daily] wages amounted to 5–10 piastres. Each establishment averaged over 20 persons, attesting to a relatively high concentration of hired labor.

At its apogee, Syrian industry marketed wares not only in Syria, but throughout the Ottoman Empire. These external markets helped promote development of manufactorial production especially in weaving and soap boiling, i.e., those branches whose products were widely marketed. Division of labor was insignificant in the remaining branches of industry in the nineteenth century and the use of hired labor was only rudimentary.

Manufactorial production, because of the size of its output, was destined for a large market and any contraction of this market affected it adversely. "Manufactory in general could not survive without protection, because the slightest change in other countries would suffice to deprive it of its market and bring about its ruin. . . . No country can afford to risk the loss of its manufactory by allowing free competition."[113]

Favorable conditions for the development of manufactorial production were absent in the Ottoman Empire. As a result of the Capitulations, European industrial goods were put in a better position than locally produced goods. When Syria was flooded by cheap factory-made fabrics during the second quarter of the nineteenth century, local weaving manufactories could not survive under this pressure. According to K. M. Bazili's reports, the number of workers on Damascus weaving looms decreased from 8,000 to 2,000 between 1820 and 1840, and those in Aleppo, from 10,000 to 1,000.[114] In 1820, 80,000 pieces of *alaja* were shipped from Damascus to Salonika and were profitably marketed at

[109] C. B. Houry, *De la Syrie considérée sous le rapport commercial* (Paris, 1842), pp. 68–70. The data apparently apply to the mid-1830's.
[110] *Ibid.*
[111] *Ibid.*, p. 88. [112] *Ibid.*, p. 87.
[113] Marx and Engels, *op. cit.*, p. 58.
[114] AVPR, ll. 99, 100.

fairs in Rumelia. In the 1840's hardly 100 pieces were sold annually throughout Rumelia.[115]

The changes observed in industrial production at the end of the eighteenth century and at the beginning of the nineteenth, and the mass ruin of a number of industrial branches during the second quarter of the nineteenth century, left an imprint on the development of Syrian towns. According to K. D. Bazili's calculations, in Syria urban population accounted for one-fourth of the total.[116] This ratio is high, yet does not testify to a high level of industrial development in Syrian towns. Certain features, characteristic of an eastern medieval town, were inherent in these towns. The majority, even in the nineteenth century, maintained their importance as administrative centers of their provinces and regions. The characteristics of an eastern medieval town—headquarters of a feudal lord—still applied to Syrian towns of that period. A relatively large percentage of the urban population consisted of permanent domestics and part-time workers in the households of the pasha, his retinue, Turkish officials, Arab and Turkish notables, wealthy merchants, etc.

The relatively large size of Syria's urban population is not indicative of a high degree of separation between industry and agriculture. On the contrary, in most towns a substantial portion of the population engaged in agriculture. Many inhabitants of Beirut owned mulberry plantations adjoining the town. This was also true of Aleppo and Damascus, not to speak of Antioch, Latakia, and Tripoli. Most of the population in towns of secondary importance like Gaza, Zahleh, Lydda, and Ramla, were engaged in farming. This feature was the second characteristic of Syrian towns. Nonetheless, the commercial-industrial aspect of these towns cannot be ignored, especially that of Damascus and Aleppo. The prosperity of Damascus and Aleppo

in the sixteenth through the eighteenth centuries was essentially due to their role in transit trade between Persia, India, and Europe. In the seventeenth century Aleppo rivaled Constantinople and Smyrna. [See Part II, chap. 2.] But the increasing importance of the trade route to India around the Cape of Good Hope and the frequent Turkish-Persian wars substantially reduced Damascus' transit trade, and still more that of Aleppo. Nevertheless, at the close of the eighteenth and during the first half of the nineteenth century, the famous caravan routes from Persia through Diyarbakir to Aleppo, from Baghdad to Damascus, and from southern Arabia through Mecca and Medina to Damascus, had not yet lost their importance.[117]

In the nineteenth century the country's development of a trade-monetary nexus was accompanied by a growing domestic trade, the foci of which were the towns. By the close of the eighteenth and the beginning of the nineteenth century internal ties among Syrian towns, as well as those between towns and adjoining regions, were strengthened. These were new elements in urban life. By the middle of the nineteenth century the urban social composition noticeably changed, the role of the commercial-industrial bourgeoisie grew, a new stratum of hired laborers emerged, and the process of differentiation among artisans evolved further.

Manufactorial production and the presence of workshops employing hired labor presupposed a relatively developed stratum of hired laborers; moreover, a large number of journeymen was employed in the domestic service of well-to-do townsmen. Turkish authorities in the 1860's (already during the period of the decline of manufactories) singled out a particular layer of the urban population, designating them as "journeymen with no capital" or those who support themselves only by the daily wages they receive for their labor.[118] A large number of artisans, impoverished as a

[115] Ibid., l. 100.
[116] K. M. Bazili, "Siriia i Palestina pod turetskim pravitelstvom v istoricheskom i politicheskom otnosheniiakh," Statisticheskie zametki, Part II (St. Petersburg, 1875), p. 137.
[117] Charles-Roux, loc. cit.
[118] AVPR, case 1308, ll. 68–70.

result of the capture of the market by European commodities, approximated the stratum of hired labor in this economic status.

These strata of the population suffered most from the ruin of manufactorial and craft production in the nineteenth century, which was accompanied by acute impoverishment, and even by the perishing of many families. During the famine year 1846, K. D. Bazili wrote of this part of the Damascus population: "There is not enough work for all, and almost one thousand families of our faith (only Orthodox) are now dying of starvation."[119] Upon losing their jobs, some of the artisans and hired laborers became *Lumpenproletariat*; many, apparently, returned to their villages and some moved to coastal towns. The economic situation of the remaining artisans and hired laborers was so unstable that any price increase, the introduction of new taxes or conscription brought poverty and hunger.

Craft and manufactorial production was burdened by the fiscal policy of direct taxes (poll tax, taxes collected from workshops and shops) and indirect taxes levied by the Turkish government on industrial products (as well as on agricultural raw materials) which, according to K. D. Bazili, reached and even exceeded 40 per cent of the value of the product in the mid-nineteenth century.[120] These immense feudal levies

[119] *Ibid.*, case 817, l. 100.
[120] *Ibid.*, case 872, l. 245.

on Syrian industry reduced its ability to withstand foreign competition.

Thus, in the first half of the nineteenth century, Syria, Lebanon, and Palestine were countries where a feudal mode of production prevailed. However, this mode of production was in a state of disintegration and a capitalist structure originated within it.

The disintegration of the barter economy, the growth of a market-oriented peasant economy, the emergence of hired labor in villages, the elements of progressing stratification of the peasantry, the appearance of craft workshops employing hired labor, and the rise of capitalist manufactory were indicative of a development of new relations of production.

The process of disintegration of the feudal mode of production in Syria evolved under the conditions of a growing influx of foreign capital and of the subjection of the country's economic development to the interests of foreign capital. The legacy of this process was the ruin of industry and the impoverishment of the peasant economy.

The growing feudal oppression, along with exploitation by foreign capital, delayed the development of new relations of production. Feudal forms of exploitation were preserved under these conditions and this led to an even greater aggravation of economic and political contradictions and to an intensification of the class struggle.

CHAPTER 4

Railways, 1888–1914

The railways of "Greater Syria" present a striking example of an inadequate and uncoordinated system. The reasons for this—the nature of the terrain, the lack of government interest in the development of the area, the intense international rivalries, and the disintegration of the region after 1918—have been discussed in the Introduction to Part IV.

The first modern transport facility introduced in the region was the Beirut-Damascus road, started in 1859 and completed in 1863 by a French concessionary company. The daily coach service on this road took thirteen hours, instead of the three days formerly required on horse-back, and the road attracted to Damascus much of the Baghdad caravan traffic, which had previously gone to Aleppo and Alexandretta. The road also established Beirut as the main harbor on the eastern seaboard of the Mediterranean, a supremacy that was confirmed when the first modern port in the region was built there in 1890 by another French company.

The granting of a concession to a British concern for a railway from Acre to Damascus presented a danger to Beirut that was countered by a French company (D.H.P.) which built lines connecting Beirut with Damascus and the latter with the grain-producing region of the Hawran, at Muzairib. The same company also laid lines connecting Damascus with Aleppo, and Homs with Tripoli.

Meanwhile two other developments had taken place. A modern road was built from Jerusalem to Jaffa,[1] in 1869, followed in 1889 by a railway between the two towns; both were designed mainly for Christian and Jewish pilgrims and tourists. The Hijaz Railway, serving Muslim pilgrims, was built in 1900–1908; this competed with the French line in the Hawran and, since it had a branch to Haifa, also in export trade. Presenting an even greater competitive threat was the Berlin-Baghdad–Bahn which was approaching northern Syria. However, the Ottoman Bank, which had interests in both railways, brought about a secret agreement under which the B.B.B. would build a line connecting Aleppo with Alexandretta and also with the main Mesopotamian line, while the D.H.P. would build one

---

[1] Earlier, in 1859, the Jaffa–Jerusalem road had been considerably improved by the voluntary labor of the villagers, in anticipation of a visit by the sultan (A. Kayat to Lord John Russell, September 15, 1859, F.O. 78, no. 1449).

connecting Homs with both Tripoli and Dayr al-Zur; provisions were made for coordination of tariffs and sharing of revenue.

During the First World War the B.B.B. reached Aleppo, and in Palestine the British forces laid a line linking the Egyptian railways with Haifa. Since then there has been no important railway construction in Lebanon, Syria, and Jordan, and little in Israel. The lack of coordination of the main lines, and the differences in gauges, continue to constitute a major handicap. This has been largely overcome, however, by the extensive use of motor cars and trucks, on which the region has become heavily dependent, and the building of a very good network of highways.

(See also works by Elefteriades, Ruppin, Verney and Dambmann, Grant and Himadeh [*Economic Organization of Syria* and *Palestine*] listed in the Bibliography.)

[From M. Hecker, "Die Eisenbahnen in der asiatischen Türkei," *Archiv für Eisenbahnwesen* (Berlin), XXXVII (1914), 789–91, 797–98, 1062–69, 1306–7, 1310–11,1315–16.]

PROMOTED PRIVATE ACTIVITY

... With the concession of the Ismit-Ankara Railroad a new era began in the construction of railroads in Turkey. The government, and particularly Abdul Hamid himself, increasingly recognized the importance of railroads and now made an effort to have them built. But, in order to attract sound private capital, the government, which was flooded with dubious offers, had to offer a special security by means of a kilometric guarantee system. The Public Debts Administration was put forward, to guarantee the commitment assumed, and its successful and unimpeachable activity eliminated the distrust of Turkey felt by private capital. Only this important expansion of the activities of the Debts Administration made possible the great development of the railroads. The effect was a surprising one; numerous applications were received from leading financial centers, relating not as previously to small branch lines, but to expanded sections of many-sided importance. The government now gave out concessions with open hands. However, it attached an excessive and onesided importance to military value, and gave its guarantee only for lines of strategic interest; in particular,

it did not offer this privilege to narrow-gauge lines.

In the years 1888–93 no less than sixteen railway concessions were granted in Turkey: of these only two were in the European and the remaining ones in the Asiatic part of the country. Their total length amounted to about 5,350 kilometers (4,820 km. in Asia). The four narrow-guage lines were only 376 kms. long, and the remaining ones were of standard gauge. Of these nine (seven), of 4,370 kms. (3,540 kms.) in total length, were granted a kilometric guarantee that fluctuated between 10,300 and 18,000 francs per kilometer. Three of the concessions were unsuccessful, one remained unused, and the others came to completion, although some not until a later date. The source of the capital was almost exclusively French and German. Shortly after, three of the old lines were transferred to foreign hands, and two new British lines did not last long [*Waren ohne Bestand*]. The causes of this are related mainly to the changed political position of Britain in Turkey, which also had negative economic effects. Britain itself felt the repercussions of this setback and tried to combat it, but in vain.[1] Although the political influence of France had declined long ago, the extraordinary power of its capital[2] gave it a leading role also in

[1] A sign thereof was the study trip of Major Law, undertaken at the suggestion of the ambassador in Constantinople.

[2] The French capital invested in Turkey amounts to well over 2 billions (milliarden) [francs], of which almost half a billion is in rail-roads.

rail-roads. On the other hand, Germany was capable, in spite of a lack of tradition and preparatory work, to reach in a short time a place of importance in Turkey. The Deutsche Bank, in particular, not only achieved a predominant role in the railway system, but also won a decisive influence over the railroads of European Turkey. The results of this fruitful period can be quickly seen. The length of the Asiatic rail network rose in nine years from 642 to 2,500 kilometers. The beneficial effects of this growth were naturally felt only gradually. The burden that the state had undertaken through its guarantee was, however, most strongly felt in the initial periods. Therefore the Public Debts Administration warned the government against an overextension of its financial activity. The advice was followed, and a decision was made in 1894 not to issue any new guaranteed concessions until the increasing revenues of the existing railroads, and the induced new tax yields, had liberated sufficient new funds. However, in order not to block the possibilities of expansion of the transport network, the government was later more willing to consider narrow-gauge lines.

Based on the Concession Agreement of the Anatolian Railroad (October 4, 1888) the "Société ottomane des chemins de fer d'Anatolie" was founded, on March 23, 1899. Von Kühlmann, until then director of the Oriental Railroads, became director general. The company took over from the government the old Haidar Pasha-Ismit line and the uncompleted extension works for a price of 6 million. The concession also included the right to expand backwards to Scutari and to build branches to Bursa and Kutahya, although without guarantee, as well as a priority for eventual connecting lines past Ankara. The concession was for ninety-nine years—a period that was from then on used for all lines. . . .

SYRIAN RAILWAYS

The 1890's were also very fruitful for Syria, which until then had not gone beyond some unused concessions. An Ottoman subject, Yusuf Navon, had already for some time proposed the project of a link between Syria and Egypt and formed an association with an Egyptian, Lutfi Bey, for its implementation. The results, however, were only a small line between Jaffa and Jerusalem. On October 28, 1888, Navon obtained a concession for seventy-one years for a narrow-gauge line, together with a four-year priority for a branch line to Gaza and Nablus. He passed the concession on to the "Société du chemin de fer ottoman de Jaffa à Jérusalem," which was founded in Paris in December, 1899, under the direction of Collas. The construction work was executed by the "Société des travaux publics et constructions" under the direction of a Swiss, Eberhard. Work began on April 1, 1890; the first section to Ramleh (23 km.) was opened to traffic in April, 1891, the second (23 km.) on December 4, 1891, and the last section (41 km.) on September 26, 1892. Construction was defective and operations were far from meeting expectations; and as a result, by 1894 the company had to suspend operations. By means of a reorganization it was able to survive, but it never overcame its initial handicaps.

In central Syria, France retained its leading political influence and succeeded in expanding it to the field of public works. The upsurge of Beirut was set in motion by the French armed intervention in Lèbanon against the Druze massacres in 1860, which led to the concentration of many Christians in that town. The construction of the road between Beirut and Damascus, by a French company headed by the Comte de Perthuis, originated in this period. The very active traffic and high profitability of the enterprise brought forward the idea of replacing the road by a railway, especially in view of the constant growth in importance of Beirut. The concession of a line from Beirut to Damascus was obtained only after great difficulties, since different competing projects were at hand, e.g., a line from Tripoli to Homs, with branches to Aleppo and Damascus, and another for a line between Acre and Damascus.

The "Compagnie des chemins de fer ottomans économiques de Beyrouth-Damas-Hauran en Syrie" was founded on June 4, 1892, with French and Belgian capital, after a 99-year concession had been secured. It also obtained in the following year, under the name "Société ottomane des chemins de fer de Beyrouth-Damas-Hauran et Biredjik sur l'Euphrate," the highly disputed concession for the Damascus-Aleppo-Birejik line, with an eventual extension to Telek to connect with the future Baghdad railroad; furthermore it also obtained the privilege for all branches to the coast that might be claimed by other parties, as well as several other benefits. Notwithstanding the narrow gauge utilized for the old line, military requirements imposed a standard gauge for the extension. The kilometric guarantee, with an upper limit of 12,500 francs, was to be determined within two years by a committee.

During those protracted negotiations, work started on some lines under previous concessions, such as the Damascus-Muzairib line which was begun at the end of 1891 by the "Société d'entreprise des chemins de fer en Syrie" of Brussels, and the Beirut-Damascus line at the end of 1892 by the Batignoles Company of Paris. Work on the first line began too quickly, in order to anticipate the British line. When it was opened, on August 3, 1894, it constituted a torso without destination, and could not be fully utilized until the main line was also opened to traffic on August 3, 1895. Although the first line operated fairly well, the financial results of the second were very unfavorable. The construction of the English line between Acre and Damascus was also begun in 1892, but abandoned in 1898 after completion of only 8 kilometers. . . .

The granting of the preconcession for the Baghdad Railway also hurt the Damascus-Hama company, since the connecting point was transferred back from Birejik to Aleppo. Still the government gave no sign of issuing the final permit for the construction of the extension, and only through the intervention of the French ambassador was the company able to reach an additional convention for compensation (May 28, 1900, *ferman* of September 29). Through this convention the construction of the initial portion, from Rayaq to Hama, was definitely authorized for a three-year period, and the kilometric guarantee, that had been set at a maximum of 12,500 francs, was increased by 2,500 francs until such time as the extension and connection with the Baghdad line would take place. This, however, was left to the undetermined future. The company, which changed its name to the present one at that time, was then in difficult circumstances, which were ended by a reorganization. Simultaneously, the construction of the new line was transferred to the "Régie générale des chemins de fer," which also leased the operations for twenty-five years, in joint administration. This company also took over at that time the operation of the Lebanon narrow-gauge line. After work started under Kapp, in September, 1901, the opening of the first part to Ras Ba'albek took place on June 20, 1902, and the full line was inaugurated on August 16 of the same year. The important extension from the main station in Beirut to the harbor was also built in the winter of 1902-3. This line had long been planned, but had not been built owing to the high costs involved. Through renewed intervention by the French ambassador, it was possible to obtain on May 18, 1905, as compensation in a dispute with the government relating to the Hijaz Railway, the concession for the final stretch; this, however, was to extend now only to Aleppo. The guarantee was now set for the whole line at a uniform 13,600 francs per kilometer. Operations to Aleppo were inaugurated on October 15, 1906.

HIJAZ RAILWAY

A great work that the Turkish state itself undertook, with unexpected success, belongs to this period, namely the Hijaz Railway. The moving spirit of this enterprise was Abdul Hamid himself. He early recognized the political importance of railroads, and vigorously promoted their construction. He was especially aware of his position as caliph; as the religious leader of all Believers, he was the strongest promoter of the Pan-Islamic movement. Thus the thought of a closer link with the Holy Cities (Mecca and Medina) which were of great importance for the caliphate, suggested by 'Izzet pasha, his second secretary, fell on fertile ground. The threatening position of Britain toward Arabia, which was gradually manifesting itself, gave the railway project political importance. The main impulse, however, was the consolidation of the sultan's internal power and of his religious authority in the whole Islamic world—this impulse is appropriately manifested in the nickname given the railroad by the beduins: "*Jahshat al-Sultan*" ("riding donkey of the sultan"). Externally, the religious aspect was given first importance: the railroad would eliminate the dangers and inconveniences of the pilgrimages, thus strengthening Islam. In reality, the benefits for the pilgrims were limited, since most used the sea route to Jidda.[3] Nevertheless, the road from Damascus had a special official character.

On May 2, 1900, on the occasion of the forthcoming twenty-fifth accession anniversary, an *iradeh* of the sultan was issued, ordering the construction of the Hijaz Railway and soliciting voluntary contributions for this religious work, which was to be carried out. without any Christian participation. In Europe, the plan encountered only mockery and distrust which, in view of previous experience with state construction of railroads in Turkey, were understandable. The reaction of Muslims, on the other hand, was one of great enthusiasm, not only within the limits of the state but also in far-distant places. From all countries in which Believers lived, plentiful funds poured from rich and poor, amounting, in the next few years, to nearly 20 million francs. Not only money but also materials were donated. The sultan also

knew how to tap other sources to cover construction expenses: the revenue from a special stamp and passport tax, a 10 per cent payroll tax on employees, compulsory payments for decorations and promotions, the considerable proceeds from the sales of lambskins from the Bairam feast—even the sale of old stamps was not neglected. The land, as well as much material (stone, ballast, wood, etc.), was available without payment, and labor costs were, as we shall see, reduced to an absolute minimum. Construction was also to be done by Muslim engineers and workers and, as far as possible, with local materials. A railroad unit, comprising two battalions, was established and started construction in the autumn of 1900. Tracks and cars were to be made in government workshops, wooden ties were to be obtained from the forests of Asia Minor, bridges were to be built throughout without the use of iron; only for locomotives was dependence on other countries foreseen. A "general commission," with its seat in Constantinople, organized the construction work; it was headed by the grand vizir, while 'Izzet pasha continued as the driving force. Construction itself was conducted by a "local commission" in Damascus, with the commanding general of the Fifth Army, Kiasim pasha, acting as director general. It was soon realized that the religious limitation proposed could not be maintained. The Turkish engineers and officers had no experience, the troops had no training, the track material was not very useful and much too expensive; confusion and bad administration were soon the order of the day. So as not to endanger the enterprise, European engineers were called; at their head was a German, Meissner (from the Régie générale), who supervised construction. He succeeded, with his ability and energy, in conducting the construction work in an exemplary fashion, and, what was particularly difficult, in gaining the confidence of the Muslims. The administrative monopoly of work was given up and some operations, particularly such constructions as bridges, tunnels, etc., were

[3] There are only estimates for the pilgrim traffic, between 5,000 and 10,000 for the outward trip, and 15,000 to 20,000 for the return trip.

disposed of to small enterprises, mostly Italian and Austrian. Gradually, however, the local forces under Meissner's guidance acquired such a training that in the later stages of construction foreigners could be increasingly dispensed with. This was convenient since, with increasing distance from settled regions, non-military working forces became scarcer and more expensive. On the last stretches, where the use of Christians was barred anyway because of the proximity of the Holy Cities, only Muslims were active, under the technical direction of Mukhtar Bey. The number of soldiers utilized grew gradually, and reached in the last stages some 9,500. Infantry labored on earthworks and other side activities, railroad troops on the bedplate and roadbed, and a special company of artisans on bridges and superstructure. Camel riders were active in the preliminary surveying. Sappers built a telegraph line and administrated the locomotive operations and workshops, and eventually a special unit was created for the operation of the telegraph. The expenditures for the troops were met by the war ministry, and the railroad itself carried only the extra pay.

The General Commission originally intended to link the railroad with the Damascus–Hama line at Muzairib and to purchase the section from Damascus to Muzairib; however, this project failed owing to the very high price demanded by the company, 7 million francs. A quick decision was taken to build a parallel line from Damascus to Der'a, which was already connected with Muzairib. In order to achieve complete independence from the French railroad, it was decided to create a separate, and more favorable outlet to the sea. Haifa was chosen as a starting point, and in 1902 the works completed up to 1898 by the "Syrian Railway Company" were purchased at 925,000 francs. Construction work on the connecting line began on April 11, 1903. The French company presented damage claims; the dispute lasted until 1905, when a compromise was found by the payment of 3,400,000 francs and the

granting of the concession for the Hama–Aleppo line.

The different stages of the construction work can be seen in Table 1 showing the inauguration dates, which were usually set on the first of September, the anniversary of Abdul Hamid's accession to the throne.

TABLE 1

Date	Extent	Length (km.)	Construction in year (km.)
Sept. 1, 1901	Muzairib (French R.R. Station)–Der'a*	14	14
Sept. 1, 1902	Der'a–Ain Sirka	80	80
Sept. 1, 1903	Damascus–Der'a	123	...
Sept. 1, 1903	Ain Sirka–Qatran	124	247
Jan, 14, 1904	Haifa–Baisan	59	...
May 27, 1904	Baisan–Jordan bridge	17	...
Sept. 1, 1904	Qatran–Ma'an	132	208
Sept. 1, 1904	Ma'an–Mudawara	113	...
Oct. 15, 1904	Jordan bridge–Muzairib	73	186
Sept. 1, 1906	Mudawara–Tabuk	120	120
Sept. 1, 1907	Tabuk–al-'Ula	287	287
Sept. 1, 1908	Al-'Ula–Medina	323	323
		1,465	183

*The connecting line between the Hijaz Railway and the French station in Muzarib (2 km.) was later put out of operation.

The progress of construction work was not always constant; technical difficulties, irregularities in supplies of funds, interruptions in the delivery of materials, and other impediments often caused delay. The opening of partial sections of the Haifa line took place ahead of schedule, even before the construction was finished, in order to obtain additional revenue. This was detrimental to traffic, as well as to the supply of materials. For that reason in the spring of 1906, after an unusual flood had caused damage in the Yarmuk Valley, public service was discontinued and reopened definitely only in the autumn, after full completion of the works.

The first official inauguration of a section took place on September 1, 1904, in Ma'an, with great festivities to which, for the first time in Turkey, representatives of the press were admitted. The same thing happened later in al-'Ula (1907) and Medina (1908). When, after the opening of the lines as far as Ma'an, regular operations were established, Europeans were again called upon to lead them. In the same period, the General Commission studied the feasibility of the construction of a branch line from Ma'an to Aqaba, which would provide a second outlet to the sea, in order to reduce the cost of transport of construction materials. This line would have provided Turkey with permanent benefits through the bypassing of the Suez Canal, with its extremely high tolls. The establishment of the railroad, however, had to be abandoned owing to British opposition.

As the Hijaz line advanced, its difficulties increased: growing distances from the starting point, the emptiness and desolateness of the traversed regions, high temperatures, scarcity of water, difficulties in supply of provisions, etc. Such an enterprise would have been impossible without military personnel. Nevertheless the speed of construction increased as Medina was approached, although at the expense of performance. The last parts were completed only in their groundwork, the superstructures lagged behind. It was possible, however, after indescribable efforts, to reach the first of the Holy Cities, Medina, and to inaugurate the whole line on September 1, 1908. A railroad 1,465 kilometers long had been completed in eight years, in great part through desert and difficult terrain. The average yearly construction amounted to 183 kilometers, and rose to 323 kilometers in the last year. This was an admirable effort for Turkey, mainly because it was financed fully through its own means and executed—with the exception of the direction—with its own manpower.

BAGHDAD RAILWAY

The revolution created by the establishment of the new constitution and the fall of Abdul Hamid started a new era in Turkey. Two wars led the kingdom into disorder and damaged its external standing. Immediately before this political revolution, the Baghdad-Bahn enterprise was able to take a decisive step forward. Through the unification of the state debt in 1904 [see Part II, chap. 11] a part of the considerable surplus of the Debts Administration [*revenus concédés*] was transferred to the state. In the following years efforts were made to use these funds as a guarantee for the Baghdad Railway. After a long struggle, these efforts succeeded, and thus opposition to the continuation of the work was removed. Large advances, amounting to nearly 15 million francs eliminated the last obstacles. On June 2, 1908, an additional agreement was concluded, authorizing the continuation of the railroad to Helif (840 km.) including the branch line Tell Habash–Aleppo, within eight years. As collateral for the guarantee the surplus of the *revenus concédés* was assigned to which would be added the sheep tax of the *vilayet*'s of Konya, Adana, and Aleppo. Simultaneously a financial agreement was concluded with the Deutsche-Bank, which took over the second and third series of the Baghdad loan in the amount of 108 and 119 million francs, through an international syndicate headed by that bank. The loans were partly issued in the following years, mainly in Germany itself. The preliminary work and construction projects were speeded up, and the plans were submitted as early as April, 1909, and accepted in October. The layout of the line was still subjected to many changes, especially the north Syrian part and the connection with Aleppo. Parliament suggested extending the line to Alexandretta, passing through Aleppo. The company was willing to agree to this economically valuable change, in spite of its high construction costs, but the war ministry would not abandon its strategic objections to an open line along the seacoast. Thus the line remained inland; however, later it was brought closer to Aleppo and the branch reduced to 14 kilometers, so that through traffic could now pass through this center.

Since, under this design, Aleppo remained too far away from the nearest port, Mersin, a new plan was put forward linking Alexandretta, which was to retain its position as Aleppo's port, with the main line. It was also agreed not to draw the line directly from Dorak to Adana, but instead to connect with the Mersin-Adana line at Yenije, and to utilize part of that line, with the necessary rebuilding.

Meanwhile negotiations for an extension past Helif had not stopped. They had to fight partly against growing British opposition, and partly against competing projects that would reach Baghdad either from Suez or from Homs—this last project being a revival of the old Euphrates Valley line [see Part III, chap. 2]. Finally the Potsdam Conference, in 1910, removed Russian opposition and opened the way for further progress, leading to a supplementary convention on March 21, 1911. The Baghdad Railway obtained authorization for the prolongation of the line from Helif to Baghdad, and the construction, without guarantee, of the branch line from Toprak-kale to Alexandretta, where the Haidar Pasha Harbor Company would build a harbor. The guarantee is provided by the existing security of the Anatolian Railroad and the Baghdad Railroad, augmented by a new rise in tariffs. On the other hand, the company gave up its claim for the construction of the last portion, from Baghdad to the Persian Gulf, which was to be given to a newly founded Turkish company. Thus, through a wise restraint, the Baghdad-Bahn Company cleared the way for a final agreement with England too, which would be concluded in the spring of 1914.

Meanwhile, on December 1, 1909, the "Gesellschaft für den Bau von Eisenbahnen in der Türkei" was founded in Frankfurt am Main. Construction began in several places in 1910. After the death of Mackensen, the four sections into which the work had been divided were placed under independent contractors. On June 10, 1912, the branch line to Alexandretta was also begun, and on July 27, 1912, the Helif–Baghdad section.

Since then the following portions have been opened to traffic:

	Kilometers
Oct. 25, 1904, Konya–Bulgurlu	200
July 1, 1911, Bulgurlu–Ulukishla	38
Apr. 27, 1912, Dorak–Yenije	18
Apr. 27, 1912, Yenije–Mamure	97
Dec. 15, 1912, Raju-Aleppo-Jerablus	203
Dec. 21, 1912, Ulukishla–Karapinar	53
Nov. 1, 1913, Toprakkale–Alexandretta	60
June 2, 1914, Baghdad–Sumaika	62

The effects of the two wars were, of course, also felt on railroad construction, partly through the withdrawal of labor forces, and partly owing to the weakness of the money market; but in the meantime the difficulties have been to a great extent removed. . . .

. . . For most railway lines, the determination of the costs of construction is difficult. The data are contradictory or non-existent; in most cases it is not possible to determine whether costs of establishment, the purchase price of land, rolling stock, etc., are included. For the Anatolian Railway, the existence of reliable data make an exact estimate possible. . . .

The original cost [*Anlagekosten*] of the entire railway (Haidar Pasha-Ankara, Eskishehir-Konya, and the Arifie-Adapazar branch) was: 168,463,317 francs or 163,200 French francs per kilometer, without rolling stock; 176,580,563 francs or 171,100 French francs per kilometer, including rolling stock.

DAMASCUS-HAMA

. . . Published figures on construction costs of the old narrow-gauge lines (248 km.) also show considerable discrepancies. According to an explanation given by the management of the railroad company, in Paris,[4] total construction costs amounted to: 24,204,948 francs or approximately 98,000 French francs per kilometer, without rolling stock; 26,770,626 francs or 108,000 French francs per kilometer, including rolling stock.

These however do not include the considerable costs of establishment, obtaining

[4] In *Z.V.D.E.*, LVII (1908), 905.

of concession, and purchase of land. According to Verney and Dambmann[5] the total original costs amounted to 37,098,000 francs (or approximately 150,200 francs per kilometer). The plausibility of these estimates is increased by later references regarding amounts in building accounts, which are in general agreement with those given above. It should be noticed that average costs include the very easy Damascus–Muzairib stretch which was relatively cheap, whereas the kilometric costs of the mountain sectors were considerably higher. Construction costs of the Rayaq–Aleppo line (332 km.) are given in the Annual Report for 1906[6] as: 59,364,131 francs and 179,000 francs per kilometer not including rolling stock. If we add this, we could estimate the kilometric cost at 187,000 francs.

Each day a passenger train and a mixed train circulate between Beirut and Damascus, and a third one between Rayaq and Damascus. Rayaq and Aleppo are connected once a day, and there is another train between Rayaq and Ba'albek. Finally Homs and Tripoli are connected daily, while the Damascus–Muzairib line is serviced four times a week. Goods trains circulate according to traffic needs. The traveling speed on the Rayaq–Aleppo line is the highest, with an average of 28 kilometers per hour; in the Anti-Lebanon it amounts to only about 22 and falls, on the Lebanon line, on the journey to Beirut to 14, and even to 12.5 kilometers per hour in the opposite direction. The mixed trains are still slower. . . .

JAFFA–JERUSALEM

The line is drawn in a winding path to avoid tunnels and major groundworks. The gauge is 1.0 meter. The gradient amounts to 20 per cent, and the smallest radius is 100 meters. The tracks, originally from Belgium and France, are very light, and lie on wooden ties. The railroad has 176 bridges and passages, and of these six of the larger

ones (10–30 m. wide) have iron super-structures (Eiffel, Paris). The station installations are very simple. The locomotives are from the Baldwin works in Philadelphia, the cars from Dyle and Bacalan. The rolling stock, as well as all the installations, are in rather bad condition. Construction costs are given differently (Report of the British Foreign Office, No. 288, 1892): 8,500,000 francs, or 97,799 francs per kilometer; approximately 100,000 francs per kilometer (Courau);[7] 10,000,000 francs, or 115,500 francs per kilometer (Cuinet);[8] 10,500,000 francs, or 121,300 francs per kilometer (*Engineer*, 1893). Since the initial capital amounted only to 9,850,000 francs, the latter figures are too high. It seems appropriate to make an approximate estimate at an average value of 110,000 francs per kilometer.

Two passenger trains circulate daily in each direction, at a speed of 23 kilometers per hour. A cargo train runs every night. Special trains for pilgrims circulate according to demand. . . .

HIJAZ RAILWAY

Costs of construction have been relatively low. This can be explained by the fact that most of the work was performed by soldiers, who were paid, clothed, and maintained by the war ministry. The railroad paid only incentive extra pay; ground and roadbed workers received for diligent work an average of 0.70 to 0.90 franc per day, builders and other handworkers 1.30 to 2.30 francs. On the other hand, certain circumstances made the work more expensive: the difficulties in water supply, the long haul for all construction materials, and others. According to a report[9] for the financial year 1328 A.H. (ending in February, 1913) total costs of establishment to that date amounted to 95,000,000 francs for 1,528 kilometers, or approximately 62,000 francs per kilometer.

[5] Verney and Dambmann, *Les Puissances étrangères dans le Levant en Syrie et en Palestine* (Paris, 1900).
[6] *Nachr. f. Handel u. Industrie*, 1908, No. 8.

[7] *La locomotive en Turquie* (Brussels, 1895).
[8] *La Turquie d'Asie* (Paris, 1892–95).
[9] In the Turkish newspaper *Tasviri Efkar*, Jan. 1, 1914.

Of the latter, according to the annual report for 1322 A.H., the Haifa–Der'a line alone accounted for 12,795,000 francs or 78,500 francs per kilometer.[10] The Damascus–Medina line on the other hand required only 79,595,790 francs or 58,100 francs per kilometer.

Regular traffic is still very limited. Between Haifa and Damascus two trains circulate daily, with an average speed of 25 kilometers per hour. Between Damascus and Medina, as well as between Der'a and Bosra, only three times a week. The complete journey requires a traveling time of 2 days and 7 hours, which—including long stays in some stations—amounts to an average speed of 23.5 kilometers per hour. Pilgrim trains have reached their destination, in the last year, in 50 hours. They leave three times a day, and consist of ten cars, with 350 passengers each. On the Haifa–'Affuleh–Janin line lately a new pair of trains have been put in circulation, and between Haifa and Acre there are three trains daily. Goods trains circulate according to demand; there are also occasional special trains. On Lake Tiberias, a regular shipping service has been established from Samakh. The Turkish system of reckoning the hours of the day, previously in use, has been replaced by the European. The service personnel consists exclusively of native Muslims. In the beginning it was difficult to train these people. But at present they have reached a generally satisfactory level in the performance of their duties. . . .

[10] The steep slope of the Yarmuk Valley, approximately 30 kilometers in length, cost an average of 175,000 francs per kilometer.

CHAPTER 5

The Frontier of Settlement, 1800–1950

A leitmotiv in the long history of Syria—and indeed that of the whole Middle East—has been the struggle between the desert and the sown, between Abel and Cain, between the livestock-raising nomad and the sedentary peasant-farmer. The balance of power between the two, and hence the location of the margin of cultivation, has depended on the strength of the government. For, unless checked by firm government action, the nomads have always sought to thrust into the settled areas, terrorizing and exploiting the villagers and eventually causing them to give up cultivation and flee. This process has been described and analyzed, with unrivaled depth and vividness, by the fourteenth-century historian and sociologist, Ibn Khaldun. In Roman times a system of excellent roads and fortifications, supplemented where necessary by judicious alliances with tribal chieftains, pushed the *limes* and the frontier of settlement deep into the Syrian steppe, in Hawran, Jabal al-Druze, and Trans-Jordan. By contrast at the end of the eighteenth century, following the emigration of the ʿAnaza tribes from Central Arabia, the nomads ranged up to the Mediterranean coast of Palestine and between Tripoli and Latakia, large portions of the country went out of cultivation, and hundreds of villages were depopulated[1] (see Part IV, chap. 1).

In the nineteenth century, as described in the following selection, the frontier of settlement began to move once more eastward, making possible a large increase in the cultivated area and a marked growth in the population.[2] A new thrust began

[1] See the vivid account by the British consul in Aleppo, Skene to Bulwer, May 12, 1860, F.O. 78, no. 1538.

[2] For a depressing but probably true picture of conditions as late as the 1850's, see a note presented by the British consul in Damascus to the Ottoman authorities. The ʿAjlun area is described as having "extensive arable lands" but "roving Arabs [Bedouins] have laid it completely waste" and the same is said of Irbid. Hauran and Jabal Hauran because of "the incursions of the Arabs is subjected to large losses." The Biqaʿ is "neglected by the government and is gradually falling into decay." In central Syria, the Hama, Homs, and Maʿarra districts are described as "extensive and exceedingly fertile lands, but they have been turned to wastes by the Bedouins, who overrun them and rule paramount over the land and its inhabitants" (Wood to Clarendon, February 12, 1855, F.O. 78, no. 1118). Two years later, the consul-general in Beirut painted an equally somber picture: "Her Majesty's Consuls in Syria agree in representing the state of their respective Districts as being at the worst. . . . The Pashalick of Saida is no exception; the towns on the sea coast are alone quiet, being accessible to Foreign Ships of War" (Moore to Clarendon, November 24, 1856, F.O. 78, no. 1219). And in 1861 the consul in Damascus reported that "within the pashalik of Damascus there are more than two thousand ruined and deserted villages, of which about one thousand were cultivated and have been deserted within the memory of man" (Roger to Bulwer, August 20, 1861, F.O. 78, no. 1586).

during the Second World War in the Jezireh region and continued to the end of the 1950's. Greater security, improved transport, high prices for wheat and cotton, and increasing use of tractors combined to bring under cultivation hundreds of thousands of acres that had lain fallow for centuries. This process now seems to have come to an end, with the exhaustion of available supplies of land, and Syria has turned to the intensification of cultivation rather than its extension, a process that had started some decades earlier in Lebanon and Palestine; this is taking the form of irrigation works, like the Ghab and Euphrates schemes, greater application of chemical fertilizers, use of better seeds, and other improvements.

(See also works by Volney, Gibb and Bowen, Cuinet [*Syrie*], Ruppin, Himadeh [*Economic Organization of Syria*], and I.B.R.D. [*Syria*], listed in the Bibliography.)

[Norman N. Lewis, "The Frontier of Settlement in Syria, 1800–1950," *International Affairs*, XXXI (January, 1955), 48–60; reproduced by kind permission of the author and the Royal Institute of International Affairs.]

Syria in the early years of the nineteenth century was a half-empty land. Centuries of misgovernment and economic near-stagnation had brought about a recession in population and a great diminution in the extent of cultivated land. The recession was not equally apparent all over the country; in much of the west, in Lebanon for example, numerous peasants maintained themselves in comparative prosperity. The process of depopulation and abandonment of agricultural land had gone furthest in the eastern parts of the country, where the plains adjoining the desert had been largely abandoned by the peasants who had formerly farmed them, and had been occupied by nomadic and semi-nomadic tribesmen. Thus hundreds of square miles of the fertile Jezireh—that part of Syria north and east of the Euphrates—lay fallow, the grazing ground and occasional battle-field of Turcoman, Kurdish, and Arab tribes. There were few villages anywhere to the east of the Sultan's road from Aleppo to Damascus, and half the villages of the Hauran (between Damascus and the present Jordanian frontier) were ruined and practically deserted. The course of the decline had been immensely long drawn out—the Jezireh, for example,

had been largely deserted by sedentary peoples since the Mongol invasions. It is impossible here to examine the course or causes of the decline at any time before the eighteenth century, but some important features of the situation as it then was stand out clearly.

The most fundamental and obvious defect of late Ottoman rule in the provinces was its inability to provide security. At the end of the eighteenth century or the beginning of the nineteenth the forces at the disposal of the local governors were derisory. A few hundred ill-armed, ill-disciplined Turcoman and Kurdish horsemen, and a similar number of wretched Maghrabi infantry were all the force at the command of the Pasha of Aleppo—the janisseries had become worse than useless. If a little more strength were available in Damascus it was still insufficient to attempt to control the outlying areas of the big province south of the Hauran.

As in the seventeenth and eighteenth centuries the power and effectiveness of the central government and its agents had diminished, so that of local forces had increased. The eastern plains felt in particular the effects of the influx of numerous and powerful bedouin tribes who, in this period, drifted north from Arabia—notably the Shammar and 'Anizeh groups. The beginning of the movement was due to obscure causes. Arabia has always periodically overpeopled herself and, at this time, the emptiness of the Syrian plains and their almost absolute lack of defences tempted the northernmost Arabia tribes. Once the movement was under way, this attraction communicated itself to other tribes; whilst from the mid-eighteenth century the disturbances accompanying the rise and fall of the first Wahabi State in Northern Arabia caused further tribal migrations. The result was a long period of strife and movement in the Syrian desert and the plains that adjoin it. Tribes like the Fadl and Mowali who had been in Syria for centuries fought with and were defeated by the new-comers, and were forced to retreat into confined areas on the fringes of the desert. The new tribes fought each other in their turn, for water and grazing and influence. Raiding and robbery were intensified, trade interrupted, the crops of desert-edge villages eaten or ruined by the flocks and herds of the nomads, and the burden of *khuwa* ("protection money") paid by villagers to shaikhs became ever greater.

Even so, many more villages might have survived in the eastern plains if the nomads had been the sole menace. But the pressure of the tax collector was as great. Every traveller describes the crushing weight of the tax-farming system. The peasantry were taxed to, and sometimes beyond, the limit. A drought, an attack of pest or disease, a special *avania* by the Pasha, the demand of a detachment of soldiers for hospitality, a bedouin raid—such calamities turned the scale. A family, a group of families, or a whole village, would abandon its lands and flee. They might go to swell the indigent population of the cities, they might seek out an area of secluded ground where they could hope to sow and reap undisturbed for a few years, they might go to another village. Probably they would go to one of the larger villages, which by reason of their size were resistant at least to nomad attacks and the excesses of irregular soldiery, and which disposed of considerable resources in the shape, perhaps, of springs. Springs would not only make possible irrigated agriculture, a form of agriculture which binds farmers closely to the soil, but

would provide a precious summer watering for the flocks and herds of the nomads. A strong village with such resources could usually survive. Others might be sited in good defensive positions, or enjoy a special function as trading centres. Many such places, therefore, acted as hosts to people from smaller and weaker places, and were, in the late nineteenth century, to play the opposite role, becoming the "mothers" of numerous "daughter" settlements. Such were Qaryatein (south-east of Homs), Jibrine (just beyond the eastern gates of Aleppo), and Fiq (four miles east of the Sea of Galilee).

Many parts of the eastern plains, as described above, lost almost all their peasantry. In others, somewhat to the west, the recession was great but not total. Two examples may be cited; the first, the Aleppo region, as described by Volney, who travelled in the seventeen-eighties:

In consequence of such wretched government, the greater part of the Pachilics in the empire are impoverished and laid waste. This is the case in particular with that of Aleppo. In the ancient deftars, or registers of imposts, upwards of three thousand two hundred villages were reckoned; but at present the collector can scarcely find four hundred. Such of our merchants as have resided there twenty years have themselves seen the greater part of the environs of Aleppo become depopulated. The traveller meets with nothing but houses in ruins, cisterns rendered useless, and fields abandoned. Those who cultivated them are fled.

The Hauran, Jebel Druze, and neighbouring areas were in a similar condition. They were full of ruined villages, many of them containing numerous houses and other buildings of Byzantine date, often in a good state of preservation. Few of these villages contained more than three or four hundred inhabitants, and many were inhabited only by two or three or half a dozen families. These might live in the old houses, or in tents pitched amongst the ruins. They might be "permanent" inhabitants, but the peasants of the Hauran were very prone to cultivate an area for a year or two and then move.

Burckhardt, for example, records that when he passed through the village of Merjan in 1810, he found one family in it. In 1812 when he visited it again he found eight or ten families, most of them Druzes, who had come from Shaara, a well-peopled village in 1810, but deserted in 1812. The south-eastern part of Jebel Druze, most remote, with the lowest rainfall, and most exposed to bedouin raids, was in the worst condition. The following figures, extracted from Burckhardt's *Travels in Syria and the Holy Land* (1822), show this clearly, and a comparison with the modern figures indicates the scale of Druze immigration into the area during the second half of the nineteenth century.

nevertheless, considerable genuine progress, especially in the last thirty years of the century and up to 1914. The primary factors making for progress were the slow, sporadic, unequal, but nevertheless real improvements in the efficiency of the administration, particularly as regards security; and the increase in trade and economic activity which went on during the century. In some cases government policy was directly responsible for specific developments: for example, Circassian and other colonists were deliberately planted on the frontier of settlement, especially from 1870 onwards. Other developments had little or no con-nexion with government activity: for instance, many of the tribal groups which

Village	Population 1810 or 1812 (Burckhardt)	Population c. 1940	
		Druze	Total
Salkhad	Nil. (Upwards of 800 ruined houses)	2,499	2,970
'Urman	Nil. (A few Druze and Christian families were in these two villages till about 1795.)	1,864	2,015
El Kraiye	Four families. (500 ruined houses)	1,641	2,053
Bekka	Nil. (a ruin)	811	818
Samad	Nil. (a ruin)	539	594
Sahwat el Khudr . .	Nil.	801	801

Much other evidence strengthens the im-pression given by these figures.

There is little sign of change in the provinces at the beginning of the nineteenth century, but as the century went by the trends described above were reversed. Security, administration and economic con-ditions improved, the population grew, the frontier of settlement was pushed forward, and semi-nomad tribes began to settle down. All this started slowly, and little change was perceptible in the first half of the century. Progress was interrupted by long or short periods of regression, and many of the evils which afflicted the country continued little abated until the end of the century. Taxation, for example, remained heavy and inequitable, and taxation and usury together continued a crippling burden on the peasants. Until 1920 deserted fields and villages were common. There was,

suffered at the hands of the 'Anizeh and other incoming tribes in the seventeenth, eighteenth, and nineteenth centuries, and were pushed into agricultural regions on the edge of the desert, naturally tended by degrees to become agriculturalists. Such were some of the Kurds and Turcomans of the northern frontier, the Naim and many Mowali sections of the Homs-Hama area, and the Fadl between Mount Hermon and the Sea of Galilee. Yet other developments only owed their origin in an indirect or partial way to government action: thus the emigration of many Druzes from Lebanon to Jebel Druze, east of the Hauran plain, was due to several causes, of which one was some measure of over-population in Lebanon, another civil strife, and a third punitive and repressive measures taken by the authorities against the community in Lebanon.

The reforms of Sultan Mahmoud II (1808–39) had little visible or immediate effect, and their ultimate results were postponed by the nine-year interregnum when Ibrahim Pasha of Egypt ruled Syria (1831–40). Their real importance lay in the fact that they were the starting point for the later reforms which were gradually to become effective. Mahmoud's most important measure was to do away with the corps of janisseries and begin the formation of a new "model" army. The results of Ibrahim Pasha's vigorous policies were more immediately apparent. The rule of law was imposed, agriculture and trade encouraged. Over 150 abandoned villages were re-settled in the Aleppo area, and a similar number in the Hauran. When Ibrahim Pasha left, there was a serious reversion and the eighteen-forties were a period of particularly bad administration, bedouin incursions, strife and unrest in various parts of the country. Many of the villages re-settled in his day, and others, were deserted again. But the results of his most important work were considerable and long-lasting: it was he who opened up the country to European commercial and other enterprise, and it was in his day that the beginnings of an expanding economy were first seen in Syria.

"Reforming Pashas" begin to make their appearance in the provincial cities of the Turkish Empire in the eighteen-fifties. Their efforts at reform were, of course, frequently misguided and unsuccessful, often carried out for the wrong motives and in the wrong way, but the ultimate and cumulative result was considerable. The policy of centralization and direct rule was of particular importance: local notables were weakened and as much power as possible concentrated in the hands of government officials. Colonization by indigenous peasants and landowners and by immigrants was encouraged, and special attention was paid to the areas near the desert fringe. Details of some aspects of these developments may be of interest. As an example one may cite the development

of government policy vis-à-vis the nomadic and semi-nomadic tribes. It should first be said that the old faults and weaknesses of Ottoman administration persisted in some measure till the end. Thus tribes would sometimes be brutally maltreated, at other times favoured and flattered. Sometimes shaikhs would be entrusted with the responsibility of maintaining security in an area, but they might well be treated traitorously, perhaps to be supplanted by a rival. The pashas could seldom resist an opportunity of playing off one tribe against another.

More fruitful policies, however, became apparent in the second half of the century. In its later decades considerable and well-armed forces were sent on punitive expeditions, or on expeditions to pacify hitherto unadministered areas and to subjugate rebellious tribes. In the eighteen-sixties and after, such expeditions worked down the Euphrates valley and into the northern desert. Little forts and police posts were established, with larger garrisons at Deir ez Zor and Palmyra. By the end of the century the Euphrates road was secure and much used, whilst foreign visitors could reach the ruins of Palmyra with relative ease. At the same time the area of "Transjordan" was being brought under direct Turkish administration. A Turkish *qaim maqam* was established in Ajlun in 1851. In 1867 an expedition penetrated the Belka (the Salt-Amman-Madeba area) and a governor was installed in Salt. Two years later the Beni Sakhr suffered at the hands of a punitive expedition, made their submission, and promised to pay the costs of the expedition. From this time onwards the country was gradually pacified, there was much peasant immigration from Palestine and elsewhere, and agriculture was greatly extended. In the eighteen-eighties other police posts or detachments of soldiery were established on the imperial domain lands east of Homs and Hama.

Why were such measures successful, when similar efforts at an earlier date had not been? The answer is partly to be found in the general circumstances of the time, and in the fact that the expeditions were mounted with more determination and system than previously, that a network of military and police posts and civilian administrators was gradually built up, that more men were used and that many of them were regular soldiers. Part of the answer, however, lies in the fact that the Turkish forces began to be equipped with modern rifles in the late eighteen-sixties, whilst the bedouin, with few exceptions, remained armed only with lance, sword, and crude flintlock. Troops on the 1869 expedition against the Beni Sakhr had breech-loading Sniders; and repeating Winchesters, which were "much dreaded," were in use by the late eighteen-seventies. For the first time the Turkish soldier found himself superior to the bedouin warrior, and the whole balance of force was changed. Companies of mule-borne riflemen, operating from the new garrison centres and posts, proved very effective. In 1872 the Wali of Damascus and other notables paid an official visit to the Rualla and other 'Anizeh shaikhs and tribesmen camped not far from the city—the first such visit ever to be paid. "One and all," it was said at the time, "considered the 'good old times' of bedouin pillage and wanderings as at an end!"

At the same time agriculturalists were increasing in number and strength near the fringe of settlement, and this too did much to restrain the tribes and to lead them to modify their way of life. Some of the peasant groups were of doughty stock. The Druzes, for example, usually got the better of their encounters with the bedouin, and effectively protected their own lands and villages. The peasant colonists of the Aleppo, Hama, and Homs areas fought off or bought off the bedouin, and frequently settled to relatively peaceful and fruitful relations with the semi-nomadic and more peaceful tribes such as the Naim and Haddedin. Some members of these tribes became agriculturalists, and others found a good livelihood acting as shepherds to the flocks of townspeople and villagers. The

most aggressive group of colonists was the Circassians. They were Muslims who had fled from their homeland during the Russo-Turkish wars and the Russian occupation of the Caucasus. From 1870 onwards they built themselves villages near the desert fringe all the way from the northern frontier down to Amman, itself founded by these people in 1878. They effectively fulfilled the role allotted to them: to occupy and cultivate land, to weaken and to act as a buffer against the bedouin. The end of the "good old days" was finally hailed at the turn of the century, when the railways, with all their economic and military potential, and with each station a little fortress, were driven triumphantly through the territories of Kurd and Arab, Mowali, Beni Sakhr, and Shammar. The tribes were to remain important for decades to come, but their power had been very greatly reduced.

At the same time, tribal settlement was encouraged. Attempts to settle the 'Anizeh and other completely nomadic tribes failed, but many smaller, semi-nomadic tribes took to a largely sedentary life. This tendency was very marked in the Aleppo region which may be taken as an example. About 1860 several hundred tents of the Wulda tribe crossed the Euphrates and eventually settled down about thirty miles south of Aleppo, in Jebel Samaane. Sections of other tribes, such as the Bu Shaikh, Lheib, and Aquedat also drifted west, usually after being defeated in raids or wars, half fleeing from the powerful desert tribes and half attracted by the possibilities of settlement. Many of them settled in the same general area. Near them were other groups, like the Sakan who had long been tent-dwelling farmers and shepherds, and who now began to build villages. Some of the Haddedin, both north and south of Aleppo, and of the Mowali did the same. (It should be noted that both then and now some sections and shaikhs of these and other tribes were completely nomadic, others tent-dwelling but engaged in farming, and others completely sedentary. The last and second named groups are now much more numerous than they were, but the evolution of tribes from the nomadic to the sedentary state is a very long process.)

Very little later, similar small groups began to settle east of Aleppo. The first of the Ferdoon, for example, ploughed and sowed in 1859, and built houses shortly after, gradually creating a line of a dozen villages along the Nahr el Dhahab, some twenty-five miles east of Aleppo. As time went on so did such groups become more completely sedentary, and so did others somewhat more remote begin to go through the same process. At the same time the first stage towards the sedentarization of the bedouin proper was reached when Jeda'an bin Muheid, a famous shaikh of the great Feda'an ('Anizeh) tribe was awarded the income from some twenty villages in Jebel Shbeit by the Pasha of Aleppo in 1865. He and other shaikhs of his tribe gained control of other lands near the Euphrates. The intention of the authorities was that the tribesmen should be settled on these lands. What in fact happened was that the shaikhs had the lands registered in their own names, and thus became big landowners. Peasants and men of semi-sedentary tribes were eventually imported to work much of the land, and associations were formed with Aleppine men of affairs. The great majority of the tribesmen remained nomads, but a number of them were to be attracted to agriculture in the boom years of the nineteen-forties and early nineteen-fifties.

The same processes which led to the sedentarization of tribesmen encouraged peasants and landlords to take new land under cultivation. Peasants emigrated, either from neighbouring villages or from a distance. They might develop lands on their own account, or for a city landlord, bedouin shaikh, or other notable under a crop-sharing agreement. Certain villages, as mentioned above, threw off many satellite settlements. The peasants of the Hauran plain gradually filled their villages. Palestinians crossed the Jordan, Alaouites went to lands east of Hama, peasants of the Aleppo region mingled with the tribesmen

in the wide plains between the city and the Euphrates. It is clear that the new security, governmental encouragement, relative over-population in the West, and rising prices, were chiefly responsible for the movement in most areas, but other factors were involved in some cases.

Such a case was the movement of the Druzes to the mountainous area east of the Hauran plain known now as Jebel Druze and formerly as Jebel Hauran. There were few or no Druzes in the Jebel until towards the end of the seventeenth century, and the villages were inhabited by peasants of Sunni Muslim or Christian faith. These were few in number and decreasing, and many villages were half-ruined and half-deserted. The area was also used by a number of small semi-nomadic tribes, and, as time went on, by the incoming 'Anizeh—first the Wuld Ali and then the Rualla. The main Druze area was, of course, south-central Lebanon, but they also had villages scattered round the flanks of Mount Hermon, and must have known of the situation in Jebel Hauran and of its possibilities.

The Lebanese Druzes were divided into two factions, the Qaisis and the Yemenis. The Yemeni faction suffered a final defeat at the hands of the Qaisis at Ain Dara in 1711, and some of the defeated fled, to make their way to Jebel Druze. A few others had probably preceded them, and thereafter new-comers frequently joined them, often the weaker party in family disputes, and others who had reason to flee from Lebanon. They were joined too by lesser numbers from Galilee, and from Jebel el Ala, west of Aleppo. These last had suffered some degree of discrimination and persecution at the hands of the authorities in Aleppo and of their Muslim neighbours. In order to establish and maintain themselves in Jebel Druze they sometimes had to deal with the opposition of the Muslim and Christian villagers and frequently with that of the semi-nomadic and nomadic tribes. They were usually successful in their clashes with these groups, and were eventually able to gain a complete ascendancy over them. By the beginning of the nineteenth century their numbers were estimated at six or seven thousand, and they continued to receive reinforcements. Emir Bechir "The Great" of Lebanon (reigned 1789–1840) made a determined and largely successful attempt to break the power of the Lebanese Druze chiefs, and many fled to Jebel Druze. Larger numbers followed them in the late eighteen-thirties, fleeing from the conscription and forced labour of Ibrahim Pasha (who also tried and failed to subjugate the Jebel Druze), and in the eighteen-forties, as a result of Druze-Christian civil strife, and especially in and immediately after 1860, consequent upon the attempt of the authorities to punish the Lebanese Druzes severely for their part in the Druze-Christian civil war of that year.

Most of their early settlements were in the vicinity of Soueida, which was to become their chief town. Especially from 1860 they expanded north and south, filling the Jebel and its south-eastern fringe, and building villages along the edge of the Leja (a lava-flow to the north, practically impenetrable by regular forces, and a Druze "fortress"). They now number some 80,000, in about 120 villages. Despite their feuds, they have a strong sense of group loyalty and difference from others. They have always resented authority and have tried to maintain a semi-autonomous State within a State in the Jebel. They are ready to fight in defence of their community and their "homeland" and the modern history of Syria is full of Druze revolts and attempts by the government to suppress them. They have several times inflicted grave losses on regular troops, Egyptian, Turkish, and French, sent against them, and are proud that a Druze revolt early in 1954 proved the beginning of the end of the rule of General Shishakli, the Syrian dictator. The Druze migration thus differs in many respects from the movement of other peasant groups to unoccupied lands on the frontier of settlement. It owed little to economic motives, and a good deal to political

factors. On the other hand, economic and social change in Lebanon lay behind much of the political and sectarian strife there. The Christians were successfully pressing for emancipation, economic, social, and political, the old feudal-type agrarian order was breaking up, and a Christian emigration westwards to the coastal cities and to countries abroad matched that of the Druzes eastwards to Jebel Druze.

Two other areas, that of Amman and that of Selemieh, provide good examples of the type of development which took place. Before the expeditions of 1867 and 1869, referred to above, there were no villages in the country to the east of Salt. Doughty, as he passed through the area in 1876, travelling south with the great Hajj caravan, was moved to write: "The desert . . . shall become a plough-land, so might all this good soil, whose sun is gone down whilst it was yet day, return to be full of busy human lives; there lacks but the defence of a strong government." He also referred, however, to the recent humbling of the Beni Sakhr, and in fact development was beginning in his time. Peasants from Palestine cultivated land for the shaikhs of the Beni Sakhr or other tribes, both partners in the contract taking a proportion of the crop. Most of these cultivators were poor, and completely dependent on the shaikhs. But about 1870 a certain Saleh Abu Jaber established himself at Yadudeh (9 miles south of Amman). He had made money as a merchant trading with the bedouin, and was on good terms with them. He associated himself with the Beni Sakhr shaikhs, brought in Palestinian peasants, cultivated a considerable stretch of territory, and became a wealthy notable. A few years later, between 1875 and 1880, a colony of Christians established themselves on the site of Madeba (about 25 miles south-south-west of Amman). They came from Kerak, fifty miles to the south, after bloody disputes with the ruling notables of that area. They secured permission from the government to settle at Madeba, but only made good their claim in the face of the bitter opposition of the Beni Sakhr shaikh who claimed the land. In 1878 the first Circassians arrived, first to shelter in the ruins of the Roman theatre at Amman, then to build and cultivate. Two years later a second group settled at Wadi Sir, eight miles to the west. Now the land was beginning to fill up. Between 1900 and 1905, said Gertrude Bell, the limit of cultivation was pushed forward two hours' ride to the east. In 1902 the railway reached Amman and was then pushed south towards Medina. Some twenty farms or villages were founded near Madeba in ten years around the turn of the century.

Selemieh lies twenty miles east-south-east of Hama, in Central Syria. In 1845 a group of Ismailis (dissident Shi'ites) moved to Selemieh from the districts of Qadmous and Masyaf in the Alaouite mountains. Selemieh was then a ruin and the land round it uncultivated. During the next twenty years the settlers brought most of the land within a radius of about eight miles under cultivation. They then began to throw off daughter settlements: two in the eighteen-sixties, seven in the eighteen-seventies. They dealt with the nomads by diplomacy, bribery, or force of arms. By 1894 they were at work thirty miles to the north-east of Selemieh. The process continued during and after the first world war, and still goes on. The Ismaili population of the area has grown in a hundred years from nil to approximately 30,000. Semi-desert lands fifty miles to the east are now being brought under the plough. In 1885 Circassian immigrants arrived, to found three villages a few miles to the north of Selemieh. Other villages were settled by independent Alaouite and other peasants. Much of the west of the area fell into the hands of Hama landlords, who brought in farmers from the Alaouite mountains of the Hama plains. Some of the lands in this area had been crudely farmed by semi-nomadic tribesmen who lived in or near the ruined villages of earlier epochs in summer, and who moved towards the desert in winter. The majority of these tribesmen were evicted, and became for a few decades largely nomadic. Many of them still are, but numbers of them have settled down further to the east. Beyond and among the Ismaili villages are those of these tribes—Turki, Bshakim, and others—founded in the late nineteen-twenties, nineteen-thirties and nineteen-forties. The process continues.

The government looked with favour on such developments and sometimes assisted settlers by granting tax remissions and other privileges. Vast areas near the frontier of settlement were declared imperial domain in the eighteen-fifties and eighteen-eighties, and settlers on these properties were granted particularly favourable terms. At the same time the operations of the Turkish land laws, from 1858 onwards, made it easy for landlords and speculators to gain control of disproportionately great areas of land. Colonization by independent peasant groups such as the Druzes and Ismailis was therefore somewhat less common than that by landlords bringing in peasants and former semi-nomadic tribesmen to work on their land. Furthermore, many peasants and former semi-nomads who had settled failed to maintain their economic independence, and fell prey to the usurer. Such problems have remained serious to this day, and have unfortunately arisen also in newly developed areas such as the Jezireh.

The mandatory period, between the first and second world wars, saw a definitive subjugation of the bedouin, and the introduction and maintenance of higher standards of public security in Syria and Transjordan than had been known for many hundreds of years. Improvement in all departments of administration, the further development of communications, the popularization of the car, bus, and lorry, and continuing economic development hastened the processes of agricultural extension, peasant colonization, and the settlement of former nomads. The frontier of settlement continued to advance, and there was a great deal of consolidation and "filling up" in the areas first developed in Turkish days. It is impossible to make any but the crudest and most approximate estimate of the amount of new land cultivated and new villages established between about 1850 and the second world war, but the following conservative estimates may be hazarded. In the area of the present Republic of Syria, excluding the Jezireh (for Jezireh figures see below), about 10,000 square miles of new land were ploughed up and about 2,000 villages established on this land; in Transjordan, perhaps 1,500 square miles and 300 villages. During the same hundred-year period an enormous amount of land must have been brought into regular cultivation, having in the past been at best infrequently used; and hundreds of places developed from hamlets to sizeable villages.

The second world war brought Syria a greater measure of prosperity, and the country has continued to flourish since the war. The same processes continue, but in more dramatic fashion. New lands are more likely to be broken by tractor-drawn steel ploughs than by the donkey-drawn wooden ploughs of the peasants. The contrast between old and new is striking: in 1944 the present writer saw new American combine-harvesters at work in the Jezireh. The crop they were reaping grew on land unploughed for centuries till that year, land where the boundary between a Kurdish and an Arab tribe was a matter of dispute. Nothing could have been more "modern" than the great machines at work—but round one there circled a defensive screen of fully armed bedouin horsemen and by the other, a mile or two away, rode a similar group of Kurds. One finds saloon cars and tractors "stabled" in bedouin tents, and shaikhs count their wealth in terms of such machines, bales of cotton, and tons of wheat. Fortunes are made, and some lost, in the rapid development of Syria's last great area of frontier land: the Jezireh.

The Jezireh is traditionally defined as that part of Syria which lies north and east of the Euphrates. This area is today divided into two provinces: Euphrates and Jezireh. The figures given in the following paragraphs refer only to the Jezireh province, the more easterly of the two.

Cultivation crept outwards from Aleppo in the nineteenth century, as described above. By 1860 the frontier lay half-way between the city and the Euphrates, and by 1900 had reached the river. The French pacification of the area beyond the river was delayed and made difficult by the persistence of bad relations with Turkey until the late nineteen-twenties, the remoteness of the area, and the resistance of its bedouin inhabitants. Hassetche remained the most advanced French military and administrative post until 1922 (only founded a year or two earlier, it is now a town of some 10,000 people). The site of Qamichlie, which has become the centre for the development of the fertile north-east part of the Jezireh, and is now a town of 30,000 people, was not occupied until 1926, and the final occupation of the north-eastern extremity was delayed until 1930. The area was initially very scantily peopled, and development owed a good deal to immigration. Large numbers of Kurds crossed the frontier from Turkey, particularly after the Kurdish insurrection of 1925 in that country. The majority of these new-comers settled down in the vicinity of the frontier, where numerous Kurdish and mixed tribes already lived. Most of these groups were already semi-sedentary, and adopted agriculture seriously in the next few years. Smaller numbers of Armenians and other Christians provided a valuable element: shopkeepers, clerks, craftsmen, mechanics, and entrepreneurs. In 1933 some 9,000 Assyrians (Nestorian Christians) crossed the frontier as refugees from Iraq and the government and the League of Nations collaborated in settling them in some twenty villages on the banks of the river Khabour. Other immigrants came from western Syria, and this movement continues.

Many new farms and villages were established in the late nineteen-twenties and nineteen-thirties, but the second world war provided the stimulus for development on a much bigger scale. Allied policy was to encourage the production of foodstuffs in the countries of the Middle East, and an official agency was formed to assist the development of the Jezireh as a grain-growing area. Prices were good enough to encourage local enterprise, and "the great plough-up began." In 1942 there were about thirty tractors and twenty thrashing and harvesting machines in the province. By 1950 there were 500 tractors and 430 combine harvesters. In 1942 only about 50,000 acres were cultivated out of the Jezireh's total cultivable area of about two-and-a-half million acres. By 1946 about 783,000 acres were cultivated, by 1949 a million acres, by 1951 perhaps a million-and-a-quarter acres. Estimates of the number of villages founded between 1920 and 1954 range as high as 2,000, and the total population is about 160,000. There are few true nomads left, most of the tribal shaikhs and tribesmen now have an interest in agriculture, even if only to the extent of collecting a yearly rent from the tractor owner who ploughs and uses "their" land.

There is still uncultivated land in the Jezireh which can be cultivated without irrigation, and there is a little in other parts of Syria, but the days of the easily expanding frontier are over. Great development possibilities exist, notably in the field of irrigation, but the grave social and political problems with which the country is faced are as important as, and will probably prove harder to solve than, the physical and economic difficulties attendant on development.

[The article included a map showing the extension of cultivation, which has not been reproduced here.—EDITOR.]

CHAPTER 6

Migration from and to Syria, 1860–1914

At various times in their long history the inhabitants of Syria, especially those of the coastal regions, have emigrated in pursuit of trade or other means of livelihood. The Phoenicians established colonies in North Africa, Sicily, and Spain. The Hebrews migrated in large numbers, first to Egypt and then to other Mediterranean countries, and were subsequently dispersed in the Diaspora. Syrians also settled in many parts of the Roman Empire, causing Juvenal to complain that the Orontes was flowing into the Tiber, and as late as the sixth century there was an important group of Syrian traders in France. But with the coming of Islam the Mediterranean was transformed into a hostile frontier between two civilizations, and peaceful migration across it ceased. A large number of Syrians settled in Spain under the Omayyads, and at the beginning of the fifteenth century Timur Lenk deported an appreciable number to central Asia; otherwise there does not seem to have been any significant movement out of Syria.

In the nineteenth century large-scale emigration was resumed. A few hundreds of Syrians went to Egypt under Muhammad Ali, and several thousands under Ismail and his successors; by the 1920's the number of Syrians in Egypt was over 50,000. Far more important was the stream to the Americas, described in the following selection. It was sparked by the tensions accompanying the economic and social transformation (see Part IV, chap. 3); by the imposition of conscription; by the spread of foreign education; by the improvement of transport; and by the massacres of 1860. In 1860–1914 total migration from what are now Syria and Lebanon was estimated at 330,000, and in the period 1900–1914 the annual average reached 15,000. This high rate was regained in the 1920's, when West Africa absorbed a large number of immigrants, but thereafter fell off sharply because of unfavorable economic conditions and restrictions on immigration in the receiving countries. After the Second World War emigration was directed mainly to the Persian Gulf oil countries; it has averaged some 5,000 per annum. Emigrants have played a very important part in the life of Lebanon, and certain parts of Palestine and Syria, through the money they have sent to their relatives and the new ideas they have brought back with them, and are now playing an important part in that of Jordan.

As for immigration, under the Ottomans a large number of Turcomans settled in the northern parts of Syria and Iraq. In the nineteenth century some 30,000 Circassians and other Caucasians, who had fled before the Russian advance, settled in Syria and Trans-Jordan. Tens of thousands of Armenians fled from Turkey, before and after the First World War. The only other important stream was the Jewish immigration described in the following selection, which reached large proportions in the 1880's, and by 1914 had raised the Jewish population of Palestine to about 90,000. During the First World War many Jews left Palestine, bringing the number in 1920 down to about 67,000, but under the British Mandate immigration rose sharply, totaling 450,000, and by 1947 one-third of the population of Palestine was Jewish.

(See also works by Himadeh [*Economic Organization of Syria* and *Palestine*], Nuss, and Safa listed in the Bibliography.)

[From A. Ruppin, *Syrien als Wirtschafts-gebiet*, Beihefte zum Tropenpflanzer, XVI, No. 3/5 (Berlin, 1916), 191–96; reproduced by kind permission of Mrs. H. Ruppin.]

... Exact information regarding immigration and emigration is lacking, just as it is regarding natural increase. I have obtained the following figures on arrivals and departures from the port authorities in Beirut [see Table 1].

TABLE 1

Year	Arrivals	Departures
1329 [A.H.] (1912–13) . .	18,131	18,904
1330 [A.H.] (1913–14) . .	9,387	16,739
1331 [A.H.] (1914–15) . .	350	6,109
Total	27,868	41,752

The figures do not, however, permit any general conclusions to be drawn; for the war, and the consequent departure of enemy aliens, created completely abnormal conditions. In addition, a large proportion of departing passengers fail to register with the port authorities.

In general, migration in Syria in the last three decades has been characterized by emigration, to America, of Christian Lebanese; by that of Mohammedans from Lebanon and the *vilayet*'s of Beirut and Damascus who have participated in this movement during the last decade; and by the immigration of East European Jews to

Palestine, particularly to Jerusalem. The number of immigrant Jews in the last thirty years may be put, with a fair degree of accuracy, at 40,000, of whom 12,000 to 15,000 left the country in 1914–15, following the outbreak of the war. The number of emigrants is variously estimated. In the *mutasarriflik* [province] of Lebanon, where emigrants are listed separately in the population registers, I obtained the official figures regarding emigrants (up to the year 1915) [see Table 2].

TABLE 2

Caza*	Emigrants
Batrun	26,124
Kisrwan	14,895
Shughr	16,961
Zahleh	2,332†
Kura	7,204
Matn	19,853
Jezzin	8,061
Dair al-Qamar	5,327
Total:	100,757

* [district.]
† The figures for Zahleh and Dair al-Qamar have probably been transposed—see next paragraph.—Translator.

Since the total population of Lebanon is estimated at around 400,000, the figures in Table 2 indicate that one-quarter of the population has emigrated. In certain districts the percentage of emigrants is still higher, e.g., in the *caza* of Zahleh, emigrants (5,327) equal 42 per cent of those remaining behind (12,658). In the areas adjoining the *mutasarriflik* of Lebanon emigration is also considerable. It is reported that of the emigrants sailing from Tripoli only 20 per cent are Lebanese, 40 per cent being Christians and a similar number Mohammedans from the *mutasarriflik* of Tripoli. From the town of Homs and its environs 40,000 persons are believed to be living in America. From Hama 300 persons are estimated to emigrate to America each year. Weakley[1] reports that, in the year 1909, the number of emigrants leaving on Italian ships was 1,807 from Tripoli and 4,002 from Beirut, or 5,809 in all; and the number on French ships, 3,759 and 4,280, respectively, or 8,039 in all; the grand total of emigrants from Tripoli and Beirut was therefore 13,848. In the reports of the German consul in Beirut for 1911 and 1912, the number of emigrants from Lebanon and the *vilayet*'s of Beirut and Tripoli was estimated at 14,000 in 1911 and 24,000 in 1912. In the report for 1912 the number of Syrian emigrants living in North and South America was put, on the basis of official inquiries, at 500,000, of whom 250,000 were Lebanese. The difference between the latter figure and the one of 100,757 given to me by the Lebanese authorities may perhaps be explained by the fact that the 250,000 include children born to emigrants in America. On average, the annual outflow of emigrants may be estimated at 15,000 to 20,000.

The main season for emigration runs from April to October. The fare from Syria to South America is 250 to 230 francs. The shipping lines, principally the French Messageries Maritimes and the Italian Rubattino Line, thus earn from the 20,000 emigrants about 6 million francs a year for the outward passage. A considerable proportion of the emigrants, about a third or a half, return to the homeland as soon as they have saved enough money in America. The Lebanese use the money, as a rule, for the purchase of land or the building of fine houses, thanks to which Lebanese villages present a very stately appearance. Other Syrians, especially Mohammedans, generally

[1] *Report upon the Conditions and Prospects of British Trade in Syria* (London, 1911), p. 11.

use it to establish a petty trading business. Most emigrants in America devote themselves to peddling, while a smaller number earn their livelihood in industry or agriculture. The report of the German consul in Tripoli for 1912 states: "It is astonishing how swiftly the great majority of emigrants attain a certain measure of prosperity in their new fields of activity and how infrequent are failures, especially if it be borne in mind that the majority of emigrants are completely uncultivated and that most of them can hardly read and write their mother tongue."

Usually emigrants succeed in saving 10,000 to 20,000 francs after a stay of five to ten years in America; this is attributable both to their inborn intelligence, as descendants of those ancient skilled traders the Phoenicians and Syrians, and to their unpretentiousness and thriftiness. They send back a large part of their savings to their homeland, where this money plays an important economic role. According to A. A. Naccache, inspector of public works and agriculture in Lebanon, the total incomes of the inhabitants of the *mutasarriflik* of Lebanon are as follows:

	Piastres
Remittances from America	90,000,000
Income from silkworm breeding . . .	60,000,000
Income from agricultural produce . .	30,000,000
Income from silk spinning	15,000,000
Income from foreign visitors	15,000,000
Income from industry (tanneries, alcoholic drinks, production of soap, cigarettes, matches)	10,000,000
Total	220,000,000
	or about 50 million francs

Thus remittances from America constitute no less than 41 per cent of the total income of the Lebanese people. I was told by the mayor of the Lebanese town of Batrun that the income of its population is as follows: from crops 60,000 to 80,000 francs, from trade 200,000 francs, and from America 200,000 francs; here, too, remittances from America account for 43 per cent of total income. Every economic crisis in America, making the earning of money more difficult there, has its repercussions on Lebanon.

Not only Lebanon but also the *vilayet*'s of Beirut and Damascus receive remittances from America, but it is said that, in general, emigrants from Beirut and Damascus, and more particularly Mohammedans from Hama and Homs, are less successful in America than are the Christian Lebanese. In the years preceding the [First] World War the annual sum sent to Syria amounted, according to information gathered by me from the banks, to not less than 30 million francs; of this about 15 million was remitted through banks in Beirut, 12 million through banks in Tripoli, and 3 million through banks in Homs.

A consequence of this annual inflow to Lebanon of large sums, which are used to acquire land, is an enormous rise in the price of land. The Lebanese buy land only within the *mutasarriflik* of Lebanon. Hence whereas in Tripoli, which lies outside the *mutasarriflik*, old olive trees cost 20 francs; in Lebanon 40 to 60 francs are paid for them. A mulberry plantation costs in Tripoli 2,000 francs per faddan (5,000 square ells, or 2,812.5 square meters) but in Lebanon 4,000 francs. However, the high land values in Lebanon are due not only to the love of the Lebanese for their native soil but also to the fact that land taxes in the *mutasarriflik* of Lebanon are considerably lower. Outside Lebanon the 'ushr equals 12.63 per cent of the crop and in addition a 0.4 per cent *werko* must be paid on the value of the land [see Part III, chap. 7]. In the *mutasarriflik* of Lebanon, on the other hand, an evaluation made in 1864 and guaranteed by the Great Powers fixed the total amount payable in land tax and military service tax at 35,000 Turkish pounds; this is a considerably lower tax burden than the above-mentioned 'ushr and *werko* which are levied in the rest of Turkey. Other reasons inducing the Lebanese not to go beyond the boundaries of the *mutasarriflik* are the relatively greater influence over the administration which is guaranteed to them and the freedom from military service which they enjoy.

Emigration also takes place, on a smaller scale, to North and South America, from the predominantly Christian localities of Bethlehem, Bait Jala, and Ramallah, near Jerusalem. In many South American cities there are what may be truly termed colonies of Bethlehemites, who remain in touch with their native land, some of them returning to it. These people are employed exclusively in trade. The report of the American consul in Jerusalem (*Daily Consular and Trade Reports*, June 6, 1914) puts emigration from the *mutasarriflik* of Jerusalem in 1913 at 3,000, mostly young men, of whom 30 per cent were Christians, 35 per cent Jews, and 35 per cent Mohammedans. The fare from Jaffa to New York is about 190 francs.

Emigration from the *vilayet*'s of Beirut and Damascus to Egypt also deserves mention. It consists mainly of Mohammedans, who go to Egypt on business and frequently stay there. There are, for example, numerous Mohammedans from Homs in Tanta, in Egypt, who lend money to cotton planters at rates of up to 20–25 per cent—an interest rate which cannot be obtained at such small risk in Syria. The passing of the Five-Faddan Law in Egypt[2] has, however, made this business much more difficult and many moneylenders have returned to Homs.

Immigration of East European Jews to Palestine, like *emigration* from Lebanon, has resulted in a considerable monetary inflow from abroad. For several hundred years there have been in Europe associations which have helped old Jews who wished to end their days in Palestine, by facilitating their migration and by regularly sending them money, thus permitting them to devote themselves in Palestine exclusively to religious studies. Many welfare establishments for the benefit of Jews living in Palestine are also supported from Europe, such as homes for the aged, hospitals, soup kitchens, orphanages, and schools. The total amount of money sent yearly to

[2] This law, passed in 1913, exempted farms of 5 faddans or less from seizure for debt.—Translator.

Palestine by Jewish associations and by relatives may be put at a minimum of 5 to 7 million francs. In addition, during the last three decades, Jews from Europe have settled in Palestine as bankers, merchants, or farmers, either bringing their own capital with them or being supported by Jewish charitable institutions; the consequent inflow of capital in the last prewar years may be estimated at not less than 3 to 5 million francs per annum. The total [annual] inflow of capital to Jews from abroad thus amounts to about 10 million francs.

Jewish immigration from Europe is accompanied, although to a much smaller extent, by that of Oriental Jews, driven to Jerusalem by religious sentiment. Thus in the last decades Jews from Morocco, Persia, Bukhara, and Yemen have settled in Jerusalem. Whereas the Moroccan and Persian Jews are very poor, and weak in body, the Bukharan are tall and well built, recalling the ancient Assyrians, and as a rule are well off or even rich. They have built their own quarter in Jerusalem, with very handsome houses. The Yemeni Jews, whose immigration started some 30 years ago [see Part V, chap. 7], are as poor and feeble as the Persian, but they are more accustomed to manual labor; they have settled not only in Jerusalem but also in Jaffa and, in recent years, as farm workers in Jewish farms in Palestine. The total number of Moroccan together with Persian Jews may be put at 5,000, of Bukharan at 1,000, and of Yemeni at 4,000; of the latter 2,000 are in Jerusalem.

In connection with capital inflow due to migration to or from Syria, mention may be made of the money sent to Syria by the Christian churches for the numerous clergymen and institutions (churches, monasteries, hospices, hospitals, orphanages, and schools) supported by them; a total estimate of 10 million francs per annum is more likely to err on the low than on the high side. . . .

CHAPTER 7

Syria in the 1900's

The picture of Syria on the eve of the First World War given in the following selection shows, on the one hand, the continuation of certain trends that operated throughout the second half of the nineteenth century and, on the other, the beginning of new ones that developed fully only after the Second World War.

Population growth, which must have started around the middle of the nineteenth century, has continued at an accelerating rate, with a temporary setback caused by the disruption and famine of the First World War. By 1932 the total population of Syria, Lebanon, Palestine, and Trans-Jordan was a little over 4 million. The concomitant increase in the population of the coastal towns—Beirut, Latakia, Tripoli, Haifa, Jaffa, Tel Aviv—relative to the inland towns also persisted until fairly recently.

The extension of the cultivated area was halted during the period 1914–39 but resumed at a rapid pace thereafter (see Part IV, chap. 5). The introduction of new crops, notably fruits in Palestine and Lebanon, and of improved methods of cultivation began in the 1920's and has gained momentum; particularly noteworthy is the growth of cotton production in Syria in the 1950's, after unsuccessful attempts in the interwar period.

Although increasingly suffering from foreign competition, Syrian handicrafts were still active at the turn of the century, and played an important part in the country's economy. In the interwar period, however, they declined rapidly. Thus by 1931 the number of handlooms in Aleppo had fallen to 1,500–2,000, in Homs to 1,500, in Damascus to 550, and in Hama to 300; the number of silk-reeling factories stood at 35, compared to 194 in 1910–11; and the number of establishments making soap was only 60, compared to about 100 before the First World War.[1] Attempts to modernize the handicrafts met with little success, and factory industry had hardly gained a foothold at the outbreak of the Second World War. Thus in 1939 there were no modern factories in Trans-Jordan, a half-dozen in Syria, and a handful in Lebanon; only in Palestine had the Jewish immigrants started a significant number of industries. Rapid industrialization came to this region after the Second World War.

[1] Himadeh, *The Economic Organization of Syria and Lebanon*, pp. 124–27.

Motor transport, whose halting beginnings are noted in the following selection, advanced rapidly in the 1920's and soon absorbed the greater part of the traffic.[2] This was made possible by the building of a very good road system under the French and British mandates, a task that has been successfully continued by the successor governments. Several new ports were also built during the interwar and postwar periods.

Improved transport and communication helped to promote trade, which has always played a leading part in Syria's economy. Against this must be set the harmful effects of the breakup of the Ottoman Empire. The latter had constituted a large free-trade area in which Syrian traders could operate, and the numerous boundaries and tariffs that were established after 1918 presented serious obstacles. So far, however, the growth of the economy of Arab Asia, particularly after the discovery of oil, has more than offset the restrictive effects of political disintegration, and the resultant increase in commercial and financial transactions has been especially beneficial to Beirut.

(See also works by Samné, Huvelin, Burns, Himadeh [*Economic Organization of Syria and Palestine*], and I.B.R.D. [*Syria*] listed in the Bibliography.)

[2] The first motorcar in the interior of Syria reached Aleppo, from Alexandretta, in 1909 (Gharaybeh, *Suriya*, p. 156). By 1939 there were 9,000 trucks, buses, and passenger cars in Palestine, 6,300 in Lebanon, 4,100 in Syria, and 600 in Transjordan, a total of 20,000.

[From E. Weakley, "Report on the Conditions and Prospects of British Trade in Syria," Great Britain, *Accounts and Papers*, *1911*, LXXXVII, 7–23, 54–68, 81–85, 126–33, with omissions.]

. . . .

Administrative Divisions.—Syria and Palestine are, for administrative purposes, divided into three vilayets or provinces and two sandjaks of the first class, that is privileged districts. The first, in the north, is the vilayet of Aleppo, subdivided into the sandjaks or districts of the Aleppo sandjak, Marash sandjak, and Ourfa sandjak, on the east of the Euphrates.

The superficies of the two first districts is roughly calculated to be about 24,000 square miles, containing 3,500 villages and a total population estimated at 800,000, exclusive of the nomad Bedouin tribes. The Ourfa sandjak has a superficies of about 7,000 square miles, with a population of 140,000 souls. Second is the vilayet of Damascus, or "Surieh," which is composed of the following sandjaks:

	Superficies Sq. Miles
Sham (Damascus)	10,000
Hama	9,200
Hauran	11,000
Kerak	5,400

with a total population of about 1,150,000. The Beyrout vilayet, with its sandjaks of

	Superficies Sq. Miles	Villages
Beyrout	1,700	400
Tripoli	2,300	640
Lattakia	2,000	1,100
Akka	3,000	230
Nablous	2,600	200
	11,600	

the total population being estimated at close on 800,000.

The Lebanon sandjak has a superficies of about 3,000 square miles and a population of 450,000, whilst the superficies of the sandjak of Jerusalem (Kudas) is estimated at 7,700 square miles, and has a population of about 400,000.

The figures just given are, however, only approximate, and according to them the total area of the country, exclusive of the Ourfa sandjak, will therefore be about

70,000 square miles, with three million and a half of inhabitants. . . .

Agriculture.—The extensive plains of the Aleppo, Hama, Homs, Damascus, and Hauran districts, as well as those in the southern region, as far down as Gazza, are very fertile, but only a small portion of their area is cultivated. Farming is carried on with primitive simplicity, modern agricultural implements are almost unknown, and the agriculturist is mainly dependent on the rainfall for the irrigation of his land; besides, a scanty population, insecurity especially on the eastern side towards the desert, and the absence of communications, greatly hinder all agricultural development. Notwithstanding the many difficulties and backwardness of the peasant class, the country produces fairly large quantities of wheat, barley, maize, lentils, chick-peas, beans, rice, sesame. The olive groves of the slopes of the mountains around Antioch, near Killis, Tripoli, Beyrout, as well as on the hills of Palestine, yield large quantities of olives, and vineyards, which are found everywhere, on mountain slope, valley and plain, cover a large area and produce grapes in abundance. Large tracts of land in the neighbourhood of towns and along the banks of rivers and streams are laid out in gardens and orchards; oranges are grown at Jaffa, Haiffa, Saida, Beyrout, and near Alexandretta, and form a most important branch of the export trade of the country. Lemons, apricots, figs, pomegranates, walnuts, pistachio nuts, almonds, and melons are produced in large quantities, besides which vegetables of many varieties are found everywhere.

It has been difficult to obtain some idea of the total yearly production of the staple crops grown in the country, and the following figures can only give a very approximate estimate of the annual yield. Given a good year, the crops in the Aleppo province—including the district of Ourfa—will average about—

6 to 7,000,000	bushels of wheat.
4 to 6,000,000	barley.
200,000	maize.
800,000	dari seed.

The Beyrout vilayet—

	4,000,000 bushels of wheat,
1 to 2,000,000	barley,
1,000,000	maize,
3,000,000	beans (broad and small varieties).

In the Damascus vilayet—

6,000,000	bushels of wheat.
5,000,000	barley.

Sandjak of Jerusalem—

1,000,000	bushels of wheat.
1,000,000	barley.
300,000	beans.
400,000	sesame.

The country frequently suffers from drought, and during the last few years the crops in the districts of Homs, Hama, and all the country near Aleppo and the lands bordering on the Euphrates have suffered so much from the ravages of swarms of locusts which came up from the desert, that fears of scarcity compelled the authorities to take precautionary measures, such as the prohibition of the export of cereals from the affected districts.

Recent indications point to the awakening of Government to the necessity of taking some steps for the improvement of agriculture and of familiarising the peasant with the modern methods and implements. As a first measure the Agricultural Department of the Ministry of Mines, Forests, and Agriculture has undertaken the establishment of small depots of agricultural implements in the chief farming centers of the Empire, where these implements can be seen and examined by the farmers before purchasing them. A small depot has been open at Homs, and the intention is to open others at Aleppo, Beyrout, and Damascus in the course of the year 1911. The implements bought by the Department for stocking such depots consist in light ploughs of German make such as— . . .

This Government measure has much to commend it, and is certainly a step taken in the right direction; the peasant is slow, and cannot be easily persuaded to give up his primitive ways, and no results can possibly be expected from the existence of these depots for some time to come. These stores will certainly, however, have a good influence, and will do much towards the introduction of better methods of farming, increase the area of cultivation, and will give an impulse to the sale of agricultural machinery . . .

Harbours.—With the exception of the port constructed at Beyrout, which is protected by a breakwater, and the natural harbour at Alexandretta, the coast at no point offers any safe shelter to shipping. Vessels have to lie far out at the road-stead of Lattakia, Tripoli, Akka [Acre], Haiffa, Jaffa, and Gazza, and the operations of taking and discharging cargo and passengers are generally attended with difficulties and some risk, and become quite impossible during bad weather. The construction of a breakwater and port at Haiffa is to be undertaken by the Hedjaz Railway Administration, but the matter has not yet taken definite shape, as the necessary financial arrangements have still to be made. Surveys for harbour works at Tripoli have been carried out on behalf of the Public Works Department, and in all probability the work of construction will, eventually, be undertaken by the Concessionnaires of the Tripoli–Homs Railway. Schemes have from time to time been mooted for building a protected port at Jaffa, but in view of the projected harbour at Haiffa and the construction of a line branching off from the Haiffa–Deraa section of the Hedjaz Railway to Jerusalem (*see* chapter on projected railways) [see Part IV, chap. 4], it is likely that all idea of improving the Jaffa roadstead will, if not abandoned, be set aside for the present. . . .

. . . *Foreign Trade.*—Regular and frequent communications between the coast and Marseilles, Trieste, Genoa, Hamburg, and Antwerp, maintained by the services of the Messageries Maritimes, Austrian Lloyd, Italian Steam Navigation Company, and the various steamship companies which form the Antwerp Combine (see chapter on shipping), with cheap freights and rapid transit, offer great assistance in the development of the trade of the countries to which

the ports mentioned belong. German, Austrian, Italian, and Belgian trade has been and is pushed with great energy by manufacturers themselves, and their commercial travellers are constantly to be met with in every large trading centre in the country.

Principals of large foreign trading or manufacturing firms also pay frequent visits to these markets, come into personal contact with their customers, exercise a wholesome control over their local agents, and have ample opportunities for studying, at first hand, local conditions and requirements, as well as the class of trade done by other countries. The bulk of the trade of Syria, like that of the rest of the Turkish Empire, is low class, cheapness in the price of every required article being an almost essential condition, and foreign manufacturers have, with great perseverance, endeavoured to adapt both the goods they offer as well as their mode of business to the tastes of their customers and to the conditions of the market in which they desire to trade. Customers' wishes are carefully carried out, whether it be in the matter of quality, length of piece, colour, shape, design, etc., small as well as large orders receive equal attention, and the facilities of payment, in the shape of long credits which are given, are very attractive to purchasers even if the price, though reasonable enough, may be a trifle higher than that which would be paid for cash.

It may here be remarked that, with the exception of the trade in few articles, all transactions between the native wholesale importers and the small retailer, shopkeeper, or the small trader in interior towns are based on credit, and this being the case, importers in their turn expect certain financial facilities to be given them by European firms. An important question is that of language; French is the language most spoken, and is understood in all principal commercial centers, and foreign firms, German, Austrian and Italian conduct their correspondence with Syrian customers in French, besides which, commercial travellers of any of these three nationalities who visit this country are generally conversant with that language.

Besides the advantages secured through shipping those also acquired by the result of continuous and close study of local needs, foreign, and especially German and Austrian trade, benefits in no small degree by the activities of the several German and Swiss business houses long established in Beyrout and Aleppo, and who are largely, if not wholly, engaged in the import trade. Essentially German or German-Swiss, these firms have from long experience acquired a thorough and intimate knowledge of the people and their business ways; they rightly enjoy the respect and confidence of all classes, and although they act as agents for French, Italian, Belgian, and even some British firms, their efforts and activities are naturally more directed towards the promotion of the considerable German and Austrian commercial interests with which they are entrusted by home firms. The few French firms in Beyrout pay more attention to the export trade, silk, either in the shape of cocoons or spun silk, being the principal item. Whilst the development of foreign trade is in some measure due to the generous terms of credit foreign merchants and manufacturers are able to grant to their customers, owing to the accommodation they receive from their own banking institutions, the success in obtaining a good footing in Syrian markets, as also in those of other ports of the Levant, is admittedly the result of hard work and sustained endeavour to study and to satisfy the tastes, likes, and pockets of their customers. It is the trader and manufacturer who now seek out the native customer and are eager to do business with him.

Although a small trade is done in a higher class of goods, the chief demand is for low class and cheap articles. British manufacturers do not appear to have given this branch of trade sufficient attention, for, with the exception, perhaps, of cheap cotton and woollen goods, cheap articles having a large sale, and which are of British origin, are rarely met with. In fact, it may be said that in such articles as hardware, glass, and earthenware, porcelain, cutlery, steel and iron, the competition is entirely between foreign makers, since similar British articles anywhere near competition prices are not seen in the market. The market for cheap goods is a large and growing one. British manufacturers would undoubtedly participate in the trade to a larger extent if goods are manufactured to suit local requirements. . . .

STATISTICS OF TRADE

It has not been possible to obtain any figures for a consecutive number of years which would show the fluctuations in the volume of trade; the bases necessary for comparative purposes are lacking, and the task of collecting data of imports and exports has not been easy, owing to the numerous ports through which traffic enters and leaves the country. It has, however, been possible to procure official returns of imports and exports for one year—the Turkish financial year of 1324, beginning with the 1/14th March, 1908, ending February 28/13 March, 1909—for each port on the coast. These returns have no pretensions to accuracy, but they convey very approximately an idea of the volume of trade of foreign countries with Syria. The total value of gross imports for the whole coast, according to these returns, was £ stg. 3,948,517 for the year ending March 13th, 1909, and of this amount £ stg. 1,422,621 or 36 per cent., was contributed by the United Kingdom. Next in importance is Austria, with 12.73 per cent., whilst imports from Egypt stand third, at 11.39 per cent. of the total amount. The figures of imports from Egypt are, however, misleading, for the greater part of the goods from Egypt are of foreign origin—principally British and Indian—in transit through Alexandria or Port Said for Syria.

With regard to exports, Egypt and France are the two countries which come first as Syria's best customers—respectively 34 and 28 per cent. of total exports—France taking nearly all the silk produced, Egypt obtaining large supplies of purely native products, provisions, fruit, etc., whilst the United Kingdom occupies the third place with 15 per cent., the exports being principally cereals.

As is clearly shown by the detailed lists,[1] Beyrout and Alexandretta are the two ports through which the greatest quantities of imports pass through into the country— Beyrout the great distributing centre for the hinterland and coast, and Alexandretta the port of the towns in Northern Syria, and to some extent also of those on the east of the Euphrates.

BANKING

Syria is exceptionally favoured by the number of banks and financial establishments which are found in the principal towns and which have been able to create a wide range of business.

The following are the banking establishments found in the country:

Agencies of the Imperial Ottoman Bank.—At Beyrout, Damascus, Aleppo, Tripoli, Homs, Jaffa, Jerusalem, with some agencies at Aintab and Haiffa.

Crédit Lyonnais.—Agencies at Jaffa and Jerusalem.

Deutsche Palestina Bank.—Agencies at Beyrout, Haiffa, Jaffa, Jerusalem.

Anglo-Palestine Company, Limited.—Agencies at Jaffa, Jerusalem, Beyrout, Haiffa. This is a Jewish Bank, founded by the Jewish Colonization Association, and is registered under the Company's Act, with head offices in London.

Banque d'Athènes.—Agency at Beyrout (newly opened).

Banque de Salonique.—Agency at Beyrout (newly opened).

Deutsche Orient Bank.—Agency at Aleppo.

[1] These lists, compiled from consular figures, may be summarized as follows (£000):

		1906	1907	1908
Beirut . .	Imports	...	1,694	1,693
	Exports	...	1,029	919
Alexandretta .	Imports	2,394	2,326	1,891
	Exports	1,466	1,448	1,467
Damascus .	Imports	920	929	853
	Exports	643	639	657
Jaffa . . .	Imports	660	809	803
	Exports	500	484	556

Detailed breakdowns by trading partner, are given for each town.—Editor.

Besides these regular banks, there are a number of private bankers in the large towns, especially at Beyrout and Aleppo. The exceptional situation enjoyed by Beyrout in particular, as a collecting centre for exports and as a storing centre for imports of European manufacture, has led to the creation of a number of really sound private banking establishments, which do an important business, chiefly connected with the discounting of bills, or promissory notes drawn on, or endorsed by, merchants in the interior for the value of imported goods.

The agencies of the Imperial Ottoman Bank have, however, the lead in all banking operations in the country, and the local rates of exchange with Europe and with Turkish towns are fixed by them. These rates are established, as a rule, about twice in the course of the week, unless any abrupt change in the rates of the principal European money markets should occur in the meantime. The rates quoted in Syria, where the basis of currency is the Turkish lira, rise and fall in accordance with those ruling in Constantinople, the slight margin existing between local rates and those of the capital being due to the state of supply and demand of the local market, and, so far as bills expressed in £ stg. are concerned, to a certain extent by the rates ruling in Alexandria. (See tables of rates.)

The banks discount local bills, which have to bear three signatures, and a great deal of paper bought by private bankers is rediscounted by the bigger establishments. The discount rate, which was between 7 per cent. and 8½ per cent., has now been reduced to 5 per cent. and 6 per cent. Advances are also made on the promissory notes which merchants known to, and dealing regularly with, the bank receive from their customers for goods which have been sold on credit.

The collection of the value of goods imported from abroad, the shipping documents of which are sent to the bank by manufacturers and others, forms a very large item in banking transactions. . . .

Amongst the various financial arrangements undertaken with a view to the development of banking operations, and also to giving facilities to traders, is the introduction of the system of making advances on goods, practised so very largely in other towns in Turkey by the Imperial Ottoman Bank. The principal agencies of the bank at Beyrout and Aleppo have developed this branch of the Bank's transactions very considerably, and importers of Manchester cotton piece goods and yarns, copper, Austrian and Russian sugar, gunnies and petroleum, and exporters of grain and wool avail themselves very largely of this financial facility, which has materially assisted the development of trade. . . .

NATIVE INDUSTRIES

SILK INDUSTRY

The rearing of silk has always been a very important industry in certain parts of Syria, and it is in the Lebanon province where it has now attained a high development, whilst the districts near the seaboard to the south, at Saida, Tyre, Acre and Tripoli, and Lattakia on the north, all in the Beyrout Province, produce large quantities of cocoons. Silk is also raised at Antioch, Swedia and Arsous, in the Aleppo province. The industry, which was a very thriving one about fifty years ago, was seriously affected by the disease of the silk worm and was greatly reduced, but it has revived rapidly owing to the aid of scientific research, which has made the detection and prevention of disease possible, and it is now a very prosperous one, and is one of the important factors conducing to the wealth and prosperity of the country. The cultivation of the mulberry tree, already very extensive in the Lebanon, has been greatly extended within the last few years in the anti-Lebanon, as well as in the plains and hill slopes around Saida, Acre, Mardjaoun, Hasbieh, as well as in the northern parts around Tripoli, Lattakia, and Antioch.

The indigenous breed of silk worm has entirely disappeared, exterminated by disease, and its place has been taken by a foreign kind, produced from eggs imported chiefly from France. The eggs are imported in well-ventilated cardboard boxes, each box containing 25 grammes (an ounce), and about 150,000 to 180,000 boxes are imported annually through Beyrout and some 32,000 through Alexandretta for distribution in the interior; some 20,000 to 30,000 boxes are also produced locally, from cocoons obtained from imported eggs. A box of 25 grammes is sold at from 2 to 3 francs.

The eggs begin to hatch about the latter part of April in the plains and about 20 days later on the hill slopes, the cocoons being produced in from 33 to 40 days. There is only one kind of cocoon and silk grown in the country, but the quality naturally varies according to the amount of care and labour bestowed on the rearing of the silk worm, for, when properly raised and fed, it produces a full cocoon, from which a good quality of silk is obtained.

The following are the calculations upon which native silk growers base the production of silk:

(1) A box of 25 grammes of eggs should, under normal conditions, produce from 25 to 30 kilos. of green cocoons. (This yield is much below that obtained by the silk growers of France and Italy.)

(2) Three okes of green cocoons (3.850 kilos.) equal 1 oke dried cocoons (1.28 kilos.); and

(3) Five kilos. of dried cocoons are required to produce 1 kilogramme of spun silk; and

(4) 850 to 900 okes (1,089½ to 1,153½ kilos.) of green cocoons produce 100 kilos. of spun silk.

Statistics giving the total annual yield of cocoons are lacking, but fairly accurate estimates have been worked out, which show that the total production is not less than from 4,000,000 to 6,000,000 okes of green cocoons per annum, of which 2,070,000 okes alone are produced in the Lebanon district.

Spinning.—The spinning industry is also centred in the Lebanon, and there are to-day no less than 152 factories, with a total of 8,560 pans (Bassines), scattered over different parts of the mountain. Most of these factories belong to natives, and a few are owned by Frenchmen; many of the factories are fitted up with modern machinery, and the system of spinning is known as the "Système Lyonnais," that is, the recognized French standard. There are also three modern spinning factories, with a total of 250 pans, in the immediate outskirts of Beyrout, one is found near Tripoli, and another not far from Swedia. The greater part of the cocoon production of the Lebanon and of the Beyrout district is absorbed by these factories, and the annual production of spun silk is reckoned to be between 4,000 and 4,500 bales, of 100 kilos. each. Owing to its good quality, none of the silk produced remains in the country; Lyons takes about 90 per cent. of the total production, Marseilles and Genoa receiving the remainder. Silk spun from double and inferior cocoons—which is much coarser in fibre—is used in the country and is worked up with Chinese silk into the cloths and stuffs made at Damascus, Homs, and Aleppo. . . .

SOAP INDUSTRY

The production must necessarily vary according to the quantity of oil available from year to year, but the following figures show very approximately the quantities of soap manufactured in the various districts in an ordinary year:

	Okes
Beyrout	500,000
Lebanon	2,000,000
Tripoli and district . . .	2,000,000
Lattakia	300,000
Haiffa and district . . .	250,000
Nablous	4,000,000
Jaffa	3,000,000
Damascus	600,000
Aleppo	1,400,000
Antioch	1,220,000
Idlib	360,000
Nezib, Killis, Aintab . .	1,000,000
	16,630,000
	or about 20,000 tons.

Markets.—Besides supplying local wants, this special industry finds a much wider market for its products in Mesopotamia, many of the inland towns of Asia Minor, and Egypt. Some of these outside markets prefer the products of one particular Syrian district to another, so that each soap-producing locality has, besides the general market, some special region to supply, where its products are appreciated and preferred to another. Thus the soaps produced in the Jaffa and in the Nablous districts find a ready sale in Egypt, the Hedjaz, and the Yemen, about 70 per cent. of the total production being taken by these countries. . . .

Transactions with these markets are conducted as much as possible on a cash basis, but local soap merchants, as distinguished from soap manufacturers, give long credits to their customers, which sometimes extend to 12 months.

The exports by sea of soap through the Syrian ports for other parts of Turkey and Egypt for the three years 1906, 1907, and 1908 are approximately:

		1906	1907	1908
Jaffa	Tons	3,810	3,165	4,511
Alexandretta .	Tons	532	765	832
Beyrout . . .	Cases	6,200	6,250	4,800
Tripoli . . .	Cases	7,700	9,350	11,200
Lattakia . . .	Cases	...	...	120

WEAVING INDUSTRY

The weaving of silk and cotton cloths is an old-established industry of Northern Syria, and is, with the manufacture of soap and the production of silk, one of the important industrial resources of the country. It is, like the soap industry, essentially a home industry, established for supplying home needs and to suit special native tastes. The products of the looms of Northern Syria, Damascus, Homs, and in a lesser degree, those of Hama and the Lebanon, are well known throughout Turkish territory, and everywhere find a good sale. The introduction of cheap European imitations, of native cloths especially, has very sensibly affected the cotton weaving branch of the industry, and this competition, as also the development of native tastes for purely European goods, has been the cause of a perceptible decrease within the last 20 years in the sale of native cotton cloths and has resulted in a diminution in the number of looms. The industry, however, still shows vitality and could doubtless be developed, and would perhaps more than regain its former position were modern methods of manufacture adopted for cheapening the cost of production. As far as it has been possible to ascertain the number, the looms at present at work in the country are:

	Cotton Only	Cotton and silk	Silk	Total
Aleppo . . .	5,500	2,000	2,500	10,000
Aintab . . .	4,000	...	...	4,000
Marash . . .	1,000	...	...	1,000
Ourfa . . .	100	...	...	100
Homs . . .	6,000	3,000	1,000	10,000
Hama . . .	1,000	...	...	1,000
Damascus . .	1,000	500	1,000	2,500
Lebanon (Bekfaya), Deir el Kamr, Beiteddin	2,000	...	...	2,000
	21,100*	5,500	4,500	31,100*

* *Sic.*

The looms, which are of wood and of primitive construction, are generally found in houses occupied by the weavers, but a great many are set up in small hans, called "kaiserliks." They are mostly owned by the weavers themselves, small weavers possessing perhaps two or three, and those working in the kaiserliks from 10 to 15 looms. The cloths produced, whether of cotton or silk, are known under the generic name of "saih," but different qualities and varieties of material manufactured have each their special Arabic designation. A feature noticeable in the majority of the cloths manufactured is the short lengths of the pieces, the generally accepted standard being from 8 to 11 "dras" (of 27 inches), viz., 6 to 8½ yards, and three-quarters of a dra (or 20¼ inches) in width. The explanation is that one piece contains just enough material to make a "gumbaz," the long outer garment fitted with sleeves, which is the common dress worn by Moslems and Christians all over Syria and Mesopotamia, as well as in many parts of Asia Minor. A characteristic which is also observed is the

sameness of pattern worked into the cotton or silk cloths, coloured stripes with black or white grounds being the generally accepted design.

Cotton goods woven with imported yarn form the great bulk of the trade and are made in white grounds, the pieces being striped with either black, blue, or green stripes on dark-blue or black grounds, having white or green, red or yellow stripes. The varieties are known under the following names: "Tchaktchak" (the cheapest kind), "djoura" (a heavier cloth), "aladja," "kutni," "hattata" (head coverings), towels, native bed sheets, dimmehs, large bath towels (bournouz). . . .

Besides the ordinary looms, there are [in Aleppo] about 50 jacquard machines, which have been made locally, and they produce:

Shawls (pure wool) . . .	20 looms
Habaras (Coverings) silk . .	6
Karawit (soft coverings) . .	10
Figured silks	14
	50 looms

It is estimated that on an average some 20,000 pieces of all kinds of cloth are woven daily in Aleppo, and some idea of the rate of daily production may be gathered from the following indications:

Weavers of tchaktchak, djoura, and kutnis can make from 15 to 18 dras (11¼ to 13½ yards) per day.

Hattatas of 39 to 43 inches in breadth and 40½ inches in length can be produced at the rate of 2 to 5 pieces per day.

Of curtains and sofa coverings of 26¾ to 35½ inches wide, from 10 to 15 dras (7½ to 11¼ yards) can be produced.

In *Menoush* figured silk cloths of 64, 100, and 110 centimetres wide, weaving is very slow, the native looms only being able to turn out 2 dras (54 inches) daily.

The daily capacity of jacquard looms is:

In woollen shawls of 1 metre square, 4 to 12 shawls.

Silk habara 120 centimetres wide, from 3 to 4 dras (2¼ to 3 yards).

Karawit (silk sofa coverings) 68 centimetres wide, from 12 to 16 dras (9 to 12 yards).

As regards wages:

	Piastres per day	
Weavers of tchaktchaks . . .	earn from 5 to	6
djoura	8	10
kutnis	9	12
hattatas	9	12
curtains, sofa coverings	9	12
menoush	9	12
jacquard looms . .	10	15

Children engaged to assist the weavers receive from 1 to 3 piastres a day.

Aleppo cloths, especially those made of cotton, have a wide and extensive sale throughout the whole of Syria, Palestine, and Mesopotamia; they are sent to the most eastern parts of Asia Minor, to Erzeroum, Van, Bitlis, besides the coast towns, including Smyrna and Constantinople, and are also exported to Egypt.

Prices vary from 7 piastres to 20 to 25 piastres per piece.

Aintab produces the inferior cotton cloth called "aladja," and no silk material worth mentioning is woven in the district. The "aladja" is of the usual pattern of cloth, with coloured stripes and is very light in weight, a piece of 8 to 9 dras in length and three-quarters of a dra in width weighing not more than from 70 to 80 drams (8 to 10 ozs.). Some 12,000 to 14,000 pieces are turned out by the weavers daily. The selling price varies from $5\frac{1}{2}$ to 11 piastres per piece, cloths costing from 7 to 9 piastres having the largest sale. Aintab "aladjas" are sold in every part of the country as far as Bagdad, and are known pretty well nearly everywhere in Asia Minor. Weavers' wages average 4 to 6 piastres per day, but some of the best workers are paid as much as 8 piastres . . .

Homs produces in cotton goods "dimmehs," kutni, hamidieh (striped cloth), but the workmen pay more particular attention to the weaving of mixed cotton and silk goods, and manufacture aladjas, habaras, hamidieh, and mellis, the latter a fine cotton and silk cloth, much used by the better-class natives for shirts. The same class of cloths are also procured in pure silk.

Cotton cloths are woven in pieces of 9 to 10 dras ($6\frac{3}{4}$ to $7\frac{1}{2}$ yards) and of a width of $20\frac{1}{4}$ inches. Silk and mixed silk and cotton materials are made in pieces of 12 dras (9 yards) and of $20\frac{1}{4}$ inches in width, for the Egyptian market, and are also made in $9\frac{1}{2}$ to $10\frac{1}{2}$ dras lengths (7 to $7\frac{7}{8}$ yards) and $27\frac{1}{2}$ to $29\frac{1}{2}$ inches in width. It is estimated that from 18,000 to 20,000 pieces of all classes of material are manufactured daily. Homs cloths are dearer and finer than those of Aleppo and they find a sale in Egypt especially, also in the Soudan, Beyrout, Aleppo, Damascus, Palestine, Salonica, and Constantinople; and it is reckoned that fully 70 per cent. of the total production is taken by Egypt alone and the rest distributed throughout Turkey. The cloths are very much appreciated, and are bought by the better class of natives.

The prices of cotton cloths range from 2s. to 5s. per piece, mixed cotton and silk from 4s. to 20s., and of silk from 20s. to 60s.

Damascus.—The pure silk and mixed cotton and silk cloths are a specialty of the Damascus weaving industry, and a fine striped cloth of silk and cotton called "misri" is woven specially for the Egyptian market. A cotton and silk cloth, the "aladja," somewhat similar in design to the cotton "aladja" of Aintab, is woven in fairly large quantities, and is bought for the Medina and Mecca markets, as also for some of the towns in Central Arabia.

Twenty or thirty jacquard looms have been introduced within the last few years, and very fine silk figured cloths are now woven for the Egyptian and Hedjaz markets; seven more looms of an improved type have recently been added. They have been purchased in Switzerland, and work with four shuttles; they are used for weaving the coloured waistbands made of silk and cotton worn by natives in Syria and Egypt. Cotton piece-goods represent, perhaps, half of the total production, the rest being Dimmeh cloth, imitation Cashmir waistbands, and other cloths.

A considerable number of looms are employed in weaving cotton curtains, and pillow and sofa coverings. These have generally a white ground, with Arab designs woven in, in red and blue colours, the better qualities having besides a certain number of gold or silver threads woven in the cloth.

"Misri" cloth is woven in pieces of 9 dras (6¾ yards), and is sold at from 12s. to 32s. and 50s. per piece.

"Aladjas," cotton and silk, sell at 8s. to 24s. Dimmehs, of pure cotton, sell at 1s. 7d. to 4s. the piece.

The annual production of the Damascus looms, if not very great in quantity as compared with that of the large weaving centres of Aleppo and Homs, is of considerable value owing to the good material employed, especially in the manufacture of cloths for the Egyptian market, and it is estimated that £ stg. 400,000 worth of goods are produced per annum. Besides the Egyptian market, Damascus stuffs are sent to the Hedjaz and Yemen, Constantinople, Smyrna, Salonica, and many of the larger towns of Anatolia.

Hama.—The weaving industry of this town is comparatively very small, and only cotton goods, such as dimmehs, towels, native bed sheets, and large bath towels, called "bournouz," are manufactured.

Beyrout and Lebanon.—The industry in Beyrout itself is insignificant, and weaving, which in former times was one of the most important occupations in the Lebanon, especially in the villages of Deir el Kamr, Beiteddin, and Bekfaya, has fallen into decay, owing, perhaps, as much as anything, to the scarcity of hands which has been brought about by the constant emigration of numbers of the population of the Lebanon to North and South America, and also to the development of the industry in other localities.

Work at the looms is carried on for about eight months of the year, the rest of the time being devoted to the raising of silk, and about 300,000 pieces represents the maximum production per annum. The cloths, which are all of cotton and mostly in dark colours, are exported to Salonica, Smyrna, and Egypt. . . .

ROADS

The construction of railways in the country has to a very large extent reduced the value of some of the trunk roads which penetrate into the interior. The only two which really still continue as main arteries of traffic are the high road between Aleppo and Alexandretta and the chaussée between Tripoli and Homs. Local and provincial roads, those which have been built to connect towns in the interior of the provinces themselves, are still all important, but they, as well as all the principal arteries, have been so neglected that wheeled traffic can pass over very few of them.

Subjoined is a list of the trunk and provincial roads existing or only partially built in the provinces of Aleppo, Damascus, Beyrout, Lebanon, and Jerusalem.

These provinces have, between them, the following:

In trunk roads or main arteries communicating with adjoining provinces:

Aleppo, 435 kilometres, of which 261 kilometres are not built.
Damascus, 211 kilometres, of which 38 kilometres are not built.
Beyrout, 268 kilometres, of which 68 kilometres are not built.
Jerusalem, 135 kilometres, of which 75 kilometres are not built.

In provincial, that is, local roads in the interior of the provinces, there are

Aleppo, 530 kilometres, of which 344 kilometres are not constructed.
Damascus, 596 kilometres, of which 231 kilometres are not constructed.
Beyrout, 328 kilometres, of which 103 kilometres are not constructed.
Jerusalem, 238 kilometres, of which 73 kilometres are not constructed.

No attempt has for some years been made to repair any of these roads, and with the exception of the Tripoli-Homs-Hama road, which was built and is kept up by the National Company of Tripoli, every one of these roads practically requires reconstruction. . . .

MOUNT LEBANON

Considerable attention has been given by the Government of the "Mountain" to the establishment of road communications within the province, and it is now possible for wheeled traffic to circulate in almost every part. With the exception of the main trunk road from Beyrout to Damascus, which is entirely out of repair, the roads, especially in the vicinity of Beyrout, and those leading up the slopes to the principal villages and townships on the "Mountain," are, as compared with those in the neighbouring provinces, very well kept. The number of main roads is as follows:[2] . . .

MACHINERY

The importation of certain kinds of machinery, such as petroleum motors, pumps, milling plants, has been going on slowly but steadily for some years past, and natives of the country now realize the advantages and real benefits which are to be derived by the use of modern appliances in many of their occupations. In regard to this question some pains have been taken to obtain particulars regarding the kinds and quantity of machinery which now exist in the country, and the results are not without interest.

Jaffa.—The great increase in orange tree cultivation in the district has rendered the question of irrigation a very important one, and modern appliances have almost entirely taken the place of the old water wheels. Pumps, mostly chain and bucket, of an improved pattern, as well as oil motors to work them, have been imported, and the following figures show as nearly as possible the number of oil motors of British make found in this district: . . .

There are therefore

187 Petroleum motors, of 1,235 aggregate horsepower;
1 Portable steam engine, 10 horsepower;
9 Suction gas plants, of 174 aggregate horsepower;

all of British make, and it is possible that a number of others may exist, which it has not been possible to trace.

A German firm has also placed 305 motors of 1,638 aggregate horse power, but no particulars have been obtainable.

Some 502 motors have therefore been imported into Jaffa, and as the development of orange tree cultivation progresses, more of these engines will be required.

Haiffa.—The engines of the Haiffa district are distributed as follows.[3] . . .

The small engines are employed for raising water, and the larger sizes for working flour mills. Wood is the only fuel obtainable for the steam engine.

Beyrout.—Beyrout is an important centre for the sale of machinery in the interior and in some of the towns of the coast, and local agents and correspondents of British makers of motors and suction gas plants have been able to introduce these engines into the town itself, the Lebanon, the Hauran, and, in one or two instances into Aleppo.

In the town itself and neighbourhood, about 15 British suction gas plants, representing about 500 aggregate horse power, are used in the local gas works and flour mills. Of gas and oil motors of from $1\frac{1}{2}$ to 23 horse power, some 35 in number (of which five are gas) are employed in the town and neighbourhood, including Saida, in printing offices, brick yards, and one or two silk factories, confectioners, flour mills, and carpenters' shops, but by far the greatest number are employed in raising water to irrigate gardens and mulberry-tree plantations. American oil motors to the number of 10 have also been sold in Beyrout.

The German engine, especially the petroleum motor, has found a good sale, and the number introduced is considered to be greater than that of British make. Suction gas plants made by the same firm are now coming into notice, and the very favourable and easy terms on which two plants were sold during the last year and a

---

[2] The list shows 205 kilometers of main roads and 658 kilometers of district roads—Editor.

[3] 27 petroleum motors, of 369 horse power, and 12 steam motors of 148 horse power, with the highest concentration in Nazareth.—Editor.

half have attracted considerable attention in the locality.

Damascus.—The river Barada, which flows through the town, furnishes considerable water power; this has been largely utilised for working the numerous flour mills found in and around the city, and consequently the need for engine power has been less felt. Moreover, since the construction of the electric tramway and the introduction of electric light in the town, electricity as a motive power has come into con iderable use. Small electric motors have been introduced, and as many as 150 of from ¼ horse power to 2 horse power are now employed in the gardens for raising water. Besides these, seven large electric motors of from 19 to 35 horse power have been set up and are working in weaving sheds, wood-carving shops, and in a brass-work factory. These motors are supplied exclusively by the Electric Tramway Company of Damascus, a Belgian concern, but the motors as well as the pumps are made by a Berlin firm. Petroleum motors and suction gas plants are consequently few in number, there being three suction gas plants, two of which have been supplied by a German firm (25 and 30 horse power respectively) and one of 40 horse power by a French firm. Besides these, four small oil motors, two of German and two of British make, have been traced. Whilst few engines have been sold in Damascus itself, a good number are to be found in the large district of the Hauran, which lies to the immediate south and forms part of the province of Syria. The district has hitherto depended upon Beyrout, and it is calculated that from 40 to 50 oil motors of from 6 to 24 horse power, all British, have been set up in various parts of the Hauran, such as Hosh, Sarih, Irbid, and Deraa, during the past ten years. Purchases are now mostly made through agents in Damascus, and some 15 engines have been imported through these channels during the last few years. The German firm have also been successful in selling a considerable number of motors in this district through their Beyrout agency, many of them being set up in the villages situated along the line of the Hedjaz Railway.

Damascus agents have also supplied the following British motors since 1907: [4] . . .

Aleppo.—The demand for machinery in the Aleppo district has been insignificant, and that is attributable principally to the want of communication and the impossibility of transporting heavy weights up country from the coast. The establishment of railway connections with Beyrout, and the possibility of now transporting heavy pieces of machinery easily and rapidly, has greatly simplified matters, and the question of the introduction and use of machinery has now been put upon a practical footing. Although there has yet been no marked inclination, as at Beyrout and other places, to adopt the use of machinery, interest in the question has been awakened, and this may later on develop into practical results. So far, two suction gas plants of 58 and 40 horse power respectively have been erected, one to drive a flour mill and the other working an ice factory in the town, and seven oil engines and one small steam engine have, besides, been imported. All these are of British manufacture. The south-western part of the province, the Harim, Jesr-Shour, Idlib, as well as the Antioch districts, are in touch with British engineering firms through their agents in Adana and Smyrna, and a few motors have been purchased through these channels besides those purchased through Damascus. . . .

Agricultural Machinery.—Efforts which have from time to time been made to introduce modern agricultural implements and machinery into Syria have so far met with poor success. Farming in all its branches is still pursued throughout the country on primitive lines; the attitude of the Government hitherto in the matter of encouraging the development of agriculture has, as in other important economic

[4] 5 motors with 125 horse power and 5 other motors. "Two or three engines are found at Homs and Hama" and 5, with 100 horse power at Tripoli.—Editor.

questions affecting the prosperity of the country, been one of complete indifference, and although a few model farms were some years ago established under Government auspices, ostensibly for the purpose of instructing cultivators in the application of modern methods, they have signally failed in their object.

Nothing in the way of improvement can be expected of the peasant farmer at present, and any change which has to take place must depend on the initiative of the large landowner, whose interest must first be awakened to the material advantages he would derive by the adoption of rational methods of farming suitable to the country and soil. The general indifference shown by the landed class of Syria to the study of new systems of farming is due to conditions and circumstances which are common to other parts of Turkey. Absence of communications and cheap transport to the coast have, in years past, been the chief obstacles to agricultural development; taxation of land and produce has been vexatious, and to these must be added the natural indolence of the native, who, besides, generally entertains strong prejudices against innovations. The easy-going Moslem proprietor finds the cultivation of his land by "métayers" the simplest way of obtaining a revenue from his land; it gives no trouble and, above all, requires little, if any, expense. In a country like Syria, where the rural population is entirely Mohamedan, the Christian land-owner is at a disadvantage, and for many reasons has been debarred, except when his property is situated near some large center or seaboard, from taking an active interest in the development of his land, and has therefore also been obliged to adopt the métayer system.

Since the partial opening up of the country by the Beyrout–Damascus and other railway systems, a few rich Moslem land-owners have given serious attention to the advantages which might be derived from the use of agricultural machinery on their estates, but they show great hesitation and seem unable to come to any decision in the matter. This state of mind is natural and comprehensible, for no technical advice can be obtained as to the kind of machinery to be purchased suitable for the work and soil, machinery itself is costly, no one can be found locally to work or understand such machinery, and should breakages occur, competent mechanics and means of effecting repairs are lacking.

Abdulrahman Pasha, a rich notable of Damascus, was persuaded a few years ago by the agent of an American manufacturing firm to purchase a steam plough, a thrasher, and several other implements, the whole order involving an outlay of some £ stg. 4,000. No expert advice could be obtained as to the class of machinery to be purchased, and it was found, after repeated trials, that the machinery was unsuitable for the work. The steam plough was subsequently sold at a considerable loss, and the remainder of the machinery was condemned as useless. The Pasha is intelligent enough to recognise the unfortunate mistake which was made in ordering the wrong kind of machinery, but the failure has, all the same, sufficiently discouraged him, and it is not likely that he will be easily persuaded to make a second venture. The trials were watched with keen interest by the people of the district, and doubtless, had they been successful, some proprietors would have followed the Pasha's example. The failure has been unfortunate, and it can only strengthen native prejudice and must tend to confirm a fixed idea, very common amongst the people, that European methods of farming and agricultural implements are unsuited to their country.

The recent attention paid to the growing of cotton in the districts around Haiffa and the Jordan Valley has created possibilities for the use of machinery, especially steam ploughs, for opening up large tracts of land needed for this special kind of cultivation. Enquiries regarding the different systems of ploughs and machinery have been numerous during the last twelve months, and catalogues and specifications from British and foreign firms have been obtained, but no practical results can as yet be recorded. . . .

Small agricultural implements have been introduced on one or two farms situated between Rayak and Baalbek, and some of the Jewish colonies in Palestine, established by the Jewish Colonisation Association, also have European implements at work on their farms, besides which one of them has also a threshing machine of British make.

The northern part of Syria, as well as the Hauran and the whole country as far as the Euphrates, is essentially agricultural, but there has yet been no demand for European agricultural implements even of the simplest kind. The peasant farmer is accustomed to the native plough, which costs little and is easily made, and has neither the means nor the inclination, at present, to make a change. Native ploughs also differ in form, especially in the shape of the steel point which takes the place of the share, in different districts, and investigations which were made by a member of a small British engineering firm in Beyrout revealed the curious fact that no less than 164 varieties or shapes are to be found in the country between Aleppo and the Hauran. Local prejudices with regard to the use of these shapes are strong, just as strong as the general prejudices against the use of European implements, and a Baalbek farmer, for instance, could not be induced to use a plough made in Damascus, nor could one made in Aleppo be sold for use in Homs or the Hauran, each locality having its own special shape of share.

The British engineering firm at Beyrout has found it worth while making these different kinds of native shares, and the head of the firm was confident of the annual sale of a large number.

Motor cars.—Great interest has been taken in the possibilities of the motor car as a profitable means of conveyance of passengers and goods. Undeterred by the bad state of the roads and thoroughfares in country and town, a few cars have been imported at Beyrout, Tripoli, and Aleppo by enterprising natives. The cars were, with few exceptions, all picked up second-hand in Egypt. Eight motor cars, five of which

are new—four of French make, and one American—besides four motor buses, two of French make, were imported at Beyrout. Three of the new cars were imported for private use, whilst the others were intended for the conveyance of passengers. The new cars are in fair condition, but cannot be much used, whilst the others are little better than scrap iron.

Two German cars, second-hand, have been imported at Tripoli for service on the Chaussée between Tripoli and Homs, but they have been put aside as unsuitable and costly.

Three cars and one large motor dray, all second hand, of French make, were brought with some difficulty over the Alexandretta road to Aleppo; they were purchased for establishing a passenger service between Aleppo, Killis, and Aintab, but the bad state of the roads has prevented them running, and they are consequently all but useless.

The only car at Damascus has been imported by a livery stable proprietor, specially for conveying tourists across the desert to the ruins of Palmyra.

Native enthusiasm and eagerness to purchase motor-driven vehicles have cooled down considerably, and it is very clear that no development in the sale of motor cars can be expected until the roads have been attended to and put in good repair. The re-building of the old main road from Beyrout over the Lebanon and on to Damascus has been already decided upon, and, as soon as this is carried out, motor traffic, especially for the conveyance of passengers, between Beyrout and the villages on this road and situated on the Lebanon slopes, is certain to develop, and a trade in cars will spring up. Cheapness being the chief point, purchasers will no doubt again look to Egypt for second-hand cars. French manufacturers will stand a fair chance of securing orders, as French firms offer such easy conditions of payment.

In view of the developments which are sure to take place, the movement in the Syrian market merits some attention on the part of British firms, for, as soon as the roads which are to be taken in hand this year are put into a good state of repair, the trade in motor cars may develop into a considerable one.

Hand looms.—Weaving, one of the most important industries of Northern Syria, is entirely done with the primitive wooden loom, made in the country, and there has been no attempt to introduce a modern hand loom adapted to weave the special kinds of cloth in cotton, silk, and wool which are made in the important weaving centres of Aleppo, Aintab, Damascus, and Homs.

The native looms for weaving cotton goods are roughly made, often by the weavers themselves, and cost from 2 to 3 medjidiehs (6s. 8d. to 10s.) each; they are slow to work, and cannot possibly turn out more than 15 to 18 draas (11 to 13 yards) of plain, striped cloth 20¼ inches in width per day.

The looms—not Jacquard—for weaving silk cloths with figures or flowers are slower and much more complicated. Jacquard looms and the perforated cardboard of patterns are now made locally, and they cost from £ stg. 5 to £ stg. 8 per piece.

One instance only has been noticed—at Damascus—where an enterprising commission agent has been in correspondence with loom manufacturers in the United Kingdom with a view to the introduction of suitable machinery in Damascus.

Power looms.—A small power loom, made by a well-known British firm, was bought second-hand by a weaver of Aleppo, and set up, but the owner has not been able to use it because of his want of sufficient technical knowledge. Four small power looms of Chemnitz make were bought second-hand by the Government three years ago for use in the industrial school at Aleppo. The only other looms run by power which have come under observation are the Jacquard looms, about 20 in number, at Damascus, which are worked by electric motors; the looms, working with four shuttles, are Swiss, and the electric motors

have also been supplied by Switzerland. . . .

Ice-making machinery.—The ice-making plants in Beyrout and Aleppo, the only towns which, so far, have these installations, are of French and Belgian manufacture. The large plant in Beyrout has been set up and is worked by the Beyrout Gas Company; it is of Belgian make, the production of ice being obtained by the sulphuric acid method, and the machinery is capable of making 20 tons per day. Aleppo has three ice factories, one has a capacity of 12 to 15 tons per day, and is of Belgian make and on the sulphuric-acid system. The second, producing eight tons daily, has French machinery, using sulphuric acid, and the third, a small French plant working with ammonia, produces four tons. In each case the driving power used is of British make. . . .

Knitting machines.—These machines have been introduced into the country by German houses established in Aleppo and Damascus, and by native agents. They are of the long-beam type, worked by hand, the yarn being moved backwards and forwards between two banks of needles. The machines are made in Dresden, Chemnitz, and Mulhouse, and are readily sold at from £T.5 for the small size to £T.15 for those of larger dimensions, but the price paid for the moderate-sized machine, which is the one most used, is between £T8 and £T.10. As in the case of sewing machines, a great many knitting machines are sold by payment on the instalment system, and it is estimated that between 5,000 and 6,000 have been sold and are in use in the town of Aleppo alone. Only two British-made machines of the circular type were met with in the bazaars; they cost a good deal more than those of German make, and the owners stated that they were harder to work and not such quick knitters as the foreign-made machines, but the class of work made on them was of better type and sold at a slightly higher figure.

About 1,500 to 2,000 machines are at work in Damascus, and a few British knitters, both of the circular and beam types, are to be found. German knitters are extensively advertised in the bazaars and shops by attractive posters, and much of the success of sale of so many machines is due to the facilities of payment offered to customers, as well as judicious advertisement. There is undoubtedly a trade to be done in these machines, but the system adopted by German firms is the only one which will ensure a fair share of the sales. . . .

PART V

Arabia

ARABIA
Introduction

Throughout history the economy of Arabia has been dominated by the extreme aridity of the greater part of the peninsula. Some four-fifths of the area receives less than 5 inches of rain a year, an amount insufficient for any form of cultivation, and another tenth receives 5–10 inches, and in this area only a few crops can be grown. Two regions alone have a higher precipitation: the mountains in the hinterland of Muscat, and those in the southwest corner of the peninsula known to the ancients as Arabia Felix and lying mainly within the borders of present-day Yemen. In the former up to 20 inches of rain may fall and in the latter, which is watered by the Guinea monsoons, 30 or more.[1]

This aridity has meant that, with the exception of Yemen, the Arabian lands have never been able to grow all the food they consume and have been heavily dependent on imports. The lack of an agricultural surplus in the countryside and the sparseness of the population have also prevented the growth of large cities and the emergence of a developed handicraft industry. Arabia has therefore generally imported textiles, metal goods, and other manufactured articles from the neighboring countries: India, Iran, the Fertile Crescent, and Egypt. Large quantities of timber have also had to be brought in—generally from southern India and East Africa—for use in ship and house building, and, since well before the Christian era, Arabia has imported slaves from Africa.

Only three groups of exports were available: pastoral products such as horses, camels, wool, and hides; pearls from the Persian Gulf; and first incense and then, starting in the seventeenth century, coffee from southern Arabia. But it seems clear that these items fell far short of paying for the imports, and the balance was met by a variety of "services." Since the rise of Islam, pilgrimage has brought tens or hundreds of thousands of Muslims each year to the Holy Cities, and their disbursements have always played a major part in the economic life of the Hijaz. To this may be added smaller items, such as the *waqf* endowments set up in various parts of the Muslim world for the benefit of the Holy Places or the expenditures

[1] See *Oxford Regional Economic Atlas: The Middle East and North Africa*, p. 27.

of the Ottoman and other Muslim rulers on public works and charity in Mecca and Medina. Another service provided by the inhabitants of the northern Arabian desert was the guiding and protection of caravans between Arabia, Iraq, and Syria, an alternative source of income being the looting of such caravans. On the fringes of the desert income was supplemented by the extortion of *khuwwa* (goodwill tax) from cultivators.

In the coastal areas the sea offered many opportunities: fishing in all the surrounding waters, pearl diving in the Persian Gulf, and coral fishing in the Red Sea. A flourishing shipbuilding industry developed in many areas, based on timber imported from India and East Africa. No less important was the vast commercial network linking the shores of the Indian Ocean. Here too legitimate trade could be supplemented, where necessary, by less peaceful activities for, as Mephistopheles pointed out:

> Krieg, Handel und Piraterie
> Dreieinig sind sie, nicht zu trennen.

Up to the sixteenth century the "Arabs remained the leading traders and mariners of the Indian Ocean,"[2] though "Indians, Persians, Jews, and no doubt other races and religions participated in it," i.e., the Indian and Far East trade.[3] The two Middle Eastern termini were the Persian Gulf and the Red Sea. In the former the main commercial center was at first al-Ubulla, then Basra; subsequently, with the weakening of the Abbasids and the Mongol invasions, it shifted further east, first to Siraf (ninth through eleventh centuries), then to the island of Kish (Qais) and finally, in the fourteenth through the sixteenth centuries, to that of Hormuz.[4] For the Red Sea, which gradually gained importance as Egypt replaced Iraq as the political and economic center of the Arab world, the main ports were Jidda and, above all, Aden. On the other side of the Arabian Sea, the Arabs had agents in Calicut and other towns on the Malabar coast, and at various times even established small colonies in Ceylon, Malaya, and China. The main imports from the east were silk fabrics, spices, and wood; these were paid for by the export of "costly fabrics of linen, cotton or wool, including rugs; metal work, iron ore, and bullion."[5] The list of goods traded shows that in both directions the Arabs acted merely as middlemen.

A flourishing trade had also been established with East Africa. "Secure in their fortified islands, their maritime supremacy unquestioned, the Muslims exchanged Asiatic textiles . . . metalwork, and beads, all of which they imported, for native produce, ivory, gold, ambergris and slaves," as well as timber.[6] Regarding the slave trade, it has been estimated that, in the fifteenth through the nineteenth centuries, Europeans were "responsible for the removal from Africa of at least 12

[2] George Hourani, *Arab Seafaring in the Indian Ocean*, p. 83.
[3] Serjeant, *The Portuguese off the South Arabian Coast*, p. 3.
[4] Wilson, *The Persian Gulf*, pp. 92 ff.
[5] Hourani, *op. cit.*, p. 70.
[6] Serjeant, *op. cit.*, p. 10.

million Africans . . .; and certainly a great many more, perhaps an equal or even higher number, perished in the process. . . . But the Arab slave trade began . . . before the Christian era, and it did not stop till some fifty years ago; and though its output in any single year can never have reached the highest figures of the European trade, the total number of Africans it exported must have been prodigious."[7] The slaves were sent on to various parts of Arabia, the Middle East, India, and even further afield.

The irruption of the Portuguese into the Indian Ocean in 1487 marks a turning point in the history of Asia, the beginning of what K. M. Panikkar had termed the "Vasco da Gama era." For the Arabs and other Muslim traders of the Indian Ocean it spelled disaster. By 1508 the Portuguese had established complete control over the Persian Gulf and forbade "any native vessel to trade in the Gulf without a pass." Although their repeated attempts to capture Aden failed, largely because of the Ottoman fleets in the Red Sea, they were well established in East Africa, India, and some of the islands and thus dominated the whole ocean. As the Portuguese chronicler Barros noted: "This busy trade [to Malacca] lasted until our arrival in India, but the Moorish, Arabian, Persian, and Gujarati ships, fearing our fleets, dared not in general now undertake the voyage and if any of their ships did so it was only by stealth, and escaping our ships." Although the Portuguese were never able completely to enforce their prohibitions, they did succeed in diverting most of the spice trade around the Cape of Good Hope. The effects on the economy of South Arabia were soon felt (see Part V, chap. 1).

The weakening of Portuguese power after 1550 led to a temporary revival of the spice trade through both the Red Sea and the Persian Gulf.[8] Moreover, thanks to the combined efforts of the Iranians, British, and Dutch, the Portuguese were eventually ejected from the Persian Gulf, their last important base, Muscat, falling in 1650. But with the establishment of the Dutch in the East Indies, soon to be followed by the British in India, the Arabs encountered even stronger competition. By 1638 Mandelslo reported that the Dutch "furnish all Persia with pepper, nutmegs, cloves and other spiceries. The English do sell or truck their English cloathes, Tinne, steel, Indico, silk-stuffs, and cotton out of the Indies."[9]

The prosperity of Iran in the seventeenth century, which had attracted both the Dutch and the British to its southern ports of Bandar Abbas and Bushire, was short lived. Early in the eighteenth century civil wars and the Afghan and Russian invasions led to a sharp decline in exports of silk, both overland to the Mediterranean[10] and through the Persian Gulf. In Iraq the Turco-Persian wars and increasing anarchy prevented the growth of any considerable commerce through Basra, although sporadic trade was carried on first by the Portuguese and then by

[7] Coupland, *East Africa and its Invaders*, p. 35.
[8] Fernand Braudel, *La Méditerranée et le monde méditerranéen à l'époque de Philippe II* (Paris, 1949), p. 421.
[9] Wilson, *op. cit.*, p. 163.
[10] Masson, *XVIIIᵉ siècle*, pp. 520 ff.

the Dutch, British, and French.[11] And on the Arabian side conditions were even worse. From the last decades of the seventeenth century, the privateers and pirates of Muscat and Oman ranged freely over the waters of the Persian Gulf, they sacked Diu on the Malabar coast, took back part of East Africa from the Portuguese, and founded a small empire including Zanzibar and parts of southern Iran (see Part V, chap. 2). Their depredations were supplemented by those of British and other European privateers and pirates, whose activities reached their peak during the great wars at the end of the seventeenth and beginning of the eighteenth centuries. Bahrein, the richest island in the Gulf, was alternately occupied by Arabs and Persians (see Part V, chaps. 4 and 5). And at the close of the eighteenth century the rising Wahhabi state broke through to the Persian Gulf, in the course of extending its control over the greater part of the Arabian coastline.

In 1800 Malcolm estimated the total trade of the Persian Gulf, i.e., exports plus imports, at

160 lakhs of [Bombay] rupees a year [i.e., 16 million rupees, about £1,600,000], mostly with India. The annual imports from India into Persia were estimated at 20 lakhs of rupees, with return exports of 12 lakhs in goods and 8 lakhs in specie and bullion. The Indian imports into Turkish Iraq amounted to 30 lakhs annually, paid for by merchandise to the value of 20 lakhs and by specie and bullion to the value of 10 lakhs. Bahrain and the rest of the Arabian coast of the Gulf took 10 lakhs' worth of Indian goods and exported pearls to an equal extent. The volume of the Arabian coffee brought to the Gulf every year was estimated at 20 lakhs of rupees.[12]

The nineteenth century saw the slow resumption of commercial activity in the Gulf, accelerated after the Suez Canal had greatly reduced the distance between it and Europe. The re-establishment of order in Iraq and the development of steam navigation on the Euphrates made possible a large increase in trade through Basra (see Part III, Introduction). Iran also enjoyed a long period of peace, reasserted its authority over its southern coast, established a steamer service on the Karun River, and expanded its foreign trade; another important development was the laying of telegraph lines and cables linking the south Iranian coast with India and Russia.[13]

[11] Longrigg, *Four Centuries of Modern 'Iraq, passim.* The disturbed conditions in southern Iraq promoted the development of Kuwait. The town had been founded, at the beginning of the eighteenth century, by migrants from the interior of Arabia and by 1765 had a population estimated at 10,000, and 800 ships engaged in trading, fishing, and pearling. During the Turco–Persian war of 1776–79, the East India Company moved the southern terminal of the overland mail route via Aleppo from Basra to Kuwait (Lorimer, *Gazetteer of the Persian Gulf,* I, 1004). At the end of the century, however, Wahhabi attacks caused much damage, and by 1831 the population had fallen to an estimated 4,000 (Kuwait Oil Co., *The Story of Kuwait,* p. 91); imports stood at $500,000 and exports at $100,000 (Lorimer, I, 1006). Thereafter conditions once more improved, and in 1863 Palgrave (*Narrative of a Year's Journey through Central and Eastern Arabia,* II, 387) described its active harbor and commerce and stated: "In its mercantile and political aspect, this town forms a sea outlet, the only one, for Djebel Shomer and in this respect like Trieste for Austria." In the same year Pelly ("Remarks on the Tribes, Trade, and Resources ... Persian Gulf," *Trans. Bombay Geographical Soc.,* XVII, 73) put the population at 20,000, of whom 4,000 were sailors. By 1914 the population had risen to about 35,000. Imports by sea in 1905–6 were estimated at Rs. 2,769,054 (£185,000) and exports at Rs. 1,154,322 (£77,000) (Lorimer, I, 1056). (See also Part V, chap. 3.)

[12] Lorimer, *op. cit.,* I, 165–66.

[13] Great Britain, Naval Intelligence Division, Geographical Handbook Series, *Persia,* p. 292; Hoskins, *British Routes to India,* pp. 374–97.

And by the outbreak of the First World War, oil was being produced in Iran on a commercial scale.

No less significant was the establishment of Britain's power in the Gulf. At first its actions were directed against the Qawasim (Jawasim) pirates of Oman; this phase ended in the General Treaty of Peace of 1820 under which the various sheikhs, including the ruler of Bahrein, undertook to refrain from piracy and slave trading.[14] This treaty, and various subsequent agreements, with the same and neighboring rulers did succeed in suppressing piracy, but slave-trading, though much reduced, continued throughout the period under review.[15] Concurrently the Indian and British navies carried out a thorough survey of the Gulf and both its shores.[16] The expansion of Persian and Iraqi trade and the more settled conditions on the Arabian side raised the total trade of the Gulf ports to an estimated £3,600,000 in 1901.[17]

British interest in the Gulf was stimulated to a still greater degree by the impending presence of other powers. Muhammad Ali's expeditions against the Wahhabis brought Egyptian troops to Hasa in 1838, an action that was immediately followed by British naval pressure which secured their withdrawal. The Ottoman conquest of Hasa, in 1871, led to similar British action. Fear of Russian, and subsequently German, influence in the Gulf—in the form of a railway or other major enterprise—caused the British to sign a series of treaties between 1891 and 1915 under which the rulers of Muscat, Bahrein, Kuwait, and Najd undertook not to alienate any part of their dominions to foreign interests without the consent of Britain.[18] The agreements with Bahrein and Kuwait specifically mentioned petroleum concessions, a fact that shows the growing realization of the potentialities of the Gulf, which in the course of the next three decades was to emerge as the leading oil-bearing area of the world. These provisions were to play an important part in shaping the pattern of petroleum concessions in the region.[19] The intensity—and the occasional absurdity—of international rivalries in the Persian Gulf is illustrated by the history of the Wönckhaus firm (Part V, chap. 10).

The course of events in the Red Sea area was somewhat different from that in the Persian Gulf. Repeated Portuguese attempts to take Aden, Jidda, and other ports failed, mainly because of Turkish naval strength. But the struggle between the two powers ruined the trade of the region, and until the end of the sixteenth century the Red Sea remained closed to European ships.[20] By then Aden, "much

---

[14] See text in Hurewitz, *Diplomacy in the Near and Middle East*, I, 88–90.

[15] Wilson, *op. cit.*, pp. 209–30.

[16] *Ibid.*, pp. 262–63.

[17] Lorimer, *op. cit.*, I, 369.

[18] See texts in Hurewitz, *op. cit.*, I, 208, 209, 218, 272; II, 17.

[19] See Issawi and Yeganeh, *The Economics of Middle Eastern Oil*, pp. 32–39.

[20] The digging of a canal across the isthmus of Suez, initially suggested by the Venetians, was repeatedly considered by the Turks and in 1529 work actually began on the project (Great Britain, Naval Intelligence Division, *Western Arabia*, p. 258, and sources cited therein).

decayed, was visited yearly by only a few small ships from India and the Persian Gulf, bringing turban cloths and cotton goods, and returning with gum Arabic, frankincense, myrrh, and madder.... Mocha, on the other hand, ... was increasingly important, being frequented by merchants from many parts of the Middle East and from India ... during their stay they traded with the merchants who sailed from Suez to Mocha." [21]

In 1609, however, a British ship called at Aden and was soon followed by other British, Dutch, and later French and a few other European vessels, most of which went to Mokha; [22] American ships also began to call at Mokha in 1800. [23] By the end of the seventeenth century European ships were going as far as Jidda, with the connivance of the sherifs of Mecca, who wanted to increase their meager revenues. Finally, in 1775 the first British ship reached Suez and attempts were made, among others by the explorer James Bruce, [24] to develop trade between India and Egypt— then enjoying virtual independence, under the Mamluk Ali Bey al-Kabir—but they met with only limited success. [25]

In the nineteenth century power politics drew Britain into the Red Sea even more rapidly than into the Persian Gulf. Already in 1799 Napoleon's invasion of Egypt had led to a temporary British occupation of Perim, at the mouth of the Red Sea, and Muhammad Ali's expedition to Yemen was one of the main causes of the British occupation of Aden in 1839. Another important factor was the desire to establish a coaling station for a steam-navigation service between Bombay and Suez. [26] By 1840 communications were such that the British consul in Cairo could report that mails leaving England on the fourth of each month reached Alexandria on the nineteenth, Suez on the twenty-second, and Bombay eighteen days later, [27] and by 1845 the London-Bombay journey had been reduced to one month.

The opening of the Suez route, and in 1869 of the Canal, multiplied by many hundred-fold the volume of traffic through the Red Sea, but the benefits of this increase were very unequally distributed. Whereas the trade of Aden (see Part V, chap. 5) and Suez expanded greatly, that of the smaller ports—Jidda, Mokha, Hodaida—showed relatively little increase. Indeed, during the first half of the century their trade seems actually to have declined because of the general insecurity caused by the spread of Wahhabism, the Egyptian expeditions, and the

[21] *Ibid.*, p. 263.

[22] Apelt, *Aden*, p. 54.

[23] MacGregor, *Commercial Statistics*, II, 376.

[24] *Travels to Discover the Source of the Nile, passim.*

[25] Anis, *British Interests, passim.*

[26] The main landmarks in the establishment of this service were the increased flow of passengers to and from India through Suez and Quseir thanks to greater security and improved communications under Muhammad Ali (see Part VI, chap. 7); the survey by the British navy of the Red Sea, in 1829–34; the occupation of Socotra in 1835, which was soon abandoned because of the lack of water and prevalence of fever; the voyage of S.S. "Hugh Lindsay" from Bombay to Suez in 1830; and the establishment of British, French, and Austrian steam services between various European ports and Alexandria (see Hoskins, *op. cit., passim*).

[27] Campbell, "Report on Egypt."

prolonged fighting in Yemen. Thus MacGregor quotes a figure of £461,600 for imports into Jidda in 1839,[28] a 34 per cent decline from that given by Burckhardt for 1814; however, the earlier figure may have been swollen by the presence of Egyptian troops in the Hijaz. MacGregor also states: "We have little that is statistical relative to the present trade of Mocha, but, from the anarchy that has prevailed, and the greater insecurity of property and person since Mehemet Ali has surrendered the Holy Cities, Mocha has certainly declined."[29] This impression is confirmed by Botta, who visited Mokha in 1837 and reported: "This town has greatly fallen from its former state: the civil wars which have devastated Yemen and the general misery caused by them, added to the monopoly on coffee imposed by the pasha of Egypt, have dried up the sources of its prosperity, diminishing on the one hand its imports of foreign goods and on the other its exports of its own produce."[30]

Another adverse factor, which operated to a greater extent during the second half of the century, was the displacement by steamers of local sailing ships, which had carried on a lively coastal trade on both shores of the Red Sea (see Part V, chap. 4). But these same steamers greatly facilitated the entry of pilgrims, who have always been the major factor in the economy of the Hijaz, and the Canal also made it possible for the Turks to reassert their authority and impose order on the Hijaz. Consequently, by 1910, Jidda's imports had risen to about £1,000,000 in dutiable goods plus perhaps another £750,000 in goods from other parts of the Ottoman Empire, not subject to duty.

The ports lying south of Jidda saw much of their former trade drained off to Aden, and the struggle between Turks and Yemenis continued until the outbreak of the First World War; hence the trade of Mokha and the other small ports remained at an insignificant figure while that of Hodaida in 1909 was put at £650,000 for imports and £400,000 for exports.[31] (See Part V, chap. 5.)

Very little can be said about developments in the interior. From the beginning of the sixteenth century to the present day southwestern Arabia has been marked by political convulsions, tribal wars, and economic stagnation. The Portuguese attacks were followed by Mamluk and Turkish occupations, but by the end of the sixteenth century the Yemeni highlanders, under the leadership of the Zaidi Imams, were in revolt against the Turks and succeeded in keeping them out of the country from 1635 to 1849. In 1849 a Turkish expedition reoccupied the coast and, after communications had been greatly improved by the opening of the Suez Canal, in 1869 the Turks advanced into the interior and took San'a in 1872. But this second period of Turkish rule was hardly more stable than the first. Constant uprisings and punitive sorties inflicted great hardships. Turkish attempts to introduce a few elements of progress were defeated, producing almost nothing beyond

[28] MacGregor, *op. cit.*, p. 374.
[29] *Ibid.*, p. 376.
[30] Botta, *Voyage dans l'Yemen*, p. 159.
[31] Great Britain, *Accounts and Papers*, "Report on Trade of Jeddah."

the installation of some telegraph and telephone lines. Further east, in the Hadhramaut, the Zaidis of Yemen failed to impose their rule and religion, and during the seventeenth and eighteenth centuries tribal wars were endemic; however, in the second half of the nineteenth century British influence began to spread in the region, and with it came some security.

Given such instability, and the diversion of the Indian trade, it is not surprising that economic activity should have sunk to a very low level. The only important innovation was the development of coffee planting. In the Middle East coffee seems to have been used from the fourteenth century on,[32] but its extensive use dates from the beginning of the sixteenth century. By the beginning of the following century Europe had acquired a taste for coffee, and there was soon considerable export through Mokha (see above). However, the virtual monopoly of Yemen was ended early in the eighteenth century by the Dutch, who transplanted shoots in the East Indies and developed large plantations. The introduction shortly thereafter of shrubs into the West Indies and Brazil opened up even greater sources of competition.

The picture of Yemen painted by travelers at the beginning of the twentieth century is uniformly dismal (see Part V, chap. 1). The population of San'a, by far the largest town, was estimated in 1905–11 at around 20,000.[33] An estimate of 50,000 for 1891 was probably exaggerated[34] but the population may well have declined between the two dates: "The number of empty houses and the chronic commercial depression indicate a decreasing population."[35] Similarly the population of Ta'izz, described by Manzoni as "a mass of ruins," had fallen to 4,000–5,000 and the populations of Yarim, Ibb, and Dhamar, the other towns of any size in the highlands, were also about 4,000–5,000.[36] In the lowlands Zabid may have had 8,000 inhabitants and Bait al-Faqih 5,000. Hodaida, the chief port, had some 40,000–50,000 inhabitants, of whom 100 were Europeans, mostly Greeks, and 1,000 British Indians.[37] The population of Mokha, estimated in 1824 at about 20,000, had sunk to 5,000–8,000, while that of Luhaiya seems to have risen slightly to 5,000.

Bury's description of Yemen on the eve of the First World War shows widespread stagnation or even retrogression. "Most of the small growers have been in the grip of capitalists [i.e., money lenders] ever since the last shortage of rain in 1910." In the uplands "farm produce and requisites must be carried by hand, or in absurdly small loads on donkeys, which have to be half carried themselves up some of the mountain tracks. When the husbandman has got his produce to a caravan route, he is faced with exorbitant transport. . . . To crown all, the caravan

---

[32] See *Encyclopaedia of Islam, s.v.* "kahwa."

[33] Great Britain, Admiralty War Staff, *A Handbook of Arabia*, p. 167.

[34] In 1877 Manzoni (*El Yemen*, p. 129) put the population at 18,000–20,000 Arabs, 3,000 Turks, and 1,700 Jews.

[35] Bury, *Arabia Infelix*, p. 80.

[36] Admiralty War Staff, *op. cit.*, pp. 168–74.

[37] *Ibid.*, p. 171; Bury, *op. cit.*, p. 192; "Report on Trade of Jeddah."

routes themselves are beset by marauders, towards the coast, where his best market is." Hence the country "imports more than £100,000 worth of foodstuffs during a year of plenty and more than double that amount in a year of famine."[38]

Nor was the state of the handicrafts any better: "Local industries are moribund, thanks to the financial slump and over-seas competition. The dyeing industry of Zabid has been dislocated by tribal disturbances, and much of it has been transplanted to Hodeida, where there was already a small, similar, industry. There it continues steady, in spite of an increasing tendency to use synthetic indigo from Germany, instead of the home-grown product which the Zabid district used to supply. There is also a colony of weavers at Hodeida, many of whom have come in from the disturbed area between Beit al-Fakih and Zabid."[39]

Channels through which modern ideas and customs could enter the region were few and narrow: "There are few non-Moslem aliens in the interior of Yemen now. Such Greek traders as there were, have either left, or are on the point of leaving, on account of the commercial depressions and general insecurity."[40] The Jews of Yemen continued to play a significant part in the country's economy until 1950, but they do not seem to have introduced or diffused any important economic activities or processes (see Part V, chap. 7). In Hadhramaut emigrants to Egypt, the Red Sea area, India, and above all the Dutch East Indies sent back considerable amounts of money but do not seem to have started any important new business in their homeland (see Part V, chap. 6). Attempts to improve communications failed completely until the 1960's (see Part V, chap. 8). A petroleum concession was granted on the Farsan Islands before the First World War to an Ottoman subject, but experimental borings were disappointing and no oil has yet been produced in that part of Arabia, although other concessions have been granted in Aden, Hadhramaut, and Yemen to American, British, and German companies during the last three decades. The section by far the most open to modern civilization in southwestern Arabia remained the British colony of Aden (see Part V, chap. 5).

As for northern Arabia, the prosperity of the Hijaz continued until very recently to be overwhelmingly dependent on pilgrim traffic (see Part V, chap. 4). The population of Mecca in 1814 was put by Burckhardt[41] at 25,000–30,000 "stationary inhabitants . . . for the city and suburbs" besides 3,000–4,000 Abyssinian and black slaves; this figure is very close to that given by Varthema at the beginning of the sixteenth century—6,000 families. For 1885 Snouck[42] put it at about 60,000, and by the First World War the figure is believed to have risen to about 70,000, including about 12,000 Indians.[43] The population of Medina was

[38] Bury, *op. cit.*, pp. 112, 115–16.
[39] *Ibid.*, p. 123.
[40] *Ibid.*, p. 184.
[41] *Travels in Arabia*, p. 132.
[42] *Verspreide Geschriften*, p. 3.
[43] Admiralty War Staff, *op. cit.*, p. 125.

put by Burckhardt as at most 16,000–20,000, including the suburbs.[44] Burton, who visited the town in 1852, put the number of houses in the city at 800 and in the suburbs at 500, on the basis of which he estimated the population at 16,000;[45] he also refers to a Turkish "census" of 1819, giving a total of only 8,000. By the First World War the number was believed to have risen to 40,000.[46]

The dependence of Mecca on pilgrims and the business they brought is noted by every traveler. Thus Burckhardt states:

The inhabitants of Mekka have but two kinds of employment,—trade, and the service of the Beitullah, or Temple; but the former has the preference, and there are very few olemas, or persons employed in the mosque, who are not engaged in some commercial affairs, though they are too proud to pursue them openly. The reader has probably remarked, in the foregoing description of Mekka, how few artisans inhabit its streets; such as masons, carpenters, tailors, shoemakers, smiths, &c., and these are far inferior, in skill, to the same class in Egypt. With the exception of a few potteries and dying-houses, the Mekkawys have not a single manufactory; but, like the people of Djidda, are dependent upon other countries for a supply of their wants. Mekka, therefore, has necessarily a considerable degree of foreign commerce, which is chiefly carried on, during the pilgrimage, and some months preceding it, by the wealthy hadjys, who bring from every Muselman country its native productions to Djidda, either by sea or across the Desert from Damascus, exchanging them amongst each other; or receiving from the merchants of Mekka the goods of India and Arabia, which the latter have accumulated the whole year in their warehouses. At this period, Mekka becomes one of the largest fairs of the East, and certainly the most interesting, from the variety of nations which frequent it. The value of the exports from Mekka is, however, greatly superior to that of the imports, and a considerable sum of money, in dollars and sequins, required to balance them. Of these, some part finds its way to Yemen and India; and about one-fourth remains in the hands of the Mekkawys. So profitable is this trade, that the goods bought at Djidda from the merchants, who purchase them out of the ships which arrive there from India, yield, when sold wholesale at Mekka, during the Hadj, a clear gain of twenty to thirty per cent., and of fifty per cent. when sold in retail. It is not surprising, therefore, that all the people of Mekka are merchants. Whoever can make up a sum of a few hundred dollars, repairs to Djidda, and lays it out on goods, which he exposes for sale during the pilgrimage. Much profit is also fraudulently made: great numbers of hadjys are ignorant of the Arabic language, and are consequently placed in the hands of brokers or interpreters, who never fail to make them pay dearly for their services; indeed, all Mekka seems united in the design of cheating the pilgrims.[47]

The same impression is given by Snouck.[48]

Medina was much less commercial: "The people of Medina, on the contrary, are very petty merchants; and their main support depends upon the pilgrims, the yearly stipends from Turkey, or their landed property." The crops of Medina are described as "very thin . . . but of good quality";[49] however, they "were said

[44] Op. cit., p. 400.
[45] Burton, Personal Narrative of a Pilgrimage to Al-Madinah and Meccah, p. 239.
[46] Admiralty War Staff, op. cit., p. 117.
[47] Burckhardt, op. cit., pp. 187–88.
[48] Mekka, Vol. II, chap. I.
[49] Burckhardt, op. cit., pp. 354–55.

to be barely sufficient for four months' consumption; for the rest, therefore, it must depend upon Yembo, or imports from Egypt."[50] Burton stresses the importance of the *awqaf* and *sadaqat* (gifts) brought in by the Damascus caravan.[51] He too notes the absence of large-scale trade: "I heard of only four respectable houses. They all deal in grain, cloth, and provisions, and perhaps the richest have a capital of 20,000 dollars."

In these circumstances the flow of pilgrim traffic was all-important, and its volume depended largely on the security prevailing in the peninsula and the surrounding areas and the state of communications. The Wahhabi wars, and particularly the capture of Mecca in 1803, seem to have greatly decreased the number of pilgrims,[52] but following the Egyptian conquest order was re-established, and Burckhardt[53] put the number of pilgrims assembled in Mecca at 70,000; of these he estimated that only one-third went on to Medina. Snouck[54] gave a figure of 80,000 for 1885 but seems to imply that the normal figure was about 100,000.[55] The opening of the Suez Canal and the great increase in the number of ships calling at the Red Sea ports considerably stimulated the pilgrim traffic, and the British consul in Jidda put the number of pilgrims arriving by sea in 1896 at 62,000. The Hijaz railway also greatly increased the flow of pilgrims arriving by land; the total number is estimated to have risen to 200,000 by 1914.[56] However, this figure almost certainly includes pilgrims from other parts of the Arabian peninsula, who may have accounted for nearly half the total. The number of overseas pilgrims, after declining sharply during and after the First World War, was "well over the 100,000 mark in 1926–30"[57] and by 1960 had risen beyond 200,000, and their total expenditure was estimated by the Saudi Arabian government at $50–$60 million.

Both Mecca and Medina continued to be trading and distributing centers for west central Arabia: "Whenever the interior of Arabia is open to caravans, Bedouins from all the surrounding parts purchase their yearly provision of corn at Mekka."[58] Some trade was also conducted in imported goods. The opening of the Hijaz railway improved the trading position of Medina. The network of trade covered the small towns of the interior and reached the nomadic tribes. Thus Palgrave, who visited 'Unaiza in 1862 reported: "Its commerce with Medinah and Mecca on the one hand, and with Najed, nay, even with Damascus and Baghdad, on the other, had gathered in its warehouses stores of traffic unknown to any other locality of inner Arabia, and its hardy merchants were met with alike

[50] *Ibid.*, p. 377.
[51] *Op. cit.*, p. 277.
[52] Burckhardt, *op. cit.*, p. 190.
[53] *Ibid.*, p. 269.
[54] *Verspreide Geschriften*, p. 3.
[55] *Ibid.*, p. 50.
[56] Admiralty War Staff, *op. cit.*, p. 125.
[57] Philby, *Arabian Jubilee*, p. 86.
[58] Burckhardt, *op. cit.*, p. 189.

on the shores of the Red Sea and of the Persian Gulf, and occasionally on the more distant banks of the Euphrates, or by the waters of Damascus." [59] On the other hand, "The commerce furnished by Riad and the other great Nejdean centres of population is in its active part abandoned to foreigners, to merchants from Hasa, from Kateef and 'Oman, from Mecca, Wadi Nejran, and Yemen." [60] Lorimer estimated that half the imports of southern Najd came through Hasa while the other half was "almost equally divided between Kuwait and the ports of Hijaz." [61]

As for the tribes, Musil reported in 1909: "As the Rwala are occupied almost exclusively in camel breeding, it is only in exchange for camels that they can get grain, clothing, arms, saddles, and other necessities of life. They sell the camels either in the inner desert or in the settled territory, and nearly always to the same wholesale merchants who live in the larger towns on the borders of Arabia and in Egypt and India." [62] A few tribes supplemented their animal raising with some form of agriculture, and some large oases even exported dates, e.g., Jauf to Damascus and Baghdad. [63] The handicrafts were few and primitive; thus Burckhardt states: "Of the arts but little is known among the Aenezes: two or three blacksmiths to shoe the horses, and some saddlers to mend the leather-work, are the only artists found even in the most numerous tribes. . . . The arts of weaving and tanning are practised by the Aenezes themselves: the former by men, the latter by women." [64]

The precarious economy of central Arabia was subject to disruption by large-scale wars, such as those arising from the spread of Wahhabism; the decline noted by Palgrave [65] in Hofuf and Hasa may have also spread inland. The second half of the century was more peaceful, but the nomad economy began to feel, to an increasing degree, the adverse effects of greater government control of the borderlands (see Part III, chap. 4, and Part IV, chap. 5). In the present century the spread of railways and motorcars, together with more complete government control in and around Arabia, both reduced the importance of the "protection" and guidance given to caravans by beduins and sharply depressed the price of camels and horses in the neighboring countries. At the same time, the price of wool and other livestock products was brought down by competition from Australia and elsewhere. The resulting crisis in the nomadic and semi-nomadic economy is described in Part V, chapter 9. It was resolved only by the tremendous oil boom which started in the late 1930's and which has provided undreamed-of wealth and employment opportunities for the inhabitants of northern and eastern Arabia.

[59] Palgrave, *op. cit.*, I, 170.
[60] *Ibid.*, p. 461.
[61] Lorimer, *op. cit.*, II, 1356.
[62] Musil, *In the Arabian Desert*, p. 201.
[63] Palgrave, *op. cit.*, I, 60.
[64] *Notes on the Bedouins and Wahabys*, I, 65.
[65] *Op. cit.*, II, 143, 156.

CHAPTER I

Trade of Southwestern Arabia in the Eighteenth Century

The ancient prosperity of southwestern Arabia, based on an elaborate system of irrigation, on the export of frankincense and myrrh, and on entrepôt trade between India and the Mediterranean, had collapsed some time before the rise of Islam. Perhaps Yemen has never regained its pre-Islamic level, but under the Rasulid dynasty (1228–1446) the country enjoyed order and a certain amount of prosperity, as is evidenced by some of the monuments built at that time; here too the Indian trade probably played an important part. At the beginning of the sixteenth century, however, a series of disasters struck the area: the overthrow of the Tahirid dynasty by the Mamluks of Egypt, followed shortly by fierce Portuguese attacks on the coasts, Ottoman occupation, and the diversion of the Indian trade (see Part V, Introduction). The poverty to which the region had sunk by the middle of the eighteenth century is well brought out in the following selection, which is taken from the excellent survey carried out by the Danish expedition of 1761.[1]

The former staple export, frankincense, also declined owing to a drop in both demand and supply. The Bents, who visited Hadhramaut in 1889, reported extensive destruction of trees and described the remains of former groves.[2] However, exports from Dhofar to Bombay continued, in small sailing boats, and were estimated at 9,000 hundredweight in 1894.[3]

The growth of coffee exports provided a certain compensation, which was, however, soon reduced by competition from the East and West Indies and Brazil (see Part V, Introduction). Further blows were struck by the endemic civil wars and by Muhammad Ali's attempt to monopolize exports of coffee.[4] And the rise of Aden led to a diversion to it of much of the trade of Yemen, with consequent

---

[1] The handicrafts, which at one time had enjoyed a certain reputation, also stagnated or fell into decay. Thus, describing Hais in 1837, Botta (*Voyage dans l'Yemen*, pp. 58–59) stated: "It is the only place in Arabia where they know how to glaze pottery." (See also Part V, chap. 5.)

[2] Bent, *Southern Arabia*, pp. 89–104.

[3] *Ibid.*, p. 234; Great Britain, War Staff, Admiralty, *A Handbook of Arabia*, p. 279.

[4] Botta, *op. cit.*, p. 159.

damage to the traditional trading ports, Mokha and Hodaida (see Part V, chap. 5). Thus in 1877 Aden took from Yemen 1,268 tons of coffee, worth 1,812,000 gold francs, by camel caravans, and 2,505 tons, worth 5,005,000 francs, by coastal boats, or a total of 3,773 tons worth £272,000.[5] In contrast, exports from Mokha were estimated to average 800 tons in a good year and those from Hodaida were put at 8,000,000 francs or £320,000.[6] But with the restoration of some degree of security toward the end of the century, coffee exports from Yemeni ports seem to have increased. Thus in 1909 coffee exports from Hodaida amounted to 47,377 bags with a value of £592,000;[7] and in 1913–14 they were 3,425 tons, with a value of 25,160,000 piastres or £226,000.[8] Coffee has continued since then to form the main export item of Yemen.

(See also works by Serjeant, Grohmann, Manzoni, Bury, and Bent, and Great Britain, Admiralty War Staff [*Handbook of Arabia*] and Naval Intelligence Division [*Western Arabia*], listed in the Bibliography.)

[5] Manzoni, *El Yemen*, p. 260.
[6] Grohmann, *Südarabien als Wirtschaftsgebeit*, II, 84–85.
[7] "Diplomatic and Consular Reports on Trade and Finance, Turkey," Great Britain, *Accounts and Papers, 1898*, XCIX (partly reproduced in Part V, chap. 4).
[8] Grohmann, *loc. cit.*; for Aden see Part V, chap. 5.

[From Carsten Niebuhr, *Description de l'Arabie* (Amsterdam and Utrecht, 1774), pp. 245–47.]

Hadhramaut is a very large country, especially if to it be added the region of Mahra which the Arabs, unless I am mistaken, attach to Hadhramaut, just as they add the Tihama to Yemen. Hadhramaut is bounded to the west by Yemen, to the southeast by the ocean, to the northeast by Oman, and to the north by a great desert. This country includes very fertile mountainous regions, valleys watered by mountain streams, and others which are arid deserts. On its coasts lie various ports from which incense, the gum known as Arabic, myrrh, dragon's blood [resin], and aloes are exported to Muscat and India; to Yemen are exported cloth, rugs, and many of those knives known as *jambea*, which the Arabs carry at their belts [*au devant d'eux*].

The two lands of Hadhramaut and Yemen were once known as Arabia Felix. In spite of this, their inhabitants did not have a larger or more profitable trade in their own goods than do the Arabs today, since incense and aloes were the main, and apparently the only, merchandise which foreigners bought in that country.[1] Even today some aloes are exported from Mokha, as in the past from Muza, and that from Socotra still has a world-wide reputation. Arabian incense is still sold, although it is far inferior to that picked up by ships in the Arabian [i.e., Red Sea] and Persian Gulfs; for although little use of incense is made in Christian churches, and perhaps none at all in mosques, much perfume is burned in all houses in the Orient and in temples in India. Anyway, if the Arabs do not export today the same quantity of incense to northern countries, the inhabitants of Yemen make up for this, with interest, by their present trade in coffee.

When one examines why southern Arabia is no longer as rich and famous as in the past, the most obvious answer that can be given is doubtless that the peoples of the north have extended their navigation. From the earliest times known to us, Arabs traded by land with Egypt and the neighboring countries. Thus Joseph was sold to the

[1] See *Navigat. & viaggi raccolte da Ramusio*, Vol. I, fol. 284, *Periplus Maris Erythroei*, p. 14.

Ishmaelites who were on their way to Egypt, carrying spices, balsam, and myrrh on behalf of Midianite merchants (Gen. 37: 25–28). In chapter 10 of Genesis Moses mentions so many towns located in Yemen and Hadhramaut that he must undoubtedly have known and visited that country personally. The Arabs of Yemen traded with the city of Tyre (Ezechiel 37). Arrian states that the Arabs of Muza, a port on the Arabian Gulf, as well as those of Qana and other ports on the southeast coast of Arabia, traded mainly in foreign merchandise, imported from Egypt, Abyssinia, Persia, and India. He also observes that, at the time when Egyptians did not dare venture as far as India, nor Indians as far as Egypt, Arabia Felix was the entrepôt for the goods of both countries. Navigation in the Arabian Gulf was already practiced but, since it has always been considered highly dangerous, most goods were carried across the whole of Arabia by caravans. This trade must have been the source of large profits not only for the ports where Indian products were landed but also for the various inland towns and even for the nomadic Arabs who supplied most of the camels needed for transport. When Henry Midleton was in Mokha, in 1611, a large caravan of merchants arrived from Damascus, Suez, and Mecca, for the purpose of trading with Indian merchants. But things have changed: Yemen and Hadhramaut are no longer entrepôts for Egyptian and Indian goods. The Arabs of these regions do not even carry all their own goods on their own ships. It is true that the Arabs of Yemen transport the greater part of their coffee from Mokha, Hodaida, Luhaiya, and Jizan to Jidda; similarly those of Hadhramaut and Shahr carry a fair proportion of their incense and aloes to Muscat; however, ships from Oman also come to Yemen and Hadhramaut to load coffee, incense, and aloes. But the Arabs have suffered particularly heavily since the Europeans, having found a way around Africa, not only meet their own needs for Indian and Chinese goods but actually supply part of those of the western Arabs, the Egyptians, and the Turks. Nevertheless, the Arabs of this region still live in towns and villages and carry on a busy trade. . . .

CHAPTER 2

Economic Conditions in Muscat and Oman, 1904

Until the seventeenth century the Omanis played a minor role in the Persian Gulf, but the weakening of the Portuguese led to an outburst of activity on their part. Their most spectacular feat was the foundation, at the end of the century, of a small empire including Zanzibar and a stretch of the African coast. This remained formally under the rule of Muscat until 1860 and continued for long after to send the latter financial aid; it was also the starting point of an extensive slave trade to Muscat. The connection between the two countries ended only in 1964, with the revolution in Zanzibar which overthrew the sultan, massacred many of the Arabs who constituted the ruling class, and deported many more to Oman.

Other aspects of Omani naval power were the sack of Diu, the temporary capture of Bahrein, the occupation of parts of the Persian coast, and the depredations of the privateers and pirates. But no less important was the commercial activity: "In the last decade of the 18th century the proportion of the trade of the Persian Gulf that passed through Musqat was about five-eighths of the whole, or one crore of rupees per annum [Rs. 10,000,000 or about £1,000,000]; and almost every line of business then was represented."[1] Imports into the town of Muscat may have amounted to about £150,000.[2] Omani ships were active in the trade with India, Yemen, and Iran.[3] And, more generally: "Musqat by 1775 had become the principal entrepôt of trade between the Persian Gulf, India, and the Red Sea."[4]

The Wahhabi invasion, at the end of the eighteenth century, caused a setback, but with the defeat of the Wahhabis by Muhammad Ali in 1818 "'Oman recovered all her former prosperity, and even augmented it. She now became an

---

[1] Lorimer, *Gazetteer of the Persian Gulf*, I, 436.

[2] Niebuhr (*Description de l'Arabie*, p. 264) states that the customs revenue was 100,000 rupees (a figure repeated by Lorimer [I, 416, 434]), or about £10,000. Since according to Niebuhr Europeans paid a duty of 5 per cent, Muslims of 6, and Banians and Jews of 9, the average duty may be assumed to have been 7 per cent.

[3] Lorimer, *op. cit.*, I, 160, 1231, 1855.

[4] *Ibid.*, p. 417.

emporium for the commerce of Africa, Persia, and India; while numerous colonies of merchants, especially from the latter country, were encouraged by the liberal policy of Sa'eed to take up their residence in Sohar, Barka, Mascat, and other sea-ports, bringing with them a skill and a persevering industry seldom to be found among the Arabs themselves." [5]

The second half of the nineteenth century, however, saw a steady decline in 'Oman's prosperity. The suppression of piracy and privateering (see Part V, Introduction) eliminated an important source of income. The establishment of steam navigation caused trade to bypass Oman, a process accentuated by the growing rivalry of Bahrein (see Part V, chap. 3). The crafts, which seem to have been quite prosperous at the beginning of the century,[6] suffered from the competition of imported goods. Gradually Indian merchants acquired a preponderance of the country's trade.[7] As early as 1863 Palgrave had noted signs of decay and stated that the population of the town of Muscat had fallen from 60,000 to 40,000.[8] By 1889 the Bents were describing it as a "beggarly town," and estimated its population at about 20,000.[9] As the following selection shows, Muscat had become a stagnant backwater, a condition which has remained essentially unchanged down to the present time.

(See also works by Wilson, Lorimer, Pelly, Palgrave, Miles, and Hay, and Great Britain, Admiralty [*Arabia*] listed in the Bibliography.)

[5] Palgrave, *Narrative of a Year's Journey through Central and Eastern Arabia*, II, 276; see also Lorimer, *op. cit.*, I, 469.
[6] See Palgrave, *op. cit.*, II, 308, 333; Lorimer, *op. cit.*, II, 1412.
[7] Palgrave, *op. cit.*, II, 307; Lorimer, *op. cit.*, II, 1413.
[8] Palgrave, *op. cit.*, II, 369.
[9] Bent, *Southern Arabia*, pp. 53–55.

["Report on the Conditions and Prospects of British Trade in Oman, Bahrain and Arab Ports in the Persian Gulf," Great Britain, *Accounts and Papers*, 1905, LXXXV, 2–4.]

OMAN

Muscat is the capital and principal port of the Sultanate of Oman. Caravans cannot readily approach it, and commerce with the interior passes through Mutra, lying in an adjacent bay. The population of these two towns may be 30,000, and that of the territory of Oman has been estimated at 800,000, chiefly Arabs. There are British, French, and American Consuls, the last named being a British subject representing a trading firm and agent for the British India Steam Navigation Company; a French trader; a Russian trader; and British Indian subjects to the number of about 1,100.

The climate is tropical, dry, with intense heat in summer, but pleasant during four winter months.

Statistics of Imports and Exports at Muscat are given in the Annual Trade Reports to the Indian Government of the Political Agent at Muscat. These statistics do not include merchandise carried in native sailing craft trading from the smaller ports of Oman. There has been no marked increase or decrease of trade in recent years.

Total Imports (excluding specie)
Average for three years to 1900   £246,000 per annum
Average for three years to 1903   £253,000 per annum

Total Exports (excluding specie)
Average for three years to 1900   £127,000 per annum
Average for three years to 1903   £119,000 per annum
. . . .

EXPORTS

Dates are the principal produce, and are sent down to the coast ports, where they are purchased and packed by the exporters. To fix the value for payment of Customs duty all dates are auctioned on arrival at Mutra, and certain taxes and fines due from the proprietors in the interior are levied along with the duty. The ruling price in Muscat at the close of the packing season this year (January 1904) was 820 mahmoodieh per "bar."[1] The "Fard" dates are mostly exported to America, where there is a steady demand for this kind only.

Statistics show a steady increase in export of dates, but the rainfall has failed in Oman during the last five years, and the palms are said to have suffered.

A few other fruits, particularly dried limes, are exported to India and Persia.

Cotton of good quality is said to have been formerly grown with success, but is not now exported.

Pearls and Shells. Bahrein is now the headquarters of the pearl fishing industry in these regions, and little business in either pearls or shells is done in Muscat. An oyster-bed is said to exist off the island of Masorah, beyond Sur, from which fine pearls were formerly obtained.

Fish. There is a regular trade to India in sun-dried and salted fish, but no organised effort has been made to develop this industry, in which a good trade might be done. The waters of Oman abound in excellent fish, and Muscat harbour swarms with sardines and a sort of whitebait (matoot). The goldfish, tunny, and ray are abundant. The fishermen use both line and net, and wages are very low.

COURSE OF TRADE

Quite four-fifths of the trade of Muscat is with India, and in the hands of British Indian subjects working through partners or agents in Bombay. Indents for Manchester or other home goods are sent to

[1] The *mahmudia* was a unit of account, at the rate of 11½ to the Maria Theresa dollar; the *bar* was equal to about 1,480 lb.—Editor.

those agents, who place orders with shipping firms in Bombay (payment against bill of lading), and draw on Muscat at 21 days, plus commission (say 2 per cent).

Cotton tissues and other manufactures suited to the climate and condition of the people of Oman can be supplied largely from goods which are already manufactured for the Indian market, but the demand is of limited extent, and traders state, I think with reason, that for the small indents made for any one commodity it is more advantageous to place orders with Bombay shippers probably dealing in large quantities of the same goods, than to deal direct with houses in Great Britain. The consignment of perhaps only a few bales is either transshipped on arrival in Bombay at once to Muscat, or if landed in India, on declaration of re-export pays 1 per cent transit duty (plus 1/4 per cent agent's commission). The Muscat trader sells locally in rupees or [Maria Theresa] dollars, usually payable in instalments concluded in about three months. Sales to the interior are in dollars cash, delivery in Muscat, or frequently on credit to be liquidated by consignments of dates or other produce in their seasons.

Oman has commercial treaties with Great Britain, France, and other powers. I summarise the conditions of greatest interest to traders:

Foreign merchants have liberty to trade and reside in the country and purchase or rent lands, houses, and godowns, and to import or export any article of commerce.
All imports are subject to Customs duty of 5 per cent ad valorem.
Exports are not subject to duty.
Merchandise imported into Muscat under declaration of re-export by the same owner within six months is not subject to duty in transit.

The Customs were formerly farmed out at an annual rental, latterly amounting to $145,000, but since November, 1899, have been administered for account of the Sultan, with the result, it is believed, of an increase of revenue. There are Customs ports at Muscat, Mutra, Sur, and other smaller ports, but the control exercised elsewhere than at Muscat and Mutra is lax, and only nominal at Sur, which serves the most populous and fertile districts of the Sultanate and is the port next in importance to Muscat.

The development of trade with Oman is retarded by the insecurity of life and property inland. Merchandise is forwarded by large caravans with not less than 10 men in charge, under safe conduct of a man from each district traversed. The authority of the Sultan is little more than nominal beyond the coast ports, and tribal feuds and raids discourage agriculture and industry in the interior.

The simple wants and general poverty of the people offer only a limited field to foreign trade. Regular steamer service from Europe and India to Gulf ports has decreased the coasting trade formerly centring in Muscat. The inland frontiers, apparently bounded in great part by deserts, afford no access to more distant markets. Little seems to be known of the mineral resources of the interior, but some hold the country to be capable of considerable agricultural development. Behind the forbidding rock-bound coast there are reported to be wide and fertile valleys with fair water supplies from the inland mountain ranges. When law and security take the place of the disorder which now prevails in the interior, there may be considerable increase in cultivation and industry, and consequently in purchasing capacity of foreign commodities. . . .

CHAPTER 3

Pearling in the Persian Gulf

The Persian Gulf has been an important center of pearl diving and trading for several thousand years, and the technical methods and organization described in the following selection are essentially the same as those used many centuries ago. In the second half of the nineteenth century, however, thanks to greater security in the Gulf and the opening of new markets overseas, the industry expanded considerably. In 1790 the annual value of exported pearls was put at 500,000 Bombay rupees, or £50,000; by 1874–75 the figure had risen to £724,000, a peak that was not regained until 1901–2; but in 1902–3, the £1,000,000 mark was passed and before the outbreak of the First World War exports exceeded £2,000,000.[1] After the war, however, and especially in the 1930's, there was a sharp decline in demand, owing to a shift in tastes, the competition of Japanese cultured pearls, and the effects of the economic slump, and the industry has since then remained in a depressed state.[2]

The main producing and marketing center has for long been Bahrein, followed by Trucial Oman; in 1905–6 these areas accounted for Rs. 12,600,000 and Rs. 8,000,000 respectively, out of the total Gulf exports of Rs. 22,000,000.[3] In 1907 the pearling fleet in the Gulf was estimated at 4,500 boats with crews totaling 74,000; of these 1,215 boats and 22,000 men came from Trucial Oman, 917 boats and 18,000 men from Bahrein, 817 boats and 13,000 men from Qatar, 461 boats and 9,000 men from Kuwait, 924 boats and 9,000 men from Iran, and 167 boats and 3,000 men from Hasa.[4]

Following its conquest by the 'Utub tribes in 1783, Bahrein also developed into an important trading center, at first partly at the expense of Muscat (see Part V, chap. 2). The Wahhabi invasions seem to have caused a setback,[5] but under British protection expansion was rapid. In 1863 Pelly estimated Bahrein's imports at 1,600,000 rupees and its exports at 1,200,000 or about £160,000 and £120,000,

[1] Lorimer, *Gazetteer of the Persian Gulf*, I, 164, and table on p. 2252; also Great Britain, Admiralty War Staff, *A Handbook of Arabia*, p. 314.
[2] Sanger, *The Arabian Peninsula*, pp. 143–46, 175.
[3] Lorimer, *op. cit.*, I, 2253.
[4] *Ibid.*, I, 2256.
[5] Palgrave, *Narrative of a Year's Journey through Central and Eastern Arabia*, II, 215.

respectively.[6] In 1895–97 imports averaged £341,000 and exports £379,000; by 1900–1902 these figures had risen to £472,000 and £534,000, respectively (from the consular report, partly reproduced in Part V, chap. 2), and by 1911–14 stood at £2,061,000 and £2,107,000 (see Part V, chap. 5). The population, which had been put at 70,000 by Palgrave in 1863,[7] was estimated at "over 100,000" by 1914;[8] the latter figure may, however, be exaggerated, since the census of 1950 showed a total of 110,000. The development of other ports in the Gulf has brought greater competition to the trade of Bahrein, but any adverse effects have been more than offset by the great contribution made to the economy by petroleum since its discovery in 1932.

(See also works by Wilson, Lorimer, Bodianski, Pelly, Miles, Villiers, and Sanger, and Great Britain, Admiralty War Staff, listed in the Bibliography.)

[6] Pelly, "Remarks on the Tribes, Trade and Resources . . . Persian Gulf," *Trans. of the Bombay Geographical Soc.*, XVII (1863), 68–69.

[7] Palgrave, *op. cit.*, p. 211.

[8] Admiralty, *op. cit.*, p. 314; Lorimer, *op. cit.*, II, 238.

[George Rentz, "Pearling in the Persian Gulf," in W. J. Fischel (ed.), *Semitic and Oriental Studies Presented to William Popper*, University of California Publications in Semitic Philology, XI, 397–402; reproduced by kind permission of the author and the University of California Press.]

Pearling, an ancient occupation in the Persian Gulf, was until recently the chief source of income from abroad for the people living on the perimeter of this shallow sea. In all the centuries before the twentieth the Gulf had no other wares of consequence to offer the world's merchants, but oil drawn from deep strata has now replaced the fruit of the oyster's irritation in the economic life of man. The Arabs lag in their search for pearls, and the day may not be far off when other craft than those with sails will scour the banks, and the divers, should any remain, will clothe themselves in gear more cumbersome than a black loincloth.

Although much has been written about pearling in the Gulf, no Western scholar, so far as I know, has approached the subject primarily from the point of view of the Arab diver and his cant. During three years in Arabia I have made the acquaintance of many who used to visit the banks summer

after summer, and have enjoyed the intimate friendship of some of these.[1] In our conversations they have spoken in detail about life at sea and in the depths of the Gulf. These men are mostly Bedouins who once would come from as far away as Hadramaut to join their boats for the season's work. In addition to these oral sources, I had read a number of accounts of pearling by Arab writers, of which perhaps the best is the one by Muhammad ibn Khalifah al-Nabhani contained in his history of Bahrain.[2] Persons competent to judge single out the passage on pearling as the

[1] My chief informants have been Hamad ibn Hindi, son of a pearling captain and himself captain of a pearling vessel in the Gulf for many years, and Khumayyis ibn Muhammad ibn Rimthan of the tribe of the 'Ujman, Said ibn Nasir al-Mu'ammam of Bani Hajir, and Thu'ailib ibn Saqr of the 'Awamir, all beduins with long experience as pearl divers . . . .

[2] *Al-tuhfah al-nabhaniyah fi tarikh al-jazirah al-'arabiyah*, 6: *Tarikh al-Bahrain* (2d ed.; Cairo, 1924), pp. 15–20. Al-Nabhani, a native of Mecca whose family traces its descent back to Nabhan ibn 'Amr of the tribe of Tayyi, visited Bahrain at the end of 1913 and the beginning of 1914, during which time he composed a history of rulers of the island, entitled *Al-nubdhah al-latifah fi al-hukkam min Al Khalifah*, later revised and republished as cited above. Ameen Rihani (Amin al-Rihani) drew extensively upon this work for the material on pearling in his *Around the Coasts of Arabia* (Boston, 1930), pp. 277–80, and *Muluk al-'arab* (Beirut, 1935), pp. 195–98. Rihani, with the carelessness that mars much of his writing, calls the author Khalifah ibn Muhammad in both the English and the Arabic versions.

most valuable and reliable part of al-Nabhani's book. The present paper consists of a translation of this passage, with supplementary information in the accompanying notes.

Al-Nabhani says:

We have used the terms that are current among the people engaged in the pearling industry. Their vessels today are of two kinds, the *sanbuq* and the *jalbut*. In the past they had other vessels such as the *baghlah*, the *bittil*, the *bum*, and the *baqqarah*, few of which are found today, since they use the first two mentioned above almost exclusively. They refer to their vessels in general as *khashab*. The number of vessels (in Bahrain) ranges between three and four thousand.[3]

The beginning of the pearling season is called the *rakbah*, and the end is the *quffal*. Pearls (*lulu*) are referred to as *qumash*,[4] with the large variety (*jawahir*) being called *danat*. After a month (*burj*) of the season of spring has gone by,[5] the pearlers set out to sea in their vessels, each carrying as many divers as it can hold under the command of a *naukhadhah*. A diver is called a *ghais*, and the one who pulls his rope a *saib*. Their assistant is a *razif*, while one younger than a *razif* is a *tabbab*.

The vessels go out to places of varying depths that have well-known names,[6] some lying about

thirty miles off the mainland.[7] The depth of the pearling banks varies from three to fourteen fathoms; banks off Oman have depths reaching to about twenty fathoms, but the number of divers working there is small because of the difficulty of diving in such deep water.[8]

The diver goes over the side of the vessel and stays on the surface of the water until he adjusts on his nose a clip called a *fitam*, which is made of the horn of a mountain goat (*wa'l*) or of a turtleshell. This clip prevents the diver from breathing as long as he is under water; when he comes up he wrenches it off and takes a deep breath. When he goes down to the bottom, he places a piece of lead or a rock weighing from twelve to fourteen pounds (*ratl*) on one of his feet to increase the rapidity of his descent. Upon reaching the bottom he releases the weight from his foot, and the *saib* in the boat pulls it up by means of a rope called a *zaibal* that is attached to it. The weight is then hung from an oar on the side of the boat. The diver takes with him a basket called a *dayyin*, made of *kanbar* ropes after the form of a sieve, except that its openings are much larger. This basket has a loop called an *'alqah*, which the diver fastens around his neck, and a rope called a *jida'*, which runs back to the boat. The *saib* holds both the ropes in his hand. The diver usually places pieces of leather called *khabat*[9] over his fingers. While tearing the oysters loose and putting them in the basket he moves along the bottom on his hands, the buoyancy of the water raising his feet higher than the rest of his body. The basket rope is held between the

---

[3] This figure is unquestionably an exaggeration. Written records of the number of vessels operating out of Bahrain were not kept before 1923, but a reliable estimate gives it as "not less than 600" for that period. From 1926 to 1931 the number was over 500 every year, but it decreased thereafter, falling below 200 for each of the years between 1944 and 1946. (Government of Bahrein, *Annual Report for the Year 1363* [January, 1944–December, 1944], p. 11, and *Annual Report for the Year 1365* [December, 1945–November, 1946], p. 14).

[4] Strictly speaking, only the smaller pearls are called *qumash*, a term which may be derived from the practice of keeping and carrying pearls tied up in bits of red cloth. Although the grading of pearls by experts is complicated and precise, larger pearls are called in ordinary speech *hasbah* (pl. *hasabi*) or *danah* (pl. *danat*). A large and fine *danah* may fetch two or three lakhs of rupees (in Arabic of the Gulf, *lakk*, with the plural *lukuk*).

[5] The season usually begins about the middle of May and continues to the end of September. Vessels may go out for the *khankiyah* late in April or early in May.

[6] I hope to publish soon the translations I have made of two *nailahs* or pilot books of the Persian Gulf prepared especially for Arab captains and mates of pearling vessels: 'Isa ibn 'Abd al-Wahhab Al Qutami of Kuwait, *Kitab al-mukhtasar al-khass lil musafir wal-tawwash wal-ghawwas* (Bagdad, 1924–25), 88 pp., and Rashid ibn Fadil Al Ibn Ali of Darin, Saudi Arabia,

Majari al-hidayah (Bahrain; 1923), 32 pp. These works give information about all the important pearling banks on the Arab side of the Gulf.

[7] Some of the banks are even further than this from the mainland.

[8] Most of the diving in the Gulf is done in depths ranging from seven to twelve fathoms. Lieutenant J. R. Wellsted of the Indian navy, who was in the Red Sea in 1830, speaks of divers there going down to thirty or thirty-five fathoms; see *Travels in Arabia* (London, 1830), I, 238–39. The divers in the Gulf whom I have known consider about eighteen fathoms the maximum.

[9] A diver wears ten *khabat* (sing. *khabatah*) made of camel hide or cowhide, one on each finger. The cap for the thumb reaches to the base of the member; the ones for the other fingers reach about halfway down.

The diver buys his own basket, basket rope, nose clip, and finger caps, or the *naukhadhah* buys them for him and charges his account. The diver also supplies his own *shamshul*, the black loincloth he wears while diving (the color white would attract sharks), and *futah*, the towel he dries himself with upon emerging from the water. The weight usually belongs to the boat. The only article used in pearling that the *saib* has to furnish is the rope for the weight.

big toe and the next one to it.[10] When the basket is filled with oysters or the diver is about to run out of breath, he jerks the rope with his foot, whereupon the *saib* pulls him up as he holds fast to the basket rope. The act of jerking the rope with the foot is called *nabr*. When the diver comes to the surface, he removes the clip from his nose and breathes while the *saib* takes the basket and empties it in the middle of the boat. The basket is then returned to the diver, and the whole process is repeated. A diver stays under water up to about ten minutes; stories told of divers staying under about an hour are without foundation.[11]

Each descent and ascent is called a *tabbah*.[12] When the diver reaches the bottom he opens his eyes so that he can pluck the oysters. The divers are able to recognize their comrades and communicate with each other under water by humming. What is said about their placing protective devices other than the nose clip on their faces is not true.

The divers continue diving until they have collected enough oysters or the sun sets. If their catch is large enough before sunset, they start splitting open the oysters, which are called *mahar*. They keep on doing this and removing whatever pearls are found until sunset, after which they rest. The following morning they split open the remainder of the oysters, and after an interval go back to their diving. This goes on until they run out of food or water, whereupon they make port and secure enough supplies to last about a month. When summer comes to an end, they all return on a day appointed by the ruler [of Bahrein]. Whoever lingers behind is punished.

When a strong wind overtakes the pearlers during the season, the boats leave the banks and take refuge among the reefs (*fasht*) near the mainland until the wind quiets down. Then they return to the banks, each of which is called a *hair*.

The divers turn over all the pearls they get to the *naukhadhah*, who sells them and keeps one-fifth of the total for himself. He divides the remainder among the members of the crew after deducting the expenses of their food during the pearling season. A *saib* gets two-thirds as much as a diver, and a *razif* half as much as a *saib*. A *tabbab* receives nothing other than the experience he has gained in pearling and the food he has eaten.[13]

When spring arrives, the people of Bahrain send their boys out every day into water a cubit or more deep along the shore to collect what oysters they may find. This type of pearling is called *majanna*. When the boys are old enough to leave their families and go out to sea in boats for about two days, the term *'azab* is used, with reference to their being away from town. When they get their boats ready and go out to pearl for about two weeks, the time is called the *khanjiyah* [*Khankiyyah*].

When the sun has advanced part way through the sign of Taurus, the people get ready for the general season of pearling and set out on a day designated by the ruler [of Bahrein].

If one wishes to keep the oysters he has found apart from the rest and sell them himself, he is called an *'azzal*. He must then pay one-fifth to the *naukhadhah*, as well as the price of the food he has eaten.

When the sun enters the sign of Libra, the general season for pearling is at an end. The pearlers all return to town together, and the *naukhadhah* sells the pearls they have, after which accounts are settled with the *jazwa*, that is, the whole pearling crew.

Some men return of their own choice to pearl, being willing to endure the cold for a period of about a month; these are called *raddadah*. Some of the Arab merchants go out to the banks in their vessels and buy pearls from the *naukhadhah* either for cash or for provisions, such as dates and rice. It is better for the *naukhadhah* to get pro-

[10] For pearling operations the vessel is anchored with its head in the wind. From one to fifteen divers work at a time all on the same side of the vessel (on the port side if the wind is from the north, and on the starboard if it is from the south). When the divers are on the port side, each uses his left foot for the weight and his right for the basket, the reverse being the case when they are on the starboard side. If a diver wishes to reach the bottom rapidly, he holds both feet together. On the other hand, if he wishes to go down slowly, he allows the foot holding the basket to trail out acting as a brake.

[11] Ibn Battutah, to whose work al-Nabhani refers, says that there are divers who can stay under for an hour or two; see Muhammad ibn 'Abd Allah ibn Battutah, *Tuhfat al-nuzzar* (Cairo, 1928), p. 177. Al-Nabhani is himself guilty of an exaggeration: the maximum is probably under three minutes. A diver who can stay under for a long time is called *ra'i al-nafs*.

[12] When the water is still cool, the divers work in three shifts or *qahamat* (sing. *qahmah*), each consisting of six *tabbat*. When the water grows warmer, the number of shifts is reduced to two of ten *tabbat* each.

[13] Al-Nabhani sets forth the basic principles governing the division of the proceeds of the season's work. There are so many special cases, however, that the matter is actually far more complicated than this simple statement would indicate. One share in the division is called a *qalatah* (pl. *qalait*), a term not mentioned by al-Nabhani.

visions in this way and so avoid returning to port to replenish his supplies, which would cause him to lose about a week's time. These merchants, who are called *tawawish*, gather pearls and classify them. The pearls are sold to other buyers[14] until in the end they are concentrated in the hands of a few merchants who take them to India, where they are sold again. There are also *tawawish* who wait on the shores of the port and meet each ship that comes in for provisioning. They buy what they like from these ships and sell the pearls in town to European merchants or to banians who have come to Bahrain especially to purchase pearls.

[14] I hope that publication will soon be made of the translations prepared by my colleagues, Catherine Brown and 'Abd al-'Aziz Majdhub, of the Bahrain Diving Law of 1923 and the Bahrain law for the pearl trade of the same year, the year of the great reform of the pearling business carried through by the government of Bahrain. These documents contain much information on the methods of selling pearls.

CHAPTER 4

The Trade of the Hijaz at the Turn of the Century

The commercial importance of Jidda came about for two reasons. It had a "well-sheltered natural harbour, almost exactly half-way down the Red Sea coast. The entrance, through three lines of reefs, is, however, difficult."[1] And its proximity to Mecca—72 kilometers away—made it the natural landing place for the tens of thousands of pilgrims to the Holy Cities (see Part V, Introduction). At the beginning of the sixteenth century Varthema noted the large imports, through Jidda, of food from Egypt, Yemen, and Ethiopia and of spices, jewels, textiles, and other goods from India.[2] The sixteenth-century wars and the closure of the Red Sea to Christian ships must have seriously affected trade, but by the end of the seventeenth century such ships were calling at Jidda (see Part V, Introduction), and in 1698 Ovington noted that: "Jedda flourishes in a constant traffick from India, Persia, and other parts of Arabia and the Abyssinian shore. . . . Hither the Arabians bring their coffee, which is bought here by the Turks and shipped for the Suez." From Egypt the town received every year "twenty or twenty-five sail of large ships, laden with provisions, money, etc., for its subsistence and the support of trade."[3]

Burckhardt, who visited Jidda in 1814 and put its population at 12,000–15,000, gives an extensive account of its economic activities: "The people of Djidda are almost entirely occupied in commerce, and pursue no manufactures or trades but those of immediate necessity. They are all either sea-faring people, traders by sea, or engaged in the traffic with Arabia. Djidda derives its opulence not only from being the port of Mekka, but it may be considered as that of Egypt, of India, and of Arabia: all the exports of those countries destined for Egypt first passing through the hands of the Djidda merchants. Hence, it is probably richer than any town of the same size in the Turkish dominions."[4] He estimated the assets of the two wealthiest merchants at £150,000–200,000. "Several Indians have acquired

[1] Great Britain, Admiralty War Staff, *A Handbook of Arabia*, p. 122.
[2] Gerald De Gaury, *Rulers of Mecca* (London, 1951), pp. 116–17.
[3] *Ibid.*, p. 159.
[4] *Travels in Arabia*, pp. 15–19.

capitals nearly equal, and there are upwards of a dozen houses possessing from forty to fifty thousand pounds sterling."

Burckhardt distinguished "two principal branches—the coffee trade, and the Indian trade; with both of which that of Egypt is connected. . . . The price of coffee at Djidda, being regulated by the advices from Cairo, varies almost with the arrival of every ship from Suez." For example, the signing of the peace between England and the United States sent the price down, in three weeks, from $35 to $24 per hundredweight. "The trade in India goods is much safer, and equally profitable. The fleets, principally from Calcutta, Surat, and Bombay, reach Djidda in the beginning of May, when they find the merchants already prepared for them, having collected as many dollars and sequins as their circumstances admit, that they may effect bargains in wholesale at the very first arrival of the ships." The scale of operation is indicated by the following: "In Syria and Egypt it is the work of several days, and the business of three or four brokers, to conclude a bargain between two merchants to the amount of a thousand dollars. At Djidda sales and purchases are made of entire ships' cargoes in the course of half an hour, and the next day the money is paid down. The greater part of the merchandise thus bought is shipped to Suez, and sold at Cairo, whence it finds its way into the Mediterranean."

Conditions at the middle of the nineteenth century are brought out in a British consular report from Jedda.[5] Its import trade in 1857 was put at £833,510 and its import (*sic*, read export) trade at £430,850, a total of £1,264,360; of this three-quarters to four-fifths was "directly or indirectly for British account." Three types of shipping and trade were distinguished. First, "trade conducted in native craft with the latteen sail, between the other ports of the Red Sea, and those of Arabia and Persia." Second, "trade conducted in square rigged vessels with the ports of India, Singapore and Java—the last named vessels are usually commanded or navigated by Europeans." Third, "occasionally vessels arrive at Jeddah from Europe, . . . and steamers of which there are several belonging to an Egyptian Company plying regularly between Jeddah and Suez" (see p. 414, below).

With his usual insight, Burckhardt had noted two threats to Jidda's prosperity. First: "Within the last six years, the coffee trade between Arabia and the Mediterranean has suffered greatly by the importation of West-India coffee into the ports of Turkey. These were formerly supplied exclusively with Mocha coffee; the use of which has been almost entirely superseded in European Turkey, Asia Minor, and Syria by that of the West Indies." And second: "If Suez were to participate in the direct Indian trade, the present flourishing state of Djidda would, no doubt, be greatly diminished, and the town would become merely what its position makes it, the harbour of the Hedjaz, instead of being, as it now is, the port of Egypt." The following selection shows how this prediction was fulfilled, and the consequences for Jidda.

[5] Stanley to Malmesbury, May 4, 1859, F.O. 78, no. 1449.

In the latter half of the century, however, the situation began slowly to improve,[6] mainly because of the increase in the number of ships calling at the port and the rise in pilgrim traffic (see Part V, Introduction). In 1896 a total of 313 steamships, aggregating 372,000 tons, entered Jidda, as did 449 sailing ships, aggregating 14,000 tons. The upward trend is indicated by the fact that the British tonnage was 200,000, compared to an average of 169,000 in 1892–96, 133,000 in 1886, and 103,000 in 1885.[7] By 1910–11 the total number of ships had risen to 1,055, with an aggregate tonnage of 657,000.[8] The population of the town had by then increased to 30,000.[9]

After the First World War the Saudi conquest caused a temporary setback, but the upward trend was soon resumed and after the Second World War the town shared in the general boom caused by the rapid expansion of oil revenues. In 1947 a new port was built, and in 1963 the population of Jidda was 148,000.

(See also *Encyclopaedia of Islam*, s.v. "Djudda," Great Britain, Naval Intelligence Division [*Western Arabia*], and works by Philby, Wahbah, and Hamzah listed in the Bibliography.)

[6] But not without interruptions and setbacks. Early in 1858, the British acting vice-consul in Jidda reported: "The route between this and Medinah is now entirely closed [by the bedouins], and that with Mecca is far from being safe." Page to Clarendon, January 30, 1858, F.O. 78, no. 1387. A few months later both he and the French consul were murdered by the mob, and in retaliation Jidda was bombarded.

[7] Great Britain, *Accounts and Papers, 1898*, "Trade of Jeddah," p. 12.

[8] Admiralty, *op. cit.*, p. 102.

[9] *Ibid.*, p. 122.

["Diplomatic and Consular Reports on Trade and Finance, Turkey," Great Britain, *Accounts and Papers, 1898*, XCIX, 2–4, and ibid., "Jeddah," *1912–13*, C, 5–7.]

The trade of the year 1896 has been satisfactory, and no complaint need be raised as to British trade and shipping.

It is sometimes observed that the trade of Jeddah has long been falling off and is slowly but gradually disappearing; this may be true as to exportation, as only two or three articles are or have ever been really worth noticing, and these form a most trifling item in quantity and value considering the extent of the district, but the import trade is in a fairly flourishing condition.

A century ago, however, Jeddah was no doubt the queen of the Red Sea, a very considerable centre for trade, and managing a large coasting trade on both coasts; this town was by far the most influential, and, excepting Mocha for trade, and Suez for shipping, was the only important commercial port, and in fact produce from all round the Red Sea used to be collected here for export.

Steam and the development and increasing ease and rapidity of sea communications entirely changed this aspect of affairs though the coasting trade in sailing vessels continued to prosper well beyond the middle of the century, and the Arabs are still fast and very efficient sailors. There are now about 400 sailing vessels (sambooks) of from 15 to 100 tons, of which the larger run long distances to the Persian Gulf, Muscat and Zanzibar, while the smaller ply along the coast and occasionally across to Suakin and that neighbourhood. But most of their carrying trade has naturally been absorbed of late years by the Khedivié Company [see Part VI, chap. 7], and by two or three smaller steamers under the British flag. Arab merchants of this town now own only two large vessels of about 2,500 tonnage (one steam and one sailing) as it may be concluded that they were unable to withstand the competition of organised companies, and not strong or wealthy enough to combine among themselves for establishing a local company.

Hence, much of the odium of this loss is popularly, but to a large extent erroneously, attached to the construction of the Suez Canal. Ill-informed Arabs can hardly be expected to review all sides of a question, and while the benefits of the canal in establishing and developing sea communications with Europe are forgotten, as also its effects upon trade and reducing cost of transit, the imposition of heavy dues on merchandise and passengers passing through are resented as a palpable burden. The loss to local sailing craft in their dealings with Suakin and Massowah since 1870 is felt to be a real grievance, but considerations such as that, without the canal, trade in the Red Sea would never have reached its present dimensions, or that in any case Egyptian ports would have sought for and obtained eventually direct communications with foreign countries on account of the Ottoman 8 per cent. export duty, first imposed a few years ago, are little likely to be understood.

When the Soudan becomes more settled there may be expected a very considerable revival in the local trade with Suakin, and there will be need of activity on the part of Jeddah sailing craft.

Along the eastern coast of the Red Sea fish is the main support of the inhabitants, and it is roughly dried and salted for local consumption. No idea of exporting fish seems ever to have occurred to anyone, yet so abundant is the supply that it can be had practically for nothing. This sea indeed contains some 80 species not found elsewhere, and I believe about 750 in all. The great majority of Mediterranean fish are to be met with, and though generally inferior in taste grow to much larger sizes.

Wheat, rice, flour, etc., are imported for the use of the wealthier classes and of the troops, whilst the Bedouins are contented to live on dates and pulse chiefly, and are only able to eke out their wretched means of subsistence by the hire of their beasts for the conveyance of pilgrims, by robbery, and by subventions from Constantinople.

They possess but few goats, sheep, and asses, and there are not more than 80,000 camels in the Hejaz, of which many belong to relatives of the Sherif family who breed them for the tribes.

The tribal Arabs produce butter and cheese and also a little spun cloth, "abbas," strong and serviceable for their own use; they could not, of course, be expected to turn to agriculture (were there water) as yet, but some attempt is being made to forward their pursuits, and of late a considerable supply of ghee (clarified butter) is being prepared for export to Egypt and Turkey. This export, however, is every now and again suspended, local authorities fearing lest supplies should run short in the province itself.

About 20,000 camels are yearly sold and sent into Syria from Nejd at an average price of about £4, whilst the ordinary price in the Hejaz is about £7 for the load camel and £14 for riding. The animal of Central Arabia is said to be a trifle smaller than the breed found in northern and eastern Arabia. However, the Hejaz animal is sturdy and enduring, and if there be any demand for camels in any part of the world, there is no reason why Jeddah should not become a port of export, for camels are largely reared in the districts known as "Sharki," i.e., east of Medina, and could be easily bred in this neighbourhood to a much greater extent than at present. For weight carrying the Arabian is not the equal of the Bactrian camel (which at Erzeroum is valued at about £23), the average load in the Hejaz not exceeding 550 lbs.; but he is just as useful for all round work, can go longer stretches, and can bear changes of climate. The riding or swift camel that can travel 300 miles in four days is not in much request in this neighbourhood and his price is very much higher. Camels worked at Aden, I am told, are considerably smaller than the Hejaz animal, and now India produces in Scinde and Rajputana [camels] for her own use, and if in need of importing would probably turn to Afghanistan and the shores of the Persian Gulf instead of seeking here.

Profitable employment for the Bedouins might possibly be found in ostrich rearing, this bird being indigenous to, and still found in, parts of Arabia, and though probably in this neighbourhood there is too much seen of man, and in places the soil may be too salt for the ostrich to exist in a natural state, yet were Mussulmans, accustomed to artificial rearing and farming, inclined to venture on a commercial enterprise of this kind in conjunction with Bedouin Sheikhs or under Government auspices, possibly they would be rewarded with success. . . .

Imports and exports. No official statistics are obtainable, and hardly any information from local merchants. It seems certain that in 1910 about £90,000 was paid as import duties, which would give a little less than £1,000,000 worth (invoice value) of dutiable imports. There may perhaps be three-quarters as much again not dutiable, i.e., imported from Ottoman ports, so that the total yearly imports may perhaps be about £1,750,000. The figures in the appended tables [not included in this excerpt] have been obtained from the best possible sources, but seem likely to be exaggerated. Until August, 1909, invoices were not as a rule considered for the purpose of estimating duty payable, but by the reform then introduced the invoice price (plus lighterage at Jeddah) is generally accepted for that purpose. At the same time custom-house procedure was simplified, about one-quarter of the then 50 employees being removed, and the remainder being better paid. The result has been as satisfactory as could be expected, though merchants continue to complain of the custom-house. Exports being trifling, the imports are for the most part paid for by money of pilgrims (see the appended figures of pilgrimages [not included here]), as the inhabitants of Mecca, Medina, Jeddah, and Yambo, and also the Bedouin camel drivers live directly or indirectly on pilgrims. Jeddah imports for

the needs of pilgrims and of the fixed population of the Hejaz, including until lately at least the greater part of the needs of Medina, which town to some extent, not published, now imports by railway. Jeddah also imports for much of Central Arabia. The Hejaz grows practically nothing except a small quantity of vegetables and grapes, and has no minerals and practically no manufactures. Specie amounting, it appears, to over £1,000,000 a year is the great export.

In the report for 1907 appeared a statement to the effect that rice and cereals from India, piece-goods from the United Kingdom direct or via Constantinople or via Syria or via India, and from India, are the principal imports from the British Empire. And this holds good for the present report. Flour is nearly all from British India (freight from Bombay 1 rupee per sack of 90 kilos., price here from 15s. to £1 per sack). There is a little superior flour from Marseilles and Russia (price here £1.10s. to £1.15s. per sack). Rice is from British India, and also during the last seven years from Basrah. Of wheat, as will be seen from the tables, only a small proportion comes from India; of the rest, nearly all is from Basrah, freights being light, whereas freights from Egypt are found prohibitive. Of the barley, four-fifths are from Basrah and the rest from Syria, the same reason being given.

There are a sort of T-cloth—plain, grey, sized—of Bombay manufacture, called gamti, imported (price about £9 per 20 pieces of 9 lbs. weight each), and some other cotton goods of Bombay manufacture, but all to a comparatively small amount. The grey sheetings from America (erroneously called shirtings in previous reports) are being, on account of their high price, replaced to some extent by the same article from Manchester, which has, I understand, held the market here until 1895; and to a perhaps greater extent by the same article, being cheapest, from Italy (price of grey sheeting here from £9 to £10.10s. per bale of 25 pieces, each 30 yards by 1 yard). The Italian competition has for the present—1911–12—been stopped by the Turco-Italian war. Muslins and madapolams are from the United Kingdom, and so are most of the cotton prints; but fancy cotton articles, as cretonnes and imitation shawls, come from Austria-Hungary, and to a small extent from France. Mixed silk and cotton goods are of Syrian or Indian manufacture. Yarns and sewing threads—white and dyed, included under "Miscellaneous"—are imported to the annual amount, it is said, of about £6,000, exact figures not being obtainable. Yarns are generally imported of numbers up to 70 (most commonly it would seem up to 40), and perhaps three-quarters of them, including all the better qualities, are from the United Kingdom the rest being, it is said, from Belgium chiefly and some from India. Cloth comes from Belgium and the Netherlands. The import of yarn, however, is relatively small, there being no weaving industry.

The iron goods in the appended list [not included here], described as coming from India, are chiefly from Europe via India. Of enamelled goods about £5,000 worth of European (chiefly Austro-Hungarian) origin is imported, and of this about one-half from India. The superior arrangements of the port of Trieste for shipping, and of the Austrian Lloyd Company, for transhipping goods at regular intervals on to the Khedivial Company's steamers at Suez for Jeddah, are said to account for the large import from Trieste, which includes most of the coffee and perhaps one-third of the sugar (the rest of the sugar now nearly all coming from Egypt). Smaller hardware, glassware, lamps and paper, whether shipped from Trieste or from Constantinople, are said to be nearly all from Austria-Hungary.

A petroleum engine for a flour mill, turning out about 1⅕ tons flour daily, was set up in Mecca in 1909, and up to January, 1912, two others of the same size have since arrived for Mecca, but have not yet been set up; and a third, three-quarters of above

size, has arrived and is working in Jeddah. They are all of British manufacture. One of those set up in Mecca will also, it is said, be used for ice-making. There is no immediate prospect of a further demand, but this kind of flour mill is a novelty in the Hejaz, and may soon be asked for again.

Public Works. The prolongation of the Hejaz Railway from Medina to Mecca seems to have been abandoned for the present. Engineers have been surveying the proposed Jeddah-Mecca line for the last year (1911), but so far as is known there is no present prospect of construction being commenced.

The water condenser in the town continues to work irregularly, and its condensed water, being from a foul part of the harbour, often has a bad smell and taste. It can turn out about 30 tons a day. The price at the condenser is about 8s. 6d. per ton. As much again has to be paid for transport in the town in small quantities. The price of good drinking-water from wells varies down to about 10s. a ton, including transport. It is now at the extraordinary high rate of about £1 per ton. Of rain-water from cisterns there has been practically none for the last two years; its price, when there is any, is generally about 18s. per ton, including transport. There is a small condenser on the quarantine island, said to turn out about 15 tons a day, supplying not the general public but some individuals; the price of its water is £1.16s.8d. per ton, including transport to shore.

A portable hospital, made of compressed paper and well equipped, was set up by Government in 1911 outside the town at the total cost of about £4,000 for the accommodation of 100 pilgrims, and is being used in the present 1911–12 pilgrimage.

Public Health. Nothing exact is known as to mortality, but the town is exceedingly insanitary, and the mortality is probably high. Bubonic plague to a small extent is probably endemic in Jeddah. It is declared in every pilgrimage season, as is also a considerable amount of cholera in Mecca and a little in Jeddah. . . .

CHAPTER 5

Yemen, Aden, Bahrein in the 1900's

When the British occupied Aden in 1839, its population had shrunk from the 80,000 figure given by Marco Polo,[1] and the 35,000 estimated for 1513[2] to a mere 600. Its former prosperity had vanished with the disappearance of the Indian trade and the diversion of that of South Arabia to Mokha (see Part V, Introduction).

The main British objectives had been to occupy a strategic spot, located on a good natural harbor, and to establish a coaling station between Bombay and Suez. The latter function became much more important with the opening of the Suez Canal, and measures were taken to make Aden more attractive to international shipping. In 1867 water condensers were installed, in 1870 cable connections with India and Egypt were provided, and in 1888 the Aden Port Trust was established, which over the following decades steadily improved and deepened the harbor, keeping pace with the growth of traffic through the Canal and the Red Sea. Thus equipped, Aden soon became the principal bunkering station on the Far East route and already by 1875–76 it was importing 94,000 tons of coal.[3] In 1911–13, in spite of the competition of the French port of Jibuti, 40 per cent of the ships passing through the Canal called at Aden or its outpost, Perim; in 1913 Aden alone received 1,529 steamers aggregating 3,900,000 tons.[4]

The challenge imposed by the increasing change over from coal to oil fueling was met by the installation, in 1920, of tanks for storing petroleum products from Abadan. In 1954 a refinery with a capacity of 6,000,000 tons a year was opened, to process Persian Gulf crude oil. And although greater efficiency enabled an increasing number of ships to travel longer distances without bunkering, so that a smaller proportion of ships transiting the Canal had to stop at Aden, the absolute number and tonnage calling at the port steadily increased. In 1926, 1,496 steamers aggregating 5,300,000 tons entered Aden, in 1946 the figures were 1,578 ships and 5,800,000 tons, and by 1960 the tonnage had risen to 25,700,000. The refinery

[1] *Encyclopaedia of Islam*, new edition, s.v., "'Adan."
[2] Apelt, *Aden*, p. 52.
[3] Hunter, *An Account of the British Settlement of Aden in Arabia*, p. 99.
[4] Apelt, *op. cit.*, p. 101.

has, moreover, facilitated the rise of a small number of industries during the last few years.

A very successful attempt was also made to revive Aden's entrepôt trade, by making the town a free port in 1850. As a result the average value of seaborne trade rose from Rs. 1,871,000 (about £170,000) in 1843–50 to Rs. 6,028,000 (about £550,000) in 1851–58, Rs. 11,316,000 in 1858–65, Rs. 15,283,000 in 1870–71, and Rs. 27,109,000 (about £2,700,000) in 1875–76. In the latter year trade by land amounted to Rs. 2,952,000 (about £290,000).[5] By 1903–4 total trade had risen to just under £6,000,000 and by 1913–14 to £8,530,000.[6] Practically all the goods handled in Aden were of foreign origin, the only local product being salt, but the town had become by far the leading trade center of south Arabia and East Africa.

The population of Aden kept pace with its growing economic activity. By 1840 it had risen to 4,600, by 1856 to 21,000, by 1881 to 35,000, and by 1911 to 46,000.[7] The 1955 census gave a total of 138,000; of these over 48,000 were from Yemen, nearly 16,000 were Indians, over 10,000 Somalis, and over 4,000 were Europeans.

In recent years the economic activity centering on the British military base in Aden has also made an important contribution to the prosperity of the colony.

(For Yemen see Part V, Introduction and chap. 1; for Bahrein see Part V, chaps. 3 and 10. And see also works by Hunter, Apelt, and Hickinbotham, and Great Britain, Naval Intelligence Division [*Western Arabia*] listed in the Bibliography.)

[5] Hunter, *op. cit.*, pp. 89–91.
[6] Admiralty, *op. cit.*, p. 190.
[7] Hunter, *op. cit.*, pp. 21–27; Apelt, *op. cit.*, Table 4.

[From Great Britain, Admiralty War Staff, *A Handbook of Arabia* (London, 1916), pp. 154–59, 188–91, 313–15. British Crown Copyright; reproduced by kind permission of the Controller of Her Majesty's Stationery Office.]

YEMEN

. . . The inhabitants of Yemen being settled and in great part occupied in cultivation, the conditions which favour the pastoral or Bedouin type hardly exist except in the littoral plain. Yemen has always been noted for its agriculture and general fertility; but this refers chiefly to the highlands and the central plateau—not to the maritime ranges, nor to the Tihamah, which is mostly desert except where great wadis cut their way through to the sea. The principal crops of the region as a whole are coffee, maize, red and white millet, bearded wheat and barley, sesame, indigo, and cotton. The distribution of crops, according to zone, is much as follows:

The Tihamah is, in the main, sterile and saline, but gardens may be maintained near some of the larger seaports by constant irrigation, while farther inland towards the foot-hills there are broad arable tracts formed of detritus brought down from the heights. The crops of this belt are red and white millet, maize, sesame, and, around Beit el-Faqih and Zebid, a small amount of cotton and indigo. These crops, as a whole, depend on the spring rains and will ripen three months after sowing. On the inner edge of the Tihamah, where they get the margin of the summer storms, as many as three crops of millet can be obtained from one sowing.

Among the hills of the maritime range little cultivation is possible (except in valleys of considerable size where flood water comes down and can be utilized); the country is well bushed, but there is little soil to cultivate, the surface-drainage water is not enough for irrigation purposes, and the population is scanty. The crops, such as they are, are grown in the spring, as the rain falls in the same foot-hills in April. Millet is the staple crop, with maize and sesame next in importance; and grass grows plentifully after rain.

The highland zone (though the soil is not naturally so fertile as the lowlands and must be artificially renewed from time to time) is the most productive of Yemen, the rainfall, as shown in a previous section, being more abundant and regular, and the inhabitants, comparatively speaking, more virile, active, and industrious. The staple production is coffee; then follow bearded wheat and barley, and fodder and garden produce.

Coffee, as an Arabian crop, is peculiar to the Yemen highlands. The plant flourishes at any altitude between 4,000 and 8,000 ft., and is first met between Hodeidah and San'a soon after leaving Hajeilah. It is not indigenous to Arabia, but was introduced from Abyssinia during the Ethiopian invasion before the dawn of Islam. The berries used for seed are first placed in the sun to dry until the husk cracks of itself and can be easily opened, care being taken in so doing not to injure the inner skin of the bean. To produce young plants the farmer selects a patch of ground free from stones with at least one foot of good soil: he damps this and smooths it down, presses each bean to a depth of a few inches in the prepared ground, and covers them with a further inch or so of loose fine soil. Artificial shade is then provided, usually of branches, leaving an aperture at the top so that sunlight may fall for an hour or so daily on each part of the planted surface. The bed is watered every two or three days, and the shoots appear in about a month. The seedlings may be planted out about four months after they appear; the plant reaches maturity in five

years, attaining a height of from 8 to 10 ft., and is too old to be profitable after about twenty years.

The plantations are laid out in terraces up the hill-sides and following their curves; these are faced with stones, sometimes enclosing a strip only a few feet wide and sometimes an acre or so; the soil is often only a foot or two deep. Great care has to be taken to prevent the destruction of the terraces by accidental water-courses caused by thunderstorms. Every accessible and suitable spot on the mountain-side is utilized. Many terraces were constructed centuries ago, and they give a peculiar and characteristic aspect to the Yemen landscape. The watering is done from cisterns of cemented masonry, built in every cleft or ravine where surface water can be intercepted—for this reason some centres are comparatively sterile and devoid of plantations, as cisterns are not practicable. The harvest, broadly speaking, is in autumn, but the berries ripen at different intervals according to their position on the tree and the amount of sun to which a plantation is exposed. The Haraz district, west of Menakhah, produces coffee of the highest quality, and that grown by the Anis and Beni Matar is also well known. Ta'izz is the centre of the southern coffee districts.

Coffee is undoubtedly still the most important crop of the Yemen, in spite of prices dropping owing to the competition of Brazil and the present insecurity and difficulties of transport. Local consumption is enormous, but the thrifty Arabs use (and seem to prefer) the husk and keep the berry for market. The outlets for the marketable berries are Hodeidah and Aden, but increasingly the latter in consequence of the comparatively greater security of the routes to Aden. The other main crops of the highlands are barley, bearded wheat, millet, vegetables, and *kat*. The latter calls for a passing notice. The plant (*Catha edulis*), resembling the spindle-tree, is cultivated in Yemen over limited areas in such districts as suit it, at an altitude of about 5,000 ft. It is tended with zealous care in walled enclosures, and is perhaps the most *profitable* of all the Yemen products. The tender leaves and twigs are the valuable parts of the plant, and are chiefly in demand. The natives chew these for their exhilarant and stimulant properties, and the habit is almost universal among the inhabitants of this part of Arabia. The only implements used by the highland farmer are a hoe, a mattock, a reed basket (the latter for transporting soil), and an empty kerosene tin for watering purposes. As to the crops farther eastward of the plateau, the country here becomes less and less fertile, and cultivation gives way almost entirely to pastoral occupations.

The farmers of Yemen in general are guided as to seasons by the stars. They watch, for example, the movement of the Pleiades for the spring activities: the Arabs call it *Thurayya* (from a word meaning wealth), and when the cluster swings low in the West he knows the spring rains are at hand; or, when he sees Aldebaran on the western skyline at dusk, he starts his ploughing, for the spring rains have then set in and the ground is soft enough for the plough or the mattock.

Produce has to be transported from the farms by hand, or in absurdly small loads on donkeys, in consequence of the extreme difficulty in negotiating some of the mountain paths, often the merest footholds. When it has been carried to a main caravan route the husbandman is then faced by the exorbitant cost of transport, often further enhanced by difficulty in obtaining fodder. The caravan routes too are beset by marauders, more especially towards the coast, where the best, though remote, markets lie. Faced by such obstacles, production is often restricted to local requirements. Yemen is fertile enough and will produce most generous harvests, yet that it is not self-supporting seems to be shown by the fact that it imports more than £100,000 worth of food-stuffs even in years of plenty. This condition, however, is probably due not to natural causes, nor even to individual sloth, but to lack of security and co-operation, for which the

political unrest is mainly responsible. A sound system of collecting surface drainage would also give a great impetus to agricultural production.

Most industries, other than agriculture, in Yemen, are either moribund or languish from various causes, but in former days they were not unimportant. The following remnant local industries are the only ones worth mentioning:

(1) Dyeing. The indigo plant is still cultivated round Zebid and Beit el-Faqih, but the dyeing which was formerly carried on at these places has been dislocated by tribal disturbance (of the Zaranik in particular), and the industry has been transferred to Hodeidah, where indigo-dyeing had already been practised on a smaller scale. There it continues to maintain itself in spite of an increasing tendency to use synthetic dyes.

(2) Weaving. There is a colony of weavers at Hodeidah, many of whom have come from the disturbed area just mentioned. They weave a coarse cotton cloth in stripes of colour, which is retailed in lengths suitable for shawls, etc., as worn by the natives. Ta'izz was once famous for weaving, but is much less so now than formerly.

(3) Boat-building. The building of dhows is carried on at some small yards along the beach south of Hodeidah. The Yemen *dhow* or *sanbuq*—used for transporting cargo to and from vessels in the roadstead—is about 50 ft. long and sharp prowed. It has a short sturdy mast, which carries a big lateen sail on an almost perpendicular gaff of great length and well tapered. The rudder is operated by tiller-ropes leading direct to it, well below the water-line from either gunnel. Such a craft takes about three months to build and costs £100. The stem and stern posts and the knees and ribs are made of up-country acacia, which is very hard and durable, but the planking comes from the Malabar coast. Sea-going *dhows* are built on the same lines, but larger, with a small mizzen-mast well aft and also lateen rigged. They have decks fore and aft;

passengers berth aft, under an awning on the raised poop. They are outlandish-looking vessels, but very seaworthy, as they need to be on this windy coast.

(4) Tanning. Hides are dressed and made into sandals at Hodeidah, Zebid, Beit el-Faqih, and some other centres. Sheep skins are also soft-tanned in some of the larger up-country centres, chiefly for making into boots, which are there more often worn than sandals because of the cold.

(5) Milling. There is a small flour-mill at Menakhah, built by the Turks; otherwise grinding is done entirely by the hand-quern.

(6) Metal-working. San'a was once famous for its ornamental work in brass and copper; the industry is now confined to the making of domestic utensils in these metals, and is still carried on in the main at the same place.

(7) Production of minerals. There is a small amount of coarse brittle native iron, but the scarcity of fuel makes smelting impracticable. Petroleum has long been known to exist in the Farsan (*Farasan*) Islands, and a concession was granted to an Ottoman subject, but the results of the experimental borings were of doubtful value. Rock-salt occurs at Salif on the mainland opposite Kamaran Island, and the flourishing salt-works there are under the control of the Ottoman Public Debt [Administration]: the bulk of the salt goes to India, but large quantities are also sent inland. Fine stones of onyx, agate, chalcedony, and cornelian are found in the hills round San'a.

TRADE

The trade of Yemen has declined in recent years, for reasons already stated. The only port of any real importance commercially is Hodeidah, but even there, before the war, trade was not as brisk as formerly. Aden proved to be a surer outlet for products largely in consequence of the fact that the caravan-routes leading thither were less liable to tribal disturbances and raid, with the result that nearly all the coffee went there. Mocha, once the centre

of the coffee trade, no longer holds any position as a trading port. The other local coasting and fishing villages, from north to south, are Ghuleifiqah, Gah (a landing-place for slaves), Mersa el-Majalis (a good harbour for small boats), and Musa.

In 1909 the value of imports at Hodeidah was £650,000 and that of exports £400,000. The chief articles of export—in fact the only worth considering—are hides, skins, coffee, and fuller's earth; coffee was the mainstay, but is now ousted by hides and skins. For coffee, France is the best customer, then the United States with Great Britain as a bad third. Hides and skins (the latter largely from Asia) go chiefly to New York, Marseilles, and London.

By far the most important imports are cereals, rice, and other food-stuffs from India; and, a long way behind these sheetings, cotton piece-goods, and yarn from the United States and Manchester, petroleum from the United States and Russia, iron and steel for smithy purposes from Germany (before the war), general stores from Italy and (?) Austria, and silk and condiments.

Imports pay an 11% *ad valorem* duty, of which 8% may be paid in kind, but with a rebate of 10% if cash is paid; the remaining 3% must be paid in cash, without rebate. Exports pay 1% duty either in cash or in kind.

CURRENCY

Currency in Yemen is in a chaotic state: little information regarding it is available, but it appears that both the coins current and their exchange value vary greatly at different times and in different localities. Bury says: "Before the affairs of the Yemen can be placed on a sound commercial basis, her currency and customs must be overhauled; both are enough to drive a brisk business man frantic." Wavell says: "A more hopeless muddle than the present condition of the Turkish currency (in the Yemen) would be difficult to conceive. It is different wherever one goes, and the value of the principal coins fluctuates daily.

There are about a dozen different coins in common use, none of which is exactly divisible into a whole number of the next smallest."

Gold. The Turkish pound should be the standard gold coin of the country, but it is rare and is becoming rarer.

The English sovereign is readily accepted as the equivalent of 10 Maria Theresa dollars; the usual quotation in Turkish piastres is 112 P.T.

The French napoleon is also in circulation.

Silver. There are two opposition silver standards:

(a) The Maria Theresa dollar, or riyal = ±
     12 piastres
(b) The Turkish Mejedieh dollar = ± 17
     piastres

The latter used to be the only legal tender in silver and the importation of the Maria Theresa was prohibited for some time but the prohibition was withdrawn in 1910; the Mejedieh dollar will only be accepted by the Arabs of the towns, and even there the Maria Theresa is accepted more readily.

The smaller silver coins in use are the 4 piastre and 2 piastre pieces. The 1 piastre is a nickel coin = 4 hilal (copper).

The merchants of Hodeidah use Indian rupees much as currency, and they base their exchange calculations on the value of 100 riyals in that currency, the rate of exchange being guided by the rate at Aden. . . .

ADEN

TRADE

Practically the whole of the trade of this region is centered in Aden—local trade as well as general. The trade of the only other notable port of this littoral, Shughrah (and even that of Makalla in Hadhramaut), is restricted and purely local in character, and is entirely subservient to that of Aden.

The total value of the trade of Aden (import and export), in round numbers, for the last two years has been:

1913–14.	£8,530,000
1914–15.	£6,940,000

This falls into two categories: Transhipment trade, and Inland (or local) trade. Comparative figures for the year 1914–15 were:

Transhipment.	£6,682,000
Inland	£258,000

From these figures it may be noted how greatly the transhipment trade exceeds the local in amount and importance. The following are the details of the two categories taken separately.

(1) *Transhipment trade.* The principal articles of import, in 1914–15, taken in their order of value were: Cotton goods of various kinds, £580,000; hides and skins, £520,000; grains and pulse (including flour), £490,000; coffee, £320,000; coal, £210,000; tobacco, £150,000; sugar, and confectionery, £90,000; provisions £70,000; oils, gums and resins, silk goods, and ivory.

The principal articles of export were: Hides and skins, £640,000; cotton goods, £530,000; coffee, £380,000; grains and pulse, £360,000; tobacco, £110,000; salt, £76,000; sugar, £75,000; gums and resins, £35,000; provisions, £30,000; dyeing and tanning materials, shells and ivory.

The movement and distribution of the trade of Aden with different countries and localities was as follows in 1914–15: total trade with India, £1,180,000; Jibuti and Obok (French Somaliland), £780,000; the United Kingdom, £700,000; the United States, £600,000; Arabian Red Sea ports (chiefly Hodeidah, Jiddah, and Mocha), £400,000; Somaliland, £340,000; Arabian Sea ports (Muscat, Makalla, Shiheir, etc.), £260,000; France, £190,000; Italian Red Sea ports (Musawwa', Assab), £140,000; Abyssinia, £130,000; Independent Somali ports, £115,000; Egypt, £80,000; Mozambique, £35,000, etc.

(2) *Inland trade.* Though the foregoing facts are instructive in a general way, it is more essential, for the particular purpose of this book, to consider in detail the trade

of Aden with the interior. The movement in 1914–15 was as follows:

Imports from the interior   £140,000
Exports to the interior   £120,000

The principal articles that passed out, arranged in the order of their value were: coffee, £30,000; fodder, £29,000; drugs (*kat*, and charcoal), £14,000; animals (chiefly bullocks, sheep, and goats, and, in a less degree, camels), £6,000; provisions (including native food products such as *ghi*, eggs, and honey), £8,000; vegetables and fruits (the latter chiefly dates), £5,000; oils (chiefly *jinjili* or sesame-oil), £3,000; dyeing and tanning materials (including saffron and henna), £1,000; and other less important products such as reeds (for building purposes and mats), sesame, madder, wax, potash, and rose-water.

The principal articles which passed into the interior were: Cotton (piece goods and yarns), £30,000; grains (jowari, bajri, rice, and wheat flour), £30,000; tobacco (unmanufactured), £25,000; spices, £16,000; seeds, £6,000; provisions (including dates), £5,000; sugar, £4,000; oils (chiefly petroleum and jinjili), £1,900; metals (wrought iron and copper), £1,000; turmeric and indigo, soap, and matches.

From the figures of the *total* trade of Aden, given at the outset, it will be noted that there was considerable decline in 1914–15 as compared with 1913–14, mostly due to prohibitions and restrictions consequent on the war. Trade has in fact been temporarily thrown back five years, the total value of trade in 1909–10 having been £6,900,000.

Aden was made a free port in 1850. Previous to that year the average total yearly trade of the town was about £120,000; in 1903–4 it had risen to just under £6,000,000; in 1913–14 (the most recent normal year) it had attained more than £8,500,000. On the opening of the port in 1850 much of the valuable trade between Arabia and the eastern coast of Africa, formerly monopolized by Hodeidah and Mocha, was attracted to it; but this marvellously rapid development has, undoubtedly, been mainly due to the opening of the Suez Canal. During the seventy odd years of British rule, the population of the town has multiplied sevenfold, and Aden now forms, normally, not only the chief centre of the Arabian trade with Africa, but an entrepot and distributing centre for an ever increasing European and Asiatic commerce.

In the year ending March 31, 1915, 2,481 vessels, of an aggregate tonnage of about 3,100,000, entered the port, including 1,300 local craft of 38,000 aggregate tonnage—as compared with 3,000 vessels of just under 4,000,000 aggregate tonnage in 1913–14. Of the 1,181 merchant vessels cleared in 1914–15, about 660, with an aggregate tonnage of $1\frac{1}{2}$ millions (or about half the total tonnage) were British; the rest were of foreign nationality and native craft.

The coffee trade, which now finds its principal outlet at Aden, was formerly almost entirely in the hands of the Hodeidah merchants; but the heavy dues of the Turkish authorities at the latter place, coupled with the insecurity of the routes under Turkish control, have diverted a large part of the coffee to Aden. Much is shipped from Hodeidah to Aden direct by sea; the coffee which reaches Aden direct is brought down by caravans from the highlands of the interior. A very considerable quantity is also brought across from the African coast, being shipped from Zeila, one of the Somali ports; it is carried thither on camels from the highlands of Harrar and the Galla country, which, like the Yemen highlands, are suitable to the growth of the coffee bush. Food-stuffs are imported from India and from the African coast, as well as from the interior of Arabia. Sheep and goats are shipped weekly in large numbers from Berbera, Bulhar, and Zeila; while oxen, fodder, vegetables, and fuel come mostly by caravan from Lahej and the surrounding country. Ostrich feathers reach Aden from the Somali and Danakil country; mother-of-pearl shells from the Persian Gulf and Red Sea fisheries; ivory from Somaliland and Abyssinia. . . .

BAHREIN

INDUSTRIES AND TRADE

The most important occupation in Bahrein is pearl-fishing, and the fisheries are the most valuable in the Gulf next to those of Trucial Oman. Were the fisheries to cease, most of the urban population would have to leave the country. They employ more than 900 boats, each with a crew of about 20, the total crews amounting to nearly 20,000 men. The pearling season opens in May, and some boats continue operations until about October. Special measures had to be taken in 1915 by the Sheikh, in conjunction with the British Resident, to enable the pearl-fishing population to tide over the crisis caused by the stoppage of the pearl-trade during the war. Sea fisheries are also extensive, the fish being taken in nets and in tidal weirs or enclosures (hadhrahs) made of reeds, some of which surround large areas in the shallow waters round the coasts; 500 lb. of fish a day were supplied without difficulty to the Indian Expeditionary Force in 1914. Agriculture is carried on by irrigation, the chief products being fruit (dates, citrons, limes, melons, figs, etc., but few of the first quality), lucerne, and a few vegetables; a great belt of date-groves on Bahrein Island runs S. from Manamah to the village of Buri, a distance of about 7 miles. Domestic animals include about 2,000 donkeys, less than 100 horses owned by the Sheikh and his family, about 100 camels, chiefly used in carrying water to Manamah for sale, and a small but fine local breed of cattle, in high repute for their milking qualities. Of the donkeys some 200 are of the famous breed imported from Hasa, from 12 to 13 hands, and white in colour.

The chief handicrafts are sail-making, weaving of abbas, lungis, and checked sheeting, and the manufacture of mats from Hasa reeds. Palgrave described the *Baharinah*

as excelling in the crafts of the weaver, the tailor, the dyer, and the worker in metal, wood or leather. Boat-building, with timber imported from India, employs about 200 carpenters; Bahrein builders can turn out an excellent forty-ton boat in less than a month. Many boats are sold to purchasers in El-Qatar and Oman.

Trade at the port of Manamah was for years hindered by the unsatisfactory arrangements for handling cargo, distribution being delayed, and goods left to deteriorate without any proper protection. In 1910 the control was given to a European, but in the following year native sentiment demanded native control, and two Arabs were appointed, with lamentable results. Since then matters have improved; a Hindu has been placed in charge, and the construction of a jetty and storage-shed has modified the worst of the former defects. The Sheikh is entitled by treaty to an *ad valorem* duty of 5 per cent. on merchandise. Bahrein is the principal market for the pearl-industry, the export of pearls in a good year attaining about £2,000,000. But it is also an important emporium for the east coast of Arabia, distributing merchandise from India and from countries bordering on the Persian Gulf, to El-Qatar, Qatif, and 'Oqair, from which last two ports goods are carried into the oases of Hasa and Qatif, and beyond into southern Nejd. This local trade is carried in native boats without manifests, so that exact statistics cannot be obtained.

The total average imports of Manamah for the three years 1911–14 amounted to £2,061,038, and exports £2,106,766. During the same period the figures under the three main heads averaged as follows:

	Imports	Exports
Pearls	£810,000	£1,826,430
Specie	461,280	60,970
General merchandise	789,740	219,350

The principal commodities imported are rice, piece-goods, *ghi*, coffee, dates, sugar, tea, tobacco, spices, fuel, and animals for slaughter. Real exports other than pearls are of small value and importance, Bahrein being a distributing and not a producing centre; a few textiles and a little sail-cloth almost complete the tale of local manufacture. The principal share of the Bahrein trade falls to the lot of India, which is responsible for more than half of the total, though many goods arriving from that country are really of European origin, sent there for reshipment owing to the lack of direct facilities, and to the fact that Bahrein has grown accustomed to placing orders in Bombay. Next to India come Persia, and Iraq, less than 10 per cent. falling to all other countries. The natural result of this preponderance is that trade is largely in the hands of Indian and Persian merchants. Besides legitimate commerce, there is a contraband traffic with the South Persian coast. In 1914 there was but a single British firm in Bahrein, Gray, Paul and Co., who are agents for the British India Steam Navigation Co.; the only other European commercial house was that of R. Wönckhaus & Co., of Hamburg, which had been established for some years [see Part V, chap. 10]. On the outbreak of war there were two resident members of the latter, the manager, who was arrested and interned at Karachi, and his assistant, who belonged to the active reserve of the German Army, and escaped to Basra. The branch was then closed. There are no banks, and transactions are largely carried out by means of Indian currency notes.

Steam communication is chiefly in British hands, the British India Steam Navigation Co. maintaining a weekly service up from Bombay and Karachi, and a fortnightly down to Karachi and Bombay. The Arab Steamers, Ltd., a line started in 1911 in opposition to the British company, call from Bombay about once every three weeks, and again on the return voyage from Basra. The boats of the Persian Gulf Steam Navigation Co. from Bombay call on the outward voyage once a month, and again on their return. Before the war, the steamers of the Hamburg-Amerika line called about once a month on the outward voyage, thus providing the only regular direct access to Bahrein from Europe. . . .

CHAPTER 6

Population in South Arabia in the 1900's

Present-day knowledge of the demography of Arabia is hardly more advanced than when the following selection was written. During the First World War an official British publication stated:

The population of Arabia cannot be estimated with any approach to accuracy. It is usually guessed to be from five to eight millions. The lower of these figures is probably nearest to the truth. If we allow two and a half millions of settled and nomadic folk to the whole Red Sea slope from Midian to Yemen (the last-named, with Asir, holding two-thirds of the total); one and a half to the southern districts and Gulf littoral, inclusive of Hadhramaut (Oman alone has about half a million); half a million to all the Central settled districts together; and one million Central nomads, we are probably over the mark.[1]

This estimate may be compared with one made by the leading authority on the peninsula, George Rentz: "In view of the extensive areas inhabited solely by scattered nomads and the relatively light density of population in most of the settled areas, one may doubt whether the total approaches 10,000,000, and it may well fall several millions short of this figure."[2] The figures given in the *United Nations Statistical Yearbook, 1961*, are: Saudi Arabia 6,036,000, Yemen 5,000,000, Aden Protectorate 650,000, Muscat and Oman 560,000, Kuwait 223,000, Bahrein 147,000, Aden Colony 138,000, Qatar 45,000, and Trucial Oman 28,000.

Throughout history Arabia has been a country of emigration, mainly to the Fertile Crescent, the Sudan, and East Africa. But some foreign Muslims, generally attracted by the pilgrimage, tended to settle in the Holy Cities and Jidda, and the growth of Aden owed much to the immigration of Indians and Somalis, who in 1955 numbered some 26,000. In the last three decades the rapid expansion of the petroleum industry has attracted nearly 50,000 non-Arabs—Iranians, Indians, Pakistanis, and Somalis—to the Arabian oil-producing countries, as well as tens of thousands of Arabs from Iraq, Palestine, Lebanon, Syria, Egypt and elsewhere, and several thousands of Americans and Europeans.

[1] Great Britain, Admiralty War Staff, *A Handbook of Arabia*, p. 18.
[2] *Encyclopaedia of Islam*, new edition, *s.v.* "Djazirat al-'Arab."

As mentioned in the selection, Hadhramaut has been a center of active emigration to Mecca,[3] the Red Sea area as far north as Egypt (where some important commercial houses were active in Cairo up to the Second World War), and to India and the East Indies. Emigration to the Dutch East Indies started on a very small scale at the end of the eighteenth century and accelerated during the second half of the nineteenth, when the islands were opened to private enterprise. In 1860 the number of Arabs was estimated at 9,000, of whom 6,000 were in Java; by 1900 the figure had risen to 27,000 and 18,000, respectively, and by 1952 they were 85,000 and 65,000. During the 1930's Arab immigration into Indonesia averaged 3,000–5,000, and the rest of the growth was accounted for by natural increase and intermarriage.

In 1939 it was estimated that there were 70,000 Hadhramis in Indonesia and another 30,000 in Malaya, East Africa, Hyderabad, and elsewhere. The remittances sent home by these emigrants played an important part in the economy of southern Arabia: thus those from Indonesia alone were put at £600,000 per annum.[4] But since the Second World War, and especially after the independence of Indonesia, this flow of funds has been sharply reduced.

[3] See Snouck Hurgronje, *Mekka*, II, 4.
[4] Ingrams, *Economic and Social Conditions in the Aden Protectorate*, p. 37.

[From Adolf Grohmann, *Südarabien als Wirtschaftsgebiet* (Vienna, 1922), pp. 47–49; reproduced by kind permission of the author.]

NUMBER OF INHABITANTS

All statements about the number of inhabitants of the region under study are unfortunately extremely unreliable; the figures often vary by millions. Only those for the Turkish province of Yemen and Aden are halfway trustworthy: for the former, Turkish and British statistics give a figure of 750,000 inhabitants[1] and for the latter the British figure[2] is 46,165 (31,290 males and 14,875 females), to which should be added some 12,000 for Socotra. As against these modest official figures, there are the much higher estimates made by scholars and travelers, which I will quote without attributing to them any more value than, perhaps, sheer interest for the history of statistics. Thus for 1886, Edward

[1] *Taqwim al-Bashir* (1916), p. 92; *The Statesman's Yearbook*, 1916, p. 1405.
[2] *The Statesman's Year-Book*, 1916, pp. 104 ff.

Glaser[3] put the population of the Turkish province of Yemen—which was then, however, considerably larger—at 1,800,000; E. Behn[4] gives a figure of not quite 1,000,000; the British consular report[5] on Hodaida, 3,000,000; Supan,[6] for Yemen and 'Asir, 750,000, for Aden, 44,000, Kamaran, 100, and British South Arabia, 140,000; Zwemer,[7] for Yemen 2,500,000; A. Zehme,[8] for Yemen and 'Asir, 2,252,000 (following Reshid-Bey). A. Beneyton[9] gives for Yemen a figure of 4,500,000 and A. Bardey[10] goes as high as 8 to 10 million, while Ibrahim Hilmi[11] puts the population

[3] *Tagebuch*, VIII, p. 45. [4] *Jemen*, p. 53.
[5] Diplomatic and consular reports on trade and finance, "Trade of Jeddah," reports for the years 1890–97.
[6] [*Bevölkerung der Erde*], p. 24.
[7] S. M. Zwemer, *Arabia: The Cradle of Islam* (new ed.), p. 29.
[8] A. Zehme, *Arabien und die Araber seit hundert Jahren* (Halle, 1875), p. 407.
[9] ["Mission d'études au Yemen," *La Géographie*, XXVIII (1913)], p. 208.
[10] "Rapport sur el-Yemen et partie du pays d'Hadramaut (Arabie)," *Bulletin de Géographie historique et descriptive*, 1899, p. 29.
[11] [*Mamalik-i-Othmaniyye Jeb Atlasi* (Constantinople, 1323 A.H.)], p. 260.

of Yemen at 3,500,000 to 7,000,000.

For the regions lying east of Yemen there are no official estimates at all. The only attempt at providing systematic statistics was undertaken by W. Hein,[12] who studied the region of Qishin and came up with a figure of 2,686 inhabitants. According to C. Landberg[13] the round total for Baihan al-Qasab, Harib, Wahidi and Jirdan, Dathina, Upper 'Awaliq, and al-Hadina is 12,500 men. The figures given by H. von Maltzan and A. von Wrede seem much too high. L. van den Berg[14] estimates the population of Hadhramaut at 150,000 and A. Zehme[15] following Reshid-Bey, at 1,550,000.

Given the uncertainty surrounding estimates of both population and area, the density of population can be estimated only with great reservations. According to the Turkish statistics, the figure is 4 per square kilometre.

MOVEMENT OF POPULATION

Even the most elementary information on births, marriages, and deaths is lacking.[16]

We are somewhat better informed regarding emigration, though here too we lack quantitative data. Whereas the Yemenis do not apparently leave their native soil easily,[17] unless forced to do so by the direst necessity, the inhabitants of Hadhramaut, Yafi', 'Awaliq, and the south in general, are both mobile and enterprising. The Hadharim [people of Hadhramaut] can be found as porters or petty traders in all the more important ports of Arabia, e.g., in Jidda and also in Abu 'Arish; they even have a colony in Cairo.[18] They pursue their activity as traders in all south Arabia, as also in Jauf and the surrounding regions. Moreover many enter the service of Indian princes, such as the Nizam of Haiderabad, or go on to Singapore and the East Indian archipelago, where they have already constituted large colonies of emigrants from Hadhramaut. Immigration into the Dutch Indies is still progressing uninterrupted.[19]

[12] "Ein Beitrag zur Statistik Südarabiens," *Mitteilungen der geographischen Gesellschaft in Wien*, XLVI (1903), 219 ff.
[13] *Arabica*, IV, V.
[14] [*Arabica*, V], p. 42.
[15] *Op. cit.*, p. 407.
[16] Only for Aden are there accurate reports. According to the *Statesman's Year-Book*, 1916, p. 126, Aden had, in 1911, 46,165 inhabitants, against 43,974 in 1901, i.e., an increase of 2,191 persons and a density of population of 577 per square mile.

[17] According to C. Ritter, *Vergleichende Erdkunde von Arabien*, I, 660, the Hashid Arabs often serve as warriors in India, while the opposite is asserted of the Yafi'. Idrisi reports, incidentally, that Yemenis emigrated as far as Spain; thus there were some in Silves (Shelb), see A. Jaubert, *Géographie d'Edrisi*, II, 21.
[18] See H. von Maltzan [*Reise nach Südarabien*], pp. 48, 20 ff.; J. R. Wellsted [*Reisen in Arabien: Deutsche Bearbeitung von Rödiger*, II (1842)], pp. 329 ff.; Ritter, *op. cit.*, I, 1019; M. J. de Goeje, *Hadhramaut*, p. 1.
[19] L. Hirsch [*Reisen in Süd-Arabien*], p. 13 *n*; L. W. C. van den Berg [*Le Hadhramaut et les colonies arabes dans l'Archipel Indien*], pp. 104 ff.; Th. Bent, *Southern Arabia*, p. 76; S. B. Miles and W. Munzinger ["Account of an Excursion into the Interior of Southern Arabia," *Journal of the Royal Geographical Society*], p. 234.

CHAPTER 7

The Yemeni Jews in the Twentieth Century

It is generally believed that the first Jewish settlements in Yemen date from the early part of the second century A.D. Jewish influence in the country reached its zenith in the fifth century, with the conversion of the royal house to Judaism. In the six centuries following the advent of Islam, Judaism disappeared from the peninsula, except for Yemen, where a large community survived under fairly severe social disabilities but enjoying a certain degree of economic well-being.

By the beginning of the nineteenth century the number of Jews in Yemen was estimated at some 30,000, and their economic life had settled into the pattern described in the following selection. Except for peddlers, few were engaged in trade; however, in neighboring Aden Jewish merchants played a leading part.[1] On the other hand, Jews had a near monopoly of silver and goldsmith work and made an important contribution to the economy as potters, smiths, carpet-makers, weavers, and tanners. Some Jews also served as royal minters.

Emigration to Palestine began in 1882 and accelerated after 1909 (see Part IV, chap. 6). By 1948 there were over twenty Yemeni settlements in the country and a total immigrant population of 16,000. Following the establishment of the state of Israel, all the Jews remaining in Yemen, about 50,000, moved over to Israel.

(See also works by Niebuhr [*Description*] and Brauer listed in the Bibliography, and *Jewish Encyclopedia* (1905) *s.v.* "Yemen," *Encyclopaedia Judaica* (1931), *s.v.* "Yemen," *Universal Jewish Encyclopedia* (1943), *s.v.* "Yemen," and *Statistical Abstract of Israel, 1960*.)

[1] Hunter, *An Account of the British Settlement of Aden in Arabia*, p. 26.

[From Joseph Kafih, *Halikhot Teman* (*Yemenite Paths*) (Jerusalem, 1961), pp. 227–29; reproduced by kind permission of the Ben Zvi Institute.]

HANDICRAFTS AND OCCUPATIONS

. . . Most handicrafts, particularly those requiring specialization, were in the hands of Jews. Although on occasion one encountered Arab craftsmen, they were not experts in their crafts.

On the other hand, Jews had very little share in wholesale trade. In Yemen commerce was totally uncontrolled, every merchant having the right to export or import whatever he wished and, for that matter, to sell at whatever price he chose. His only obligation was to pay the tariff. In cases where the customs inspectors overrated the value of goods, the merchant was permitted to pay the import duty in kind. Yemen receives goods from all over the world through Aden. The exports of Yemen include coffee, kidney-beans (*athar*), almonds, raisins, wheat, butter, skins, small fish, and so on.

The Arab population earns its livelihood through agriculture. Apart from wheat, barley, and beans, vegetables and fruits are also raised. In San'a and its environs wheat is a very common crop. In the south of Yemen *dhurah* [sorghum] is commonly raised and represents practically the sole diet of the population there. In the west of Yemen, *dukhn* [pennisetum] and *dhurah* are raised, both of these comprising the basic diet of that area. In the east of Yemen *tahaf* (seed very much like sesame) is raised in addition to these other crops.

Throughout the year the Arab farmer borrows on the basis of the crops of the following year; accordingly, the crops are always utilized for the payment of debts. The Jewish villager served the Arab farmer all year long in any number of handicrafts, such as cobbling, tailoring, smithery, carpentry, and other such skills, and received payment at the time of the harvest. On occasion the Jew would make an arrangement with the gentile whereby the Jew would undertake to perform all necessary forms of labor for him with the understanding that he would receive as payment a certain proportion of the annual crop, regardless of the extent to which the gentile farmer had made use of the Jew's services. Other arrangements also obtained whereby the Jew was to be paid only in accordance with the amount of work which he performed, the amount being reckoned as a debt until harvest time, when payment would be made from the crop itself. Each Jew earned his livelihood by maintaining such a working relationship with several gentiles.

The Jew was called by the Arab "*usta*,"

i.e., "expert." For any matter of consequence, one repaired to "*al-usta*." If the Jew was known by name, his name was appended to the title and he was addressed, for example, as "*al-usta* Yusuf." If his name was unknown he was addressed simply as "*al-usta* Salim." The latter name was the one given to any Jew who was not known personally. A Jew who was totally unknown was addressed by gentiles as "*usta*." Jews dwelling in villages also served as astrologers and fortune-tellers as well as domestic and family counselors.

Viticulture is an important segment of agriculture here. Part of the crop was sold to Jews for the production of wine and beer, whereas the rest was sold as food or for the making of raisins, either for local consumption or for export.

Most Arab farmers own their own land, while the minority are tenant farmers. In more recent years the number of tenant farmers rose, owing to the fact that the title to many farms was transferred to *bait al-mal* (the state treasury) in payment of taxes and tithes which landowners owed to the state. Official appraisers coming to evaluate the annual crop at harvest time were received upon their arrival by the local *shaikh*, whose advice was usually followed in the evaluation of the harvest. Any man who had displayed recalcitrance and defiance toward the government found his crops appraised at an exorbitant value; a field which would normally be expected to produce one hundred qadah would be appraised as productive of two hundred, thus doubling the tithe which the farmer would have to pay. In that way, he was progressively impoverished from year to year until he was totally crushed. This was how difficult persons were dealt with until they were liquidated automatically. Of course, this paved the way for the corruption of *shaikh's* and appraisers by limitless bribes. Those unable to pay their taxes in accordance with the rate at which their crops had been appraised were not pressed for immediate payment. Instead, they were given extensions and their taxes reckoned as a debt, which, of course, increased from year to year until one's debt amounted to the value of his landholding. At that point the man involved would be brought to trial, and in view of the fact that he would be unable to pay, having been progressively impoverished, his property would be confiscated and transferred to the state treasury.

Most villagers do their work and attend to their affairs in the morning hours. The afternoon hours are dedicated to the smoking of narghilas and to the chewing of qat [see p. 326, above]. The inhabitants of a small town or village usually gather for the qat hour at the *shaikh*'s or *'aqil*'s, where they spend the afternoon hours. Very few persons work during the afternoon, except during the seasons of plowing and harvesting, when the whole day is spent in work. All members of the village behave as members of one family and follow a uniform schedule. They are, accordingly, to be found together every day for many hours and spend their time in groups. The subjects of conversation in these gatherings are matters pertaining to plowing, planting, women, and general gossip.

Currency is referred to in Yemen by the inclusive name of *zalat*. The largest and most serviceable is the Maria Theresa *riyal* [dollar] which is called *rial faransi*. The *rial* is made of forty *buqsheh*. The smallest coin is a quarter of a *buqsheh*. This is a local coin with no impression on it except for the legend on one side, "There is no God but Allah and Muhammad is the apostle of God. Minted in San'a in the year . . ." and on the other side the legend "Yahya ibn Muhammad, whom God gave victory in the year 22, prince of the believers, who trusts in God the master of the universe." Yemen has no banks, and every man keeps all his money in his own house. The best way to guard funds is to hide them as our rabbis of blessed memory said, "The only way to safeguard funds is to hide them underground" (Babylonian Talmud, Baba Mezia 42a). The transfer of currency outside of Yemen is effected by means of exchange between exporters and importers or by purchase of a check from the government in the capital city of San'a to be sent to governmental agents in Aden or in Hodaida, the port cities and centers of foreign trade. Funds themselves are also transferred as shipment on the backs of asses as far as Aden. However, merchandise is shipped to the interior of Yemen by camel, which is a far cheaper conveyance.

JEWISH OCCUPATIONS

The Jews of Yemen were engaged in many different types of occupation. Indeed, one might say that apart from a small number of Jews who derived their livelihood from petty trade such as shopkeeping and salesmanship of various types (major merchants and wholesalers were very rare among Jews), the vast majority of them were craftsmen. What is more, for the most part they bequeathed their crafts to their children and their children did the same to their children, and so on for generation after generation. Very often the name of a particular trade became associated with the whole family of the man engaged in it, or indeed displaced his family name. In the following chapter we shall list the various crafts in which Yemenite Jews were engaged by name and type. However, first we should like to describe in detail the craft of the goldsmith, which was particularly characteristic of the occupations of Yemenite Jews. Indeed a number of Yemenite Jewish scholars and rabbis were engaged in that pursuit. With the craft of goldsmithery there were associated a number of skills in the workmanship of hard and soft metals which were supplementary to the craft of the goldsmith, or which were quite within the purview of the smithery trade itself.

The prevalence of smithery and the various crafts in metal associated with it can be explained in several ways:

1. It stands to reason that the ancestors of the Jews of Yemen, who, according to one tradition, came of their own accord or were brought during the reign of King Solomon[1]

[1] There are, to be sure, variant traditions, among them one which states that the Jews came to Yemen toward

were selected particularly from the crafts-men in metalwork in general and from among the silver- and goldsmiths in particular. Inasmuch as these people be-queathed their skills to their children generation after generation, we find them engaged in these crafts down to our own days, even as their ancestors had been.

2. These occupations more than others enabled them to work at home, near their hearth and their families. As a result, they were able to apportion regular hours for the study of Torah and for prayer in the same synagogue or the same house of study which they customarily attended, to partake of their meals along with all of their house-hold, and finally to maintain a careful watch over the way of life of their sons and daughters and teach their sons religion along with handicraft, thus making them partners in the task of maintaining the house and in the regulation of the way of life of the family.

3. These occupations, like trade, were considered most respectable, whereas other handicrafts were considered less honorable.

The Jews of Yemen were especially sensitive about their honor and about the genealogy of their families, not only with respect to their station in the Jewish community but also as far as the gentile community was concerned. The occupation of the Jew established not only his pedigree, since he was often addressed as "X the son of Y, the goldsmith son of a goldsmith,"

but also served to establish his honor and station in the eyes of the gentile who required his manufactures. The gentile invariably treated the more skilled worker with greater respect and always addressed him with the honorific form of address reserved for the Jew, "*usta*," or "craftsman." If a gentile came to a Jew to purchase silver and gold ornaments for himself or his wife and found these ornaments to be pretty, thus moving him to have full confidence in the Jew with regard to the work of silver or gold, he would obviously be warmly predisposed and would treat the Jewish artisan with great respect. This was not the case when he came to buy a pair of shoes from a Jewish cobbler or in similar situations.

The occupation of the smith was con-sidered most respectable especially because it required great intelligence and expertise, and, what is more, considerably more judgment than was necessary in other handicrafts. Because of all these character-istics many families clung to this trade and would not relinquish it, even in times of economic depression, when there was obviously no market for their produce, such as in the days of drought or war when neither the heart nor pocket are inclined toward the acquisition of silver and gold jewelry. These men, as we indicated, bequeathed their skills to their children. Indeed the members of families who were engaged in other kinds of occupations and who wished to improve their social station —we emphasize their *station* and not necessarily their livelihood— sent their children to become apprentices in the workshops of renowned smiths. . . .

the end of the days of the Second Temple. However, the tradition which attributes the arrival of the Jews to the days of the destruction of the First Temple was par-ticularly widespread among the Jews of Yemen.

CHAPTER 8

Railway Project in Yemen, 1909–1912

The first railway line built in the Arabian peninsula was the 1,465-kilometer Hijaz Railway linking Damascus with Medina, which was completed in 1908 (see Part IV, chap. 4). Projects were considered for extending it to Mecca and Jidda, and some preliminary surveying was begun (see Part V, Chap 4), but no actual construction was done. During the First World War the line was blown up in several places by the Arab forces, with technical assistance from T. E. Lawrence, and since the early 1920's the section south of Ma'an has been out of use. Various schemes for reconstructing the railway have been studied in the last few years, and in 1963 a £10 million contract was awarded for this purpose by the governments of Saudi Arabia, Jordan, and Syria.

The second line was built in 1915 to facilitate British military operations against the Turks in the vicinity of Aden. It connected that town with Lahj, 42 kilometers away, and in 1918 was extended by a few kilometers to Habil, but in 1936 traffic was suspended.[1] The only railway now in operation—the Dammam-Riyad line—was completed in 1951. Its length is 560 kilometers and its cost was $52.5 million.

The following selection describes the attempt to build a railway in Yemen shortly before the First World War. The line was no doubt designed for military purposes as it would have helped the Turks keep Yemen under control. But it would also have opened up the richest part of the country and have greatly promoted its economic development. The 200-mile line, together with some simple port works at Ras al-Katib, designed to give "five-fathom anchorage to a dozen vessels, beside providing a stone quay where three such vessels could tie up and discharge simultaneously," were estimated to cost £2 million. By the time work was suspended in 1912, about £500,000 had been spent, including the cost of imported materials, and five miles had been laid down.[2]

Earlier the Turks had built a road between Hodaida and San'a. "This, however, is of more strategic than commercial value, for its surface and gradients forbid

---

[1] Apelt, *Aden*, p. 110; Great Britain, Naval Intelligence Division, *Western Arabia*, p. 537.
[2] Bury, *Arabia Infelix*, pp. 127–28.

ordinary vehicular traffic, and even camel caravans avoid its mountain passes, preferring longer but less arduous routes."[3] Between 1902 and 1908 stone jetties and a breakwater were built at Hodaida, at a cost of £14,000. "After the moles were constructed it was found that the water was not deep enough to allow loaded lighters to come alongside, so the stevedores have to wade, and merchandise for shipment, or just landed, is dumped down on the beach. Large vessels anchor about 2½ miles off in four fathoms; merchandise is transferred in native craft."[4] In 1892–96 an average of 125 steamers aggregating 85,000 tons and 455 sailing ships aggregating 11,000 tons called at Hodaida.[5]

With very minor improvements the transport system of Yemen remained unchanged until the early 1960's, when the Soviets completed port installations at Hodaida, the United States laid a main road linking Ta'izz, Mokha, and San'a, and the Communist Chinese built another road between San'a and Hodaida.

(See also works by Hecker, Schmidt, Saint-Yves, and Lawrence, and Great Britain, Admiralty War Staff [*Handbook of Arabia*] listed in the Bibliography.)

[3] *Ibid.*, p. 126.
[4] Great Britain, Admiralty War Staff, *A Handbook of Arabia*, p. 171.
[5] Verney and Dambmann, *Les Puissances étrangères dans le Levant*, p. 391.

[From A. Beneyton, "Mission d'études au Yemen," *La Géographie*, XXVII, No. 4 (October, 1913), 200–204; reproduced by kind permission of the Société de Géographie de Paris.]

One of the first signs of interest the new regime in Turkey showed in technical and financial collaboration with France was the concession granted to a French group for a railway in Yemen. In August, 1909, the Ottoman parliament ratified the convention concluded between the Imperial Ottoman government and the French group for the study, construction, and exploitation of a railway between Hodaida and San'a, with branches, and of a port on the Bay of Jabana which would serve as its terminus. The consulting engineer of this group, Mr. A. Zaborowski, under whom I had already served twice, in Turkey and in China, had suggested my name as director of studies as early as February, 1909. I was asked to direct the work of the first study mission, which lasted from August, 1909, to June, 1910. The result was a project for a railway starting at the Bay of Jabana, serving Hodaida, Bajil, and Ubal and reaching

San'a by the valley of the Siham and Farsl and through the lowest pass of the Sera chain at a height of 2,450 meters; from San'a the line was to be prolonged to 'Amran.

The Imperial Ottoman government approved the project as far as Ubal and requested that the line be prolonged to Hajileh, i.e., as close as possible to Manakha. It reserved for later consideration the section between San'a and 'Amran and entirely rejected the one passing through the Siham and Farsh, since it could not undertake to guarantee security and the exploitation of the line in those regions.

I was once more, in January, 1911, put at the head of a second study mission, which was assigned the task of finding a passage through the region of Ta'izz, passing through an area which was at once quieter and richer. The result of this second mission was the drawing-up of a scheme which, starting in Hodaida, served the richest and most important centers of Yemen: Bait al-Faqih, Zabid, Hais, Ta'izz, Ibb, Yarim, Dhamar, and Ma'bar [and from there to San'a]. This project was satisfactory to the government, to the natives, and also to the

French group in charge of construction and exploitation. In this scheme the Serat chain was to be crossed by the pass of Fijre Gaitan, at a height of 3,000 meters. The profile of the projected line did not show gradients higher than 25 millimeters per meter nor radii below 100 meters—in other words it was the profile of a first-class, though mountain, railway. . . .

A beginning was made on building the projected railway after the issue, in 1911, of an Ottoman loan designed to cover the costs of construction of the Jabana-Hajileh portion and of the port of Jabana. Work was interrupted in February, 1912, by the blockade imposed by the Italian naval forces on the coast of Yemen. This blockade inflicted no damage on Ottoman power and brought no benefit to the Italians, but it seriously hurt the private interests of fishermen, traders, and the builders of the railway. . . .

CHAPTER 9

The Nomad Economy

The following selection describes, with the usual Marxist slant, what may well have been the first major, and was certainly by far the most important, change in the economy of the nomads and semi-nomads of northern Arabia during the last two or three thousand years. This resulted from the slow but relentless pressure exercised by increasing government control around, and in, northern Arabia; competition from overseas suppliers of livestock products; and the development of mechanical transport (see Part V, Introduction). All these trends have continued, at an accelerating rate, down to the present.

Information on the number of persons living in northern and central Arabia is even scantier than that on other parts of Arabia (see Part V, chap. 6). Palgrave provides a "numerical list taken partly from the government registers of Riad, partly from local information, and containing the provinces, the number of the principal towns or villages, the population, and the military contingent, throughout the Wahhabee empire."[1] This shows 316 settlements, with a population of 1,219,000, of which 72 and 260,000, respectively, were in the eastern provinces of Hasa and Qatif. To this Palgrave adds "the Bedouin population, a much diminished element of Central Arabia," totaling 76,500. Elsewhere he puts the population of the Jauf province at 40,000–42,000 and that of Hayil at 20,000–22,000.[2] It should, however, be added that serious doubts have been cast on the accuracy of Palgrave's account.[3]

Two extracts from Burckhardt's *Notes on the Bedouins and Wahabys* (pp. 69, 72) shed further light on the nature of the nomad economy, and the economic stratification within the tribes.

An Arab's property consists almost wholly in his horses and camels. The profits arising from his butter enable him to procure the necessary provisions of wheat and barley, and occasionally a new suit of clothes for his wife and daughters. His mare every spring produces a valuable colt, and by her means he may expect to enrich himself with booty. No Arab family can exist without one camel at least; a man who has but ten is

[1] Palgrave, *Narrative of a Year's Journey through Central and Eastern Arabia*, II, 83–85.
[2] *Ibid.*, I, 61, 103.
[3] See H. St. J. Philby, *Arabian Days* (London, 1948), p. 167.

reckoned poor: thirty or forty place a man in easy circumstances, and he who possesses sixty is rich. I do not, however, make this statement as applicable to all the Arabs: there are tribes originally poor, like the *Ahl Djebel* Arabs; among whom, from the possession of ten camels, a man is reckoned wealthy. Some sheikhs of the Aenezes have as many as three hundred camels. . . .

The richest sheikh lives like the meanest of his Arabs: they both eat every day of the same dishes, and in the same quantity, and never partake of any luxury unless on the arrival of a stranger, when the host's tent is open to all his friends. They both dress in the same kind of shabby gown and messhlakh. The chief pleasure in which the chief may indulge, is the possession of a swift mare, and the gratification of seeing his wife and daughters better dressed than the other females of the camp.

This may be supplemented by a family budget[4] for "an Arab in easy circumstances. . . . He said that in ordinary years he consumed:

	Piastres
Four camel-loads of wheat	200
Barley for his mare	100
Clothing for his women and children . .	200
Luxuries as coffee, *kammerdin*, *debs*,*, tobacco, and half a dozen lambs . .	200
	700

(about 35 or 40 pounds sterling)

* Kammerdin, dried apricot jelly from Damascus—Debs, a sweet jelly made of grapes."

A more typical family budget, estimated by Auhagen[5] in 1905 for Syrian desert tribesmen, shows total expenditure at 402.50 francs, of which 240 were for food, 70 for tobacco, coffee, sugar, and candies, and only 17.50 for clothing.

The deterioration caused by the changes described below was sharply reversed by the development of the oil industry in eastern Arabia. By the late 1950's the Arabian American Oil Company alone estimated that it had employed, in the course of its operations, over 100,000 Saudi Arabs. By the early 1960's Aramco's wage rates for Arab labor had reached the West European level. And the hundreds of millions of dollars received each year by the various governments of Arabia from the oil companies have led to the development of many branches of the economy and are providing great opportunities for employment. Thanks to oil, the transition from a traditional to a modern economy is being greatly accelerated.

(See also works by Philby, Burckhardt, Musil, Palgrave, Lawrence, Twitchell, and Issawi and Yeganeh, and Arabian American Oil Company [*Handbook*] listed in the Bibliography.)

[4] Burckhardt, *op. cit.*, p. 20.
[5] Auhagen, *Beiträge zur Kenntnis der Landesnatur und der Landwirtschaft Syriens*, p. 40.

[A. I. Pershits, "Khozyaistvenny byt kochevnikov saudovskoi Aravii" ("The Economic Life of the Nomads of Saudi Arabia"), *Sovietskaya Etnografia* (Moscow), I (1952), 104–12.]

Saudi Arabia, extending over the entire northern and central desert of the Arabian peninsula, was known only twenty years ago as one of the classic regions of nomadic livestock raising, and to a lesser extent for oasis farming. In the 1930's, Saudi Arabia also became known as an oil country, an arena of unrestrained expansion for American oil monopolies which seized the country. In these circumstances the economic life of the population of "the country of sand and oil" is particularly interesting, and indicative of the manner in which the United States spread imperialism in its colonies and semi-colonies.

In the late nineteenth and twentieth centuries, up to the First World War, no less than two-thirds of the population of what is now Saudi Arabia was engaged in nomadic animal husbandry. Camel drivers predominated among the nomads and, unlike the semi-settled sheep herders of Iraq, Syria, and Palestine, were named beduins in Arabia, i.e., "dwellers of the desert." The Arabian dromedary, which was at the very basis of the beduin economy, was utilized by the beduins in the most diversified manner. Camel milk and meat were used for food, hair for outer clothing and sacks, hide for footwear and reins, dung for fuel, and even urine was used for washing and medicinal purposes. The annual sale of camel offspring made it possible for the beduins to buy grain, dates, and handicraft wares from the towns. But many beduins lived almost exclusively on camel's milk, fresh or sour.[1]

At the same time, until the First World War, the camel was the sole means of transport not only for the beduins but also for numerous trade caravans and those of the pilgrims. This allowed the beduins to hire themselves out as guides and lease their animals and, most important, created an extensive market for camels. The purchase of camels was handled by the 'Uqail, an ancient, widespread corporation of camel traders, centered in Baghdad, with representatives in nearly every large tribe.

The place held by camels in beduin life is illustrated by the fact that their classification into age and sex and quality includes more than 100 terms and by the fact that the

words "camel" and "beauty" originate from the same root. Unfortunately exact figures on camels in the beduin economy date only from the beginning of the nineteenth century: 300–400 in a sheikh's herd; 60 for a wealthy nomad; 30–40 for a well-to-do person; and 10 for a poor man.[2] Bourgeois authors at the end of the nineteenth century and the beginning of the twentieth, ignoring the stratification of property among the beduins, give only average figures: 50 camels per household for the Anizah beduins,[3] 20 for the Shararat and Huwaitat beduins.[4]

Beduin livestock raising is bound up with seasonal migrations in search of pastures. Almost all beduin tribes had three quarters: winter, spring, and summer. In winter, during the rainy season, the desert waste of the Arabian peninsula grows verdant especially with *khadda*, a reddish bush with pulpy green leaves, rising 1.5 meters above the ground. This is the camels' favorite forage, and during a heavy rain season they often overfeed and become sick, so that the herders have to muzzle them. The damp, green fodder permits the camel to go without water for as long as three or four weeks. People use camel's milk to make up for the lack of water, as a result of which beduin tribes are not dependent upon springs for their water supply during the winter season. In spring (April–May) the green pastures are scorched by the sun. The camel needs to be led to a water hole approximately every fourth day, and the tribe moves to its spring quarters in the proximity of temporary pools or to an artificial reservoir. The reservoirs, more often than not, are hewn from stone and are a few meters deep; often they are large underground reservoirs, accessible by well and ladder. When these water supplies are finally exhausted, the tribe moves on to its summer quarters where a permanent supply of water is available in the farm zone. The

[1] Euting, *Tagebuch einer Reise in Innerarabian* (Leiden, 1896), I, 94; A. El-Aref, *Beduin Love Law and Legend* (Jerusalem, 1944), p. 172.

[2] J. Burckhardt, *Bemerkungen über die Beduinen und Wahaby* (Weimar, 1831), p. 56.
[3] Ch. Grant, *The Syrian Desert* (London, 1937), p. 21, *Handbook of Arabia* (London, 1920), p. 50.
[4] *Handbook of Arabia*, p. 61.

beduins remain here during the two dryest months, July and August. The camels graze on the outskirts of the steppe regions and, according to ancient custom, on the peasants' harvested fields. Here the beduins sell their camel produce and stock up on grain, dates, and other indispensable goods. With the first autumn rains (end of August, beginning of September) the tribes return to the desert and the cycle repeats itself.[5]

The way of life among the nomadic beduin tribes in central Arabia, about which little is known, appears to be somewhat different. Here climatic conditions differ: both subtropical winter and tropical summer rainfalls prevail on the latitude of Mecca, and further south the latter prevail.

Moving along the traditional, strictly observed route, the larger beduin tribes in Arabia crossed the vast desert wasteland. These migrations by the Suba'a group of the Anizah tribe covered 1,200 kilometers at the beginning of this century; the Ruwala and Amarat of the Anizah tribe covered even greater distances.[6] This type of migration greatly hampered the beduins in raising other forms of livestock. Sheep and goats cannot survive long without water, and so the beduins could not take them into the desert. That is the reason why beduins, as a rule, did not raise livestock other than camels and were even obliged to buy material from sheepherders for tents, which are made from goat, not camel, hair. The number of horses was also small among nomadic beduins. The horse was used only for riding purposes and was considered a symbol of the not inconsiderable wealth of its owner.[7] Until the First World War the beduins did not practice agriculture. Referring to the large beduin tribes of Anizah in northern Arabia, an official

British handbook states that even in 1920 "the plough had not touched a single inch of their territory."[8] Exceptions could be found among the ruling clique of the tribes, the sheikhs, who often owned fertile tracts of land, palm tree groves, and sometimes entire oases, as for example the Jauf oasis, owned by the sheikhs of the Ruwala, of the Anizah tribe.[9] In some cases these lands were the personal property of the Sheikhs. In others they were considered to be the collective property of the beduin clan or tribe, but in fact they always belonged to the Sheikhs. However, in all cases the land was cultivated, during the period described, not by ordinary beduins, who minded the livestock, but by the sheikhs' Negro slaves, emancipated slaves, or tenant *fellahin*. Such a system existed in the first two decades of this century among the Anizah tribes of Awlad Sulaiman and Ruwala,[10] the Suba'a Beduins of Najd,[11] the Shammar beduins,[12] and others.

As already noted, the beduin camel raisers made up the great majority of all nomadic livestock raisers in northern and central Arabia. Semi-nomadic sheep herding, which was widespread in Syria, Iraq, and Palestine, did not develop significantly in Arabia owing to the absence of grass pastures and meager water resources. However, here too could be found some semi-nomadic sheep raisers (in Najd, Jabal, Shammar) and goat raisers (in the mountainous areas of Hijaz).

The economic life of semi-nomadic tribes combined nomadic livestock raising with more or less intensive cultivation of the land. Sheep and goats were the main livestock raised; they held the same position in the life of semi-nomads as did camels in that of the beduins. Cattle was not raised in the majority of tribes. The number of camels was small; sometimes there were

[5] A. Shcherbatov and S. Stroganov, *Kniga ob arabskoi loshadi* [Book on the Arabian Horse] (St. Petersburg, 1909), p. 52, A. Musil, *The Manners and Customs of Rwala Beduin* (New York, 1928), p. 338.

[6] A. Boucheman, "Matériaux de la vie bédouine Sbaa," *Documents des Etudes Orientales*, IV, 8.

[7] C. Guarmani, *Northern Najd* (London, 1938), p. 16; *Arabia*, p. 68; K. Raswan, *Im Lande der schwarzen Zelten* (Berlin, 1934), p. 151.

[8] *Handbook of Arabia*, p. 46.

[9] Musil, *op. cit.*, p. 58.

[10] *Arabia*, pp. 67, 81; cf. C. Guarmani, *op. cit.*, p. 82.

[11] H. St. J. Philby, *The Heart of Arabia* (London, 1922), I, 171.

[12] R. Montagne, "Contes poétiques bédouins," *Documents des Etudes Orientales*, V, 38, 115.

none at all. Stolid Arabian donkeys and mules were used for transportation purposes. There were horses, in larger quantity than among the beduins, but of poorer stock. Migrations took place only in winter, during the season of heavy rains. The herders took their livestock into the desert for a few months, driving the herds from one water hole to another. The distance traveled never exceeded 200–300 kilometers; some tribes and clans with smaller herds, and limited in their possibilities of pack transport, roamed up to 20 kilometers away. Remaining in places with permanent water supplies for the greater part of the year, hence in places suitable for farming, most sheepherders combined livestock raising with cultivation of the soil. In the fall, before moving to winter pastures, they tilled and sowed a small tract of land, which was guarded by a few families left behind. Large tracts of land were owned only by the heads of tribes, who used freed Negro slaves, tenant *fellahin*, and impoverished members of the tribes to till the land.[13]

Depending on the ratio of animal husbandry to crop cultivation, semi-nomads can be divided into two groups: Shawia ("scattered," "separated") and Ra'ia ("herd"). Sheep raising (less frequently goat raising) was at the core of the Shawia economy, while farming was of secondary importance. The Shawia had large herds, strictly adhered to nomadic traditions, lived all the year round in woolen tents, and did not have any permanent lodgings even in the summer grounds. Their rather limited agrarian culture consisted only of cereal crops: barley, rye, and wheat. The Ra'ia consisted of tribes which concentrated on farming rather than on livestock herding. A characteristic of theirs was the maximum cultivation of arable land, diversified crops, a narrow radius of migration, and the replacement of the camel for transport

purposes by the donkey or mule. They kept an insignificant number of sheep and goats but this was partly compensated by the presence of cattle and poultry. The Ra'ia used tents no more than two or three months out of the year; the rest was spent in permanent constructions: mud houses or huts made out of straw or palm leaves.[14] It is necessary, however, to note that not all semi-nomadic tribes can be identified with either the Shawia or the Ra'ia. The way of life in many north Arabian tribes varied to such an extent that some were of the Shawia type, others of the Ra'ia, and still others led a sedentary life.[15] This economic heterogeneity within the same tribe thus corroborates Marx's words that "one can establish a correlation in all eastern tribes between a settled way of life on the one hand, and on the other, a nomadic life which goes back to the beginning of history itself."[16]

The basic traits of the economic life of nomadic livestock raising tribes, as described above, were typical of the overwhelming majority of peoples in northern and central Arabia up to the second decade of this century. That this situation prevailed despite the millenary process of settling of nomads in the Arabian peninsula can be explained by two facts. The first, and in our opinion the most important, reason was the lack in northern and central Arabia of any significant water supply; hence, those nomadic tribes which took up goat raising and later settled down to farming had to move to neighboring regions of the peninsula, namely Syria and Iraq. This is borne out by the historical dispersion of Arabian tribes, which shows an invariable trend from south to north, from Arabia to the Syrian desert and southern Mesopotamia. A specific example is the history of the Bani

13 *Arabia*, pp. 68, 74; Musil, *op. cit.*, p. 44; cf. El-Aref, *op. cit.*, p. 23; A. Boucheman, "Notes sur la rivalité des deux tribus moutonnières—Mawali et Hadedijjin," *Revue des Etudes Islamiques*, VIII (1934), 31, 46; *Review of the Civil Administration of Mesopotamia* (London, 1920), p. 21.

14 Musil, *op. cit.*, p. 44; cf. El-Aref, *op. cit.*, p. 22; M. F. Jamali, *The New Iraq; Its Problem of Beduin Education* (New York, 1934), p. 67.
15 I. Van Ess, *Meet the Arab* (New York, 1943), p. 65; cf. H. Field, *The Anthropology of Iraq* (Chicago, 1940), p. 27.
16 K. Marx and F. Engels, *Sbornik izbrannykh pisem* [Collection of Selected Letters] (Moscow-Leningrad, 1931).

Tamim[17] and Tai[18] tribes, the Mesopotamian Shammar[19] and the Anizah tribes of Awlad 'Ali, Fedaan, and Suba'a.[20] The second reason is the reverse process—repeatedly witnessed by a number of authors—that of switching over from a semi-settled and settled status to nomadic camel raising;[21] this is due to a shortage of fertile land, a breakdown in the irrigation system, or oppressive taxes. This reverse trend of "beduinization" neutralized, to some extent, the process of settling down, thereby justifying the relation noted by Marx between settled and nomadic modes of life.

The first significant blow to established relations was dealt in the nineteenth century, when the backward, naturally isolated countries of the Arabian peninsula were drawn into the world capitalist market and began to feel more strongly the competitive effect of capitalist livestock exports from Australia, Argentina, and the Union of South Africa. The slow breakdown of nomadic livestock raising was reflected in an increased gravitation of nomads toward the farming of land, but this propensity was not general, and did not reach the scale of a mass movement. The situation radically changed in the 1920's, when the gradual disintegration of livestock-raising economies became catastrophic.

The world agricultural crisis in the 1920's dealt a heavy blow to all the types of economies of the north Arabian tribes, but was especially shattering to the beduin camel raisers. After the First World War, the imperialist colonialists in the Near and Middle East, seeking to exploit captured markets and sources of raw materials to the fullest, while preparing

strategic lines and bases for a new world war, began building highways and later railways. Highways were constructed not only in Iran, Iraq, Turkey, Syria, Egypt, and so on, but along nearly all the ancient pilgrim-trade caravan routes in Arabia: Medina-Tabuk-Damascus, Jidda-Mecca-Riyad, Riyad-Kuwait, Riyad-Qatif, Jidda-Medina-Hail, Hail-Najaf, and others.[22] Already in 1923 the first highways which cut across the Syrian desert made it possible to complete in twenty hours a trip that had required thirty days by camel caravan, not to mention the fact that highway transport was a good deal cheaper. It is understandable that the thousand-year-old method of pack transportation could not compete with contemporary methods of transportation, and camel drivers were not only deprived of hiring their animals and escorting caravans, but were faced by an enormous fall in prices and demand for camels. Whereas, previously, the Baghdad 'Uqail bought camels in large numbers throughout northern and central Arabia, they now no longer found markets even for their own Iraqi camels. "Prior to the War," reported an inspector in Iraq, a British administered mandate, "there were good markets for Iraq's camels in Syria, Turkey and Persia, in addition to the large numbers required for transport purposes in Iraq itself. Since the War [many railways have been constructed throughout the Middle East] and the road systems of all countries have been greatly extended and improved. These roads are now well served by a large and increasing number of motor cars and lorries, which have to a very great extent taken the place of camel transport, thus practically removing the income to the Bedouins from their sale of camels."[23]

According to El-Aref a good pack camel in the Near East before the war cost 20–30 pounds sterling, 50–100 pounds during the war, and fell in the twenties to 3–6 pounds.

[17] *Hudud al-'Alam* (London, 1937), p. 146; D. Guarmani, *op. cit.*, p. 89; A. Musil, *The Middle Euphrates* (New York, 1927), p. 139.
[18] Montagne, *op. cit.*, p. 37.
[19] *Ibid.*, pp. 40–41.
[20] Guarmani, *op. cit.*, p. 90; *Handbook of Arabia*, p. 45; A. Musil, *Arabia Deserta* (New York, 1927), p. 116.
[21] Guarmani, *op. cit.*, p. 56; H. Sykes, "Journeys in North Mesopotamia," *Geographical Journal*, XXX, 250; Longrigg *Four Centuries of Modern Iraq* (Oxford, 1925); *Palestine and Trans-Jordan* (London), p. 40; Jamali, *op. cit.*, p. 37.
[22] A. Mac-Kie Frood, "Recent Economic and Social Developments in Sa'oudi Arabia," *Geographie*, XXIV, p. 164.
[23] Jamali, *op. cit.*, p. 63. [The words in square brackets were omitted, without indication, in the Russian text.]

The same was true of horse breeding. The price of a thoroughbred horse of average stock fell from 100 to 20 pounds.[24]

A critical evaluation of the tendentious information given above by the representative of the British administered mandate, who flagrantly exaggerates by listing mechanization of the means of transport under other imperialist colonialist "achievements," clearly reveals that under these new conditions the beduin camel-herding economy entered a stage of real crisis. The shattered nomadic economy could not be saved by the attempted transition from camel to sheep raising,[25] for the latter was also harshly affected in the 1920's by the world agricultural crisis.[26]

The economic crisis and the replacement of pack transport by automobiles was the essential factor in the disastrous disintegration of the nomadic livestock-raising economy of the north Arabian tribes, and in their massive striving toward sedentary agriculture. The policy of the new Saudi Arabian government, which united all the northern and central regions of Arabia in the 1920's, also played no small part in settling the nomads.

In 1921, the Amir of Najd, Abd al-Aziz Ibn Saud, once and for all disposed of his long-standing enemy and rival, the Amir of Jabal Shammar, and annexed his territory. In 1922 he took possession of the Jauf oasis, which had belonged to the Anizah tribes, and in 1924 captured the mountainous region of 'Asir. The conquest of Hijaz in 1926 transformed the then relatively small emirate into the kingdom of Hijaz, Najd, and its dependencies, which, in 1932, was renamed Saudi Arabia. The new kingdom covered a territory of one and half million square kilometers and, according to the most conservative figures, included a population of more than four million, two-thirds of which consisted of nomadic tribes[27]

ruled by insubordinate, separatist-minded, and almost independent tribal sheikhs. Collecting taxes from these "elusive beduins" was anything but easy, especially since the ruined miserable herdsmen not only wished to avoid payment but did not have the means to pay. Thus Ibn Saud, anxious to centralize his feudal kingdom and to build up a sizable royal treasury, had to begin by dealing with the dislocated economy which, owing to the acute nomadic economic crisis, meant transforming the nomads into sedentary farmers. The beduins, writes the Arab author Amin al-Rihani in a fit of overenthusiasm, "were the most difficult problem" confronting Abd al-Aziz. "He solved it in an original manner, along modern lines, and herein is Ibn Sa'oud The Sultan 'Aziz a reformer whose like Arabia has not seen since the days of the Prophet. . . . He would (1) conquer the Bedu, (2) make good Wahhabis of them, and (3) chain them to the soil."[28]

The first attempt to transform the beduins from pastoralists to crop cultivators was initiated by Ibn Saud as early as 1912, when the first *hijra* (Wahhabi agricultural community) was founded, on the basis of well irrigation, by the beduin tribe of Mutair. The experiment proved successful. Some other small *hijra*'s were formed by the 'Ujman and 'Ataiban tribes. But the extensive development of new lands and the reorientation of large beduin groups to farming was undertaken by Ibn Saud in the 1920's, and only owing to the abovementioned circumstances. A. Rihani, who visited Riyad in the late twenties, lists approximately sixty *hijra*'s organized by the Saudi government in various beduin tribes in Arabia.

Mutair *hijra*'s: Irtawia, Fraisan, Mulaih, al-'Imar, al-Ithla, al-Irtawi, Miska, al-Shib, Dhuraia, Qaria the Upper, Qaria the Lower, Sudair, Nukair, Imbayedh.
'Ujman *hijra*'s: al-Sirrar, Hunaiz, al-Sihaf, al-'Ujair, 'Uraira.
Banu Hajir *hijra*: 'Ain Dar.

[24] El-Aref, *op. cit.*, pp. 190–91.
[25] Raswan, *op. cit.*, p. 152.
[26] See Boucheman, "Notes," *loc. cit.*, pp. 43–45, and Jamali, *op. cit.*, p. 136.
[27] Mac-Kie Frood, *op. cit.*, p. 162; H. St. J. Philby, *Arabia* (London, 1930), p. 222.

[28] A. Rihani, *Ibn Sa'oud of Arabia, His People and His Land* (London, 1928), p. 191.

'Awazim *hijra*'s: Thaj, al-Hasi, al-Hannat, al-Afiq.

'Utaiba *hijra*'s: Gatgat, Dahna, as-Sawh, Sajer, 'Arja, 'Usaila, Nifai, 'Urwa, as-Sanam, ar-Rawda.

Hutaim *hijra*: Binwan.

Banu Murra *hijra*'s: Benak, Ubairiq.

Dawasir *hijra*'s: Mushairqa, Wusaita.

Qahtan *hijra*'s: Haiathim, Jufair, Hisat, al-Rayn the Upper, al-Rayn the Lower.

Harb *hijra*'s: Dukhna, Shubaiki, Dulaimia, Qurain, Al-Sadqa, Hulaifa, Hunaizal, Burud, Qibah.

Shammar *hijra*'s: al-Jafr, Rowd-al-'Uyun.[29]

The number of *hijra*'s multiplied in the early thirties with the further centralization of government in Saudi Arabia. In 1934 there were 140 *hijra*'s, half of which were centered on newly tapped water reserves. The first Irtawia *hijra* included 12,000 people at that time, and the total number of beduin sedentary farmers was 200,000. There was not one beduin tribe in Arabia that had not established one or several *hijra*'s and had not been converted, in greater or lesser degree, to farming.[30] Statistics on the growth of *hijra*'s are not available after 1934.

In converting beduins to a settled way of life by means of the *hijra* the Saudi Arabian government pursued primarily fiscal and military objectives. The inhabitants of a *hijra*, called *ikhwan*, or "brothers," were divided into three categories: the Wahhabi clergy or *mutawwa*'; the merchants; and the masses who were mostly farmers, but some of whom were also herdsmen in locations distant from the agricultural community, since many *hijra*'s had their own pastures. The latter two categories were in the military reserve and were classified into *jihad*, a regular armed demobilized force recruited from herdsmen, who were the first to be called up, and the merchant and farmer group who followed them.[31] The *ikhwan*, under the strong influence and the constant surveillance of

the *mutawwa*''s, were the most reliable taxpayers and military contingents in Saudi Arabia—relatively speaking, for Wahhabi propaganda did not prevent a large number of *ikhwan* from actively participating in the 1928–29 uprisings.

Thus, the feudal government of Saudi Arabia, acting in its own narrow class interests, converted a certain number of beduins to farming in the 1920's and 1930's. However, not all who sought to settle on land had the opportunity to do so. Owing to the scarcity of arable land, a very large number of beduins were obliged to continue camel husbandry. The mass impoverishment of the rank and file beduins, which coincided with the acute and intense feudal and tax oppression in centralized Saudi Arabia, led in the late twenties to a series of uprisings of beduin tribes against the government. Such was the nature of the uprising by the Harb tribe of the Hijaz in 1927 and the 'Ujman tribe of Hasa in 1929. The 1928–29 uprisings of the Mutair and 'Ataiban beduins of Najd were also of an anti-feudal nature, although these revolts were provoked by England, which exploited this "incident" to seize the neutral territory bordering Iraq.[32]

The uprisings of nomadic tribes were brutally put down by Ibn Saud, by massacring entire beduin clans, but no really radical steps were taken to improve the situation of the impoverished nomads. The rank-and-file nomads, who became poorer and poorer each year, fell *en masse* into bondage to their own sheikhs and feudal lords, and were transformed into semi-serf pastoralists and small tenant farmers. Another significant portion of impoverished nomads moved to industrial centers in the country in search of a living and fell into the clutches of imperialist monopolies which had long since gained entry into Saudi Arabia. . . .

[29] *Ibid.*, pp. 198–99.
[30] Mac-Kie Frood, *op. cit.*, p. 162.
[31] Rihani, *op. cit.*, pp. 194, 223; Mac-Kie Frood, *op. cit.*, p. 166.

[32] Rafik Musa, "Reformy v Gedzhase" ["Reforms in Hijaz"], *Musulmanskii mir*, 1928, No. 1, p. 55; E. Veit, *Araviia* (Moscow, 1930), pp. 81–82; cf. *Report by His Majesty's Government in the United Kingdom of Great Britain and Northern Ireland to the Council of the League of Nations on the Administration of Iraq for the Year 1939*, p. 34.

CHAPTER 10

International Economic Rivalries in the Persian Gulf, 1896–1914

The elimination of Portugal as the dominant power in the Persian Gulf was followed by intense political and commercial rivalry between the British and Dutch, but by the eighteenth century the former had established their supremacy. Attempts by the French to gain substantial influence, especially during the Napoleonic era, were fairly easily warded off. In the nineteenth century British control was so complete (see Part V, Introduction) that the Gulf could well be called an "Anglo-Indian lake."

Given Britain's political hegemony in the Gulf, its industrial, maritime, and financial leadership in the world, and the Gulf's traditional ties with India, it is not surprising that the British Empire dominated the trade of the region. As early as 1800 Malcolm had stated that the Gulf's trade was "mostly with India."[1] A hundred years later an estimate by Lord Lansdowne put the total trade of the Gulf ports, in 1901, at £3,600,000, of which £3,300,000 was accounted for by the British Empire.[2] Thus in Basra, at the beginning of this century, Britain and India took some 90 per cent of the exports and supplied three-quarters of the imports.[3] In Bahrein, in 1903, 83 per cent of exports went to the British Empire, which supplied 66 per cent of imports.[4] More generally, to quote a British commercial report (see Part V, chap. 2): "The bulk of the foreign trade of Oman, Bahrein, and the Arab coast of the Gulf is transacted through India, and is in the hands of British Indian traders, who obtain most of the manufactured goods they require from British shipping houses in Bombay." Britain's predominance in shipping was even greater, as is shown by the fact that all the steamers entering Bahrein and Dibai in that year were British, as were 96 per cent of those entering Basra.[5]

Toward the end of the century, France, Russia, and Germany made repeated, and increasingly successful, attempts to challenge the almost complete British monopoly. A French steamer service between Marseilles and Basra, inaugurated

[1] Lorimer, *Gazetteer of the Persian Gulf*, I, 165. See Part V, Introduction.
[2] Lorimer, I, 369.
[3] Saleh, *Mesopotamia*, pp. 194–202, 230–34.
[4] Bodianski, *Bakhrein*, p. 91.
[5] Lorimer, II, 246, 1440, and 805.

in 1881, had to be discontinued in 1885. "The line, though heavily subsidized by the French government, had carried principally British goods; and if British ship-owners had suffered its competition, British merchants had benefited by the lowering of its freights."[6] But, as related in the following selection, Russian and German attempts were more successful. More generally, the industrial and commercial efficiency of Germany, its increasing economic penetration of the Ottoman Empire (see Part II, chaps. 10 and 11, and Part III, chap. 9), and the growing imperial rivalries between Britain, Germany, and Russia, created an atmosphere in the Gulf in which the smallest incident was magnified to enormous proportions and was likely to produce grave diplomatic repercussions. After the First World War Britain retained a predominant, though steadily declining, position in the Gulf, but entry of the American oil companies, the growing economic competition from other European countries, Japan, and the United States, loss of control over the subcontinent of India, and the increasing nationalism and greater independence of most of the countries bordering on the Gulf have greatly reduced Britain's power in the region, both political and economic. However, it still exercises control over the eastern and southern coasts of Arabia.

(See also works by Wilson, Saleh, Sykes, and Lorimer listed in the Bibliography.)

[6] *Ibid.*, I, 1738.

[From Eugene Staley, "Business and Politics in the Persian Gulf: The Story of the Wönckhaus Firm," *Political Science Quarterly*, XLVIII (1933), 367–85; reproduced by kind permission of the editor.]

... At the time when the Wönckhaus firm commenced its activities the political interests of Germany were beginning to extend through Asiatic Turkey along the line of the proposed Baghdad Railway. This grandiose project for railway construction, planned and financed under the leadership of the *Deutsche Bank*, carried forward with the enthusiastic cooperation of the Kaiser and the German Foreign Office, hailed by German publicists (often to the annoyance of those in charge of its execution) as a potential threat to other powers, as well as a symbol of Germany's rising prestige, was the embodiment of German imperial ambitions. It carried the political interests of Germany toward the Persian Gulf, where they clashed with those of Britain.

As the Wönckhaus firm prospered and developed in this focal point of imperial policies it inevitably took on a political importance. The first recognition of this fact came from the Russians. About 1899 Russia decided to pay more attention to what was passing in the Persian Gulf ports. First she sent out travelers and warships, then opened consulates and trading posts, and soon organized a subsidized maritime service between Odessa and the Gulf.[1]

[1] Some details show the Russian zeal and methods. In 1899 Dr. Chevanowky began to practice medicine at Bushire. He treated free of charge the natives who came to see him, not forgetting to question them about local affairs. His inquiry finished, he returned to Russia. In 1900 several Russian travelers visited the Gulf, two of them sent by the Russian Trade and Navigation Company of Odessa, a high Russian delegation called on the Persian official in charge of the Gulf ports and islands, and Russian gunboats appeared. In 1901 a consulate-general was established at Bushire and a consulate at Basra. The Consul-general arrived in great pomp with two Mohammedan merchants who were Russian subjects; the aim was to set up a Russian consular and economic organization. There were no Russians there at the time, and the Russian business was at first carried on by a Dutch house, Hotz, which represented the Odessa company. In 1902 a director of a

Several governments were establishing consulates along the Gulf about this time, but that of Russia at Bushire was particularly pretentious and well equipped, although there were no Russians in the region. The Russian government was trying its best to construct out of whole cloth a commercial interest in the Gulf. Russia wanted to have interests which could be pointed to as justification for demanding that England discuss Persian Gulf questions with her. "An officer of the Russian Volunteer Fleet, Gorski," says Mr. Wönckhaus, "was sent into the region to build up a Russian trade. He was paid, of course, by the Russian government, and the whole campaign was a government enterprise. It failed, because from start to finish it was such an artificial construction. They shipped in sugar, for instance, for which there was no market, and most of the business they did was conducted at a loss." . . .

The English in the Gulf at the time, from the Political Resident down to the clerks of commercial houses, believed that the Wönckhaus firm was not merely an energetic business rival but a direct representative of German political imperialism. That its rapid expansion and prosperity were explained by a subsidy from Berlin was considered a matter of universal knowledge. According to Mr. Wönckhaus, the main circumstance which confirmed the English in their belief that he received a subsidy was his success in a number of business fields where their firms could not make a profit. It is not human nature to ascribe such a defeat to incapacity, and the natural reaction of his competitors was, "Well, of course, *he* can do business there—the German government makes up his losses. We can't expect to compete with a

subsidized firm." When Mr. Wönckhaus did not deny such stories—"and why should I deny them?" he asks, "for as long as they believed that there was no profit in my operations I had the field to myself"—the English trading and political community became sure of their truth.

"The real grounds for my success, which was inexplicable to the English except on the supposition of a subsidy, were simple enough," Mr. Wönckhaus relates. "My people and I worked harder than they. Often we would be hard at it in the office while they were out playing tennis, though I liked to play tennis, too, when I had the time. Sometimes we used to send telegrams at three o'clock in the morning in order to have answers the next afternoon. My market information from Europe was nearly always about a day ahead of that of other firms. I applied myself to the language and learned to speak Persian fluently. I maintained close contact with the natives and had native buyers gathering wheat and barley—our chief exports—in the cheapest markets, inland, not just along the coast. Furthermore, I think I knew my wares better than my competitors, for I had worked with them in Hamburg and was familiar with all the types and qualities. Finally, I was the chief of my own firm while the English commercial community was made up mostly of subordinates employed by firms with headquarters in London; I could make important decisions on the spot, adapt myself to new conditions, close a contract immediately, while they had to consult London." . . .

It was in 1906, partly at the instigation of Mr. Wönckhaus, that the Hamburg America Line actually established a regular service to the Persian Gulf. The Wönckhaus firm became the agent of the steamship company. The assertion is often encountered in English sources that the Hamburg America Line received a substantial subsidy from the German government for its Persian Gulf service, but this Mr. Wönckhaus denies categorically. "I was connected with all the negotiations, and I know for a certainty

Moscow bank came to study the territory, but no Russian bank dared to set up in southern Persia. In 1903 a regular steamship service was inaugurated by the Russian Trade and Navigation Company and continued until 1914. The Russian government allowed it 200,000 roubles yearly for four round trips between Odessa and Basra. The Russian consular service was also enlarged. (R. Vadala, *Le Golfe Persique*, published by *La Dépêche Coloniale et Maritime*, Paris, 1920. Vadala was consular officer of France in the Gulf.)

that there was not a single penny of subvention," he says.[2] The new line and the Wönckhaus firm handled shipments for the construction of a portion of the Baghdad Railway. . . .

In the eyes of English officials, anything undertaken by a foreign power or its nationals in the Persian Gulf had political importance. It is easy to understand, then, why they resisted with particular vigor every attempt by Germans to secure concessions which might have had the effect of settling them permanently on a bit of Gulf territory. The Koweit incident has already been alluded to. When the first intimations came that Germany might attempt to secure facilities at Koweit for a Persian Gulf terminus of the Bagdad Railway, and when rumors of a Russian railway concession from Tripoli in Syria to Koweit were abroad, the British government acted promptly. On January 23, 1899, a secret agreement was signed by the Sheikh of Koweit, who pledged himself to cede no territory and receive no foreign representative without the sanction of Her Majesty's Government. Subsequently a British cruiser thwarted an effort by the Sultan of Turkey, backed by Germany, to assert Ottoman sovereignty over Koweit, and the German government was informed that a terminus

on the Gulf could be had only on the basis of a previous understanding with Great Britain.[3]

Sometime later the Wönckhaus firm tried to obtain from an Arab Sheikh rights to pearl fisheries in the neighborhood of Bahrein; this was prevented by the English.[4] Thereupon the firm is said to have begun negotiations in Constantinople for pearl-fishing rights and for lease of Halul Island, a center of the industry. Again England intervened, fearing that the island might ultimately be used as a coaling station.[5] A third incident, which could easily have attained major importance, occurred on the island of Abu Musa.

An English firm, F. C. Strick and Company, had contracted for and was working a deposit of iron oxide on an island called Ormuz. Mr. Wönckhaus looked about and found a similar deposit, not quite as good, but worth working, on the nearby island of Abu Musa. The Sheikh of Shargah, whose territory it was, had conceded to three Arabs[6] the right to exploit the iron oxide of Abu Musa, and in 1906 two of them transferred their rights to the Wönckhaus firm, which then prepared to start operation. At this stage the Sheikh canceled the concession, influenced by the English,[7] who had a treaty dating

---

[2] Dr. Friedrich P. Seigart, of the *Institut für Weltwirtschaft und Seeverkehr*, Kiel, author of *Die Subventionen der Weltschiffahrt und ihre sozialokonomischen Wirkungen* (Berlin, 1930), informs the writer that the North German Lloyd received government aid but that the Hamburg America Line received no subsidies for any of its lines before the war.

Huldermann in his biography of Albert Ballin merely mentions the Persian Gulf line in passing and says nothing about a subsidy: the year 1906 "brought about the founding of a line to the Persian Gulf in cooperation with the growing German interests in that part of the world." (Bernard Huldermann, *Albert Ballin* (Berlin, 1922), p. 151.)

A study of state aid to shipping made by the U.S. Dept. of Commerce reports that, "The largest of the German lines, the Hamburg-American Line . . . has developed rapidly without government aid." "For a time it shared with the North German Lloyd a subvention paid for the carriage of mails to China and Japan, but the amounts received in this manner were small." (U.S. Dept. of Commerce, Bureau of Foreign and Domestic Commerce, Special Agent Series No. 119, *Government Aid to Merchant Shipping*, by Grosvenor M. Jones, 1916, pp. 23, 17.)

[3] *British Documents*, vol. I, pp. 333–34.

[4] The writer is informed by an Englishman of long experience in the Gulf that this action was taken on grounds of policy and that any such project, even by a British firm, would have been similarly quashed. "Modern methods" would have resulted in over-production and destruction of the industry, according to the official view.

[5] Cf. *Times History of the War*, vol. III, ch. 52; Franz Stuhlmann, *Der Kampf um Arabien zwischen der Türkei und England*, Hamburgische Forschungen, I. Heft, April, 1916; Sykes, *History of Persia*, vol. II, pp. 431–33. The writer is unable to find any mention of these incidents in the diplomatic archives published since the war. The following grossly prejudiced account from the *Times History of the War* is given to show how commercial activities may attain deep political significance in an atmosphere of chauvinist suspicion . . . .

[6] "Two of the men, father and son, resided at Lingah, and it is supposed that they applied for the concession on German instigation." (*Times History of the War, loc. cit.*)

[7] The Sheikh had nothing but negative opinions on such matters, which he did not understand, says Sir Percy Cox. He was open to persuasion by English or Germans.

from 1892 with him and other Arab chieftains to the effect that he would enter no relations with any government but Great Britain and would dispose of none of his land to any other power. The French vice-consul, Vadala,[8] writes that the red-oxide of Abu Musa would have made an ideal freight for the steamers of the Hamburg America Line, which arrived in the Gulf laden with construction material destined for the last section of the Bagdad Railway but lacked return cargoes. This was one reason why the English were determined to prevent Wönckhaus from exploiting the deposits. There may have been more weighty reasons, however, including the apprehension that if Abu Musa proved to be commercially valuable claims to sovereignty might be made by Persia.

The Wönckhaus firm took no notice of the Sheikh's revocation of the concession. In October 1907 the British warship *Lapwing* appeared at Abu Musa towing a number of sailing boats loaded with three hundred of the Sheikh's armed followers. The warriors disembarked, seized the workers employed by Wönckhaus, and removed them to Lingah. Two hours later, when a representative of Wönckhaus arrived, he was fired upon, but luckily not killed, by these same native warriors.[9]

There was a cry of indignation in the German press.[10] Mr. Wönckhaus protested to the German government, which passed on his protest to the British government through the Embassy in London. According to Mr. Wönckhaus, however, the German Foreign Office induced him to lower his claims for compensation below the amount to which he believed himself justly entitled, made his original protest much milder, and did not press the matter very energetically.[11] The question dragged on, was postponed and repostponed, until finally in 1914, some months before the outbreak of the war, the British government agreed in principle that Wönckhaus was entitled to compensation.[12] The determination of the actual amount was further postponed. Then the war came, and in the end Wönckhaus received no compensation at all.[13]

The checks administered to the Germans at Koweit, Bahrein, Halul, and Abu Musa did not discourage the "politico-com-

---

[8] *Op. cit.*

[9] Interview with Mr. Wönckhaus. Also: *Times History of the War*; R. Vadala, *op. cit.*; Franz Stuhlmann, *op. cit.*; Skyes, *op. cit.*

[10] "The *Cologne Gazette* was mild and said that the German purpose was commercial. The *Neuste Nachrichten*, rather more severe, spoke of the 'incomprehensible violation of German rights.' The *Berliner Tageblatt* grew a little violent, and announced that Great Britain was trying to undermine German prestige and to demonstrate her own supremacy. It said that the English 'seem to have had the intention to show Germany that she can do nothing in the Middle East without Great Britain's consent,' . . . declared that 'commerce and politics can no longer be divided,' and that Germany could only attain commercial success by 'energetic political action.' . . . The hubbub was reflected in the London press, but it soon ceased." (*Times History of the War*.)

[11] At the India Office in London the writer was informed that the papers on the Abu Musa affair and the Wönckhaus claim for compensation cannot be made available, but an official very kindly volunteered to look them through and to answer what questions he could without violating official discretion. His impression from a reading of the documents was that Germany had done everything proper in pushing the claim and had not been at all soft about it.

[12] This may have formed part of the general settlement of outstanding Anglo-German differences relating to the Bagdad Railway and other subjects which was negotiated on the eve of the war (letter to writer from von Kuhlmann, who was secretary of the German Embassy in London in 1914). Dr. von Kuhlmann says he remembers that the friction connected with the Wönckhaus firm formed a part of his diplomatic work from time to time, but he cannot recall the matter in detail, since a huge mass of such episodes passed through his hands.
The Abu Musa affair is not mentioned in the collection of *British Documents on the Origins of the War* nor in *Die Grosse Politik*.

[13] Interview with Mr. Wönckhaus. The India Office official who looked through the papers informed the writer that apparently some sort of compromise was reached just before the war, Mr. Wönckhaus claiming that he ought to have compensation at least for the iron oxide he had already mined and lost. This official agreed that to accept the version given by Mr. Wönckhaus and used above in the text "would not be far off the mark."
Sykes in his *History of Persia* is mistaken when he says that though there was a storm in the German press the position was too weak to be defended by the Berlin Foreign Office and was dropped after a formal protest. Likewise the *Times History of the War* comment that "the German case had not a leg to stand on" is inaccurate. The *Peace Conference Handbook* (No. 76, Persian Gulf) prepared by the Historical Section of the Foreign Office says that "the question was still unsettled on the outbreak of the war in 1914."

mercial" firm of Wönckhaus, writes the French vice-consul Vadala.[14] It turned its interest to the region of the Karun River and set up a steamboat service in competition with the English firm of Lynch Brothers which lasted until 1914.

On the whole, however, the Wönckhaus firm was reduced to occupying itself with commerce as such—the import and export business in the large ports of the Persian Gulf. It also had a river transportation service on the Karun and a maritime service from Hamburg to Basra, but it was never able to succeed with its special enterprises because the preponderant influence of the English with the Arab sheikhs always crushed the politico-economic plans of Wönckhaus, who, for that matter, was out not only to make money but also to supplant the prestige of the English.

Thus, continues this French observer, German dreams had to remain unfulfilled, and during the war all German influence was driven out of the Gulf by the British.

[14] *Op. cit.*, p. 36.

Wönckhaus himself maintains to the end that his actions in the Gulf were inspired purely by commercial, not by political, motives, and that the story widely believed in the Gulf and printed in some British newspapers to the effect that Germany was trying to get a footing on the island of Abu Musa which might serve as a sort of base for future German operations was all nonsense. Nevertheless, as it often happens in politics that beliefs, even if mistaken, are just as important as facts, the operations of the Wönckhaus firm actually acquired great political importance and did as much as any other factor outside of the Bagdad Railway itself to make the Persian Gulf "one of the principal theatres of British and German rivalry before the war."

The writer believes that we can accept Mr. Wönckhaus' version of his purposes and activities in the Gulf as substantially accurate. . . .

PART VI

Egypt

CHAPTER I

The Economic Development of Egypt, 1800–1960

The following selection is a survey of the economic history of Egypt since 1800, centered on the development of its foreign trade and ending just short of the socialist revolution of 1961–62. Although the revolution has completely transformed the institutions of the country, and noteworthy progress has been achieved in several fields, the resource patterns and the consequent difficulties discussed in the selection are basically unchanged.

(See also works by Crouchley [*Economic Development*], Arminjon, Fridman, and Issawi [*Egypt: An Economic ... Analysis* and *Egypt in Revolution*] listed in the Bibliography.)

[Charles Issawi, "Egypt since 1800: A Study in Lopsided Development," *Journal of Economic History*, XXI (1961), 1–25; reproduced by kind permission of the editor. Most of the footnotes have been omitted.]

One of the main points at issue between economists from advanced and those from underdeveloped countries is the role of foreign trade in economic development. The former see in the expansion of foreign trade the main motive power of development, while the latter pin their hopes on other sectors, notably manufacturing. The answer would seem to be that foreign trade is a necessary but not a sufficient condition of development. Economic growth of underdeveloped countries can be achieved most smoothly if they can build up a substantial export trade that is sufficiently closely linked to the rest of the economy to exert upon it some form of multiplier effect so that a rise in exports leads to a more general and diffused expansion. In other words, over a long period of development, foreign trade is the engine that provides the motive power, but this engine cannot move the economy unless it is provided with adequate transmission lines. Or, to change the metaphor, other branches of the economy can be vivified and developed by grafting on to them some of the capital created and the skills generated in foreign trade.

If this is so, it follows that economic growth can be retarded by one, or both, of two causes: insufficient expansion of exports, or isolation of the export sector from other sectors of the economy. Isolation may be due to one or more of several factors. The export sector may have been developed by foreign capital, and the income earned by that capital may be reinvested in the country of origin, making no further contribution to the economy of the producing country; in other words, the export sector may constitute a foreign enclave in the economy. Or else such income may accrue to a small number of wealthy residents of the producing country, who spend or invest it abroad, with the same result. Or the benefits of the growth of the export sector may be more widely diffused, but are dissipated in greater consumption (mainly of imported manufactured goods, locally produced food, and services) and thus once more fail to be reinvested in other sectors. Or finally, the export sector may have little backward linkage with the rest of the national economy, in that it purchases few inputs from other local industries; or forward linkage, in that only a small proportion of its output is taken up by other local industries. This is likely to occur if the export sector consists of primary production for foreign markets.

Some light may be shed on this subject by examining the historical experience of underdeveloped countries. It would seem that, in the course of development, most countries outside Europe and North America tend to pass through three stages: from a subsistence economy to an export-oriented economy and thence on to what, for lack of a better term, may be called a complex economy. It would also seem that, making allowance for certain frictional adjustments and lags, each of these stages is marked by higher real national income than the preceding one and, in most cases, by higher per capita income.

In a subsistence economy, primitive techniques are used in all sectors; the proportion of output marketed is small, since few branches produce a surplus and means of transport are poor; monetary transactions are few; and foreign trade plays a very minor part. The characteristic of an export-oriented economy is that one sector—usually some form of mining or the production of a specialized crop—is developed far more intensively than the rest of the economy, for purposes of export. This brings about a large increase in both the absolute and the relative importance of foreign trade in the economy and leads to an improvement of techniques in the export sector. To move the export product and handle the imports which are bought in return for it, a network of transport, commercial, and financial services is established, directed predominantly or exclusively toward foreign trade, but the rest of the economy remains largely unaffected by these developments. In some countries, for example the oil producers of the Persian Gulf, the gap between the export and domestic sectors is so great that one may even speak of a "dual economy."

A complex economy is characterized by the development of other sectors, notably manufacturing. At that stage, the use of progressive methods tends to be widespread in all sectors, though this does not, of course, preclude the persistence of pockets of underdevelopment, especially within agriculture. Production for the market, rather than for subsistence, becomes the rule in all sectors, and money replaces barter in all transactions. Transport, commerce, finance, research, and other tertiary activities now tend to serve the needs of the whole economy and not only those of the export sector. Lastly, exports and imports, though increasing in volume and value, may fall relative to the gross national product. Whether they do so depends on a number of factors; the size and population of the country, its natural resources, its level of development, and its particular pattern of growth.

Parallel to these developments, there occur important demographic changes. In the transition from a subsistence to an export-oriented economy, population grows fairly rapidly because of larger food supplies, improved transport, and, above all, better health. Urban populations increase and large towns, usually sea or river ports, develop. Little change takes place in the distribution of labor among primary, secondary, and tertiary industry; however, the proportion engaged in secondary industry may fall because the establishment of a few mechanized processing plants and factories is unlikely to offset the combined effect of the decline in the handicrafts and the growth of the total labor force. In the transition from an export-oriented to a complex economy, urbanization is accelerated. Total population continues to grow, but the rate of increase may slow down because of the effects on birth rates of urbanization and rising levels of living. Last, there is a sharp rise in the proportion engaged in secondary industry. The proportion engaged in tertiary industry may also increase, and there will be an important change in its composition; whereas in the first two stages it consists predominantly of petty traders, hawkers, porters, and domestic servants, in the third stage it will include large numbers of professional people and employees of "modern" transport, commercial, and financial establishments.

A word may be said about the social and political context of these changes. The transition from a subsistence to an export-oriented economy is accompanied by a breakdown of traditional feudal, communal, or tribal structures. The ties binding the individual to the village or tribe are gradually loosened or violently snapped, and labor becomes a mobile marketable commodity; similarly, land ceases to be the inalienable property of the group and becomes a commodity which can be bought and sold by individuals. This process continues during the transition from an export-oriented to a complex economy. As for the political framework, the first transition usually takes place either under direct foreign rule or at least under strong foreign political influence, while the second transition is accompanied by a nationalist revival and is usually carried out by a national government that enjoys either full independence or at least a great measure of autonomy.

Egypt's economic development during the past century and a half conforms to the general pattern described above but presents certain peculiarities which deserve attention. First, at the very beginning of this period, Egypt made an unsuccessful effort to leap from a subsistence economy directly to a complex economy. Following that failure, the transition from a subsistence to an export-oriented economy was consummated very swiftly. The passage from an export-oriented to a complex economy was greatly delayed, and has begun to gather momentum only in the last few years. This delay has resulted in the accumulation of severe difficulties, notably a rapid population growth, which are hampering the transition and may perhaps be overcome only by extra-economic measures.

II

The "Founder of Modern Egypt," Mohammad Ali (1805–49), attempted to effect a transition from the subsistence economy prevailing at the beginning of the nineteenth century [see Part VI, chap. 2] to a "modern" complex economy. In this he failed, but instead started Egypt on the road leading to an export-oriented economy. The methods pursued by him are very reminiscent of those used in the Soviet Union and elsewhere in the last forty years.

First, there was a revolution in the system of land tenure. Tax farming was abolished and peasants paid their taxes directly to the government; large estates, often of uncultivated land, were granted to relatives or followers of Mohammad Ali; and the prevailing method of communal ownership was replaced by one in which peasants enjoyed *de facto*, though not yet legally recognized, rights of ownership. [See Part VI, chaps. 3 and 4.]

Second, irrigation works were undertaken, which appreciably increased the land under cultivation and, what was more important, made it possible to produce valuable crops that require summer water.[1]

[1] It is difficult to determine the extent of the increase in cultivation. Al Hitta (*Al-zira'ah*, pp. 9 and 83) puts the cultivated area at 3,054,710 faddan in 1813, about 3,500,000 in 1835, 3,856,226 in 1840 and 4,160,169 in 1852. (A faddan is equal to 1.038 acres or 4,201 square metres.) On the other hand, Rivlin (*Agricultural Policy*, chap. ii) points out that during the French occupation (1798–1801) the cultivated area was 4,038,177 faddan and that by 1844 the area of village land, which probably included a small amount of uncultivated land, was 4,293,164 faddan, an increase of only 254,987; over the same period of time the amount of taxed land decreased

Third, the planting of long staple cotton was started on a commercial scale in 1821, and it found ready markets in Europe. By 1824, over 200,000 qantars of cotton were being exported, and in 1845 the figure of 345,000 was reached.

Fourth, communications were developed, mainly in order to facilitate foreign trade; especially notable were the improvement of the port of Alexandria and its linking by canal to the Nile. [See Part VI, chap. 7.]

Fifth, trade was conducted under a system of monopoly. Mohammad Ali bought crops from farmers at low fixed prices and resold them to foreign exporters at great profits. He also directly imported about two fifths of the goods brought into Egypt.

A similar monopoly was used to build up a modern industry. [See Part VI, chap. 5.] Machinery was imported from Europe, together with technicians, and by 1830 factories were turning out cotton, woolen, silk, and linen textiles, sugar, paper, glass, leather, sulphuric acid and other chemicals. A well-run foundry met the needs of the government armament plants and arsenal, and simple machinery and spare parts were produced. Investments in industrial establishments up to 1838 amounted to about £12 million. Some 30,000 to 40,000 persons worked in the factories, an impressive figure in a total population of 3 to 3.5 million, and the number engaged in handicrafts was considerably greater.[2]

The productive apparatus thus built up, with its very large bureaucracy, as well as the army and navy, required men trained in modern techniques. To meet this need, over three hundred students were sent to Europe, and several times as many studied in the newly opened schools of medicine, engineering, chemistry, accountancy, and languages and in the military and naval colleges.

In brief, Mohammad Ali was trying to carry out a program of forced industrialization. His success was due primarily to the administrative protection that he gave to his infant industries, which did not, however, outlive that protection. The capital required for establishing those industries was obtained from the profits of his monopoly of internal and export trade and from taxation [see Part VI, chap. 6] and forced loans, and the losses of industrial enterprises were covered from the same sources. The necessary unskilled labor was conscripted and paid low wages, while foreign technicians and skilled workers were attracted by high salaries. A market for the output of the factories was provided by the armed forces, by import substitution, and by displacing some handicrafts.

Other points of resemblance with recent programs of rapid development should be mentioned. First, the level of living of the population certainly did not rise, and more probably declined, as a result of Mohammad Ali's intensive and often mismanaged investment and of the consequent inflation; the hardships entailed by this and by militarization caused thousands to flee the country in spite of his efforts to seal the frontiers. Nevertheless, a very good case can be made for Mohammad Ali; perhaps unwittingly, but judging from some of his remarks quite possibly consciously, he was trying to lay the foundation for a balanced, diversified economy that in time would have greatly

by 400,862 faddan. Her conclusion is that "any improvements made by Mohammad Ali were qualitative rather than quantitative." Of course the two sets of figures can be reconciled on the very reasonable assumption that cultivation shrank greatly in the chaotic period following the withdrawal of the French troops.

[2] Estimates of Egypt's population at this period are unreliable and show considerable variations. Volney put the total in the 1780's at 2,300,000. For the year 1800, Jomard gives the figure of 2,489,000, and Chabrol that of 2,400,000; Jomard's estimate is discussed in Mahmoud El-Darwish, "Analysis of Some Estimates of the Population of Egypt before the XIXth Century," *L'Egypte contemporaine* (March, 1920); Chabrol's estimate is judged to be too low by Gibb (*Islamic Society*, I, 209). For 1821, Mengin gave a figure of 2,536,000. For 1836 Cadalvène gave one of 2,213,000; Duhamel one of 2,500,000; Clot one of 3,000,000; and Mohammad Ali one of 3,500,000. In 1840, Bowring

stated that the official estimate was 3,200,000 but that in "the opinion of the best informed" the number was from 2,000,000 to 2,500,000. In 1846 a census of houses showed a total of 4,543,000, but this figure is also not very reliable.

raised the level of living. Unfortunately, his prime interest was in building up a modern army and navy to safeguard his position and extend his influence. Hence, the compulsory reduction of his armed forces in 1841 following his defeat at the hands of the Great Powers, removed most of the incentive that had made him seek to industrialize Egypt. At the same time, the enforcement of the Anglo-Turkish Convention of 1838 [see Part II, chap. 3] permitted foreign traders to buy and sell anywhere within the Ottoman dominions, including Egypt. Simultaneously deprived of Mohammad Ali's protection and encouragement and exposed to the competition of European industry, his factories began to decline and did not survive his death in 1849.

The collapse of Mohammad Ali's schemes points out one of the major obstacles to economic development in Egypt, an obstacle that was not removed until the 1930's: the lack of political autonomy. Economic development usually requires considerable aid in the form of tariff protection, tax exemptions, rebates on transport rates, cheap power, special credit facilities to certain sectors, educational policies, etc., which only a government enjoying a large measure of political and fiscal independence can provide. Now except for a brief period when Mohammad Ali managed, by various subterfuges, to carry out his own economic policy, Egypt did not enjoy such independence until very recently. The tariff was fixed by conventions concluded between the Ottoman government and the Great Powers. No direct taxes could be imposed on foreigners without the consent of their government, because of the Capitulations. And, more generally, until 1882 the Egyptian government was subject to great international economic and financial pressures, and after that date it was under British control.

III

With the failure of Mohammad Ali's industrial plans and the abolition of his monopoly system, the first phase of Egypt's modern economic history came to an end. The attempted leap from a subsistence to a complex economy had failed, and instead the country had landed on the road leading to an export-oriented economy. Egypt could now be integrated, as an agricultural unit, in the world-wide economic system.

The extent of this integration may perhaps best be gauged by measuring the growth of Egypt's foreign trade. The first reliable figures refer to 1823 and put imports at £E. 656,000 and exports at £E. 1,455,000, giving a total of £E. 2,111,000. These figures probably represent an advance over the level attained at any time during the previous fifty years or more.[3] By 1838 the total value of trade had risen to £E. 3.5 million and by 1850 to £E. 3.7 million. In 1860 the total stood at £E. 5.1 million, in 1880 at £E. 21.8 million and in 1913 at £E. 60 million. If one assumes that at the beginning of Mohammad Ali's reign the value of trade

[3] For the year 1800, Bréhier gave the figures of £E. 269,000 for imports and £E. 288,000 for exports (as quoted by Crouchley, *Economic Development*, p. 266). In 1784, Volney (*Oeuvres* [Paris, 1825], II, 166) estimated Egypt's exports at not over 15 million livres (or £600,000) on the assumption that exports to France, which amounted to 3 millions, constituted at least one fifth of the total; according to him, Egypt's imports from France amounted to 2½ million livres. In this context, it is worth noting that Crouchley (*ibid.*, p. 269), apparently misled by Bréhier, quotes the figure of 15 million as representing total trade. Volney also reproduces a report prepared by the Chamber of Commerce of Marseilles putting French exports to Alexandria in 1784 at 2,311,637 livres and French imports at 2,465,630 livres (*Oeuvres*, II, 339–40). [See Part II, chap. 2.]

Masson, 1911 (pp. 595–99) gives the following figures for average annual French imports from Egypt: 1715–30, 2 million livres; 1730–43, 2 million; 1749–55, 2.5 million; 1764–69, 2.7 million; 1769–74, 3.56 million; then followed a decline because of anarchy in Egypt, and in 1787–89 the average was 2.68 million.

French exports to Egypt averaged 2 million until 1750, rose to over 3 million in 1764–76, and fell back to 2.76 million in 1787–89.

France was by far Egypt's most important trading partner among European countries. Raynal put Egypt's trade with France in 1776 at 7.1 million livres, with the whole of Europe at 12.89 million and with the whole world at 80.4 million, or £3.2 million, but his estimate for non-European trade is exceedingly rough. Abbé Raynal, *Settlements and Trade of the Europeans in the East and West Indies* (London, 1787), V, 152.

was about £E. 1.5 million, the expansion in the course of the hundred years preceding the First World War would be about forty-fold. Since Egyptian trade figures are officially stated to have been undervalued until 1911 and since the British price level in 1800–1815 was about twice as high as in 1913, an estimate of a fifty- or sixty-fold increase is not likely to err on the side of exaggeration.

The integration of Egypt into the world system necessitated a number of structural changes. First, the remaining restrictions on private ownership of land were gradually removed. By 1858 collective responsibility for land taxes had been abolished; the right of inheritance by both males and females had been fully affirmed and so had the right to sell or mortgage land; finally, foreigners were authorized to acquire any kind of land. This last provision was of particular importance, since it enabled foreign capital to enter Egyptian agriculture by means of mortgage and other loans.[4] During the following two decades, various measures were taken removing remaining restrictions, improving the machinery of registration, and by the establishment of the Mixed Courts in 1875 setting up a legal framework that gave foreigners the widest measure of rights. Land had become a commodity like any other, easily bought and sold. Concurrently, labor was freed from all the ties binding it to the soil and also became a mobile, marketable commodity.

Second, there was a vast expansion in the irrigated area. Under Ismail (1863–79), 13,500 kilometers of canals were dug, and under British rule (1882–1922) the Aswan dam (at the time the largest in the world) and other major irrigation works were built. Consequently the cultivated area increased from 4,160,000 faddan in 1862 to 4,743,000 in 1877 and 5,283,000 in 1913. This made it possible not only to grow more

crops, but also to concentrate more fully on such cash crops as cotton and sugar cane, in which Egypt had a comparative advantage because of soil and climate.

Third, there was a great improvement in transport. The first railway was opened as early as 1853, and by 1858 Cairo was linked to both Alexandria and Suez. In 1877, there were 1,519 kilometers of standard gauge railways and by 1913 this figure had risen to 2,953; at the latter date there were also 1,376 kilometers of light railways. Moreover, not only the Nile but also many of the irrigation canals were navigable the whole year round. A network of telegraph lines, some 5,200 kilometers long, covered the country. Thus Egypt, whose total inhabited area is only 35,000 square kilometers, had built up an internal system of transport and communications comparable to that of many European countries at a much higher level of development.

Nor did external communications lag behind. The port of Alexandria was repeatedly enlarged and improved, to become one of the two or three best in the Mediterranean, and the new ports of Suez and Port Said were built on the Suez Canal. The opening of the canal in 1869 served to channel a vast flow of international traffic through Egypt and to multiply the links binding it to the outside world.

The strengthening of the financial link binding Egypt with the international community constituted a fourth development. The currency reform of 1835 placed Egypt on a bimetallic standard, and in 1885 there was a shift to the gold standard. At the outbreak of the First World War, a shift to a sterling exchange standard occurred so that to all intents and purposes, Egypt became an extension of the London money market, with large movements of funds to and from London each year. A spectacular growth of banking activity started in the 1850's; by 1877 eight banks were providing telegraphic exchange on Paris and London. In 1880 two foreign mortgage banks were opened, and expansion continued during the next thirty years.

---

[4] Between 1876 and 1883, the mortgage debt of farmers rose from £E. 500,000 to £E. 7,000,000. Lord Dufferin, in a report to Lord Granville dated Feb. 6, 1883, quoted by I. G. Levi, "La distribution du crédit en Egypte," *L'Egypte contemporaine* (February, 1918). By 1914, mortgage debts stood at about £E. 60 million.

The fifth development, which cast a dark shadow over the progress achieved, was the accumulation of a huge public debt beginning in 1858. Part of the capital expenditure mentioned above was financed out of government revenue, but the greater part came from foreign loans. Other factors contributing to swell the debt were the fantastic extravagance of some of the monarchs, the corruption of their subordinates, and the usurious terms on which most of the loans were contracted. [See Part VI, chap. 9.] The Law of Liquidation of 1880 fixed Egypt's public debt at £98,377,000, and during the next twenty years a further £18,210,000 was borrowed. In addition, foreign private capital investment rose rapidly after 1900, reaching £E. 92 million in 1914. The debt service and tribute to Constantinople absorbed just under £E. 5 million per annum, or over half the budget. [See Part VI, chap. 10.] The addition of interest on private capital raised Egypt's liabilities to foreigners to £E. 8.5 million per annum by 1914. Clearly, this could be met only if the country succeeded in building up a large export surplus.

This surplus was obtained by greatly developing the production and export of cotton (partly at the expense of wheat, which suffered from American and Australian competition), thus converting the economy into a highly specialized one-crop economy. Stimulated by the high prices prevailing during the "cotton famine" provoked by the American Civil War, output of cotton rose from 501,000 qantars in 1860 to 2,140,000 in 1865. [See Part VI, chap. 8.] Thereafter progress was swift, output rising to 3,124,000 qantars in 1879 and 7,664,000 in 1913. Table 1 shows the corresponding increase in cotton shipments, and their overwhelming share in the country's total exports. Cotton was the main beneficiary of the government's investment on public works and the magnet drawing private foreign capital to Egypt. All the other sectors of the economy, such as transport, commerce, and finance, had as

their main function the moving of the cotton crop. Most of the capital investment that did not directly serve cotton was used for providing amenities, such as tramways, gas, electricity, and water, suitable to the level of income generated by the increase in cotton. And the greater part of the imports paid for by cotton exports consisted of consumer goods demanded by the beneficiaries of this rise in incomes. In other words, the large increase in production and exports achieved during this period was absorbed partly by the population growth (see Table 2) and partly by a sharp rise in the level of living of the upper and middle classes and a small rise in that of the mass of the population;[5] little of it was reinvested.

The question that comes to the mind of any student of this period is why this vast influx of capital, the large-scale immigration of foreigners,[6] and the less spectacular but nonetheless real rise in the cultural level of the Egyptians did not lead to the development of other sectors of the economy. Granted that the government was unable or unwilling to help actively and directly beyond providing certain overhead facilities,[7] why is it that a group of foreign or

[5] For sidelights on this, see G. Douin, *Histoire du règne du Khedive Ismail* (4 vols.; Rome, 1933–38), I, 239; and M. Rifaat, *The Awakening of Modern Egypt* (London, 1947), p. 102. As an indication of the rise in mass consumption during the latter half of the period, it may be noted that imports of coffee increased from an average of 3,600 tons in 1885–89 to 6,900 in 1910–12, of tobacco from 3,100 to 8,700 tons, of cotton textiles reckoned by weight from 13,000 to 21,000 tons and of cotton textiles reckoned by length from 4.3 to 61.2 million metres. Egypt, *Annuaire statistique*, 1913. None of these imports displaced domestic production. There is also good evidence that consumption of wheat increased considerably.

[6] The total number of foreigners rose from about 3,000 in 1836 to over 68,000 in 1878 (J. Heyworth-Dunne, *An Introduction*, p. 343) and to 147,000 in 1907. For a vivid picture of the immigrants, see Landes, *Bankers and Pashas*, chap. iii, entitled "Klondike on the Nile."

[7] In addition to the public works mentioned above, Ismail set up some sugar and textile units and a few other factories, enlarged, with private capital, a shipping company founded by his predecessor and sponsored a mixed trading company. All these enterprises were eventually liquidated or disposed of to private interests. See 'Abd al-Rahman al-Rafi'i, *'Asr Ismail* (Cairo, 1948) I, 188–90, and II, 12–13, and Landes, *Bankers and Pashas*, *passim*.

native entrepreneurs did not emerge?
In the absence of research on this subject, any answer can only be highly tentative. As to the foreigners, it may be surmised that during the cotton and financial booms under Ismail the opportunities for making enormous and rapid gains in speculation, in banking, or at best, in trade were so great that more prosaic occupations were, with few exceptions, neglected. Under the British, the hostile attitude of the government to industrialization may have inhibited foreign enterprise in that field. As for the Egyptians, it is a strange fact, but one which had its counterpart in Turkey and other countries, that they left business almost entirely to foreigners. Not only did foreigners control finance and large-scale commerce, they even dominated petty trade. As Lord Cromer put it, "Bootmending, as well as bootmaking, is almost entirely in the hands of Greeks and Armenians. The drapery trade is controlled by Jews, Syrians, and Europeans, the tailoring trade by Jews."[8] And the same holds true for the professions—practically all physicians, pharmacists and engineers were foreign, as were a very large number of lawyers. [See Part II, chap. 13.]

Wealthy Egyptians bought land, and a few enterprising members of the royal family or aristocracy experimented with agricultural machinery, better varieties, and new methods of culture. Educated Egyptians flocked to the rapidly expanding civil service, those with technical skills finding ready employment in the irrigation and railway services.[9] But practically none showed any interest in industry, trade, or finance, beyond the occasional purchase of stock in existing companies, and it was not until the 1920's and 1930's that an Egyptian business and professional class even began to emerge, not till the 1950's that it became dominant. Even today, foreign technicians continue to play a vital part in several

industries, but foreign capital is no longer very important.

A partial explanation of this lag may be found in the fact that, under the Capitulations, foreigners enjoyed a fiscal and judicial immunity which gave them a great advantage over Egyptian competitors. Another advantage was provided by their financial and commercial links with European markets. But other causes must also be sought, probably in the historical and cultural fields.

IV

The First World War marks the end of the period of rapid expansion. Owing to the fact that all readily available land had by then been reclaimed, the cost of extending cultivation was sharply rising. Hence, although several large-scale works were subsequently built,[10] the resulting extension in cultivation was slight, the total cultivated area being 5,845,000 faddan in 1952 compared with 5,280,000 in 1912, but the crop area rose from 7,700,000 to 9,300,000 faddan in 1952 and 10,050,000 in 1957.[11] Attention therefore shifted to a new direction, that of intensification of production.

Even before the war, cotton yields had begun to decline, dropping from a peak of 5.8 qantars per faddan in 1897 to as little as 3.13 in 1909. Among the causes of the decline were attacks by insect pests, overcropping and soil exhaustion, and a rise in the water table due to inadequate drainage and to the fact that farmers tended to use too much water, since there were no irrigation charges. In the 1920's these handicaps were overcome by the provision of drains, selection and control of cotton seed, better methods of cultivation, and the

---

[8] *Annual Report for 1905*, Cd. 2817.
[9] For a descriptive list of early Egyptian engineers and natural scientists, see Rafi'i, *'Asr Ismail*, I, 264–78.

[10] See Egypt, Ministry of Public Works, *Irrigation and Drainage in Egypt* (Cairo, 1950). Total expenditure on capital irrigation works from 1927 to 1937 inclusive amounted to £E. 32.5 million. M. M. Hamdy, "A Statistical Survey of the Development of Capital Investment in Egypt since 1880" (Ph.D. thesis, University of London, 1943).
[11] This was achieved by extending perennial irrigation, thus making it possible to grow three crops in a two-year cycle on a given patch of land.

use of pesticides and fertilizers; by the late 1930's, Egypt was using 600,000 tons of chemical fertilizers a year, giving a higher figure per cultivated acre than any other country in the world. These measures raised yields again, from a low of 3.06 qantars in 1916 to 5.52 in 1937, but also increased costs of production. This rise in cotton and other yields, together with the extension of cultivation, increased output appreciably; between 1924–28 and 1935–39, a weighted index of the fourteen main crops showed a rise of 15 per cent. After a setback during the Second World War, the rise was slowly resumed in the postwar period, and in 1954–58 the quantum index for all crops (1934–38 = 100) stood at 114. Attempts were also made to diversify the pattern of agriculture, but although some success was achieved, in 1955–56 fruits and vegetables accounted for only 7 per cent of gross agricultural output, and livestock, dairy, and poultry products for 22 per cent, as against 25 per cent for cotton. And in foreign trade Egypt is as heavily as ever dependent on its cotton crop.

The total purchasing power of that crop on world markets has, however, shown very little change since 1912. From the average price of Egyptian cotton [see Part VI, chap. 11] and the index of the price of exports of manufactured goods from the United Kingdom, it is possible to determine a rough index of Egypt's terms of trade until 1938 (or more accurately an index of the external purchasing power of a unit of Egyptian cotton), and a reliable semi-official index is available for subsequent years. This shows an improvement of Egypt's terms of trade from 1850 to 1870, a deterioration from 1870 to 1895, an improvement till 1913, sharp fluctuations during the First World War and immediate postwar years, and a marked deterioration from 1925 to 1938. A further deterioration of the terms of trade during the Second World War (when, however, Egypt was a large creditor on current account owing to Allied expenditure) was followed by a sharp rise in 1948 and an equally sharp drop after 1951, leaving the index a little above the prewar level.

Of more interest is the last column of Table 1, which shows Egypt's import capacity or the buying power of its exports, in effect, of cotton, which accounts for over 80 per cent of the total. It will be seen that there was a very sharp rise until the First World War, a decline during the war and immediate postwar years, another rise in the middle and late twenties, a sharp fall in the early thirties, a gentler rise in the middle and late thirties, a sharp drop during the Second World War, a sharp rise in the late forties and an equally sharp drop in 1952, followed by a leveling off at the prewar level. It will also be seen that the curve seems to bump against a ceiling, represented by the figure of £E.50 million in 1938 prices, and that only during the Korean war did it succeed in momentarily breaking through that ceiling.

The fact that the buying power of exports failed to increase after 1914 may be explained by both supply and demand factors. On the supply side was the small rise in output and the sharp increase in domestic consumption of cotton; from under 50,000 qantars until 1930, annual consumption grew to over 500,000 by 1939. By 1958 it stood at 2,240,000 qantars, or one-fourth of the crop, and only a small part of this (about one-sixth) finds its way abroad in the form of exports of yarn or cloth. On the demand side was the competition of other producers and of synthetics, which prevented cotton prices in terms of other goods from rising.[12] In other words, three assumptions on which arguments for strict international specialization implicitly rest have proved dubious. First, in the last fifty years, in spite of the great rise in world industrial production, demand for agricultural raw materials has not increased as much as the spectacular growth of British imports in the nineteenth century would have led one to expect.

[12] All the cotton offered by Egypt has sooner or later succeeded in finding export markets, but in some years the crop was cleared only by a drastic reduction in the premium which, because of its superior quality, it normally enjoys over other staples.

Second, and largely because of the amazing increase in agricultural productivity in some of the larger and newer countries, such as the United States, Canada, and Australia, world agricultural output has greatly expanded. These two factors explain why, taking the world as a whole, the effect of diminishing returns has been repeatedly staved off and why the terms of trade did not move in favor of agriculture, as the earlier economists had expected. Third, some countries, such as Egypt, have approached the limits of their agricultural productive capacity sooner than had been anticipated; this has meant that they have simultaneously suffered from the inelasticity of their supply and the unfavorable terms of trade for their exports.

Nor does there seem much hope for considerable improvement in the near future. The competition of other growers and of synthetics will certainly not decline, and prospects for a large increase in Egypt's output of cotton are poor. Appreciable expansion of the cultivated area can be achieved only by such gigantic schemes as the projected High Dam, which was estimated to cost £E.275.5 million and to require twenty years for completion.[13] Further intensification is of course possible, but when it is remembered that Egyptian cotton yields are higher than those of any other country and that Kendall's ranking coefficient, an index of physical output per unit area based on nine cereals and pulses, gave Egypt seventh place in the world in 1946, it will be seen that Egypt, unlike most underdeveloped countries, has already had its agricultural revolution and that the scope for improvement is not immense. Nor does agricultural diversification offer much promise. Egypt's soil is much too precious to waste on grains, beyond what is required by present rotations. Ideally, Egypt should become Europe's fruit and vegetable garden, but the prevailing feelings on both sides are

hardly conducive to such a form of integration. Clearly, as far as agriculture is concerned, Egypt may be said to have ended its period of rapid growth in 1914. All subsequent efforts have carried it little beyond the level of that period and future prospects are not bright.

V

In the meantime, another factor had begun to make itself felt: population pressure. Until close to the end of the nineteenth century Egypt suffered from a shortage of labor and as late as the 1860's plans for large-scale immigration of Italians, Chinese, and other laborers were seriously considered. By the turn of the century, however, the labor supply was fully adequate; since then the population has increased rapidly and in recent years the rate of growth has been accelerating.[14] It is now estimated at 2.5 per cent per annum, and further improvements in hygiene—for which there is great scope— may raise it to 3 per cent or over.[15] The combined effects of very slow economic growth and rapid population increase have been disastrous. The amount of cultivated land per capita declined from 0.2 hectares in 1907 to 0.11 in 1952 while the cropped area decreased from 0.29 to 0.18 hectares, one of the lowest ratios in the world. The per capita income, which had risen fairly rapidly till the First World War, is today certainly lower than it was at that time.[16] The level of living fell in the interwar

[14] In addition to the general factors accounting for population growth in underdeveloped countries, one specific to Egypt may be mentioned, viz., cotton. For cotton requires not only much labor but also much child labor, and therefore is best suited to a dense and growing population.
[15] The government has just begun to show an interest in birth control, and recently opened a few clinics. The effects of such measures on population growth can, however, make themselves felt only very slowly.
[16] Per capita income, in 1913 prices, has been put at £E. 7.6 in 1880–97, £E. 12.4 in 1913, £E. 12.2 in 1921, £E. 8.2 in 1930–33, £E. 9.6 in 1935–39, and £E. 9.4 in 1940–59. A. El Sherbini and A. F. Sherif "Marketing Problems in an Underdeveloped Country —Egypt," in *L'Egypte contemporaine* (July, 1956). While such estimates are subject to caution, they seem well in line with other available information.

[13] For details, see United Nations, *Economic Developments in the Middle East, 1954–1955* (New York, 1956), pp. 113–16. The dam will also provide flood control and 8 billion kilowatt hours of electricity per annum.

period, and today is not above the 1939 level. And Egypt which, until the Second World War, had an export surplus of grain is now a net importer.

VI

Not unexpectedly, awareness of these difficulties lagged well behind their emergence. It was not until the depression that Egypt's ruling class, which until then had been doing very well out of cotton, began to be even dimly conscious that the economy had taken an unsatisfactory turn, and the first study pointing out the existence and consequences of population pressure was published, by an American, in 1936.[17] Men's minds now began to turn to industrialization.

After the liquidation of Mohammad Ali's factories, no interest had been shown by either foreign or local capital in the unprotected Egyptian market. Mohammad Ali's monopoly system had borne very hard on the handicrafts and killed whatever spirit of enterprise may have survived in them. For their part, subsequent governments were precluded from offering tariff protection, because of international conventions fixing the level of customs duties. [See Part VI, chap. 13.] Moreover, the British administration had no desire to industrialize Egypt.[18] Hence, although a few food-processing, textile, and building-materials industries were established, in 1927 total employment in manufacturing plants employing ten persons or over was only 95,000 and manufacturing and mining

probably accounted for less than 5 per cent of the gross national product.[19]

In 1930, however, Egypt recovered its tariff autonomy and in 1936 its fiscal autonomy. Industry was provided with tariff and other forms of protection and began to grow rapidly. The Second World War provided further stimulation and in recent years government support has been intensified. As a result, by 1954 employment in establishments with ten persons or over (excluding repair shops) stood at 265,000, an increase of 180 per cent over 1927, and industrial output had probably risen in a higher proportion.[20] At present, the share of manufacturing and mining in the gross national product is over 15 per cent.

Other measures taken to strengthen and diversify the economy may be briefly mentioned. Especially since 1952, improvements have been made in the transport system. Highway building, begun on a large scale after the Anglo-Egyptian Treaty of 1936, has recently been accelerated; special attention is being paid to desert roads to facilitate prospection for and production of minerals. The land reform of 1952 both improved the lot of tenants and small farmers and removed some of the institutional and political factors impeding development. More important have been the financial measures. In 1939, exchange control was established, and by now it is largely effective. In 1947 Egypt left the sterling area, and since then various measures have given the government, acting through the Central Bank, extensive control over the money

[17] Wendell Cleland, *The Population Problem in Egypt* (Lancaster, Pa., 1936). An earlier warning had gone unheeded. "If the rate of increase elicited at last census is maintained, it is not difficult to show that, in 50 years time, the population will be about 29 millions. The cultivable land will then be 7.7 millions of feddans cropped twice a year and so equivalent to some 15.4 million feddans of land.... Now 4.4 million feddans at present barely support 13.1 million of people; will 8.7 [*sic*] million feddans support the 29 million of 1967? Yes, if the yield of the crops is improved; no, if it is not." J. I. Craig, "The Census of Egypt," *L'Egypte contemporaine* (April, 1917).

[18] For details, see C. Issawi, *Egypt at Mid-Centruy*, p. 37, and A. A. I. al Gritly "The Structure of Modern Industry in Egypt," *L'Egypte contemporaine*, 1947.

[19] A list of manufacturing enterprises operating in 1916 shows that the total number was 15 and total employment about 30–35,000. René Maunier, "L'exposition des industries égyptiennes," *L'Egypte contemporaine* (November, 1916). The sugar industry accounted for the bulk of employment.

[20] For details see United Nations, *The Development of Manufacturing Industry in Egypt, Israel and Turkey* (New York, 1958). Figures on employment in establishments with 10 persons or over tend to exaggerate the rate of growth since total industrial employment rose by only 53 per cent from 248,000 to 379,000. However, increased mechanization and better organization have greatly raised labor productivity, and available data on output fully support the statement that industrial production increased more than threefold between 1927 and 1954.

market. At the same time some of the more glaring gaps in the credit system have been filled, by the provision of cheap credit to small farmers and by the institution of an Industrial Bank. The tax structure has been reformed by the imposition of progressive income taxes and death duties, which however still account for only 15 per cent of total revenues. Last, mention may be made of the fact that the two world wars enabled Egypt to accumulate large sterling balances, thus converting it from a debtor to a creditor country; in recent years these balances have been heavily drawn upon to meet deficits in the balance of payments.

Other possibilities also suggest themselves. Egypt's location and climate should enable it greatly to increase the scope and variety of the services it provides foreigners, such as tourism, international air traffic, and entrepôt trade, but in the political atmosphere prevailing at present not much can be expected in this direction. Hence, hopes for diversifying the economy are pinned on further industrial development, and the government is trying to stimulate industry in every possible way. The tariff and exchange control, as well as import licensing, have been increasingly used to reduce imports of manufactured goods to a minimum, and at the same time to facilitate imports of raw materials, machinery, and spare parts. Power is being provided on reasonable terms, and more will be available in the near future with the completion of various thermal stations and of the Aswan dam hydroelectric scheme, which came into operation in 1959 and will provide 1,500 million kilowatt hours annually. Increased facilities for technical training are being supplied. Credit is being advanced through the Industrial Bank. Various forms of encouragement have been offered to local and foreign investors through the Mining and Investment laws passed since 1952. Finally, the government is participating directly in many projects. Whereas until 1952 manufacturing had been left entirely to private enterprise, many of the larger plants now under way or recently opened include a large proportion of government capital (for example, a petroleum refinery, a steel mill, fertilizer, motor car and railway truck plants), and the share of the government in industrial investment is rising steadily; in 1957, government agencies accounted for 66 per cent of capital issues of industrial enterprises. The scope and variety of Egyptian industry has greatly increased; total output rose by 64 per cent between 1952 and 1958 and in recent years the annual rate of growth has been over 13 per cent.[21] A large-scale program of industrialization is being carried out, with the help of a Soviet loan of 700 million rubles and a West German loan of 545 million marks. It aims at a total investment of £E. 277 million over five years (1958–63) with an anticipated increase in employment of over 70,000, in gross output of £E. 202 million, and in net output of £E. 84 million. It is expected that the share of manufacturing and mining in the gross national product will rise to 22 per cent by 1965.[22] The transition to a complex economy seems to be in sight.

VII

Some important considerations should be kept in mind, however. First, the productivity of Egyptian industry, though rising rapidly in some sectors, is still very low compared to that of more advanced countries; a study by an Egyptian statistician suggests that net output per person employed in manufacturing in 1947 was much less than one-third of the British level in 1935 less than one quarter of the German level in 1936 and less than one-eighth of the American level in 1937. Many Egyptian industries survive only through heavy protection, and protection partly accounts for the fact that output per man employed in industry is about twice as great as output per man in agriculture.

[21] United Arab Republic, *Al taqaddum al sina'i fil iqlim al misri* (Cairo, 1959), p. 67.
[22] For full details on the Plan, see *ibid*. In addition the Soviet Union has opened credits equivalent to about $370 million for aid in building the High Dam.

Second, the labor-absorptive power of industry is low, compared with Egypt's needs. The 1947 census put the number employed in manufacturing and mining at 722,000, or 8.5 per cent of the economically active population. Now Egypt's labor force is growing at the rate of some 2 per cent per annum, that is over 160,000 persons. Moreover, there is a large surplus rural population, whose number runs into millions and whose marginal productivity must be close to zero. The growth of manufacturing would have to be phenomenal to make a dent on this large reserve of manpower, even assuming, as does the government, that an industrial job creates three additional ones in transport, distribution, etc.[23]

Third, many Egyptian industries are heavily dependent on imports of raw materials, while the country as a whole has in recent years been importing about one-third of its fuel needs and practically all its machinery. It is true that some, though not many, of the agricultural raw materials now imported might be grown domestically and that intensive prospection will probably reveal unsuspected mineral and fuel resources—indeed some significant petroleum discoveries have already taken place and output is once more rising. Moreover, in time, Egypt may meet some of its needs for machinery and spare parts. Nevertheless, it seems safe to assume that further industrialization will result in greatly increased dependence on imports.

Last, it may be noted that by far the greater part of the growth of Egyptian industry is attributable to import substitution. Egyptian exports of manufactured goods are small, consisting mainly of cotton yarn and cloth. Under normal conditions, Egypt stands little chance of competing in export markets with countries already established, and it should not be forgotten that other underdeveloped countries are also heavily protecting their nascent industries. Moreover, unless income levels should rise, import substitution cannot go beyond certain well-defined limits. For "in 1953–1955 imports of manufactured goods other than machinery and equipment into Egypt amounted to only one third of the gross value of its manufacturing production.[24]

From these considerations, two depressing conclusions follow: first, that industrialization will not, by itself, greatly raise the per capita income from its present low level of little over $100 per annum; second, that industrialization may, at least in the short run, present Egypt with a major foreign-exchange problem.[25] For a country which is already a net importer of food and fuel, this can be a dangerous situation; the difficulties with which Turkey is struggling, despite her richer natural resources and much

[23] The existence of surplus agricultural labor in Egypt, or indeed in other countries, has been denied by very distinguished economists. However, in addition to the arguments adduced in the above-mentioned citation, the following may be found cogent. In the last forty-five years the Egyptian rural population almost doubled but agricultural output showed little increase, in spite of the above-mentioned improvements (fertilizers, better seeds, expansion of perennial irrigation, etc.), which have probably offset any soil exhaustion that may have taken place. Cotton production in 1953–55 was some 5 per cent *below* that of 1912–14, while the output of the five leading grains and pulses (wheat, maize, rice, beans, and barley) was less than 20 per cent above that of 1913–15, the earliest period for which figures are available. Now considering that in 1913 the average, and therefore presumably the marginal, productivity of Egyptian agricultural labor was already very low, its present marginal productivity must be close to zero, or perhaps even zero.

[24] United Nations, *The Development of Manufacturing Industry*, p. 69.

[25] In these circumstances, it may well be questioned whether there are any *short-term, purely economic* arguments in favor of industrialization. The answer is that capital investment in industry is justified wherever the "value added" by labor using that capital is greater than the value added by a corresponding amount of labor using an equal amount of capital would have been in agriculture. In a country like Egypt, where new land can be brought under cultivation only at great cost and where intensification of agriculture has been carried very far, this may well occur even if all machinery, fuels and raw materials used in manufacturing have to be imported.

It will be noticed that this argument focuses on the scarce factor, capital, and not on the abundant factor, labor. No assumption regarding zero productivity of labor in agriculture is made. Where, however, this does hold true, as it may in Egypt, there are also powerful arguments for using labor in public works designed to create "overhead capital." The long-term economic, as well as the social and political, arguments for industrialization are well known and, in the opinion of the present writer, cogent.

higher land-man ratio, give a glimpse of what may lie ahead for Egypt. Hence, although Egypt may well achieve the desired transition to a complex economy within the not-too-distant future, its problems will be far from solved. Its economy will still be a low-income economy, suffering from chronic balance of payments difficulties. Means must therefore be found for increasing the country's availabilities of foreign exchange. The normal "economic" ways of achieving this would be by promoting exports or the inflow of foreign private capital. The first has already been discussed and the second may be ruled out. Not since the 1907 crisis has Egypt succeeded in attracting significant amounts of capital,[26] and recent events such as the nationalization of the Suez Canal and the Egyptianization of foreign companies have hardly enhanced its attractiveness. Only if great reserves of oil or some other valuable mineral should be discovered is large-scale private foreign investment in Egypt conceivable. It would, of course, be foolish to build excessive hopes on such an eventuality.

VIII

It is now possible to interpret Egypt's historical experience in the light of the pattern indicated above. Until the 1820's, Egypt had a subsistence economy in which exports were very small and could not exert a significant effect on the economy. Between 1820 and 1840, an attempt was made both to build up the export sector and to create a mechanism for transmitting the expansion generated by exports to other sectors of the economy. Upon the failure of that attempt, Egypt entered the phase of an export-oriented economy, in which it subsisted until the 1930's; during most of that period exports grew fairly rapidly, but this did not lead to a parallel growth in other sectors because of insufficient investment in them. This in turn was partly due to the

[26] For the reason pointed out by several economists, namely that capital tends to be attracted by abundant resources, not cheap labor, for the latter implies low incomes and narrow markets.

fact that incomes earned by foreign capital were not reinvested in the country, partly because a large part of the rise in rents and other income of the richer classes in Egypt was spent abroad and partly because of the growth in mass consumption due to rapidly increasing numbers and, until the 1920's, a rise in the level of living. Since the 1930's, and more particularly during the last few years, Egypt has been trying to develop a complex economy, by large-scale investment in manufacturing, mining, power, and other sectors. Now, however, it is faced with a major difficulty: prospects for increasing exports are poor, while import needs are due to rise. In other words, at the very time when adequate transmission lines have been set up, the engine that provided the original motive power shows signs of failing, and the auxiliary engines are not sufficiently powerful to replace it.

The question cannot be closed at this point, however, for there remain what may be described as "extra-economic" possibilities. Of these, three may be considered.

First, there is the prospect of a technical advance which will make it possible to distill sea water at low cost by means of solar energy or other methods. Experiments are being carried out in many parts of the world and success may not be far off. Such a breakthrough would, of course, drastically alter Egypt's man-land ratio and offer possibilities of increasing agricultural output and exports very considerably.

Second, Egypt can continue to make use of its political position to obtain large-scale assistance from the Soviet Union, or the United States, or both. Possibilities in this direction seem to be promising!

Last, Egypt can put its leadership of the Arab countries to economic use, by promoting some form of integration. Such a measure would give it a twofold help in dealing with its foreign exchange difficulties. First, Egypt could become the workshop of the Arab countries, supplying them with manufactured goods; secondly, it could draw on the vast inflow of foreign exchange resulting from exports of Arab petroleum.

TABLE 1

FOREIGN TRADE, 1848–1956
(Yearly Averages)

	Volume of cotton exports (millions of qantars)[a]	Average price of cotton (talaris per qantar)[a]	Value of cotton exports including seed (millions of Egyptian pounds)[a]	Value of all exports (millions of Egyptian pounds)	Index of import prices (1938: 100)[b]	Buying Power of Egyptian exports[c] (millions of Egyptian pounds at 1938 prices)
1848–52	0.36	9.6	—	2.2[d]	58.8	3.7
1853–57	0.50	9.4	—	2.8	66.5	4.2
1858–62	0.57	13.2	—	3.1	66.5	4.7
1863–67	1.69	32.2	—	10.9	84.7	12.9
1868–72	1.59	19.9	—	9.9	75.6	13.1
1873–77	2.49	17.4	—	13.5	74.2	18.2
1878–82	2.52	14.2	9.3[e]	12.1	60.2	20.1
1883–87	2.78	12.9	8.7	11.7	54.6	21.4
1888–92	3.89	11.9	9.6	12.6	56.0	22.5
1893–97	5.20	9.0	10.7	12.9	51.8	24.9
1898–1902	5.89	9.3	12.9	16.1	56.7	28.4
1903–7	6.28	14.4	19.5	23.1	60.2	38.4
1908–12	6.72	16.8	24.9	28.1	64.4	43.6
1913–17	6.28	21.3	28.0	32.0	84.8	37.7
1918–22	5.10	46.5	50.8	58.3	198.4	29.4
1923–27	7.24	32.4	50.1	54.5	130.1	41.9
1928–32	7.06	19.6	33.4	37.6	105.4	35.7
1933–37	8.02	12.7	25.9	33.0	90.8	36.3
1938–42	6.72	15.3	20.5	26.0	171.2	15.2
1943–47	4.27	37.4	32.4	48.6	296.0	16.4
1948–52	7.36	87.2	130.7	158.6	339.0	46.8
1953–56	6.58	61.3[f]	115.3[f]	137.6	397.8	34.6

[a] Cotton season ending in year specified. A talari is one fifth of an Egyptian pound.
[b] Until 1938, index of price of exports of manufactured goods from the United Kingdom; 1938–56, index of price of all imports into Egypt.
[c] Value of all Egyptian exports divided by price index of imports.
[d] Average of 1850–52.
[e] Average of 1880–82.
[f] Average of 1953 and 1954.
SOURCES: *Annuaire Statistique* (Cairo); A. E. Crouchley, *The Economic Development of Modern Egypt* (London, 1938); Werner Schlote, *British Overseas Trade* (Oxford, 1952); *The Economist* (London); National Bank of Egypt, *Economic Bulletin* (Cairo).

TABLE 2

EGYPT: GROWTH OF POPULATION, 1800–1960[a]

Year	Population	Percentage increase during decade
1800	2.4–3 million	—
1836	3–3.5 million	—
1871	5,250,000	—
1882	6,804,000	—
1897	9,715,000	—
1907	11,287,000	16.2
1917	12,751,000	13.0
1927	14,218,000	11.5
1937	15,933,000	12.1
1947	18,947,000	18.9
1960	26,080,000	36.8[b]

[a] Estimates until 1871; census figures for 1882–1960, census figures exclude nomads, numbering 55,000 in 1947.
[b] Increase over 13 years.

One may, of course, question whether the other Arab countries would welcome an arrangement which offers them few economic advantages in return for their contribution to a solution of Egypt's problems. It would, however, seem that many Arabs are willing to pay an economic price for the political and other advantages which they hope to gain from unity under the leadership of Egypt.

Finally, if everything else fails, there remains what may be called "the economics of neo-barbarism," or the "Chinese way." This consists of squeezing the surplus from groups which are above the subsistence level and the leisure time of groups on the subsistence level, mobilizing all available labor power, and by these means greatly raising the rate of investment and accelerating economic growth. Of course, a small country like Egypt, with relatively few untapped resources and with a very intensive system of agriculture which leaves little "technological slack" to be drawn upon, is far less well placed to practice such a system than is China, or even India.

Whether, and to what extent, these extra-economic possibilities will materialize is not within the scope of this article. They have been mentioned merely to illustrate its central thesis: that the combined effect of an early transition to an export-oriented economy and a late transition to a complex economy has presented Egypt with problems which are well-nigh insoluble by ordinary economic means. The remarkable development achieved during the second half of the nineteenth century gave fair promise for the future, but it blinded Egypt's rulers to the fact that reserves of cultivable land were running out; that the economic surplus was being dissipated in consumption instead of being used to create new sources of income; that the progress achieved was localized in the export sector and showed no signs of spreading to other sectors; and finally that population had begun to grow quite rapidly following the breakdown of the subsistence economy and, failing a drastic social change, would continue to increase until it had outstripped existing resources. Today we can see what a heavy price Egypt has paid for overspecialization and exclusive reliance on the world market.

CHAPTER 2

Agricultural and Industrial Techniques
in 1800

Few surveys of any country at any time can be compared, in either breadth or depth, with the *Description de l'Egypte*. This monumental work, carried out by the brilliant team of scholars who accompanied Napoleon on his Egyptian expedition, covers almost all aspects of Egypt: flora and fauna, history and archeology, political, social, economic, and financial structure. It constitutes the richest single source on any part of the area and period covered in this book.

The first extract brings out one of the most important facts about Egypt's agriculture: the relative profitability of such "summer" crops as cotton and sugar cane. Now, unlike "winter" crops, which can be sown in November after the recession of the Nile flood and harvested in April–May before the river rises again, summer crops have to be grown during the flood period. This means that the traditional system of "flood," or "basin," irrigation, practiced since the earliest times, under which the river is allowed to inundate the surrounding lands, must be replaced by "perennial" irrigation. The latter implies the building of dikes to keep the water off the fields in summer; the digging of canals to irrigate the crops during this period; and the provision of devices to raise the river level and feed the canals: regulator barrages, water wheels, pumps or manually operated *shaduf*. As the French scientists correctly foresaw, Egypt's agricultural expansion in the nineteenth century was based on the extension of the cultivated area by the provision of perennial irrigation. It was only in this century that intensification—the application of fertilizers and the improvement of seeds—began on a large scale.

The second extract points out one of the main obstacles to the industrialization of Egypt, an obstacle that is just being overcome: the lack of cheap motive power. Until the development of turbines to generate electricity, the Nile could not be used to provide power on a significant scale, and Muhammad Ali's attempts to use some of the barrages for this purpose met with little success. The complete absence of forests deprived Egypt of another source of power, firewood. And, in spite of the optimism of the French scientists, windmills never assumed any importance in Egypt.

It is surprising that such acute observers, writing at the beginning of the nineteenth century, should have ignored the potentialities of coal-generated steam. They may have judged that transport costs would raise the price of imported coal to a prohibitive level—as indeed they did until the middle of the nineteenth century. And in fact the greater part of the motive power used in Muhammad Ali's factories was generated by animal power, steam being reserved for only limited uses. Thereafter coal was relied upon almost exclusively until the Second World War, after which oil and hydroelectricity reduced its share to a very small fraction.

(See also works by Baer, Rivlin, Hitta, Sami, Atsamba, Giritli, and Fahmy listed in the Bibliography.)

[From P. S. Girard, "Mémoire sur l' agriculture, l'industrie, et le commerce de l'Egypte," *Description de l'Egypte, état moderne* (2 vols.; Paris, 1809–22), I, Part 1, 688–91, 618–20, and 701–11.]

AGRICULTURE

... The annual phenomenon of the Nile flood and the regularity of the seasons free the Egyptians from most of the operations which the soil elsewhere demands from those who till it. Since only little effort is required to obtain a rich produce, it is natural that agricultural practices should have remained stationary.

Hence we see before us today what ancient sources relate regarding irrigation, sowing, and crops; with few exceptions, the same cereals, leguminous crops, and textile fibers are still cultivated. We have observed earlier that agricultural weights and measures have remained unchanged since the remotest antiquity; the soil receives the same amount of seed; and if some difference may be observed between present-day yields and those related by ancient chroniclers, it must be attributed to the exaggeration of some of them who, amazed by a fertility which demanded so little work, exalted it beyond measure.

How indeed could they not have been astonished by the fertility of the soil, which often does not even need to be plowed before taking in the seed entrusted to it; which, until the harvesting of that crop, seems to repel all other vegetation; and

which, consequently, needs neither the help of manure nor the labor of weeding!

The only work required of farmers is that of watering the soil when the latter has not been flooded by natural processes or when it is made to produce several crops in the course of a year. It is by measuring the work put into this watering that we have been able to evaluate the average power of Egyptian men. Whether because of continual perspiration in the hot sunshine which weakens them, or because the food they eat lacks substance, or perhaps because the desire to improve their lot cannot excite their activity in an order that allows them no hope of a better future—the laborers employed in watering provide only two-thirds of the power that would be produced in our climate by men of comparable build working for the same amount of time. It is true that the same difference may be observed in the work of animals: in Egypt an ox harnessed to a machine for raising water in cisterns is only two-thirds as efficient as an ox of similar size harnessed to a similar machine in Europe.

By extending this comparison to plowing operations, and expressing the results in French units, we have found that in Egypt two oxen and their driver plow a hectare in three days and a third, a day's work being assumed to be ten hours; in those French provinces where oxen are used, however, four days are required to plow the same area. This conclusion, which seems to contradict the one we have just given, may be easily explained by the extreme lightness of the Egyptian plow and the shallowness of its furrows—indeed it only scratches the soil.

The average money cost of a working day in Upper Egypt is 35 centimes and that of a laborer employed in irrigation is below 22. The food consumed by these laborers does not cost more than 12 centimes a day; it consists of *dura* [sorghum] bread, milk products, and vegetables, except during the month of Ramadan. Generally speaking, the annual cost of the food and upkeep of a man employed in agricultural work may be put at 120 francs.

The data we have given on the purchase price, daily fodder, and upkeep of the animals raised by farmers make it possible to compare costs of breeding in Egypt and France. We shall add here only that Egyptians do not know how to fatten either livestock or poultry. Should this ignorance be attributed to their abstemiousness, which leads them not to value highly the quality of the meat they eat? Or to the lack of natural meadows? The latter circumstance alone would force them to reduce the number of domestic animals they raise to what is strictly necessary, for they could not increase their herds unless they devoted a larger area to fodder crops—which implies a corresponding reduction in cereals; yet in fact they must expand the cultivation of cereals as far as possible for, in addition to the amount indispensable for the consumption of the inhabitants, a further quantity of grain is required to meet the taxes in kind which are levied on the land and to pay for part of the foreign goods consumed in the country.

In Upper Egypt, the proportion of the total cultivated area planted to fodder crops may be put at one-sixth, in the Delta at one-third. It is the latter province which supplied the ox and buffalo hides sent to France and Italy. The only lands in Egypt which are allowed to rest are those that do not receive natural flooding or artificial irrigation.

As for fertility, each hectare receives 155 liters of wheat seed and yields, in an ordinary year, 2,325. In our most fertile departments in France, 2 hectoliters of seed are used per hectare and the yield is 20 hectoliters. In other words, land in Egypt yields 14 or 15 for every 1 sown whereas our best provinces yield only 10 and our worst 3. Thus, estimating the fertility of land by the ratio of crops to seeds per given area, the fertility for Egypt may be put at 15 and the average for France at 6.5; in addition it should be noted that our lands need artificial fertilization whereas the countryside along the Nile needs only natural flooding.

The average price per hectoliter of wheat in Egypt is about 4 francs 30 centimes; in France it is today[1] 14 francs 59 centimes. The average ratio of prices is therefore 10 to 33.

The picture we have given of the fertility of Egypt agrees with that drawn by ancient writers; we may add that it is difficult to see how it could be changed appreciably. What improvements, indeed, can one expect by introducing new methods of cultivation in a country where nature renders superfluous fertilizers and sometimes even plows the fields! The simpler the art, the less can be done to improve its practice.

But if one must abandon hope of obtaining a greater fertility from the land, it would still be possible to increase prodigiously the extent of the fertile land. All that would be necessary would be to control, suitably, the waters of the river, by digging new canals and raising new dikes—in a word by establishing a system of irrigation which would allow the largest possible area to benefit, as long as possible, from the flood. That would enable all lands to yield two or three crops a year, which now takes place only in certain privileged spots.

Such multiple crops will always require artificial irrigation, the technique of which it is essential to improve. Because of the rudimentary condition of the instruments employed today, the men and animals who set them in motion use up a notable

---

[1] End of April, 1822 [*sic*; the volume from which this extract is taken bears the date 1812].

TABLE 1

Costs, Proceeds and Profits of Different Crops on an Area of 10 Faddan*

Crop	Costs of Production†	Proceeds of Output‡	Difference
Barley, *al-bayadi*	28.14	85.49	57.35
Barley, *al-shitwi*	94.61	139.61	45.00
Lentils	18.25	80.75	62.50
Chick peas	27.63	75.38	47.65
Lupins	27.80	81.30	53.40
Onions	68.02	235.30	167.28
Fenugreek	23.32	93.74	70.51
Vetch	30.87	90.87	60.00
Field peas	42.04	111.60	69.56
Colza.	16.65	101.60	84.85
Lettuce	39.04	119.75	80.71
Cotton	374.10	534.00	159.80
Sugar§	939.04	2,110.00	1,170.86
Tobacco	69.30	288.80	219.50

* In *abu taqa* and *medin*; one *abu taqa* equaled 90 *medin* and its value was put at 3 francs 21 centimes (see Appendix II).
† Includes transport to warehouse.
‡ Includes by-products, e.g., straw.
§ Includes costs and value added in refining.

proportion of their power in overcoming the obstacles caused by their poor construction. The effective output could be doubled if the workmen who made these machines became more skillful. We do not say if they had better models, for the swinging pails, the pot- and scoop-wheels, are the simplest irrigation apparatus for those who do not have inanimate motors at their disposal. Everything leads one to believe that this equipment, which has been used in Egypt since time immemorial, formerly attained a higher degree of perfection. It is even certain that the screw for drawing water, known as Archimedes' screw, was formerly used; it can no longer be found today because, with the retrogression of civilization, the habit of using various instruments, the making of which demanded a certain degree of skill, has been successively lost.

Undoubtedly the agricultural production of Egypt could be increased by establishing a good irrigation system and improving the instruments used for irrigation. But what would especially increase output would be some institution that allowed the *fellahin* to participate in the ownership of land. At present they till the soil only to live and pay taxes but they soon would till it to live better: the assurance of benefiting from

their labors would make the crops on which they work more abundant.

The idea of dividing part of the territory of the Sa'id [Upper Egypt] among the cultivators was one to which General Desaix gave much thought. He considered its implementation as the surest means of accelerating the civilization of this country and allowing it promptly to enjoy the main improvements of which it is capable. For indeed it is only owners who can undertake the planting of such costly crops as sugar and indigo, however high the potential returns may be. That is why the profits made from these crops accrued exclusively to the *bey*'s and *kashif*'s who owned certain villages the land of which was suited to this kind of cultivation. . . .

[The memoir is followed, on pages 701–11, by a detailed analysis of costs, returns, and profits for different crops, which is summarized in Table 1 (compiled by the translator). It indicates the profitability of cotton and onions, which were to become Egypt's leading exports in the nineteenth and twentieth centuries, and of sugar cane, which for a long time was the second most important crop. For various reasons, including fiscal ones, tobacco never became widespread in Egypt, in spite of its profitability.]

INDUSTRY

... What we have said so far regarding the various crafts practiced by the modern Egyptians shows the state of infancy to which they have returned. They consist merely in the production of articles of first necessity for the feeding, clothing, and lodging of man. It can easily be imagined that in a land which has to import wood and metals from abroad, and whose absolute government renders uncertain the enjoyment of private wealth, it is impossible to exercise advantageously any of those industrial professions which can be supported only by luxury and on which one's superfluity can be safely spent.

In Egypt, human and animal labor is much less expensive than would be the use of most of our machines. Many machines are, indeed, used there but only for one object: the raising of water to irrigate land or feed cisterns. We have described these machines under the names of scoop-wheels and pot-wheels. Although they are rudely built, they preserve the original concept of a gear which transforms into a rotary movement on a vertical plane the horizontal movement of the harnessed animals that provide motive power.

Transformation of movement also takes place in flour mills and in the system of cylinders used to crush sugar cane. One can easily recognize in these cylinders, and in the smaller ones used for separating cottonseed from the lint surrounding it, the idea underlying metal-rolling mills. Nevertheless, Egyptians have not applied it to the latter use, and the metal sheets from which coins are made are hammered [by hand] into the desired thickness. This leads one to believe that the art of sugar making, which was imported to Egypt together with the cultivation of the sugar cane, has been known for only a few centuries, whereas the minting of coins, which is much older, has been preserved without any of the improvements that have been introduced elsewhere by the progress of civilization.

Mills for crushing oilseeds are also, as we have said, put in motion by animals harnessed to them; the same applies to mills used for pounding plaster. One may note that the latter process has reached a higher degree of perfection than in France, where plaster is pounded by hand on a flat floor; this is certainly less efficient than to subject the calcinated plaster to the pressure of a vertical stone cylinder moved by an animal-driven mill.

In a country where human and animal foods are very abundant, and where consequently the price of their labor can never rise to a high level, it is natural that such forces be employed rather than those of any other agent. One should also remember that this country has no streams which could be used for motor power and that the canals which could be dug from the Nile and equipped with hydraulic wheels would meet this need imperfectly, since they would have to remain dry part of the year.

But if industry in Egypt cannot use water power effectively it can draw on the regularity and strength of the winds. It is known that westerly, northwesterly, and northerly winds blow the whole year round. The artificial hillocks on which the villages are built provide convenient locations for the erection of windmills. Such mills will therefore be the first machines to be installed in this country when, owing to greater agricultural and commercial prosperity, the price of human and animal labor will rise to such an extent that it will be advantageous to replace them by inanimate motors. We say the first machines that will be installed, for one should not take into account the seven or eight windmills to be found in Alexandria on the island of Pharos. The latter have been there for a long time, but their use has not spread to the interior of the country; they are to be found only on that shore where, it would seem, they were introduced by Europeans. This would prove, be it noted in passing, that the ancient Egyptians had no knowledge of this ingenious machine. ...

CHAPTER 3

The Revolution in Land Tenure, 1801–1815

By the eighteenth century most of Egypt's land was held under the *iltizam*, or tax-farming system (see Part II, chaps. 8 and 9). The tax farmer (*multazim*) acquired the land by public auction, upon payment of a sum of money (*hulwan*). The differences (*faiz*) between the taxes raised by the *multazim* from villagers and the land tax (*miri*) he paid to the government was kept by him. Tax farms were granted for many years and could even be sold to other persons or passed on to heirs. The area granted was divided into two parts: the *wasiya*, worked directly for the *multazim*; and the village land (*ard al-fallah*) cultivated by the peasants who paid land tax on it to him. Peasants enjoyed no legal rights but in practice were allowed to cultivate the land, as long as they paid taxes, and to transmit their portion to their heirs.

Another form of tenure, covering about a sixth of the cultivated area, was mortmain—endowments in favor of a religious or charitable institution (*waqf, rizaq ahbasia*); the persons connected with such institutions, who were often the descendants of the donor, received pensions from the revenues of the land so endowed.

As the following extracts show, the Ottomans, on re-entering Egypt following the withdrawal of the French in 1801, attempted to question the titles of holders of *iltizam* and *rizaq* and to increase their taxes; in so doing they were probably trying to implement the reformist ideas of Selim III (1789–1808). But it was left to Muhammad Ali to carry out a real revolution in Egypt's land tenure. In successive moves between 1806 and 1814 he appropriated part of the *faiz*; subjected the *wasiya* to taxation; abolished the *iltizam*, granting some of the former tax farmers a life pension equal to the whole or a part of the *faiz*; and confiscated most of the *rizaq*, again paying compensation to some but not all beneficiaries.

Muhammad Ali's reforms had several objectives: to increase his revenue; to break the power of the *multazim*'s—many of whom were connected with the former Mamluk nobility—and the *'ulama*, or Muslim learned men, clergymen, and lawyers; and to ensure a more efficient use of the land. Some aspects of the last-mentioned are discussed in the following selection; the evolution of Egypt's land tenure system in the nineteenth century is described in Part II, chapter 9.

The following extract is taken from the massive chronicle of al-Jabarti (1753–1825 or 1826), which represents an extremely important source on the late eighteenth and early nineteenth centuries; it is available in a rather faulty French translation. The author, a distinguished *'alim* and descended from a long line of Ethiopian *'ulama*, was naturally opposed to Muhammad Ali's reforms, and some scholars have attributed his sudden death to the pasha; at any rate the Egyptian government held up the publication of the chronicle for fifty years after his death. (See also *Description de l'Egypte* and works by Gibb and Bowen, Mouelhy, Artin, Rivlin, Baer, Hitta, Shaw, Clot, and Hamont listed in the Bibliography.)

[From 'Abd al-Rahman al-Jabarti, *'Ajaib al-athar fi al-tarajim wa al-akhbar (The Marvellous Remains in Biography and History)* (4 vols.; Cairo, 1297 A.H./A.D. 1879), IV, 93–94, 141–42, 154, 183, 208–9.]

And in [1224 A.H./A.D. 1809] they began to prepare a register for the taking of half the *faiz* from the *multazim*'s and another for the imposition of taxes on *rizaq ahbasia* devoted to mosques, fountains, alms, and charitable works; the same applied to the *wasiya* land of the *multazim*'s. Proclamations were dispatched to the villages and countryside and officials were sent by the various provincial governors (*kashif*'s) with power to investigate the *rizaq* belonging to mosques or used for charitable works. Each person controlling such land was ordered to present his title deed to the central government office (*diwan*) and replace it with a new one; a delay of forty days was allowed for this, after which the title to the property could be taken away and given to another person. The pretext used in the proclamation was one which had never been advanced before, viz., that when a sultan died or was deposed his orders and decrees ceased to be valid, and that the same applied to the sultan's deputies, and that therefore they had to be renewed by the new governor—and other such statements!

It should be remembered that these endowments dated back to Saladin's time—in the fifth century A.H. [*sic*, read sixth, i.e., twelfth century A.D.]—who paid for them out of the central treasury (*bait al-mal*) to facilitate matters for those who were entitled to receive allowances from the treasury. His example was followed by kings, sultans, and princes until our day: they built mosques, hospices, inns, asylums, and fountains, endowing them with land taken from their own *wasiya*, the taxes (*kharaj*) or revenues of which were used for that purpose. Similarly they would make endowments in favor of scholars or poor people, as a charity, enabling them to live and pursue learning; and when the beneficiary died the judge or the supervisor would appoint some deserving person in his place. The beneficiary's name would then be put down in the records of the judge and also in the register of the sultan's office, which were kept by a special official known as the clerk (*katib*) of the *rizaq*. This official would deliver a title deed, under the terms of the decree, called *ifraj* and would put on it his seal and that of the pasha and the chancellor (*defterdar*). Each district in Upper and Lower Egypt had its own register, with a stamp on the outside bearing the name of the district to facilitate bookkeeping, inspection, and audit in case of doubt, and the recording of the shares of the beneficiaries.

And thus the office of the *rizaq ahbasia* remained preserved in perfect order in all the lands of Egypt, generation after generation. . . .

The French occupied Egypt but did not touch this institution. But Sharif Effendi, the chancellor, who came shortly after the arrival of Yusif pasha, the vizir [in 1801], ordered all *multazim*'s to pay to the government a new *hulwan*, on the basis that the government had devised to extort money by any means. Their pretext was that the French occupation had rendered Egypt a war area (*dar harb*) which had been reconquered and whose lands had therefore become the property of the government; therefore anyone who desired to take possession of a piece of land or other property had to buy it from the sultan's deputy by payment of the prescribed *hulwan*. [Tax returns were also scrutinized and rates were increased.] . . .

In [1227 A.H./A.D. 1812] Ibrahim Bey [*sic*], the son of the pasha [Muhammad Ali] went to Upper Egypt, followed by Ahmad Agha Laz, the governor of Qina and Qus and the other *kashif*'s; they carried out a cadastral survey of the lands of Upper Egypt and imposed on them a tax of 7 rials per faddan, a very high rate. They also made a survey of all the *rizaq ahbasia* devoted to mosques, alms and charity in Upper and Lower Egypt; the total amounted to 600,000 faddans. They then proclaimed that mosque *rizaq* would pay half the assessed rate, i.e., $3\frac{1}{2}$ rials. The beneficiaries of the *rizaq* were greatly disturbed and many of them appealed to the sheikhs, who went off to speak to the pasha on this subject. They said to him that that would lead to the ruin of the mosques, whereupon he replied: "Where are the flourishing mosques? If anyone is not satisfied with this arrangement let him raise his hand and I will restore the ruined mosques and provide them with the necessary means." Their protests were of no avail and they returned to their homes. . . .

And he [Muhammad Ali] seized all the *iltizam*'s, leaving something to their former owners only in exceptional cases, and even so only in very small amounts. His pretext was that the Mamluk princes had seized these lands when they fled from Cairo [after the massacre of the Mamluks in 1811] to Upper Egypt and that he had fought and chased and killed them and therefore had inherited all their possessions, whether legitimately or illegally acquired [by them]; and such land was known as *al-madbut*.

Lands which belonged to local *multazim*'s, resident in Upper Egypt or Lower Egypt, at the time of the influx of the Mamluks, and with whom he wished to keep on good terms, were treated differently. If the owner made an appeal and asked for permission to continue in possession and declared that he had been free of obligations at the time of the Mamluk influx, and if he proved that with documents—drawn from the archives (*ruznameh*) or other offices—he would either be allowed to continue in possession or told he could get compensation in the form of land in Lower Egypt. But the pasha would then procrastinate and let time slip by, or else he would refer the matter to his son, Ibrahim pasha, saying he had nothing to do with Upper Egypt, which was under the authority of Ibrahim pasha. And if the claimant then went to Ibrahim pasha the latter would say: "I will give you the *faiz*," if he consented to this he would get a very small amount, with promise of more, and if he did not he would be told: "Bring an authorization from our Lord." And both [Muhammad Ali and Ibrahim] would either be traveling or absent—or one of them would be present and the other absent and the claimant would be left hanging in the air like a dangling participle! . . . And in [1229 A.H./A.D. 1814] the chief of the archives (*ruznamji*) and the other officials came, after the Coptic clerks had filled in, at their dictation, the registers with the names of the *multazim*'s and the extent of their shares. Then Mahmud Bey and Master Ghali and their retinue of Coptic clerks appeared and the people realized what they had contrived and devised in the matter of the cadaster. For, owing to the fact that they had used a measuring unit (*qasaba*) smaller than that previously employed [see Part VI, chap. 6] the extent of the land showed an increase of a third or a quarter. And they measured the *rizaq ahbasia*, noting the names of their beneficiaries and cultivators, and the *wasiya* lands separately, including the threshing floors, and land not fit for cultivation, and lands which could be reclaimed but were not actually being cultivated or were uncultivable. When this was done they reckoned the land in the new faddan, showing an increase in area, and proceeded to tax it at the rate of 15, or 14, or 12, or 11, or 10 rials per faddan, according to the nature of the region and the quality of the soil. The result was an enormous increase: thus the village which had formerly paid 1,000 rials in taxes (*firda*)—a sum that had given rise to complaints on the part of *multazim*'s and peasants and had resulted in uncollectable arrears—was now assessed at between 10,000 and 100,000 rials, more or less.

And the pasha's lieutenant [*kutkhuda*] bade Ibrahim Agha al-Razzaz and Sheikh Ahmad Yusuf come into his presence and gave them robes of honor. A special office was set up for them. Those who undertook to pay the taxes assessed on the share to which they were entitled received a title deed confirming their possessions, in return for which they engaged themselves to pay a stipulated sum at designated dates. This done they could dispose of their share—but only of *wasiya* land—cultivating it directly if they wished or else leasing it to others; and they were entitled, from the *kharaj*, to only that *al-mal al-hurr* which had been stipulated in the title deed delivered by the government office, and known as *taqsit*. And all the excess land resulting from the new cadastral survey, whether village land (*tin al-filaha*) or *wasiya*, was taken over by the ruler (*miri*).

As for the *rizaq ahbasia* devoted to alms and charity, and to the upkeep of mosques, fountains, libraries, and other philanthropic works, they too were measured with the new unit and all the resulting excess was taken over by the government (*diwan*). The remaining part was registered in the name of the actual beneficiary and the original maker of the endowment and the actual cultivator—or such information as was provided by the cultivator at the time of measurement or elicited by questioning the overseers. Such land was subjected to the same tax as village land. If the beneficiary could show satisfactory title, or had a new deed dating from the time of the vizir and Sharif effendi or later, half the rental value of the land would be registered in his name, the other half going to the government.

The clerk of the *rizaq* was ordered to set up a special office for that purpose, staffed by a large number of clerks. People would come to him with their title deeds and those who had new deeds would receive a copy of the entry in the register, which he would then take to the *diwan*, where it would be entered after investigation and much argument on both sides. Doubts often arose regarding the names of the title-holders or those of the blocks or plots; in such cases the claimant would be asked to prove his claims, and orders would be given to him to carry to the local judges and district headmen, asking them to help him provide the evidence. He would then have to travel back to the village, incurring trouble and expense, as well as encountering the difficulties created by the judges and headmen; after that he would return to the *diwan* with the required answers, where, however, he might be met by a counterclaim. And all this trouble and toil might be for a faddan or so! And the people crowded in on the office of the clerk of the *rizaq*. This opened a door for abuse, for the clerk would not issue a deed until he had received a certain sum of money, the amount of which depended on the size of the land in question, the position of the claimants, the state of their deeds, etc. . . .

CHAPTER 4

Agriculture under Muhammad Ali

The following selection is taken from the report presented by the economist and administrator Sir John Bowring to Lord Palmerston in 1840. Although not free from errors, and sometimes presenting too favorable a view of Muhammad Ali's system, it constitutes an important source on the period.

The extract brings out the salient features of the prevailing agricultural pattern: the spread of irrigation by canals, small barrages, and water-lifting devices; the extension of cotton cultivation (see Part VI, chaps. 1 and 2) and the heavy burden of taxation which, added to conscription, made many thousands of peasants flee the country.

It also gives a picture of the system of agricultural monopoly practiced by Muhammad Ali: the government determined what crops were to be grown, advanced funds, and purchased the crop at fixed prices. Muhammad Ali resold the produce to Egyptian consumers or foreign merchants at much higher prices. Table 1 shows the spread in local purchase and sale prices and the consequent profit to the pasha in 1821; in that year agricultural and industrial monopolies provided 67,000 purses (£E.335,000) out of a total government revenue of 240,000.

TABLE 1*

Crop	Purchase Price (Piastres per ardab)	Sale Price (Piastres per ardab)	Profit (£E.)
Wheat	30	50	50,000
Beans	20	30	30,000
Maize	20	32	3,600
Peas	20	27	1,750

* From A. E. Crouchley, "The Development of Commerce in the Reign of Mohammed Ali," *Egypte contemporaine*, February–March, 1937.

Other figures, for an unspecified date, show the wider spread between local and export prices (see Table 2).

TABLE 2*

Crop	Unit	Purchase Price (Piastres)	Sale Price for Local Consumption	Sale Price for Export
Wheat	ardab	27	56	90
Maize	ardab	16	27	61
Rice	dariba	60	...	247–270
Sugar	qantar	41	...	150
Flax	qantar	74	...	180

* Amin Mustafa Afifi Abdullah, *Tarikh misr al iqtisadi* (Cairo, 1954), pp. 294–95.

(See also works by Rivlin, Baer, Hitta, Campbell, Clot, Hamont, and Crouchley [*Economic Development*] listed in the Bibliography.)

[From John Bowring, "Report on Egypt and Candia," in Great Britain, *Parliamentary Papers, 1840*, XXI, 12–21, 45–47.]

The lands in Egypt are by no means apportioned according to the supply of agricultural labour. A survey has been made of the greater part of the cultivated districts, but it is neither complete nor correct, and a more accurate cadastre is understood to be determined on. There are many villages to which a far greater portion of land is allotted than they can find labourers to cultivate; and others have less than their fair portion. Both the insufficiency and the excess are injurious to the revenue and to the peasantry. I had occasion to represent more than once, to the pacha, the desirableness of apportioning the lands according to the population, and of showing the unequal pressure of the existing state of things, which his highness said he felt ought to be changed and proposed to take early steps for that purpose. . . .

M. Linant informs me that he calculates there are in Lower Egypt 50,000 sakiahs [water wheels] for asnaf (cultivation by irrigation), not to reckon shadoofs; each sakiah may be estimated as having three oxen (say 150,000 oxen) and two men (being 100,000 men in all). They work, on an average, 180 days in the year, the oxen costing 1½ piastre each, making 40,500,000 piastres, or 405,000 *l.*; the men at 1 piastre, making 18,000,000 piastres. A sakiah costs for erection an average of 1,200 piastres;

so that 50,000 represent a capital of 60,000,000 piastres. An ox is worth 900 piastres, which represents a capital of 105,000,000 piastres [*sic*]; thus the interest of 165,000,000 of piastres, which must be calculated at 12 per cent. per annum, M. Linant estimates in all at 65,520,000 piastres [*sic*], or 650,000 *l.* sterling per year—an enormous outlay for the charge of irrigation alone. This heavy expense, it is imagined, would be got rid of by the barrage of the Nile (of which I shall speak hereafter), at a short distance from the fork of the Delta—a work, no doubt, of stupendous magnitude of whose probable success I do not feel authorized to hazard an opinion. But it is certain the outlay on canals and sakiahs is immensely great; 20,000 purses, or 100,000 *l.* sterling, have been spent in the small canal of Serdawi, which only water, even with the assistance of sakiahs, 8,000 feddans of land; and two ponts barrages are about to be made at the mouths of Shibin and Moeze. . . .

I was not able to obtain a general account of the whole number of canals excavated; but the extent is very considerable.

Beyond the valley of the Nile wells have been completed for the supply of water. Two English engineers repaired or excavated, in 1831 and 1832, a considerable number of wells. There are eight wells between Keneh and Kosseir, four of which have been put into a good condition.

In the distribution of agricultural productions the government generally takes the initiative, by determining what quantity of a particular article shall be cultivated in a given district, and at a price fixed upon before the time of delivery. By this arrangement most of the produce of the land comes into the hands of the government on terms determined by itself; and, in fact, the government, considering itself possessed of the fee simple of the lands, looks upon the fellahs as labourers under its direction, who may abandon, as indeed they frequently do abandon, the lands whenever the conditions of cultivation are not satisfactory to them. When the fellah is poor, the prices paid by the government scarcely allow him to exist; but when the holder of the lands has capital for seed, and can afford to wait for the returns, I believe the price allowed by the government will give from 15 to 20 per cent. on the outlay of capital; at least such was the assurance I had from some of the natives, who were cultivating lands on an extensive scale. In bad and sterile years the government furnishes to the fellah his seed. Certain quantities are placed for this purpose in the hands of the authorities, who distribute them among the poorest peasants, according to the quantity of land they hold. They repay the advances with interest after the harvest. When the produce is large, the fellah usually lays aside a sufficient provision of seed.

The excuse alleged for forcing a particular cultivation in Egypt is, that the lazy habits of the fellahs would induce them to abandon cultivation altogether, or at all events only to produce the articles necessary for their own consumption, and such as required the smallest application of labour, were not the despotic stimulant applied. On one occasion, when I suggested to Mahomet Ali that a greater latitude left to the cultivator would lead to an increased production, he replied, "No! my peasantry are suffering from the disease of ignorance to their true interest, and I must act the part of the doctor. I must be severe when anything goes wrong." . . .

But of all the agricultural produce of Egypt cotton[1] is incomparably the most

[1] I am much inclined to believe that the *Byssos*, mentioned by Herodotus as the growth of Egypt, was

important, and it is an article whose introduction is wholly due to the enterprise of Mahomet Ali. The average growth of this article, as regards her relations with foreign countries, may be said to fluctuate from 100,000 to 150,000 bales per year, the bale being about 2 cwt., the price varying from 8 dollars to 20 dollars per quintal [*qantar*]. Years have been when the whole quantity has not exceeded 50,000 bales.

Cotton is not willingly cultivated by the fellah, and would probably be scarcely produced at all but through the despotic interference of the pacha. When the grower is rich and influential enough to protect himself against the exaction and the dishonesty of the collectors and other agents of the government, cotton production at the price paid by the pacha is profitable; but when the poor fellah is at the mercy of the officers of the state, his situation is frequently most deplorable, and he is pillaged without mercy; often when the cotton he produces is of superior quality he gets only the ordinary price, he is cheated in weight, and cheated by being kept out of his money; indeed, the functionary too often dreams of nothing but to extort from the suffering fellah whatever he can get hold of.

Another cause for the unwillingness with which cotton is cultivated is, that it produces only one crop per year, while many other fruits of the soil give two or three harvests.

It is not believed that the average produce of cotton exceeds two cantars per feddan, and in many parts not more than one cantar; but I am informed that, with proper attention to irrigation, to cultivation, and to gathering the wool, seven or eight cantars would be a fair average production at a price of 200 piastres per cantar. I believe

the cotton plant. I found no small quantity of raw cotton employed for wrapping round the bodies of children among the mummies at Abydos and other places. It is an interesting and a remarkable fact, that this article should have gone almost wholly out of cultivation through the whole of Egypt, and that the finest quality should have been introduced by a Mahomedan governor after a neglect of 20 centuries. The cotton plant has been found growing wild on the banks of the Blue Nile.

the cultivator is not badly paid: much, however, depends upon the cost of irrigation, which is the principal expense. . . .

No advances are ordinarily made to the fellah by the pacha; he requires the payment of the miri [land tax] after the harvest; the fellah is obliged to deliver all his produce to the pacha, who pays the cultivator from 112 to 150 piastres, the quintal of 120 pounds, according to the quality, the fellah being required to deliver it in the principal town of the district. He receives a document for the value of the cotton; if he have not paid his contributions, the amount is deducted from them; if he have, he gets his money little by little at the convenience of the director of the district. The price of labour in the Said [Upper Egypt] is from 20 to 30 paras a-day for field labour. In lower Egypt it is 30 to 40. The expense of living is about half the price of labour. There are abundance of fellahs whose expenditure is scarcely ½d. per day. The cotton grounds should be removed from the inundations of the Nile, either by dikes, or their elevated position. On the contrary, wheat, pulse, etc. succeed best in the inundated lands. For these, the sowing takes place in the month of November, after the retreat of the waters; but of cotton in March or April. There the introduction of cotton has interfered little with the means of producing wheat, etc., but has principally driven maize out of cultivation. The arrangement for cultivation is, that the commanders of the provinces, according to the orders of the pacha, direct the quantity of feddans to be sown with cotton in each village, after an examination of the localities. The head of the villages sub-directs to each fellah the quantity of feddans he is to sow. When produced, the cotton is delivered as above described. There was at first some resistance on the part of the fellahs to cotton cultivation; but as it really interfered little with other produce, they have willingly adopted it, as the pacha has assisted them with wells and water-wheels, which have greatly tempted them. The first price paid by the pacha was 175 piastres; but the reduction of

that price has led to a diminished zeal and an increased neglect. . . .

The principal source of receipt is the *miri* or land tax, which appears to be considered throughout Egypt as an equivalent for rent. It is levied according to the estimated value of the soil, though in that valuation there is much of favouritism and abuse. The maximum land-tax is 64 piastres, about 13s. per feddan, the lowest in the cultivated districts is 38 piastres, 7s. 6d. per feddan. In the Delta and in Lower Egypt the higher rent is generally paid. In Middle Egypt, I found the average rate to be about 42 piastres, say 8s. 6d. A native proprietor of 208 feddans in the neighbourhood of Cairo told me he paid 25 purses—125 l. sterling, which makes about 12s. per feddan. The owner informed me he had paid for his tenure of the land about three years' purchase, and considered the fee-simple as vested in him. There is nothing to prevent the land-tax being increased to any extent, except, of course, the power of the land to pay it with profit to the holder; but at the present rate of the land-tax there is little difficulty in obtaining grants of land from the government.

Two millions of feddans are subjected to the miri, of which in 1833, 1,850,000 were in cultivation.

In many districts the fellahs are much in arrear; there is generally a year's taxes due, and in some districts two or three years. When the irrigation of the Nile is insufficient, or excessive, it is often impossible for the cultivator to discharge the demands of the government, but a favourable year allows him to get rid of the arrears.

Of late many tracts of land have been transferred to capitalists who have consented to pay the arrears due, and who in consequence employ the fellahs as day labourers, taking from them the responsibility of discharging the land-tax, and of delivering the stipulated quantity of produce at the prices fixed by the pacha. In such cases the wages paid to the fellah seldom exceed 40 paras per day, or 2½d. I visited some districts in which from 300 to 800 feddans had been taken by capitalists, and I have reason to believe the investment had been profitable.

When the burden of arrears is increased to an intolerable weight, the peasants, frequently abandon the spot, and the lands are granted to applicants on such conditions as the government may think fit to impose. . . .

It is not difficult to account for the unproductive speculations of the government of Egypt. There is in the mind of the viceroy a boundless fund of curiosity, and an eager desire to avail himself of every thing which represents European civilization; hence he frequently lends a willing ear to the suggestions of adventurers proposing one and another scheme of improvement, wholly inapplicable to the condition and circumstances of Egypt. Whatever seems to promise additional strength or wealth is too suddenly adopted, and, as a natural consequence, often too suddenly abandoned, when the first experiments have failed. I heard the pacha estimate the cost of the different attempts he has made to introduce improvements from Europe at 60,000,000 of dollars, or 12,000,000 *l.* sterling. The efforts to improve the country, and to advance its manufacturing and agricultural development, are no doubt meritorious in a high degree; but many of them required for their success means and instruments such as Egypt is not at present in a condition to furnish.

Heavy as are the amount of taxation and the expenses of government, it is impossible to estimate the extent of pillage, and the losses which occur in the transfer of the taxes from the pockets of the people to the public treasury.

It may be estimated that a sum of little less than 4,000,000 *l.* sterling is paid by the cultivators of the land, which makes an amount of taxation of more than 2 *l.* per head. This is as much as is paid by the population of Great Britain, nearly twice the average amount paid by the people of France, and four times that contributed by the Spanish nation to the expenses of their government.

There can be no stronger evidence, however, of the productive powers of the Valley of the Nile; and were nothing taken from the payers of taxes but the amount which really reaches the public coffers, there might be an accumulation of property in the hands of the producer. . . .

CHAPTER 5

The Commercial, Financial, and Industrial
Policy of Muhammad Ali

As in agriculture (see the previous two selections), Muhammad Ali's policy in industry moved rapidly through successive stages to almost complete monopoly.

At the beginning of the nineteenth century Egypt's industry, which had stagnated and even retrogressed for several hundred years, remained essentially medieval in its techniques (e.g., in the complete absence of inanimate motive power) and its structure (e.g., in the prevalence of a guild system). But there were a few large workshops employing scores, or even hundreds, of workmen and producing for the market, a phenomenon which has led one scholar to discern the germs of capitalistic development.[1]

In his search for revenue Muhammad Ali at first (1816–18) tried to monopolize all existing industries, supplying the craftsmen with raw materials, buying their products at fixed prices, and reselling at huge profits. But the requirements of his armed forces, the advice of foreign experts, and the desire both to develop Egypt's productive power and to conserve foreign exchange led him, after 1818, to build up a modern industry. Thus by 1828 there were thirty cotton spinning and weaving mills, with 1,960 mule jennies and 1,750 looms; and by the 1830's annual output of cotton yarn in factories was about 2,500 tons and of cloth over 1,000,000 meters. Modern woolen and linen factories were also established, and the refineries produced over 1,000 tons of sugar a year. Other modern industries included glass, paper, tanneries, sulphuric acid and other chemicals. The output of the foundry was nearly 1,000 tons per annum, and in the 1830's the arsenal of Alexandria launched seventeen warships and five steam vessels.[2]

Three further points may be noted. First, many handicraftsmen were ruined by factory competition; however most seem to have survived, though government monopoly and regulations made life increasingly difficult for them. Second, a very small number of modern plants were set up by private interests, notably in

[1] F. M. Atsamba, "Sostoyanie promishlennosti," in V. B. Lutskii (ed.), *Ocherki po istorii arabskikh stran*, pp. 6–9.

[2] Moustafa Fahmy, *La révolution de l'industrie en Egypte et ses conséquences sociales au 19ᵉ siècle (1800–1850)*, pp. 24–49.

rice bleaching. Lastly, Egypt exported a significant quantity of industrial goods, especially textiles, to neighboring countries.

(See also Part VI, chaps. 1 and 13; and *Description de l'Egypte* and works by Atsamba, Bowring, Crouchley [*Economic Development*] and Fahmy listed in the Bibliography.)

[From Ali al-Giritli, *Tarikh al-sina'a fi Misr* (*The History of Industry in Egypt*) (Cairo, [1952]), pp. 40–51, 97–104, 141–50; reproduced by kind permission of the author.]

GENERAL ECONOMIC POLICY AND RELATION TO INDUSTRIALIZATION

It is necessary to relate Muhammad Ali's industrial policy to his general economic policy, information on which can be found in his letters to his assistants and his conversations with Bowring, Boislecomte, and other foreign travelers and emissaries. In these letters and conversations we find a kind of economic thinking which resembles to a great extent the concepts of the Mercantilists. . . .

Muhammad Ali's economic views manifested themselves in his interest in obtaining precious metals, encouraging local production and exportation, and endeavoring to limit imports whenever possible.

a) Interest in metals. Muhammad Ali was extremely interested in searching for metals, for there was an urgent need for precious metals to increase the quantity of money in circulation, to keep pace with transactions in a society rapidly changing from a barter to a monetary economy. This was the more necessary in that Egypt was not acquainted with other methods of payment, which could reduce the use of coins, such as paper money whose velocity of circulation is higher than that of coins. He therefore attempted to retain the precious metals in Egypt by prohibiting their exportation.[1]

His interest in prospecting for other metals was no less than for precious metals, because the process of industrialization and construction requires the importation of great quantities of metals at an exorbitant

[1] *Taqwim al-Nil*, 1829, II, 347.

cost. In 1830, Muhammad Ali learned of "the existence of iron ore in the area between Wadi Halfa and Isna which, blended with the scrap iron of cannons and shells, resulted in a yellow metal. He therefore ordered continuation of prospecting under the supervision of the engineers Dalmas [?] and Galloway, the dispatch of an expedition to the above-mentioned area, and another one to the place where the metal had been discovered, and the assaying of both with the use of coal."[2] In 1831 he ordered "assistance for Mr. Ganzira [?], the Swede, in his search for iron on the shores of Suez."[3] Mining problems in the eastern desert attracted his particular attention, because of the chronicles of historians regarding its rich mines. He issued an order to the supervisor of military supplies to "examine the four kinds of metals reported by the prospectors in Tor . . . and as the location of those metals is one and a half days from the Red Sea, their extraction requires no expense; and, moreover, the work is easier because of the proximity of water."[4]

Muhammad Ali's interest in mining was not confined to Egypt alone, but extended to the Sudan and Syria. He asked his assistants to send "those who have some knowledge of chemistry to Kordofan to search for metals."[5] In 1831 information reached him about the "presence of lead at Zaila, in a spot 200 hours south of Massawa, on the Red Sea." He ordered a study of the subject in order to "avoid having to import this product, if that one proved serviceable."[6] He also sent expeditions to prospect in Jabal al-Druze and in the Adana area.

[2] *Ibid.*, 1830, II, 365.
[3] *Ibid.*, 1831.
[4] *Ibid.*, 1830, II, 375.
[5] *Ibid.*, 1822, II, 293.
[6] *Ibid.*, 1831, II, 382.

Bowring states that the government discovered a silver mine in Lebanon as well as a coal mine in which 114 laborers were employed.[7]

b) Encouraging local production. Muhammad Ali did his utmost to encourage the various kinds of local production and to reduce imports. His objectives are clearly demonstrated in his letters concerning the establishment of a fez factory: "In view of the great need of the people and the army for fezzes, which we are forced to import from foreign countries for considerable sums, it has been decided to establish a factory to manufacture this commodity. Recommendations have been made to import the necessary machines and appoint employees to operate them."[8] In another decree he says: "as fezzes are among the foremost needs of our country, especially military ones, they should rather be manufactured by factories in the country, and therefore of widespread benefit to all. . . . we have started to recruit skilled personnel and to make the necessary preparations, with the advice of Ahmad al-'Azbi [?], a notable of Alexandria, and his brother Muhammad al-'Azbi as well as writing to Europe on this subject."[9] He also wrote to the director of factories urging him to develop factories "to the appropriate level and increase their profits and production day after day, which would increase the wealth of the Egyptian people and spare them the use of the produce of foreign countries, so that their wealth should not leak out."[10] Likewise, he discussed the matter with Baron de Boislecomte.[11]

Muhammad Ali attempted to restrict imports by various means of "administrative protection," for, like other Ottoman governors, he was forced to follow an "open-door" policy. It was, therefore, not in his

power to protect his nascent industry by imposing high customs duties. He always urged on his assistants the need to dispense with imported goods and replace them with local products, even when the latter were higher in price and of inferior quality. He gave instructions that "rope should not be imported any more from foreigners because there is plenty of hemp in Egypt."[12] He also issued an order to the supervisor of buildings prohibiting "the use of European glass, since glass is being produced by the Alexandria factory, even though the latter is crude, for one should prefer the fruits of one's own labors to those of others." When the glass factory faced some difficulties in selling its products he asked the governor of Alexandria to "tell the glass merchants not to import it, but to draw their requirements from the said factory in order to ensure its continued operation."[13]

Muhammad Ali wore clothes "made by his country," and hoped that his people would follow his example. This is of course an instance of "administrative protection" and the encouragement of national industry; similar examples were the [British] propaganda to "buy British" products, and the campaign to encourage Egyptian products which appeared twenty years ago under the slogan: "Egyptian for Egyptians."

In some of Muhammad Ali's orders he expresses scorn for officials who violated his strict orders regarding preference for Egyptian manufactures; we believe that he was attempting to overcome their inherent tendency to prefer everything foreign. Thus he read the report of a committee stating that "the ink which is currently used in the khedivial office and other offices is inadequate, and should be imported from Constantinople; but the *oke* of that ink costs two piastres and is being used by the government offices; why then is it not fit to be used by them?" He therefore charged the members of the committee with aiming,

[7] J. Bowring, *Report on the Commercial Statistics of Syria*, p. 19.

[8] *Taqwim al-Nil*, 1825, II. 317.

[9] Court Register 19, Turkish, document 62, 11 Ramadan 1240 A.H.

[10] Department of factories, operations, and steam engines, document 11/12, 27 Jamadi al-ula 1257 A.H.

[11] G. Douin, *La mission du Baron de Boislecomte, L'Egypte en 1833*, p. 93.

[12] Court Register 44, document 478, 6 Jamadi al-ula 1248 A.H.

[13] *Al-waqai'al-Misria* (Official Gazette), no. 185, 13 Rabi'al-awwal 1246 A.H.

by their report, "at benefitting the importer, and accordingly, he advises the cancelation of the committee's resolution and the use of Egyptian ink as in other offices." [14] Muhammad Ali, also urged government offices to buy local products even if they were more expensive than similar foreign ones, claiming that "the difference in the price is offset by the difference in quality." Once he read the report of a committee that "it has been decided to distribute a hundred European imported fezzes from warehouses to the students of Faraskur school . . . yet, although the European fez is less expensive it is known to be less durable. . . . does the committee's recommendation, then, to distribute this kind of fez, because of the unavailability of the Fuah fezzes or of the cheaper price, indicate clearly the quality?" [15]

Another time he wrote to the officials of government buildings, regarding the encouragement of the local glass industry: "the glass manufactured by the Alexandria factory has become unsalable, it is criticized for being unbaked, and the needs of government buildings are being met by buying European glass despite the fact that the Qasr al-Iskandaria glass is manufactured by the Alexandria factory, and none of its products that we have seen are unbaked. If, therefore, the desire not to buy this glass is based on these statements, they should be rejected as sheer fantasy. . . . If, however, the refusal to buy it is due to its high price, and is not based on those statements, you should notify us accordingly." [16]

The pasha did not only encourage industrial production in Egypt; he urged his assistants to increase the output of primary products in Egypt and the regions attached to it. When he introduced the woolen industry, he urged the recruitment of shepherds to raise sheep in Egypt, and when the use of alcohol in the factories showed a constant rise, he wrote to the supervisor of factories asking whether it was possible to distill that kind in Egypt and save the government from having to buy it at a high price abroad. [17]

However, he did not persist in the production of such products once it had been proved to him that they did not reach an acceptable standard. For instance, he realized that "the caustic soda produced in Egypt is not suitable for use in the fez factory at Fuah, as we have been informed; therefore, it should be imported from abroad through the Zananiri firm." [18]

Muhammad Ali realized that industry had no future unless production of consumer goods was accompanied by production of some machinery and equipment; hence, spindles and looms, even complex ones, were produced locally. He often urged his assistants to increase local production of machines. An example was his order to the Katkhuda Bey to "discuss with Mr. Bokti the question of the looms which he recommends be imported from Europe, and whether wooden looms could not be made in Egypt by Egyptian hands." [19] He also wrote to Adham Bey that "he does not approve the importation from Europe of iron scoops used to take smelted copper out of kilns," ordered him to "discuss the matter with Mr. Dalmas [?] and find a way to make them in Egypt, even if the cost is high." Another aspect of Muhammad Ali's commercial policy was the encouragement of ship-building.

The aim of the pasha in all this was to stimulate local production, even high-cost production, in the hope that industrial expansion would reduce unit costs and develop auxiliary industries. This kind of reasoning is very similar to the theory of protection of growing industries put forward by the German economist Friedrich List in the middle of the nineteenth century.

From all this, we see that Muhammad Ali pasha spared no effort to achieve self-

14 *Taqwim al-Nil*, II, 453.
15 *Ibid.*, 1835, II.
16 Court Register 19, Turkish, document 252, 7 Rabi'al-awwal 1241 A.H.

17 Court Register 49, Turkish, document 79, 12 Rajab 1248 A.H.
18 Court Register 59, Turkish, document 184, 24 Jumada al-akhira 1250 A.H.
19 Court Register 3, document 149, 1234 A.H.

sufficiency in important manufactured goods, expecially those widely used, such as cotton textiles. He even hoped to increase production and export the surplus to Turkey and other Near Eastern countries. He also ordered the exportation of linen and calico textiles to Europe "to be sold on an experimental basis." [20]

He harbored ideas about extending the export of industrial products to the United States of America. As a result, he instructed the Supervisor of Sales that "in connection with the appointment of Gliddon as United States Consul in Alexandria, and the opportunity of discussing the trade between Egypt and the United States during his interview with him, the consul suggested that he should be informed of the price of linen and other Egyptian textiles before forwarding them to America; therefore he orders the forwarding of five pieces of each kind with their prices." [21] He also sought assistance of agents, whom he appointed in "all the sea-ports, even in France, England, Malta, Izmir, Tunis, Naples, Venice, Yemen and India" [22] to dispose of the products.

The viceroy used different means to encourage exports of industrial products and ordered their exemption from custom duties despite the implied violation of international agreements. He wrote to the chief of the Alexandria customs "not to collect customs duties on sailcloth woven in Rosetta. . . . and exported to Constantinople and other places for sale." [23] Likewise, he sent a circular to the farmers of customs about the "necessity of overlooking the collection of customs duties on the fezzes made at Fuah and exempting the products of other Egyptian factories from such duties." He expressed concern at the decline of exports of some commodities. On one occasion he wrote, "there is good evidence that the production of sugar is far less than that of previous years; in the past output

was sufficient for local consumption in the Egyptian regions, and a large surplus was exported to European countries for sale; at present, however, not only is it insufficient to meet the needs of the Egyptian country, but nearly 10,000 to 15,000 qantars are imported from European countries."

Muhammad Ali granted his favorite merchants the monopoly of purchasing the products of government factories for export and personally approved the conditions of sale. In a decree issued to the revenue department we read: "I have perused the conditions made with Mr. Maracini [?] granting him all of the gray calico produced by the factories for one year for the sum of 180,000 Egyptian pounds." [24] On another occasion we find him approving the sale of "270,000 rolls of gray calico at a price of 40 piastres in bills of exchange and 31 piastres in cash," [25] and that none of the offered calico should be sold to anyone else, and that he should be given an export license for the quantity which he will forward to foreign countries. Following the huge losses to the government resulting from the bankruptcy of its agents, however, it insisted that payment at both retail and wholesale levels should be in cash or "50 per cent in cash and 50 per cent in bills drawn on the treasury according to the kind of merchandise."

Finally, the pasha believed that the state should have a surplus in its balance of trade. This is shown by his demand that Hekekyan prepare a statement on United States exports and imports "for it exports more than it imports; therefore, its trade must be profitable." [26] Bowring explained to him the fallacy of this primitive reasoning.

A last word may be said regarding Muhammad Ali's customs policy and its influence on industrialization. The pasha was not free to choose the customs policy

[20] *Taqwim al-Nil*, II, 501.
[21] *Ibid.*, II, 390.
[22] Jabarti, *'Ajaib al-athar*, Vol. IV.
[23] Court Register 6, Turkish, document 15, 1236 A.H.

[24] Decree issued to Revenue Department, 1843, *Taqwim al-Nil*, p. 525.
[25] Department of Imports, Folder no. 2, document 169, 27 Safar 1259 A.H.
[26] Bowring, *op. cit.*, p. 148.

that suited the country's needs for he was always bound by the agreements which the Sublime Porte concluded with the Great Powers. In 1820 an order was issued to him that customs duties on imports should not exceed 3 per cent. Mengin mentions that in 1823, i.e., at the very beginning of industrialization, duties on imports from Turkey were 5 per cent and on those from other countries 3 per cent; additional duties of 4 per cent were imposed at Bulaq. The consuls had a direct interest in ensuring the application of those rules, for they were themselves big merchants and importers. It was not, therefore, in Muhammad Ali's power to protect the nascent industry from foreign competition by imposing protective customs duties, even though he enjoyed a natural protection as a result of the high transport costs. In addition, the monopolized goods were exempt from customs regulations. But, realizing the importance of government monopoly in the economic system established by Muhammad Ali and the increased revenue he derived from them, the Porte granted the Powers customs privileges and exemptions in order to embarrass the pasha, create discord between him and the Powers, and impede the consolidation of the Egyptian economy.

It is probable, however, that the industrialization policy was not greatly affected by the low customs duties on imports. As has been previously mentioned, Muhammad Ali was able to evade the restrictions imposed on him by the authorities in Constantinople by using what has been termed, by recent economists, administrative protection. He gathered in his hands the reins of both production and trade. Most exports came from the government's storehouses, and the government handled the greatest portion of imports,[27] through the pasha's delegations abroad or indirectly through local merchants. For monopsony offered him the opportunity of directing the demand of government administrations toward local production and restricting the

import of commodities which threatened to compete with national products.[28] Furthermore, the pressing need for the importation of tools, equipment, ships, fuel, and metals induced him to restrict that of ordinary consumer goods. Therefore, the list of imports at that time included many of those goods which are greatly needed by countries in the process of large-scale industrialization. Nevertheless, the pasha, again and again, complained about the intensity of foreign competition and insisted that factory managers and departmental directors give preference to national products whenever possible.[29]

At the end of Muhammad Ali's reign, however, the progress of sea transport and the fall in freight rates led to the increase of imports; this eliminated the natural protection enjoyed by local production for some time. While Egyptian industry was deprived of customs protection, the European states, after the Napoleonic Wars, endeavored to encourage their developing industry and placed high barriers in the way of imports from countries which had outstripped the others in industrialization and investment. The idea of protecting growing industries also found support from some economists like Fichte, Müller, and List in Germany, and Carey and Hamilton in the United States.

The Sublime Porte endeavored to whittle down the pasha's power and destroy the sources of his income from monopolies in the hope that that might lead to the weakening of his military power. What helped the Porte in this regard was Britain's[30] desire to ensure freedom of trade throughout the vast Ottoman Empire, secure markets for her industrial products, and remove discriminatory treatment against her subjects.

The campaign started in 1834, with the issuing of a *ferman* abolishing government

---

[27] Forty per cent of total imports in 1840.

[28] Court Register 71, document 316, 14 Dhi al-qa'da 1215 A.H., "Concerning the procurement of gunpowder and salt petre from abroad."
[29] Department of Imports, Folder no. 2, document 40, 1 Jumada al-akhira 1245 A.H.
[30] Britain at that time practiced trade protection and imposed the corn laws for the protection of agriculture.

monopolies in Syria. Britain then concluded, in 1838, the commercial agreement with the Porte known as the Balta Liman or Anglo-Turkish Commercial Convention. . . . [See Part II, chap. 3.]

This agreement struck the monopoly system a mortal blow. At first the pasha tried to continue his previous policy but, after 1840, he had neither sufficient power nor authority to enable him to ignore the commercial agreements concluded by the Porte; he therefore yielded to superior power. In 1840 he wrote to an assistant, "Although permission has been given to the owners of rice produced by private plantations to export their crop and sell it abroad as they please, according to the new rules, a 12 per cent customs duty should be imposed on exported products. It is therefore necessary to inform the provinces of Damietta and Rosetta of the situation and authorize them to collect the said tax. The same decision applies to linseed, sesame, and other grains."[31] Thus Egypt entered the stage of free trade, which continued until 1931. . . .

The financing of industry. Muhammad Ali raised the necessary capital for industrial investment from various sources, of which the most important were: (1) profits from trade, monopolies, and existing industrial projects; and (2) taxes, compulsory loans, and debasement of the currency.

1. The monopoly of internal and external trade was a source of enormous profits for Muhammad Ali. In view of his strong monopolistic position, he bought agricultural products at a low price and sold locally produced and imported commodities at a high price. At the same time, agricultural produce was sold abroad at many times its purchase price.

At the beginning of Muhammad Ali's reign, al-Jabarti described "the seizure of crops . . . their purchase by the pasha and the selling of 200,000 ardabs for 100 piastres while the price in Egypt was 18 . . . and received the price from the Europeans in different kinds of gold coins such as the Venetian, Hungarian, and French as well as different kinds of broadcloth, cochineal, lead, and various American goods."[32] Boislecomte[33] relates that the export price of wheat in 1833 was double that paid to the farmers, while that of rice was three times the local price. The continuation of war in Europe and the imposition of the Continental Blockade gave him a precious opportunity for profitable trade. He provided the British armies in Spain and Portugal with grains and pack animals, in spite of the opposition of the Porte. The government also exploited farmers in different ways. Taxes in arrears and loans advanced to them were deducted from the sale price when settling their accounts; part of the price was paid to them in cash and part in treasury bills which they had to discount with usurers at high rates. But it should be noted that not all the burden of government exploitation fell upon the farmers, since the government took the place of the merchants and brokers in exploiting the weakness of the farmers and their ignorance of marketing conditions. Similarly, industrial products were sold to consumers at high prices, and profits from existing industries were used to finance new ones.

2. At the beginning, Muhammad Ali raised money by the sordid methods practiced in the time of the Mamluks, such as the *firda*, or arbitrary impositions on the villages in cash or kind, and compulsory loans "payable immediately"; these led the people to complain to the *'ulama* of al-Azhar "of stagnation, the reduction of the means of living, the desolation of villages, and the impoverishment of their inhabitants."[34] Likewise, the imposition of taxes on commodities increased with the

[31] *Taqwim al-Nil*, II, 509.

[32] Jabarti, *Akhbar*, 1225 A.H.

[33] Douin, *op. cit.*, p. 90.

[34] Jabarti, *Akhbar*, 1221–27 A.H. It should be noted that these compulsory loans were not loans in the true sense of the word, since the government had no intention of repaying them. They were a means of acquiring money quickly in a country lacking an organized financial market.

growing need for funds to finance wars, agricultural and industrial investment, and the construction of palaces. Bowring stated that indirect taxes were constantly increasing, which raised the price of goods. But it may be observed in this regard that the increase in the burden of direct taxes did not affect the majority of the people because the former *multazim*'s had squeezed the utmost from the taxpayers, and Muhammad Ali simply shared in their illegal gains.

In his last days, however, Muhammad Ali did realize the enormity of his taxes and reduced them somewhat. Thus, we read in one of his orders that "the position of the rich and the poor with regard to the paying of taxes is similar; there is no doubt that this practice contradicts the principles of justice, according to which taxes should be proportional to the condition and ability of each person. It is necessary to levy the *firda* according to existing conditions in order that nobody should have reason to complain. Therefore, the poor whose tax is from 15 to 150 piastres should not be touched, while the *firda* of the rich, which is in excess of that figure, should be increased according to their wealth and ability."[35]

Some contemporary descriptions have exaggerated the degree of misery in which the people lived as a result of taxes and monopolies. But we should not forget that the nineteenth century was a transitional period, and Egypt had lived for many centuries in semi-isolation; hence its price level was not affected by the fluctuation of prices in the outside world. When, at the beginning of the nineteenth century, local prices began to be related to world prices, because of the improvement in the means of transport, the price of grains in Egypt rose as a result of the tendency to export in order to benefit from the price differentials [see Part VI, chap. 12]. This was one of the causes of the inadequacy of local supply in meeting consumption needs.

We should mention that the burdens laid upon the Egyptians represented the forced

savings which accompanied the increase of government investment. It was hoped that increased investment would lead to a rise in national income and production. This did take place, as may be seen from the survey of cultivated lands and the figures on production and exports. But it was not accompanied by a rise in the level of the living of the masses, since the government's share in production was high. In addition, supplying the army with provisions exhausted a substantial share of the resources and led to the diversion of a large part of the means of production to the unproductive war effort.

A last word must be said on currency and inflation under Muhammad Ali. At the beginning of the nineteenth century several foreign currencies were in circulation in Egypt, in addition to Egyptian and Turkish. This plurality of currencies led to widespread anarchy and fraud and hindered trade. Since 1808 the pasha had thought of improving the currency system and ordered "the renovation of the Egyptian mint because of the scarcity of the necessary currency, which does not meet the needs of the people."[36] He also "imposed drastic punishments on those who dare to increase or decrease the established values of the different currencies or to clip coins." But, despite repeated attempts to control prices and cruel punishments for hoarders of goods and speculators, the inadequacy of the supply of consumer goods, compared with the demand for them, affected prices. The inevitable result of price control was the disappearance of goods from the market and their diversion to what we call today the black market.[37] Documents indicate

---

[35] *Taqwim al-Nil*, 1839, p. 495.

[36] *Ibid.*, 1808.

[37] In addition to the irregularity of currency, which is the medium of circulation and the standard of value, anarchy also prevailed in weights and measures. Muhammad Ali attempted to regulate them and had some success. An order was issued stressing the necessity "of stamping the weights under supervision of the director of the Baqirkhaneh." Another order stated that "the weight of the qantar, of whatever kind, is 125 ratls (*Al-waqai' al-misria*, no. 66, 10 Rabi' al-Thani, 1245 A.H.). On 29 Shawwal, 1250, an order was issued to Boghos Bey, the gist of which was that "in view of the

that the viceroy altered the values of currencies and attempted to increase his monetary income by debasing gold and silver coins, by alloying them with other metals, or reducing their fineness. He also attempted to manipulate the value of the different currencies, raising the price of those of which he had a surplus, and decreasing that of others which he needed to pay for imports. Likewise, he sometimes lowered the exchange rate of currencies in which taxes were paid and raised that of currencies paid by the treasury in settlement of claims upon it. He also attempted to manipulate the value of currencies in Egypt and abroad. Thus the exchange rate of some currencies was higher in Egypt than in Syria, since there was greater demand for them in the former country, while that of others was higher in Syria. The pasha "sent to his agents in Syria, each month, a thousand sacks of silver coin to be exchanged for francs, to which he added three times as much copper and struck new silver coins, thus making huge profits." [38]

The quantity of money in circulation in Egypt was much less than that needed for transactions, especially in view of the increased commercial contacts between the different parts of the country and the radical changes introduced by the pasha in the agricultural system and the increase in crop production. To this should be added the rise in the demand for money for the payment of wages in industrial establishments and the army. Consequently, treasury bills were discounted at high rates by usurers, and the government was forced to pay wages and salaries partly in kind. What made things worse was the hoarding of coins, since the monetary system was primitive and the use of other means of payment and credit, such as promissory notes and other substitutes for money, was not practiced. Moreover, a class of brokers did not develop in Egypt to facilitate transfers of capital, like the one that emerged in the financial markets of England and the Netherlands.

The currency inflation continued for a long time as may be seen by comparing the ratio of foreign gold and silver currencies to the piastre and its subdivisions. The value of the *talari* (thaler), for instance, rose from 400 paras in 1817 to 560 in 1820, and that of the Spanish real from 150 paras in 1805 to 250 in 1823. During the same period the value of the *zar mahbub* [39] dropped to one-third. With the passage of time, the precious metal contents of the currency decreased, and by 1815 silver coins contained only one-fourth of their value in silver. Boislecomte estimates that the value of money in circulation in 1833 was one-fifth of what it had been at the beginning of the century. [40]

To remedy this general confusion, Muhammad Ali [41] issued a decree to use the *abu taqa* alone as a monetary unit and fixed its value at 20 piastres. He also fixed official rates for the various European currencies and prohibited their circulation at other rates. The intention of this decree was to keep in line with states which had adopted bimetallism, and the exchange rate between gold and silver was fixed at 15.5. But experience showed the difficulty of maintaining this system for long; it failed in Egypt, as in Europe, and finally gold alone was used as the currency standard.

Contemporary writers greatly praised the monetary reform, but Muhammad

irregularity of weights and measures and the conflicting values of each type given by the people and the government, and as it is necessary to create a uniformity of measures in order to have an established rule, the Royal Assembly had deliberated ... to consider the qantar which is 100 ratls and 36 okes as a unit for weights and the ardab, which equals 24 rub's the unit for measures of capacity, and the piastre the unit for transactions in order to eliminate frauds and deceptions, and this is for perusal." In 1251 A.H. an order was issued to punish "he who dares to sell commodities with shortweights with flogging." Finally a committee was formed by Muhammad Ali's order and estimated the length of the qasaba at 3.55 meters. [But see p. 404, below.]

[38] *Taqwim al-Nil*, 1815, p. 259.

[39] See Jomard's memorandum in *Histoire de l'Egypte sous Mohamed Ali*, I, 450.

[40] He ascribes that decline to the eagerness of the wealthy to acquire buildings and lands, the result of which was that investment in real estate became the most important kind of private investment.

[41] 27 Dhu al-huja 1251 A.H.

Ali's orders and the observations of travelers show that it had little effect. In 1842 Wilkinson noted the continuous fluctuation of currencies and the consequent loss borne by those who held them.[42] The pasha himself complained that "some cashiers of the government treasury resorted to the use of fraud towards those to whom sums were due, by forcing them to receive foreign currencies standing at a discount instead of Egyptian currency and profiting from the difference between the two."[43]

The extensive investment by the government was accompanied by a monetary inflation which was inevitable in the circumstances. The pasha was forced to obtain the necessary resources by any means. He was unable to raise internal loans in his primitive money market and did not wish to contract foreign loans for fear of the resulting political complications[44] and the consequent intervention by creditor states in the internal affairs of borrowing countries. Therefore, the increase of government investment was not accompanied by voluntary saving, that is, a decrease in individual expenditure; nor was it accompanied by an increase of resources by the formation of a surplus of investment goods which could be paid for from the proceeds of loans. Hence, he resorted to direct seizure of resources, *corvée*, compulsory loans, and other violent means to restrain private consumption and investment. Monetary inflation also played an important part in bringing about compulsory saving. . . .

CENTRAL DIRECTION OF INDUSTRY
INTRODUCTION

Muhammad Ali was right in his belief that conditions in Egypt at the beginning of the nineteenth century necessitated a policy of government intervention. It is certain that modern industry could never have started had the government not undertaken direct investment, the establishment of factories, the training of workers, and the search for raw materials and fuel. In conversations with emissaries who came to Egypt for research and investigation, Muhammad Ali repeatedly used this argument to justify his intervention. Often the argument became heated, since most of them held the new ideas of Adam Smith and his followers in England or those of the Physiocrats and their disciples in France. . . . He repeatedly asserted to his visitors that the main reason for the government's intervention was the idleness of the Egyptians and their disinclination for productive work. The Egyptian laborer, he claimed, worked only as long as was necessary to secure an income barely sufficient for his subsistence and that of his family; having obtained that income, he refrained from work and enjoyed the sweet taste of laziness.[45] Muhammad Ali set out to "change the nature of the Egyptians and to accustom them to work in industry. Until that was achieved, it was necessary to direct and guide the people like children."

Both the number and the activity of government establishments in the various branches of industry increased in order to supply the armed forces with arms and ammunition and to provide the local market with goods. With the increase and diversification of establishments, the problems of central governmental administration and supervision became increasingly difficult and complicated, compared to the problems of production under the individualist capitalist system. . . .

Muhammad Ali closely supervised the operation of this diversified production despite his absorption in political and administrative problems. By nature he was not one of those who delegate authority to subordinates and avoid going into details, devoting themselves to the direction of higher policy. Hence, we find the pasha controlling the administration of many different enterprises and supervising the

---

[42] Wilkinson, *Modern Egypt and Thebes*, p. 102–3.

[43] Department of factories, operations, and steam engines, document 8/7, 17 Rabi' al-awwal 1257 A.H.

[44] Campbell mentions that some European financiers offered the pasha immense loans, but he refused all such proposals.

[45] Douin, *op. cit.*, p. 98; Bowring, *op. cit.*, p. 147.

provision of each with raw materials and fuel, in addition to distributing their products and supervising their costs and quality. Such extensive bureaucratic supervision in a primitive administrative system undoubtedly involved many difficulties, which we shall study in the following order:

1. *The difficulty of co-ordinating production in the factories.* The rapid industrial expansion under centralized supervision led to much disorder in the administration of factories. Reports, decrees, and minutes of the General Council are full of complaints of maladministration. One aspect of this disorder was the inability of the factories to obtain, at the required time, the necessary quantities and kinds of primary products to enable them to continue production without interruption. We often read that factories stopped work because primary products and supplies were not provided to them regularly. On many occasions the pasha demanded that officials deliver hides at the appointed time in order "to protect the shoe factory as well as the military equipment factory from stoppage."[46] There are also hundreds of letters in which he urges managers and contractors "to expedite the delivery of necessary provisions to eliminate the delay of operations"[47] or to "expedite the delivery of broadbeans and hay needed for the cattle" [used as motive power in the factories]. Likewise, factory managers complained that the governors of provinces did not fulfil their contracts "to supply laborers at the appropriate time." We also find an order to the district governors and officers "urging them to expedite the delivery of the necessary wool for the making of carpets because the workers have been idle for four months."[48] Another directive was sent to the province of Rosetta to "make all efforts in preparing the means of work at Rosetta factory since the factory machinery has stopped for lack of

workers."[49] He wrote frequently to the agha supervisor of merchants "to endeavor to send linen instead of excuses."[50] He also asked for "pressure on Arab sheikhs to provide the wool needed for the factories."

There are many other examples, some of which are noted here as evidence of the difficulties facing factory operations. Very often imported machinery stayed idle for a long period for want of experts to assemble it. For instance, "a sprayer has been imported from France, costing 3,557 purses, which is still in crates; it is difficult to count or make an inventory of its parts without its first being assembled. However, if permission were granted to assemble it, the expense would be high and it would still be unfit for operation; therefore it should be kept in the warehouse until an expert in such machines be found."[51] Also, "the spindles of the silk factory have stopped because the required machinery is not available."[52] Again, the manager of the armoury states that "if the barrels needed for the manufacturing of guns do not arrive within a few days, the factory will stop completely."

It was also difficult, in the circumstances prevailing at that time to achieve co-ordination between the factories and the arsenals which made the tools needed by them, or between factories producing primary commodities, such as indigo and yarn, on the one hand and the textile and dyeing plants on the other. Very often these factories stopped because their stocks of wool or dyes had been exhausted and their allocations of these materials had not yet arrived. Moreover, the delay in transporting goods from factories in the provinces to the

[46] Court Register 44, document 507, Jamadi al-Ula 1248 A.H.
[47] See, e.g., High Decree no. 1245.
[48] Court Register 16, Turkish, document 490, 1240 A.H.

[49] Court Register 25, document 335, 1245 A.H., order to the Province of Rosetta.
[50] Court Register 5, Turkish, document 423, 1253 A.H.
[51] Court Register 71, 23 Rabi' al-Akhir 1245 A.H.
[52] Court Register 15, document 36, 1238 A.H., order to the manager of factories. There are also complaints "of the inability of the fez factory to deliver the required number to the army and navy, estimated at 11,000 fezzes a month, in addition to civilian consumption, due to the negligence of Boghos in buying wool and cochineal."

main sale stores in Cairo, or between the latter and the export warehouses in Alexandria, due to the difficulty and slowness of transport, caused an accumulation of goods in some places and a shortage in others. There is an order to the director of the arsenal to deliver boats to all the factories in Upper Egypt in order to transport their stocks of cloth immediately . . . in view of the great demand of merchants willing to pay cash for them.[53] Finally, there was the difficulty of co-ordinating the production of different goods with the demand for them; this caused overproduction in some branches, and therefore an order would be issued to stop production temporarily until the stored goods had been disposed of.[54]

2. *Methods of central supervision.* Reports indicate that the departments supervising the factories employed some of the methods of central supervision which were current at that time in Europe to regulate production in large factories. But their application in Egypt was not successful because of the ignorance of the administrative supervisors, the difficulty of transport, and the fact that factories were dispersed. The pasha demanded from the managers detailed estimates of their future needs for primary products and fuel, which would be taken into account in drawing up production plans and would give the government an opportunity to "import what is demanded from abroad, if necessary." Some managers, however, were negligent in the execution of those instructions and did not "bother to provide the annual estimates" of their needs, which led to shortage of materials and interruption of production. While some factories suffered from a shortage of materials, others stocked much more than their needs. Moreover, as a result of the difficulty of co-ordination between the numerous factories and the lack of information at the central administration, large quantities of primary products were

purchased although they were available at the main warehouses. There was much correspondence between the administration and the factories designed to ascertain which factories had surplus quantities of primary products. On a certain occasion, the pasha issued an order to the managers of the fez factory indicating " the existence of shortage of twine in the fez factory at Fuah, and advising him to make an estimate of the quantity for a year."[55]

The shortage of primary products caused great embarrassment, forcing factories to buy them from local markets immediately, and thus exposing themselves to exploitation by merchants who realized their straits and charged high prices. For instance, factories were forced to buy "from Mr. Dimitri Zaraq the cochineal needed for the fez factory, lest work stop."[56] Very often the delay in obtaining materials was caused by the plurality of responsible authorities. The manager of the woolen factory, for instance, had to get in touch with the supervisor of the war department (*Jihadia*),who contacted the department of commerce, which, in turn, requested the pasha's agents in Europe to forward the needed commodity, or endeavored to procure it locally. All this, of course, would take a long time, during which the factories would remain idle, or be forced to use local primary products instead of imported ones.[57] The pasha often complained of the negligence of managers in holding adequate stocks which prevented their factories from delivering contracted products to the war department and to the public.

In his book on public works in Egypt, Linant de Bellefonds[58] gives a detailed description of the development of the construction of the Delta Dam, which reveals defective co-ordination among the

[53] Unnumbered Record, document 71, 1250 A.H., order to the Director of Warehouses.
[54] Court Register 6, document 762, 1236 A.H., "an order to stop the looms temporarily due to the excessive quantities of calico and to endeavor to dispose of them."
[55] Court Register 8, document 99, 1252 A.H. There is also an order blocking the cotton required for use in 22 factories . . . in one year ending in Muharram 1245 A.H.
[56] Court Register 8, document 1560, 8 Ramadan, 1245 A.H.
[57] *Al waqai' al-Misria*, no. 106, 1 Sha'ban, 1245 A.H.
[58] *Mémoire sur les principaux Travaux d'utilité publique exécutés en Egypte*, p. 437.

different administrations and their inability to carry out public works. For instance, a great number of laborers was recruited to work on the construction of the dam without the necessary measures being taken to provide them with food or lodging. At the beginning, the laborers dug with their [bare] hands and slept in the open air; the number recruited far exceeded that needed in the preliminary stages of work.

3. *The objectives of production.* Muhammad Ali granted factory managers little authority and kept for himself the right to direct and take decisions even in relatively insignificant administrative matters. He did not, however, give any opinions on purely technical matters. Thus he wrote to the manager of the fez factory rebuking him for consulting him in purely technical matters of which he had no knowledge. He mentioned in that letter that he knew nothing about "the mixing or non-mixing of the different kinds of wool," and that he held the manager responsible if the fezzes were spoiled as a result of "the non-mixing of the wool."[59] But, despite his many problems, Muhammad Ali's assistants apprised him of the contents of the reports sent by the factories, on which he commented and gave instructions similar to those issued by a general manager or managing director of a corporation nowadays to the manager of a factory belonging to that corporation.

The pasha also determined the goals or "norms" for the different machines, based on general average production, or on output in factories which had good management and gave satisfactory results. In the light of the reports which he received, he wrote to factories whose production did not reach the determined goal, asking for an explanation of the causes of failure. For instance, he wrote to Mahmud Bey, supervisor of the war department that "he had perused the monthly list for the manufacturing of guns, and had been informed that the number of guns made monthly amounted to 500 and a fraction and that it had been resolved that 800 guns should be

manufactured by the factory and another 800 at that of al-Hawd al-Marsud, provided that repair work were moved from the latter to Bulaq; total monthly production would thus be 1,600 guns. . . . what then was the reason for not moving the repair work to Bulaq? and for the shortage in the number of guns?"[60] In 1837 he wrote to the governors of both Upper and Lower Egypt that "the factories of the two districts have been assigned the weaving of 6,745,269 military and other uniforms, and that he had learned from the report of the director of the khedivial office that the quantity delivered was 1,367,150 and that this number, compared to the required number, is insignificant; it is therefore required that the delivery of the assigned quantity be expedited, because it is urgently needed."[61]

It is evident from all this that those in charge of drawing up plans were overoptimistic, as are their counterparts in centrally planned countries nowadays. We do not know the grounds on which the figure was based; it may have been exaggerated as a result of a colossal error in estimation. However, the great difference between the goal and actual production might be attributable to exceptional circumstances or negligence in execution. . . .

4. *Supervision of quality, costs, and methods of production.* We find in Muhammad Ali's letters to the factory managers many directives concerning improvement of the quality of goods, accuracy in accountancy, reduction of costs, and regulation of supervision. In a letter to the general manager of factories, he protested that the goods produced in the factories under the latter's supervision "do not reach the desired degree of excellence"—and repeated his complaint that local products had not yet reached the "standard of European goods." He also wrote to the general manager of factories that "the yarn used in the factories under his supervision is of inferior quality," and

[59] *Taqwim al-Nil*, 1836, p. 474.
[60] *Taqwim al-Nil*, 1837.
[61] Court Register 44, document 303, 7 Rabi' al-awal, 1248 A.H.

threatened him with severe punishment for his negligence, and as an example to others "for if he is unable to use the yarn, let him inform him [i.e., Muhammad Ali], that he might replace him with another person; he should devote his attention to the yarn or be punished by execution."[62] He also wrote to the manager of the fez factory about the "necessity of paying attention to the manufacturing of fezzes demanded of him."[63] In a letter to the manager of tanneries he stated that "there is a great difference between some of the saddles currently produced by the War Department and those made in Europe, for the latter are white and firm," he demanded that he "look to the improvement of hides, or else he will be sorry and will not be left unpunished."[64]

Further examples are his complaint to the governor of Damietta that "the two garments woven at the Damietta factory and sent [to Muhammad Ali] are of poor workmanship; therefore draw the attention of the factory workers to exert an effort in producing goods of better quality."[65] He also warned Adham Bey that "the axes produced by the government factories are not fit for chopping wood because they are badly made." . . .

[62] Court Register 44, Turkish, document 487, Jamadi al-ula, 1248 A.H.

[63] Court Register 3, 1247 A.H.

[64] *Taqwim al-Nil*, II, 458.

[65] Court Register 11, document 121, 1252 A.H.

CHAPTER 6

Public Revenue and Expenditure,
1790–1842

The rapid growth in public revenue during the reign of Muhammad Ali, shown in the following selection, may be explained by five sets of causes. First, there was the growth in Egypt's national product due to the development of agriculture, industry, and transport (see Part VI, chaps. 3, 4, and 5). Second, the pressure of taxation did not decrease and may have increased. Third, the replacement of tax farming by direct collection meant that a greater proportion of the total raised found its way to the treasury. The government monopolies imposed a large degree of "forced saving" on the population and diverted a substantial proportion of the national income to the government. Last, the rapid rise in prices raised both revenue and expenditure.

Under Muhammad Ali, as under his predecessors and successors until the end of the nineteenth century, land tax was the leading source of revenue, usually accounting for well over half the total. Customs duties constituted the next most important item, and by the end of the period covered by this book had outstripped land tax. Under Muhammad Ali government monopolies, and, under his successors, the state railways, made further contributions to revenue.

Military and civilian administration absorbed the greater part of the expenditures, but under Muhammad Ali large sums were spent for the development of industry, transport, and agriculture, and his successors also invested large sums in the two latter fields. Starting with Said, the servicing of the foreign debt became a heavy charge, and by the 1880's public debt and tribute to Constantinople accounted for half the total expenditure. In both the raising and expenditure of government revenue methods continued to be chaotic, wasteful, and inequitable until order was imposed during the British administration (see Part VI, chaps. 9 and 10).

The total figure for the budget reached a high level by the end of Muhammad Ali's reign that was not surpassed until the close of the 1850's. By 1862 Said's loans had made it possible to raise expenditure to £E.8,868,000, compared with a revenue of £E.3,707,000, and by the end of Ismail's reign revenue approached the £E.10 million mark, while expenditure exceeded it greatly. During the first twenty years of British rule the budget was balanced at around £E.10 million, but by 1914 it had risen to £E.17 million. The First World War doubled the budget, but there was no structural change until the 1930's, when protective tariffs and certain schedular taxes on income were imposed.

The book from which this extract has been taken is a rich source on the administrative and economic history of Egypt during the nineteenth century.

(See also works by Crouchley [*Economic Development*], Hitta, Shaw, Bowring, Mengin, and Douin listed in the Bibliography.)

[From Amin Sami pasha, *Taqwim al-Nil* (*The Almanac of the Nile*) (Cairo, 1928), II, 570–72.]

... Muhammad Ali pasha took over the reins of government in Egypt three years and nine months and thirteen days after the end of the French Occupation. At that time government revenue was only £E158,725 and expenditure was £E135,888, leaving a surplus of £E22,837, which was sent to Constantinople, as may be seen from the research on Egypt's finances undertaken by Count Estève, the editor of the Egyptian official journal [*Le Courrier de l'Egypte*].[1]

According to him, until 1205 A.H. (A.D. 1790–91) revenue was the same as in 1213 (1798–99), i.e., 116,651,727 medins; using a conversion rate of 28.35 medins to the franc, he obtained a total of 4,114,699 francs, or £E158,724. Expenditure amounted to 99,868,276 medins, i.e., 3,522,691 francs or £E135,888; the balance, which was sent to Constantinople, was 16,783,451 medins, i.e., 592,009 francs or £E22,837.[2]

When Ismail Bey died and power reverted to Murad Bey and Ibrahim Bey, they found various excuses for diminishing the amount sent to the Sublime Porte. From the surplus of 16,783,451 medins sent to Constantinople they deducted: 1,000,000 for the purchase of clothing; 1,000,000 for the purchase of sugar; 3,000,000 for the repair of the fortifications in Cairo; 1,500,000 for the repair of fortifications in other parts of

Egypt; 2,783,451 to be kept at the disposal of the Sheikh al-Balad [governor of Egypt]; i.e., a total of 9,283,451 medins, leaving 7,500,000 medins, i.e., 264,550, francs or £E10,205, using a rate of 28.35 medins to the franc.

After that the budget grew constantly, reaching a figure of £E2,926,625 in the year 1258 A.H. (A.D. 1842) as may be seen from Table 1.[3] A review of the budgets of the Egyptian government, noted in this book and summarized in Table 1, shows that the average [annual] rate of growth between the years 1233/1818 and 1237/1822 was £E94,841. This growth is attributable to many causes, chief of which was the policy of reform and development; the imposition of land which had previously been cultivated without payment of taxes; and the increase in the size of the cultivated land subject to taxation following the standardization of the qasaba at 3.55 meters.[4] For previously its length and the size of the faddan had varied in different parts of the country; in most of the land the faddan was equal to 400 qasabas, but in some parts it was 432 and in others 310 or 200.

The average growth between the budgets of 1237/1822 and 1249/1833 was £E45,014, which is a normal amount and one within the capacity of the country and the people. The same may be said of the average

[1] See *Description de l'Egypte* (Paris, 1823), XII, 243–48.
[2] All figures have been rounded to the nearest unit.—Translator.

[3] Rounded to the nearest pound; discrepancies in figures for 1818 and 1822 in original.—Translator.
[4] Following the cadastral survey of 1813–14; according to Rivlin (*Agricultural Policy*, p. 125), and Hitta (*Tarikh al-zira'a*, p. 35), the length of the qasaba was fixed at 3.64 meters; previously it had ranged between 3.75 and 3.99 meters; see Appendix I.—Translator.

TABLE 1

Year	Revenue	Expenditure	Balance
1213/1798	158,724	135,888	22,837*
1233/1818	1,502,134	355,149†	1,148,985‡
1237/1822	1,881,499	266,123†	1,615,371‡
1249/1833	2,421,671	1,927,079§	494,592‖
1258/1842	2,926,626	2,176,860§	749,765#

* Surplus sent to Constantinople.
† This figure refers to expenditure on collection of taxes; other government expenditure is included under "Balance."
‡ Other government expenditure and tribute (*werko*) to Constantinople.
§ Includes appropriation for tribute.
‖ Reserve at disposal of viceroy.
#From this should be deducted £E170,733, representing losses of *arzaq* [charitable endowments]; balance, i.e., £E579,032, is reserve.

growth between 1249/1833 and 1258/1842, viz., £E45,905. If we assume that the latter annual increment continued, and add to the figure for revenue in 1258/1842, viz., £E2,926,626, six times the annual figure of £E45,905, viz., £E275,430, we obtain a figure for 1264/1848 of £E3,202,056; this represents the maximum revenue attained in the budget.

Thus government revenue rose to 20.17 times its level at the time Muhammad Ali pasha took power. And it is truly a miracle that, with such sums, Muhammad Ali pasha was able to run the country with its armies and navies, its schools, numerous government departments, factories, and workshops and to expand its irrigation and agriculture and to defend other countries such as Morea, Crete, Syria, Hijaz, and the Sudan. Truly it is a miracle!

CHAPTER 7

The Development of Transport, 1800–1870

Egypt is unique among Middle Eastern countries in having a navigable waterway which crosses the entire length of the country. From the earliest times the Nile has served as the principal means of transport and has played a most important part in promoting political unity and economic activity. Its usefulness is increased by the fact that the prevailing winds blow from the north, which means that ships can sail upstream, and float downstream with the current.

The developments in transport noted in the following selection had two primary objectives: to facilitate Egypt's external trade and to improve communications on the route between Europe and the Far East. The first aim was attained by the Mahmudia canal, which linked the Nile to the re-created port of Alexandria and provided cheap water transport to export Egypt's agricultural products and import coal, wood, machinery, and other bulky or heavy commodities. Later, railways running parallel to the Nile and its branches supplemented, and competed with, water transport. The second aim was achieved first of all by improving the Cairo–Suez road, thus connecting the Mediterranean and the Red Sea by Nile and road; then by building the Alexandria–Cairo and Cairo–Suez railways; and lastly by digging the Suez Canal; moreover, in the 1860's Egypt was linked by submarine cables to both Europe and India.[1] By the 1870's additional railway construction and port improvement had given Egypt a transport system which was hardly matched outside Europe and the United States, and further progress was made under British rule.

In the 1930's air transport was developed and an impetus was given to road construction, and both these forms of transport received further attention after the Second World War. During this period Egypt became a nodal point on the air routes linking Europe to Africa and Southeast Asia. As for the Canal, its importance grew steadily, with brief interruptions during the Depression, the

---

[1] The railway projects aroused intense international rivalries, with Britain strongly advocating the schemes and France strenuously opposing them. See the correspondence of Consul C. A. Murray with Lord Palmerston, F.O. 78, nos. 875–77, 887, and 915–19; and Helen A. Rivlin, "The Railway Question in the Ottoman-Egyptian Crisis of 1850–52," *Middle East Journal*, 1961. Over the Suez Canal project, the roles of Britain and France were reversed, France advocating the project and Britain opposing.

Second World War, and the nationalization crisis of 1956–57, and was greatly increased by the expansion of oil production in the Persian Gulf. In 1870, the first full year of operations, 486 ships aggregating 436,000 tons passed through the Canal, but by 1877 the figures had risen to 1,663 and 3,419,000, respectively, and by 1910 to 4,533 and 16,600,000. The 1960 figures were 18,734 and 185,300,000, the bulk being accounted for by tankers. In 1955 it was estimated that some 13 per cent of the world's seaborne trade passed through the Canal and for tankers the figure was 19 per cent.

(See also *L'Egypte: aperçu historique* and *L'Egypte contemporaine* and works by Hoskins, Wiener, Hallberg, Charles-Roux [*Autour d'une route* and *L'isthme*], and Marlowe listed in the Bibliography.)

[From Ahmad Ahmad al-Hitta, *Tarikh Misr al-iqtisadi* (*The Economic History of Egypt*) (Cairo, 1957), pp. 219–43; reproduced by kind permission of the author.]

ROADS

... During that period [the first half of the nineteenth century] the government devoted some attention to strengthening the dikes along the Nile, the canals, and the basins; these dikes were built for irrigation purposes but also served for transport, since they provided leveled and firmer roadways, more suitable for traffic.

At the beginning of the reign of Muhammad Ali order was enforced and roads were secured against attacks by bandits and highway robbers; this led to an increase in traffic. Among the highways to which the government paid particular attention under Muhammad Ali were the Qina-Qusair and the Cairo-Suez roads. It promoted the former, enforced order along it, and looked after travelers using it; the reason for this was that the growing power of the East India Company led to a constant increase in the movement of officials, travelers, mail, and merchandise between India and Britain. The route usually taken was that between Qina and Qusair, which was crossed by caravans.

The Cairo-Suez route, although shorter, was at first less frequently used because, during most of the year, the prevalence of strong northerly winds in the Red Sea prevented sailing vessels from reaching

Suez. But the situation changed when, in 1834, the East India Company started to use steamships between Bombay and Suez, for such vessels could sail up to Suez against the wind. This led to an increase in passenger and goods traffic through Cairo, and to an abandonment of the Qina-Qusair road in favor of that between Suez and Cairo.

The government accordingly began to take an interest in the Cairo-Suez road, enforcing security and facilitating the movement of camel caravans transporting coal from Cairo to Suez; this led to a drop in the price of coal in Suez. In 1834 a project was put forward for the building of a railway from Cairo to Suez, to eliminate the inconveniences of caravan travel, but this scheme was abandoned and attention shifted to the improvement of the road. In 1837 the transport department for the utilization of the Suez road was established in Cairo, under the supervision of the East India Company. The company opened three offices, in Alexandria, Cairo, and Suez, and in the same year Muhammad Ali granted it the right to establish stations along the Cairo-Suez road for a period of ten years. In addition, the government leveled the road from Cairo to Suez, rendering it suitable for wheeled traffic, and set up sixteen towers between the two towns, for use in semaphore telegraphy. Stations were built, at ten-mile intervals, and passengers were now able to travel in horse-drawn carriages. In 1841 and 1842

Muhammad Ali authorized the Peninsular and Oriental Company to run two steamships on the Rosetta branch [of the Nile] as well as steam tugs on the Mahmudia Canal; this reduced travel time between Alexandria and Suez to three days. However, fearing the extension of foreign influence in Egypt, Muhammad Ali decided to eliminate foreign supervision of transport; he therefore established the Traffic Department in 1844, to administer passenger and goods traffic through Egypt, and bought out the stations and installations on the Cairo-Suez road as well as the steamers on the Rosetta branch and the Mahmudia Canal.

The improvement of the Suez road led to an increase in transit trade through Egypt and the number of passengers passing through rose from 275 in 1840 to 2,300 in 1845 and to over 3,000 in 1846. The journey from London to Bombay, which took four months by sailing ship around the Cape of Good Hope, was reduced to forty days on the route through Egypt. The success of the Suez route in transporting mail, passengers, and goods also led the British to plan a railway between Cairo and Suez; but Muhammad Ali, [again] fearing the extension of foreign influence in Egypt, rejected such a scheme in 1845 and, for the same reason, a French scheme for the digging of a canal through the isthmus of Suez, presented in 1847.

At the beginning of the nineteenth century land traffic was confined to pack animals, but during the reign of Muhammad Ali carriages[1] and carts made their appearance. But their number was very restricted and their use confined to the viceroy and his family, high officials, consuls, and prominent European merchants; in 1840 there were thirty carriages in Cairo and somewhat more in Alexandria. As for carts, Muhammad Ali imported a large number for the transport of construction materials for factories and buildings and for the removal of the earth mounds surrounding Cairo. Their use spread rapidly and they became the sole means of transport to and from factories and construction sites; Egyptians quickly took to these carts and many were made locally for the carrying of goods and crops or for the conveyance of people. Nevertheless, carriages and carts did not gain a predominant position in Egypt at that time; the most widespread means of transport continued to be pack animals, i.e., camels, horses, mules, and donkeys. . . .

During the reign of Abbas I [1849–54] the Cairo-Suez road was improved and paved with stones, which greatly facilitated the movement of carriages. The flow of passengers, mail, and goods over that route expanded to such an extent that the necessity of building a railway—or a canal that would replace the land route—made itself increasingly felt. And indeed during the reign of Said [1854–63] a railway was laid down between Cairo and Suez, following the completion of the Alexandria-Cairo line initiated under Abbas. Abbas also made an effort to improve security by taking action against highway robbers, thus further aiding land transport. Under Said a paved country road, ten meters wide, was built along the Mahmudia Canal, using the silt excavated from the canal in the process of dredging. In 1891, during the reign of Tawfiq [1879–92] a decree was issued for the construction of country roads to facilitate movement between towns and villages. The use of motorcars greatly improved communications and reduced travel time on these roads. Nevertheless, in 1917 Egyptian highways were not, strictly speaking, fit for transport because of both restricted mileage and inadequate maintenance. As for country roads, their absence began to be noticed only lately, after the increasing use of motorcars.

INTERNAL WATERWAYS

At the beginning of the nineteenth century, ships navigating the Nile and the

---

[1] The first carriage seen in Egypt was the one received by Ibrahim Bey, one of the Mamluk princes, from France. The second was that used by Napoleon Bonaparte during the French expedition, and the third was Muhammad Ali's.

canals were preyed upon by pirates, which greatly impeded water transport. But at the beginning of the reign of Muhammad Ali order was enforced, which constituted a first step in the progress of water transport in Egypt.

The second step was the linking of Alexandria and the Rosetta branch at 'Atf, by means of the digging of the Mahmudia Canal in 1819. For this 313,000 peasants were employed, of whom some 12,000 died during the ten months of construction work. The canal connected the main waterway with Alexandria, Egypt's most important port on the Mediterranean, facing Europe and the country's leading trade partners. Alexandria was more suitable than Rosetta and Damietta, whose harbors were difficult of access; in particular that of Rosetta was the scene of many shipwrecks. The Mahmudia Canal thus promoted the expansion of foreign trade and that of agriculture, especially cotton, and stimulated traffic on both the land route from Cairo to Suez and on the Nile and the canals.

At first the Mahmudia Canal had weirs at either end, which prevented Nile boats from entering the canal and canal boats from sailing out to sea. Hence, goods from the interior had to be trans-shipped twice which raised costs and exposed the merchandise to certain risks. In 1842, the weirs were therefore removed and were replaced by two locks at each end of the canal, one for small boats and the other for large.

The third step in the progress of internal navigation was the increase of sailing boats on the Nile and navigable canals, caused by the growth of foreign and transit trade, and the expansion of agriculture, particularly cotton. From 1,600 at the time of the French Expedition, the number rose to 3,300 around 1840, of which the government owned 800. In addition, Muhammad Ali founded a Nile Navigation Company in 1846.

The government's monopoly of most agricultural goods and the products of some small industries, as well as its disposal of the output of government factories, led to its monopolization of river transport. However, the latter monopoly ended with the abolition of agricultural and industrial monopoly and the closing down of government factories. . . .

STEAMSHIPS

Steam navigation on the Nile did not spread, owing to the high costs entailed by the scarcity of fuel. Muhammad Ali, however, had an iron steamer which sailed on the Nile.

Such were the various kinds of ships during the reign of Muhammad Ali. Thanks to the increase in the number of sailing boats, the Nile and the navigable canals—such as the Mahmudia, Bahr Muis, and Bahr Shibin—became the best means of transport for agricultural produce and passengers. The improvement of water transport contributed to agricultural and commercial progress by facilitating the movement of cotton and other agricultural produce to Alexandria, from whence they were exported abroad. It also led to a rise in the price of Egyptian produce, which could now be more easily moved about the country and shipped abroad, and to a decline in the price of imported goods, owing to the reduction of internal transport costs.

Usually boats could go upstream only under sail; navigation was helped by the northerly winds which blow during some six months of the year. At times the winds were not strong enough and the boats could not pursue their course; in such cases the crew would jump ashore and tow the boat with ropes—but such methods were usually resorted to only when the passengers were Europeans, who were known for their lack of patience and their desire to shorten travel time! In the Mahmudia Canal another method was very successfully used, namely, having the boats towed by horses. When sailing downstream the boat was borne by the current, but speed could be increased by having those on board pull at the oars. The Nile sailors were familiar with the difficulties of navigation from their childhood and acquired much strength, resistance, and experience, thus becoming proficient in their craft and well versed in matters of wind and weather; skilled navigators bore witness to their competence.

Such were the conditions of internal water transport under Muhammad Ali. Under Abbas the government continued to enforce order, which had favorable repercussions on water transport in Egypt. Under Said the Mahmudia Canal was dredged of the silt which had accumulated in it and which rendered navigation almost impossible. The operation was completed in twenty-two days, by the use of 115,000 peasants, although the length of the canal was no less than 80 kilometers. In addition, its openings on the Rosetta branch and the Mediterranean were widened and pumps were installed at 'Atf to supply it with water and facilitate navigation.

During the same reign, in 1854, the Egyptian Steam Navigation Company was founded, with a fifteen-year concession, for the transport of merchandise and passengers by steamships on the Nile. Whereas sailing ships carrying goods from the interior by way of the Nile and the Mahmudia Canal took fifteen days from Cairo to Alexandria, steamships covered the distance in thirty-six hours. The establishment of the company facilitated communication by water but it was a foreign company, most of its capital being foreign and the only Egyptian member of the board being Dhulfiqar pasha, the minister of finance, who was its honorary president; nevertheless, its charter stipulated that conflicts between it and the government should not come before the consular courts but be resolved by arbitration [but see below, p. 414], and that its ships should sail under the Egyptian flag.

During the reign of Said the shipyards at Bulaq were dismantled, the government thus losing the boats it had for internal transport.

Under Ismail railways began to compete

with Nile transport, since trains were swifter than boats, and some Nile traffic was diverted to the railways. Nevertheless there were, at that time, regular steamer services carrying goods and passengers to and fro; in 1872 there were 53 steamers on the Nile in Egypt and 9,563 sailing boats, the steamers being used mainly for towing the sailing boats, the capacity of which was 117,286 ardabs. The government granted the 'Azizia Company a monopoly of steam navigation on the Nile for passenger transport and the towing of boats. During the same reign the Nile was improved south of Wadi Halfa, by the blowing-up of rocks and other obstacles which impeded navigation; that stretch of the river was thus made navigable for steamers and sailing ships, and communications between Egypt and the Sudan were facilitated. In addition some of the *sudd* [blocks of thick Nile vegetation] on the upper Nile were removed; the shipyard established in Khartoum by Muhammad Ali was also improved and the number of Nile steamers using it increased.

During the Mahdist revolt some of the Nile steamers belonging to the government were destroyed; most of the others were sold, during the British Occupation, to the British firm of Thos. Cook and Son, and only a small number remained, viz., those which were handed over to the department of public works. The Bulaq dockyard was also transferred, during the British Occupation, to the department of public works, which sold most of the steamers, keeping only a few for the use of British inspectors. By 1917 there was no modern river port in the whole of Egypt, navigation in shallow or narrow stretches of the canals was fraught with danger during the low Nile season, and merchants transporting their goods on the Nile were subject to the arbitrary and capricious behavior of the ship masters.

RAILWAYS

The first projects for the construction of railways in Egypt were put forward during the reign of Muhammad Ali. In 1834 the viceroy decided to build one between Cairo and Suez, in order to improve communications between the two towns and to eliminate the inconveniences of travel by camel caravans across the desert; his objective was to increase the flow of passenger and goods traffic on the Cairo-Suez route, following the use of steamers between Bombay and Suez. A British engineer, Galloway, employed by the Eygptian government, studied the route and pronounced the project feasible. Muhammad Ali thereupon sent him to England to buy rails and make the necessary arrangements. But the British government refused to provide the financial guarantees necessary for the project, so Galloway returned from London to Egypt in 1836, with five shiploads of rails. Muhammad Ali subsequently abandoned the scheme, owing to French opposition and also because of the many financial burdens then weighing on the Egyptian budget. Had it been implemented at that time it would have been the first railway line outside Europe [and the United States], and one of the very first in the world.

In addition to the Cairo-Suez scheme, Muhammad Ali thought of laying down a railway from the western end of the Delta to the eastern, at Mansura. Detailed plans were drawn up and the route was traced on the ground, but the scheme met the same fate as the preceding one. And when passenger and goods traffic on the Cairo-Suez route increased, the British supported the project for a Cairo-Suez railway but, starting in 1845, Muhammad Ali rejected the scheme lest foreign influence spread in Egypt.

. . . By the beginning of the second half of the nineteenth century the flow of traffic on the land route from Europe to India and the Far East had reached a level that necessitated the construction of a railway or the digging of a canal—Britain supported the first alternative and opposed the second owing to its belief that a canal would make it easier for the other imperialist powers to move their warships to the Red Sea and India, threatening British interests; France, on the other hand, supported the canal and opposed the railway.

The railway project succeeded because the British consul-general in Egypt, Murray, had much influence over Abbas I, which made that viceroy carry out the wishes of Britain and oppose the French scheme. Abbas had the Cairo-Suez road improved and began construction on a railway from Alexandria to Cairo. On July 12, 1851, he signed an agreement with Robert Stephenson, the British engineer [son of the famous inventor], for the drawing-up of the designs and the supervision of construction in return for a fee of £56,000. The line from Alexandria to Kafr al-Zayyat, 112 kilometers long, was completed in 1853, during the reign of Abbas, while the Kafr al-Zayyat to Cairo stretch was opened in 1856, under Said. The Alexandria-Cairo line was thus the first railway in Africa and the east and one of the first built outside Europe.[2]

Under Said a railway was built from Cairo to Suez, and opened for traffic in 1858. This provided a railway connection between Alexandria and Suez, which increased the flow of passengers, goods, and mail on the east-west route through Egypt and led to a rise in government revenue. Railways replaced carriages on the Cairo-Suez road and boats on the Alexandria-Cairo water route, which increased the speed and comfort of travel.

In addition to these two lines, the following railways were built under Said:

1. Tanta–al-Mahalla al-Kubra–Samannud
2. Banha–Mit Birah
3. Banha–al-Zaqaziq

The total length of the railways built in Egypt during that reign was 336 kilometers. Under Ismail the Railways Administration, which had become disorganized during the previous reign, was reformed, the Cairo–Alexandria line was double-tracked, and the following lines were constructed:

1. Tanta–Mahallat Ruh
2. Banha–al-Zaqaziq [*sic*]

[2] Under Muhammad Ali, the Mahmudia railway had been built in [the port of] Alexandria, but it was a short one, only 300 meters, and was used solely for merchandise.

3. Barrage-Qaliub
4. Barrage-al-Zaqaziq
5. Al-Zaqaziq-Mansura
6. Al-Zaqaziq-Ismailia
7. Disuq-Zifta
8. Tanta-Shibin al-Kom
9. Talkha-Samannud
10. Abu Kabir-al-Salihia
11. Mansura-Damietta
12. Ismailia-Suez
13. Alexandria-Rosetta
14. Alexandria-Sidi Gabir
15. Al-Ma'mura-Abu Qir
16. Qallin-Kafr al-Shaikh
17. Bulaq al-Dakrur-Itiai al-Barud
18. Bulaq al-Dakrur-Asiut
19. Al-Wasta-Abu Kisah

The total length of these lines, including the doubling of the Cairo-Alexandria railway, was 1189 kilometers.

The following lines were also constructed under Ismail:[3]

1. Cairo-Sarai al-Qubba
2. Cairo Station-'Abbasia-Citadel-Hilwan
3. A line from Wadi Halfa south, for a distance of 57 kilometers

As a result of this new construction during the reign of Ismail the main towns in the Delta were joined by a network of railways and the growth of the sugar industry in Upper Egypt was stimulated by the Bulaq al-Dakrur-Asiut line. However, until 1891, the latter remained disconnected from the terminal of the Delta railways at Cairo, for lack of a bridge over the Nile linking the two lines.

Railway expansion under Ismail was undoubtedly one of the main causes of the economic and social progress registered during that period; it also helped the expansion of cotton cultivation by providing swift transport for the crop to Alexandria, whence it was exported.

However, the opening of the Suez Canal to navigation in 1869 diverted the east-west flow of passengers, mail, and goods from the railways to the Canal, thus leading to a loss of the profits that Egypt previously derived from the transit traffic. The annual

profits of the railways from transit traffic before the opening of the Canal amounted to £E750,000. But in 1869 operations on the Cairo-Suez line ceased, following the opening of the Canal and of the Cairo-Ismailia-Suez railway, while revenue from the Cairo-Alexandria line fell drastically. Thus the railway which had originally been built to serve east-west traffic became dependent on passenger and goods traffic within the confines of Egypt.

Under Tawfiq the Banha-Al-Zaqaziq line was doubled and the following lines were built:

1. Bab al-Luq-Al-Ma'adi
2. Shirbin-Bilqas
3. Al-Rahmania-Damanhur
4. Shibin al-Kom-Minuf
5. Asiut-Girga
6. Al-Fayyum-Sinuris
7. Kubri al-Limun-Al-Qalg
8. Sidi Gabir-Al-Nuzha
9. Cairo-Bulaq al-Dakrur

The total length of these lines, including the doubling of that from Banha to Al-Zaqaziq, was 234 kilometers.

During the reign of Abbas II [1892–1914] the following lines, totaling 806 kilometers, were built:

1. Al-Maks line [from Alexandria]
2. Al-Dikhila-Ras al-Tin
3. Mariut-Al-Dab'a
4. Al-Busili-Idfina
5. Bilqas-Kafr al-Shaikh
6. Al-Zaqaziq-Zifta
7. Barrage-Minuf
8. Minuf-Al-Shuhada
9. Al-Qalg-Shibin al Qanatir
10. Ismailia-Port Said
11. Girga-Al-Shallal
12. [Western] Oases railway
13. Bani Suaif-Al-Lahun

In addition, the Imbaba-Itlidim line was doubled, a railway was built between the quarries of Al-Qanawia and Asiut, railway stations were improved, and new ones were built. The government also bought out the following lines:

1. The Mariut line [from Alexandria]

2. The additional lines bought by the Sugar Company in 1903 from the Daira Sania Company
3. The Oases line
4. The Ismailia–Port Said line, under the agreement concluded between the government and the Suez Canal Company ...

Such were the lines built in Egypt during the second half of the nineteenth century and up to 1914. However, railway transport costs remained very high for bulky but light and low-priced agricultural goods. The fact that the north-south main line ran along the Nile also meant that many centers of production remained separated from the railway by the river. ...

Maritime Transport

... Thus was born the Egyptian merchant fleet in the Mediterranean.[4] The number of ships increased to seventeen by 1817. Muhammad Ali's interest in merchant shipping in the Mediterranean continued even after his conflict with the sultan had been resolved, in 1841; thus in 1845 he founded a steam navigation company, between Alexandria and Constantinople. In addition, Egypt was linked to other lands by several foreign lines. ...[5]

Egypt was one of the first countries in the world to benefit from the use of steamships in maritime transport, being connected by steamship lines with Europe, India, and the Far East. In 1834 the East India Company started a regular steamer service between Suez and Bombay; this was later replaced by a service from Suez to India and the Far East operated by the Peninsular and Oriental Steam Navigation Company. In the Mediterranean there were the following steamship lines: a British company, Oriental Steamship Company, with sailings to Egypt and Syria starting in 1836; a French line, Messageries Maritimes, with a service between Marseilles and

Alexandria starting in 1837; an Austrian line, Lloyd, in 1838; and another British line, the above-mentioned Peninsular and Oriental, starting in 1840.

The port of Alexandria was improved under Muhammad Ali, being enlarged and deepened so as to enable ships to dock instead of having to anchor far from the shore. European ships, which had hitherto been restricted to the eastern port, were now authorized to enter the western; this led to an increase in traffic. A quay for merchandise was built in the port; a railway connected it with the warehouses where grains and other goods were stored, to facilitate their transport to the ships; and storehouses, a customshouse, and dwellings for officials were built in the port area. Buoys ('*alamat*) were placed at the entry of the Alexandria harbor, to guide incoming and departing ships, and a lighthouse was built on the peninsula of Ras al-Tin. In 1844 construction of a repair dock was initiated in Alexandria.

The improvement of maritime transport during the reign of Muhammad Ali stimulated agricultural and commercial development, by facilitating the export of cotton and other goods; opened the country to foreign influences and new, progressive ideas; raised the price of Egyptian produce, which could now be more easily shipped abroad; and reduced that of imports, because of the greater ease and lower cost of sea transport.

Such was the situation under Muhammad Ali. Under Abbas I, the number of vessels calling at Alexandria in 1850 was 1,807. The government decreed that ships should leave the port of Suez only in a certain order; this led to an increase in freight rates and a costly delay in the movement of merchandise through Suez.

Under Said the Majidia Company was founded, in 1857, by Egyptian and foreign capital. Its purpose was steam navigation in the Mediterranean and Red Sea, and its period of concession thirty years. Its ships carried the Egyptian flag and any disputes in which it was involved were to be

---

[4] In 1812, when Muhammad Ali's ships started sailing from Alexandria to Constantinople on the one hand and Malta on the other.—Translator.

[5] In the year 1833–34, 634 foreign ships called at Alexandria, and in 1840, 1,079 ships; the highest figure recorded between those dates was 1,240.—Translator.

brought before the Egyptian commercial courts, not the consular courts. The company had depots and stations in Suez, Qusair, and Massawa. Its steamers sailed between Suez, the ports of Hijaz and Yemen, Qusair, Suakin, and Massawa, carrying pilgrims to and from Hijaz; it also had a Mediterranean service. But toward the end of Said's reign the company began to decline, because of bad administration, and it was liquidated under Ismail.

The government also sought to improve the port of Suez, in view of the increase in traffic caused by the opening of the Cairo-Suez railway and the founding of the Majidia Company. A contract was signed with the French firm of Dussaud[6] for the enlargement of the port and the building of a floating dock for ship repairs. Work began on two ports, one for warships and the other for merchant ships, surrounded by a breakwater with a channel for the passage of vessels; construction of a floating dock was also started. The work of improvement of Suez harbor was completed under Ismail.

Under Said the restrictions on ships leaving Suez and regulations in other ports impeding trade were abolished; this led to an appreciable decline in freight rates. During the same reign excavation began on the Suez Canal, which was opened to navigation under Ismail, in 1869, and had a great effect on navigation, as will be described later. The number of ships calling at Alexandria was 1,996 in 1860 and 2,576 in 1862; between 1853 and 1862, 72 per cent of Egypt's exports passed through Alexandria.

In 1863, under Ismail, a steamship company, the 'Azizia Company, was founded by Egyptian and foreign capital. Its object was the transport of passengers and goods in the Mediterranean and Red Sea, and it replaced the Majidia Company, which had been liquidated. The company improved Egypt's sea communications with other countries and competed successfully with

[6] Dussaud was actually a contractor, acting on behalf of Messageries Impériales.—Translator.

foreign lines. In 1873 Ismail bought the shares of the company and converted it into a government department, under the name of Khedivial Mail Line [Administration de Paquebots Postes Khédiviaux]; its scope expanded and it came to operate twenty-six steamers, flying the Egyptian flag and carrying passengers, cargo, and mail between Egypt and the Mediterranean coasts of Syria, Anatolia, and Greece; the Dardanelles and Bosphorus; such Red Sea ports as Suakin, Massawa, Yanbu', Jidda, and Hodaida; and the ports of Berbera and Zaila, beyond the straits of Bab al-Mandib. The floating dock in Alexandria was put under this department and a workshop for the repair of ships was assigned to it in the arsenal of Alexandria.

The government also bought, in addition to these steamers, large sailing ships for the transport from Anatolia of the timber required by the departments of war and the navy; under Ismail Egypt had a merchant fleet of 555 sailing ships, aggregating 30,919 tons.

In 1872 Egypt was directly connected with several foreign ports, by the following steamship lines:

1. Three Egyptian lines, two between Alexandria and Constantinople and one between Suez and Massawa
2. Five British lines, two between Alexandria and Southampton, two between Suez and Calcutta, and one between Suez and Bombay
3. Five French lines, of which one linked Alexandria and Marseilles and one linked Marseilles with Hong Kong by way of Port Said and Suez
4. Four Austrian lines, one from Alexandria to Trieste, one from Alexandria to Constantinople, and one from Trieste to Bombay, passing through Port Said and Suez
5. Two Italian lines, one between Alexandria and Genoa and the other from Genoa to Bombay, by way of Port Said and Suez
6. A Russian line, from Alexandria to Constantinople and Odessa
7. A Turkish line between Constantinople and Basra, by way of Port Said and Suez.

In addition to these scheduled services,

many steamers, especially British, sailed at irregular intervals between Egyptian and European ports.

Under Ismail the improvement of the port of Suez, begun under Said, was completed and that of Alexandria was undertaken by the British firm of Greenfield and Elliot, for a sum of £E2,542,000; a larger iron floating dock replaced the stone dock built under Muhammad Ali, which was no longer adequate for repair work, especially on big ships; a breakwater was constructed between the peninsula of Ras al-Tin and Agami, with a channel for the passage of ships; and within the port a quay for loading and unloading, as well as other quays, were built.

Maritime traffic in Alexandria increased and its share in Egypt's exports in 1863–72 rose to 94 per cent, from 72 in 1853–62. During those ten years, 31,909 merchant ships, aggregating 12,462,703 tons, called at Alexandria; in 1875 the number of ships was 2,589, displacing 832,127 tons; and between September, 1877, and August, 1878, the number of sailing ships was 1,233 and that of steamers 751. The average annual number of ships calling at all Egyptian ports in 1863–72 was [5,909, aggregating 2,038,098 tons; of this 3,190, aggregating 1,246,270 tons called at Alexandria; 970, aggregating 384,474 tons, called at Port Said; and 440, aggregating 312,352 tons, at Suez]. . . .

CHAPTER 8

Egyptian Cotton and the American Civil War, 1860–1866

The development of cotton as Egypt's major crop came in two spurts. In 1819 a French engineer, Jumel, who was employed in Muhammad Ali's textile works, started to experiment with a new type of cotton he had discovered in a Cairo garden.[1] The viceroy quickly realized the potentialities of the new crop, both as a raw material for his mills and as an export product. Suitable land was allocated to cotton, instructors were brought in from Syria and Asia Minor, and the peasants were given the necessary orders and at the same time provided with credit, seeds, and cotton gins. Simultaneously, markets were opened for Egyptian cotton in Lancashire and elsewhere by British and other European merchants resident in Alexandria. By 1824 output had risen to 225,000 qantars, and cotton exports brought in nearly £500,000. After that, production and exports fluctuated —in response to changes in world prices, labor supply, cotton diseases, and other factors—but the general trend was upward, and continued so even after Muhammad Ali's monopolies were abolished and his control over agriculture had been ended. For by then private growers had discovered the great profitability of the new crop, while the government played its part by providing canals and other simple irrigation works. By the 1850's exports had passed the 500,000 qantar mark and cotton was accounting for well over a third of total export proceeds.

The next impulsion came during the American Civil War and is described in the following selection. The immediate effect of the "cotton famine" was to raise prices sharply,[2] a process that provoked an almost immediate response among

[1] An alternative version is that Muhammad Ali, having seen a piece of cloth woven from Sennar cotton, asked the governor of that Sudanese province to send him a sample of the cotton together with a consignment of seeds. The governor's successor, Mahu Bey, complied with the order and thus gave his name to the first variety of cotton bred in Egypt by Jumel (Richard Hill, *Egypt in the Sudan, 1820–1881*, pp. 51–52). However, the viceregal order in question is dated December 9, 1824, and is thus three years later than the beginning of cotton cultivation in Egypt.

[2] On November 5, 1862, the United States consul in Alexandria, William S. Thayer, reported: "The fluctuations of prices vary principally in accordance with the spirit of the daily telegrams from the Liverpool market and the impressions as to the probability of peace in America entertained by the mercantile community of Liverpool and Alexandria. A decided victory on the part of the Union forces tells ordinarily in a depreciation of price" (U.S. Department of State, *Papers Relating to the Foreign Relations of the United States*, 1863, p. 1102). See also dispatch of July 20, 1861).

Egyptian growers. Exports passed the 1,000,000 qantar mark in 1863 and reached 2,000,000 in 1865. The end of the Civil War brought cotton prices down sharply, and with it Egyptian acreage and production, but the upward trend was soon resumed and continued at an accelerating pace until the First World War (see Part VI, chap. 1). The rapid extension of irrigation, both before and especially during the British occupation, was the main factor at work, but the decline of world wheat prices in the late 1870's, because of increased supplies from the Americas and Australia, and rising cotton prices after the turn of the century also played their part (see Part VI, chap. 11). By then cotton and cottonseed accounted for 90 per cent of Egypt's exports. Subsequent developments, including a slowing-down in the expansion of cultivation and the consumption of over a quarter of the crop in local mills, have reduced the predominance of cotton in Egypt's exports, but it is still by far the most important item.

(See also works by Charles-Roux [*Coton en Egypte*], Rivlin, Hitta, Crouchley [*Economic Development*], and Landes listed in the Bibliography.)

[From E. R. J. Owen, "Cotton Production and the Development of the Cotton Economy in 19th Century Egypt" (unpublished thesis, Oxford University, 1965); printed by kind permission of the author.]

THE COTTON BOOM, 1861–66

The years 1861 to 1866 mark an important turning point in the history of Egyptian cotton production. When the period began some half a million cantars were being grown on perhaps 250,000 feddans; five years later the harvest had increased four times in size, the area by five, and from then on cotton became once and for all the crop which absorbed the major portion of Egyptian energies and the overwhelming share of its export earnings.[1] The cause of this sudden metamorphosis was the American Civil War which, by depriving the European textile industry of the greater part of its supplies of American cotton on which it was largely dependent, drove up the price of cotton to enormous heights and conferred great prosperity on those countries which, like Egypt, were able to take advan-

tage of the favourable situation. In England, for example, where 80 per cent of raw cotton requirements came from the Southern United States and where the Liverpool price of Middling Orleans (an average variety) rose from 7.5–8 pence a pound in 1861 to a high of 31.5 pence a pound in July, 1864, Jumel was able to increase its share of the market from 3 per cent to 12 per cent during the war period and its earnings from £1.5 to £14 million.[2]

... [By the summer of 1862] alternative sources of supply were urgently sought, and European imports from India, Brazil, and Turkey [see Part II, Chap. 7] as well as Egypt were rapidly expanded in an effort to make good the deficiency.

Among these countries, Egypt was particularly well placed to increase its production, although this was not the opinion of most contemporary observers. Henry Lockwood, writing in 1858, had pointed to the fact that the fellah cultivator was "improvident" and "the enemy of improvement" and that, except for the estates of the royal family and a few of the richer pashas, Egyptian cotton was badly produced; and he had concluded that "it

[1] Estimates for both weight and value of Egyptian cotton exports vary ... The figures chosen are those provided in the '*Statistique de l'Egypte*' published in 1873. ... [See W. O. Henderson, *Lancashire Cotton Famine* (Manchester, 1934), pp. 122–23, and Part VI, chap. 11 for cotton prices in Alexandria and Liverpool—Editor.]

[2] £14 million was the peak of British imports of Egyptian cotton. In the following ten years their value varied between £6 and £8 million.

may be questioned whether the annual exports of cotton from Egypt would admit of any extension, as long as the present system of culture and preparation is continued, even were the social system of the peasantry to improve." And even someone so well acquainted with local conditions as Ninet was able to maintain, on the eve of the war, that the chronic shortage of agricultural labour would prevent even the smallest increase in the area sown with Jumel. Perhaps neither man could have been expected to foresee the high prices which the American war was to bring but they also overlooked the very important changes which had occurred in the agricultural sector of the economy in the previous ten years. During this period contact between merchant and cultivator had been re-established, the fellaheen were once again used to producing cash crops for immediate sale; facilities for the provision of agricultural capital, albeit at a high rate, had spread throughout the lower Egyptian provinces. Meanwhile numerous cotton-ginning establishments had been built, the Alexandria-Cairo railway completed, and the Delta barrage brought to a point where it was able to raise the level of water in a number of major canals.[3] Then unlike India, where cotton changed hands so many times between cultivator and exporter that it was impossible to fix responsibility for dirty or adulterated cotton, the Egyptian system, whereby the Alexandria merchants sent their agents to buy cotton at the main Delta collection points and made payment according to grade, allowed some control to be exercised over quality. In this respect Egypt also benefited greatly from the presence of a few rich proprietors who traditionally were concerned to produce cotton by the most up-to-date methods and who set a standard and an example for other cultivators to try and emulate. In what is admittedly a very rough piece of calculating,

[3] The barrage was completed in 1861 and first used to hold up water in 1863. Dangerous cracks then appeared in its superstructure, but the level of water in some of the Delta canals was, in fact, raised.

Thayer, the American Consul, estimated that two-thirds of the Egyptian crop was classified (according to colour, cleanness, strength of staple) as "average" at this time and only 47,000 to 56,000 cantars, or approximately 10 per cent of the total, as "inferior."

Another advantage Egypt possessed was that in the year before the war was declared cotton production had once again begun to rise after having remained static throughout the previous decade. Exports of the 1860 crop reached almost 600,000 cantars and in 1861 this increased to well over 700,000 (a figure which would have been even higher had not a portion of the harvest been carried away by the high Nile flood of that year). The reasons for this movement are uncertain but it may have been connected with the construction of ginning factories which made preparation of cotton for export easier and the slight rise in prices at the time of spring sowing in 1860. Another important factor was undoubtedly the new market which had been established for cotton seed in the late 1850's. For every five cantars of ginned cotton there were roughly 3.5 ardebs of seed, which at 1861 prices would have provided an additional income of 25 piastres for each cantar produced or 2.5 dollars per feddan (given the average Jumel yield of 2 cantars per feddan), augmenting total earnings by 10 per cent. That cultivators were quick to profit from this situation is shown by the fact that nearly 75 per cent of the seed from the 1861 crop was exported. Finally, it is possible that when sowing their cotton in March, April, and May, 1861, many of the cultivators were sufficiently aware of the increase in demand which would accompany an interruption of American supplies that they extended the area devoted to its cultivation still further, even though prices at this time were no higher than they had been a year earlier. But whether this is true or not, once war was actually declared and the price of Jumel started to climb, cultivators were quick to grasp the potentialities of their position, and by July Thayer was reporting that "in expectation of scarcity in England some of the commercial houses in Alexandria are sending agents into the interior to buy cotton in advance of the harvest. But so well understood is the condition in the cotton-growing region in the United States, even by the poorest fellahs, that it is difficult to persuade them to sell on terms which heretofore they would have been delighted to accept." Jumel, he went on, was then being quoted at 13.75 dollars a cantar "but some of the largest growers insist on 17 dollars, and are holding back for this unheard of figure." And such was the demand that cotton was sold and resold several times between Alexandria and the interior.

Prices continued to rise during the autumn and winter and by the spring of 1862 had reached 16 to 18 dollars a cantar. More land was then placed under cotton; amounting to a total of perhaps 500,000 to 600,000 feddans as against some 350,000 feddans the previous year. Gregoire mentions a particular increase in cotton sown in the Cairo area and also in Behera province where previously it had been thought that manpower was too scarce to make it attractive. Meanwhile, Ismail, the heir to the throne, was instrumental in planting 4,000 feddans with cotton in Upper Egypt, the first time Jumel had been successfully introduced into this region. Money was abundant following the completion of arrangements for a state loan in March and the number of moneylenders, Muslims as well as Europeans, proliferated. The result was a crop of 1.2 million cantars which was sold for nearly £9.5 million. In addition seed worth £475,000 was exported, much of it going to Turkey and other neighbouring countries which were also trying to expand their production of cotton.

Said himself grew 40,000 cantars of cotton on his estates in 1862, while he and other members of the royal family, in particular his brother Halim and nephew Ismail, were active in importing machinery and improving methods of cultivation. It was said of Ismail "that buyers fought to purchase his cotton because he paid special attention to tilling the soil so as to produce the best crops and to realize the best prices for them." But there is little evidence of direct government action to increase the area of cotton planted.[4] "Prices alone will prove a sufficient stimulus without any effort on my part," Said had told a visiting Englishman in 1861, and on the whole he was perfectly right. The common pattern was almost certainly very like that described by Wallace, writing of a village in the Delta where the fellaheen had returned gratefully to cereal production after having been forced to grow Jumel during Mohamed Ali's reign, but whose prejudices vanished in the face of the prospect of large profits. One peasant planted a little cotton and got a good price for it; the others then followed, with help from several Greeks who had arrived in the district and who offered to provide the seeds and money required. Nevertheless, as the cotton shortage in England became more severe, Lancashire pressure on Said to use his influence to expand production still further became increasingly intense. This was particularly the case during his short visit to Manchester in July, 1862. After being shown a number of mills he was presented with an address from the Manchester Chamber of Commerce urging him to take action. "The Directors of this Chamber," it began, "have watched with great satisfaction the encouragement afforded by your predecessor and yourself to the cultivation of the cotton plant and they indulge in the hope that the knowledge obtained by your Highness of the value and importance of the manufacturing industry of this district will make an enduring impression upon your mind and enable you to foresee the vast benefits which must accrue to both producer and consumer from the more extended cultivation of that most valuable material." In

---

[4] Some sources say that the duty on exported cotton was reduced from 10 per cent to 1 per cent in 1862, but it is not clear why it was originally so high when the rate fixed by the Anglo-Turkish Commercial Convention of 1838 was 12 per cent. [See Part II, chap. 3.]

reply, Said assured his audience that the next crop would be at least half as large again as the one just planted. And on his return to Egypt he urged all proprietors to sow a fourth of their land with cotton, a suggestion which according to Thayer was tantamount to a command, while occupying himself with organizing the cleaning of the canals and the better distribution of water.

Pressure and encouragement on Said to increase production also came from the Manchester Cotton Supply Association. The Association had been founded in 1857 but its origins went back much further and lay in the fears of such men as a Liverpool correspondent of the president of the Board of Trade who as early as June, 1828, had written of "the precarious situation of the cotton trade of this country from our too great dependence on the United States for the raw material." Subsequently, alarm at the thought of a Negro revolt or the partial or total failure of the American crop, and the increasing use of Southern cotton in Northern [U.S.] mills had led John Bright and Thomas Bazley to urge both the Government and Lancashire business men to do all in their power to encourage the growth of good, cheap cotton in the Empire, particularly India and the West Indies, and Brazil. This movement led to the foundation of the Association whose primary aim, as set out in an editorial of its newspaper, *The Cotton Supply Reporter*, in November, 1858, was to increase the sources of cotton supply "by bringing its influence to bear upon our own and other governments for the removal of restrictive duties or legislative obstructions to cotton growth or exportation in the British Dominions and elsewhere; by obtaining and diffusing all available information as to countries capable of growing cotton, with a view to stimulating and directing private enterprise in its production; by circulating printed instructions as to the best methods of cotton farming and the preparation of cotton for the market; by grants of cotton-seed, cotton gins, and machinery of the most improved kinds or construction as inducement to private persons or associations to enter upon cotton culture; . . ." and by a variety of other means.

The attention of the Association, both before and after 1862, was directed mainly towards India, which seemed to offer the best prospects for an immediate large increase in supply, but the possibilities of other areas were also investigated.[5] A number of reports on Egyptian conditions were prepared and in August, 1861, Haywood, the secretary of the society, paid a brief visit to the country. In an interview with Said he offered the Association's assistance in increasing cotton production and discussed with him a project to which the Viceroy attached great importance: the establishment of a system of government-guaranteed advances by English capitalists which would relieve the cultivator of his dependence on rural money-lenders who charged high rates of interest. Haywood then went on a tour of the main cotton-growing areas and ended his stay by writing a letter to the Viceroy in which he outlined his findings. These included the need for more mechanical gins, better seed, and for more intelligent management of some of the farms he had visited. He also spoke once again of the plan to establish a cotton bank to provide loans for cultivators. On Haywood's advice a number of packages of New Orleans seed were later sent to Egypt by the Association and distributed among the larger cotton growers with full instructions as to their cultivation. Several improved hand gins were also presented to the Viceroy and a dispatch from Thayer suggests that a start may have been made in lending British money to cotton growers in the spring of 1862. However, the impact of these innovations was small. The New Orleans seed was never successfully grown, while the cotton bank scheme was given up after Said's death in January, 1863, its abandonment necessitating no loss as the money-lenders as well as some Alexandria

[5] Between 1860 and 1862 the Indian share of the British cotton market increased from 14 per cent to 71 per cent.

banks and credit institutions continued to supply all the money the cultivators needed. More machinery, including steam ploughs, cotton gins, and packing presses worth £71,000, was sent to Egypt in 1863 in conjunction with the Manchester Chamber of Commerce but by this time British manufacturers no longer needed convincing that Ismail's government was doing all in its power to increase production, and thereafter the Association confined itself to occasional verbal exhortation.[6]

Ismail's accession in 1863 was a signal for renewed optimism in Egypt's continuing prosperity. He was known as "a model farmer." His first speech to the foreign consuls, in which he expressed a desire to develop Egypt's resources in an orderly and diligent manner, produced a very favourable impression; while to a correspondent of the Manchester Cotton Supply Association writing in February, 1863, he seemed "alive to the importance of extending the cultivation of cotton still further." Meanwhile cotton prices had reached 31 to 34 dollars a cantar and more land than ever was devoted to Jumel, many of the larger proprietors increasing their crop area by a third. However, almost at once Ismail was called upon to face a series of crises which threatened to undermine all Egypt's agricultural efforts. The first was the plague which began attacking cattle in the Delta some time in the early summer. Once the serious nature of the outbreak was realized, in June, a number of measures were announced in an attempt to isolate the affected districts; it was forbidden to move animals from village to village, fairs were cancelled, orders were given that corpses should be burned rather than thrown in the river. However, these restrictions were largely ignored and by September it was said that most of the Lower Egyptian provinces were swept clean of cattle, the only exception being the Wadi district

where an energetic European director with considerable local influence was able to save about a quarter of the total. Ismail at once began to encourage the introduction of replacements from abroad. He sent his own agents first to Syria, Libya and Crete, then further afield to Marseilles, Trieste and Odessa to purchase new animals; he also lifted the duty on imported cattle. Oxen as well as horses and donkeys began arriving in large numbers in the autumn and were immediately sold to the cultivators. But many were weak and small and failed to acclimatise, others died from over-work, while those from Russia brought new diseases with them. Finally a second outbreak of the murrain in November and December killed off most of those who remained and a new series of imports was necessary. As in 1843 the cattle plague also provided a great stimulus to the introduction of steam-ploughs and steam-pumps. Once again Ismail led the way: "We must look to machinery to supply the grievous loss the country has experienced in its cattle," he told the British Consul General. "My object is to set an example to my countrymen. I can afford to do so now. . . ." He himself purchased machines on a large scale both for his own estates, where by May, 1864, he was said to possess 200 steam-ploughs, and for re-sale to other proprietors. The European merchants soon followed suit, and in 1864 and 1865 the value of agricultural engines imported from England alone amounted to well over £650,000. . . .

While the cattle plague was running its course a second crisis occurred, this time from the highest Nile of the century, which during the night of September 25 infiltrated the dike along the Rosetta branch 6 miles above Kafr al-Zayat. The waters spread rapidly across the countryside, destroying much recently harvested cotton and cutting the Alexandria-Cairo railway line for a month. By great personal exertion Ismail prevented further damage. At the same time he requisitioned all the steamers on the river and organized a temporary service between Cairo and Kafr al-Zayat

---

[6] The Association echoed the strong protest of the British merchants in January–February, 1864, about conditions on the railways and at the port of Alexandria.

to cope with the large quantities of cotton awaiting transport.

Nevertheless, in spite of both flood and murrain, exports of the 1863 crop reached 1.7 million cantars, or 50 per cent above the previous year. Estimates of the size of the crop made before June put it at a possible 2 million cantars and losses may have been something in the nature of 200,000 cantars as a result of the murrain, and 100,000 from the flooded fields, although such a calculation can only be the very roughest approximation. That the loss was not larger was due to the fact that the crop had been planted before the shortage of animals began to make itself felt and also that the majority of the cultivators employed the Bali method by which the cotton was watered by flow irrigation and shadoof once the Nile started to rise rather than by an oxen or buffalo-turned sakia.

The effects of the murrain continued to be felt in 1864. Prices were almost at their peak during spring sowing but whether the area under cotton was extended it is impossible to say. Fellaheen, in particular, must have found the effort of preparing the ground for the new crop a difficult one and contemporary accounts speak of them yoking themselves to their ploughs like animals. Of the remainder, many left their plants in the ground for another year. As for the larger proprietors some compensation was provided by imported machinery although the great bulk of the steam-ploughs did not begin to arrive until after the sowing season was over. And cattle were not entirely unobtainable; according to the *Times* correspondent 4,500 beasts were sold at the main Tanta fair during the summer.[7] The result was a crop of 2 million cantars but almost certainly a decline in yield. During 1862 and 1863 the average number of cantars per feddan can be assumed to have been rising as this was generally the case when cotton was first extended to new areas. However, by 1864, many of the Delta fields had been under

Jumel for three years and in some of the districts the soil was beginning to show signs of exhaustion. Again, owing to the scarcity of animals much of the land was insufficiently ploughed and watered, while plants which were not uprooted at the end of a season but left for another inevitably produced less lint.

The murrain and flood had even more serious repercussions on Egyptian food production. Ismail was first forced to import butter and meat and then, on March 8, 1864, when a large deficit in the coming cereal harvest seemed certain, to issue an order suspending the duty on imported wheat and flour from that day on and forbidding the export of the same articles from April 8.[8] A low Nile made matters worse and during 1864 and again in 1865 Egypt became a net importer of grain, although not on a large scale. At the time it was common to blame this situation on the "avidité sans bornes" of the fellaheen who were prepared to sacrifice everything for cotton, but this is not entirely fair. In 1863, when it is likely that almost as much land was devoted to cotton as in 1864, exports of wheat and beans were above average, and the difference between the two years lay not so much in the fact that Delta cereal producing land was diverted to Jumel but that owing to the flood a large part of the millet crop on which the fellaheen were dependent was destroyed, forcing them to eat more wheat. Again, the murrain left few animals for harvesting and transporting the cereal crop grown in the autumn of 1863. As for 1864, the peasants were faced with a choice: They could devote their now depleted resources to preparing the ground for cotton or they could forgo a portion of their prospective profits to concentrate on a winter cereal crop of the normal size. In the event, they appear to have chosen the first course, although at the same time ensuring their own personal food supplies, the small amounts of imported grain going largely to the urban population. In Upper Egypt

---

[7] 25,000 were sold in 1863.

[8] The prohibition on exports was extended several times and not finally lifted until July, 1866.

cotton production was not on a sufficiently extensive scale to make much difference to the cereal harvest.

The rapid increase in Egyptian trade at this time imposed a severe strain on Egypt's harbour facilities and transportation system. In particular the railway administration found it difficult to cope with the large quantity of cotton to be taken to the coast for shipment. Basic shortcomings such as the lack of sufficient trucks and the fact that there was only a single track between Cairo and Alexandria were aggravated by inefficient management and irregular service. Some delays were first experienced in the winter of 1862–63, and soon after his accession Ismail was forced to send government boats to assist in moving the harvest. At the same time he promised to accelerate work on doubling the main line which had been begun in 1860. The following winter conditions worsened. Not only was the crop larger than ever but the flood, by interrupting rail services in October, caused more and more cotton to pile up at the intermediate stations while large numbers of cattle and machines accumulated at Alexandria for delivery to points in the interior of the Delta. Service became increasingly uncertain—there were 16 collisions in March, 1864, alone, passengers had to be refused, and to judge from a series of complaints from Taylor, a British merchant, sizable consignments of cotton were often lost, burned, or delivered to the wrong person, without payment of compensation. Another source of hold-up and confusion was the Alexandria dock area; here there was only one wharf so that the majority of ships had to be loaded and unloaded by lighter, "always a work of much delay and frequently of danger." Customs house facilities were inadequate and the streets between the harbour and the town and railway station were unpaved and often deep in mud. Irritation at such conditions produced a long series of protests from the mercantile community. These became particularly virulent in the winter of 1863–64 when in addition to the usual complaints about delays and losses it was felt that Ismail, in his position as the largest cotton grower and chief merchant in the country, was beginning to use the transport system for his own ends. A strongly worded memorandum drawn up after a meeting of leading members of the British community in January, 1864, accused him of monopolising the railway for the carriage of his own goods and taking over all the lighters and labourers in Alexandria to unload the coal and machinery he was then importing in such quantity. While in April, after this first protest had been rejected, the same group claimed that one of their number, wishing to send a consignment of goods into the interior, had been told by a railway employee that "so long as there remained for transport a single package of the merchandise belonging to His Highness, the Viceroy, the goods of private persons could not be forwarded." Nevertheless, it should be noted that by April perhaps three-quarters of the cotton crop had been exported. Nor did the protests go unheeded. A new director of the railway administration was appointed ("the most able man in Egypt") with an Englishman, Rouse, as chief engineer, more rolling stock was ordered, and work on doubling the Alexandria-Cairo line finally completed. Meanwhile a personal inspection of the customs area by Ragheb Pasha, the senior minister, led to a rapid clearance of the piles of goods accumulated there. Ismail ordered the construction of an iron screw-pile jetty and an extra shed for merchandise awaiting inspection but there were insufficient funds for any more comprehensive improvements and his good intentions were further hindered by what the *Times* correspondent referred to as "The stolid and inert obstinacy of the chief customs officer and his perverse tribe of subordinate" men "who instead of aiding by prompt dispatch of business, create the most vexatious delays, and obstruct the measures of the merchants to clear their goods and disembarrass the customs house, and so confusion and difficulty magnify with every additional store."

In each cotton season between 1863 and 1865 over one million feddans or about 40 per cent of the total cultivated area of Lower Egypt was placed under cotton. And it follows that if some cultivators used a biennial, others a triennial rotation, at some stage during this period cotton must have been grown in almost every Delta field.[9] Methods used do not seem to have varied much from those described in earlier chapters. The majority of proprietors were peasants who owned land at some distance from the main summer-water canals and for them the Bali method, which delayed the irrigation of the growing plant until the Nile began to rise in July, was not only less labour and animal-intensive but essential. Some change in rotation may have occurred, however. In the years before 1861 many cultivators used a two- or three-year cycle in which Jumel followed the berseem of the previous summer; then land lay fallow from June until it was prepared for sowing the following March. But as the extension of cotton meant a diminution of the area available for food crops it was no longer possible to leave the soil unoccupied for so long and maize was grown in the early autumn in the space of time between the two other crops. Another way of maintaining the food supply was to intensify the practice of sowing wheat and beans between the rows of cotton but this may not have proved so popular, as the harvesting of the former inevitably injured the young Jumel plants.

A little more is known of the conditions on the larger estates. There, the preparations for sowing cotton began in the middle of March when the land was ploughed, watered, then ploughed again. Planting began early in May, the seeds being placed in rows three feet apart. The cotton was irrigated approximately four times during growth and weeded every thirty days. Harvesting commenced in September. Figures from an American consular dispatch of March, 1863, give some indication of the cost of cultivating one feddan in the Mansourah district. . . . Assuming a yield of four cantars a feddan, total expenses of P.T. 480 would work out at 6 dollars (£1.2) a cantar. Later, however, the expenses of those using sakia-irrigation almost doubled as agricultural wages rose and new cattle had to be hired or purchased to replace those killed in the murrain. Machines were, at least in theory, less expensive to buy and operate but contemporary calculations were generally based on an unrealistically low figure for the price of fuel. According to Ninet, coal which cost only 12.5 francs a ton f.o.b. Newcastle or Cardiff, retailed at 75 to 100 francs in the interior of the Delta. Even then regular delivery could not be assured. Because of the uncertainty of the railway service, consignments of fuel which reached Alexandria in April often did not arrive at their final destination until August or September, when the cotton season was almost at an end. In addition, Egypt did not have the industrial organization to keep machines in good repair and the full-time employment of a European mechanic was almost essential.

The money necessary to finance the cultivation of cotton came from a variety of sources. In the case of the peasants they borrowed the cash they needed from the rapidly multiplying number of village usurers.[10] The latter, in turn, either had links with Greek and other mercantile houses in Constantinople or Alexandria or had made their capital as village traders, selling manufactured goods to the fellaheen. The estate owners, on the other hand, were able to obtain advances from banks and other credit institutions against land or cotton. The ease with which money was provided, first to finance, then to move the crop was a vital factor in allowing the extension of cotton. As the majority of its cultivators would only accept payment in gold, large amounts of bullion had to be imported each year, there being insufficient

---

[9] Such calculations are open to serious doubts. Many cultivators used the same field year after year.

[10] Loans were also made to pay the taxes which during Ismail's reign were often levied in advance of the harvest.

coinage in circulation even for normal needs.

By the end of 1862 at least a third of the Egyptian cotton crop was being ginned in steam-ginning factories of which there were then nearly eighty.[11] Later, this number increased still further. Charges were high, being anything from one to four dollars a cantar, as well as a right to keep the seed, which was generally worth much more. Nevertheless, the demand for their services was so great that even working night and day they were often unable to cope with their commitments. "During last season," Thayer wrote in March, 1863, "I have seen many of these establishments entirely barricaded with cotton waiting to be cleaned." The ginned cotton was then pressed into 500 lb. bales and sent to Alexandria for sale to the merchants, the majority of whom were now acting as brokers, receiving commissions from abroad, importing the necessary gold, and purchasing the amounts required on commission; while the remainder of the crop was bought up by their agents stationed at the main Delta collection points. Cotton seed was also purchased for export. In addition, a small portion of the total was crushed into oil at a factory built on the edge of the Mahmudiah canal at Alexandria by a company under the control of Edward Dervieu.

There were many opportunities for profit at each stage of the production process. Ginning was such a lucrative business that many owners were able to regain their initial outlay within two years; money-lenders obtained anything from 1 per cent to 5 per cent a month for their loans, while in 1862 it was said that most of the Alexandria merchants doubled or tripled their capital. But it must be supposed that in the first instance the bulk of the proceeds from the sale of their cotton— some £40 to £50 million between the

years 1861 and 1866—went to the cultivators themselves. As far as the fellaheen were concerned much of the gold they received was at once buried or converted into ornaments for their wives. Some, however, used their earnings for such traditional purposes as feasts or dowries or, in a few cases, for making the pilgrimage; others to purchase silks, jewelry, silver, pipes, furniture, and slaves.[12] Maize flour was widely replaced by wheat and many villages saw the erection of ovens owned by Greek and Maltese for making bread. Imports do not seem to have played an important part in increased peasant consumption, with the possible exception of cotton goods and the animals introduced after the murrain.

Less can be deduced about the pattern of expenditure of the richer cultivators. But in so far as the majority were as yet little acquainted with European ways of life it can probably be assumed that they too spent only a small portion of the increased income on imports. A study of British exports to Egypt during this period would seem to bear this out.[13] . . . Very tentatively it may be suggested that with the exception of agricultural machinery the items in which a large increase occurred between 1861 and 1865 were unlikely to have been purchased by rich Muslims in any quantity. The iron and copper were destined mainly for the government and for the construction of European-owned buildings, the cotton textiles were for the fellaheen or for re-export to Africa, while the carriages and other luxury goods were mainly for sale to foreign residents.[14]

---

[11] The fact that so much cotton was steam-ginned meant that the harvest was forwarded to Alexandria more quickly than before, imposing a consequent strain on the limited transport facilities.

[12] Wallace tells of a fellah who purchased a white Circassian slave, a "white elephant" in every sense of the phrase—not only was she very fat but she nearly bankrupted him by getting him to buy expensive household appliances.

[13] British export figures have to be used as Egyptian import figures are almost wholly misleading: methods of calculation were primitive, there was widespread smuggling, and none of the goods imported on government account even passed through the Customs House.

[14] Further evidence of the low import content of Egyptian consumption during the boom comes from the fact that British exports of such goods as cotton manufactured articles, woolens, haberdashery, etc.,

The fact that a large part of the cotton profits was devoted to the purchase of locally produced goods had two important results. In the first place it was instrumental in spreading the prosperity into other areas of the economy, to the wheat growers of Upper Egypt, for example, and to the artisans in the towns. And, secondly, it was partially the cause of a rapid inflation in the price of all major food items, a situation made worse after 1863 by the murrain and the consequent shortages of butter, meat, and cereals. "There is a large rise in every article of living," wrote Colquhoun, the British Consul General in September, 1863. "Our daily household expenses have doubled in a year. . . . the enormous fortunes realized during the past two years have caused money to be abundant, and the merchants have adopted a style of luxury and extravagance that enables them to command the daily market and have forced up the price of articles of daily necessity to a ruinous height." And in the following year he forwarded a list showing the increase in the price of various staples during the previous four years. Wheat, he said, had gone up from 25/- to 42/8 a quarter (64½ per cent), beef from 5.8 pence to 15.4 pence a pound (165 per cent), eggs from 1.9 pence to 4.25 pence a dozen (124 per cent), and geese from 12.8 pence to 42.3 pence each (230 per cent). Consuls never considered their salaries adequate and are thus not always the best of guides to changes in the cost of living but in this case figures from other sources tend to bear him out. Those who suffered the most were the urban poor; not only was their food more highly priced but it was often unobtainable and in June, 1864, the Privy Council was forced to ask Ismail's permission to use Government transport to supply the townspeople with the vegetables upon which they largely subsisted.[15] Conditions in the villages were

less difficult. The fellaheen were more or less self-sufficient in food and were able to sell any surplus at a tremendous profit. They also benefited from the concurrent rise in agricultural wages which in some areas reached 10 to 12 piastres a day compared with approximately two piastres before 1860. Others to prosper from the inflation were the importers of much-needed goods—it is significant that coal, the one imported item on Colquhoun's list, increased by 100 per cent in price between 1860 and 1864—and local middlemen who were able to use their position to force prices still higher.

Apart from the purchase of agricultural machinery by some of the richer cultivators only a small portion of the profits from cotton was spent on works of agricultural improvement. Thus once the boom was over and taxes began to rise few had anything to show for their sudden prosperity. But it is difficult to see how it could have been otherwise. The greater part of the cultivated land was owned by peasants who had neither the means nor the mechanical aptitude to buy steam engines even had they wished to do so and no effort was made to provide simpler but more efficient tools which might have proved attractive to them. In general the true dimensions of the problem were wholly misunderstood, especially by European commentators who tended to talk as though the fellaheen were no different from European farmers and equally receptive to the use of new machines. A good example of this is the facile assumption of the *Times* correspondent writing in March, 1864, that the creation of the Société Agricole et Industrielle to supply and install steam pumps on the large estates would in some way "assist the fellah in improving his system of agriculture and extending the area of cultivation."

continued to increase through 1867 even though agricultural incomes had diminished sharply because of lower cotton price and heavy taxation.

[15] Some compensation was provided for a few townspeople by the rise in the wages of workers in cotton ginneries. In 1863 at a ginning establishment in Mansourah a night operative received 5 piastres a shift while the boys and girls who worked during daylight hours received 2 piastres, the equivalent of an agricultural labourer's salary before the boom.

On only one occasion was any serious attempt made to examine this issue. This was in a paper read by J. Lattis to the Institut d'Egypte in December, 1862.[16] Lattis began by pointing out how important it was that the gains made as a result of the boom should not be immediately dissipated. The peasants, temporarily enriched by circumstances which would not last, were at that moment accessible to the idea of progress and amelioration, and the main aim of those interested in Egyptian agriculture should be to make them understand that all their energies should be devoted to increasing the yield of their land to compensate for the lower prices they would receive for their crops in the future. To this end it was necessary to improve the tools they used and also to perfect their animals. As a result of Lattis' initiative a committee of members of the Institute was set up to examine his proposals in detail and to suggest practical measures which could then be recommended to the Government. Later, however, Ismail's accession was thought to make its work superfluous and the whole idea was dropped.

Two further points should be noted. One is that even had the Government agreed to furnish simple tools the cattle murrain would have greatly hampered its efforts to distribute them. After the summer of 1863 the only agricultural investment which a fellah could have been interested in was the replacement of his dead animals at prices which were then over £50 an ox compared with £5 twenty years earlier. And secondly, seen in longer perspective, the peasants who benefited most from the boom were not those few who spent money on improving their fields but those who by the purchase of land and other means were able to use their wealth to join the ranks of the village nobility. During Ismail's reign an alliance with the shaykh or money-lender was the one means by which a small fortune might be preserved. The sign of this move into the local hierarchy was generally the con-

struction of a house at the edge of the village, away from the huts of the peasants.

The cotton boom greatly accelerated the process which had begun in the 1850's of growing European interest in Egypt's financial possibilities. One manifestation of this was the large inflow of foreigners. Some idea of the size of this movement can be obtained from the figures provided for Sacre and Outrebon by the Alexandria passport administration, which show that between the beginning of February and the beginning of August, 1864, there was an excess of arrivals over departures of nearly 12,000 foreigners, including 1,873 Greeks, 1,650 Englishmen, 1,187 Frenchmen, and 1,061 Austrians, bringing the total European population of the country to roughly 100,000. Most of the newcomers stayed in Alexandria, but an increasing number spread out into the Delta towns or settled in Cairo, a city of rapidly growing importance because of Ismail's plans for its development and its position at the centre of the Delta retail trade.[17] The arrival of so many foreigners created many investment opportunities. There were houses to be built, wood and other construction materials to be imported, and new tastes to be catered to. In addition a number of valuable public utility concessions were awarded for the provision of Alexandria and Cairo with gas-lighting and supplies of domestic water. . . .

Cotton prices reached their peak in the summer of 1864, then began to decline just as the Egyptian crop began to reach the market, falling from 52 dollars a cantar in August to 37 in December. In reaction many of the cultivators, including the Viceroy, kept hold of their cotton, preferring to borrow rather than to sell at what they considered to be an inferior price. A number of ginning factories had to stop work but those who were hardest hit

[16] Lattis had come to Egypt in the mid-1850's to try to interest Said in an improved method of rice culture.

[17] Cairo's position began to be encroached on by Alexandria in the early 1860's as better communications were established between the main Delta towns and the coast. Previously goods had first been shipped up the Nile to the capital.

were the banking houses and credit companies who had lent money against Jumel and who were forced to take up their now depreciated security. The crisis continued and was at its worst in April, 1865. Prices were at their lowest as the American Civil War came to an end; business in Mansourah, the centre of the most important Delta cotton-growing district, was at a standstill even though it was estimated that a third of the local harvest remained in the fields; and on April 9, C. Joyce and Co. of London, East Indian and Egyptian merchants, collapsed unexpectedly. Few other firms followed however, although most showed losses (the Bank of Egypt valued these at £2 million) and then, almost at once, business revived. On the one hand, Southern [American] stocks of cotton were revealed to be far smaller than anticipated nor was there any immediate prospect of a return to the large American crops of pre-war years, and prices began to rise again. This, combined with the fact that the crop was 300,000 cantars larger than the previous year, meant that there was no decline in gross income from cotton. On the other hand, Ismail was persuaded by a committee of local financiers to assist those firms who had lent money on land, now a worthless security following the collapse of the Egyptian property market. According to the plan proposed and accepted, the Government took over the "village debts" as they were called, paying the European creditors with bonds carrying 7 per cent interest while arranging to collect the money from the debtors over a period of 7 years at 12 per cent.[18] To Ismail not only did this provide him with an opportunity to make some money but by this means "the government would be spared the confusion and recriminations which would inevitably follow a general expropriation." The total of such debts was fixed at 17 million francs (£680,000). As

they comprised only those loans made on land they represented only a small portion of total indebtedness. Nevertheless their prompt repayment provided much needed relief for many of the Alexandria business community.

In the meantime the sowing of the 1865 cotton crop was in progress. In an attempt to compensate for lower prices many cultivators extended the area they devoted to Jumel, Ismail himself increasing his cotton fields by half. Others, particularly peasants, sowed their cotton more closely together. Thus, although agricultural credit was more difficult to obtain and the shortage of draft animals still persisted, it is probable that the total amount of land placed under Jumel was augmented considerably.[19] Partly in consequence there was a further decline in yield, there being neither workers nor cattle enough to cope with such a large area, and in spite of all the efforts made the harvest was some 30 per cent to 40 per cent less than that of the previous year. Its sale coincided with the final collapse of the boom. Trade had remained steady throughout the rest of 1865 but most firms were working from capital or by means of loans and when the London Stock Market crash of May, 1866, finally put an end to the credit which it had been possible to obtain from Europe many of them were unable to continue. A large number of Egyptian houses went bankrupt; the Anglo-Egyptian Bank lost £205,000 on its second year's activities, when it proved impossible to issue more than a small part of a projected Government loan of which it was the contractor and was forced to re-organize; the Trading and Agricole were finally forced to suspend operations.[20] In addition several ginning establishments were abandoned for lack of work, some owners attempting to sell their machinery at a third or a half of its

---

[18] The use of the term "village debts" is a further indication of contemporary failure to understand rural conditions. In fact no European financier would have been prepared to lend money on peasant land, and the debts in question must refer to those contracted by the more well-to-do.

[19] Figures provided by an Egyptian correspondent of the Manchester Cotton Supply Association give the areas placed under cotton as: 1864, 1 million feddans; 1865, 1.5 million; 1866, 1 million.

[20] The Agricole had actually discontinued operations in February. A few months later it was forced to suspend payments.

original cost. As for Ismail himself, surrounded on all sides by eager creditors and unable, temporarily, to borrow the sums he needed, he began a series of increases in the land tax which in a few years were to wipe out most of the profits of the boom years which still remained in the hands of the cultivators.

The period of the cotton boom in Egypt has a special flavour all its own, one which can be best summed up in a quotation from the *Times* correspondent written at a time when optimism about Egypt's economic potential was at its height and there was a feeling in the air that all things were possible.

An extraordinary revolution is rapidly proceeding in this country. Europe has finally understood the immense future of Egypt and is eager to develop her budding resources. Every steamer is pouring a new population and a golden stream on our shores; energy and capital are taking possession of the land, and urging it forward in the path of civilization and wealth. Not only are the cities of Alexandria and Cairo receiving so great an influx of inhabitants that, although whole quarters are rising on every side, house room is still insufficient, and rents are always increasing, but the inland towns and villages are over-run, and factories with high chimneys and long lines of black smoke cut the clear sky of our flat landscape through the length and breadth of Lower Egypt. . . . The Viceroy has expressed his conviction that, although the cattle murrain has been a grievous present calamity, it will confer a lasting benefit, by compelling the adoption of an improved system, which will civilize his people while enriching them.

Meanwhile, "Halim Pasha has found, in conversing with his farm labourers, that the intellects of the lads who have grown up since the new mechanical appliances, is greatly in advance of that of men who had grown to manhood under the former primitive system of cultivation when the ox was the all-in-all to the fellah and when his mind had no stimulus and no cause for thought and enquiry."

Nevertheless it would be wrong to look at the boom period only in isolation. In so far as Ismail himself was concerned it was only a prelude to even larger schemes for Egypt's economic development which he had in mind and which he proceeded to attempt during the next ten years. New firms came forward to undertake public works contracts; the amounts of money borrowed from Europe became larger and larger; imports remained at a high level. To an Egyptian living in 1875 looking at the changed face of his country, the modern city of Cairo, the railways linking every major Delta town, the harbour works at Alexandria, 1865 must have seemed as far away as 1845 or earlier. The only lasting effect of the boom was the fact that it caused the cultivation of cotton to spread into every corner of Lower Egypt and to remain there, firmly entrenched in the rural rotation of crops in spite of the falling prices and high taxes which marked the remainder of Ismail's reign.

CHAPTER 9

Progress and Indebtedness under Ismail, 1863–1875

The report from which the following extract is taken was written in December, 1875, by a group of four British experts, headed by Stephen Cave, a junior member of Disraeli's ministry. The initiative for this mission had come from Ismail pasha, whose rapidly accumulating difficulties had led him to ask the British government for a financial adviser, probably in the hope of getting financial assistance and support from Britain. The British government, which had just purchased Ismail's holdings of Suez Canal shares and wished to strengthen its hold on Egypt, responded by sending the Cave Mission to conduct an enquiry into the state of Egypt's finances.

Although the mission received very little co-operation from the Egyptian government, it was able to reach some sound general conclusions. Pointing out that Egypt's difficulties were due to extravagance and waste, and to the highly unfavorable terms on which loans had been contracted, it drew attention to the progress achieved during the previous twelve years and judged that the country's credit could be restored by retrenchment and reform. For this, however, it deemed it necessary that the khedive engage, and follow the advice of, foreign experts.

At Ismail's request publication of the Cave report was withheld, but this fact was revealed in answer to a question in Parliament, causing a sharp loss in confidence in Egypt, and the report itself appeared in March, 1876. Two weeks later, on April 8, the khedive suspended payment of interest on treasury bonds, following the example set by the Ottoman government the previous October (see Part I, chap. 11). But whereas in Turkey bankruptcy resulted only in foreign financial control, in Egypt it eventually led, by a complicated and unforeseen process, to the deposition of Ismail, the Urabi revolt, armed intervention, and occupation. In the meantime, the Law of Liquidation of 1880 had fixed Egypt's debt at £98,377,000, mostly bearing 4 per cent interest.

Thanks to the research carried out by an Egyptian scholar, more reliable figures on expenditure and revenue during the period 1863–74 are now available.[1] Expenditure amounted to £158,200,000, of which administration absorbed £48,592,000, tribute £7,593,000, and interest and sinking funds £41,529,000, giving a subtotal of £97,714,000. Public works, including railways, canals, ports, shipping, compensation for expropriated land, and other items accounted for £31,103,000; however, this figure should be compared with the one of £39,394,000 given by Crouchley.[2] Expenditure on the Suez Canal amounted to £9,412,000, to which should be added £6,663,000 paid in interest on funds raised because of the convention with the Canal Company. Tax receipts and other ordinary revenues amounted to £94,300,000, and the balance was made up by the effective proceeds of foreign loans—£35,100,000, a figure lower than that given in other sources; the sale of the Suez Canal shares for £4,000,000—which, however, was not effected until 1875; the contraction of a floating debt, and other sources of revenue.

It may be added that an estimate in the *Investor's Monthly Manual* of December, 1875, put Egypt's per capita public debt at £14, with an annual service charge of £1 15s. 10d., both figures being among the very highest in the world.[3] Between 1880 and 1914 interest on the debt absorbed half the budget and equaled a quarter to a third of exports (see Part VI, chap. 1).

(See also works by McCoan, Cromer, Rafi'i [*Ismail* and *Al-thawra al-'Urabia*], Hamza, Landes, and Crouchley listed in the Bibliography.)

[1] Abdel Maqsud Hamza, *The Public Debt of Egypt, 1854–1867*, pp. 278–81.
[2] A. E. Crouchley, *The Economic Development of Modern Egypt*, p. 117.
[3] Hamza, *op. cit.*, p. 212.

[From "Report by Mr. Cave on the Financial Conditions of Egypt," Great Britain, *Accounts and Papers*, *1876*, LXXXIII, *Egypt*, No. 7, 1876, pp. 1–10]

The critical state of the finances of Egypt is due to the combination of two opposite causes.

Egypt may be said to be in a transition state, and she suffers from the defects of the system out of which she is passing as well as from those of the system into which she is attempting to enter. She suffers from the ignorance, dishonesty, waste and extravagance of the East, such as have brought her Suzerain to the verge of ruin, and at the same time from the vast expense caused by hasty and inconsiderate endeavours to adopt the civilization of the West.

Immense sums are expended on unproductive works after the manner of the East, and on productive works carried out in the wrong way, or too soon. This last is a fault which Egypt shares with other new countries (for she may be considered a new country in this respect) a fault which has seriously embarrassed both the United States and Canada; but probably nothing in Egypt has ever approached the profligate expenditure which characterized the commencement of the Railway system in England.

The Khedive has evidently attempted to carry out with a limited revenue in the course of a few years works which ought to be spread over a far longer period, and which would tax the resources of much richer exchequers.

We were informed that one of the causes which operates most against the honesty and efficiency of native officers is the precarious tenure of office. From the Pashas downwards every office is a tenancy at will, and experience shows that while dishonesty goes wholly or partially unpunished, independence of thought and action, resolution to do one's duty and to resist the peculation and neglect which pervade every department, give rise to intrigues which, sooner or later, bring about the downfall of honest officials; consequently those who begin with a desire to do their duty give way before the obstructiveness which paralyzes every effort . . . .

The tenure of land varies. All land theoretically belongs to the State, as in feudal times in Europe, and similarly large estates were parcelled among the conquering races, and charged only with a fixed quit-rent called the dime or ouchour. The remainder of the land is held from the State by communities or individuals on payment of a tax called karadj, which is really a rent, and which was variable, and might at anytime be augmented at the will of the Government. This land could not originally be leased, alienated, or devised, but relapsed to the State at each termination of ownership. More liberal and humane laws have been enacted by the present Ruler, and the land passes as easily as copyhold in England. Where land belongs to communities, the Sheykh distributes it to families for a year only, which is a great obstacle to industry. Nubar Pasha informed us that he let some land for rent in the ordinary way. Some he worked with labourers for hire; some in a sort of partnership with the labourers, who paid him a certain portion of the produce, he finding seed, implement, etc.

Labourers for hire are difficult to be obtained in many places. Almost every man has a small parcel of land to cultivate, consequently contractors agree to take a piece of work for so much, and to bring a certain number of hands from various places. They make their terms with the landowner, who knows no one but the contractor, and it often occurs that the latter, though well and punctually paid, starves and defrauds the labourers in his gang, and great misery and oppression take place, whether the gangs so brought together are of the better sort, who feed themselves and earn, say, 5 piastres a day,

most irregularly paid, or whether they are the poorest Fellaheen, obtained by help of the Mudir or Head-man of a district, who are paid nothing, but work from sunrise to sunset for their bare food, and run away at every opportunity. This uncertainty, whether as to labour and taxes by the proprietary or as to pay and position by the peasantry, lowers the value of land to such a degree that we were informed that good land in the Delta might be bought for five years' purchase. Some time ago the Khedive established a "Crédit Foncier," or land bank, for the purpose of lending money to the peasantry at moderate rates, and lost a large sum of money by it. His motives were doubtless good, but he evidently began at the wrong end, and tried to palliate the evils of a system he ought to have reformed. There have been projects lately on foot for the introduction of Chinese into Egypt, and proposals have been made to the Khedive to send people to China to organize a system of emigration, but he objects that the introduction of Chinese will be very expensive, and that there will be much trouble in enforcing their contracts. If they come of their own accord, he will be glad to employ them and to settle them on unoccupied land. We were informed that all the labourers employed in the sugar-factories were paid regular money wages, and that the soldiers who are settled in military colonies or encamped near the sugar-estates are paid about 1s. a day, or by the task, besides their military pay; and as they work under their officers, it is said that twenty-five do as much work as sixty ordinary labourers. Besides these there are undoubtedly *corvées* and people working out the land tax paid for them by the Khedive.

The Daira Samieh [Saniya], or private estate of the Khedive, consists of some 350,000 feddans of good land, chiefly in Upper Egypt, besides 100,000 feddans of poor land not under cultivation. Of the former he lets about half and keeps about half in hand. The net revenue of the whole is estimated at 422,000 £, in round figures. About 15,000 acres of what the Khedive keeps in hand are planted in cotton, and 120,000 in what is called winter cultivation, i.e., corn and vegetables of various kinds. But the most important industry is the cultivation of the sugar-cane and the manufacture of sugar: 40,000 acres are planted with canes, and there are 12 large factories with most elaborate machinery at work.

The fault here, as in so many other instances, has been that this industry has been established without due consideration. Very large factories were built before the land was ready to supply them. They have not been placed in the middle of the estates, but near the main railway; consequently the canes have to be brought many miles by locomotives to the factories, involving a large consumption of coal, and making supervision more difficult. Some factories, full of costly machinery, have been abandoned, others left unfinished with the machinery already on the spot; steam machinery for irrigation has been erected and never used.

The manufacturing accounts can be accurately kept. Those for cultivation are complicated by *corvées* and military labour, and labour in payment of debts. We have heard the cost of cultivation, including the cutting of the canes, estimated at 5 *l.* per acre. The sugar-estates, we feel convinced, bring in a return beyond their working expenses, and this will increase year by year as the cultivation improves, as more land is brought under canes, and the full power of the machinery brought into play. Much economy has already been effected by the utilization of the refuse of the factories for manure, and by the better management of the megass, or cane-stalks, which now almost wholly replace coal, both in driving the machinery and evaporating the sugar. It would therefore be unadvisable that these estates should be given up. But the original faults can hardly be remedied, and it seems impossible that there should ever be an adequate return for the capital, especially as so much was provided by loans at a high rate of interest.

It is therefore with great apprehension that we hear of the capital account of the Daira being still open, and of vast schemes of irrigation costing millions being under consideration.

We were informed before leaving England that Egyptian sugar had been sold in London for less than cost price. This might have been owing to a faulty system by which merchants were favoured at the expense of the grower, or pressing debts discharged in sugar at prices below the market value, or to buyers who had combined to make a monopoly, having been obliged to realize at a loss. A deceptive mode of sampling had also given a bad name to Egyptian produce. A very much better system now prevails and will soon produce good effects. The sampling is honestly and carefully performed; the sugar is sold at public sales, and a genuine competition is commencing, so that Egyptian sugar, which is of excellent quality, may be expected to give better returns. A fact has been mentioned to us by a high authority here, in confirmation of his opinion that sugar does not pay and ought to be given up, namely, that French refined sugar in Alexandria competes with native sugar, notwithstanding an 8 per cent duty. But this has been explained by practical people in two ways. First, there is no refined, i.e., loaf sugar, sent to Alexandria for sale as a regular system (not more than 2,000 tons are made at present altogether, namely, at Minieh); the highest of the three qualities made for the market is white crystallized sugar. Secondly, the bounty in form of drawback given by the French Government enables French sugar in Egypt, as in England, to compete unfairly with other sugar, though with regard to Egypt there is this excuse—that Egyptian sugar is protected by a customs duty unbalanced by an excise on native produce.

It has been said that the public accounts, as well as those of the Daira Samieh, have been made with a view to deceive. It seems possible that an intricate statement may be preferred for the purpose of retaining power in the hands of the Finance Minister, in whose office no European is at present employed, or even allowed to enter. But we can hardly imagine that a designedly fictitious statement would be published year after year, and yet that it should be proposed that an inspection of accounts should take place by an experienced financier to remain here for at least five years with access to all the records.

That the accounts are kept in a slovenly imperfect manner is evident on the face of them. Take for instance the Budget for 1876, and the "Compte Rendu" for 1875, which contains items jumbled together in a most extraordinary way, such as a railway in Soudan and a canal in Egypt in one sum. If we examine the account of the Customs, which are under the Finance Minister, we shall find no complete official table of the imports and exports of each Custom-house in Egypt, specifying the kind, the quality, the value, the place from whence they come, or their destination. Moreover, the returns of quantity are made on no principle whatever, being sometimes according to weight, sometimes according to number, size of parcel, so many pairs, etc., and the periods are sometimes according to the Coptic, sometimes according to the Gregorian calendar, which, it is scarcely necessary to say, do not correspond.

Table No. 8 in the Appendix [not included in this excerpt] may serve to show how much reform is required in this branch of the service, upon which so important an amount of revenue depends.

According to a calculation made from the imperfect data accessible to the public, it has been estimated by a high independent authority, that the receipts from the Custom-house of Alexandria alone for the year 1872 ought to have amounted to 558,727 *l*., whereas the return of receipts from all the ports reached only 541,215 *l*., or 17,510 *l*. less that it ought to have been from Alexandria alone.

Again, the receipts and expenses of railways for the year 1874–75 (1591 Coptic) give the receipts at the different stations with great minuteness, even to an entry of 4 piastres. But the salaries and wages, amounting to 195,297 *l*., are comprised in one sum, with no particulars of the payments to any particular class, nor even of the number of officials or servants employed; the same may be said of a single entry of 137,010 *l*. for repairs of engines and carriages. It is therefore easily to be understood that the receipts of the railways are generally supposed to be one fifth lower than they ought to be under efficient management.

It may be mentioned here that all construction of new railways, except that of the Soudan, is suspended [see Part VII, Introduction]. . . .

According to the documents handed to us by the Khedive, and to information furnished verbally by His Highness, and tested by such means as were in our power, the present position of the Egyptian finances is as follows:

The revenue of Egypt has increased from 55,000 *l*. a year in 1804, 3,300,000 *l*. in 1830, and 4,937,405 *l*. in 1864, the second year of the Khedive's administration, to 7,377,912 *l*. in 1871, the year previous to the changes caused by the law of Moukabala. Under this law all landowners could redeem one half of the land tax to which they were liable by the payment of six years tax, either in advance in one sum or in instalments. Those who paid down this contribution in one sum received an immediate reduction of their tax; those who elected to make the payment in instalments received a discount of $8\frac{1}{3}$ per cent. on their advance, and the reduction only takes place on the completion of their contribution. . . .

The revenue has certain elements of elasticity in it, but these are not likely to be very active in operation.

The principal of these is the Land Tax, which, after its reduction under the operation of the Moukabala Law, will probably grow with the increasing area of cultivation, an increase likely to receive an impulse from the reduction of the tax. At present 4,805,107 feddans pay tax as under cultivation, which, compared with the 4,051,076 feddans cultivated in Said Pasha's time, shows an increase of 18½ per cent. during the present Government. 352,350 feddans have also been brought under cultivation and will shortly be assessed for taxation. As this will be effected gradually no immedi-

Khedive's accession, making therefore in all an addition of 33½ per cent. during his rule of thirteen years.

There are still 1,098,000 feddans of cultivable ground which have been registered but not yet cultivated.

TABLE I

Loan of	To be Paid off in	Nominal Amount of Loan, but Real Debt of State	Charge on Nominal Amount			Amount Realized	Real Charges on Amount Realized			Remarks
			Interest	Sinking Fund	Total		Interest	Sinking Fund	Total	
		£	Per cent.	Per cent.	Per cent.	£	Per cent.	Per cent.	Per cent.	
1862	1892	3,292,800	7	1	8	—	—	—	—	No particulars of amount realized.
1864	1879	5,704,200	7	3.87	10.87	4,864,063	8.2	4.5	12.7	
1866	1874	3,000,000	7	—	—	2,640,000	8	18.9	26.9	Railways loan, repaid by six annual payments of 500,000 *l.*, equivalent to a sinking fund of 18.9 per cent.
1868	1898	11,890,000	7	1	8	7,193,334	11.56	1.68	13.25	
1873	1903	32,000,000	7	1	8	20,740,077	10.8	1.56	12.36	
						35,437,474				
Daïra taken over by the State.										
★ ⎧1865	1881	3,000,000	9	3.27	12.27	3,000,000	—	—	12.27	⎫ No particulars of
⎩1867	1881	2,080,000	9	3.4	12.4	2,080,000	—	—	12.4	⎬ amounts realized, but ⎭ probably the whole.
						5,080,000				
The Daïra Loan of His Highness the Khedive										
1870	1890	7,142,860	7	2.35	9.35	5,000,000	10	3.36	13.36	

★ The return of the Finance Minister does not include these loans, which were probably expended on lands.

ate increase of revenue will take place, but an addition of 180,000 *l.* a year from this source may be expected in the course of the next five years.

A further area of 267,650 feddans will become liable to taxation after it has been surveyed, from which an additional 140,000 *l.* a year may be expected.

These two additions to the cultivated area amount to 620,000 feddans, or 15 per cent. of the land under cultivation at the

The net revenues of the railways have increased from 750,000 *l.* a year in 1873 to 990,800 *l.* in 1875 but this rate of increase cannot be entirely relied upon, as more of the gross receipts will necessarily be required for maintenance and renewal as a permanent way becomes worn, and deficient crops would cause diminished traffic. Still, even after making these allowances, an honest and intelligent administration of the railways would probably produce a larger revenue.

The extent of railways in 1873 was   1,110 miles
were added in 1874-5   100 miles
                          ————————
                          1,210 miles

These lines have been constructed at an average cost of about 11,000 *l.* per mile. Other lines have been projected, but the only important one actually in the course of formation is that in the Soudan. This is not the original Soudan line, but, as explained above, a section of it only, required to pass the worst cataracts.

The Customs duties may also be expected to improve. There has been a steady and gradual increase of the exports of cotton, which have risen from 1,253,593 quintals [qantars] in 1867 to 2,615,120 quintals in 1874.

In the thirteen years of Ismail Pasha's rule, the quantity of cotton exported has been 3.6 times that of the exportation of the preceding thirteen years, or an increase of 257 per cent. The fall in price has caused disappointment, and may check production, it being now doubted whether corn does not pay better. At the same time improved machinery enables cotton to be more effectually separated from the seed, from which oil and cake are now largely made.

In the general returns of exports and imports there is also a marked improvement. The total value of imports from 1863 to 1875 amounts to 61,939,736 *l.* against, from 1850 to 1862, 29,641,155 *l.*, showing an advance of 100 per cent. in thirteen years.

Exports have quadrupled during the same period, having increased in value from 36,339,543 *l.* to 145,939,736 *l.*

During the thirteen years the growth of the population of Egypt has been considerable, the births having exceeded the deaths by 636,809.

Education has been carefully attended to, the number of schools established on an European model having increased from 185 in 1862 to 4,817 in 1875.

In the latter year there were 4,817 schools, with 6,048 masters and 140,977 pupils, being an augmentation on the previous year of 1,072 schools, 1,615 masters, and 27,722 pupils.

The quality of the education given necessarily varies, but it has on the whole decidedly improved, and is in some cases of a very superior character.

These statistics show that the country has made great progress in every way under its present ruler, but, notwithstanding that progress, its present financial position is, for the reasons that have already been stated, very critical. Still the expenditure, though heavy, would not of itself have produced the present crisis, which may be attributed almost entirely to the ruinous conditions of loans raised for pressing requirements, due in some cases to causes over which the Khedive had little control. . . .

From [Table 1] it is seen that none of the Egyptian loans cost less than 12 per cent. per annum, while some cost more than $13\frac{1}{2}$ per cent. per annum and the railways loan even 26.9 per cent. per annum, including sinking funds.

A Return furnished by the Minister of Finance sets the amount paid for interest and sinking funds of the public loans to the end of 1875 at 29,570,994 *l.*[1]

According to the same Return, the revenue received from 1864 to 1875 inclusive amounted to 94,281,401 *l.* During the same period the expenses of administration, including tribute to Constantinople, were 56,461,363 *l.*; and the Government expended on the Suez Canal, on different works specified in the subjoined list, and on certain compensations and transactions 56,654,722 *l.*

The debtor and creditor account of the State, from 1864 to 1875, stands thus:

Receipts	£
By revenue	94,281,401
loans	31,713,987*
sale of Suez Canal shares . . .	3,976,583
floating debt.	18,243,076
	148,215,047

* Excludes greater part of 1864 loan.

[1] According to the Loan Contracts the service of the loans should only have cost 27,923,716 *l.* to the end of 1875. This sum may have been swollen by extra charges.

Expenditure.	£
Administration	48,868,491
Tribute to the Porte	7,592,872
Works of utility, etc..	30,240,058
Extraordinary expenses—some of questionable utility, and others under pressure of interested parties . . .	10,539,545
Interests and Sinking Funds	34,898,962
Suez Canal	16,075,119
Total	148,215,047

Two striking features stand out in this balance-sheet, namely, that the sum raised by revenue, 94,281,401 *l.*, is little less than that spent on Administration, Tribute to the Porte, works of unquestionable utility, and certain expenses of questionable utility or policy, in all amounting to 97,240,966 *l.*, and that for the present large amount of indebtedness there is absolutely nothing to show but the Suez Canal, the whole proceeds of the Loans and Floating Debt having been absorbed in payment of interest and sinking funds with the exception of the sum debited to that great work. It is to be further observed in connection with this subject that the necessity of paying large amounts to the Suez Canal Co. obliged the Egyptian Government to resort to its earlier loans in 1864 and 1868. . . .

It may be expected that if the gravity of the situation is explained to the bond-holders they will consent to an arrangement for securing to them a fair return on their money, and saving them from the heavy loss inseparable from a financial collapse.[2]

As regards the floating debt, it may be supposed that the holders of Treasury Bonds, which have been frequently renewed and now represent a value far in excess of the amount paid to the Khedive, would willingly take bonds for the present nominal amount of these bonds with an assured interest and repayment.

It remains to examine whether the resources of the country are equal to the payment of the necessary annuity for covering this payment of interest and sinking fund.

[2] It must be observed that, by clause 19 in the contract of the Loan of 1873, the Khedive engages to make no fresh loans before 1878, except to the extent of 10,000,000 *l.* sterling for public works. It is alleged, however, that this engagement would not be broken by a loan for the purpose of funding existing debts.

	£
As above shown, the amount of Funded and Unfunded Debt to be paid off, independently of the three small Loans, is	72,000,000
If to this be added, for the expense of the Abyssinian War	1,000,000
And for the cost of this operation . . .	2,000,000
We have a total amount of	75,000,000

For the interest and sinking fund of which provision would have to be made. The annuity to repay this sum in fifty years with interest at 7 per cent. per annum would be 5,434,425 *l.*, but as the Daïra Loan and Floating Debt have been taken into the operation a proportion of this charge will fall on the private estate of the Khedive and not on the State; this proportion would be 672,608 *l.*,[3] leaving 4,761,817 *l.* to be furnished by the State.

The permanent charges of the Budget are:

	£
Tribute to Constantinople	685,308
Interest on Suez Canal Shares till 1895 .	198,829
Administration (including Civil List of His Highness and family)	3,067,560
	3,951,697
Say	4,000,000
The Revenue of 1876 to 1885 should be	10,689,000
Less the Moukabala (which we propose to deal with separately)	1,531,000
	9,158,000
Deduct the permanent charge . . .	4,000,000
	5,158,000
The charge for interest and Sinking Fund	4,761,817
Leaves a working surplus of	396,183
But in 1886 and subsequent years we have shown that the Revenue will be only (except the growth that may be expected in the future)	8,473,000
Deduct permanent charge	4,000,000
	4,473,000
Service of Debt	4,761,817
Leaving a deficit of	288,817

This deficit might be dealt with by reserving the produce of the Moukabala receipts. These receipts will be 1,531,818 a year until the end of 1885. . . .

[3] The Loan alone, without the interest of floating debt, now costs the Khedive 668,000 *l.* a year so that this sum can be well borne; as shown by His Highness' Daïra account.

It would appear from these calculations that the resources of Egypt are sufficient, if properly managed, to meet her liabilities but that as all her available assets are pledged for the charges of existing loans, some fresh combination is necessary in order to fund at a moderate rate the present onerous floating debt.

The annual charge upon the people of Egypt is heavy, and has increased; but the power of meeting it, that is, the wealth of the country as indicated by its exports, has increased in a far greater degree. And it must be remembered that this annual charge includes not only a sinking fund for the redemption of debt, but a very large proportion of what we should call local taxation. It also includes the cost of much that is done in this country by private enterprise, such as railways, canals, harbours, docks, etc., besides actual rent of funds belonging to the State, and repayment of advances during periods of scarcity and murrain.

We gather from all the information that we have been able to obtain that Egypt is well able to bear the charge of the whole of her present indebtedness at a reasonable rate of interest; but she cannot go on renewing floating debts at 25 per cent. and raising fresh loans at 12 or 13 per cent. interest to meet these additions to her debt, which do not bring in a single piastre to her Exchequer. . . .

Public Finance under the British
Administration, 1882–1901

In his *Modern Egypt* Lord Cromer distinguished two kinds of reforms: those that could be carried out by administrative action and those that required a social revolution.[1] Naturally no attempt was made to introduce radical reforms in land tenure, *waqf*, Muslim law, education, and other fields where changes can come about only as part of a far-reaching social revolution. But the British administration did carry out many reforms of the first category, e.g., in irrigation, sanitation, and prisons, and the abolition of *corvée* labor. But it was in administrative organization, and more particularly in the fiscal field, that British rule rendered its greatest benefits. Financial reform took two main forms: centralization and simplification of administration and accounts, and collection of taxes just after the marketing of crops; and abolition of vexatious or unproductive taxes. The following selection gives some details of this process.

The figures on expenditure also illustrate Cromer's declared policy of "balancing the budget . . . on the basis of maintaining the *status quo*." Nearly half the expenditure was for tribute and debt service and most of the rest was absorbed by administration. But it should be added that, in view of the intense international rivalries and the high probability that another bankruptcy would lead to a new foreign intervention, the British had no choice but to pursue financial solvency, whatever the cost in economic and social development.

Peace, order, and good administration gave full scope to the country's recuperative powers, and a remarkable advance took place in agricultural output and foreign trade. At the turn of the century world cotton prices rose (see Part VI, chap. 11) and the terms of trade moved sharply in Egypt's favor. The resulting growth in national product raised Egypt's real per capita income to a peak which has only just been regained. Available evidence on the standard of living shows a great increase, to a level that is also just being matched (see Part VI, chap. 1).

But the British policy of reliance on a one-crop agriculture was fraught with

[1] II, 397.

danger. For one thing, the potential increase in agricultural output was over-estimated; thus in 1906 an output of 10 million qantars of cotton was forecast within ten to fifteen years;[2] but, except in 1937, this figure has never been attained by Egypt. For another, the ominous implications of the continuing population growth were ignored. Finally the deterioration in Egypt's terms of trade after the First World War drove home the dangers of one-sided specialization and the need for industrialization (see Part VI, chap. 13). By then the general growth in the economy, the fall in the real burden of the debt due to the general rise in prices, and the continued improvement in fiscal administration had relegated budgetary problems to the background.

(See also works by Cromer, Owen, Arminjon, and Issawi [*Egypt at Mid-Century*] listed in the Bibliography.)

[2] *Annual Report*, 1906.

[From "Report by H. M. Agent and Consul-General on the Finances, Administration and Condition of Egypt and the Soudan in 1902," Great Britain, *Accounts and Papers, 1903*, XXXVII, *Egypt*, No. 1, 1903, pp. 4–8.]

... It is perhaps as well to remind residents in Egypt, both European and native, that but a short time separates them from a period when the complaints now occasionally heard against the Government, mainly on the ground of parsimony, would have been considered almost trivial, for the very sufficient reason that other and far more serious complaints were capable of being substantiated. The Commission of Enquiry, of which I was a member in 1878, and whose report formed the starting-point of most of the subsequent reforms, summed up the situation which then existed in the following terms: "Il s'agit, en effet, de créer tout un systeme fiscal, et cela avec un personnel très restreint; à présent presque rien n'existe de ce qui doit exister." The Commission, in fact, found that the abuses which had grown up in every branch of the Egyptian body politic were so general and so deep-rooted as to defy the application of any remedy which would be effectual and, at the same time, speedy. They had to deal, not with a patient suffering from a single malady, but with one whose constitution was shattered,

and whose every organ was diseased. Finance, instead of being used as the most powerful of all engines for the social and material improvement of the people, had degenerated into a series of clumsy and often cruel devices, conceived with the object of first extracting the maximum amount of revenue from unwilling contributors and then spending the proceeds on objects which, for the most part, conferred no benefits whatever upon the contributors themselves. Lady Duff Gordon, whose letters give a faithful account of the state of Egypt some thirty-five years ago, wrote in 1867: "I cannot describe the misery here now—every day some new tax. Every beast, camel, cow, sheep, donkey, and horse is made to pay. The Fellaheen can no longer eat bread; they are living on barley meal mixed with water, and raw green stuff, vetches, etc. The taxation makes life almost impossible: a tax on every crop, on every animal first and again when it is sold in the market; on every man, on charcoal, on butter, on salt.... The people in Upper Egypt are running away by wholesale, utterly unable to pay the new taxes, and do the work exacted. Even here (Cairo) the beating for the year's taxes is awful."[1]

It must further be remembered that it was

[1] "Last Letters from Egypt," pp. 108 and 166. Matters got worse subsequent to the period when this was written.

not till 1890, that is to say, twelve years after the Commission of Enquiry expressed itself in the terms quoted above, that I was able to report that "after a long struggle, during which the future solvency or insolvency of the country remained doubtful, financial equilibrium was secured."[2]

During the early years of the British occupation, seeds were, indeed, sown which ultimately produced good fruit; but it is only during the last ten or twelve years that, the fear of bankruptcy being removed, the Egyptian Government has been able to devote itself seriously to the work of reform. Before that time, the funds, without which no reform, whether of a fiscal or administrative character, could be accomplished were, for the most part, not forthcoming.

Under these circumstances, it can be no matter for surprise that only the most pressing improvements have been effected and that in many directions the hand of the reformer has as yet not been adequately felt.

In the second place, it is perhaps doubtful whether the financial policy which has been steadily pursued ever since the British occupation commenced is sufficiently understood. Whether that policy was the best of which the circumstances admitted may be a matter of opinion. I shall presently show that an alternative course of action was possible, and may, indeed, be defended by strong, though, in my opinion, inconclusive, arguments. There can, however, be no doubt whatever that the policy which was actually adopted, whether wise or the reverse, has been perfectly clear; and, moreover, that, although it has been liable to temporary interruptions owing to the vicissitudes of the seasons and to adventitious circumstances, of which the reoccupation of the Soudan was by far the most important, it has been persistently followed for a long series of years. More than this, I venture to assert, as a fact capable of the clearest proof, that it has fully answered all the expectations with which it was conceived.

[2] "Egypt No. 1 (1890)," p. 1.

In the third place, the execution of the financial policy to which allusion is here made, though not complete, is approaching completion. I shall presently point out the direction in which a change may with advantage be gradually effected.

I trust that these reasons may be considered adequate for introducing an historical retrospect into the present Report. Some general appreciation of the past is, indeed, necessary in order to obtain a clear appreciation of the present, and also in order to enable some forecast to be made of the direction which future action may advantageously assume.

I will now explain the nature of the financial policy which was actually adopted.

Amidst the chaos and confusion which existed after the Arabi revolt had been quelled, three points were clear:

The first was that the people were overtaxed, and that the fiscal system, although it had undergone some material improvements during the period of the Control (1876–82), was, to say the least, extremely defective.

The second was that a large capital expenditure, more especially in the direction of drainage and irrigation, was very necessary if the Egyptian people were to derive the full amount of benefit possible from the fertile soil and exceptionally favorable agricultural situation conferred on them by nature.

The third was that reforms, all involving considerable expenditure, were necessary in every Department of the State.

It was clear that the attainment of all these objects simultaneously was impossible; they were, in fact, for the time being, mutually destructive. It was necessary, to a certain extent, to choose between fiscal and administrative reform.

I have said that an alternative policy was possible. It is capable of defence on logical grounds. It is permissible to argue that the taxes ought, generally speaking, to have been maintained at the level at which they stood in 1882, in order to enable the administrative reforms to be accomplished, and that then, and not till then, fiscal relief should have been given to the tax-payers.

The counter-arguments which were allowed to prevail were that the mass of the people generally were far more interested in obtaining fiscal relief than in the execution of administrative reforms, however desirable these latter might appear to European eyes; and, further, that, by allowing a large portion of the money heretofore collected in taxes the Treasury would, in one form or another, gain in the end, and the administrative reforms, although in some degree postponed, would eventually be carried out far more thoroughly and with a greater amount of popular concurrence than would have been the case had they been originally placed in the first rank of the Government programme.

The question of expending capital on public works, notably on irrigation, stood on an entirely different footing to that of spending money on administrative reforms. Apart from the fact that expenditure on irrigation was far more comprehensible, and far more popular in the eyes of the mass of the Egyptian people, than expenditure of any other description, it was to be observed that it was distinctly remunerative. One, though not of course, the sole, object with which it was undertaken was to enable the funds necessary for administrative, and, I may add, sanitary, reform to be eventually provided.

The policy which was actually adopted may, therefore, be described as follows: fiscal reform, accompanied by substantial relief to the general body of tax-payers, was placed in the first rank. All the large sums of money which the Government could spare were devoted to remunerative public works, notably irrigation and drainage. Administrative reform, in so far as it was impossible without incurring heavy and immediate expenditure, was relegated to the third rank.

It would, of course, be a great error to suppose, when I say that administrative reform was relegated to the third rank, that nothing has been done in this direction,

and that matters which lie outside the scope of the main portions of the programme have been neglected. Such is very far from being the case. I have shown, in my successive annual Reports, that in the Judicial, Medical, Educational, and other Departments, great improvements, involving considerable extra expenditure, have been effected.

The expenditure on the Judicial Department, in all its various branches, has grown from £E.255,000 in 1882 to £E.407,000 in 1901; that on Prisons, from £E.20,000 to £E.60,000; that on the Medical and Sanitary Department, from about £E.70,000 to £E.105,000; and so on.

It is, however, none the less true that grants to these and other Departments have been, in some degree, subordinated to the exigencies involved in the execution of the main portions of the policy so far adopted—namely, fiscal reform and expenditure on remunerative public works.

I now proceed to explain the extent to which the financial policy adopted by the Government of Egypt has attained its objects.

In the first place, the corvée system has been practically abolished at a cost of about £E.400,000 a year. This system of taxation, though not altogether indefensible in theory, gave rise to very numerous and very cruel abuses in practice. It weighed heavily on the country. The burthen of taxation was notoriously evaded by the rich and by their dependents. It fell with excessive severity on the poorest classes.

The land-tax has been reduced by about £E.570,000 a year. At the same time, the productive powers of the soil have been greatly increased by improved irrigation and drainage. When the re-assessment now in course of progress is finished, the tax will be more equitably distributed than heretofore.

The professional tax has been entirely abolished at a cost of about £E.180,000 a year. It was a form of taxation which, though perfectly justifiable in principle, was little suited to the circumstances and requirements of Egypt. In former times it fell exclusively on the native population; Europeans resident in Egypt were exempted from payment.

The sheep and goat tax, yielding £E.40,000 a year, which weighed heavily on the agricultural population, and the collection of which gave rise to numerous abuses, has been suppressed.

So also has the weighing tax, which yielded £E.28,000 a year, although, inasmuch as this form of taxation was also somewhat specially liable to abuse, a considerably larger sum was probably paid by the tax-payers than ever found its way into the Government Treasury.

A number of petty and vexatious taxes, yielding in the aggregate about £E.53,000 a year, have been abolished.

The navigation of the Nile has been freed, at a direct loss to the Treasury of about £E.46,000 a year.

The Octroi duties, which in the past yielded a varying revenue amounting generally to about £E.200,000 a year, have been everywhere abolished.

The system under which a revenue is derived from fisheries has been reformed in such a manner as to afford relief to the tax-payers to the extent of about £E.40,000 a year, and, at the same time, to free this industry from some of the shackles by which it was formerly crippled.

External trade has been relieved by a reduction of the light-dues, at a cost which, in the first instance, amounted to £E.33,000 a year.

The salt-tax has been reduced by 40 per cent., with the result that the consumption of salt has risen from 24,000 tons in 1886 to 50,000 tons in 1901.

Large reductions have been made in the postal rates. The number of letters passing through the Post Office has risen from 4,354,000 in 1882 to 17,256,000 in 1901. In spite of the reduction in the rates, the Treasury has gained. The net receipts have increased from about £E.13,000 in 1883 to £E.26,000 in 1901.

A very similar course has been adopted as regards the Telegraph Department. The rates have been reduced by about 50 per cent. A large development of telegraphic correspondence has, in consequence, ensued. The number of telegrams passing over the wires increased from 680,000 in 1882 to 4,251,000 in 1901. The loss of revenue caused by the reductions was speedily recouped. The net revenue in 1901 was £E.12,000, as compared to £E.11,000 in 1883.

Large reductions have also been made in the railway rates, but the loss of revenue has been covered by increased traffic. In 1883, 2,761,000 passengers and 1,176,000 tons of goods were conveyed over the lines. By 1901, these figures had increased to 13,040,000 passengers and 2,975,000 tons of goods. The net receipts during the same period rose from £E.693,000 to £E.1,165,000.

The house-tax, which was formerly only paid by Ottoman subjects, is now paid by all residents in Egypt, irrespective of nationality. The receipts under this head have risen from about £E.60,000 in 1882–83 to £E.145,000 in 1901.

The only increase of taxation has been in the duty on tobacco, which has been raised from P.T.14 to P.T.20 per kilo.

To sum up, it may be said that, irrespective of the relief afforded by reducing the salt duty and by lowering the postal, railway, and telegraph rates, taxation to the extent of about £E.1,600,000 [3] annually, has been remitted during the last twenty years. The rate of taxation per head of population has sunk from £E.1.030 (1*l.* 1*s.* 1½*d.*) in 1882 to £E.0.789 (16*s.* 2*d.*) in 1902.

Nothing, I venture to think, shows more clearly the remarkable recuperative power of Egypt than these two facts, namely, first, that this large remission of taxation has been possible in spite of an extra charge of over £E.300,000 a-year being thrown on the Egyptian Treasury by reason of the re-occupation of the Soudan; and, secondly, that concurrently with the relief of taxation the Egyptian revenue has increased by about £E.2,000,000 to £E.2,500,000.

[3] In this figure account is taken of the recent abolition of the Octroi duties in Cairo and Alexandria.

Twenty years ago, the ordinary revenue was about £E.9,000,000. It was collected with difficulty. Forced sales of land, on account of non-payment of taxes, were numerous. Large arrears of land tax always remained due at the end of the year. In the early days of the occupation, arrears to the extent of £E.1,000,000 were remitted by a stroke of the pen. The ordinary revenue may now be taken at from £E.11,000,000 to £E.11,500,000. Sales of land, by reason of non-payment of taxes, are, relatively speaking, matters of rare occurrence. Out of a total taxpaying area of 5,540,900 acres, only 592 acres were sold by the Government in 1901. On a total assessment of £E.4,698,000, arrears to the amount of only £E.18,278 were due at the end of the year.

Turning now to the second object which the financial policy of the Egyptian government purported to attain, namely, the construction of remunerative public works, I have to observe that, up to the end of 1902, extraordinary expenditure to the extent of about £E.9,000,000 has been devoted to drainage and irrigation.[4]

The beneficial results are everywhere apparent. The disastrous effects which would otherwise have ensued from a series of low Niles have been averted. Stability has been given to the whole situation. Egyptian credit has been restored. European capital has been attracted to the country. Financial equilibrium no longer depends on the vicissitudes of the seasons. There has been a very large rise in the value of land. The area assessed to the land tax has increased from 4,758,474 acres in 1882 to 5,540,900 acres in 1901. In spite of a great fall in prices,[5] the value of the imports has increased from about £E.8,000,000 in

1883–84 to over £E.15,000,000 in 1901. During the same period, the value of the exports has grown about £E.12,000,000 to about £E.16,000,000. The cotton crop, which, twenty years ago, generally amounted to about 2,500,000 to 3,000,000 kantars (of 50 kilog.), now varies from 5,000,000 to 6,000,000 kantars. The amount of sugar exported, which formerly varied between 20,000,000 and 25,000,000 kilog., rose to as much as 73,500,000 kilog. in 1896, and although there has since been a diminution, the amount has never fallen below 49,000,000 kilog.

These facts and figures are, I venture to think, conclusive. They show beyond all manner of doubt that the financial policy— which, as I have explained, was deliberately adopted—has achieved the objects which it was intended to achieve. Very substantial fiscal relief has been given to the tax-payers of Egypt. Remunerative public works on a large scale have been constructed, with the most beneficial results.

With a view to the further elucidation of this interesting and important subject, I invite attention to the following Table.

The total receipts of the Egyptian Government during the twenty years from 1882 to 1900, both inclusive, have been as follows:

1. From ordinary revenue	204,816,420
2. From loans and other sources—	
(a) Guaranteed loan of 1885, raised to pay the Alexandria Indemnities, etc.	9,495,911
(b) 4½ per cent. Loan of 1888 (raised principally for commutation of pensions and of a portion of the Civil List), subsequently converted into Preference Stock.	2,158,304
(c) New Issue of Preference Stock in 1890, for irrigation, commutation of pensions, and expenses of conversion.	2,162,567
(d) Other sources, principally balance in hand at the commencement of the period	982,921
	14,799,703

---

[4] This figure includes the expenditure on the Nile Reservoir. For further details in connection with this subject see my despatch to the Marquess of Lansdowne of the 19th June, 1901 ("Egypt No. 2 [1901]," pp. 1–3). Since that despatch was written further expenditure has been incurred.

[5] Average Prices: £E.:

	1882	1901
Cotton	2.900	2.137
Wheat	1.045	.854
Barley	.582	.483
Sugar (first quality)	1.102	.477

3. Economies from the conversion of the Daira and Domains Loans, and interest on the investment of the Economies Fund — 1,584,020

4. Proceeds of sales of lands, and interest on the investment of the General Reserve Fund — 1,948,484

5. Miscellaneous receipts paid into the Special Reserve Fund, the most important of which was a sum of £E.779,000 paid by the British government in aid of the Soudan campaign of 1898 — 1,057,524

Total — 224,206,151

The Egyptian tax-payers have a right to know how these large sums of money have been spent by their trustees. I lay stress on the word "trustees," for the conception that the Government are the trustees of the tax-payers is not yet fully realized in this country, or, indeed, generally in the East; neither, looking to the history of the past, can it be any matter for surprise that the idea that the interests of the governing body and those of the governed are not only divergent, but even antagonistic, should still linger. Time and experience can alone disabuse the Egyptian people generally of this error.

The following Table gives the information required:

I. Ordinary expenditure— £E.
  1. Khedivial Civil List — 5,919,917
  2. Justice — 7,054,503
  3. Public Works — 10,419,807
  4. Education — 1,822,547
  5. Medical and Sanitary Department — 1,852,515
  6. Other Administrative expenditure — 22,152,310
  7. Expenses of revenue-earning administrations — 20,769,036
  8. Army — 12,368,109
  9. Pensions — 8,655,745
  10. Tribute — 13,393,910
  11. Interest on Debt — 79,448,786
  12. Suppression of corvée — 5,977,454
  13. Soudan — 3,678,889

  Total ordinary expenditure — 193,513,528

II. Extraordinary expenditure debited to General and Special Reserve. Funds, loan and other resources:
  A. Final expenditure—
    1. Alexandria Indemnities — 4,143,956
    2. Irrigation and drainage* — 4,120,121
    3. Emission of loans — 988,014

    4. Commutation of pensions and allowances — 3,633,612
    5. Public buildings — 943,183
    6. Postal steamers — 210,569
    7. Railways — 966,727
    8. Soudan — 2,618,827
    9. Miscellaneous — 759,943
    — 18,384,952

  B. Advances made from the General Reserve Fund, and repayable by the Government—
    1. Public buildings — 38,209
    2. Railways — 907,618
    3. Miscellaneous — 24,367
    — 970,194

    Total extraordinary expenditure — 19,355,146

III. Paid into sinking fund — 896,741
  Total expenditure, ordinary, extraordinary, and sinking fund — 213,765,415

* This is exclusive of the amount spent on the Nile reservoirs.

It has been shown that the total resources placed at the disposal of the Government during the period under review amounted to £E.224,206,151. The total expenditure amounted to £E.213,765,445. There remains, therefore, a balance of £E.10,440,736. This is accounted for in the following manner.

I. Sum carried forward from year to year, since 1890, owing to a change in the date of the settlement of the revenues assigned to the Debt — 1,253,914
II. Balance of the Conversion — 4,490,500
III. Balance of the General Reserve Fund — 3,794,785
IV. Balance of the Special Reserve Fund — 1,287,352
  Less surplus of the years 1880–81 — 385,815 — 901,537
  Total — 10,440,736

The first point which calls for observation in connection with these figures is that every farthing which has passed through the Government Treasury during the last twenty years is accounted for. I need hardly add that the accounts of which I have only given a brief summary, might be given in the fullest detail. This, of itself, is a great innovation. The Commission of Enquiry reported in 1878 that large sums had been sent to Constantinople "dont on n'a pu rendre compte." This special form of abuse has long since entirely disappeared. . . .

CHAPTER II

The Movement of Cotton Prices, 1820–1899

Soil, water supply, and climate, together with abundance of labor, have combined to make Egypt the producer of the world's finest cotton. To these factors should be added the great care in selecting and developing new varieties and in controlling grading and packing in the last seventy or eighty years. As a result, save in very exceptional circumstances such as the American Civil War, Egyptian cotton has always been sold at a price above that of American, Indian, Brazilian, and other varieties. This is brought out clearly in the following selection.

Various studies have shown that there is only slight correlation between the *size* of the Egyptian crop and the *price* of Egyptian cotton. For the latter is determined by total world supply and demand, and the main factor influencing supply has been the size of the American cotton crop. There is, however, a marked negative correlation between the *ratio of the sizes* of the American and Egyptian crops on the one hand and the *ratio of their prices* on the other. In other words the size of the Egyptian crop determines the extent of the premium it commands over other varieties; the larger the size, the smaller the premium.

Since, however, the size of the Egyptian crop exerts very little influence on world prices, and hence on the basic constituent of the price of Egyptian cotton, Egypt sought, until after the First World War, to maximize its cotton crop and hence, since there is a positive correlation between the size of the Egyptian crop and its *total value*, its export proceeds.

In the 1920's various attempts were made by the Egyptian government to raise the price of Egyptian cotton by restricting its acreage, but they all ended in failure. During and after the Second World War rectrictions on cotton acreage were designed mainly to increase the supply of grains, with which cotton competes for the available land.

(See also Issawi, *Egypt: An Economic . . . Analysis* and *Egypt in Revolution* and sources cited therein.)

[From Mahmoud el Darwish, "Note on the Movement of Prices of Egyptian Cotton, 1820–1899," *L'Egypte contemporaine* (Cairo), XXXII (1931), 641–44; reproduced by kind permission of the Société d'Economie Politique, de Statistique et de Législation, Cairo.]

1. The tables show the movement of prices of Egyptian cotton at Alexandria as well as those of American cotton in U.S.A. in the eighty years from 1820 (earliest on record for Egyptian) until the close of the nineteenth century. For Egyptian cotton, prices are taken from *Cotton. History, Development, etc.* by G. C. Dudgeon, No. 3A of the series "Egyptian Agricultural Products." Those of American cotton are taken from *Cotton Statistics* by J. A. Todd.

2. In the tables, quotations for Egyptian and Brazilian cotton at Liverpool are also given. The original figures (Todd's *Cotton Statistics*) were given as maximums and minimums; those tabulated are very crude averages of the grades given in the original series.

3. The chart and tables speak for themselves. The parallelism of the two lines plotted on the chart is quite evident, but some deviations need a few words of explanation:

a) American cotton was actually higher than Egyptian on more than one occasion. This was the case in 1824, 1846, 1847, 1849, 1850, and 1852–54. But it was during and after the American Civil War that the disparity was most noticeable. With the exception of 1871, prices of American kept above those of Egyptian for the whole period 1861–72. The war reduced the American crop to very small dimensions. The average annual crop for the years 1857–61 had been about four million bales of 500 pounds each. It dropped to 1.6 million bales in 1862, to 400,000 bales in 1863, and to 300,000 only in 1864. And the dislocation continued long after the close of the war. The average annual crop was, in the years 1865–69, two million bales, and it reached prewar dimensions only in 1873.

b) But it should be noticed that even during the Civil War American cotton did not fetch higher prices at Liverpool than did Egyptian.

c) It is interesting to notice how Brazilian cotton, supposed to be the mother of Egyptian, fetched higher prices at Liverpool than Egyptian in the earliest recorded period (1824–32) but soon fell below and has kept its inferior rating ever since.

Years	American Upland (Cents per Pound)*	Egyptian in Alexandria (Dollars per qantar)	Egyptian in Liverpool (Dollars per qantar)	Brazilian in Liverpool (Dollars per qantar)
1820	14.3	16.00	...	...
1821	14.3	15.50	...	...
1822	11.4	15.50	...	...
1823	14.7	17.00	...	...
1824	18.6	13.00	21.89	23.14
1825	12.2	13.00	34.97	34.97
1826	9.3	13.00	17.60	21.63
1827	10.3	13.00	15.33	19.11
1828	9.9	12.00	15.85	16.86
1829	10.0	12.00	14.47	14.97
1830	9.7	10.50	16.60	16.86
1831	9.4	15.00	16.60	15.59
1832	12.3	25.00	16.60	17.99
1833	12.9	30.75	...	...
1834	17.4	25.25	...	...
1835	16.5	18.50	...	...
1836	13.2	13.00	...	...
1837	10.1	15.00	22.13	19.62
1838	13.4	18.25	30.18	18.61
1839	9.9	13.00	23.38	20.12
1840	9.5	13.25	21.63	18.61
1841	7.8	10.00	16.86	17.34
1842	7.2	7.75	15.33	14.97
1843	7.7	18.00	14.08	13.08
1844	5.6	6.00	13.08	12.45

Years	American Upland (Cents per Pound)*	Egyptian in Alexandria (Dollars per qantar)	Egyptian in Liverpool (Dollars per qantar)	Brazilian in Liverpool (Dollars per qantar)
1845	7.9	10.25	15.59	13.20
1846	11.2	10.00	16.10	13.84
1847	8.0	7.25	...	...
1848	7.5	10.00	...	...
1849	12.3	11.75	...	...
1850	12.1	8.75	...	...
1851	9.5	10.25	...	...
1852	11.0	10.00	...	...
1853	11.0	9.00	...	...
1854	10.4	9.25	...	...
1855	10.3	10.75	...	...
1856	13.5	16.25	...	...
1857	12.2	12.75	...	...
1858	12.1	12.00	...	...
1859	11.0	12.25	...	...
1860	13.0	14.00	...	...
1861	31.3	23.00	...	...
1862	67.2	36.25	...	...
1863	101.5	45.00	50.30	48.79
1864	83.4	31.75	54.08	57.84
1865	43.2	35.25	39.48	38.73
1866	31.6	22.50	40.24	34.45
1867	24.9	19.00	24.91	23.88
1868	29.2	23.00	...	...
1869	24.0	19.50	...	...
1870	17.0	15.75	...	...
1871	20.5	21.56	...	...
1872	18.2	16.16	...	...
1873	17.0	14.94	...	...
1874	15.0	18.84	...	...
1875	13.0	13.68	...	...
1876	11.7	12.25	...	...
1877	11.3	13.59	...	...
1878	10.8	14.06	...	...
1879	12.0	14.34	...	...
1880	11.3	13.75	...	...
1881	12.2	15.00	...	...
1882	10.6	13.50	17.10	14.20
1883	10.6	12.56	16.10	11.95
1884	10.5	11.41	15.09	12.45
1885	9.4	12.00	12.07	11.69
1886	10.3	12.19	12.96	10.68
1887	10.3	13.00	14.08	11.19
1888	10.7	12.94	13.58	11.57
1889	11.5	13.61	14.97	12.69
1890	8.6	13.94	13.96	12.69
1891	7.3	12.06	11.81	10.68
1892	8.4	9.62	9.68	9.06
1893	7.5	9.44	10.56	9.56
1894	5.9	9.44	9.56	8.06
1895	8.2	11.19	11.69	8.06
1896	7.3	10.09	12.19	9.36
1897	5.6	7.87	9.94	8.56
1898	4.9	8.91	8.94	7.42
1899	7.6	12.28	10.94	7.94

* Since after 1835 the qantar was equal to 99 pounds, a price expressed in cents per pound was practically identical with one in dollars per qantar.—Translator.

The Trend in Prices, 1800–1907

The rise in prices discussed in the following selection was the resultant of many forces.

In the first place, the ending of Egypt's long period of isolation and its increasing trade relations with Europe, during the first half of the nineteenth century, forced its price level upward, more in line with that prevailing outside. Cheaper transport and the removal of prohibitions (see Part II, chap. 3) led to a large increase in exports of foodstuffs and a rise in their prices. On the other hand, until the 1840's cheap foreign manufactured goods could not enter Egypt freely, and the downward pressure they could exert on the price level did not make itself felt until the second half of the century.

Two other inflationary factors during the reign of Muhammad Ali were the debasing of the currency and the very large government expenditure on the army and on economic development (see Part VI, chaps. 5 and 6). As a result the currencies issued by the Egyptian government depreciated sharply in terms of foreign exchange. An attempt at currency reform in 1835, setting up a bimetallic system, had very limited results, since government expenditure continued to be very high, and since Ismail tried to take advantage of the fall in silver prices by issuing large quantities of silver coins; however, in 1885 Egypt shifted to a gold standard and thus obtained a stable currency.

Under Said and Ismail the large influx of foreign capital operated as another inflationary force (see Part VI, chap. 9). The sharp rise in cotton prices in the 1860's also worked in the same direction, since it greatly increased the value of Egypt's exports and expanded its income. By the same token the decline in cotton and other agricultural prices during the last quarter of the nineteenth century exerted a downward pressure on Egypt's price level. The fall in the unit price of Egypt's imports (see Part VI, chap. 1) also pushed prices down.

A factor noted in the following selection—the sharp rise in house rents in the large cities—is explicable in terms of the rapid growth of the urban population and the shift to the European kind of housing.[1] It is also to be presumed that the price of services rose appreciably.

[1] Janet Abu-Lughod. "Tale of Two Cities: The Origins of Modern Cairo."

At the very end of the century new inflationary forces began to make themselves felt. The world price of cotton rose sharply, and this, together with the increase in the quantity produced and exported, greatly expanded Egypt's income. At the same time foreign capital began to enter the country in large amounts. The movement culminated in the speculative boom of 1903–7, which witnessed a sharp rise in prices and which ended in the crash of 1907. It may be added that since then Egypt's price level has moved in line with the world level, rising sharply during the two world wars and the Korean War.

The author of the following selection was one of the small group of Armenians who attained eminence in Egyptian government service under Muhammad Ali and his successors and during the British occupation; he was Under-Secretary of State for Education and wrote some important works on education, as well as a useful book on land tenure.

(See also works by Douin, Bowring, Crouchley, and Société égyptienne, *Buhuth*, listed in the Bibliography.)

[From Yacoub Artin Pacha, *Essai sur les causes de renchérissement de la vie matérielle au Caire au courant du XIXe siècle (1800–1907)*, Mémoires de l'Institut Egyptien, V, fasc. 2 (Cairo, 1908), 57–58, 106–8, 131.]

For some years past the increasing prosperity of Egypt, which has manifested itself in all branches of human activity, has had as one of its consequences a rise in the price of all the necessities of material life. This rise in prices, which until 1903 had made itself felt gradually, has since that date accelerated sharply, and it is precisely since then that complaints have been heard, especially in large cities like Cairo and Alexandria. The complaints soon became widespread in the whole of Egypt, coming mainly from those classes of the population that live on fixed salaries and wages.

The government, which is the largest employer with the greatest number of wage and salary earners, was moved by these complaints to appoint commissions charged with examining their validity and with studying the question with a view to raising the emoluments of officials and employees, from the highest to the lowest grades. Agriculture, commerce, and the general public, influenced by the same causes, had to follow the government and were compelled also to raise the salaries and wages of their employees, domestic servants, and workmen.

Since the time when foodstuffs started their upward trend, i.e., since 1903, everyone has racked his brain searching for the causes of this state of affairs. . . .

The first striking fact in this table is that the price of all import goods has fallen, or at most has risen very slightly, between the beginning of the nineteenth century and our times. This is no doubt due to the progress achieved in manufacturing in Europe, where costs of production have fallen, and in great measure also to the change in means of communication resulting from the reduction in freights, insurance, customs duties[1] and other expenses. As a result, the price of colonial goods, lighting, heating, fruits, clothing, textile products, etc., has declined. The goods that have risen most are the produce of the soil, meat, poultry, construction materials, etc.[2]

[1] Until 1865, I believe, customs duties were 12 per cent ad valorem of prices prevailing in Egypt. After that date they were reduced to 8 per cent of net price in the country of origin. As for export duties, they too were 12 per cent until 1865; after that date they diminished by 1 per cent each year until they fell to 1 per cent, at which level they have remained until today. [See also Part II, chap. 2 and Part III, chap. 7.]

[2] Large-scale exports of onions, eggs, etc., have contributed in no small measure to raise the price of

TABLE IV

RATIO OF INCREASE OR DECREASE

Materials and Objects	1800–1882		1882–1907		1800–1907	
	From	To	From	To	From	To
Animals, sundry	1	1.5	1	1.7	1	2.5
Cereals, sundry	1	4	1	1.5	1	5
Crops	1	2.5	1	2.6	1	6.5
Colonial goods	1.7	1	1	1.4	1.1	1
Heating and lighting	1.8	1	1	1.5	1.2	1
Fresh and dry fruits	1.6	1	1	1.7	1	1.1
Clothing	1.3	1	1	1.4	1	1.4
Oils, sundry	1	2	1	1.8	1	2.3
Textiles	1.1	1	1	1.5	1	1.2
Vegetables	1	1.4	1	1.2	1	1.8
House rents	1	12	1	2.5	1	29
Construction materials	1	1.3	1	5.1	1	6.5
Metals	1	1.2	1	2	1	2.3
Animal fodder	1	4	1	2	1	8
Peasants' food	1	4	1	1.6	1	6
Hides and leather work	2	1	1	2.6	1	1.3
Foodstuffs	1	3.6	1	1.7	1	6
Workers' wages	1	2.3	1	2	1	4.7
Domestic servants' wages	1	2.7	1	2.1	1	5.4
Poultry	1	3	1	2.3	1	7.5

TABLE V

RATIO OF INCREASE OR DECREASE

Materials and Objects	1800–1882		1882–1907		1800–1907	
	From	To	From	To	From	To
Food	1	2.7	1	1.8	1	5.7
Animals, sundry	1	1.5	1	1.7	1	2.5
Manufactured goods	1	1	1	1.8	1	1.5
House rents	1	12	1	2.5	1	29
Construction materials and metals . . .	1	1.3	1	3.5	1	4.4
Agricultural produce	1	1.4	1	1.8	1	3.6
Wages	1	3.2	1	2	1	5
General average	1	3.2	1	2.1	1	7.4

But the item that has risen most rapidly, the ratio increasing from 1 in 1800 to 29 in 1907, is the one given under the heading "House rents in Cairo." . . .

this kind of produce, which began to be exported only ten or twenty years ago, thanks to the improvement in transportation in regard to both speed and lower freights. The following figures show the considerable increase in the export of these goods between the first year of export and 1906.

Onions
1855 . . . . . 7,110 tons
1906 . . . . . 80,597 tons
Tomatoes
1889 . . . . . 1,690,416 kilograms
1906 . . . . . 1,884,975 kilograms
Eggs
1896 . . . . . 14,475,000 units
1906 . . . . . 62,483,000 units

The price of wheat, barley, beans, etc., has risen (1) because the number of consumers, human and animal has increased, and (2) because the area planted to cotton having greatly increased, that under grains has necessarily been reduced. Production [sic, read exports] in the two periods indicated below was as follows:

Wheat (ardabs)
1884. 618,288
1906. 23,352
Maize
1884. 407,363
1906. 3,788
Barley
1884. 141,787
1906. 140
Lentils
1884. 95,483
1906. 6,913

The following figures show the progress in cotton exports since 1821 . . . . [See Part V, chap. 1.]

Beginnings of Industrialization, 1916

After the liquidation of the factories set up by Muhammad Ali (see Part VI, chap. 5) no serious attempt was made to industrialize Egypt until the 1920's. In the first place, agricultural expansion seemed to offer unlimited prospects for economic growth. Second, there was no native entrepreneurial class interested in industrialization—Muhammad Ali's monopoly system had killed whatever spirit of enterprise had existed among craftsmen—and foreign businessmen were interested in the more immediately profitable fields of speculation, finance, and trade. Third, Egypt met few of the objective prerequisites for industrialization: its population was small and with heterogeneous tastes; its capital availabilities were meager; its labor force was unskilled; except for cotton, it had few raw materials and no fuels. Lastly, the Capitulations and the international trade conventions (see Part II, chap. 3) made it impossible for the government, even had it so desired, to provide the initial protection and help without which industry cannot make a start in underdeveloped countries.

Under the British occupation the government's attitude to industry was positively hostile. Lord Cromer's opinion was that "it would be detrimental to both English and Egyptian interests to afford any encouragement to the growth of a protected cotton industry in Egypt"[1] and that it was "not desirable to impair the considerable revenue derived from customs duties on cotton goods."[2] As a result, the same duty, 8 per cent, was paid on coal as on any other imported material, and local cotton goods were subjected to an 8 per cent excise duty. On the other hand mining was encouraged and many concessions were granted, leading to the discovery of several deposits; but actual production remained negligible until the First World War. During this period, however, a few modern industries were set up. Ismail had established a sugar industry, which was subsequently developed, as well as a few textile plants; and during the British occupation two salt factories, two spinning mills, two breweries, some cigarette factories, and plants for the ginning and pressing of cotton and the extraction of oil from cottonseed and its use in soap manufacturing were founded. Nevertheless, by

[1] *Annual Report, 1891.*
[2] *Ibid., 1901.*

1916 total employment in the fifteen modern manufacturing enterprises operating in Egypt was only 30,000–35,000. For the handicrafts the period was one of steady decline, but a few held their own, or even expanded, during the British occupation, notably weaving, which was helped by imports of yarn.[3]

The First World War demonstrated vividly Egypt's great dependence on foreign sources of manufactured goods, and a commission on commerce and industry was set up, part of whose report is reproduced below. Its two leading members were Ismail Sidqi, future Prime Minister and president of the Federation of Industries (established in 1922), and Tal'at Harb, who in 1920 founded and presided over the Misr Bank. Subsequent developments have been discussed in Part VI, chapter 1. It may, however, be added that under the Five Year Development Plan of 1959–64 industry received a greater share of investment than any other sector and that by 1965 its contribution to the gross national product was expected to exceed that of agriculture.

(See also works by Gritly, Fridman, and Issawi [*Egypt: An Economic . . . Analysis* and *Egypt in Revolution*] listed in the Bibliography.)

[3] See several articles in *L'Egypte contemporaine*, 1910, 1911.

[From *Rapport de la Commission du Commerce et de l'Industrie* (Cairo, 1922), pp. 43–52.]

PRESENT CONDITION OF INDUSTRY IN EGYPT

GENERAL OBSERVATIONS

Among the ills from which Egyptian industry suffers one of the least deserved is the sentiment of indifference, and sometimes even of contempt, which industrial questions generally arouse.

The majority of the public, including the enlightened class, seems to have accepted as a dogma the assertion—which both is unjustified and shows a lack of reflection—that Egypt cannot seriously count on any resources other than the natural produce of its soil and its agriculture.

This superficial opinion has paralyzed the desire to seek, in the field of industry, a solution for the country's economic problems. And the belief that Egypt is, in this respect, afflicted with an irremediable incapacity has been such that it influenced even the governmental authorities; in spite of its deep solicitude for all that concerns the economic progress of the country, the government has for long given industrial matters only passing and inadequate attention. And industry, struck in its vital organs by numerous factors, was perforce doomed by this general indifference to neglect and failure. This has been its fate since the day when it was deprived of the care with which it was treated by Muhammad Ali.

It is true that, since the middle of the last century, when foreign goods began to flood the Egyptian market, it became difficult for the national industry to fight against an external competition which disposed of more powerful means; whose modern, scientific, and co-ordinated methods surpassed the primitive industrial methods of Egypt; and whose products were often more attractively packaged [*mieux présentés*] and less expensive.

But this does not justify the general inaction in the face of those new factors which exerted such a harmful influence on Egyptian industry. One must deplore the fact that both the Egyptian public and the various government authorities since Muhammad Ali did not seek to preserve such an important national patrimony by adapting it to new conditions and thus ensuring its maintenance and progress.

This task would have been facilitated by

the fact that during that period European industry was still searching for the right path and that it was still possible to use it as a model, instead of completely giving up to it the ground won by local industry at the cost of considerable sacrifice. This situation could only deteriorate from day to day. While other countries advanced economically, here each new progress made by European industry corresponded to a step backward by local industry. The most insignificant goods soon ceased to be made in Egypt and, in the humblest households, foreign junk replaced Egyptian goods, which seemed to be condemned to extinction. And while Egyptian tastes became more and more Europeanized—without, however, succeeding in being penetrated by the western spirit —traditions and old habits were lost, and with them the use of goods which were no longer suited to modern life. So much so that, not long ago, speaking of Egyptian industry in one of his annual reports Lord Cromer stated: "The difference must be apparent to anyone whose recollection of Egypt goes back for some ten or fifteen years. Quarters that were formerly hives of busy workmen—spinning, weaving, braiding, tassle-making, dyeing, tent-making, embroidering, slipper-making, gold and silver working, spice crushing, copper-beating, water-skin making, saddle making, sieve making, wooden-bolt making, lock making, etc.—have shrunk to attenuated proportions, or have been entirely obliterated. Cafés and small stores retailing European wares are now to be found where productive workshops formerly existed."[1] For lack of encouragement and control, Egyptian industry soon lost the rank it had previously occupied, thanks to the talent and well-known taste of its workers. The qualities which, in the past, had distinguished Egyptian products gave way to the most serious defects. The Egyptian worker, although endowed with qualities of dexterity, temperateness, and capacity for assimilation which can render him the most useful element in industrial progress, acquired, over time, such defects that a new education has become indispensable if he is to enter on a better path.

What are the characteristics of the Egyptian handicraftsman? We see him by nature averse to exertion and working just enough to earn sufficient to meet his needs, which have been reduced to a minimum. We observe with regret that his taste, which in the past inspired so many masterpieces, has been perverted by a long period of inertia; hence it is not surprising that he feels nothing but indifference toward the beautiful and the "finished." The Egyptian worker of today cannot understand the art which his predecessors carried to such heights, and consequently cannot love it. His work is inspired by the "almost" and he is no longer disturbed by defects, poor workmanship, or lack of taste. What can be more picturesque than the following sketch of the Egyptian worker by M. Bourgeois, which may be a little overdrawn but is accurate in essentials? "When it becomes necessary to repair a bicycle or a motorcar, turn to a native worker. He will repair it all right, he will even show much skill. But he will replace a cotter-pin by a nail, or a nail by a piece of wood; Ma'alesh (never mind!)." Here then are the two ills that have to be corrected, first of all, in order to have a renaissance of Egyptian industry: the indifference of the people and of the public authorities, and the defects in the character and education of the Egyptian worker.

The Egyptian government has not failed to accept the evidence of the preceding truths, and although its action has been belated it has definitely shown that it intends to cast away the hestitations of the past and resolutely to face the economic problem. The attention it has directed during the last ten years toward professional instruction and its greater interest in industry—especially since the present war proved that the power of nations and their influence in the world are related to their productive power and wealth—are happy portents of an industrial future conforming to the favorable condi-

[1] For 1905, Great Britain, *Accounts and Papers, 1906*, CXXXVII, 90.—Translator.

tions prevailing in the country. The Egyptian public, whose complete lack of interest we have been criticizing, seems to be giving up many of its prejudices against industry. The recent success of a large number of industrial enterprises, the anxiety caused by the persistence of diseases attacking agricultural produce and, lastly, the lessons of the war have all been factors making for a fairly deep revision of currently accepted ideas.

The following pages will provide a picture of the present, the perspectives and needs of the future, and, lastly, the remedies we deem applicable to the present situation if better use is to be made of the resources and capacity for work of Egypt.

PRESENT STATE OF INDUSTRY

The general census of 1907 showed that the industrial population of Egypt consisted of 380,000 persons, of whom about 360,000 were males and only 20,000 females. It is highly probable that these figures understate the present level, in view of the general increase in population, on the one hand, and the impetus which the war has, by and large, given to industry. The number of persons engaged in industry represents about 3.4 per cent of the total population. This is a very low ratio when measured against that of other countries; thus in the United Kingdom, for example, it is 24.5 per cent, in Switzerland 8.5 per cent, and in Argentina, an agricultural country comparable to Egypt, 4.12 per cent. Closer observation shows that the proportion is even smaller, for whereas in other countries use of machinery and co-operation considerably increase the output of human effort, here the defective methods and individualism which still characterize Egyptian industry limit this output to a minimum.

The above-mentioned industrial population of Egypt is subdivided into those working in small and those in large industry. The former occupies the vast majority of working men and the second a much more limited number. The 1907 census gives a distribution of the industrial population, by branches (Table 1).

TABLE 1

Industry	Population
Extraction of minerals	4,112
Textile industries	83,238
Hides, skins, other materials drawn from the animal kingdom	1,218
Wood	7,506
Metallurgy	30,111
Ceramics	9,653
Chemical products and analogous . . .	690
Food industries	40,669
Clothing and toilet industries	76,409
Furniture industries	5,420
Building industries	94,925
Construction of transport equipment . . .	3,866
Production and transmission of physical forces	8,601
Other industries	14,035
Total	380,453

These data refer to very wide groupings and can give only an incomplete idea of the respective importance of the various and multiple industries existing in Egypt. The Commission hopes that the data which will be provided by the 1917 census will excel those of previous censuses not only in greater accuracy but also in more complete details on the various crafts, thus making possible a more balanced and thorough judgment of the situation.

SMALL-SCALE INDUSTRY

We have already defined, in a previous study, what is meant in Egypt by "small-scale industry." As we said, it is the one carried on in workshops with a very limited number of workers, or in booths by handicraftsmen working on their own, with the help of a few apprentices. In fact, and in spite of its name, it is the most important category, for it employs the greatest number of workers and spreads its network over all the towns and large villages [*bourgades*] of Egypt.

The research undertaken by the Commission has of necessity covered all crafts practiced at present. But we have judged that the framework of this report lent itself rather to discussions of general developments, in order not to distract the attention of the reader and to guide his thoughts towards general solutions from which more particular measures can ordinarily be deduced. We have, however, published, in the form of an Annex to this report, notes on the main groups of industry, showing their present state, their prospects for the future, and the recommendations concerning them which the Commission has deemed it useful to suggest. . . . From these notes it is clear that the main industries at present are: building, weaving and its derivatives, dyeing, metallurgy and ironworks, wood and its derivatives, tanning, shoemaking, milling, chemical industries (soap, oil, candle-making, etc.), and artistic crafts (jewelry, fine carpentry, embossing, etc.).

These industries are practiced all over the country, but there are certain centers where some are particularly acclimatized. Cairo, which has always led in industrial and artistic activities, is certainly the Egyptian city with the greatest variety of industries, and the most important ones. The town of Mahalla specializes in the weaving of silk and cotton cloth, Damietta in silk-weaving, shoemaking, and carpentry, Qaliub and Akhmim in cotton cloth, Asiut in weaving, inlaid-work, and shawls, Qina in pottery, and Naqqada in the weaving of cotton and silk cloths designed for the Sudan. On the other hand there are certain industries which are not so localized. One example is the weaving of woolen cloth, whose raw material is available to craftsmen in the smallest villages, thus making it a widespread industry. Another is tanning and the preparation of hides, which are carried on wherever there are important slaughterhouses. Dyeing, ironwork and woodwork are also to be found everywhere, because of their constant and widespread use, whereas jewelry and artistic crafts are hardly practiced outside the capital and the large towns.

In a country where particularism is held in such great respect and where the benefits of co-operation are almost entirely unknown, it is naturally rare to see any of the industries under discussion arise from a principle of association. Each workshop is established and managed by its owner, and although in most cases he works alone, or is helped by one apprentice, there are several workshops which employ a certain number of workmen. In Cairo, Qaliub, Mahalla, and Damietta there are some hand-loom workshops which employ up to a hundred workers. The great impetus given by the war to most industries has helped in many cases to increase the number of workers employed in small workshops.

The premises of these industries are usually in a very poor state. In the villages handicraftsmen work in their own mud hut, surrounded by all the filth commonly found in village dwellings. In the towns workshops are very often relegated to dirty quarters; moreover the industrialists pay no heed to questions of order, tidiness, or hygiene. The urge to find very cheap premises overrides all other considerations, and it would seem that industrialists are far from aware that a decent installation, seen by the public to be clean and in order, may more than compensate for the extra costs involved by the confidence it inspires. The poor conditions of the premises are such that very often they constitute a danger for the workmen, who spend the greater part of their existence in them. And it is often very painful, when visiting town workshops, to notice the sickly expression of those who work there. The largest weaving shed in Cairo, located in a remote quarter, consists of a succession of shanties, more or less in ruin, lacking light and air. The owner, who has been making large profits—especially since the war—did not seem to us to have the least desire to improve these conditions, however slightly. In another, very prosperous, workshop making trimmings—a workshop using an ox-driven mill—the premises are so small that men and beasts work, so to speak, side by side, in the most uncomfortable and unhygienic conditions.

If, leaving aside the question of premises, we look at current methods of work, a painful impression is made by the inveterate attachment to old practices which seems to constitute the basis of the character of the Egyptian workman. In all branches of industry he shows recalcitrance, and even hostility, toward reforms and innovations. He is averse to using new tools, even where these would facilitate his task or improve the quality [*façon*] of his work. He unendingly repeats the models and patterns bequeathed to him by his predecessors and in this matter his obstinacy is rendered less curable by the fact that it generally rests on an exaggerated opinion of his own worth. This frame of mind is generally the fruit of ignorance, for a man who has experienced the blessings of education aspires continually to a better use of his faculties, whereas an ignorant man limits himself and takes delight in his atavistic immobility. And this reproach, which one is compelled to direct at the Egyptian craftsman, is the very one whose echoes are heard every time mention is made of agricultural reform. The progress of the latter, like that of industry, will be achieved by a greater degree of culture and a judicious diffusion of instruction.

This attachment to old methods of work is often the reason why native goods are much more expensive than similar ones made in Europe. The slowness of the work processes and the use of a greater amount of raw material, a matter which is particularly striking in weaving, lead to an exaggeratedly high level of prices, thus making it difficult to market the goods, especially silks. This was one of the observations made by the Alexandria import merchants who, having visited the exhibition recently held there, announced their regret at not being able, because of high prices, to participate in the marketing of these goods, for whose excellent quality they expressed appreciation.

In this country where commercial organization, especially in native trade, lends itself to many improvements, the question of the marketing of industrial products demands serious attention. In most cases the Egyptian industrialist is also a trader. He manufactures his goods and markets them himself, either wholesale or retail. And it is a constant fact that, since he keeps no books or has only the most rudimentary accounts, he is unaware of the cost of production of the goods he makes and is consequently exposed to all

the risks that flow from inexact estimates in this matter. As his main concern is to ensure his livelihood and that of his family, he limits his horizon to satisfying that need and neglects all that could promote the progress and vitality of his business. Instead of watching the market in order to acquire his raw materials and supplies on the best terms, he buys when he can and is thus exposed to the exigencies of intermediaries. Ignoring saving, he is equally at the mercy of buyers and sellers, and that is why industry not only remains stationary but yields such low profits to those who practice it in such deplorable conditions.

The picture sketched above is well exemplified by an industrial center like Akhmim and Qina. The former town used to be able to market a large part of its textile products, thanks to the annual visit of tourists. The cutting-off of this traffic since the war has caused a depression; yet no serious effort has been made to find new outlets, and the town of Akhmim, whose reputation is as justified as it is ancient, is now undergoing a real crisis. In Qina, the main center of pottery, one is struck by the condition, bordering on poverty, of those pursuing this industry. To the makers of *qulla* (water jugs), whose use is so widespread, the idea of co-operation is alien; they therefore waste their time and money in costly manipulations and transport, whereas if they associated in common work and used more modern and expeditious forms of transport they would receive a higher price for their labor. Far from being masters of a market which they in reality monopolize, they ruin each other by competition in which profits accrue only to the intermediaries.

This cut-throat competition among people of the same condition, or exercising the same craft, is a real affliction from which Egyptian industry, and probably the whole country, suffers; instead of seeking by a noble emulation to attain a better status, they use, in their mutual dealings, methods of competition which bring losses upon them all and hurt the industry or craft they pursue. We have been assured that this is the case in certain centers, and that such practices have been the main cause of the stagnation existing in them.

In Egypt small-scale industry is usually practiced by the indigenous population. In certain instances, however, especially in Cairo and Alexandria, foreigners take part in it. These foreigners work more methodically and thus constantly succeed in improving quality and raising the output of their workshops. Proof of this may be found in the soap industry, in tanning, shoemaking, shirtmaking, and clothing which, under the skillful management of foreigners, have gained great momentum during the war.

In Egypt the small workshop is the rule and will remain so for very long. Its survival is helped by the lack of capital and reserves. Human labor will therefore continue to be the main factor of production, and if evolution does take place it will necessarily be slow enough to let the illusion survive of a crystallized and immobile society. This has been true even in Europe, and this prospect should not lead to any feeling of discouragement regarding the future of industry.

The picture we have sketched of the defects of small-scale industry and of the failings of both masters and workers may perhaps seem too blackly pessimistic to warrant the hopes we have for the renaissance of industry in Egypt. However, we have come across many cases where the Egyptian industrialist has shown a spirit of order and progress, and the ill, deep-rooted as it is, does not seem to be irremediably recalcitrant to measures of improvement and wise reforms. For together with grave defects, Egyptian industry contains latent elements of progress from which with judicious nurture one could reap, in the course of time, the most splendid harvests. . . .

LARGE-SCALE INDUSTRY

This designation covers, in Egypt, industry which processes a large amount of materials in fairly big factories, using mechanical power and employing a more or less considerable number of workmen. Just as for small-scale industry, we provide in an Annex notes summarizing the present situation in each of the industries on which the Commission has been able to gather information. . . .

One may readily deduce from these data that, contrary to current opinion, there exist in Egypt industries of great scope, whose exploitation constitutes an important source of wealth for the country. A few figures illustrate this: the Filature Nationale d'Alexandrie, which consumes 50,000 qantars of Egyptian cotton a year, makes 3,500,000 pounds of yarn and 8 to 9 million yards of cloth; the annual production of the Sucreries is 100,000 tons [of refined sugar], and this company employs 17,000 workmen; the alcohol industry presently produces 11,000,000 kilograms a year, and the oil presses in Egypt, which absorb a quarter of the total cottonseed crop, produce over 100,000 tons of cottonseed cake, which corresponds to an output of 140,000 barrels of oil.

Alongside these industries, whose size and power are comparable to those of the largest European industries, there are several others which meet the various needs of Egyptian consumers, thus rendering signal services. These industries are: metallurgy, cigarettes, cement, salt and soda, fezzes, brickmaking, earthenware pipes, brewing, rubber, canning, etc. There are also the important industries of cotton ginning, rice-polishing, and wheat-milling, which are indispensable adjuncts to agricultural production.

All these industries, almost all of which are organized in company form, have required for their establishment and upkeep the investment of considerable funds. The capital of industrial companies, together with the bonds they have issued [*obligations qu'elles ont contractées*], amount to a figure close to 9,000,000 [Egyptian] pounds.

In general, large industries in Egypt were founded relatively recently. Many of them have overcome the particular difficulties that arise during the period of creation and schooling [*écolage*], which in Egypt give rise to much greater expenditure and disappointments than elsewhere and the risks and consequences of which must always be borne by the industrialist alone. In the absence of all fiscal aid, privilege, and other encouragement, having to sacrifice much time and money to pioneering and initiation, the industrialist seldom receives a reward proportionate to his efforts.

The existing enterprises, some of which are being temporarily favored by the economic circumstances arising from the war, render great services to Egypt, both in normal times and in times of crisis. The perseverance and vitality they have shown call for and justify a benevolent attitude on the part of the government and the giving of direct or indirect aid which all states desirous of industrial progress grant, in varying but reasonable proportions, to these important cogs of national prosperity.

There were other industries born as a result of the influx of capital and the feverish business conditions that marked the first decade of this century. Their constitution and installation showed the marks of the haste and improvidence with which they were launched. Their promoters, who only too often sought merely the immediate gain resulting from the resale of securities, paid little heed to the future of these companies; thus, because of both their conception and management, many of these companies bore in themselves the seeds of their inevitable ruin. This is the reason why a certain number of industries began in stagnation, after which they either collapsed or continued to subsist in precarious conditions.

In time, however, things began to improve. For some industries this was because the period of initial difficulties and schooling was over; for others, because the initial errors and the results of poor management provoked the adoption of energetic measures of improvement; and, for still others, because other companies with a smaller capital and a more intelligent management took over the older ones, which were being liquidated or were collapsing. The result was that large-scale industry, having eliminated

as far as possible its elements of weakness, took on a new impetus full of hope and promise.

But this period of failure—and almost of debacle—could not but greatly injure the country's industrial reputation. Capital, which was already suspicious, shrank further, and the assertion that funds invested in industry were exposed to adventurous risks became generally accepted. From there there was only a step to saying that industry could not succeed in Egypt, and that step was quickly, and very rashly, taken.

In the following pages the Commission will not only attempt to erase the impression still remaining from such allegations, but will above all try to prove that for this country industrial expansion constitutes an immediate necessity. In the meantime, we beg leave to render homage to the present leaders of Egyptian industry who, surrounded by innumerable reefs, have to the greatest possible extent been able to steer their enterprises safely. For one must remember that, in this country, nothing has been done to aid industry. Indeed unfavorable factors often thwart or block its progress. Is it not the rule that foreign goods are always, and even without scrutiny, more appreciated than local ones? And is it not a cause for regret that, in order to market their merchandise more easily, Egyptian industrialists often feel compelled to give it a foreign label?

The notes appended to this report show the range of grievances expressed by industrialists. Although allowance must be made for exaggeration in some of them, it remains true that in Egypt industry has always lacked the elements which are indispensable for success, namely, the good will and protection of the public authorities and, we should add, the control exercised by them.

Nothing of what has been established in other countries, especially those in which industry is nascent, has been attempted in Egypt. Some industries are subjected to, or threatened by, excise duties; no favor is shown to them in the matter of import [*entrée*] or transport of their raw materials; no preference is given to them in supplying the needs of the government; no measure has been taken to prevent or attenuate the effects of the competition of similar foreign goods; and so on. Granted the absence of positive help, industrialists are seldom received with an encouraging welcome which could, at a pinch, replace that help; in the absence of a government administration charged with protecting the interests of trade and industry, it is difficult for them to turn with profit to an authority which could help them with advice or deal with their complaints. We believe, however, that the lessons of the war will help to put an end to this state of affairs. Egyptian industry, which, we readily admit, has greatly profited from the exceptional circumstances created by the war—circumstances which have been described in an earlier report—has been a real boon for the country. The effort made by small industrialists as well as big ones has rendered it possible not only to relieve the shortage or absence of several goods but also to prevent the enormous rise in prices which in other countries upsets economic conditions. What fantastic prices would we not have had to pay for our sugar, oil, cement, alcohol, fezzes, soap, furniture, etc., if the industries producing these goods had not existed in Egypt? And, on the other hand, how much inconvenience and loss would we not have been spared if we had had industries producing crockery, glass, paper, chemicals, fertilizers, etc.?

In brief, and reserving for later our remarks and recommendations concerning the future of large-scale industry, we believe that the present state of this important branch of economic activity justifies the best hopes and calls for the most helpful assistance. We wish only to express our regret that Egyptians, save for a few exceptions, have always hestitated to participate in large industrial enterprises and to invest their capital in them. But we hope that, thanks to the diffusion of practical and technical education and to the confidence which a better organization of industry will not fail to arouse, this attitude will soon be only a memory of the past.

PART VII

Sudan

SUDAN
Introduction

As far as can be judged from the available evidence, the centuries that preceded the Egyptian conquest of 1820–21 saw very little change in the economic life of the Sudan. The most important developments were the slow but steady spread of Islam, particularly after the fourteenth century, which tightened not only cultural but also economic relations with neighboring Egypt and Arabia; the flow of pilgrim traffic from central and west Africa across the Sudan to Hijaz, especially after the seventeenth century, which may have stimulated trade; and the influx of large numbers of camel-owning Arab tribesmen, who reinforced the existing nomadic elements. Politically, the country consisted of three areas. The Fung sultanate of Sennar ruled the eastern part of the Sudan until the Egyptian conquest but gradually lost control of the outlying provinces. The sultanate of Darfur emerged as the dominant power in the west and survived until 1874. And the Ottomans established some control over Lower Nubia and occupied the Red Sea ports, but their grip over both areas gradually relaxed with the decline of the Ottoman Empire.[1]

The main economic regions corresponded to these political centers: the Nile Valley from Sennar to the Third Cataract, where a number of market towns existed, notably Arbaji and Shendi; Darfur; and the area around Suakin, which lived solely by trade. In all of these areas, and in all branches of the economy, conditions were extremely primitive. In agriculture the simplest techniques were used to sow and harvest crops in the rain-fed zone—thus in Sennar "ploughs were not in use, the ground being tilled with a hoe."[2] Along the Nile banks, however, as far south as Sennar, water wheels (saqia) were used for irrigation, and Burckhardt's description of conditions in 1813 is worth quoting:

In poor villages one Sakie is the common property of six or eight peasants; but the wealthier inhabitants have several. The number of water-wheels between Assouan and Wady Halfa, or between the first and second cataract, is from six to seven hundred. The ground watered by one Sakie, which requires the alternate labour of eight or ten

[1] P. M. Holt, *A Modern History of the Sudan*, pp. 23–25.
[2] O. G. S. Crawford, *The Fung Kingdom of Sennar*, p. 277.

cows, comprises from three to five Egyptian Fedhans. In fruitful years, the winter wheat and barley irrigated by one wheel yields from eighty to one hundred Erdebs (twelve to fifteen hundred bushels); the proportions sown of these grains are generally one fourth wheat and three fourths barley.[3]

The principal crops were millet, wheat, and *dukhn* (*Pennisetum typhoideum*), but cotton grew in northern Sudan, some tobacco was exported from Sennar, and gum arabic was picked from wild trees. Animal husbandry has always played an important part in the Sudanese economy, especially the breeding of Arabian horses in the Halfaya, Gerri, and Dongola districts for export to the Arabian Peninsula.[4]

Handicrafts were also few and primitive. Here again Burckhardt may be quoted:

Small looms are frequently seen in the house of the Nubians; with these the women weave very coarse woollen mantles, and cotton cloth, which they make into shifts. From the leaves of the date-tree they also form mats, small drinking bowls, and large plates on which the bread is served at table; and though these articles are formed entirely by hand, they are made up in so very neat manner, as to have every appearance of being wrought by instruments. The above are the only manufactures in Nubia; everything else is imported from Egypt.[5]

Nor were conditions better in other parts of the country. In Shendi the only craftsmen Burckhardt saw were blacksmiths, silversmiths, tanners, potters, and carpenters, but cotton-spinning and mat-weaving were carried on in homes; here, too, heavy reliance was placed on imports. The Fung capital, Sennar, had iron-workers—who made such simple articles as nails, spears, and knives—masons, shoemakers, tanners, and cotton weavers.[6] Bruce states that in Halfaya "their principal gain is from a manufacture of very coarse cotton cloth, called Dimmour,"[7] while Browne makes no mention at all of handicrafts in his detailed account of Darfur. The only minerals exploited were some iron and copper, which were extracted and smelted in Darfur,[8] and gold dust, which was exported.

Given the extremely low productivity of agriculture and the very restricted number of handicrafts, it is not surprising that no big towns were to be found in the Sudan. The largest, Sennar, probably contained 10,000–15,000 inhabitants at the beginning of the nineteenth century—earlier estimates of 100,000 must be considered completely unreliable.[9] Shendi, the most important town in the north and the hub of the caravan routes, may have had 800–1,000 houses and some 6,000 inhabitants in the eighteenth century; by 1833 these figures had declined to 600–700 houses and 3,000–3,500 inhabitants, respectively;[10] Bruce, however, gives the

[3] John Lewis Burckhardt, *Travels in Nubia*, p. 126.
[4] James Bruce, *Travels To Discover the Source of the Nile*, V, 284–88.
[5] Burckhardt, *op. cit.*, p. 135.
[6] Crawford, *op. cit.*, p. 277.
[7] Bruce, *op. cit.*, p. 276.
[8] W. G. Browne, *Travels in Africa, Egypt, and Syria, from the Year 1792 to 1798*, p. 267.
[9] Crawford, *op. cit.*, pp. 277, 319–21, 325.   [10] *Ibid.*, p. 62.

low figure of 250 houses for 1773.[11] Of Kobbeh, "one of the most populous towns" of Darfur, Browne states: "I cannot persuade myself that the total amount of both sexes, including slaves, much exceeds six thousand"; as for the total population of Darfur, "The number of souls within the empire cannot much exceed two hundred thousand."[12] Regarding the other towns, Burckhardt[13] gives a figure of 500 houses for Damer, and Bruce[14] one of 300 houses for Halfaya; Caillaud, however, states that the latter had had a population of 8,000–9,000, reduced by nomad raids to 3,000–4,000, by 1821.[15]

Another factor impeding both the growth of towns and the general development of the economy was the lack of transport facilities. Very little use was made of the Nile, which in the nineteenth century was, over long stretches, the main traffic artery. Again quoting Burckhardt: "There is no communication by water between Sennar, Shendy, and Berber; boats are used only as ferries, but even these are extremely scarce, and the usual mode of passing the river is upon the Ramous, or small raft of reeds."[16] For long distances, camel caravans provided the sole means of transport.

The Darfur and Sennar caravan routes (see Part VII, chap. 1) carried the bulk of the Sudan's international trade. However, there was a caravan route from Suakin to Sennar and another from Suakin to Berber, and a small amount of trade also flowed between Sennar and Gondar, in Ethiopia. Through the Turkish-occupied Red Sea ports of Suakin and Massawa some trade was conducted with Yemen and India.[17] Gold from the more westerly parts of central Africa was tapped by the Murzuq and other Trans-Saharan caravans.[18]

The articles enumerated in chapter 1 bring out clearly the nature of the Sudan's trade. Slaves[19] and gold constituted the main articles of export, as they had done for centuries, followed by such items as ivory, ostrich feathers, and skins. In addition horses, tobacco, and occasionally grain were exported to Arabia. Imports, whether bought in Cairo or in Suakin, consisted of European and Indian goods, but some products of Egypt and other Middle Eastern countries, e.g., textiles and soap, were also in demand. Among the goods shipped from Jidda to Suakin and carried into the interior by the Suakin caravan were Indian spices, coarse muslins, and "blue cotton cloth from Surat,"[20] as well as European hardware arriving by way of India.[21]

The isolation of the Red Sea area after the sixteenth century because of the

---

[11] *Op. cit.*, p. 243.   [12] Browne, *op. cit.*, pp. 284–85.

[13] *Op. cit.*, p. 265.   [14] *Op. cit.*, p. 270.

[15] Crawford, *op. cit.*, p. 69.

[16] *Op. cit.*, p. 314.

[17] 'Abd al-Jalil al-Shatir, *Ma'alim tarikh Sudan wadi al-Nil* (Cairo, 1955), p. 71.

[18] Browne, *op. cit.*, p. 268.

[19] Burckhardt (*op. cit.*, p. 290) puts the number of slaves annually sold at Shendi at about 5,000, of whom 2,500 were sold to Suakin merchants, 1,500 to Egyptians, and the rest to Dongola and the beduins of eastern Sudan.

[20] Bruce, *op. cit.*, p. 243.

[21] Burckhardt, *op. cit.*, p. 286.

diversion of trade and the exclusion of Christian ships (see Part V, Introduction), must have contributed to the backwardness of the Sudan. For whereas in the fifteenth and sixteenth centuries some Venetians seem to have traded in Suakin, between the mid-seventeenth century and 1814 no European visited the port except for a few missionaries.[22] Burckhardt, who entered the town in 1814, described its commerce as being in the hands of local Turks and Arabs from Hadhramaut[23] (see Part V, chap. 6). In Darfur, most of the merchants were North Sudanese, or Egyptians, and a few were Tunisians and Tripolitanians.[24] North Sudanese were also active in the Sennar trade. Burckhardt made some very interesting observations on the organization of trade between Egypt and Sudan:

The Egyptian trade is, in general, carried on with very small capitals. I do not believe there is a single merchant, the whole amount of whose stock exceeds fifteen hundred Spanish dollars. . . . The common class of merchants have from two to three hundred dollars; even this money is seldom their own property; in general, it is either borrowed by them in Upper Egypt, at high interest [50 per cent for the duration of the journey],or their merchandise is bought at Esne, Kenne, or even at Cairo, upon credit: the reason is, that no truly respectable merchant of Egypt ever engages in such enterprises. . . .

It may easily be conceived, from what I have already said of the prices of several articles of trade, that the profits of the Egyptians are very great. In fact, there is not a single article of Egyptian, or European manufacture, which is not sold in Shendy at double or triple its prime cost in Egypt, and the products of the southern countries yield as great a profit when sold in Egypt. The rapacity of the chiefs through whose territories the caravans pass, the expense of transport across the desert,[25] the feeding of the slaves, the tribute paid to the Ababdes, and the duties laid upon the trade by the Pasha of Egypt,[26] are indeed heavy drawbacks, but still the profits are very considerable; and I am certain that a well chosen assortment of goods carried from Daraou to Shendy, leaves, after the sale of the return cargo at Daraou, a clear gain of one hundred and fifty per cent, according to the most moderate calculation. I have heard of Zamales, or camel loads of Sembil and Mehleb, which, after having been exchanged at Shendy for slaves, produced at Cairo a profit of almost five hundred per cent. . . .

The entire amount of the capital invested by the Egyptian merchants in the Soudan trade, I calculate to be from sixty to eighty thousand dollars, but as this sum produces a profit twice, and sometimes thrice in one year, according to the number of journeys, the whole value of the imports into these countries from Egypt may be computed at about fifteen hundred, or two thousand dollars per annum [*sic*]. No dollars are re-exported from the Negro countries; they are dispersed or hoarded by the chiefs and other persons, and thus Soudan becomes a continual drain for a part of the silver of Europe.[27]

The absence of local coins does not seem to have greatly hampered the flow of

[22] Crawford, *op. cit.*, pp. 122–25.

[23] *Op. cit.*, pp. 390–91.

[24] Browne, *op. cit.*, p. 241.

[25] The expenses of the outward journey are three times as much as those attending the transport back from Berber to Daraou, on account of the cheapness of camels at Berber.

[26] Upon every slave imported into Upper Egypt, Government exacts at present a duty of sixty piastres. The most important articles of the trade, as slaves, Erdeyb, ostrich-feathers, natron (from Darfour), are besides exclusively bought up by the Pasha, who fixes a maximum to the Soudan merchants, and resells them at pleasure, with a great profit.

[27] Burckhardt, *op. cit.*, pp. 272–73.

international trade. Thalers were imported in large quantities from Egypt. "The common currency at Berber, and all the way from thence to Sennar, is Dhourra (millet) and Spanish dollars. . . . another substitute for currency is the Dammour, a coarse cotton cloth. . . . In Cordofan, besides Dhourra and Dokhon, the usual currency is small pieces of iron, which are wrought into lances, knives, axes, etc.; besides these pieces of iron, *cows* are used as a representative of money in large bargains, and are thus continually transferred from one person to another." [28] Browne reports that in Darfur thalers were mainly used as ornaments and that at al-Fashir the closest approximation to money was "certain small tin rings, the value of which is in some degree arbitrary," [29] and in other places beads and salt. The limited amount of internal exchange could presumably be easily achieved by barter or by these substitutes for money.

Among the most powerful motives that had led Muhammad Ali to the conquest of the Sudan were the lure of gold, the hope of supplementing Egypt's meager timber supplies, and the desire to draft black slaves for his expanding army or to sell them abroad. All these expectations were frustrated: gold proved elusive, the available timber was too hard, and slave raids brought in disappointingly small numbers, while the attempt to make the Sudanese pay their taxes in slaves threatened to disrupt the existing economic and social order and resulted in serious revolts against Egyptian rule.[30] Similarly, the imposition in 1824 of an export monopoly like the one prevailing in Egypt (see Part VI, chaps. 1 and 4) had to be abandoned in 1843. And although taxes were so high as to cause much discontent (see Part VII, chap. 3), they usually failed to meet regular administrative and military expenditure; however, until 1843, net profits from monopolies covered at least part of the deficit.[31]

But although Muhammad Ali's conquest brought scant profit to him and little immediate economic advantage to the Sudan, it did lay down the basis of progress. In the first place, security, the prime condition of economic growth, was enforced throughout the vast area under Egyptian rule and was maintained until the final collapse in the 1880's. Second, the country was opened up to foreigners. In the wake of the conquest, came Egyptian petty traders, soon followed by skilled workmen sent by Muhammad Ali and peasants fleeing his rule.[32] The breakdown of the monopoly system in 1843 led to "the development of a European trading community, at first mostly Greek and Italian, in Khartoum." [33] That town was founded by the Egyptians and by 1840 had a population variously estimated at 13,000–50,000,[34] by far the largest in the Sudan. Moreover many minor improvements were made in agriculture, such as the introduction of new

[28] *Ibid.*, pp. 215–17.
[29] Browne, *op. cit.*, p. 290.
[30] Holt, *op. cit.*, pp. 43–44.
[31] Henri Déhérain, *Le Soudan égyptien sous Mehemet Ali*, pp. 181–87; see also 'Abd al-Jalil, *op. cit.*, pp. 138–42.
[32] Richard Hill, *Egypt in the Sudan*, pp. 49–59.
[33] Holt, *op. cit.*, p. 61.
[34] Hill, *op. cit.*, p. 162; Déhérain, *op. cit.*, p. 123; Walkley, in *Sudan Notes and Records*, 1935.

crops and the restoration or amelioration of the irrigation system, and a few factories were established. (See Part VII, chap. 2.) No less important, a large fleet of sailing boats was launched from three government shipyards, and seasonal connections were established between all parts of the country; year-round sailings were possible on the sections of the two Niles which were free of cataracts, i.e., above Khartoum.[35] The Sudan was thus at last enabled to make use of the cheapest and most convenient form of transport available to it.

Under Said (1854–63) and still more under Ismail (1863–79) economic progress accelerated. Perhaps the main factor at work was improved communications. By then regular steam services had been established between Suez and Bombay, and several steamers, including after 1857 those of the Egyptian line (see Part VI, chap. 7), called at Suakin and Massawa. This connection with the outside world, which was reinforced by the opening of the Suez-Cairo-Alexandria railway in 1858 and the Suez Canal in 1869, had a stimulating effect on the Sudanese economy, by greatly reducing the distance along which goods had to be transported by caravan. Still more beneficial was the introduction of a fleet of river steamers in the early 1860's, which considerably increased the volume of traffic on the Nile.[36] But since steamers could not sail over the cataracts between Khartoum and Wadi Halfa, except during high flood, and since caravan transport to Egypt and the Red Sea was slow and expensive, various railway schemes were put forward. Muhammad Ali toyed with the idea of a line between Suakin and Shendi, as well as one from the White Nile to Kordofan.[37]

In 1863 Ismail set up the Compagnie du Soudan, with a paid up capital of £2,000,000; among its objectives were trade, the launching of river steamers, and the building of railways, but nothing came out of the latter two and the company soon went into liquidation.[38] In the following years surveys were made for railways connecting Shendi with Aswan on the one hand, at an estimated cost of £9,000,000, and Suakin on the other. The 1870's saw further projects; in 1873 work actually started on a ship incline at Aswan, to facilitate water communication with Wadi Halfa, and in 1875 the first rails of a line designed to connect Wadi Halfa with the center of the country were laid down. By 1878, when the Cave report (see Part VI, chap. 9) recommended that further work be discontinued, a total of 33 miles had been constructed, at a cost of £600,000.[39] The implementation of other railway projects (see Part VII, chap. 3) was stopped first by the bankruptcy of the Egyptian government and then by the advance of the Mahdist forces.

In the absence of railways, caravan traffic continued to develop. In the late 1870's, 30,000–40,000 camels made the journey to Egypt each year, at a dollar a

35 Hill, *op. cit.*, pp. 61–62.
36 Hill, *op. cit.*, pp. 99–101, 132, 156–60.
37 *Ibid.*, p. 67.
38 *Ibid.*, p. 122; David Landes, *Bankers and Pashas*, pp. 151–54.
39 Hill, *op. cit.*, pp. 133, 158–60; L. Wiener, *L'Egypte et ses chemins de fer*, p. 588.

load and "security improved with lowered rates and increased traffic."[40] In addition a postal service was established, and over 3,000 miles of telegraph lines were laid down, providing adequate communications with the various parts of the country. Telegraphic links with the outside world were available through Suakin and Egypt.

The improvement of transport and communications, the influx of a few dozen European merchants, and the removal of restrictions on trade in the Upper Nile region in 1853 led to a decided increase in the country's commerce. At first the most flourishing branch was the slave trade, developed by Europeans as a by-product of the ivory trade but soon taken over by northern Sudanese. The government's repeated efforts to suppress the slave trade achieved some results but created great discontent, which was to contribute powerfully to the overthrow of Egyptian rule (see Part VII, chap. 4). But other exports were also developing: gum arabic, which was increasingly demanded for use in paper-making, and cotton, which was developed during the boom of the 1860's (see Part VI, chap. 8). In 1873 the gum yield was put at 14,000 tons and the cotton yield at 12,000.[41] In 1875 a visitor to Suakin, Junker, noted: "Export dues [are] over £60,000 up to exchanges of over £1,000,000. The best traffic is in slaves." By 1879 French, German, Italian, and other traders had settled in the town, whose population had been put at 18,000 by Baker in 1869.[42]

Taken as a whole, the Egyptian period was one of distinct economic growth, as is indicated by the following authoritative judgment:

We know that there was a great increase in the cultivated area of the Sudan; we may safely deduce a parallel increase in the total population of the northern and central regions. Of the population of the Southern Sudan we know too little even to speculate. The acceleration in the settlement of emigrants from the western sultanates in the almost empty lands between the Blue Nile and the Setit denuded the forests and began to change the face of the Southern Butana.[43]

But high taxes, harshly and arbitrarily levied, and forced labor inflicted great hardships on large sections of the population. The weakening of government control, due to increasing financial embarrassments in Egypt, the Urabi revolt, and the intervention of the Great Powers, made it possible for the Mahdists to harness this discontent and overthrow Egyptian rule.

The Mahdist period (1881–98), and more particularly that of the Revolutionary War (1881–85), was one of intense disruption and of economic retrogression in the Sudan. Some of the capital equipment installed under the Egyptians, such as the telegraph, was destroyed, and the rest gradually ran down, e.g., the few steamers that survived the war. Tribal levies and movements of population contributed to disorganize agriculture, and the years 1888–90 were marked by

---

[40] Hill, *op. cit.*, p. 129.
[41] *Statistique de l'Egypte*, 1873.
[42] Bloss, in *Sudan Notes and Records*, 1936.
[43] Hill, *op. cit.*, p. 153.

crop failures, famine, and pestilence.[44] It is probable that the population sharply declined, but Lord Cromer's estimates[45] of 3.5 million "swept away by famine and disease" and another 3.25 million killed in war seem highly exaggerated. Similarly, little value can be attached to his statement: "During the last few years, the population has been increasing but it is possible that it does not now exceed 2 million." The latter figure is probably far too low, for it would imply, over the period 1907–56, when net immigration was very small, a more than fivefold increase compared with just over a doubling in Egypt, where hygienic conditions were far superior. The figure of 8–8.5 million often quoted for the population in the 1870's seems, on the other hand, much too high, and when the "Khalifa's apologists deny that the pre-Mahdist population can have been more than 4 to 4½ million"[46] they may well be closer to the mark. After all Egypt's population at that time, after half a century of rapid growth, was probably around 6 million.

It may be added that the Mahdist period saw two population shifts: that of the inhabitants of Khartoum to Omdurman,[47] which grew to be by far the largest town in the Sudan (see Part VII, chap. 5), and the enforced migration of some western tribes to the region around the new capital.

Regarding the economic policy of the government, the burden of taxation seems to have somewhat diminished, but its irregularity became even greater.[48] The issue of a national gold and silver currency was soon followed by debasement.[49] Commerce was regarded with suspicion; because of the opportunities it presented for foreign infiltration, and was strictly regulated and taxed. Further obstacles to trade were the state of the currency, the border warfare with Egypt and Ethiopia, and the fact that throughout this period Suakin remained in Anglo-Egyptian hands. Figures available for the thirteen-month period, from December 20, 1892, to January 27, 1894, show Sudanese exports to Egypt to have been only £8,207 and imports £18,429; exports to Suakin totaled £90,909 and imports £47,297. The chief exports were gum and ivory.[50]

After the overthrow of the Mahdists and the Anglo-Egyptian reconquest of the Sudan, the task facing the British government may be described as follows: in a huge country, with considerable long-term potentialities but almost totally devoid of capital equipment and skills and living in a low-level subsistence economy, to bring into being an exchange sector that could generate the money income required both to run modern administrative and social services and to create the savings needed for development. This in turn presupposed the production of exportable raw materials and the establishment of a transport network and a marketing system to move those materials. Moreover the determination to

[44] P. M. Holt, *The Mahdist State in the Sudan, 1881–1898*, pp. 172–74.
[45] *Modern Egypt*, II, 545.
[46] K. D. Henderson, *Survey of the Anglo-Egyptian Sudan, 1898–1944*, p. 13.
[47] See Walkley, *op. cit.*
[48] Holt, *Mahdist*, p. 186, and Part VII, chap. 5.
[49] *Ibid.*, pp. 112, 192.
[50] *Ibid.*, p. 237.

avoid two features that had marred the development of Egypt—the concentration of landownership (see Part VII, chap. 7) in a few hands and foreign control over large sectors of the economy (see Epilogue), together with the absence of initial opportunities for large-scale private investment—meant that foreign private capital would play only a minor part. The burden of getting the economy started had therefore to be shouldered by the small but efficient civil service (consisting of a core of British officials aided by Lebanese and Egyptians), with the help of the few hundred foreign merchants who had settled in the major towns.

But for various reasons connected with international politics, the Sudanese government could not raise large sums abroad and its own revenues were tiny, £35,000 in 1898 and still only £804,000 by 1906.[51] A temporary solution was found by channeling subsidies from the Egyptian budget to the Sudanese. In 1899–1912 Egypt made a total contribution of £2.8 million for civil expenses, and in 1901–14 it advanced interest-free loans of £5.5 million, to which should be added Egyptian army expenditures in the Sudan aggregating £6.4 million in 1899–1924.[52] Starting in 1909 the Sudan government began to borrow abroad, in the London money market; by 1914 its foreign debt stood at £1.3 million and by 1924 at £12.1 million.

These sums, together with some budgetary appropriations (by 1913 ordinary revenue had risen to £1.7 million and in 1929 it reached a peak of £7 million) were largely used to improve transport. Already by the end of 1899 the railway built by the advancing Anglo-Egyptian army had reached Khartoum, 931 kilometers from its starting point at Wadi Halfa. By 1912 it had been extended to al-Obaid, 687 kilometers farther south, tapping the Sennar region. In the meantime the long-projected railway connecting the Nile valley with the Red Sea (see Part VII, chap. 6) had been built in 1906, between Atbara and the country's first modern harbor, Port Sudan.[53] And between 1922 and 1929 the Kassala Railway Company had financed the construction, by the state, of a line connecting Haiya, on the Atbara–Port Sudan line, with Kassala, Gedaref, and Sennar, on the other main line, at a cost of £2.1 million. At the same time the Sudan Plantations Syndicate built a small network of light railways in the Gezira (see Part VII, chap. 8). Moreover, from the very beginning, great use was made of river navigation. Steam services were established on the main Nile between Wadi Halfa and Shellal, providing a connection between the Sudanese and Egyptian railways, and between the Third and Fourth Cataracts; on the Blue Nile between Sennar and Rusairis; on the White Nile between Kosti and Juba; and on the Bahr al-

<hr>

[51] Cromer, *op. cit.*, II, 549.

[52] G. Marzouk, "Sudan's Balance of Payments."

[53] The effect of the Red Sea connection on the economy of the Sudan may be judged from the following figures: steel girders cost in Khartoum £10 and cement £6 to £7 a ton when imported through Egypt; these prices fell by £3 a ton when shipment was made through the Red Sea and Port Sudan (Great Britain, *Accounts and Papers, Egypt*, 1906, Vol. CXXXVII). Previously it had been stated by the Governor-general that "wheat can be sent from Chicago to Liverpool at practically the same freight as from Khartoum to Wadi Halfa" (*ibid.*, 1904, Vol. CXI).

Ghazal between Jur and Sobat. By the end of 1929 river services covered a distance of 3,340 kilometers and the railways totaled 3,213 kilometers. The capital of the State Railways was £7.2 million, of which £5.3 million was accounted for by the railways and the balance by river shipping and Port Sudan.[54] At the same time as it provided transport, security, and minimal educational and health services,[55] the government sought actively to develop the production of cotton, which in the absence of easily accessible minerals provided the most suitable raw material. Initial experiments having been successful, an arrangement was made with two British companies for a large-scale scheme (see Part VII, chap. 8). The First World War held up implementation but the project was carried through in the 1920's and became the backbone of the country's economy.

The progress of cotton is reflected in the composition of the country's exports. The slave trade had diminished under Mahdist rule and practically disappeared under British rule. The other traditional items, gold and ivory, greatly decreased. In 1907–13, gum arabic provided 33 per cent of total exports, followed by cotton and cottonseed making up 11 per cent. But by 1929 cotton exports, which had risen over sevenfold in quantity, accounted for 70 per cent of exports. The Second World War and the Korean War raised cotton prices to unprecedented heights, and the steady expansion of output in the Gezira and elsewhere greatly increased the quantity available for export. In 1946 the Sudan was thus enabled to launch its first large-scale development plan, and growing revenues together with substantial foreign aid and loans have led, in the past few years, to the implementation of many important schemes in the fields of irrigation, transport, power, industry, education, health, and social welfare. Thus the Sudan seems at last to be in the process of developing its enormous potentialities.

[54] Wiener, op. cit., p. 631; Morrice, in Sudan Notes and Records, 1949.
[55] Holt, A Modern History, pp. 119, 131.

CHAPTER I

Foreign Trade: The Darfur Caravan, 1800

The Darfur caravan followed one of the two main routes connecting the Sudan with Egypt, its size varied with each trip. In the following selection the number of slaves carried each year was put at 5,000–6,000, but Browne estimated that the caravan in which he traveled in 1796 consisted of nearly 500 camels and that "they esteem two thousand camels and a thousand head of slaves a large caravan."[1] In that same year the value of the merchandise carried to Egypt was about £115,000. Its frequency also varied: most authors have referred to it as an annual expedition, but Browne noted that both it and the Sennar caravan "are extremely various in their motions; sometimes not appearing in Egypt for the space of two or even three years, sometimes two or more distinct caravans arriving in the same year." These fluctuations were attributed to "the perpetual changes in their several governments, and the caprices of their despots" and to the insecurity of the roads.

The route traveled by the Darfur caravan was known as Darb el arba'in, or Route of Forty, probably because of the approximate number of marching days required. From Asiut to its terminal at Kobbeh, near al-Fashir, the total distance was nearly 1,100 miles.[2] The route avoided the Nile Valley up to Asiut, because of the great insecurity prevailing there.

The other caravan between Sudan and Egypt was usually referred to as the Sennar caravan, although in fact it "comprised the caravans from Sennar, Shendy, Berber, Mahass and Seboua."[3] It passed through Ibrim, in Nubia, to its terminus at Isna or Darau, in Upper Egypt, and the total traveling time from Sennar to Darau was estimated at thirty-three days. Girard says that "the Sennar caravan is smaller than that of Darfur, but sometimes several caravans arrive [in Egypt] in the course of the year."[4] The number of slaves carried by the Sennar caravan was estimated by him at not over 500. The second most important item was gum arabic; 3,000 qantars was an average load and 8–10 funduqlis an average price.

---

[1] W. G. Browne, *Travels in Africa, Egypt, and Syria, from the Year 1792 to 1798*, p. 249.
[2] Shaw, in *Sudan Notes and Records*, 1929.
[3] John Lewis Burckhardt, *Travels in Nubia*, p. 217.
[4] P. S. Girard, in *Description de l'Egypte*, II, 637.

Other goods included ostrich feathers (8–10 qantars), ivory (45–60 qantars), whips, and some gold dust. On its return to the Sudan the caravan took various spices, soap, cotton, woolen and silk cloth, mirrors and other glassware. Like the Darfur, the Sennar caravan sold some of its camels in Egypt, at prices ranging from 15 to 36 zar mahbubs.

(See also works by Bruce, Burckhardt, Déhérain, Crawford, and Holt [A Modern History] listed in the Bibliography, and Shaw in Sudan Notes and Records, 1929.)

[From P. S. Girard, "Mémoire sur l'agriculture, l'industrie et le commerce de l'Egypte,"Description de l'Egypte, Etat Moderne (Paris, 1809-22), II, Part I, 632-36.]

. . . Each year five or six thousand slaves come to Egypt from Darfur. Of these four-fifths are women aged from six or seven to thirty or forty years; the largest number is ten to fifteen years old. Each caravan is led by a man belonging to the king of Darfur and attached to his household. This leader receives as wages, from each of the merchants making up the caravan, 23 paras per camel and 45 paras per Negro. The merchants and the men employed by them, such as camel drivers and other servants, usually number four or five hundred.

Before reaching Cairo, the caravans spend some time in Asiut, Bani Adin, Manfalut, and the surrounding localities, where they sell part of their merchandise. The reduced price of slaves is, in an ordinary year, 35 zar mahbubs. The value of those who have been made eunuchs is usually two or three times as high; this is why the leaders of the Darfur caravan stop at Abutig, a small town in Upper Egypt where there are barbers who are accustomed to castrate children. One might add that this operation is not carried out on children over eight or ten years old. An account of this may be found in the memoir written by Doctor Frank, on the trade in Negroes in Egypt.[1]

The Darfur caravan also usually brought to Cairo 150 camel loads of elephant teeth, each load weighing 3 qantars of 110 ratls

[1] Collection de mémoires sur l'Egypte, ed. P. Didot, vol. IV.

each. A qantar is sold at 30 to 60 funduqlis, according to the size and beauty of the ivory. It also brought about 600 qantars of Tamr hindi (tamarind, Tamarindus indica) sold at 15 to 30 abu taqas per qantar of 110 ratls; from 1,000 to 2,000 qantars of gum arabic, with a weight of 150 ratls and a price of 20 funduqlis per qantar; about 600 qantars of chishm [a kind of lentil], the price of a qantar of 110 ratls being 20 abu taqas; and in addition two or three hundred kurbags (whips), usually sold at 45 to 60 medins apiece.

The ostrich feathers imported to Egypt by the Darfur caravan are sold by weight and may amount to 20 to 30 qantars. White feathers are the most highly valued, and the finest of these may fetch up to 1,500 abu taqas per qantar; those of inferior quality, the black ones, fetch hardly 200 abu taqas. This kind of merchandise is transported from Darfur to Egypt in leather bags; it is bought in Cairo only by Jews and Christians, who send on practically the whole amount to Europe.

In Egypt rhinoceros horn is used for making sword or dagger hilts. The Turks, and particularly the Mamluks, hold the superstitious belief that it gives courage to those who handle the weapon where it is so used; this raises its value, according to its degree of scarcity. Two thousand pieces used to come each year, and were sold at 5 to 7 abu taqas; the price rose to 15 during the French Expedition.

The Darfur caravan brings to Egypt about 4,000 pairs of water-skins, made of ox or camel skin; each pair is sold at 10 to 12 abu taqas; to these various imports must be added about 1,000 qantars of natron; the qantar of 120 ratls is sold at 14 to 15 abu taqas.[2] On its way the Darfur caravan collects in the desert a certain quantity of alum, which it carries with it to Cairo. From the information given to me on this subject by Haggi-Sultan, the sheikh of the Gallabi, it would seem that, like natron, alum is extracted from the bottom of certain lakes where it crystallizes; the following year more is found in the same spots. The weight of the alum imported into Egypt through this channel was usually 200 qantars of 150 ratls each, and the price 3 to 4 abu taqas.

Immediately upon arrival in Egypt, where most of the goods enumerated could be shipped by Nile, the Darfur caravan would try to get rid of the camels for which it no longer had any use; usually it sold sixteen- or seventeen-twentieths of those it had brought along; the price ranged from 8 to 20 zar mahbubs, depending on the age and strength of the camel. It will be readily understood that, since slaves are the main article imported by the caravan to Egypt, a much larger number of camels is required on the outward than on the return trip, to transport the water and food provisions required during the journey.

Upon its arrival at Asiut, the caravan paid the resident *sanjaq* (governor) a duty of 4 zar mahbubs per slave and 2.5 per camel, whether laden or not. In old Cairo a duty of 1.5 abu taqas per camel was levied. Finally, upon arrival in Cairo, a further duty of one zar mahbub per slave was paid to the customs and half a zar mahbub for the use or rent of the *okel* or market where they were displayed for sale.

Exports [from Egypt to the Sudan]

The business transactions of the members of the Darfur caravan in Egypt usually compel them to prolong their stay for six or eight months; hence, not infrequently, a caravan reaches Cairo before the departure

of the preceding one. These caravans buy, in exchange for what they brought into Egypt, local products, European merchandise, and so forth.

Among the Oriental products they take are: Egyptian and Syrian silk and cotton fabrics, cotton and linen cloth from the Delta and Asiut, other cloths known as *alaga* [alaja], muslins and white shawls from India, equipment for horses, coats of mail, coffee, sugar, a little rice, and sometimes a few horses.

Foremost among the European goods bought by the Darfur caravan in Egypt comes the glassware of Venice, especially that with red, white, and black grains; glass rings of various colors, used as bracelets; amber and coral beads (*grains*); a certain kind of bells worn as ornaments by women; woolen fabrics; velvet; razors; files; tin; lead and copper; rifles, pistols, swords, and gunpowder; finally, cowrie shells (*Cypraea moneta*) used as money in the interior of Africa.

As may be imagined, the quantity and value of merchandise taken out by the Darfur caravans vary with circumstances. It is therefore necessary to consider details in terms of averages of several years: Rolls of silk and cotton, known as *qutni*, the main article exported from Egypt by the caravan, number about one thousand; each is 12 piks [the *dira'*, about 58 centimeters] long and costs 10 to 15 abu taqas. Secondly there are twenty to twenty-five thousand rolls of cloth from al-Mahalla al-Kubra; each is 18 piks long and costs 135 paras. The third item of local manufacture consists of one to two hundred rolls of cloth known as *alaga*; each costs 5 abu taqas. To this should be added five to six thousand rolls of linen cloth from Asiut, each 27 piks long and costing one and a half abu taqas. A fourth article is 2,000 qantars of *shaiba* or stalks and leaves of wormwood (*Artemisia judaica*, according to Linnaeus), which is used as a medicine or as a perfume when burned with aloe wood; the price per qantar of *shaiba* is 2 abu taqas.

It is known that Egyptians and Arabs

[2] See the list of goods imported into Egypt by the Darfur caravan during the French Expedition, drawn up by M. Mercure-Joseph Lapanouse (*ibid.*, IV, 88).

place the saddle of their horses on a piece of felt, of varying thickness, folded several times; the Darfur caravan takes about three hundred pieces of felt, each of which is sold at 90 medins. It also takes a hundred to a hundred and fifty coats of mail, at a price of 50 zar mahbubs. It seems that warriors in this part of Africa still use this defensive weapon.

As for the merchandise of India and Asia, the ones exported from Egypt by the caravan are: one to two thousand rolls of silk cloth, each at 6 to 8 abu taqas; about eight hundred rolls of muslin, at 7 to 10 abu taqas apiece; two thousand shawls, at 5 to 6 abu taqas apiece; fifty qantars of coffee from Yemen, each weighing 100 ratls and costing 20 to 25 piastres; and one hundred qantars of Egyptian sugar. The rice taken by the caravan is exclusively for its own travel needs.

In an ordinary year it takes one hundred camels loaded with Venetian glassware; each camel load is 5 qantars of 105 ratls, at 12 zar mahbubs per qantar. It also takes fifty camels loaded with *sembal*, or *Spica celtica* (*Valeriana celtica* according to Linnaeus); this dried plant comes from Trieste and, among other uses, is mixed with oil to form a cosmetic ointment; each load weighs 2.5 qantars of 150 ratls each, at a price of 30 or 32 abu taqas.

European merchandise is also exported from Egypt by caravan as follows: (1) 10 qantars of amber beads; a qantar of this merchandise weighs 100 ratls, at 7 to 8 abu taqas per ratl; (2) 4 qantars of coral beads, each ratl being sold at 15 to 20 zar mahbubs; (3) five hundred to a thousand units [mesures] of a kind of small bell which, like the two preceding items, are used as women's ornaments; the usual price is one abu taqa per unit.

The caravan does not take woolens in rolls, but takes about a thousand ready-made garments [béniches] each consisting of 4 to 5 piks of cloth at 5 to 6 abu taqas the pik, or a total cost of 30 abu taqas. The most sought-after colors are rose, green, red, yellow, and other bright hues; generally speaking, dull or dark colors are not suitable for Africans. To this woolen clothing should be added 500 piks of velvet, at 5 or 7 zar mahbubs a pik. This kind of velvet is used for the clothing of notables and to cover the saddles of some horses.

The hardware bought by the caravan in Egypt consists of: (1) twenty crates of razors, containing 4,000 packages at one zar mahbub apiece, and (2) about a thousand packages of files, each of which, consisting of four files, is sold at 90 medins. It also takes 200 to 500 qantars of potters' lead; each qantar weighs 140 ratls and is sold at 6 to 10 abu taqas.

The only metals which the caravan buys in Cairo are tin, lead, and old copper: each year 500 qantars of tin, at a price of 30 abu taqas, are bought; 500 qantars of lead, at 20 to 22 abu taqas; and 1,000 qantars of old copper, at 20 to 25 abu taqas. The last named is worked up in Darfur into ornaments for women.

As for arms, the caravan buys only 20 or 30 European rifles at 5 to 6 zar mahbubs each, a score of pistols, and about a hundred sword blades for cavalrymen made in Germany; each blade is usually sold at 2 abu taqas and they are mounted in the country. Lastly, it takes 50 qantars of gunpowder, made in Cairo, in the form of cartridges at 1,000 paras per qantar.

Each camel loaded with merchandise pays, on leaving Bulaq for Darfur, a duty of 38 paras.

Generally speaking, the various articles brought from Darfur to Egypt are exchanged for other goods. Out of a total value of 1,000 piastres of imported goods, 900 are used for this kind of exchange; the remaining 100 piastres are exported in the form of specie [en nature], for transformation into bracelets and other silver ornaments.

CHAPTER 2

The Sudan under Egyptian Rule, 1821–1881

The greatest service rendered to the economy of the Sudan by Egyptian rule was order and security, which were imposed by harsh but effective methods. The second service was the improvement in communications (see Part VII, Introduction and chap. 3). The following selection, which is taken from a publication primarily designed to establish Egypt's claim to the Sudan, dwells on the benefits of Egyptian rule. In fact the Egyptian government improved the irrigation system of the northern Sudan; introduced new crops such as sugar cane, indigo, and several kinds of fruits; and installed a sugar refinery and distillery and a soap factory. The influx of Egyptian petty traders, skilled workmen, and peasants helped to develop the economy, as did the few dozen European merchants. But attempts to exploit iron and copper deposits were frustrated by technological backwardness and very high transport costs; gold, which had lured Muhammad Ali into the Sudan, proved elusive; and the available timber was much too hard for the uses for which it was intended. Egypt absorbed, or re-exported, increased quantities of the traditional Sudanese exports: ostrich feathers, ivory, gum, live-stock, leather, camels, and—in the 1870's—cotton (see Part VII, chap. 3).

(See also works by Hill, Shukry, Holt [*A Modern History*], Douin, Shibeika, Déhérain, and Sabry listed in the Bibliography.)

[From M. Sabry, *Le Soudan égyptien (1821–1898)* (Cairo, 1947), pp. 107–11.]

EGYPTIAN CIVILIZATION

. . . Speaking of the condition of Dongola after its reconquest, in 1897, Dr. Abbate pasha, president of the Geographical Society of Cairo, wrote: "The territory of the province of Dongola was thickly populated and fertile under the domination of Egypt, before the fatal invasion of Mahdism. These river banks were strewn with *saqias* [water wheels], which are indispensable during the dry season of the Nile. Formerly there were up to 8,000, today hardly a thousand. This is a disaster for a region whose livelihood depends on water and irrigation. Where are the productive crops today? Everything is in confusion and ruin. It is to be hoped that the Egyptian government will be able to safeguard these provinces—fortunately reincorporated in its domains—against further anxiety by gradually leading them back to their former well-being and prosperity."[1]

[1] *Aegyptica* (Cairo, 1909). "During the five months which I spent in the Province of Dongola in 1897 I saw the most abject misery everywhere. Four-fifths of the population had been destroyed, the greater part of the

As for Khartoum, after its fall and the death of the Mahdi, which occurred on June 22, 1885, his successor, the Khalifa Abdallah, moved his residence to Omdurman, since Khartoum had become uninhabitable.[2]

Khartoum, like Kassala in the Sudan proper, Berbera on the Gulf of Aden, and Ghildessa in Harrar are towns founded and developed by Egyptians. Before the Egyptian conquest Khartoum was a fishing village, consisting of a few tents and scattered huts. In 1823, following the establishment of a permanent camp, the tents were replaced by native *tuqul*'s and the huts slowly gave way to houses made of sun-dried bricks and to a few better buildings for officers. There followed a mosque, then a bazaar and other buildings. In 1830 Khurshid pasha, governor-general of the Sudan (1826–39), made it the official capital. He built a palace, public buildings, and two dockyards on the White and Blue Niles and laid out some gardens.

---

land had gone out of cultivation, the palm trees had been so greatly neglected that the date crops barely supported the remnant of the population which struggled for a living, most of the waterwheels had been burnt or were broken, and the Dervishes had eaten the cattle which had worked them. There was no trade and no money, the young men had been slain in the wars of the Mahdi and Khalifa, and the young women had been carried off to fill the harims of the Bakkara.

"The condition of the country between Abu Hamed and Khartum was even more terrible, as I saw for myself when I visited the Island of Meroe three months after Lord Kitchener had captured Omdurman. Every here and there a few wretched people, chiefly old men and women, had gathered together and were trying to form a village, and how or on what they lived were things to marvel at. Thorns and briars and brambles had taken possession of nearly all the land which had been formerly fertile fields, and the few natives who had straggled back from their flight before Mahmud sowed the seed for their scanty crop on the mud flats in the river and on the moist mud of the banks. In the courtyards of the ruined houses of the old villages were to be seen the stones on which the women were grinding their dhurra when Mahmud's soldiers appeared, and the scattered grain which lay under the grinders testified to the suddenness of their flight. Ruin and desolation were everywhere, man and cattle were rarely seen, and even the dogs had been wiped out" (E. A. Wallis Budge, *The Egyptian Sudan* [2 vols.; London, 1907], pp. xiv–xv). One may add that the population of the Sudan was included in the general ruin, having been decimated by revolution, war, and disease: from 8,500,000 in 1882, it fell to 1,900,000 in 1905, after six years of peace.

[2] This statement is inaccurate.—Translator.

When Muhammad Ali visited the town, in 1838, it contained barracks, a hospital, and four to five hundred houses. Khurshid was, moreover, the first governor who urged the native population to give up their cowskin and reed huts and build brick houses. However, most of these huts were in danger of collapsing, especially during high Nile floods. A physician, Dr. Toscanelli, was crushed under the ruins of his house in Khartoum, in 1841, during an exceptionally high flood.

"Little by little," wrote Abbate pasha, "sturdier buildings began to rise here and there—the Governor's residence, the Government offices and a few houses of baked bricks, belonging to officials or traders, which seemed imposing when contrasted with the surrounding dwellings. Later an arsenal was built, as well as barracks, a gunpowder magazine, two mosques, and an establishment for [Christian] missionaries; in the gardens fig trees, orange, lemon and banana trees and palms were gradually introduced and a large number of vegetable gardens surrounded most of the better buildings, as well as the wretched huts of the soldiers who constituted the garrison."

In 1856, Brun-Rollet put the population of Khartoum at 40,000–45,000; according to Abbate, by 1882 it had 50,000–55,000 inhabitants. In fact, since the time of Muhammad Ali, Khartoum had become, in the words of the eminent historian Emile Bourgeois, "the bridgehead of civilization in Africa."

The town of Kassala grew up near an old village in that district. The village was inhabited by the Halenga tribe, which claims to have migrated from the southern shores of Arabia six centuries ago. The arrival of the Mirghania family in 1840 brought about noteworthy changes, for it was in that year that Egyptian troops took possession of the district and reduced the turbulent Hadendowa to obedience. Order and security also reigned in the eastern Sudan, to a degree which caused astonishment to S. Baker.

The general annexation of the Soudan and the submission of the numerous Arab tribes to the Viceroy have been the first steps necessary to the improvement of the country. Although the Egyptians are hard masters, and do not trouble themselves about the future well-being of the conquered races, it must be remembered that, prior to the annexation, all the tribes were at war among themselves. There was neither government nor law; thus the whole country was closed to Europeans.[3] At present, there is no more danger in travelling in Upper Egypt [the Sudan] than in crossing Hyde park after dark, provided the traveller be just and courteous. At the time of my visit to Cassala in 1861, the Arab tribes were separately governed by their own chiefs or sheiks, who were responsible to the Egyptian authorities for the taxes due from their people: since that period, the entire tribes of all denominations have been placed under the authority of that grand old Arab patriarch Achmet Abou Sinn, to be hereafter mentioned. The Sheik Moosa, of the Hadendowa tribe, was in prison during our stay in that country, for some breach of discipline in his dealings with the Egyptian Government. The iron hand of despotism has produced a marvellous change among the Arabs, who are rendered utterly powerless by the system of government adopted by the Egyptians; [unfortunately, this harsh system has the effect of paralysing all industry].[4]

The cultivation of cotton in Kassala flourished during the period 1840–74. After thirty years of [Egyptian] occupation in Kassala, wrote Mr. Fleming in 1922, cotton cultivation had gone beyond the experimental stage and the pasha, Ahmad Mumtaz, who had already established the cotton industry in Tokar, decided to introduce mechanical ginning in Kassala. In the eastern Sudan cotton cultivation is still associated with the name of Ahmad Mumtaz:

The growing of cotton over the Eastern Sudan is even now associated with the name of Ahmad Mumtaz. Until quite recent times the people of Kassala grew the strange plant, which went, not by the name of cotton, but of Mumtaz, and the cultivator on the Rahad still grows Mumtaz from which he spins a damur of fairly good quality.

He also had the enterprise to introduce machinery for the spinning of cotton in Kassala, and the building of the ginnery and spinning shed was commenced in 1821 and the work of construction put by him into the hands of Munzinger pasha.

The work went forward with considerable vigour. . . .

Be that as it may, the work, which he left undone in Kassala, was never completed and on the fall of Kassala into the hands of Dervishes in 1885, the peaceful instruments of commerce, brought with infinite pains over the mountains to Kassala, were beaten into implements of war.[5]

In his report to Malet, dated July 23, 1883, Stewart announced that he had visited Kassala and the cotton ginnery, the cost of which was £20,000–£30,000. "The Factory," he reported, "is complete in all respects, with motors aggregating 100 horsepower and 21 ginning machines."[6]

Thus, during the Egyptian supremacy, the Sudan had enjoyed security, well-being, and the benefits of a civilization adapted to the country and its needs. . . .

---

[3] In 1882 there were 10,000–15,000 Europeans in the Sudan.

[4] Sir Samuel Baker, *The Nile Tributaries of Abyssinia* (Philadelphia, 1869), p. 52 [sentence in square brackets omitted in Sabry's quotation].

[5] *Sudan Notes and Records*, Vol. V, No. 2, 1922.

[6] British Archives, F.O. 78-3556.

CHAPTER 3

Taxes, Trade, Railway Projects on the
Eve of the Mahdist Revolt, 1882

The report from which the following selection is taken was the last major survey of the Sudan before the Mahdist takeover; though signed by Col. J. D. H. Stewart, it was the joint work of Stewart and G. B. Messedaglia.

The first point it raised was the heavy, and growing, burden of taxation. Under Muhammad Ali the tax assessment rose from £E125,000 in the early 1820's to £E165,000 in 1838–42.[1] Under Said the figure dropped to £100,000, but it increased again to an estimated £232,000 in 1864–65.[2] The subsequent rise in tax rates and growth in government revenues is shown in the tables.

In addition to the tax on water wheels (*saqia*) the following are mentioned by Stewart: on wells (*amtar*), 175–350 piastres per well; on irrigation buckets (*shaduf*), 250–350 piastres; land tax on land that gradually dries up as the Nile level falls, 52.20–60.10 piastres per faddan; on riverain land (*garuf*) cultivated as the level of the river falls, 22.20–45 piastres per faddan; on rain-fed lands (*karwah*), 15–56.20 piastres per faddan; date tax, 2 piastres per palm tree.

The chief non-agricultural taxes were the following: *werko*, or trade and profession tax; *'ataba*, or house tax, estimated at one-twelfth the annual rental; stamp duty, 23 piastres per document; stamp duty on receipts, 2 piastres per 1,000; tobacco duty, 200 piastres per faddan; succession duty, 5 per cent; transit dues, 4 piastres per camel load; market dues of 5 per cent on certain commodities; and a graduated boat tax.

But perhaps more burdensome than the actual weight of taxation was the method used for collection, by the irregular Bashi-Buzuq troops. These were described by Stewart as "mostly swaggering bullies, robbing, plundering, and ill-treating the people with impunity. Probably for every pound that reaches the treasury these men rob an equal amount from the people."[3] (See also Part VII, chap. 4.)

---

[1] Arnoud, quoted in Henri Déhérain, *Le Soudan égyptien sous Mehemet Ali*, p. 182.
[2] Richard Hill, *Egypt in the Sudan, 1820–1881*, p. 107.
[3] Stewart, "Report on the Soudan," p. 13 (see following selection).

The report also outlines alternative schemes to connect Khartoum with the Red Sea. In the previous few years such projects had frequently been discussed in both Egypt and England (see Part VII, Introduction). In 1882 a "Suakin-Berber syndicate" met in London and estimated costs at about £1,500,000 and annual profits at £180,000.[4] In 1885 the British government actually ordered construction to be started, but the northward sweep of the Mahdists caused it to abandon the attempt a few months later. The scheme was, however, taken up again immediately after the reconquest (see Part VII, chap. 5).

(See also works by Hill, Shibeika, Douin, and Shukry listed in the Bibliography.)

[4] Richard Gray, *A History of the Southern Sudan, 1839–1889*, p. 189.

[From Lieut.-Colonel J. D. H. Stewart, "Report on the Soudan," Great Britain, *Accounts and Papers, 1883*, LXXIV, 14–15, 21–23.]

. . . Previous to 1881 these taxes were all considerably higher but in consequence of a Report drawn up during that year a reduction to their present rate occurred. It is, however, probable from what I hear that they are still too high, and notably so in the Province of Dongola, where it is quite notorious that the people would be quite unable to pay the tax if they were not assisted by other members of the family who are employed in other trades.

I gather from this Report, which appeared in April 1881, that his Highness Said Pasha, when he visited the Soudan in 1857, issued an order fixing the tax on sakiyes at 200 piastres, and that this tax was gradually raised by successive Governor-Generals until, at the time of Jaafar Pasha, it was fixed at 500 piastres. This officer stated openly that he was quite aware the tax was excessive, but that he had fixed it at that rate to see how much the peasant would really pay, and that he hoped after three years' trial to be able to arrive at a just mean. He was, however, removed long before his three years were over, and his successors, either through ignorance or indifference, allowed the tax to continue. In the Report just quoted a melancholy account is given of the ruin this excessive taxation brought on the country. Many were reduced to destitution, others had to

emigrate and so much land went out of cultivation that in 1881, in the Province of Berber, there were 1,442 abandoned sakiyes, and in Dongola 613.

Included in this Report are the proceedings of a Commission of Dongola Notables, presided over by the Mudir, and assembled to report on the condition of that province.

They proceed to state that they had begun by carefully calculating the earnings and cost of working of two sakiyes irrigating fair average land, and that, after deducting all expenses, including the maintenance of the cultivators, they had found that the net returns, exclusive of taxes, were for one sakiye 391 piastres, and for the other 201 piastres.

They then state how the cultivator, in order to meet the tax, is compelled either to depend on other sources, to sell his cattle, or to borrow. Their Report is rather long and involved, but shows how, in 1856, Said Pasha had fixed the following rates of taxation:

	Piastres
1. Sakiye	200
2. Land on Islands	25
3. Riverain lands	20
4. Date palm	1

and how the tax had been again gradually raised till, at the time the Report was drawn up, the taxes on a first class sakiye were as follows:

	Prs.	para.
Tax in 1862	350	00
Increase by Jaafar Pasha	150	00
Share per sakiye of all the arrears due between 1862 and 1869, and which were estimated at 1,000 purses	64	20

	Prs'	para.
Share per sakiye of the taxes on ferries, boat-building, etc., which were remitted by the Government . . .	27	23
Share per sakiye of the salaries of tax-gathers and other officials . . .	15	32
Total	607	35

And so on with other taxes

RAILWAY

Some years ago the Egyptian Government decided, for both political and commercial reasons, to connect Egypt with the Soudan by a line of railway. Of the several projects they selected the one follow-

	Expenditure £E.	Revenue £E.
Central Government at Khartoum, Courts, etc. . .	22,878	1,452
Province of Khartoum	55,193	69,510
Arsenal, Khartoum	15,706	2,709
Printing Office	1,266	8,149
Telegraph, Soudan	10,082	3,866
Province of Senaar	26,809	39,775
Dongola	10,304	55,118
Berber	14,411	40,684
Taka	151,434	51,806
Kordofan	46,305	74,405
Railway	9,647	7,564
Province of Fashoda	18,455	7,816
Fasher	33,975	16,395
Dara	19,788	20,332
Kolkol	18,680	10,826
Bahr-el-Ghazelle	14,302	12,198
Equator	42,450	52,239
Total	511,684	474,843
Deficit	36,841	

The Committee conclude their Report by making some proposals, of which the following are the chief: . . .

. . . For the sake of comparison I append the Budget of 1881:[1]

For further information, at the end of the Report I append Tables of the Revenues of the Provinces of Dongola, Berber, Khartoum, Senaar, and Fazoglou and Taka for the years 1870 to 1879, and of which the following is a summary:

ing the Nile Valley. The scheme was actively taken up, but beyond wasting a great deal of money in contracts, salaries, etc. but little was done.

About the time Colonel Gordon became Governor-General a line had been made 8 kilom. in length from Assouan to the village of Shellal, south of the First Cataract, and another of 52 kilom. along the east bank of the Nile from Angash, 2 miles north of Wady Halfa, to the village of Seres. Colonel

September 1869 to September 1870.	378,585	315,492
1870	1871.	359,662	257,373
1871	1872.	356,995	240,340
1872	1873.	363,003	301,227
1873	1874.	369,337	319,292
1874	1875.	370,865	321,767
1875 to December 1876.	482,986	363,819
1877	363,745	271,873
1878	392,493	283,822
1879	402,505	287,705
Total	3,840,176	2,962,712

[1] In the two tables sums have been rounded to the nearest pound.—Editor.

Gordon decided to stop the works, and it is only to be regretted that the decision was not taken earlier, as anything more preposterous than the scheme it would be hard to imagine.

Besides this scheme, there are two others designed to connect Khartoum with the Red Sea cost.

First scheme: From Souakin to Berber, a distance of some 245 miles.

From Souakin, for some 70 or 80 miles, as far as Wadi Haratri (alt. boiling point, 2,869 feet) there is a gradual and almost uniform rise.

The road lies through bare hills and shallow, somewhat wooded ravines. From this point till a few miles beyond Ariab (distant 120 to 130 miles from the sea) the general aspect of the country is that of barren level plains alternating with low ranges of bare hills and shallow defiles. Thence the road into Berber is over an open, level, and barren plain. The boiling point alt. of Berber is from 1,000 to 1,100 feet.

The main difficulty on this line would be the water supply. Judging, however, from the general character of the country, I should expect that the wells need hardly ever exceed 200 feet in depth. There are no rivers and torrents to bridge, and the only rain that falls are a few heavy showers in the winter season.

In the districts bordering the coast a considerable amount of small timber is found, which might prove useful.

According to a rough estimate, I should think the line could be made for from $1\frac{1}{2}$ to 2 millions. It would be well worth considering whether the narrow gauge might not answer.

Between Berber and Khartoum the river would be used, and a channel would have to be made at the Sixth Cataract or that of El Hajjar between the Saballoka Mountains. This offers no serious difficulty, as it would be only necessary to blast a few rocks. At present, during the months of February, March, April, and May steamers are unable to pass.

I would, however, beg to point out that even now, with the little traffic there, it is difficult to supply the steamers with sufficient wood, so that if the traffic were to increase the wood supply would have to be brought from elsewhere, or the steamers would have to burn coal.

The second scheme is that of a line direct from Khartoum, or rather from a point on the Blue Nile opposite that town, to the coast. This line would cross from Khartoum a perfectly level plain as far as Goz Redjeb, and thence to the coast at Souakin or Alik-es-Saghir, some 30 to 40 miles south of Souakin, and where there is said to be a very fair natural harbour far better than that of Souakin. About halfway between Goz Redjeb and the coast, hills begin similar to those on the Berber-Souakin road.

Of the two lines, the last is of course much the longest, but it would be a question whether the advantage it would afford of bringing such a central place as Khartoum in direct communication with the sea would not more than compensate for its extra length and the necessity of throwing a bridge over the Atbara. By running a branch to the south from Goz Redjeb to Senaar and Gallabat some of the richest districts of the Soudan would be tapped, as also a good deal of the Abyssinian trade.

TRADE, COMMERCE, AND MANUFACTURE

Although at present, owing to the rebellion, the trade of the Soudan is almost at a standstill, in ordinary times it is considerable, and shows rather a tendency to increase.

For trade purposes the country may be divided into three districts, each connected by roads with Egypt or the Red Sea.

The first district includes the basins of the White and Blue Niles with their tributaries, and also the eastern portion of the Province of Kordofan. This district is connected with Egypt by the Nile Valley, and with the Red Sea by the Berber–Souakin road. The great grain-growing districts of Karkotsch are also connected with Souakin by a road passing through Guedaref and Kassala.

Khartoum, situated at the junction of the Niles, is the centre of this district.

The trade consists chiefly of gum, ivory, ostrich feathers, tamarind, senna, hides, hippopotami hides, gutta-percha, honey, wax (fallen off), doora (kind of millet), salt (local trade), rhinoceros horns, indigo (small quantity), musk, palm-oil, and a vegetable fat used in scents.

The second district includes the Darfour and western districts of Kordofan. This district is connected with Egypt by the long and toilsome road from Kobbe to Siout, known as the "Road of the forty days' march." [See Part VII, chap. 1.]

In former years the track along this road formed an outlet not alone for the Darfour, but also for the trade of the Wadai, Bagirmi, Bornu, and other districts further west, amounting, I am told, to over 100,000 cantars. Large quantities of salt and nitre were also exported to Egypt from the plains over which the road passes. Of late years the trade along it has, however, greatly fallen off, partly because the road was closed for some time to prevent the export of slaves, and partly because the Sultans of the Wadai, Bagirmi, etc., frightened by the never-ending conquests of the Egyptian Government, had forbidden all communication with Darfour, so that the trade of those districts was diverted on to the northern road leading from Lake Tchad to Murzoukh and Tripoli. The salt trade was also stopped by order of the Government in Egypt, as it interfered with the salt monopoly.

At present only some two or more very large caravans leave Kobbe annually in September and January for Siout. On arrival at Siout they have to pay transit dues.

The trade consists mainly of gum, ostrich feathers, ivory, ebony, and hides.

The third district is that of Abyssinia, with its export centre at Massowah. Coffee, wax, and honey are the chief articles.

By an order given some years ago, the White Nile was completely closed to traders. This was done to put a stop to the Slave Trade along that river. Although, of course, the order greatly hampers trade, still, for the above reason, it should be maintained.

The natural result of the order is that the Equatorial trade has become a Government monopoly.

Of other products, cotton sufficient for local consumption is grown in the districts of Berber, Senaar, Kassala, and Ghedariff (or Guedaref).

Tobacco culture has of late sprung up about Senaar, and is, I hear, succeeding admirably.

The tax is at present 200 piastres the feddan (acre), or about 4 piastres per oke (3 lbs.). Probably, were this tax reduced, the revenue would greatly benefit.

All the districts south of Khartoum, between the Niles, and also about Karkotsch and Ghedariff, are celebrated for their corn-growing capacity, and may be said to be the granary of the Soudan. Were easy communications opened with the sea, there can be little doubt that a considerable export trade in grain would spring up. At present grain is allowed to rot in the ground in those districts, while it is perhaps at a famine price at Souakin and Jeddah.

Manufactures.—None, except a kind of light cotton cloth made at Dongola, and called "tamur."

The import trade is mostly manufactured cotton goods, cutlery, etc.

Transit dues are levied at Berber, at the rate of 4 piastres per camel-load on all articles passing through to Egypt, either via Korosko or Souakin.

Dues on all imports up the Nile Valley, at the same rate, are levied at Siout.

I append Tables of the import and export trade of the Soudan, as far as I have been able to procure them. . . .

CHAPTER 4

Economic Causes of the Mahdist Revolt

The benefits of Egyptian rule in the Sudan were numerous (see Part VII, chap. 2) but the methods employed were harsh and oppressive. This is brought out in the following selection, which is taken from one of the most useful sources on the Sudan. Among the causes of the Mahdist revolt given by the author, high taxation was discussed in the previous selection. Another cause, not mentioned by him, was the persistence of *corvée* labor in the Sudan, after its reduction in Egypt; this undoubtedly inflicted much hardship, even when the labor was used for worthwhile ends, e.g., a water-supply system for Suakin,[1] and it lent itself to much abuse on the part of officials.[2] And it may be noted regarding the reference to the hostility aroused by the nomination of Christian officials that, on the eve of the Mahdist revolt, four out of fourteen provincial governors were foreign.[3]

The capture of slaves was one of the main attractions that led Muhammad Ali to conquer the Sudan. During his reign slave raids were regularly carried out by large contingents of troops; thus in 1836 an expedition to Nuba returned with 2,187 slaves. Some of these were distributed among the troops, others were sold by the officials on behalf of the government; in 1837 prices ranged from 100 to 1,500 piastres.[4]

In 1854 Said pasha prohibited the slave trade and his successor, Ismail, continued his policy with greater vigor; in August, 1877, Egypt and Britain signed the Slave-Trade Convention which terminated the trade in Ethiopians and Negroes through the territory of the Egyptian empire and provided for the ending of the private sale and purchase of slaves in the Sudan by 1889. The results of these attempts at suppression were mixed. Private slave-raiding continued, and occasionally even regular troops participated in such activities, e.g., a raid on the Dinka in 1863–64. Indeed the opening-up of the upper reaches of the Nile, in the 1850's and 1860's, added a large source of supply to the ones already existing in the Nuba mountains, the Blue Nile regions, and the Ethiopian borderlands, and a brisk

[1] Richard Hill, *Egypt in the Sudan, 1820–1881*, p. 115.
[2] *Ibid.*, p. 124.
[3] *Ibid.*, p. 147.
[4] Holroyd, quoted in Henri Déhérain, *Le Soudan égyptien sous Mehemet Ali*, pp. 173–76.

trade in ivory and slaves continued until the collapse of Egyptian rule and through-out the Mahdist period. Although the flow to and through Egypt dried up, Arabia provided an eager market, and in 1876 it was estimated that each year some 30,000 slaves were shipped across the Red Sea from northeast Africa, sometimes in steamers owned by the Egyptian government. Of these a substantial proportion was from the Sudan; in 1875–79, according to Gordon, 80,000–100,000 slaves were exported from the Bahr al-Ghazal area.[5]

Nevertheless there is no doubt that the government's measures had some effect and were correspondingly resented by the slave traders. At first the ivory and slave trade in the southern Sudan, but not in the eastern and western provinces, was in the hands of European merchants operating from Khartoum, sometimes on behalf of larger firms established in Cairo. But by the mid-1860's all Europeans had withdrawn, leaving the field open to Arab settlers and slave raiders and traders. The latter formed a powerful group who, with their local allies such as the Baqqara tribe, bitterly opposed all attempts at suppressing the slave trade and who soon joined the Mahdist revolt.

(See also works by Gray, Hill, Holt [*The Mahdist State*], Douin, and Shibeika listed in the Bibliography.)

[5] Richard Gray, *A History of the Southern Sudan ,1830–1889*, pp. 68, 126, 127, 167.

[From Naʿum Shuqair, *Tarikh al-Sudan* (*History of the Sudan*) (Cairo, 1903), III, 110–12.]

TAXES

... Several governors came in succession after the *daftardar*[1] and laid various taxes on the people, who were not accustomed to taxation and found it burdensome. And what added to the burden was that taxes were not equitably distributed, being rigorously collected from the poor and sparingly from the rich. The degree to which the rich escaped payment was proportionate to their capacity to bribe officials and to the extent of their connections with the rulers—hence a large part of the property of the rich and of government officials was exempt from taxation.

Moreover they entrusted the levying of taxes to the Bashi-Buzuq [irregular troops] drawn from the Shaiqia [a Sudanese tribe], the Kurds, and the North Africans who had

[1] Muhammad Bey Khusraw, son-in-law of Muhammad Ali and commander of the second Egyptian expeditionary force.—Translator.

conquered the country and who used the utmost cruelty and violence in the process of collection. Thus if anyone was in arrears they whipped and humiliated him until he had paid the last penny. Still worse was a phenomenon which had no counterpart outside the Sudan, viz., that the officials were not satisfied with levying official taxes but imposed various unofficial imposts [*firda*] on the population, which they collected together with the taxes. The reason for this was that most of the Sudan's governors came there from Egypt unwillingly, in view of its distance from their country and its heat and difficult living conditions. Hence they were generally interested only in profiting from their positions, so they would exact "gifts" from the provincial governors who in turn would recoup these sums from the district officers serving under them or from the Bashi-Buzuq charged with the collection of taxes; the latter would then raise several times as much from the people, to make up for what they had paid, keeping the balance for themselves.

In raising these sums the Bashi-Buzuq used the same methods of pressure as for taxes, knowing that they need fear no reprisals in view of the collusion of the governors and provincial governors. The resentment of the people against the rulers therefore increased; their hearts were filled with sorrow and hatred, and they began to wish for the disappearance of the government, which had subjected them to merciless rulers, and its replacement by any other. An indication of their feelings is the saying which became current when the Mahdi appeared: "To the grave we'll give many—in taxes not a penny." Another sign of discontent was that many left their homes and sought refuge in the outlying parts of the country, such as Gallabat, Bahr al-Ghazal, and Darfur, as was mentioned earlier. One may also quote the following lines from the verses written by Sheikh Muhammad Sharif satirizing the Mahdi:

Sudan had ne'er a government denied
'Til tax demands from Egypt multiplied;
A third or two in taxes we did pay
And many times more officials took away;
The wretch they'd tie and pitilessly beat,
Then throw him out in the sun's blazing heat;
They'd drive their tent-pegs, and still worse
    than that
They would inflict the torture of the cat.[2]

that is, they would put a cat in the trousers of the man who was being tortured, then beat it until it had torn out his flesh; the poet claims to have seen such torture in the Khartoum district, during the governorship of Ahmad Agha Abu Zaid.

SUPPRESSION OF SLAVERY

What made matters worse, and finally made the cup overflow, was the increasing strictness of the government in suppressing the slave trade and slavery. For, as has been shown, the slave-trade was a long-established activity in the Sudan, practiced by a very large number of people, including those with most power and prestige. And

[2] The poor quality of the English verse reflects that of the original—Translator.

the owning and selling of slaves is not forbidden by the religious law of its inhabitants, who do not see in it a wrong that should be suppressed but rather think that its suppression is itself wrong; the more so because all services to Arabs in the Sudan, both within and outside the household, were provided by slaves, the Arabs themselves restricting their activity to rulership and trade, as was mentioned earlier. This was a condition to which they had become accustomed over many years and which suited them so well that it was no longer possible to deprive them of it at one blow. But the government persisted in attempting to suppress slavery forcibly, especially during the governorships of Sir Samuel Baker and Colonel Gordon. For although both men were personally convinced that enforced suppression of slavery was premature and inadvisable, they were forced to comply with the orders of the government and to use very strict methods of suppression, putting great pressure on slave traders throughout the Sudan and especially in Bahr al-Ghazal and Equatorial Province. They punished them severely and scattered them, putting some to death, sending some to prison, and confiscating the possessions of others. And Gordon emancipated many slaves, especially after the proclamation of the convention concluded between [the khedive] Ismail pasha and the British government in 1877; indeed when the slaves saw that freedom was within their grasp, they started to leave their masters for the slightest reason or for no reason at all.

Moreover the people used to meet part of their taxes by supplying slaves; but after the suppression of the slave trade they could no longer do this; so the tax-gatherers subjected them to all sorts of indignities and humiliations. And the interference of Baker, Gordon, Gessi, Giegler, and other Christians in the suppression of slavery was regarded by the common, ignorant people as an attack by Christians on their faith, which caused a deep sense of grievance and gave rise to many complaints. . . .

CHAPTER 5

Economic Conditions under Mahdism

The confidential report from which the following extract is taken was based on information supplied by Slatin pasha, the Austrian governor of Darfur who was taken prisoner by the Mahdists, after his escape from the Sudan in 1895. Naturally it was concerned mainly with military and political affairs. The few paragraphs dealing with economics show clearly the general deterioration and the rapid debasement of the currency that were taking place.

The reference to Ohrwalder is to the confidential report by Major F. R. Wingate, "General Military Report on the Egyptian Sudan, 1891, Compiled from Statements made by Father Ohrwalder" (War Office, London, 1892). Three passages from that report shed further light on trade:

Export trade from the Sudan is entirely in the hands of Jaalin merchants. Import trade to the Sudan is carried on by—
(a) Magharba Wad Ali Arabs, travelling via Bimban and Dongola.
(b) Ababdeh and sub-tribes, *via* Korosko-Abu Hamed.

Halfa-Dongola.

Assuan-Berber.

Egyptian merchants do not dare to go to the Sudan as they are not tolerated by the dervishes. Trade imported from Suakin is usually carried by Hadendowa and Jaalin merchants. . . .

The principal advantage gained by the Khalifa through trade is the imposition of the "ushr," or one-tenth tithe, and on this account he has recently made a considerable revenue. . . .

Unless a merchant is in charge of a certificate that he has paid the "zeka," or alms tax, he is obliged also to pay that (i.e., $2\frac{1}{2}$ per cent.).

Therefore the total amount claimed by the Khalifa on all imported goods is, approximately, one-eighth. . . .

Slave trade is not so flourishing in the Sudan since the southern districts have been disturbed, and since Tokar was retaken by the Government.

Every slave-owner must be in possession of a certificate from the Beit-el-Mal that his slaves have been duly purchased.

Some 60 female and young slaves are to be found daily in the Omdurman slave market.

Slaves unfit for the Jehadieh are sold at from 30 to 60 dollars each, female slaves from 20 to 100 dollars.

From 10 to 30 slaves are sold daily in the Omdurman bazaar.

(See also works by Holt [*Mahdist State*], Shuqair, Theobald, and Rafi'i [*Misr wa al-Sudan*] listed in the Bibliography.)

[From "General Report on the Egyptian Soudan, March 1895, Compiled from Statements Made by Slatin Pasha" (unpublished document, War Office, London), pp. 9–11.]

AGRICULTURE

... In the early days of Mahdiism, the entire country being under arms, agriculture was abandoned, but the great famine had the effect of dispersing the large central camps and gradually the population are reverting to their former ways, while the Khalifa himself now encourages agriculture in all districts in the vicinity of Omdurman. Grain is at present very cheap in the Soudan (see list of Bazaar prices, Appendix D), but less than half the land, as compared to the Government days, is now under cultivation.

With the exception of agriculture, there are very few industries in the Soudan; in Omdurman a certain number of persons work in the arsenal and dockyard; there is a considerable manufacture and trade in spears, and there are a certain number of masons, carpenters, weavers, tailors, shoe and sandal-makers, saddlers, and boat builders.

COMMERCE AND TRADE

Slatin pasha concurs with Father Ohrwalder's remarks regarding commerce and trade. He gives, however, the following list of money current in the Soudan:

| | Weight in Dirhems | |
	Silver	Brass
(a) The Mahdi dollar.	7	1
(b) The first dollar made by Ibrahim Adlan	6	2
(c) The second dollar made by Ibrahim Adlan	5	3
(d) The first dollar of Nur-el Gereifawi (this is known as the Makbul dollar)	4	4
(e) The second dollar of Nur-el-Gereifawi (this is known as the Abu Sidr or Makbul). . . .	3	4
(f) The dollar of Suleiman Abdulla (this is known as the Abu Kibs dollar)	2½	4½
(g) The first dollar of Abdel Mejid (also called the Makbul) . . .	2½	4½
(h) The dollar of Weki Alla . . .	2½	4½
(i) The dollar of Omla Gedida (new money)	2	5

Nur-el-Gereifawi and Abdel Mejid are now the principal coiners, and though it is given out that the new money ("Omla Gedida") is composed of two parts silver and five parts brass, as a matter of fact, there is not more than half a dirhem of silver, which serves to lightly cover over the brass dollar.

This decrease in the intrinsic value of money is an interesting indication of the decline of Dervish power and government.

The two Heads of the Mint pay 12,000 dollars a month for permission to coin money, and any money issued by them must be accepted as good money.

The present rate of exchange is:

5 Omla Gedida dollars = 1 Maria Theresa dollar
8 Omla Gedida dollars = 1 Medjidi dollar

Subsequent to the Mahdi guinea of 1885 no gold coinage has been struck. English gold is very rare in the Soudan. One oke of gold is equivalent to 170 to 180 Makbul dollars.

TRADE

Slatin Pasha affirms that the Khalifa has benefited considerably by the opening of trade with Egypt, and that the taxes taken on goods at Kokreb, Dongola, Berber, Omdurman, and El-Obeid all go to swell his private Treasury.

Stoppage of trade would no doubt be severely felt in the Soudan, but Slatin considers that, apart from the Khalifa, it is such a benefit to the Soudanese themselves that he would not recommend their deprivation of it. On the other hand, he points out the great necessity of preventing the entry into the Soudan of any sort of material which is likely to assist in the manufacture of ammunition, such as files, iron, brass, chemicals, etc.

The weights and measures formerly used in the Soudan are still employed, but most of the brass weights have been disposed of in the manufacture of ammunition, and the equivalent weight is now made up by different-sized leather bags filled with stones.

SLAVE TRADE

Slatin confirms the previous statements regarding the Slave Trade and Regulations respecting slaves; he adds, however, that should a female slave desert her master and take refuge in the Kara or in the Mulazemin quarters, inquiries are made as to who her master is; should he be a Baggari he can have his slave back on the payment of a small sum, but should he be an ordinary native, the slave becomes the property of the first soldier who claims her. The Khalifa enforces most strictly the rules as to male slaves being prohibited from going to Egypt, as he knows they are at once taken for the army.

POSTAL SYSTEM

The fifty camels attached to the Beit-el-Mal for postal purposes are always carefully looked after and well fed. These are employed solely for the Khalifa's post; ordinary letters must be sent by hand, and merchants are the usual carriers.

TELEGRAPH

A telegraph line is in good working order between Khartoum and Omdurman, but the rest of the extensive Soudan telegraph system has been long since destroyed. . . .

CHAPTER 6

The Fiscal Administration of the Mahdist State, 1881–1898

The period of Mahdist rule is marked by a decline in all branches of the Sudanese economy; in particular, trade shrank to a small fraction of its previous volume. But the exigencies of government continued to make themselves felt, and a fairly elaborate fiscal administration was eventually established, as is described in the following selection. It may be added that the sources of revenue enumerated below were supplemented by exactions from the well-to-do and by debasement of the currency [see Part VII, chap. 5].

The selection also gives a few details on the rise of Omdurman, the country's largest town, which was founded by the Mahdi; the former capital, Khartoum (see Part VII, chap. 2), had suffered greatly during the siege of 1884, and its surviving population was deported to Omdurman in 1886. Khartoum was refounded, as the capital of the Sudan, immediately after the Anglo-Egyptian reconquest of 1898 and became the country's administrative, economic, and cultural center; in the last few years its population has caught up with that of Omdurman.

(See also works by Holt [*Mahdist State*], Shuqair, Theobald, and Rafi'i [*Misr wa al-Sudan*] listed in the Bibliography.)

[From Mekki Shibeika, *Al-Sudan fi Qarn, 1819–1919* (*The Sudan during a Century, 1819–1919* (Cairo, 1947), pp. 257–59; reproduced by kind permission of the author.]

. . . Government revenues consisted of the alms tax [*zakat*] and other taxes on merchandise, waterholes, water wheels, orchards, and the spoils of war; but the main muscle of the Mahdist body politic was the legal *zakat* on crops, animals, and livestock.

Each province had its own treasury [*bait al-mal*], and in Omdurman there was the central treasury for Muslims. The latter started on a small scale in Qadir [the mountain in western Sudan to which the Mahdi fled in 1881], under the friend of the Mahdi, Ahmad Wad Sulaiman, and consisted of spoils of war. It then expanded, with the extension of conquests, because of increased spoils and the alms taxes of the conquered territories, becoming the mainstay of the Mahdist administration; and its parts increased in complexity as new sources of revenue and expenditure emerged. Thus there was the central treasury, which drew its revenues from the inhabitants of Omdurman and the surrounding villages and tribes as well as the surplus of the provincial treasuries; from it were defrayed the expenditures of the treasury officials, those of the families of the Mahdi and khalifa, and those incurred in preparing the armies for campaigns. There was, secondly, *Bait al-mulazimia*, to which were assigned the revenues of the Gezira district and which paid for the upkeep of the bodyguard of the khalifa, known as the *mulazimia* (the companions or attendants). Thirdly, there was the treasury of the military workshop, to which were assigned taxes on water wheels and orchards in Khartoum, as well as receipts from the ivory coming from Bahr al-Ghazal and Equatoria, and which paid for the making of arms and munitions. Lastly there was *Bait Mal al-khums*, which received the proceeds of taxes on boats and water holes, profits on ostrich feathers and ivory, a third of the profits on gum, and the tithes collected on goods imported from abroad [in addition to the 2.5 per cent duty formerly paid]; it defrayed the personal expenditure of the khalifa and his intimates.

A number of officials who had served under the previous administration continued to work in the treasury, using the methods of accounting and bookkeeping which they had formerly learned and practiced. This made for careful accountancy and ensured that the taxes collected from the Muslims would not be dissipated. One of the functions of the treasury was minting coins and putting them into circulation, but the country did not lack forgers who imitated them. It also stamped goods on which the tithe had been paid, which led to both smuggling and false stamping. Otherwise, the collection of taxes, safekeeping of balances, and disbursement of funds proceeded in a way that was satisfactory to all,

under the vigilant eyes and direction of Ya'qub [the brother of the khalifa]; and each provincial administration had its own treasury, into which were paid the proceeds of the alms tax and other imposts, and which bore the costs of administration and of maintaining order.

The country was divided into provinces, to facilitate administration, each of which was under a governor who supervised the army and administration and was the supreme authority for local matters and the channel through which the people communicated with the khalifa. Orders and proclamations were sent to him from the capital, for enforcement, and the khalifa's agents would descend upon him to investigate important matters, solve problems, and deal with crises. The great provinces were: Dongola, Barbar, the West, and Kasala; the rest of the central Sudan was under the supervision of the khalifa, or rather Ya'qub. Each governor had a number of assistants who helped him in his administrative work. On the frontiers were amirs whose duty was to defend what was called the *bughaz* [marches]; thus there was a garrison in Sawarda, in the extreme north, and another in Qallabat and Qadarif; each amir was under the authority of the respective provincial governor. . . .

Omdurman was transformed from a camp into a large city, with mud houses replacing the tents and reed-huts. . . . Slatin pasha estimated the inhabitants of Omdurman at over 400,000, a figure which rose during feasts and periods of pilgrimage and which is about four times its present population. The Sudan had no tradition of or experience with such large towns. Hence houses were built without any plan, hygienic conditions were of the worst, and the streets were narrow, except for Shari' al-'Arda; all this led to occasional outbreaks of disease and epidemics. . . .

CHAPTER 7

Railway Projects, 1899

In a country the size of the Sudan, about a million square miles, lack of transport has always been, and still is, a major obstacle to economic development. The Nile is navigable throughout the greater part of the Sudan, but its southern reaches are blocked by thick vegetation (*sudd*) and the stretch between Khartoum and Aswan is interrupted by six cataracts—hence various projects were devised under Ismail for connecting the center of the Sudan with Egypt on the one hand and the Red Sea on the other (see Part VII, Introduction and chap. 3).

During the campaign of 1896–98 a narrow-gauge railway was built in Dongola and another between Wadi Halfa and Khartoum. This meant that the northern Sudan was now connected to the Mediterranean by a combination of railway, river steamer, and railway. But this route was expensive, especially for bulky goods; coal cost 90–95 francs a ton in Khartoum, compared to 27–30 in Alexandria.[1] Therefore there was the need, discussed in the following selection,—taken from one of Lord Cromer's annual reports on Egypt and the Sudan—for a direct connection with the Red Sea. By 1906 this had been secured by the laying of a railway between Atbara and the newly built Port Sudan.

The other objective indicated in the selection was the tapping of the most productive region in the Sudan, the Gezira. By 1910 the main railway line had been extended to Sennar, and in the 1920's other lines were built, by private British capital, in and from the Gezira to the Red Sea.

For the reasons given in the selection, all the Sudan's railways were built by the government and the greater part was operated by it. Even the private lines opened in the 1920's were built by the government, which was reimbursed by the companies for its outlay.

(See also works by Wiener, Hill, Sayyad, Abbas, and Shibeika listed in the Bibliography.)

[1] L. Wiener, *L'Egypte et ses chemins de fer*, p. 600.

[From "Report by H. M. Agent and Consul-General on the Finances, Administration and Condition of Egypt in 1898," Great Britain, *Accounts and Papers*, *1899*, CXII, *Egypt*, No. 3, 1899, pp. 3–5.]

. . . Difficulties in connection with transport and supply were the main obstacles to rapid progress during the recent campaigns in the Soudan. Similarly, the absence of facilities for communication stand in the way of developing that portion of the country where order and tranquillity already reign. It cannot be doubted that railways constitute perhaps the greatest want of the Soudan. Nevertheless, in this, as in other matters, it is desirable to proceed with deliberation.

The first question to decide is what direction the railways should take, and which, amongst various projects which may be supported by more or less valid arguments, calls most urgently for prompt exertion.

There is water communication, which is free at all seasons of the year, between Khartoum and Fashoda. A railway connecting these two points would necessarily compete with river transport. The construction of this line is not, therefore, a matter of urgency.

It is not only probable, but almost certain, that sooner or later railway communication will be established between the Nile Valley and the coast of the Red Sea. At first sight, the most obvious course to pursue would seem to be to connect Suakin and Berber. The construction of this line has, in fact, often been suggested. So long as the Dervishes remained in possession of Berber, it was clear that any discussion on this subject was premature. This obstacle is now removed. The question may, therefore, be considered on its own merits.

The line from Suakin to Berber has never yet been properly surveyed, neither has any trustworthy estimate been made of its cost. It is certain that throughout its course it will pass through nothing but a long tract of almost waterless desert. Without venturing at present to give any very decided opinion on the subject, I may say that I incline to the view which is held, I think, by all the most competent authorities whom I have consulted on this question, namely, that connection with the Red Sea via Abu Haraz, Gedarif, and Kassala to some spot on the coast, although relatively circuitous, is to be preferred to the direct route from Suakin to Berber. As I shall presently explain, the establishment of connection with the Red Sea, though obviously desirable, is not of such immediate importance as the execution of an alternative project. Nevertheless, the question must to a certain extent be taken into consideration, in order that whatever immediate extension is undertaken shall not clash with any general plan which may ultimately be adopted.

There can, indeed, be no doubt of the direction in which railway extension is most urgently required. The territories about the upper waters of the Blue Nile were styled by Sir Samuel Baker, who visited this region many years ago, as "the granary of the Soudan." All recent accounts confirm this view. A short time ago almost famine prices ruled at Omdurman, whilst at Gedarif grain was so plentiful as to be well-nigh unsaleable. As I write, the price is P.T. 160 (I *l* 12s. 6d.) per ardeb (300 lbs.) at Omdurman, and P.T. 22 (4s. 6d.) per ardeb at Gedarif. At the latter place the price is expected to fall to P.T. 10 (2s.) when the new crop, which is almost ripe, is harvested.

I should add that Kassala is now being supplied with grain from Gedarif, the current price being P.T. 48 (9s. 10d.) per ardeb. When the Kassala crop is gathered it is expected that the price there will fall to P.T. 22 (4s. 6d.) per ardeb.

I need hardly say that these striking differences in price, occurring at localities situated at no great distance from each other, are wholly due to want of communications.

Clearly, under these circumstances, it will be desirable as soon as the railway reaches Khartoum, to make arrangements for its extension to Abu Haraz, with a view ultimately to reaching Gedarif. The distance is 122 miles.[1] The line has not yet been surveyed, but it is believed that no great engineering difficulties will have to be encountered.

The question of the agency through which this, and eventually other lines, should be constructed remains to be considered.

Rather less than two years ago some discussions took place on the question of selling the existing Soudan railways and relying on private enterprise for further extensions. These discussions were unproductive of result, and, on the whole, it is fortunate that such was the case. Further consideration leads to the conclusion that, for the time being at all events, it is desirable that the existing railways should remain in the hands of the Government, and that extensions should be executed by the Government. The reasons are manifold:

In the first place, it is at present quite impossible to make any trustworthy forecast of the future of the Soudan railways. Until further experience is gained no one can state with confidence whether they are likely to prove remunerative or the reverse. The elements are wanting to enable any conditions of sale to be settled which would be alike acceptable to the Government and to the shareholders in the undertaking. As regards the latter, it is more especially to be observed that, unless the project is to be purely speculative—a course which, on many grounds, is greatly to be deprecated— some information, based on the solid ground of acquired knowledge, should be laid before the public when they are invited to subscribe. Both on my own behalf and on behalf of other Egyptian and Soudanese authorities, I wish to state that we are not at present prepared to take any moral responsibility in the direction of furnishing such information.

I am aware that these difficulties might be overcome if the shareholders could rely for a return on their capital, not so much on

[1] Following the windings of the river, the distance is about 143 miles.

the remunerative character of the undertaking as on a Government guarantee for the payment of interest. Without in any way discarding altogether, or for an indefinite period, the use of this method for raising capital, I have to say that its adoption on any large scale is not for the moment possible. Money cannot be borrowed on the security of the Soudan revenues only. I have already explained that the Soudan Budget shows a considerable deficit. In the event, therefore, of any guarantee being given for the payment of interest on capital expenditure in the Soudan, the charge will, in reality, devolve on the Egyptian Treasury. Egyptian finance is in a thoroughly sound condition, but, however desirable it may be to push on as rapidly as possible the development of the Soudan, it would not be either prudent or just to the Egyptian taxpayers to run any risk that the present position of assured solvency, which is the result of many years of sustained labour, should be in any degree imperilled in order to provide for the necessities of the Soudan. At this moment, moreover, there is a special reason for guarding against any relaxation of that prudence in the assumption of fresh pecuniary obligations, which has been the corner-stone of the financial policy pursued in Egypt for many years past. The construction of the Nile reservoir is by far the the most important operation in which the Egyptian Government is at present engaged. When it is completed, it will, I hope and believe, furnish funds which may be applied advantageously to Egyptian, and possibly also to Soudanese, interests. Time, however, will be required before all the beneficial results, which may be expected to accrue from the construction of the reservoir, can be realized. In the meanwhile, it has to be remembered, as Mr. Gorst has very rightly pointed out in this note on the Estimates for the current year, that in 1904 a charge of £E.160,000 will fall on the Egyptian Treasury by reason of the construction of the reservoir: and further, that, under the conditions imposed on Egypt by existing laws, a real surplus, amounting to double that sum, viz., £E.320,000, must be realized in order to meet that charge.

I speak only of the actual condition of affairs. It is quite possible that, even before the reservoir is completed, so great an improvement may occur as to render the assumption of fresh financial obligations unobjectionable. But, for the time being, prudence must be exercised in this direction.

Another consideration, which points to the same conclusion, is that, if any private firm or Company undertook to construct railways in the Soudan, the difficulty of finding labour, and possibly also employees, would probably prove an insuperable obstacle. So far, the Soudan railways have all been constructed by military labour. The employees are soldiers. It is open to question whether, under any other system, it would be possible to make or to work the railways. But the amount of military labour which is obtainable is limited. This consideration affords an additional argument in favour of proceeding slowly.

I hope, therefore, that the railway to Khartoum will be finished by the end of the current year, and that it will be possible to arrange for the extension to Abu Haraz in 1900. I venture to think that, for the moment, this programme is sufficient. As events develop, the matter can of course be reconsidered.

Whether it will eventually be desirable to hand over the whole or any portion of the Soudan railway system to a Company is a matter which I need not now discuss. For the present, it seems clear that the Government must be the pioneer of railway enterprise.

So many questions have recently been addressed to me on this subject, that I have thought it desirable to treat it at some length. . . .

CHAPTER 8

Land Policy, 1906

Compared to other African countries which fell under European domination, the Sudan enjoyed three main advantages. Its harsh climate precluded white settlement. It did not contain rich and easily exploitable mineral deposits which, by attracting large amounts of capital, might have created powerful foreign vested interests. Lastly, its civil service soon established a tradition of great competence and integrity and showed a capacity to learn from the mistakes made in other parts of the British Empire.

The following selection brings out the first and third of these points. In addition to the Indian experience mentioned in the report, Governor-General Wingate no doubt had in mind the Egyptian. By 1896, 44 per cent of Egypt's cultivated land was owned by 12,000 landlords, and it was plain that the greater part of the benefit of the country's rapid development was accruing to a small section of the community. Moreover land speculation in Egypt, which was very active, spilled over into the Sudan immediately after the reconquest, and there was danger that much land would be bought up. The rapid growth of the Sudanese population, following the re-establishment of peace and order, constituted another warning sign.

The well-justified caution of the government and the slowness of the land commissions set up under the Titles to Land Ordinance of 1899, prevented the alienation of land. Thus, when it was finally decided to carry out the scheme "practically the whole of the land in the Gezira remains in native ownership divided into comparatively small holdings, so that it may be said that, not only has the foreign speculator been kept out, but also the wealthy native absentee landlord, and the whole of the land remains in the ownership of the actual cultivators that work upon it." [1] The government was therefore able to implement its tripartite arrangement without encountering opposition from native or foreign landlords (see Part VII, chap. 9). The same situation prevailed, by and large, in other parts of the Sudan.

(See also *Reports by H.M.'s Agent* . . . and works by Gaitskell, Tothill, Sayyad, and Shibeika listed in the Bibliography.)

[1] Statement by Foreign Secretary, 1924, quoted in Arthur Gaitskell, *Gezira: A Story of Development in the Sudan*, p. 45.

[From "Report by H. M. Agent and Consul-General on the Finances, Administration and Condition of Egypt in 1906," Great Britain, *Accounts and Papers, 1907,* C, *Egypt,* No. 3, 1907, pp. 123-24.]

A very full and interesting report which I have received from Mr. Bonus, the Director of Agriculture and Lands, contains the following passage: "After the date of the Report for 1905 applications, both large and small, for agricultural land continued for some time to be received in considerable numbers both at Khartoum and in the provinces. For obvious reasons, Berber and Dongola appear to be the favourite localities, though a large number are reported for land in Sukkot and near Kamlin, the latter being probably influenced by expectations of a large irrigation scheme in the Blue Nile Province. In respect of large applications for development schemes, experience has shown the impossibility of rapid action and the imprudence of haste, so applicants were warned that their proposals could not be considered before the land concerned had been surveyed and the title settled under the Land Settlement Ordinance, 1905. This state of affairs no doubt became notorious, for the number of applications sensibly decreased."

There can be no doubt of the desirability of eventually bringing in foreign capital to assist in the land development of the Soudan; but, in the first instance, the conditions under which concessions of land should be made have to be carefully considered. I am aware that delay in this matter will not improbably be attributed to a narrow officialism, which is reluctant to encourage private enterprise and is not sufficiently active in promoting the development of the country. I am, however, very decidedly of opinion that no great account should be taken of criticisms of this nature. The matter is, indeed, one of primary importance. It is scarcely an exaggeration to say that the whole future of the Soudan depends upon the treatment which this question receives. It is one which evidently requires prolonged study and great care. Not only do the facts speak for themselves, but the experience of other countries shows the harm which can be done by undue haste. For instance, in 1796, the Government of Lord Cornwallis thought that the Zemindars of Bengal were landed proprietors of the British type, instead of being, as was actually the fact, mere farmers of revenue on behalf of the Mogul Government. The result was that not only was the amount of the land tax fixed in perpetuity, but also full rights of ownership were conferred without due consideration of the consequences which would accrue. Hence arose endless difficulties, which can scarcely, after the lapse of more than a century, be said to have been settled in a satisfactory manner. I am all the more disposed to think that a similar danger has to be guarded against in the Soudan from a remark contained in the report of Mr. Bonus. He says: "Hitherto the general impression appears to have been that the native rights are easily disposed of, and present no difficulty when terms have been arranged with the concessionnaire. I am inclined to hold the contrary opinion." I go somewhat further than Mr. Bonus: I hold the contrary opinion very strongly. Until the nature of the native rights has been clearly ascertained, and until the terms which, in connection with those rights, shall be imposed when any land concessions are granted be determined, I hold that it would be in the highest degree imprudent to deal with this question. I am confirmed in this view from the fact that, in the case of some few concessions which were granted shortly after the reoccupation of the Soudan, there can be little doubt that the action of the Government was premature. Those concessions, Mr. Bonus says, "have unluckily left a crop of difficulties by which the Department of Agriculture and Lands will be embarrassed for some time to come."

It is, moreover, in the interests of bona fide investors that this matter should be dealt with in a most deliberate fashion. A good deal of land has been bought and sold in the town of Khartoum. Mr. Bonus describes the result in the following language: "Not only is the supply of suitable houses unequal to the demand, but the rents asked are beyond the means of the class of persons requiring houses. The reason is not far to seek. The land boom which began last year resulted in feverish speculations, and many of the present holders of town lands have paid prices on which no rent which they are likely to get gives a reasonable return. They have also in many cases exhausted their resources in the purchase of the land, and have con-sequently been able to comply only in the most perfunctory way with the building stipulations which have to be observed to avoid forfeiture."

Under these circumstances, I have no hesitation in saying that, in respect to the granting of land concessions in the Soudan, the same principle should be applied as has been adopted, with some success, in dealing with all other Egyptian and Soudanese questions. Slow and steady progress, after a very careful examination of the facts, is to be preferred to haste and the production of immediate, but possibly fallacious results. . .

CHAPTER 9

Preparations for the Gezira Scheme,
1904–1925

The Gezira scheme may, without exaggeration, be said to have been the main-spring of economic development in the Sudan. It has contributed the greater part of the country's exports and the bulk of government revenue and has constituted the most important segment in the cash economy. The following selection describes the experiments in both land tenure and crop rotations and irrigation which preceded the launching of the scheme. Another important aspect was the scientific research carried out in the Gezira itself as well as in the laboratories of Gordon College, in Khartoum.

The initial capital for the scheme was provided by the Sudan Plantations Syndicate, which started in 1904 with an issued capital of £80,000, raised by successive steps to £2,475,000 in 1935; the company also provided the management. But most of the investment came from the government, which spent £11,500,000 on the Sennar dam and some of the main canals and a further £21,900,000 between 1925–26 and 1950. The original owners, whose land the government had taken on a long-term lease at a nominal rent, contributed their labor as tenants of the scheme. After 1926, when the arrangement described in the selection was altered, net profits on cash crops were shared as follows: government, 40 per cent; tenants, 40 per cent; companies, 20 per cent.

The scheme nearly foundered during the depression, when it was struck by a rapid fall in cotton prices and various crop diseases. But it recovered in 1934, and during the Second World War and postwar years developed enormously. By 1950, when the concession lapsed and the government took over the companies' share, the net proceeds divided among the three partners exceeded £16,000,000, and much higher figures have been registered since then. The area of the scheme has also been considerably extended. The number of tenant families exceeds 30,000 and the total population of the Gezira area is around 650,000.

(See also Reports by H.M.'s Agent; Reports on the Finance; and works by Gaitskell, Ani, Tothill, Shibeika [*Independent Sudan*], and Abbas listed in the Bibliography.)

[From Muhammad Mahmud al-Sayyad, *Iqtisadiat al-Sudan* (*The Economics of the Sudan*) (Cairo, 1957), pp. 107–10; reproduced by kind permission of the author.]

THE PRELIMINARY STAGE

The Mahdist revolt led to the collapse of the Sudan's economic system; the many evil consequences of this breakdown were, however, accompanied by one favorable one, namely, that it gave an opportunity to the new administration to build up a new system on sound foundations. The Gezira region, with its agricultural potentialities, drew immediate attention; but a large scheme, such as the one envisaged, required preliminary experiments demonstrating its soundness and evaluating the benefits to be derived from it; this led to the carrying-out of agricultural experiments in Zaydab, Tayyiba, and Barakat.

Modern agricultural development in the Sudan has been closely bound up with the Sudan Plantations Syndicate, Ltd., one of the British firms set up to exploit the resources of the Sudan after the British had taken the country over. The establishment of that company goes back to 1904, when an enterprising American, Leigh Hunt, visited the Sudan and came back impressed with the country's potentialities as a cotton grower. This ambitious American succeeded in obtaining, through Lord Cromer, 10,000 faddans of government land for cotton-growing experiments; he also succeeded in attracting British capital to his scheme, founding the Sudan Plantations Syndicate.

The lands granted to the Syndicate were at Zaydab, about 240 kilometers north of Khartoum. The company installed pumps for lifting water from the Nile and started cultivation in 1905, letting out land to tenants drawn from that locality and neighbouring ones. In spite of its small size, this region has played an important part in the modern economic history of the Sudan, since it was the first school in which cotton cultivation was taught; the experiment proved that, given the necessary agricultural means, the Sudanese could be converted into farmers capable of tilling the soil. The success of the Zaydab experiment also stimulated orientation towards the south—to the lands of the Gezira, which later became the leading producing region in the Sudan.

Many experiments were required in the Gezira region. In 1911 the Tayyiba pumping station went into operation;[1] the government made an agreement with S.P.S. under which the former covered the cost of the pumps while the company administered the scheme. The initial area was 3,000 faddans—later increased to 5,000—divided into plots of 30 faddans each, and the agreement was to run for four years. But the success of the project led the government to conclude a new agreement with the company in 1913, on the basis which was subsequently adopted for the Gezira scheme, viz., a partnership in cultivation between the government, the company, and the farmers, who were to receive 35 per cent, 25 per cent, and 40 per cent of profits, respectively. The government undertook to pay the rent of the land to its owners and to meet pumping expenses; the company was responsible for administering the scheme and supervising agricultural operations; and the cultivator was to carry out the agricultural operations. It will be noticed that conditions differed from those in Zaydab. In the latter, the land belonged to the government and was transferred to the company, whereas in Tayyiba it was privately owned and therefore had to be bought or rented, and was in fact rented at 5 piastres per faddan. In contrast to the procedure followed later in the Gezira, no preference was given to the original owners in renting the land back from the company; the reason given was that the scheme was still in the experimental stage and had to ensure all conditions of success, which meant that the company should have a free hand in distributing land to those it believed to be competent cultivators, and not be restricted by other considerations.

[1] For details see P. F. Martin (ed.), *The Sudan in Evolution* (1927), p. 302.

The Tayyiba experiment was a success, and this spurred the government to implement the Gezira scheme in co-operation with S.P.S. However, to make sure that the scheme was a sound one, the government did not content itself with one experiment. In 1914 it opened the Barakat pumping station, which was set up by the company at its own expense, and dug canals for the irrigation of an area of 8,000 faddans; here too the company did not restrict itself by giving preference to original owners of the land. The company continued to manage the Barakat scheme, as an experimental station, until the completion of the Sennar dam in 1925.

As the First World War held up the implementation of the major irrigation schemes, the company set up two pumping stations, at Hag Abd Allah in 1921 and at Wadi al Nau in 1923; in other words,

at the time of the opening of the Sennar dam the company had four pumping stations in the Gezira, in addition to the one at Zaydab.

In the meantime the government was carrying out the essential preliminary measures for implementing the Gezira scheme: land was surveyed and registered and railways were built, directly connecting the Gezira region with the Sudan's first port, Port Sudan. And as soon as the war was over, construction began on the Sennar dam. Upon the completion of the dam, the Gezira scheme went into operation, on the basis which had been followed in Tayyiba and Barakat; the land was bought [by the government] at the price of £E 1 per faddan or rented for 10 piastres a year per faddan, but this time preference was given in the allocation of tenancies to the original owners or their nominees. . . .

PART VIII

Epilogue, 1961

Epilogue, 1961 : Shifts in Economic Power

The following paper, read in April, 1961, reviews the course of events in the Middle East during the last fifty years. The evolution described in this book reached its culmination in the period immediately preceding the First World War. After that the achievement of political independence, growing economic and social awareness, the weakening of the traditional colonial powers, the growth of the oil industry, and, in recent years, Western-Soviet rivalry, combined to reverse some of the previous trends and to develop new ones.

Two points may be added: in 1963 Iran followed the other major countries in the region and launched a large-scale land reform; and the movement toward socialism noted in the paper has greatly accelerated. In July, 1961, the United Arab Republic nationalized most of the industry, transport, finance, and foreign trade in both regions and imposed other measures aimed at the rich, such as higher income taxes and, in October, 1961, sequestration. Although many of these measures were repealed in Syria, after the breakup of the United Arab Republic in September, 1961, some have been reimposed. In July, 1964, Iraq nationalized its financial institutions and main industries, and other countries may be expected to follow suit.

(See also I.B.R.D. [*Turkey, Iraq, Syria, and Jordan*], United Nations, [*Economic Conditions in the Middle East* and *Growth and Structure*], and works by Hershlag, Karpat, Rozaliev, Himadeh, Issawi and Yeganeh, and Issawi [*Egypt in Revolution*] listed in the Bibliography.)

[Charles Issawi, "Shifts in Economic Power," paper read at the Middle East Institute, Washington, April 7, 1961.]

... In the last forty years, and more particularly in the last ten, three main shifts in economic power have taken place in the Middle East: from foreigners to nationals; from the landed interest to the industrial, financial, commercial, and managerial interests; and from the private sector to the state. I shall discuss them in that order.

FROM FOREIGN TO NATIONAL INTERESTS

The rise of foreign economic influence in the Middle East began in the 1850's with the blossoming of factory industry in Britain, and to a lesser extent in Belgium and France, with the rise of the railway and steamship and with the accumulation of vast savings available for overseas investment. Simultaneously, a group of westernizing monarchs and ministers appeared in the Ottoman Empire, Egypt, and Iran who opened their countries to foreign influences. By 1914, a vast amount of European capital had flowed into the Middle East, accompanied by a significant number of financiers, merchants, engineers, physicians, skilled workers, and the adventurers of all sorts who join a gold rush. The results may be summarized as follows:

First, although the greater part of the capital raised either never reached the recipient country at all—being lost by issues much below par or in the form of commissions—or was dissipated by the rulers themselves (Said and Ismail, Abdul Majid and Abdul Aziz, Nasiruddin and Muzaffaruddin), a large amount did get through. And this amount accounted for the greater part of the *net* capital formation that took place in the Middle East in those years. The only significant capital formation that was financed by local investment was some of the irrigation works in Egypt and Iraq, and some of the schools, roads, and other public works in the Ottoman Empire, as well as the usual private investment in agriculture, buildings, and trade.

Second, the Middle Eastern countries built up huge foreign public debts. It is true that these debts were drastically scaled down after Turkey had declared bankruptcy in 1875 and Egypt the following year. Nevertheless, in 1914 the Ottoman government had a foreign debt of £T150 million, the Egyptian of £E94 million, and the Iranian of under £E10 million. As for private investment, it was about £64 million in Turkey, about £100 million in Egypt, and a few millions in Iran. Altogether, foreign investment in the Middle East at the outbreak of the First World War must have been about $1.5–2.0 billion, probably nearer the higher figure. The charges on this foreign indebtedness were, naturally, high. In the Ottoman Empire, interest and service charges on the public debt absorbed nearly a third of the government budget and in Egypt nearly a half. The servicing of payments on capital invested in the private sector added a further strain on the foreign exchanges.

Third, practically all the main sectors of the economy of the middle Eastern countries passed under foreign control. Except in Egypt and the Sudan—and the Hijaz railway (see Part IV chap. 4)—all the railways were foreign owned and operated and the same applied to the ports. So were the other public utilities: gas, electricity, water supply, river transport, light, railways, and streetcars. So were all the banks, and practically all the mines and the few factories that had been established. So, of course, was the oil industry, which had just entered into production in Egypt and Iran at the outbreak of war. And the bulk of export and import trade was conducted by foreigners. The main foreign interests were German, French, and British in Turkey; French, British and Belgian in Egypt; British and Russian in Iran; and French in the Levant.

If to this be added the fact that much of large-scale internal trade, and many of the professions, were also in the hands of either foreigners or local minority groups, it will be seen that the bulk of the indigenous population earned its living in agriculture, in various kinds of unskilled work, in the surviving handicrafts that were increasingly feeling the impact of foreign competition, in government service, and in internal trade. The last two groups, civil servants and traders, deserve special attention since it was from their ranks that the new economic leadership was to spring. It may be added that in some countries, notably Lebanon and Syria and to a lesser extent Iran, the native bourgeoisie showed much more vigor and kept a larger sector of the economy in its hands than it did in Egypt or Turkey; by the same token, the foreign influx of people and capital into these countries was very small.

Of course this anomalous situation was the result not so much of impersonal economic forces working in a vacuum as of specific political pressures: Great Power diplomacy, armed intervention, the Capitulations exempting foreigners from taxation, the international commercial treaties regulating tariffs [see Part II, chap. 3], and other similar factors.

And what politics has made politics can unmake. The economic history of the last forty years in the Middle East is one of a continual retreat of foreign interests, a retreat which was provoked either by revolutionary pushes or by the relentless squeeze of legislative and administrative action. There is of course one exception, and a very important one: the oil industry; in that field alone foreign capital has continued to advance.

In this, as in so many other respects, Turkey—whose evolution aften seems to precede that of other Middle Eastern countries by a generation or so—set the pace. The years following the Kemalist Revolution saw a large-scale liquidation of foreign interests. First, the public debt was drastically scaled down by successive defaults and arrangements with creditors [see Part II, chap. 11]. Then the various foreign concerns in Turkey were in turn bought out: the railways, the coal and copper mines, the tobacco monopoly, and many public utilities. Stringent laws were passed regulating foreign economic activity in the country and giving local concerns preferential treatment. Fiscal and financial autonomy were regained by abolishing the Capitulations and customs agreements. And the expulsion of local minority groups left a vacuum which was filled by Turks. Not until the 1950's was Turkey once more ready to take in foreign capital in large amounts, and then only on terms very different from those it had accorded to its predecessors.

In Egypt the course of events was at first somewhat different. Two world wars enabled that country to build up huge foreign balances, which it used to buy up its public debt and a significant amount of shares and bonds of foreign companies operating in Egypt. In addition there was a movement for the Egyptianization of the economy, spearheaded by Bank Misr, which was founded in 1920, and aided in every way by government legislative and administrative pressure. In 1930 Egypt recovered its tariff autonomy, and in 1936, with the abolition of the Capitulations, its fiscal autonomy. This was used further to protect and promote local industry. During the interwar and postwar periods, the amount of foreign investment in the country was very small, being confined mainly to some industrial enterprises, usually in partnership with Egyptians, a few banks, and some oil prospecting. And, according to one estimate, whereas in 1933 only 9 per cent of the capital invested in joint stock companies operating in Egypt was Egyptian, in the period 1934–39 no less than 47 per cent of the *new* corporate capital raised was Egyptian, and the share steadily rose to 84 per cent by 1946–48. Similarly, whereas in 1920 the number of Muslim Egyptians or Copts serving on the board of directors of companies operating in Egypt was negligible, by 1951 it had risen to about 31 per cent and 4 per cent, respectively.[1]

But the main shifts in Egypt came more violently. At the outbreak of the Second World War, Italians and Germans were interned and their property was sequestered. The Arab-Israeli war led to an exodus of Jews and the loss of much of their property. And the nationalization of the Suez Canal and the war that followed resulted in the taking over of a huge amount of British, French, and Jewish property, the expulsion of thousands of foreigners, and the passing of legislation Egyptianizing all foreign banks and insurance companies. Very recently, the Congo crisis caused a break in relations between Egypt and Belgium and the sequestration of Belgian property. To all intents and purposes, the economic position once held by foreigners in Egypt may be said to have been wiped out.

Obviously a new foreign position is developing, the Soviet. The most recent

[1] [The 1960 figures were 66 and 4 per cent.]

estimates put Soviet aid to Egypt at over $700 million. This represents the line of credit opened by the Soviet Union; how much of it has actually been drawn so far we do not know, but it seems to be only a small fraction of the total credit. Of course we all know that this aid has been offered "with no strings attached." And we also know that Soviet diplomats and generals, unlike their western counterparts, never thump the table with their fists—though they sometimes bang it with their shoes. But money has a way of talking, and one cannot but feel that the linguistic ability of the rouble may be considerable.

Very recently Syria, which had already nationalized most of its foreign-owned enterprises such as the railways, electricity and water companies, has followed the Egyptian lead and Syrianized its banks. It has also received much Soviet aid and is scheduled to receive considerably more. Even Lebanon and Israel have nationalized their public utilities. The Sudan took over the only important foreign enterprise, the Gezira, when its concession lapsed in 1950. As for Iran, under Reza shah there was much investment by the state, about $500 million, and perhaps an equal amount by local private enterprise but, except in oil, hardly any by foreigners who were not given much encouragement by the suspicious shah. More recently, there has been substantial foreign investment and, of course, a large amount of United States aid.

That brings us to the petroleum industry, which accounts for practically the whole of foreign investment in the Persian Gulf countries. By 1926, gross fixed investments, at current prices, had reached about $100 million, rising to about $350 million in 1935 and $900 million in 1947. But the real increase came in the postwar period, when the figure rose to over $4.1 billion by 1960; a little over half the total consists of United States capital, the rest being mainly British, Dutch and French. These huge amounts carry with them commensurate economic power and represent the only significant foreign interest left in the Middle East.

What the fate of these investments will be, it is not for me to say. On the one hand, Dr. Mossadegh's attempt at nationalization failed and, to the surprise of most people, the revolutionary government in Iraq, another important recipient of Soviet aid, has not yet tried to take over the oil industry. On the other, the tide of nationalism is running high, even in countries like Saudi Arabia, Bahrein, and Kuwait. The least one can say is that the future is uncertain. But it is not inconceivable that the oil companies may be able to work out some agreement with the local governments—perhaps in the form of a joint international cartel!

One last question remains to be mentioned in this connection—foreign trade. For several decades Middle Easterners, along with the inhabitants of other underdeveloped countries, have complained that international trade makes them dependent on foreigners, and they have sought by various measures, such as industrialization and diversification, to decrease that dependence. Of course, in this form, their complaint is absurd: the United Kingdom or Belgium or Norway are more dependent on international trade than the majority of underdeveloped countries. But there is an underlying stratum of sense: like almost all other peoples, Middle Easterners do import some of their basic necessities and, as with other primary producers, two or three commodities account for practically all their exports. And their efforts to reduce their dependence in these two respects have been vain. Their exports remain as concentrated as ever and their industrial development and the mechanization of their agriculture and transport have merely increased their dependence on foreign fuels, raw materials, machinery, and spare parts.

But there was also one other form of dependence which they resented: dependence on one market, e.g., the United Kingdom for Egypt and Iraq, France for Lebanon and Syria, and so on. Here some important shifts, away from traditional markets and suppliers, have taken place in the last ten years. But one sometimes wonders whether the Middle Easterners have not just exchanged whips for scorpions, since several countries have now become heavily dependent on the Soviet bloc.

FROM THE LANDED TO THE BUSINESS INTEREST

The second shift, from landed interests to industrial, financial, commercial, and managerial interests, with which I shall deal more briefly, was partly a consequence of the one just described. For, as mentioned, until quite recently most nonagricultural activity was in foreign hands. But as foreign interests were liquidated and foreign business and professional men left the Middle East, room was created in which a national bourgeoisie began to develop, partly from the old commercial class, partly from civil servants and professional men, partly from other strata. This process has been at work in Turkey and Egypt since the 1920's and in Iraq since the Second World War, and particularly after the exodus of the Jewish middle class in 1950–51, and it seems to be starting in the Sudan; it has not taken place in Lebanon, Syria, or Israel, since in these countries the business community was mainly native, and in Iran only to a limited extent, for the same reason.

But, adapting the terminology of international trade, there was, in addition to middle-class substitution, middle-class creation owing to the growth of the non-agricultural sectors of the economy. The most important development in this field was the rise of factory industry. In the late 1920's, it is doubtful whether in any Middle Eastern country manufacturing and mining accounted for more than 5 per cent of the gross national product. Today, even excluding the foreign-owned oil sector, the corresponding figure is around 15 per cent in Turkey, Lebanon, and Iraq, somewhat more in Egypt, considerably more in Israel (21 per cent) and not much less in Syria and Iran, and the share of industry is steadily, and in one or two countries rapidly, growing. To this should be added the considerable expansion of foreign trade in countries like Lebanon, Israel, Iraq, Iran, Syria, and Turkey, which has reinforced the commercial and financial middle class, and the impact of the oil industry, which has brought into being a new class of contractors, merchants, and other businessmen in the Persian Gulf area. A no less important development has been the growth of a new indigenous managerial and professional class. This has been stimulated, on the one hand, by the huge expansion of the educated élite; Iran alone has some 10,000 students in foreign universities, and Lebanon over 1,500, and the number of Turkish, Egyptian, Israeli, Iraqi, Jordanian, and other students abroad runs into many thousands, to which should be added the tens of thousands in local universities. But this increased supply is barely keeping up with the demand, from government and business, for trained engineers, agronomists, physicians, statisticians, economists, administrators, and technicians. Particularly noteworthy is the growth of a new managerial group in such countries as Egypt and Turkey; this group has been called into being by the steady increase in size and complexity of the industrial and financial establishments in these countries and the development of corporate forms of enterprise, which are slowly undermining the position of the traditional Middle Eastern entrepreneur who founded a company, raised most or all of its capital, directed its policy, and supervised its day-to-day operations.

The growth of all these classes has created a weighty counterpoise to the traditionally predominant landed interest. The "New Men" have been using their influence to bring about a shift in economic policy, favoring the business sector at the expense of the agrarian. The most striking example of this is the breaking-up of large estates in Egypt, Syria, and Iraq, which has dealt crippling blows to the landowners, but the same trend may be observed in tax legislation and other economic measures taken in these and other countries. On the other hand, in Iran the position of the landed interest still seems unshaken, and the shah's attempt at introducing even a mild land reform, as distinct from the redistribution of his family estates, has been frustrated.[2] As for Turkey, the situation is more complex. During the 1930's and 1940's the urban sector was undoubtedly favored at the expense of the rural, though perhaps not more than in Ottoman times when the peasant bore the brunt of taxation [see Part II, chap. 12]. In the 1950's, however, agriculture prospered greatly, and the large and medium landowners increased their income several fold; in this they were helped both by direct government aid in the form of credits, machinery, and road building, and by the fact that they were exempt from income tax. It is also significant that the Turkish land reform of 1945, which was in many ways very successful, left the large estates practically intact. Finally, it should be mentioned that many landowners in Turkey have invested in trade or in industries located in their area. How the position will be affected by the 1960 revolution, which in some respects represented a revolt of the town against the country, is by no means clear.

It remains only to add that this general trend may be expected to continue. In the Middle East, as in other parts of the world, industry is growing much more rapidly than agriculture, and in view of the general passion for industrialization will probably continue to do so, and so are the services. Real estate, formerly almost the only source of wealth, is steadily declining in importance. And, what is no less significant, public opinion is increasingly turning against large or even medium landowners, who are regarded as functionless survivors of an out-of-date system and whose large unearned incomes are eyed as a rich source of investment—or consumption—by the state apparatus.

[2] [A large-scale land reform was carried out in Iran in 1963.]

FROM THE PRIVATE TO THE PUBLIC SECTOR

This brings us to the last shift—from the private to the public sector. Of course, state intervention in economic life is nothing new in the Middle East; on the contrary, it is private property and the control of the dominant sectors of the economy by private interests which are new. In the "hydraulic societies" of Egypt and Mesopotamia, control of the vital irrigation works was a task which the government alone could perform, and Prime Minister Joseph's buffer stock and price stabilization scheme was, I am sure, not the only one of its kind. Government supervision of the handicrafts and trade varied in intensity, sometimes taking the form of disastrous extortion, as in fifteenth-century Egypt. And it should be remembered that agricultural land was, throughout the Middle East, held on a communal or tribal tenure, except for islands of freehold in Lebanon. Finally, it is worth recalling that in the 1820's and 1830's, Muhammad Ali of Egypt attempted, and nearly succeeded in carrying out, the first state-controlled program of modern times aiming at accelerated development through forced saving and rapid industrialization [see Part VI, chap. 5]. But in the second half of the nineteenth century a different pattern evolved. To use the convenient terminology of Albert Hirschman, the state provided some of the "social overhead capital"—irrigation works, roads, and, in so far as these were not established by foreign capital, railways and ports—leaving the "directly productive activities" to private enterprise, which, except in agriculture, usually meant foreign enterprise. As for agriculture itself, it was slowly being transformed by the impact of the world market and the spread of cash crops, which helped to break down the traditional communal tenure and replace it by private ownership of land. This process was accelerated by government legislation inspired by western concepts of private ownership, such as the Egyptian land laws of 1854 and 1858 and the Ottoman Land Code of 1858 [see Part II, chaps. 8 and 9]. In brief, the general philosophy was one of private enterprise and laissez faire. This was, after all, the dominant view in Europe and therefore, as so often since, tended to be accepted uncritically in the Middle East. It was also the only realistic philosophy, given the impotence of the Middle Eastern governments, whose hands were tied by the Capitulations, commercial conventions, and foreign pressure or downright occupation.

In the last forty years, however, the power and activity of the state have grown considerably; the reasons for this, in addition to the factors operating all over the world, may be summed up under the headings of nationalism, socialism, military revolutions, oil income, and the inflow of foreign funds.

As for nationalism, it was soon felt that political independence was only a first step, one that should be followed by economic independence. The latter was taken to mean two things: first, reducing the predominant power of foreigners in the economic life of the country, the process described earlier; and, second, reducing the economic dependence of the country on the outside world by developing its resources and creating new sources of income, especially in industry and finance. The only force that could effect this economic transformation was political power, and the only machine that could set it in motion was the state. Hence we see the state gaining new economic power by its legislative and administrative regulations; by taking over several fields previously run by foreigners, such as railways, public utilities, and mines in Turkey in the 1920's and in the Arab countries after the Second World War; and by launching large-scale investment programs such as the Turkish Five-Year Plan of 1934 and the massive investment in industry and transport carried out by Reza shah in Iran.

And close on the heels of nationalism has come, in most countries, socialism—indeed Sir William Harcourt's statement made nearly seventy years ago that "We are all socialists now" seems very applicable to the Middle East today. Of course very few people have really tried to understand and clarify what socialism means, and even fewer have read the classics of European socialism. But within the amorphous entity that goes by the name of socialism in the Middle East three elements may be distinguished: (1) a drive for greater social equality, which has manifested itself in the efforts toward land reform, higher and more progressive taxation, and the provision of wider social services; (2) anti-capitalist feelings, the conviction, spreading among certain intellectuals and civil servants, that private gain is immoral—the more so as it is identified with the West; and (3) the conviction that socialist planning is the gimmick that will infallibly and simultaneously bring about national power, rapid economic development, and social well-being—and Soviet Russia is today regarded as the possessor of the magic formula just as was Nazi Germany in the 1930's and constitutionalist England and France at the beginning of the century.

The third factor forwarding state control has been the series of revolutions that put the army in power in Turkey after the Balkan and Greek wars and again last year [1960], and in most of the Arab countries after the Arab-Israeli war and even more recently. For, although it may be true that the pen is mightier than the sword, at a higher level of technology the machine gun and revolver seem to be definitely more powerful than the typewriter and fountain pen, the weapons of the businessman. By and large, the army has found little difficulty in bending the leaders of the economy to its will. Naturally, in doing so it is acting in the belief that state control, with the army in turn controlling the state, is the only means of making the economy work for the general good. But at the same time one can hardly help recalling the statement of Helvétius: "I have never understood the subtle distinctions in the different forms of government. I know only two—the good, which at present do not exist, and the bad, in which the whole art is, by different means, to transfer the money of the governed into the pockets of the ruling class." And what the governed think on the subject is shown by the following story, fresh from a Middle Eastern country. In a crowded bus a man turns to his neighbor:

"Excuse me, sir, are you in the Army?"

"No."

"Do you have a son or a brother in the Army?"

"No."

"Are any of your in-laws in the Army?"

"No."

"Then, curse your father, stop crushing my toes."

The fourth factor is oil. The huge income generated in the oil industry has gone primarily to the government, in the form of royalties and taxes. For the economy of most of the producing countries was so rudimentary that there was little the companies could buy or sell locally, and practically all the private sector gained was the wages and salaries paid to employees of the companies and the income of contractors and suppliers working for the companies. But the governments received huge revenues—about $1.25 billion a year at the present time—and, with much more justification than Louis XIV, many an Arabian ruler can say: "L'Etat c'est moi." Even in Iran and Iraq, where oil is not the only sector of the economy, the public sector has become predominant thanks to the influx of oil revenues.

For the same reason, the inflow of United States, Soviet, British, and German economic aid has strengthened the public sector, since the aid goes, of course, to the governments. And let us not forget that United States aid to the region has totaled over $3 billion, while Soviet credits opened to various Middle Eastern governments are over $1 billion, huge sums by Middle Eastern standards. To this should be added the very large amounts, over $1.5 billion, that have gone to the Israeli public sector in the form of German reparations, transfers by Zionist organizations, and other such remittances.

It may seem ironic that such staunch believers in private enterprise as the United States government, the oil companies, and contributors to United Jewish Appeal have been instrumental in expanding the public sector in the Middle East, but then history has its own, rather wry, sense of humor. And Hegel did make some cryptic remarks about *Die List der Vernunft*.

The expansion of the public sector may be illustrated by two sets of figures: the size of the government budgets relative to gross national product, and the relative shares of the public and private sectors in capital formation. Needless to say, both are highly tentative and are given only in order to illustrate trends and indicate orders of magnitude. In regard to the first, in recent years in the Arabian oil-producing countries, government expenditure has accounted for by far the greater part of GNP, in Iran for about 30 per cent and in Iraq for over 40 per cent. In Lebanon the figure is about 10–12 per cent, in Israel over 25 per cent, and in Turkey under 20 per cent. In the United Arab Republic, the share of the public sector in GNP has greatly risen—according to the 1960–61 estimates it was to be 35–40 per cent in the Syrian region and over 50 per cent in the Egyptian. For purposes of comparison, it should be pointed out that only a dozen years ago in no country except some oil producers was the figure over 20 per cent, and in most it was far lower.

As for the relative shares in new investment, here too the government's contribution has risen very sharply. In the Arabian oil-producing countries practically all investment is being carried out by the government—except of course for the large amounts being invested by the oil companies. In Iran, again excluding oil companies, the government has been accounting for perhaps 60 per cent of new investment and in Iraq for over 70 per cent. In Lebanon private investment accounts for nearly two-thirds of the total, but its share is slowly falling; in Turkey, for a little over half, with the relative shares remaining unchanged for the last decade; and in Israel, for about a half. In the Syrian region of the UAR, the bulk of investment used to come from private sources, but the present Five-Year Plan puts the share of the public sector at 63 per cent. The same shift has occurred in the Egyptian region, where the public sector now probably accounts for some three-quarters of new investment.

One last word in conclusion. I have merely described and analyzed existing trends in the Middle East, without attempting either to project or to evaluate them. As for the projection, I expect more of the same, at least for some years to come. And as for the evaluation, some of these trends would meet with widespread approval, others are far less welcome, and all consist of tangled strands of good and ill. But, after all, our role is to understand, and attempt to live with, these forces, rather than to sit in judgment on them.

For, in the last analysis, it is for the Middle Easterners themselves to decide what form of society suits them best; like other peoples they have the right to make their own mistakes, even if some of these mistakes prove fatal, and it is only from their own experience that they are going to learn the facts of life—although in some cases they may do so posthumously! And neither our approval nor our disapproval is likely to shift them appreciably from their present course.

Reference Material

Weights and Measures

No attempt will be made here to penetrate into what the leading authority on the subject has termed "the chaos" (*das Wirrsal*) of Islamic weights and measures, but only to indicate the approximate value of the ones commonly used in the Arab countries in the nineteenth century. The confusion is attributable partly to local variations and differences in historical and cultural background; partly to the frequent use of the same name to denote very different units, depending on the nature of the commodity in question; and partly to the fact that some weights and measures are based on such units as "a camel load," or "the area of land that can be plowed in a day by a team," or "the area that can be sown with a given amount of grain," and therefore cannot have an exact equivalent in metric or avoirdupois terms. To add to the confusion, in 1882 the Ottoman government decreed that certain units were to designate an equivalent in metric terms, e.g., the oke was to equal one kilogram and the qintar 100 kilograms, but this was ignored in practice.[1]

WEIGHTS

In the Islamic world the standard units of weight were the *dirham* and the *mithqal*. As units of currency these are discussed in Appendix II as the dirham and the dinar. For purposes other than currency, the standard dirham seems to have been 3.125 grams or 48.225 grains, and the mithqal (whose ratio to the dirham was in theory 10:7 and in practice 3:2) 4.464 grams or 68.888 grains.

The other main units, the *uqia*, *ratl*, and *qintar*, correspond very roughly to the ounce (28.35 grams), pound (454 grams), and hundredweight (45.4 kilograms), respectively. The Egyptain uqia equaled 12 dirhams or about 37.5 grams, the Baghdadi $10\frac{5}{6}$ dirhams or 33.9 grams, and the Meccan 27.1 grams. In Syria the uqia had a much higher value: in Damascus it equaled 50 dirhams, or 154.2 grams; in Aleppo 60 dirhams, or 190 grams; in Hama 55 dirhams, or 171.9 grams; in Homs 72 dirhams, or 225 grams; and in Jerusalem $66\frac{2}{3}$ dirhams or 208.3 grams.

The Egyptian *ratl* (often referred to by Europeans as *rottoli*) was equal to 12 uqias (144 dirhams) or 449 grams, i.e., almost exactly 1 pound; however, for certain goods and in particular localities the "large" ratl was used, of 160 dirhams or 500 grams. In Iraq the ratl usually equaled 130 dirhams or 406.3 grams; the same value held in most of Arabia, but in some localities its weight was greater, e.g., in Medina the ratl was equal to 1.5

---

[1] Georges Samné, *La Syrie*, p. 173.

Baghdadi ratls or 609.4 grams. The Syrian ratl, like the uqia, was much larger; its value varied between 800 and 1,017 dirhams, or 2.564 and 3.255 kilograms. The Constantinople ratl equaled 876 dirhams, or 2.8 kilograms.

The *qintar*, or *qantar* (usually referred to by Europeans as *quintal* or *cantar*) was in principle equal to 100 ratls. In Egypt until 1835 it was equal to $43\frac{2}{3}$ okes, i.e., 54.7 kilograms, but after that date it equaled 100 ratls or 36 okes, i.e., 44.9 kilograms or 99 pounds. In Yemen it was equal to 45 okes or 56.25 kilograms. In Syria the most widespread qintar was equal to 100 ratls or 256–288 kilograms, but other values were also used.

Seven other weights may be noted. The *qirat* (*karat*) was in Iraq equal to $\frac{1}{20}$ of a mithqal, or 0.223 grams, and in Egypt, Syria, and parts of Arabia to $\frac{1}{24}$ of a mithqal, or 0.195 grams. The *uqqa* (referred to by Europeans as *okka* or *oke*), a weight widely used in the Ottoman Empire, was equal to 400 dirhams or 1.283 kilograms; in Egypt and in Yemen it was equal to 1.25 kilograms. The *himl*, or camel load, was in principle equal to 244 kilograms but in practice varied widely according to the locality and the nature of the commodity used. The *taghar* and *wazna* were used in Syria and Iraq; in Syria the taghar ranged between 1,280 kilograms (1,000 okes) and 2,000, and in Iraq between 300 and 2,000. In Syria the wazna varied between 30 and 65 kilograms; in Kirkuk and Sulaimaniya it was equal to 100 kilograms, but in Baghdad it varied according to the commodity weighed, e.g., for charcoal it equaled about 50 and for grains and vegetables 78 kilograms. Two other common units of weight in Iraq were the *hugga*, equal to 2 pounds 3 ounces or almost exactly one kilogram, and the *maund*. For imported goods the latter had a constant value of 6 huggas, or about 6 kilograms, but for local produce it varied widely between commodities: thus in Basra it was equal to 4 huggas for soap, 10 for spices and meat, and 60 for vegetables, fruits, rice, flour, wool, and skins.

CAPACITY

The standard Egyptian unit is the *ardabb*, which is at present equal to 198 liters or 5.45 bushels, and therefore corresponds to 150 kilograms of wheat and 140 of maize. In the first half of the nineteenth century it was generally equal to 182 kilograms, but much higher values were also common. The ardabb is subdivided into 12 *kailas*, each equal to 16.5 liters, and 48 large or 96 small *qadahs*, the latter—which is the most common— being equal to 2.06 liters or 3.63 pints. In Syria the main unit was the *kaila*, or bushel, generally equal to 36–37 liters, but subject to local variations. The *mudd* was equal to half a kaila and the *rub'ia* to a quarter of a mudd. In parts of Arabia the main unit was the *sa'*, equal to 2–5 pints or 1.14–2.84 liters. A unit used exclusively for rice in husk in Egypt is the *dariba*, which is equal to 8 ardabbs and corresponds to about 945 kilograms of rice in husk.

It will be noticed that the above measures refer to grains. Liquids are usually sold by weight, not volume.

LENGTH

The basic unit of length was the *dira'*, or ell (often referred to by foreign writers as *pik* or *pike*), which varied widely according to the locality and the nature of the object being measured. In Egypt the most commonly used dira' was about 58 centimeters, but the *Constantinople dira'* of 69 centimeters and the *dira' mi'mari* of 75 centimeters were also used; in Iraq the most common values were 75–80 centimeters, and in Syria 75–76 centimeters with local variations of 63 in Damascus, 68 in Aleppo, and 65 in Jerusalem. The dira' was divided into 24 usba's (or fingers), whose length varied with that of the dira'. The Egyptian *qasaba* (rod) was equal to 3.99 meters, or slightly less, until 1813 when Muhammad Ali reduced it to 3.55 meters (see below). Long distances were measured in *mil* (mile), of 4,000 standard dira's of 54 centimeters, or about 2 kilometers. The *farsakh* (Persian *parasang*) was equal to 3 mils, or 6 kilometers.

AREA

The standard measure of area in Egypt is the *faddan*. Until the nineteenth century it was equal to 400 square qasabas or 6,368 square meters but, following the 1813–14 cadaster, Muhammad Ali reduced it to $333\frac{1}{3}$ square qasabas, and since the length of the latter was also reduced (see above), the faddan became equal to 4,201 square meters, or just over one acre. The Egyptian faddan is divided into 24 *qirats* of 175 square meters, which are subdivided into 24 *sahms* of 7.29 square meters each.

In Syria the term "faddan" had widely different connotations. In some regions it was defined as the area that could be plowed in a day by a team, or about a quarter to a third of a hectare.[2] In others it designated the area seeded with 500 okes of wheat plus 700 okes of barley, or, say, 27.5 hectares, depending on the nature of the terrain and soil;[3] other values, of 11–18 hectares, and 0.07 hectares, are also given in other sources.[4] A more uniform unit was the *donum* (Arabic *dunum*), defined as 1,600 square dira's or 919 square meters. In Iraq however, the donum, or *mishara* as it is more commonly known, is equal to 0.25 of a hectare or 0.618 of an acre. Another measure, peculiar to southern Iraq, is the *jarib*, which designates the area covered by 100 palm trees, or about 0.92 of an acre.

In recent years metric weights and measures have been displacing the traditional ones in the more advanced countries of the region. Moreover some of the older units have been standardized, on a metric basis. Thus, since the 1920's, the donum has been equal to 1,000 square meters in Lebanon, Syria, Palestine, and Jordan, and very recently Egypt has replaced the traditional qintar by a *metric qintar* of 50 kilograms.

(For further details see Great Britain, Admiralty [*Handbook of Mesopotamia*], Great Britain, Admiralty War Staff [*Handbook of Arabia*], and Government of Egypt [*Annuaire statistique*] and works by Hinz, Latron, Cuinet [*Turquie*, Vol. III], and Ruppin listed in the Bibliography.)

[2] André Latron, *La vie rurale en Syrie et au Liban*, p. 12.
[3] Vital Cuinet, *Turquie en Asie*, III, 44.
[4] Noel Verney and Georges Dambmann, *Les Puissances étrangères dans le Levant, en Syrie et en Palestine*, p. 719; Samné, *op. cit.*, p. 173.

Currencies

ARAB COINS

From the first century A.H. (seventh century A.D.) on, the two standard Islamic coins were the gold *dinar* and the silver *dirham*. The dinar was modeled on the Roman solidus, or denarius aureus, and from the time of 'Abd al-Malik (A.D. 685–705) had a weight of 4.25 grams and a fineness of 98 per cent or over. The dirham was modeled on the drachma and, until the third century A.H. (ninth century A.D.), weighed 2.97 grams.

The nominal ratio between the two coins was 1:10 or 1:12, but since gold was relatively scarce, the ratio fell to 1:15, 1:20, 1:30, and occasionally as low as 1:50. In the sixth century A.H. (twelfth century A.D.), the dinar began to disappear in the western half of the Arab world and in the seventh–thirteenth centuries in the eastern half; henceforth it was used only as a unit of account. The dirham survived longer and was the ancestor of the Ottoman and Egyptian coins. However, in the fifth–eleventh centuries, dirhams of base silver or copper were struck; this practice was extended in the following centuries and led to a sharp rise in prices.

OTTOMAN COINS

The standard Ottoman coin, taken over from the Seljuks and modeled on the dirham, was the *akçe*, or "small white one"; it was usually referred to by Europeans as the *asper* or *aspre*, derived from the Greek word for white.

When it was first minted, in A.D. 1327, it had a weight of 6 qirats, or about 1.1 grams, and a fineness of 90 per cent, but both weight and fineness were steadily reduced during the next centuries, with a few interruptions. By the middle of the seventeenth century the weight had fallen to 1.5 qirats and the fineness to 50 per cent. In addition, from the latter part of the sixteenth century, the influx of American silver caused a sharp fall in the value of silver coins relative to gold.

In the meantime the first Ottoman gold coins had been issued, in 1478, under Mehmed II; they were modeled on the Venetian sequin or Austrian ducat, which, together with other European coins, circulated widely in the Empire. Later known as the *şerifi*, they continued to be minted until near the end of the seventeenth century "with but slight variations . . . in their standard weight of 53 grains [3.4 grams] or fineness."[1] The şerifi having been driven out by debased coins minted in North Africa and Egypt, they were called in and, in 1697–1711, replaced by coins with an equivalent weight known

[1] H. A. R. Gibb and H. Bowen, *Islamic Society and the West*, I, Part II, 51.

variously as *tughrali, zencirli, funduqi* or *findikli*. By then the exchange rate of the akçe to the Turkish gold coin had declined from its original value of 40 to 360 in 1691. At the same time a smaller gold coin, weighing about 2.5–2.6 grams, was minted, the *zer-i mahbub.*

The issuing of these gold coins did not, of course, solve the problems caused by the depreciation of the silver akçe, which was the main medium of transaction. Around 1620, therefore, a new silver coin, the *para*, worth at first 4 and subsequently 3 akçes, was struck. And around 1688 another silver coin, the *kuruş*, known to Europeans as the piastre, was introduced. The kuruş was modeled on the European dollars (Austrian thaler, Spanish piastre) but was only two-thirds as heavy. Its original rate was 40 para or 160 akçes; however, when the exchange rate of the para fell from 4 to 3 akçes the kuruş followed, and the rate 1 kuruş = 40 paras = 120 akçes was maintained until the end of the eighteenth century, all three coins depreciating in the same proportion. The same is true of another silver coin introduced at about the same time as the kuruş, the *zolota*, which was equal to 30 paras or three-quarters of a kuruş.[2]

Another seventeenth-century innovation was the *kis* or *kise* (purse), a unit of account. The kise-i Rumi was the equivalent of 50,000 akçes and the kise-i Misri of 25,000 paras or 60,000 akçes, "regardless of the real values of the coins concerned."[3]

Mahmud II's reign saw further rapid depreciation of the currency, owing to both the internal confusion of the Empire and the financial difficulties of the government and to the fact that the large import surplus (see Part II, Introduction) had to be met by transferring bullion or specie abroad. Under Mahmud, "The form and name of the Ottoman coinage was changed 35 times for gold and 37 for silver issues, and the rate of the Turkish piastre or its equivalent to the pound sterling fell from 23 in 1814 to 104 in 1829."[4] The most noteworthy coins introduced were the *beşlik* (5 piastres) in 1810, and the new beşlik in 1829, and the *altilik* (6 piastres) in 1833; all three were short in weight and contained an unduly large proportion of alloy.[5] By this time the kise was reckoned as the equivalent of 500 piastres.

A more important innovation, in 1840, was the issue of paper money in the form of interest-bearing treasury bonds, *kaimeh mu'teberei nakdieh*. Although various attempts were made to withdraw them, new issues continued to swell the total circulation, and heavily to depreciate their value until 1879; between that date and Turkey's entry into the war in 1914, the only paper money in circulation consisted of the notes issued by the Ottoman Bank. During the First World War a total of 144 million Turkish pounds was issued in paper currency, leading to heavy depreciation.

In 1844 the first serious attempt to stabilize the currency was made. The government, with the help of the Ottoman Bank, withdrew the old coins and introduced a bimetallic gold and silver standard, at the ratio of 1:15.909. The new *Turkish pound* was worth 100 kuruş or 18 shillings. But this scheme was wrecked by the continued financial difficulties, aggravated by the Crimean and other wars, the deficit in the balance of trade, the issue of paper money, and the fall in world prices of silver starting in 1860, after a

[2] The akçe continued to be minted until the reign of Mahmud II (1808–39), but its value declined to such a point that it came to be used solely as a conventional unit of account.
[3] Stanford J. Shaw, *The Financial and Administrative Organization and Development of Ottoman Egypt*, p. xxii.
[4] Bernard Lewis, *The Emergence of Modern Turkey*, p. 108.
[5] A. du Velay, *Essai sur l'histoire financière de la Turquie*, pp. 56–57.

stability in relation to gold that had lasted since 1780 and that had greatly facilitated bimetallism everywhere. The Kararnameh (decree) of 1296 A.H. (1880) therefore shifted the currency to the gold standard. The Turkish gold pound of 7.216 grams, 91.65 per cent fineness, equivalent to 18 shillings, or $4.40, was the basic coin. It was subdivided into 100 gold kuruş sagh (known in the Arab provinces as qurush sahih), or sound piastres; however, the latter were used only for official transactions. The main silver coin was the mecidieh (Arabic, majidieh), which was officially equal to 20 kuruş sagh but, since the value of silver had depreciated by some 8 per cent, was worth under 19 kuruş. In an effort to stabilize the rate of exchange of these two coins, the government declared its readiness to receive the mecidieh at 19 piastres, giving an implicit ratio of 105.26 piastres to the pound; but even so it did not succeed in obtaining stability.[6]

Moreover, subsidiary coins whether silver—such as the 2-piastre, 1-piastre and 0.5 piastre—or copper or nickel—such as the beşlik (2.5-piastre), 40-para (1 piastre), 20-para (0.5 piastre), 10-para or metallik, 5-para and 2.5-para—were issued in excess of demand. This meant that their market value fell well below par, and a new unofficial unit came into being, the kuruş çuruk (known in the Arab provinces as qurush mu'ib) or defective piastre; "its value in terms of gold and silver coins varied in different places, and in certain commercial centers it had more than one value, depending upon the goods for which it was used in payment."[7] Thus in Syria in 1914 the Turkish pound exchanged for 123 kuruş çuruk in Tripoli, 124 in Homs, 124.6 in Beirut, 125 in Sidon, and 130.8 in Damascus.[8]

In Syria on the eve of the First World War Turkish gold pounds, which were the medium of exchange for large payments, were supplemented by foreign coins, notably the British sovereign, the French 10- and 20-franc gold pieces, and, to a lesser extent, the Russian ruble. Turkish subsidiary coins were used in small transactions. In Iraq the situation was essentially the same; here, however, the main foreign coins included Iranian ones, such as the gold ashrafi or tuman and the silver kran, and the Indian rupee and anna; the official rate of the tuman was 77.50 piastres, of the kran 3.15 and of the rupee 7.50. Iranian and Indian coins also circulated widely in Arabia. But the most widespread currency in Arabia—still the medium of exchange in Yemen until the year 1963— was the Maria Theresa thaler. In addition, Turkish, British, and French coins were in circulation as were Dutch coins, mainly from the East Indies, in Mecca, Medina, and Jedda. Mention may also be made of "imaginary units of account" used in Hijaz, including the 'umla dollar which was equal to 28 bad piastres.[9]

EGYPTIAN COINS

In the eighteenth century the local gold coin which was most prevalent in Egypt was the zer-i mahbub (see above). The basic silver coin was the para. "This was a direct descendant of the silver muayyadi coin used in the Mamluk Empire in Egypt since Sultan Muayyad and first minted in 818/1415-6, and it was therefore called midi colloquially and medin by Europeans throughout the Ottoman period";[10] it was also

[6] Sa'id Himadeh, Monetary and Banking System of Syria, p. 26.
[7] Sa'id Himadeh, Economic Organization of Syria and Lebanon, p. 263.
[8] Himadeh, Monetary and Banking System, p. 24.
[9] Great Britain, Admiralty War Staff, A Handbook of Arabia, p. 104.
[10] Shaw, op. cit., p. xxii.

known as the *fidda* or *nuss*. The ratio of the para and the akçe fluctuated, a figure of 4 being fairly common. The third unit of account, introduced in the seventeenth century, was the *kise-i Misri*, or Egyptian purse; in Egypt this was worth 25,000 paras or 60,000 akçes, "regardless of the real values of the coins concerned."[11] The absence of any native coin between the zer-i mahbub and the para caused much inconvenience, which Ali Bey (1763–73) tried to remove by minting a *qirsh* (kuruş) of 40 paras and a half-qirsh of 20 paras. Upon his overthrow no more qirsh were minted until 1800, when the French reintroduced them at the former rate of 40 paras. Henceforth accounts were kept in qirsh, para and purses worth 500 qirshs.[12]

However, the gap between the zer-i mahbub and the para was filled mainly by foreign coins, principally the Austrian thaler and the Spanish piastre, which were approximately equal in value.[13] They were known as *rial* or *abu taqa*, referred to as *pataka* or *patak* by European writers. The use of such coins, and subsequently of French and British ones, was greatly promoted by the continued debasement of the local silver currency; thus in 1773 the thaler was worth 90 paras, but by 1798 it was worth 150 and by 1835, 800 paras.[14] Hence foreign merchants increasingly refused to accept Egyptian or Turkish coins in payment for their merchandise and insisted on receiving European currency. Indeed the rial, or abu taqa, became a unit of account in Egypt, along with the para or medin. The above-mentioned depreciation of the para led, however, to a distinction being drawn between the rial as a unit of account equal to 90 paras and the commercial rial, worth several times as much. The rial, or thaler or *tallari* as it was called by Europeans in Egypt, also became the unit in which foreign trade prices were quoted, a practice that has survived to the present day for cotton exports.

In 1835 Muhammad Ali attempted to reform the currency by placing it on a bimetallic standard, at the ratio of 15.5:1. The unit of account was the piastre (P.T.) subdivided into 40 paras; the basic coin was the 20-piastre silver piece, equal to the thaler in silver content and market value (see above), but gold coins of various denominations (5-, 10-, 20-, and 100-piastre) were also issued, as were smaller silver coins.[15] The exchange rate of foreign gold coins was fixed in terms of the piastre, but all were slightly undervalued, thus the pound sterling, which was exchanging at 100 piastres, was officially valued at 97.5; naturally, this drove foreign currency out of circulation.

After 1860 the fall in the price of silver began to disrupt the Egyptian currency, as it did all bimetallic standards. This was aggravated by Ismail's attempt to profit from the situation by issuing large amounts of silver coins and by the strains in Egypt's balance of payments. The ensuing confusion was ended by the reform of 1885, which put Egypt on a gold standard with the Egyptian pound (equal to 100 piastres and 1,000 *'ushr al-qirsh* or *millième*) defined as equal to 8.5 grams of 87.5 per cent fineness. The chief silver coin was the 20-piastre piece, of 28 grams of 83.33 per cent fineness, and various subsidiary coins of silver, nickel, and bronze were also minted. As before, the rates fixed for foreign currencies were below their real values: the pound sterling at 97.5 piastres, the napoleon

[11] *Ibid.*
[12] A. E. Crouchley, *The Economic Development of Modern Egypt*, p. 99.
[13] Turkish coins also circulated in Egypt.
[14] Crouchley, *op. cit.*, p. 97.
[15] However, the continued depreciation of the Turkish currency (see above) soon broke the link between the Turkish and the new Egyptian para.

at 77.15 piastres and the Turkish pound at 87.75 piastres. Since, however, very few Egyptian gold coins (pound and subdivisions) were minted, the vacuum was filled by the least undervalued foreign currency, the pound sterling, which came to account for practically the whole monetary gold stock of Egypt. On the outbreak of the First World War Egypt shifted to a sterling exchange standard, and the link between the Egyptian pound and sterling was maintained until 1947; the par value between the two currencies has not been officially changed, although the Egyptian pound was *de facto* devalued in 1962.

(See also *Encyclopaedia of Islam*, *s.v.* "Akçe," "Dinar," "Dirham," and works by Lewis, Gibb and Bowen, Velay, Himadeh [*Monetary and Banking System of Syria*], 'Azzawi [*Tarikh al-nuqud*], Shaw [*Financial and Administrative Organization ... of Ottoman Egypt*], Lane, and Crouchley [*Economic Development of Modern Egypt*] listed in the Bibliography.)

APPENDIX III

Glossary

(A: Arabic; P: Persian; T: Turkish)

Agha (T): Gentleman, official

Akçe (T): Ottoman coin (see Appendix II)

Amir (A): Commander, prince

Ard al-fallah (A): "Peasant's land," i.e., the part of the *iltizam* assigned to peasants

Ardabb (A): Unit of capacity (see Appendix I)

Bait al-mal (A): Treasury

Bey (T): Rank below that of *pasha*

Cizye (T): *See* Jizia

Çiftlik (T): Farm, estate

Defter (P, T); daftar (A): Government register

Defterdar (P, T): Accountant, chancellor

Derebey (T): "Lords of the Valley," i.e., quasi-independent local rulers

Dira (A): Grazing ground of a particular tribe

Dirham (A): Unit of weight; coin (see Appendixes I and II)

Divan (P, T); diwan (A): Council

Dönme (T): Sect of Jews converted to Islam in seventeenth century

Eyalet (P, T); ayala (A): Name used for Ottoman province until 1864

Faddan (A): Unit of measure (see Appendix I)

Faiz (A): "Surplus," i.e., portion of land tax which the *multazim* was entitled to keep

Ferman (P, T): Order, decree

Firda (A): Impost, levy

Has (T); khass (A): Ottoman crown lands

Hujja (A): Title deed

Iltizam (A): Tax farm granted by government

Iradeh (T); irada (A): Decree

Jizia (A): Poll tax, paid by non-Muslims

Kashif (A): Governor of district or province

Kese, kise (T); kis (A): Purse (see Appendix II)

Kharaj (A): Land tax; in very early Arab and late Ottoman times used as synonym of *jizia*

Kharaji (A): Term used in Egypt to designate *miri* land

Lazma (A): Holding of tribal sheikhs in Iraq

Liva (T); liwa (A): Subprovince; subdivision of *vilayet*

Metrouke (T); matruka (A): "Left," i.e., land reserved for some communal purpose

Mewat (T); mawat (A): "Dead," i.e., uncultivated, land

Miri (A): "Pertaining to the *amir*"; tax; land the ownership of which belongs to the state and the usufruct to the individual

Mugharasa (A): Co-plantation

Mulk (A): Land in absolute freehold ownership

Multezim (T); multazim (A): Tax farmer, holder of *iltizam*

Musha' (A): Communal ownership of land

Muzara'a (A): Crop sharing

Para (T): Ottoman coin (see Appendix II)

Paşa (pasha) (T): Highest Ottoman rank

Qantar, qintar (A): Unit of weight (see Appendix I)

Raqaba (A): Ownership of land, as distinct from usufruct

Rizaq ahbasia (A): Term used in Egypt to designate *waqf*

Ruznameh (P, T): Department of finance

Sanad (A): Document, title deed

Sancak (T): Subdivision of *eyalet*

Saniyya (A): Pertaining to the sultan or king

Sarraf (A): Money changer; tax collector

Şeri (T); shar'i (A): Conforming to *shari'a*

Şaria (T); shari'a (A): Muslim law

Shaikh (A): Elder; chief of tribe, village, guild, or religious order

Sharif (A): Noble; descendant of the Prophet Muhammad

Sipahi (P, T): Cavalryman; holder of *timar* or *ziamet*

Tamattu' (A): Tax on professions

Tanzimat (A, T): Ottoman reform movement of 1839–77

Tapu (T): Land registration; land registration department; a type of land tenure in the nineteenth century

Tasarruf (A): Right to usufruct of land

Timar (T): Ottoman "fief" yielding an annual revenue of under 20,000 akçes

'Ulama (A); singular, 'alim: men learned in religion; Muslim "clergy"

'Ushr (A): "Tenth," i.e., tithe

Vakf (T): *See* Waqf

Vergi (T); werko (A): Tax on land and buildings

Vilayet (T); wilaya (A): Name used for Ottoman province after 1864

Wakil (A): Agent, steward

Waqf (A); plural awqaf: Endowment in favor of religious or charitable institutions

Waqf ahli (A): "Family *waqf*," i.e., one the revenues of which were assigned to the descendants of the donor

Waqf khairi (A): "Charitable *waqf*" i.e., one the revenues of which were assigned to a religious or charitable institution

Wasiya (A): Portion of *iltizam* assigned to tax farmer for his own use

Zakat (A): Alms tax, levied on capital

Ziamet (T); zi'ama (A): Ottoman "fief" yielding 20,000 akçes or more per annum

Selected Bibliography

The following list consists mainly of the books and articles cited in the introductory essays and notes and in the appendixes. Of the sources from which the selections were taken, it includes only those that are cited elsewhere in the volume. Apart from section I, "Reference Works and Bibliographies," this Bibliography is arranged in sections corresponding to the parts of the volume. Since each source is listed only once—in the section most appropriate—but may be cited in several parts of the volume, the reader will sometimes have to search through several sections of the Bibliography to find a particular title. Further references are to be found in the footnotes to the selections. Books marked with an asterisk contain useful bibliographies.

I. REFERENCE WORKS AND BIBLIOGRAPHIES

American School of Classical Studies at Athens. *Voyages and Travels in the Near East made during the XIXth Century.* Princeton, N.J., 1952.

———. *Voyages and Travels in Greece and the Near East and Adjacent Regions Made Previous to the Year 1801.* Princeton, N.J., 1953.

American University of Beirut. *A Post-War Bibliography of the Near Eastern Mandates.* Beirut, 1933–35.

Birge, J. K. *A Guide to Turkish Area Study.* Washington D.C., 1949.

Coult, Lyman H. *An Annotated Research Bibliography of Studies in Arabic, English, and French of the Fellah of the Egyptian Nile, 1798–1955.* Coral Gables, Fla., 1958.

Egypt, Ministry of Finance, Survey Department. *Bibliography of Scientific and Technical Literature Relating to Egypt, 1800–1900.* Cairo, 1915.

Encylopaedia of Islam.

———. New Edition (letters A–G).

Field, Henry. *Bibliography on Southwestern Asia*, Vols. I–VIII. Coral Gables, Fla., 1953–62.

Hill, R. L. *A Bibliography of the Anglo-Egyptian Sudan from the Earliest Times to 1937.* London, 1939.

Hinz, Walther. *Islamische Masse und Gewichte.* Leiden, 1955.

Ibrahim-Hilmy. *The Literature of Egypt and the Soudan, from the Earliest Times to the Year 1885, Inclusive.* London, 1886–88.

Koray, Enver. *Turkiye tarih yayinlari bibliografyasi, 1720–1950.* Ankara, 1952.

Lewis, Bernard, and Holt, P. M. *Historians of the Middle East.* London, 1962.

Library of Congress. *The Arabian Peninsula—A Selected Annotated List of Periodicals, Books, and Articles in English.* Washington, 1951.

Lorin, Henri. *Bibliographie géographique de l'Egypte.* Cairo, 1928.

MacGregor, John. *Commercial Statistics.* London, 1847.

Macro, Eric. *Bibliography of the Arabian Peninsula.* Coral Cables, Fla., 1958.

———. *Bibliography on Yemen.* Coral Gables, Fla., 1961.

Masson, Paul. *Eléments d'une bibliographie française de la Syrie.* Congrès français de la Syrie, 1919.

Maunier, René. *Bibliographie économique, juridique et sociale de l'Egypte moderne (1798–1916).* Cairo, 1918.

Nasri, Abdel Rahman el. *A Bibliography of the Sudan, 1938–1958.* London, 1962.

Patai, Raphael. *Jordan, Lebanon and Syria: An Annotated Bibliography.* New Haven: HRAF, 1957.

Pearson, J. D. *Index Islamicus.* London, 1958.

———. *Index Islamicus Supplement.* London, 1962.

Pratt, Ida A. *Modern Egypt: A List of References to Material in the New York Public Library.* New York, 1929.

Ramzi, Muhammad. *Al-qamus al-jughrafiy li al-bilad al-misriyya.* Cairo, 1953–55.

Thomsen, Peter. *Die Palaestina—Literatur: eine internationale Bibliographie.* Leipzig, 1911–38; Berlin, 1954–58.

Wilson, Sir Arnold. *A Bibliography of Persia.* Oxford, 1930.

II. OTTOMAN EMPIRE AND GENERAL

Belleten, 1937———. Ankara.

Istanbul University, Faculty of Economics, *Revue*, 1939———.

Aktan, Reşat. "Agricultural Policy of Turkey." Ph.D. diss., University of California, 1950.

Anhegger, Robert. *Beiträge zur Geschichte des Bergbaus im Osmanischen Reich.* Istanbul, 1943–45.

Archiv für Wirtschaftsforschung im Orient. Berlin, 1916–18.

Bailey, Frank Edgar. *British Policy and the Turkish Reform Movement.* Cambridge, Mass., 1942.

Banse, E. *Die Türkei.* Brunswick, 1915.

Barkan, Omer Lutfi. *Çiftciyi Topraklandirma Kanunu*, Istanbul, 1946.

Belin, F. A. "Essai sur l'histoire économique de la Turquie," *Journal Asiatique*, 1864.

———. "Etude sur la propriété foncière en pays musulman et spécialement en Turquie," *ibid.*, 1861–62.

Blaisdell, D. C. *European Financial Control in the Ottoman Empire.* New York, 1929.

Bonné, Alfred. *State and Economics in the Middle East.* London, 1948.

Brooks, Jerome E. *The Mighty Leaf.* Boston, 1952.

Bruck, W. F. *Die türkische Baumwollwirtschaft.* Jena, 1919.

Bursal, Nasuhi. *Die Einkommenssteurreform in der Türkei.* Winterthur, 1953.

*Chapman, Maybelle. *Great Britain and the Bagdad Railway.* Northampton, Mass., 1948.

Cuinet, Vital. *Turquie en Asie.* Paris, 1896.

*Davison, Roderic. *Reform in the Ottoman Empire.* Princeton, 1963.

Earle, E. M. *Turkey, the Great Powers, and the Baghdad Railway.* New York, 1923.

Engelhardt, E. *La Turquie et le Tanzimat.* Paris, 1882-84.

Farley, J. L. *The Resources of Turkey.* London, 1862.

Fisher, S. (ed.). *Ottoman Land Laws.* London, 1919.

Galante, Abraham. *Histoire des Juifs d'Anatolie.* Istanbul, 1937.

——. *Histoire des Juifs d'Istanbul.* Istanbul, 1941-42.

*Gibb, H. A. R., and Bowen, H. *Islamic Society and the West.* London, 1950.

Gordon, Leland James. *American Relations with Turkey, 1830-1930.* Philadelphia, 1932.

Grothe, H. *Türkisch-Asien und seine Wirtschaftswerte.* Frankfurt, 1916.

Günyüz, Süleyman. *Entwicklung und Bedeutung dem Tabakproduktion in der Türkei.* Istanbul, 1951.

Hallauer, J. (ed.). *Das Türkische Reich.* Berlin, 1918.

Hecker, M. "Die Eisenbahnen in der asiatischen Türkei," *Archiv für Eisenbahnwesen* (Berlin), Vol. XXXVII (1914).

*Hershlag, Z. Y. *Introduction to the Modern Economic History of the Middle East.* Leiden, 1964.

——. *Turkey: An Economy in Transition.* The Hague, 1960.

*Hoskins, H. L. *British Routes to India.* London, 1928.

Hourani, A. H. *Minorities in the Arab World.* London, 1947.

Hüber, R. *Die Bagdadbahn.* Berlin, 1943.

Hurewitz, J. C. *Diplomacy in the Near and Middle East.* Princeton, 1956.

Hüsrev, Ismail. *Turkiye Koy iktisadi.* Ankara, 1934.

Inalcik, Halil. "Land Problems in Turkish History," *Muslim World* (Hartford, Conn.), 1955.

——. "Tanzimat nedir'," *Tarih araştimarli.* Ankara, 1941.

Issawi, Charles. "The Arab World's Heavy Legacy," *Foreign Affairs* (New York), April, 1965.

——. "Economic Growth in the Arab World since 1800: Some Observations," *Middle East Economic Papers* (Beirut), 1964.

*Issawi, C., and Yeganeh, M. *The Economics of Middle Eastern Oil.* New York, 1962.

Junge, R. *Die deutsch-türkischen Wirtschaftsbeziehungen.* Weimar, 1916.

Kahyaoglou, H. S. *Le tabac turc et son importance économique.* Fribourg, 1937.

Karal, Enver Ziya. *Osmanli imparatorlugunda ilk nufus sayimi, 1831.* Ankara, 1943.

Karamursal, Ziya. *Osmanli mali tarihi hakkinda tetkikler.* Ankara, 1940.

*Karpat, K. H. *Turkey's Politics: The Transition to a Multi-Party System.* Princeton, 1959.

[Kay, J. E.] de. *Sketches of Turkey in 1831 and 1832.* New York, 1833.

*Lewis, Bernard. *The Emergence of Modern Turkey.* London, 1961.

Longrigg, S. H. *Oil in the Middle East.* London, 1961.

Mantran, R. *Istanbul dans la seconde moitié du XVIIe siècle.* Paris, 1962.

Masson, Paul. *Histoire du commerce français dans le Levant au XVIIIe siècle.* Paris, 1911.

*Mears, E. G. (ed.). *Modern Turkey.* New York, 1924.

Moltke, Helmut von. *Briefe über Zustände und Begebenheiten in der Türkei.* Berlin, 1891.

Morawitz, Charles. *Les Finances de Turquie,* Paris, 1902.

Novichev, A. D. *Ocherki ekonomiki Turtsii.* Moscow-Leningrad, 1937.

Nuss, 'Izzat al-. *Ahwal al-sukkan fi al-'alam al-'arabi.* Cairo, 1955.

Ohsson, Mouradgea, Ignatius, d'. *Tableau général de l'Empire Othoman.* Paris, 1790.

Oppenheim, Baron M. von. *Vom Mittelmeer zum Persischen Golf.* Berlin, 1899-1900.

Padel, W., and Steeg, L. *La Législation foncière ottomane,* Paris, 1904.

Philippson, A. *Das türkische Reich,* Weimar, 1915.

Philips, E. B. *Der türkische Tabak.* Munich, 1927.

Pressel, W. von. *Les chemins de fer de Turquie.* Zurich, 1902.

Puryear, Vernon John. *International Economics and Diplomacy in the Near East.* Stanford, 1935.

Renner, R. *Der Aussenhandel der Türkei vor dem Weltkriege.* Berlin, 1919.

Rohrbach, P. *Die Bagdadbahn.* Berlin, 1902.

Roumani, A. *Essai historique et technique sur la dette publique ottomane.* Paris, 1927.

Rozaliev, Yu. N. *Osobennosti Razvitiya kapitalizma v Turtsii.* Moscow, 1962.

Saint-Yves, G. *Les chemins de fer français dans la Turquie d'Asie.* Paris, 1914.

Sanjian, Avedis. *The Armenian Communities in Syria under Ottoman Domination.* Cambridge, Mass. 1964.

Schaefer, C. A. *Ziele und Wege für die jungtürkische Wirtschaftspolitik.* Karlsruhe, 1913.

Scherka, B. *The Turkish Mining Regulations.* Constantinople, 1917.

Schmidt, H. *Das Eisenbahnwesen in der asiatischen Türkei.* Berlin, 1914.

Senior, N. W. *Journal Kept in Turkey and Greece in the Autumn of 1857 and the Beginning of 1858.* London, 1859.

Slade, A. *Record of Travels in Turkey, Greece, etc. . . . in the Years 1829, 1830, and 1831.* London, 1832.

Shwadran, Benjamin. *The Middle East, Oil, and the Great Powers.* New York, 1959.

Testa, I. de. *Recueil des traités de la Porte ottomane. . . .* Paris, 1864-1901.

Tosbi, S. *Anonim Şirket,* Ankara, 1943.

Ubicini, Abdolonyme, and Pavet de Courteille, A. J. *Etat présent de l'Empire ottoman.* 1876.

Ubicini, M. A. *Letters on Turkey.* Translated by Lady Easthope. London, 1856.

Ulgener, S. *Iktisadi Inhitat Tarihimizin Ahlak ve Zihniyet Meseleleri.* Istanbul, 1951.

United Nations, Food and Agricultural Organization, Center on Land Problems in the Near East, Salahuddin, Iraq. Papers and Reports. October, 1955.

Urquhart, David. *Turkey. . . .* London, 1833.

Velay, A. du. *Essai sur l'histoire financière de la Turquie.* Paris, 1903.

*Ward, Robert E., and Rustow, Dankwart A. *Political Modernization in Japan and Turkey.* Princeton, 1964.

Warriner, Doreen. *Land and Poverty in the Middle East.* London, 1948.

———. *Land Reform and Development in the Middle East.* Oxford, 1957.

Webster, D. E. *The Turkey of Ataturk,* Philadelphia, 1939.

Wolf, John Baptist. *The Diplomatic History of the Bagdad Railroad.* Columbia, Mo., 1936.

Wood, Alfred Cecil. *A History of the Levant Company.* London, 1935.

Yeniay, Hakki. *Osmanli borçlari tarihi.* Ankara, 1936.

Young, G. *Corps de droit ottoman.* Oxford, 1905-6.

III. IRAQ

*Adams, Doris. *Iraq's People and Resources.* Berkeley, 1958.

Adams, Robert McC. *Land behind Baghdad.* Chicago, 1965.

Ainsworth, W. F. *Personal Narrative of the Euphrates Expedition.* London,

Ali, Hassan Mohammad. *Land Reclamation and Settlement in Iraq.* Baghdad, 1955.

Andrew, W. P. *Memoir of the Euphrates Valley Route to India*. London, 1857.

'Azzawi, Abbas al-. *Tarikh al-nuqud al-'Iraqia*. Baghdad, 1958.

———. *Tarikh al-daraib al-'Iraqia*. Baghdad, 1959.

Buckingham, J. S. *Travels in Mesopotamia*. London, 1827.

———. *Travels in Assyria, Media, and Persia*. London, 1830.

Buckley, A. B. *Mesopotamia as a Country of Future Development*. Cairo, 1919.

Chesney, F. R. *The Expedition for the Survey of the Rivers Euphrates and Tigris*. London, 1850.

———. *Narrative of the Euphrates Expedition*. London, 1868.

Chiha, M. *La Province de Baghdad*. Cairo, 1900.

Dowson, E. *Enquiry into Land Tenure*. Letchworth, 1931.

Foster, Sir William. *The English Factories in India*. London, 1906–27.

*Gharaybeh, Abd al-Karim. *Al-'Iraq wa al-jazira al-'Arabiya fi al-'ahd al-'Uthmani*. Damascus, 1960.

Great Britain, Admiralty, Intelligence Division. *Handbook of Mesopotamia*. London, 1916–17.

Great Britain, Colonial Office. *Report to the League of Nations, 1922–32*.

Great Britain, Foreign Office, Historical Section, "Peace Handbooks," Vol. II: *Arabia, Mesopotamia*, etc. London, 1919.

Haddad, Ezra S., and Fishman, Priscilla. *History Round the Clock: The Jews of Iraq*. Tel Aviv, 1952.

Haider, Saleh. "Land Problems of Iraq." Thesis, London University, 1942.

Hall, L. J. *Inland Water Transport in Mesopotamia*. London, 1921.

Hammond, F. D. *Report on the Railways of Iraq*. London, 1927.

Hasan, M. "Foreign Trade in the Economic Development of Iraq, 1869–1939," Thesis, Oxford University, 1958.

Himadeh, Sa'id. *Al-nizam al-iqtisadi fi al 'Iraq*. Beirut, 1938.

I.B.R.D. (International Bank for Reconstruction and Development). *The Economic Development of Iraq*. Baltimore, 1952.

Ionides, Michael. *The Régime of the Rivers Euphrates and Tigris*. London, 1937.

Iraq Government, Directorate General of Irrigation. *Report on the Control of the Rivers of Iraq* . . . ("Haigh Report"). Baghdad, 1951.

Jamil, M. Husayn. *Siyasat al-'Iraq al-tijariya*. Cairo, 1949.

Kemball, Sir A. *Reports on the Trade of Baghdad and Basrah*. Great Britain, *Parliamentary Papers*, 1867, Vol. LXVII.

Lanzoni, A. *Il Nuovo regime turco e l'avvenire della Mesopotamia*. Rome, 1912.

*Longrigg, S. H. *Four Centuries of Modern Iraq*. Oxford, 1925.

*———. *Iraq 1900 to 1950*. Oxford, 1953.

Mahmud, Abd al-Majid. *Al-masarif fi al-'Iraq*. Baghdad, 1942.

Olivier, G. A. *Voyage dans l'Empire ottoman, l'Egypte, et la Perse*. Paris, 1807.

Rich, C. J. *Narrative of a Residence in Koordistan*. London, 1836.

Rousseau, J. B. *Voyage de Bagdad à Alep, 1808*. Paris, 1899.

Saleh, Zaki. *Mesopotamia (Iraq) 1600–1914*. Baghdad, 1957.

Salter, Lord. *The Development of Iraq*. Baghdad, 1955.

Sousa, Ahmed. *Iraq Irrigation Handbook*. Baghdad, 1944.

Willcocks, Sir William. *The Irrigation of Mesopotamia*. London, 1911.

IV. SYRIA

Aswad, Ibrahim al-. *Dalil Lubnan.* Ba'abda, 1906.

Auhagen, Hubert. *Beiträge zur Kenntnis der Landesnatur und der Landwirtschaft Syriens.* Berlin, 1907.

Bazantay, P. *L'artisannat à Antioche.* Beirut, 1932.

Béchara, E. *Les industries en Syrie et au Liban.* Cairo, 1922.

Berkengeim, A. M. *Sovremennoe ekonomicheskoe polozhenie Sirii i Palestiny.* Moscow, 1897.

Bowring, John. "Report on the Commercial Statistics of Syria," Great Britain, *Parliamentary Papers,* 1840, Vol. XXI.

Burckhardt, J. L. *Travels in Syria and the Holy Land.* London, 1822.

Burns, Norman. *The Tariff of Syria.* Beirut, 1933.

Cardon, Louis. *Le régime de la propriété foncière en Syrie et au Liban.* Paris, 1932.

Carruthers, Douglas. *The Desert Route to India.* London, 1929.

Charles-Roux, F. *Les Echelles de Syrie et de la Palestine au XVIIIe siècle.* Paris, 1928.

Chevallier, Dominique. "Aux origines des troubles agraires libanais en 1858," *Annales* (Paris), January, 1956.

Churchill, Charles H. S. *The Druzes and the Maronites under Turkish Rule from 1840 to 1860.* London, 1862.

Cuinet, Vital. *Syrie, Liban et Palestine.* Paris, 1896.

Ducousso, Gaston. *L'industrie de la soie en Syrie.* Paris, 1913.

Elefteriades, Eleuthère. *Les chemins de fer en Syrie et au Liban.* Beirut, 1944.

Farley, J. L. *Two Years in Syria.* London, 1858.

*Gharaybeh, Abd al-Karim. *Suriya fi al-qarn al tasi' 'ashar.* Damascus, 1962.

Granott, A. *The Land System in Palestine.* London, 1952.

*Grant, Christina Phelps. *The Syrian Desert.* London, 1937.

Great Britain, Admiralty, Naval Intelligence Division. *A Handbook of Syria.* London, 1920.

Guys, Henry. *Beyrout et le Liban.* Paris, 1850.

———. *Relation d'un séjour de plusieurs années à Beyrout et dans le Liban.* Paris, 1847.

———. *Statistique du Pachalik d'Alep.* Marseilles, 1853.

Hasani, Ali al-. *Tarikh Suriya al iqtisadi.* Damascus, 1342. A.H. (1924).

Himadeh, Sa'id. *Monetary and Banking System of Syria.* Beirut, 1935.

*———. *The Economic Organization of Syria and Lebanon.* Beirut, 1936.

*———. *Economic Organization of Palestine.* Beirut, 1938.

Houry, C. B. *De la Syrie considérée sous la rapport commercial.* Paris, 1842.

Huvelin, Paul. "Que vaut la Syrie?" *L'Asie française* (Paris), 1921.

I.B.R.D. (International Bank for Reconstruction and Development). *The Economic Development of Syria.* Baltimore, 1955.

Ismail, Adel. *Histoire du Liban.* Vol. I, Paris, 1955. Vol. IV, Beirut, 1958.

Ismail, Haqqi, *et al. Lubnan.* Beirut, 1906.

Kerr, Malcolm. *Lebanon in the Last Years of Feudalism.* Beirut, 1959.

Latron, André. *La vie rurale en Syrie et au Liban.* Beirut, 1936.

Lortet, Louis. *La Syrie d'aujourd'hui.* Paris, 1884.

Mantran, R., and Sauvaget, J. *Règlements fiscaux ottomans: les provinces syriennes.* Paris, 1951.

Medawar, Wady. *La Syrie agricole*. Beauvais and Paris, 1903.

Michaud, Joseph, and Poujoulat, Jean. *Correspondance d'Orient*. Brussels, 1841.

Monicault, Jacques de. *Le Port de Beyrouth et l'économie des pays du Levant sous mandat français*. Paris, 1936.

Poliak, A. N. *Feudalism in Egypt, Syria, Palestine and the Lebanon*. London, 1939.

*Polk, William. *The Opening of South Lebanon*. Cambridge, Mass., 1963.

Qoudsi, Elia. "Notices sur les Corporations de Damas." *Actes du Sixième Congrès international des Orientalistes*. Leiden, 1884.

Ruppin, A. *Syrien als Wirtschaftsgebiet*. Beihefte zum Tropenpflanzen, Vol. XVI, No. 3/5. Berlin, 1916.

Rustum, Asad. *A Calendar of State Papers* . . . (in Arabic). Beirut, 1940–43.

————. *Materials for a Corpus* . . . (in Arabic). Beirut, 1930–34.

Safa, Elie. *L'émigration libanaise*. Beirut, 1960.

Samné, Georges. *La Syrie*. Paris, 1921.

Sauvaget, Jean. *Alep*. Paris, 1941.

Tower, Allen. *The Oasis of Damascus*. Beirut, 1935.

Urquhart, D. *The Lebanon (Mount Souria): A History and a Diary*. London, 1860.

Verney, Noel, and Dambmann, Georges. *Les Puissances étrangères dans le Levant, en Syrie et en Palestine*. Paris, 1900.

Weulersse, J. *Paysans de Syrie et du Proche Orient*. Paris, 1946.

v. Arabia

Aitchison, C. N. *A Collection of Treaties, Engagements and Sanads, relating to India and Neighbouring Countries*. Calcutta, 1909.

*Apelt, Fritz. *Aden*. Grossenhain, 1929.

Arabian American Oil Company. *Aramco Handbook*. 1960.

Bent, T. *Southern Arabia*. London, 1900.

Bodianskii, V. L. *Bakhrein*. Moscow, 1962.

Botta, Paul-Emile. *Voyage dans l'Yemen*. Paris, 1880.

Brauer, Erich. *Ethnologie der jemenitischen Juden*. Heidelberg, 1934.

Burckhardt, J. L. *Notes on the Bedouins and Wahabys*. . . . London, 1831.

————. *Travels in Arabia*. London, 1829.

Burton, Sir Richard. *Personal Narrative of a Pilgrimage to al-Madinah and Meccah*. London, 1898.

Bury, G. Wyman. *Arabia Infelix*. London, 1915.

Coupland, Reginald. *East Africa and Its Invaders*. Oxford, 1938.

Deutsch, Robert. *Der Yemen*. Vienna, 1914.

Great Britain, Admiralty War Staff. *A Handbook of Arabia*. London, 1916.

Great Britain. Naval Intelligence Division. *Western Arabia and the Red Sea*. Geographical Handbook Series. London, 1946.

————. *Iraq and the Persian Gulf*. London, 1944.

————. *Accounts and Papers*, 1912–13, Vol. C, "Report on Trade of Jeddah."

Grohmann, Adolf. *Südarabien als Wirtschaftsgebiet*. Vienna, 1922.

Guarmani, Carlo. *Northern Najd*. London, 1938.

Hamzah, Fuad. *Qalb jazirat al-'arab*. Cairo, 1933.

Hay, Sir Rupert. *The Persian Gulf States*. Washington, 1959.

Hickinbotham, Sir Tom. *Aden*. London, 1958.

*Hourani, George. *Arab Seafaring in the Indian Ocean*. Princeton, 1951.

*Human Relations Area Files. "Southern Arabia." New Haven, 1956.

*———. "Eastern Arabia." New Haven, 1956.

Hunter, F. M. *An Account of the British Settlement of Aden in Arabia*. London, 1877.

Ingrams, Doreen. *Economic and Social Conditions in the Aden Protectorate*. Asmara, 1950.

*Kammerer, A. *La mer rouge, l'Abyssinie et l'Arabie depuis l'antiquité*. Cairo, 1929.

Kelly, J. B. *Eastern Arabian Frontiers*. New York, 1964.

Kuwait Oil Company. *The Story of Kuwait*. London, 1959.

Lawrence, T. E. *The Seven Pillars of Wisdom*. London, 1926.

*Lipsky, George A. (ed.). *Saudi Arabia*. New Haven, 1959.

Lorimer, J. G. *Gazetteer of the Persian Gulf*. Calcutta, 1908–15.

Manzoni, R. *El Yemen*. Rome, 1884.

Miles, S. B. *The Countries and Tribes of the Persian Gulf*. London, 1919.

Montagne, Robert. *La Civilisation du désert*. Paris, 1947.

Mukhtar, Salah al-Din al-. *Tarikh al-mamlakah al-'arabia al su'udia*. Cairo, 1960.

Musil, Alois. *In the Arabian Desert*. New York, 1930.

———. *Arabia Deserta*. New York, 1927.

———. *Manners and Customs of the Rwala Bedouins*. New York, 1928.

———. *Northern Negd*. New York, 1928.

Nallino, Carlo Alfonso. *L'Arabia Saudiana*. Rome, 1939.

Niebuhr, Carsten. *Description de l'Arabie*. Amsterdam and Utrecht, 1774.

———. *Voyage en Arabie et en d'autres pays circonvoisins*. Amsterdam, 1776.

Palgrave, William Gifford. *Narrative of a Year's Journey through Central and Eastern Arabia*. London and Cambridge, 1865.

Pelly, L. "Remarks on the Tribes, Trade and Resources . . . Persian Gulf," *Transactions of the Bombay Geographical Society*, Vol. XVII (1863).

Philby, H. St. J. *Arabian Jubilee*. New York, 1953.

———. *Saudi Arabia*. London, 1955.

———. *Arabian Oil Ventures*. Washington, D.C., 1964.

*Proshin, N. I. *Saudovskaya Aravia*. Moscow, 1964.

Rihani, Amin. *Muluk al-'arab*. Beirut, 1929.

———. *Maker of Modern Arabia*. Boston and New York, 1928.

Sanger, Richard H. *The Arabian Peninsula*. Ithaca, N.Y., 1954.

*Serjeant, Robert. *The Portuguese off the South Arabian Coast*. Oxford, 1963.

Snouck Hurgronje, Christian. *Mekka*. The Hague, 1888–89.

———. *Verspreide Geschriften*. Bonn–Leipzig, 1923.

Sykes, Percy. *A History of Persia*. London, 1921.

Tarsisi, Adnan. *Al-Yaman wa hadarat al-'Arab*. Beirut, 1963.

Twitchell, K. S. *Saudi Arabia*. Princeton, 1958.

Vidal, L. S. *The Oasis of al-Hasa*. Aramco, 1955.

Villiers, Alan. *Sons of Sindbad*. New York, 1940.

Wahbah, Hafiz. *Jazirat al-'arab fi al-qarn al-'ishrin*. Cairo, 1961.

*Wilson, Sir Arnold T. *The Persian Gulf: An Historical Sketch . . .* Oxford, 1928.

Zehme, A. *Arabien und die Araber seit 100 Jahren*. Halle, 1875.

VI. EGYPT

Report by H.M.'s Agent and Consul-General on The Finances . . . 1880–1920.

L'Egypte contemporaine (Cairo), 1910——.

Annuaire Statistique, 1873 and 1910——.

Abu-Lughod, Janet. "Tale of Two Cities: The Origins of Modern Cairo," *Comparative Studies in Society and History.* (The Hague), July, 1965.

*Arminjon, Pierre. *La situation économique et financière de l'Egypte, le Soudan égyptien.* Paris, 1911.

Artin, Yaqub. *The Right of Landed Property in Egypt.* Translated by E. A. van Dyck. London, 1885.

Atsamba, F. M. "Sostoyanie promishlennosti," in V. B. Lutskii (ed.), *Ocherki po istorii arabskikh stran.* Moscow, 1959.

*Baer, Gabriel. *A History of Landownership in Modern Egypt.* London, 1962.

———. *Egyptian Guilds in Modern Times.* Jerusalem, 1964.

Barois, J. *Les irrigations en Egypte.* Paris, 1911.

Bowring, John. "Report on Egypt and Candia," in Great Britain, *Parliamentary Papers,* 1840, Vol. XXI.

Brown, Robert Hanbury. *History of the Barrage at the Head of the Delta of Egypt.* Cairo, 1896.

Campbell, Patrick. "Report on Egypt" dated July 6, 1840, Great Britain, Foreign Office, Archives 78, vol. 408.

Cattaui, René. *Le règne de Mohamed Ali d'après les archives russes en Egypte.* Vol. I, Cairo, 1931; Vol. II, Rome, 1933 and 1935; Vol. III, Rome, 1936.

Charles-Roux, François. *Autour d'une route, l'Angleterre, l'Isthme de Suez et l'Egypte au XVIIIème siècle.* Paris, 1922.

———. *L'isthme et le canal de Suez.* Paris, 1901.

———. *La production de coton en Egypte.* Paris, 1908.

Clerget, Marcel. *Le Caire: Etude de géographie urbaine et d'histoire économique.* Paris, 1934.

Clot, A. B. *Aperçu général sur l'Egypte.* 2 Vols. Paris, 1840.

Cressaty, Comte de. *L'Egypte d'aujourd'hui.* Paris, 1912.

Cromer, Earl of. *Modern Egypt.* New York, 1908.

Crouchley, A. E. *The Economic Development of Modern Egypt.* London, 1938.

———. *The Investment of Foreign Capital in Egyptian Companies and Public Debt.* Cairo, 1934.

Deny, Jean. *Sommaire des archives turques du Caire.* Cairo, 1930.

Description de l'Egypte, état moderne. Paris, 1809–22.

Douin, Georges. *La mission du Baron de Boislecomte; L'Egypte et la Syrie en 1833.* Cairo, 1927.

———. *Histoire du règne du Khédive Ismail.* Rome, 1933–39.

Duhamel, Colonel. *Tableau statistique de l'Egypte en 1837.* St. Petersburg, 1847.

L'Egypte: aperçu historique et géographique. Cairo, 1926.

Fahmy, Moustafa. *La révolution de l'industrie en Egypte et ses conséquences sociales au 19ᵉ siècle (1800–1850).* Leiden, 1954.

Foaden, G. P., and Fletcher, F. *Egyptian Agriculture.* Cairo, 1910.

Fridman, L. A. *Kapitalisticheskoe razvitie Yegipta.* Moscow, 1963.

Gliddon, G. R. *A Memoir on the Cotton of Egypt.* London, 1841.

Gritly, A. A. I. al-. "The Structure of Modern Industry in Egypt," *L'Egypte contemporaine*, 1942.

Giritli, Ali al-. *Tarikh al-sina'a fi Misr.* Cairo, [1952].

*Hallberg, C. W. *The Suez Canal.* New York, 1931.

Hamont, P. N. *L'Egypte sous Mehémet-Ali.* Paris, 1843.

Hamza, Abdel Maqsud. *The Public Debt of Egypt, 1854–1867.* Cairo, 1944.

Hanotaux, Gabriel (ed.). *Histoire de la nation égyptienne.* Paris, 1931–40.

Hassanaine al-Besumee. *Egypt under Mohammad Aly Basha.* London, 1838.

*Hitta, Ahmad Ahmad. *Tarikh al-zira'ah al-misria fi 'ahd Muhammad 'Ali.* Cairo, 1950.

Hunayn, Jirjis. *Al-atyan wa al-daraib fi al-qutr al-misri.* Cairo, 1904.

*Issawi, Charles. *Egypt: An Economic and Social Analysis.* London, 1947.

*———. *Egypt at Mid-Century: An Economic Survey.* London, 1954.

———. *Egypt in Revolution.* London, 1963.

Landes, David. *Bankers and Pashas.* Cambridge, Mass., 1958.

Lane, Edward William. *The Manners and Customs of the Modern Egyptians.* London, 1944.

Linant de Bellefonds, M. A. *Mémoires sur les principaux travaux d'utilité publique éxécutés en Egypte.* Paris, 1872–73.

McCoan, J. C. *Egypt As It Is.* New York, 1882.

*Marlowe, John. *World Ditch.* New York, 1964.

Mazuel, Jean. *Le sucre en Egypte.* Cairo, 1937.

Mengin, Félix. *Histoire sommaire de l'Egypte sous le gouvernement de Mohamed Ali (1823–1838).* Paris, 1839.

Mouelhy, Ibrahim el. "L'enregistrement de la propriété foncière en Egypte durant l'occupation française," *Bulletin de l'Institut d'Egypte*, 1949, pp. 187–228.

Mubarak, Ali. *Al-khitat al-tawfiqia.* Cairo, 1306 A.H. (1888).

Owen, Roger. "The Influence of Lord Cromer's Indian Experience on British Policy in Egypt," *St. Antony's Papers, No. 17.* London, 1965.

Polites, Athanasios G. *L'hellénisme et l'Egypte moderne.* Paris, 1930.

Pyritz, Karl. *Die Volkwirtschaftliche Entwicklungstendenz im Aegypten und im englisch-aegyptischen Sudan.* Berlin, 1912.

Rafi'i, 'Abd al-Rahman al-. *Tarikh al-harakah al-qawmiyah.* Cairo, 1929.

———. *'Asr Isma'il.* Cairo, 1932.

———. *Misr wa al-Sudan.* Cairo, 1948.

———. *Al-thawra al-'Urabia.* Cairo, 1937.

Rivlin, Helen A. *The Agricultural Policy of Muhammad Ali in Egypt.* Cambridge, Mass., 1961.

Rothstein, T. *Egypt's Ruin.* London, 1910.

Sami, Amin. *Taqwim al-Nil.* Cairo, 1928.

Senior, Nassau. *Conversations and Journals in Egypt and Malta.* London, 1882.

Shafi'i, Ali al-. *Al ashghal al-'amma al-kubra fi 'ahd Muhammad 'Ali.* Cairo, n.d.

Shaw, Stanford J. *Ottoman Egypt in the Age of the French Revolution.* Cambridge, Mass., 1964.

*———. *The Financial and Administrative Organization and Development of Ottoman Egypt.* Princeton, 1962.

*Shukri, Muhammad Fuad. *Bina dawlat Muhammad Ali.* Cairo, 1948.

Societé égyptienne d'économie politique. *Buhuth al-'id al-Khamsini.* Cairo, 1960.

Voisin, Bey. *Le canal de Suez*. Paris, 1902–6.
Wiener, L. *L'Egypte et ses chemins de fer*. Brussels, 1932.
Wilkinson, Sir Gardner. *Modern Egypt and Thebes*. London, 1843.
Willcocks, W., and Craig, J. I. *Egyptian Irrigation*. London, 1889.
Wilson, Sir Arnold T. *The Suez Canal*. London, 1933.
Wright, A. *Twentieth Century Impressions of Egypt*. London, 1909.

VII SUDAN

Reports by H.M.'s Agent and Consul-General on the Finances, Administration and Condition of Egypt and the Soudan. 1898–1913.
Reports on the Finances, Administration and Conditions of the Soudan. 1921–52.
Sudan Notes and Records. Khartoum, 1918——.
Abbas, Mekki. *The Sudan Question*. London, 1952.
'Abd al-Jalil al-Shatir. *Ma'alim tarikh Sudan wadi al-Nil*. Cairo, 1955.
Allen, Bernard M. *Gordon and the Sudan*. London, 1931.
Ani, Khattab al-. "The Gezira Scheme in the Sudan." Ph.D. dissertation. Columbia University, 1959.
Anchieri, E. *Storia della politica inglese nel Sudan (1882–1938)*. Milan, 1939
Baker, Sir Samuel W. *Ismailia*. London, 1874.
Browne, W. G. *Travels in Africa, Egypt, and Syria, from the Year 1792 to 1798*. London, 1799.
Bruce, James. *Travels to Discover the Source of the Nile*. Edinburgh, 1805.
Burckhardt, John Lewis. *Travels in Nubia*. London, 1819.
Crawford, O. G. S. *The Fung Kingdom of Sennar*. Gloucester, 1951.
Déhérain, Henri. *Le Soudan égyptien sous Mehemet Ali*. Paris, 1898.
Douin, G. *Histoire du Soudan égyptien*. Cairo, 1944.
Duncan, J. S. R. *The Sudan: A Record of Achievement*. Edinburgh, 1952.
*Gaitskell, Arthur. *Gezira: A Story of Development in the Sudan*. London, 1959.
*Gray, Richard. *A History of the Southern Sudan, 1839–1889*. London, 1961.
Henderson, K. D. *Survey of the Anglo-Egyptian Sudan, 1898–1944*. London, 1946.
*Hill, Richard. *Egypt in the Sudan, 1820–1881*. London, 1959.
*Holt, P. M. *The Mahdist State in the Sudan, 1881–1898*. Oxford, 1958.
*——. *A Modern History of the Sudan*. London, 1963.
Marzouk, G. "Sudan's Balance of Payments." Thesis, London University.
Petherick, John. *Egypt, the Sudan and Central Africa*. Edinburgh. 1861.
Sabry, M. *L'Empire égyptien sous Mohamed-Ali*. Paris, 1930.
Sayyad, Muhammad Mahmud al-. *Iqtisadiat al-Sudan*. Cairo, 1957.
Shibeika, Mekki. *Al-Sudan fi Qarn, 1819–1919*. Cairo, 1947.
*——. *The Independent Sudan*. New York, 1960.
Shukry, Muhammad Fuad. *Al-hukm al-Misri fi al-Sudan*. Cairo, 1945.
Theobald, A. B. *The Mahdiya*. London, 1951.
Tothill, J. D. (ed.). *Agriculture in the Sudan*. London, 1948.
United Nations, *Structure and Growth of Selected African Economies*. New York, 1958.

Index of Place Names

The following index is restricted to place names. The persons mentioned in this book who played a significant part in the economic history of the region were Muhammad Ali (see Part II, chap. 9; Part IV, chaps. 2–3; Part V, Introduction, and chap. 5; Part VI, chaps. 1–8; Part VII, chaps. 2 and 5; and Appendix II); Mahmud II (see Part II, Introduction and chaps. 5 and 9; and Appendix II); Ismail (see Part VI, chaps. 1 and 7–9; and Part VII, chaps. 2–4); Lord Cromer (see Part VI, chaps. 1, 10, and 13; and Part VII, chaps. 7–9); Midhat pasha (see Part III, Introduction and chap. 5).

Subject Index

Agriculture, 9, 11–12, 60–70, 74 ; Arabia, 4, 293, 300, 302, 305, 324–26, 330, 336, 345–49 ; Egypt, 11, 129, 361–62, 364, 366–67, 375–78, 384–87, 416–29, 434–35 ; Iraq, 3, 129–30, 133–34, 140–41, 177–78, 180, 191–97 ; Lebanon, 60–61, 74, 118, 226–33 ; Sudan, 9, 463–64, 469, 477–79, 489, 500–502 ; Syria, 3, 60–61, 205, 215, 227–33, 258–59, 265–68, 276 ; Turkey, 9, 19, 60–70, 116–18 ; cereals, 9, 32, 66, 74, 177–78, 227, 276, 377, 384–85, 419, 422, 483–84 ; cotton, 9, 19, 32–33, 37, 67–68, 133, 145, 208, 229, 287, 310, 361–62, 364, 366–68, 373, 375, 386–87, 416–29, 436, 440, 444, 446–48, 469, 472, 479, 500–502 ; irrigation, 9, 10, 21, 65, 80, 84, 129, 133–34, 164, 191–97, 285, 305, 348–49, 361, 364, 366, 368, 376–78, 385, 418, 442, 444, 463, 468, 477, 495, 500–502 ; livestock, 66, 117–18, 132, 293, 303–4, 320, 330, 344–49 ; silk, 33, 118, 208, 226, 229–30, 280 ; tobacco, 9, 19, 60–64, 67, 229, 378, 484. *See also* Land tenure
Americans, 10, 22, 94, 207, 271, 332, 343–44, 372, 393

Banking : Egypt, 11, 272, 364, 369–70, 419, 420, 424, 425, 428, 432, 453 ; Iraq, 4, 11 ; Lebanon, 232, 234, 279–80 ; Syria, 211, 234, 272, 279–80 ; Turkey, 11, 21–22, 98, 211, 250, 521
Beduins. *See* Nomads

Capitulations, 8, 15, 39, 54, 121, 245, 366, 507
Caravans. *See* Road transport

Debt, public : Egyptian, 365, 430–31, 435–38, 506 ; Ottoman, 94–106, 186–87, 190, 506 ; Sudanese, 471

Education, 10, 21, 22, 111–12, 131, 133, 207, 362, 445, 472, 500, 509
Europeans, 7, 9, 10, 28, 94–95, 184, 206–7, 217, 227, 332, 365, 419, 427, 467, 469, 486, 505–6

Foreign investment, 10–11, 21, 198–99, 506 ; Arabia, 198–99 ; Egypt, 11, 95, 364–66, 370, 435, 449–50, 505–7 ; Iraq, 198–99, 505 ; Lebanon, 210, 232, 508 ; Sudan, 471, 500–502 ; Syria, 210, 232, 505, 508 ; Turkey, 11, 19–20, 249–50, 506–7 ; American, 10,

94, 198–99, 508 ; Belgian, 94, 95, 506 ; British, 7, 9, 94, 95, 198–202, 506, 508 ; French, 6, 9, 94, 95, 198–99, 210, 249, 506, 508 ; German, 9, 65, 94, 198–202, 210, 250, 370, 506 ; Russian, 352, 370, 506, 508
Foreign trade, 7, 11, 12, 28, 30–37, 121, 182–85, 508–9 ; Arabia, 33, 281, 284, 294–99, 302, 303–7, 308–10, 312–13, 317–21, 324, 326–31, 347, 350–57, 476 ; Egypt, 33, 60, 278, 281, 284, 304, 306–7, 362–64, 367–68, 373, 391–93, 416–18, 425, 436, 444, 466, 473–76, 488–90 ; Iraq, 131–33, 135–36, 141, 171, 179, 182–85, 281, 303–4 ; Sudan, 465–66, 469–70, 472, 473–76, 484, 488–90 ; Syria, 33, 60, 63, 132, 136, 205–9, 216–19, 230, 277–79, 303–4 ; Turkey, 17, 30–31, 132, 136, 281, 284, 318 ; America, 33–34, 63, 318, 321, 327 ; Austria, 48, 208, 277–78, 321 ; Britain, 7, 10, 28, 30, 37, 48–50, 60, 132, 208–9, 278–79, 295, 310, 318, 327, 350, 416–18, 425 ; France, 10, 28, 30, 37, 48–49, 63, 208–9, 219, 277–79, 321, 327, 350, 363 ; Germany, 31, 48, 133, 277–78, 350 ; Greece, 32 ; India, 7, 34, 132, 136, 141, 294–96, 306–7, 310, 318, 331, 350, 476 ; Iran, 32, 33, 42, 132, 135–36, 143, 208, 295–96 ; Italy, 7, 15, 16, 37, 277–78, 321 ; North Africa, 34–35 ; Russia, 350

Guilds, 27, 46, 53

Handicrafts. *See* Industry

Industry, 4, 5–6, 7, 8, 9, 11, 41–59, 118–20, 509 ; Arabia, 293, 301, 302, 305, 326–27, 336 ; Egypt, 61, 362–63, 365, 366, 369–71, 376, 379, 389–93, 399–401, 421, 425, 432–33, 452–59, 509 ; Iraq, 43, 130, 136, 158–59, 180–81, 509 ; Lebanon, 51, 57–58, 233, 239, 240–43, 274, 280–81, 284, 285, 509 ; Sudan, 464, 479 ; Syria, 41, 43, 50–52, 58, 208, 216, 221–24, 231, 239, 240–45, 274, 280–86, 289–90, 509 ; Turkey, 18, 42–45, 48–53, 55–58, 509 ; textile, 5, 8, 33, 38, 41–42, 48–51, 55–58, 136, 159, 208, 221–24, 241, 280–84, 289–90, 326, 389, 457, 458, 479

Land tenure, 9, 21, 28, 71–90, 107 ; Arabia, 336, 345 ; Egypt, 79–90, 361, 364, 369, 378, 380–83, 387, 432,